союза рабочих и кресть

…ии, соединяйтесь!

…-ое Международный

…я труда!

For Zdenek Horeni and Ondrej Kadlec,
heirs of Hus and Zizka and true sons
of the February Revolution

THE ART OF REVOLUTION

The Art of Revolution

First published in the United Kingdom in 2011 by Evans Mitchell Books, 54 Baker St, London W1U 7BU, United Kingdom www.embooks.co.uk **and co-published by** GMB, 22-24 Worple Road, London SW19 4DD, United Kingdom www.gmb.org.uk

Written by Dr John Callow, Dr Grant Pooke and Jane Powell

Design by Darren Westlake, TU ink Ltd, London www.tuink.co.uk

British Library Cataloguing in Publication Data. A CIP record of this book is available on request from the British Library.

ISBN 978-1-901268-60-7

Printed in the UK by Butler Tanner and Dennis Ltd, Frome, Somerset

THE ART OF REVOLUTION

How posters swayed minds, forged nations and played their part in the progressive movements of the early 20th century

Illustrated by the collection of the Marx Memorial Library

By John Callow, Grant Pooke and Jane Powell

ЗА ВЫСОКИЙ УРОЖАЙ!

CONTENTS

PREFACE

FROM PAUL KENNY GENERAL SECRETARY, GMB 6

The GMB@WORK is a progressive union, proud to defend and advance our rights in the workplace and to be at the cutting edge of radical art and design for the good of the Movement.

The Bolshevik Revolution changed everything. Art became political. In the moment of Revolution the political poster became its most formidable expression.

The peoples of the USSR had to be mobilised behind the Collectivisation and the Five-Year Plans. Cornfields, tractors, factories and mines suddenly became the order of the day.

Soviet artists inspired resistance to fascism, and bore witness to the heroism and sacrifice of the people. Raising the Red flag over the Reichstag was their finest hour.

The victory of the Revolution of February 1948 compelled Czech artists to re-imagine the possibilities of Socialism, just as the Cold War threatened to go hot.

THE

REVOLUTION IN RUSSIA.

To express sympathy with the Russian Revolutionists,

A PUBLIC

MEETING

WILL BE HELD ON

Monday, January 22nd,

IN THE

MEMORIAL HALL

FARRINGDON STREET, E.C.

This Meeting will form one of a series of simultaneous meetings to be held in every Country at the recommendation of the International Socialist Bureau.

THE CHAIR WILL BE TAKEN AT 8 P.M. BY

WILL THORNE, M.P.

AND AMONG THE SPEAKERS WILL BE

J. E. GREGORY (London Trades Council) **G. STANDRING** **J. F. GREEN** (Friends of Russian Freedom)

B. WEINGARTZ **G. FREUND**

H. M. HYNDMAN **H. QUELCH** **W. C. STEADMAN, M.P.**

CECIL CHESTERTON (Fabian Society).

THE CHOIR OF THE COMMUNIST CLUB WILL SING.

A Collection will be made in aid of the Russian Revolutionists.

January 17th, 1906. S.D.F. OFFICE, 3, BOLT COURT, FLEET STREET, E.C. (Tel. No. 13877 Central).

A COMMON TREASURY FOR ALL

The GMB is proud of our new and progressive partnership with the Marx Memorial Library. Working together in solidarity we aim to provide the necessary resources, organisational and political support to breathe new life into the history, art and iconography of the international labour movement for a new generation of activists.

ВЫПОЛНИМ И ПЕРЕВЫПОЛНИМ НОВЫЙ ПЯТИЛЕТНИЙ ПЛАН!
ЗА ВЫСОКИЙ УРОЖАЙ!

The Marx Memorial Library contains an archive of posters, images and publications held in trust on behalf of the whole trade union and socialist movement that represents some of our greatest cultural treasures. Our project aims to make sure that as many of these treasures as possible reach a wider audience in the movement and beyond than has so far been possible - creating a new archive of images to act as a resource for unions, socialists and campaigners to use as we enter a new age of political activism.

These images are a living link to those who came before us and their achievements. They inspired generations of working people in the past and even in the age of Twitter, Facebook and digital media they have a lot to tell us about how to construct a powerful socialist message.

If you look across the page you will see that Will Thorne, the founder of our union, stood-up against the Tsarist regime in Russia and tried to stop the massacres and deportations that followed the failure of the 1905 Revolution.

The GMB was, from the first, part of this struggle.

This union exists for you: to protect you, to represent you, and to make life better for you.

But the GMB recognises cultural values alongside the 'bread and butter issues'. That is why this unique collection of labour movement images is so important for both ourselves and the Marx Memorial Library.

Paul Kenny

Борись с вредителями!

Кооперация

Кооператив

Частная торговля

Червь подтачивает хлебные всходы, торговец-кулак выматывает крестьянское хозяйство. Стройте и укрепляйте кооперацию.

Л. Е.

Издание Центросоюза Москва, тел. 2-33-25.

A REVOLUTION ON PAPER

What should not have been forgotten, had been forgotten. Hundreds of socialist posters – British and Soviet – lay overlooked in a warehouse, covered by walls of boxes, plastic carrier bags and layers of dust and fallen plaster. Piles of papers, and 'vast quantities' of books and pamphlets, from the newly defunct Communist Party of Great Britain had long since spilled over from the hastily constructed mesh and metal shelving, buckling the bookcases and tumbling to the floor.

It would take two hard summers' work, in 2005-6, to clear the scene of chaos, to sift and catalogue the discarded files, and to serve notice on the crumbling storage space, bringing useful materials back to their home at the Marx Memorial Library.[1]

Chief among the finds were the posters, rolled into thick bundles, bound tightly with age-worn string or stuffed into ubiquitous 'Sainsbury's' carry-alls. A swift glance was enough to reveal that the scope of the collection far transcended – in both numbers and importance – the handful of images reprinted for the Library, in the 1980s, in its 'Early Soviet' collection of postcards. Yet the problem of how to properly list and conserve them remained unanswered until the visit of Paul Kenny, the General Secretary of the GMB, to the Library at the beginning of February 2008.

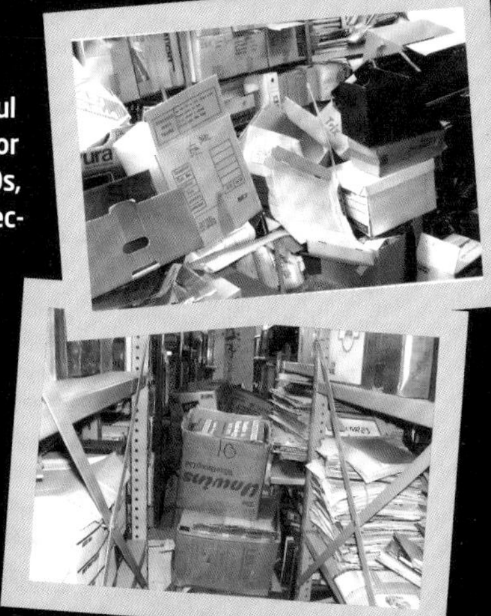

What had begun as a simple tour of Marx House soon turned into a practical discussion about the posters and the need to safeguard their long-term future. The sheer power of the images, the richness of their colours – even after more than sixty years – and their heady ideological content was immediately apparent to Kenny, and he donated sufficient funds from his union to buy-in the protective sleeves required for the first stage of their conservation. Within months, selected designs would appear as GMB posters at their Congress in Plymouth and as T-shirts for Ethical Threads and the Workers' Beer Company, to be worn at the Glastonbury and Leeds Carling festivals.

"FIGHT THE PESTS!"

Bridging the old, folk traditions of the *lubki*, and the new world of existing Socialism, this poster from 1925 seeks to link agricultural advance, increased yields and plenty, with learning, urbanisation and the abolition of private interests. Lenin's attempt to socialise the market, through the NEP, had brought an end to famine, stabilised the economy after the destruction wrought by the Civil War and done much to raise living standards.

Yet, the basic impulse of the Party was to abolish the private sector, entirely. Though NEP was still in force, this brightly coloured poster – designed to win over the peasantry – marks an opening salvo in the campaign against the kulaks and grain speculators that would eventually lead to Collectivisation of agriculture.

The towering son of the peasantry – resplendent in his folk costume and very much in keeping with Ivan Bilibin's fairy tale vision of traditional Russian life – is captured in the act of smiting the pests that threaten the crop, with a large volume bearing the emblem of a sunrise and the title *Co-operation*.

One of the parasites - the caterpillar – is identified as a kulak and a 'blood sucker', while the other – a gopher – is designated 'private trade', a capitalist out to exploit the hard work of others. The text reinforces the message that: 'The worm eats our crops, the dealer exhausts the peasants and our agriculture. Build and strengthen co-operation'.

The co-operative farms, seen at the top right, show the way forward – the meeting of town and country, and the venue for the equitable exchange of the people's resources. Already, the struggles of the late 1920s-30s to reshape the Soviet countryside and the invectives they inspired against the kulaks and 'NEP-men' have been charted.

Their realisation, in pursuit of an ideal, would plunge the land back into conflict and bring about greater equality, though at the price of hardship and suffering for millions.

„Пролетарии всех стран, соединяйтесь!"
Р.С.Ф.С.Р.
№87.
ОРУЖИЕМ МЫ ДОБИЛИ ВРАГА
ТРУДОМ МЫ ДОБУДЕМ ХЛЕБ
ВСЕ ЗА РАБОТУ, ТОВАРИЩИ!

"WE DEFEATED THE ENEMY WITH WEAPONS - WITH HARD WORK WE WILL GET OUR BREAD. EVERYONE TO WORK! WORKERS OF ALL LANDS, UNITE!"

Published in 1920, just as the tide was turning decisively in favour of Frunze's Red Army, this poster attempted to project the revolutionary enthusiasm of the Civil War into peacetime reconstruction. Significantly, it also sought to emphasise sexual equality as male and female workers contribute equally to building the future of the Soviet state.

The worker and the Red Army soldier are one and the same. The stack of rifles, beside the forge, the budenovka – the distinctive cap adopted by the Red Army – has been carefully set-down; show that the worker is constantly vigilant and ready to take up arms again. In the background, the agitprop train, which brought news, theatre groups and the political poster, to the remotest fronts during wartime, is being refitted.

Lenin's maxim that Soviet power equaled 'Communism plus electrification' is echoed in the power cables and telegraph lines up above, while the busy furnaces, wrought iron bridges and smoking chimneys are suggestive of intensive industrial productivity and rapid growth.

Though the hammer and the sickle would not be officially adopted as the arms of the Soviet Union until November 1923 – and the hammer and plough had frequently appeared on Civil War banners – these symbols were already synonymous with the Revolution and take pride of place in this composition for the 'Workers' and Peasants' State'.

At the same time, trade union support was backed by genuine academic interest through the involvement of the School of Arts at the University of Kent. Preliminary work began upon a catalogue and as the result of the broad coalition between the Marx Library, the GMB and the University of Kent, the Leverhulme Trust awarded a grant for research, conservation and development, that ran from September 2009 to October 2010. This was among the first major collaborations outside the purely academic sector for the School of Arts and one which brought immediate scholarly attention with two successful Cold War Conferences at Canterbury and London, and a showcase for a selection of the newly restored posters at the TUC Congress, in Manchester, in September 2010.[2]

The book which you now hold represents the conclusion of the first stage of that project, focusing upon Soviet and revolutionary posters between 1917-53. This poster collection is unique.

Had the collection been created by private collectors, connoisseurs or critics, it would have been very different. It accrued, instead, through the efforts of political activists - in particular Robin Page Arnot and Andrew Rothstein - who returned to London from forays into Weimar Germany, the Soviet Union and post-war Czechoslovakia with tubes full of the latest propaganda posters; intending to inform and inspire a British working class audience. Political necessity, as opposed to aesthetics served as the benchmark and the Bolsheviks lived in - and for - the day, often heedless of long term considerations in their desire to secure the survival of the first workers' state.

Consequently, the posters at Marx House do not represent an even, impartial or constant picture of Soviet graphical art and society. Rather, they throw a sudden - and frequently harsh - spotlight upon the preoccupations of the Revolutionary Soviet Government, and latterly its satellites, at particular junctures and periods of crisis. Its omissions and blind spots reflect, just as significantly, upon the relative strength of the British Communist party and the exigencies of the Cold War. Hence the dramatic break in the run of posters between 1956 and the late 1960s, when Soviet ideological hegemony was threatened; the resumption of images under Brezhnev - when the old revolutionary archetypes were resuscitated - and their gradual tailing-off as 'official art' was successfully challenged and fragmented under Gorbachev.

"CROSSED OUT BY THE OCTOBER REVOLUTION!"

Published in Moscow and Leningrad, in 1933, Viktor Deni's work re-caps many of the themes that characterised his output during the Civil War. His caricatures of the enemies of the Revolution emphasised that it was not enough to just remove the monarchy – the Tsar and Tsarina, the courtiers, clergy and the corrupt influence of Rasputin – in February 1917; but that the October Revolution was needed to finish the job and destroy Capitalism, as well.

Thus, the imperial eagles of the first panel are replaced by money bags in the second, as Kerensky – the would-be democrat, turned Napoleon – shelters beneath the corpulent industrialist and a murderous array of White Guard generals: the war criminals Kolchak, Denikin, Kaledin and Wrangel.

By the time Deni set to work on this poster, the Tsar and his family were long dead, Kaledin had been killed in action and Kolchak had been executed for his crimes in the Civil War. Wrangel had died in Brussels, in 1928, while Kerensky and Denikin were, respectively, eking out their existence in Paris and New York.

Viktor Deni (1893-1946) was one of the great poster artists of the Revolution. Described as possessing 'a sharp political mind ... a formidable artistic gift' he worked as both artist and poet. His problem was his inability to adapt to new artistic fashions and his work, by the 1930s, began to look somewhat dated.

This may not have been all bad news. His avoidance of contemporary issues and preoccupation with the values of the October Revolution enabled him to keep working, as a cartoonist for *Pravda*, when many of his contemporaries fell during the purges. He returned to political poster art, with renewed vigour, during the Great Patriotic War.

If Stalin figures large, alongside the Five-Year Plans and drives towards Collectivisation that formed the kernel of his policies, it is because of his total dominance of the Soviet political scene after 1929 and his commensurate hold on the popular imagination of the peoples of the USSR. Yet, if there was self-censorship, at times, on behalf of the members of the Marx Library – who went in and out of favour with the Soviet leadership post-1956, and whose interest in the art of the agitational poster waxed and waned – there seems to have been no attempt to 'weed' the collection in order to fit changing circumstances. Rather, the

posters were quickly but quietly removed from the walls and put into storage for another day. In this manner, the victims of the purges – Tukhachevsky, Blyucher and Ordjonikidze – stare back at us from barely creased or faded sheets that have been almost entirely destroyed in the former Soviet Republics, since 1937.

Though today we tend to view these images out of context and with the full benefit of hindsight, safe in the knowledge that the Cold War did not end in nuclear annihilation and that revolution did not sweep all before it in the West; these are still images that exude a raw – and perhaps even uncomfortable – power. The Russian Revolution of October 1917 changed everything, not least art itself, and even now the spirit of freedom and social justice it released has not been totally forced back within the bounds of a neoliberal 'Pandora's Box'.

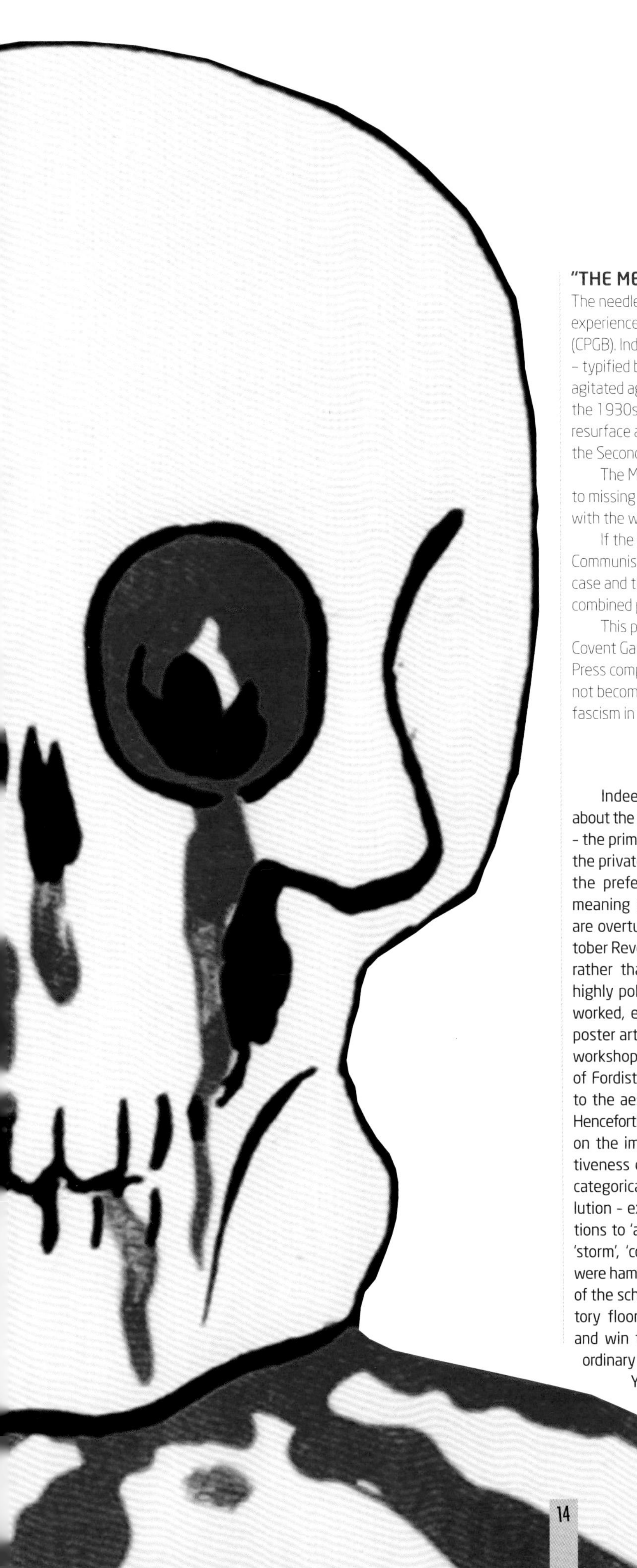

"THE MENIN ROAD OR THE LENIN ROAD?"

The needless slaughter of the First World War was the greatest formative experience for the foundation members of the Communist Party of Great Britain (CPGB). Indeed, a potent strain of pacifism and opposition to war in all its forms – typified by the career of the first General Secretary, Albert Inkpin, who had agitated against both the Boer and Great Wars – ran through the Party until the 1930s and the revolt of the fascist generals in Spain. It would briefly resurface again, between 1939-41, in the Party's volte-face in characterising the Second World War as an 'imperialist' rather than an 'anti-fascist' conflict.

The Menin Road in Flanders, and the Gate built post-war as a memorial to missing British and Commonwealth troops, were synonymous for Britons with the waste and destruction of total war.

If the Great War was fought 'as the war to end all wars', then the British Communists of the 1920s were determined to ensure that this would be the case and that the future, charted by a Leninist Party, would be one that combined plenty and peace.

This poster was issued by the headquarters of the CPGB in King Street, Covent Garden, and was printed to aid a recruitment drive by the Party's Dorritt Press company. Despite all its best attempts, the British Communist Party would not become a truly mass organisation until it took the lead in the fight against fascism in the 1930s-40s.

Indeed, all our preconceptions about the nature of artistic endeavour - the primacy of the individual artist, the private sphere of enjoyment and the preference for multi-layers of meaning and inherent ambiguity - are overturned by the art of the October Revolution. Art was now public rather than private, utilitarian and highly politically charged. The artist worked, especially in the sphere of poster art, as part of a collective in a workshop or large studio. The logic of Fordist production was extended to the aesthetics of graphic design. Henceforth, the artist would be judged on the immediacy and social effectiveness of his or her work and the categorical imperatives of the revolution - expressed through exhortations to 'advance', 'unite', 'speed-up', 'storm', 'construct', or 'strengthen' - were hammered home from the walls of the schoolroom, canteen, and factory floor in order to engage with and win the support of, millions of ordinary Soviet citizens for the Five-Year plans and collectivisation of agriculture.

'Art' according to the manifesto of the avant-garde Lef group, 'builds life' but a brief survey of the career of one of the most brilliant poster artists, Gustav Klutsis (1895-1938) clearly demonstrates the Bolshevik fusing of theory and practice. Klutsis, a Latvian, whose brother had been arrested by the Tsarist secret police after the failure of the 1905 revolution, had been drafted into the Imperial Russian Army before joining the Revolution as a member of the crack detachment of Latvian riflemen. He stormed the Winter Palace in October 1917, served as one of Lenin's Kremlin guards and fought to overthrow the Kronstadt uprising which threatened to bring all of the Soviets' achievements to dust. His preference for using red in his compositions, as 'the pigment of the epoch' was no throw-away quip but rather a statement of belief. By the late 1920s, he had begun work on a series of monumental propaganda posters celebrating the values of collective action and social solidarity. He produced hundreds of images that were intended to surpass Western propaganda and advertising in their scope, quality and integrity.

WAR or PEACE

Which do you Prefer?

MILITARISM

MENIN ROAD

OR

PEACE

COMMUNISM

LENIN ROAD

JOIN THE COMMUNIST PARTY

PUBLISHED by C.P.G.B. 16 KINGS St W.C.2.

PRINTED by THE DORRITT PRESS Ltd 68-70 LANT St S.E.1

"VOTE COMMUNIST!"

This wall poster, printed on no more than tissue paper, was issued in time for the German elections of May 1924 and seems to have been brought back to the Marx Library by Robin Page Arnot from Berlin.

These elections were the first to be fought by the KPD (Kommunistische Partei Deutschlands), which up until that time had advocated revolutionary insurrection as opposed to a parliamentary road to Socialism. However, as the poster shows, the Party was proud of its revolutionary tradition and sacrifices during the Spartakist uprising of January 1919.

The ghost of Karl Liebknecht, who had been abducted and murdered alongside Rosa Luxemburg, by the Freikorps during the abortive rising, is shown confronting the bourgeois ministers of the Weimar Republic. Outside the revolutionary wave, undeterred by the loss of its leaders, prepares to fulfill their mission marching to take power under the folds of the red flag.

The plumpest of these, toppling back in his chair, represents Friedrich Ebert, the Social Democrat Chancellor who had called in the Prussian officer class to shoot down and terrorise the workers. Indeed, the myth of these 'true German' Freikorps veterans of the First World War would be crucial to the subsequent rise of Nazism.

The diaries of his wife, Valentina Kulagina - herself a major poster artist, whose work is also included within this book - gives some idea of the tempo of the times. On 22 September 1933, she wrote that: 'My poster *Comrades coal miners!* (page 34) has turned out rather well in print. Today handed in six slogans for the transportation workers. Three have been approved at once ... Drawn posters are much more interesting to make than montage. Gustav [Klutsis'] *Politburo* has made quite a storm, it's a big success'.[3]

Perhaps what is most unsettling and inexplicable to contemporary art historians is the primary concern of these artists to celebrate the world of work and the mood of optimism, even of euphoria, in the act of constructing a new society. It seems to belie our knowledge of the human cost of the progress achieved and of the shadows cast by the Show Trials of the 1930s. Yet, poster images such as that of *Metropolis!* or *Odessa: a tourist's paradise* (pages 31 & 26) are reflected in the monumental canvas *New Moscow*, painted by Yuri Pimenov in 1937; and in the diaries of Kulagina, herself. She writes, breathlessly, on 4 February 1934, of: 'How wonderful Moscow has become. Everything is being built, torn down, torn up - everywhere there are Metro towers, trolley-buses are running, there is more of everything in the shops. Maybe things really will be different ...'.[4]

If, as Victoria Bonnell has claimed, the 'critical issue facing the Bolsheviks in 1917 was not merely the seizure of power but the seizure of meaning'; then Klutsis, Kulagina and their comrades in the Communist International had little difficulty in articulating and propagating their vision. Look, for a moment at the poster published by the Central Committee of the German Communist Party (KPD), celebrating the first ten years of the Soviet Union's formation and - against all initial probability and prediction - the survival of the Bolshevik Revolution (page 94). Promethean-like, with the globe at their feet, a Red Army soldier and an industrial worker exchange fraternal greetings, against a backdrop dominated by the Soviet Star.

Constructing an entirely new visual culture was to prove central to the nascent Soviet state which faced a host of internal and external threats in the months and years following the October Revolution of 1917. Russia's land mass covered one sixth of the Earth's surface, stretching from the Arctic to the Black Sea and from the Baltic to the Far East, and its territory encompassed over thirty five distinct nationalities and cultural groups. With uniformly high levels of illiteracy - one estimate from the early 1920s suggests that only two out of five adults could read,[5] art in all its forms (painting, posters, photography, films, sculptures, textiles and ceramics, as well as design and architecture), provided a powerful and direct visual language to propagate the ideas and aspirations of the new order.

Since before the Petrine reforms of the seventeenth century, the icon-religious images of the saints and *lubki* - woodcut and engraved images depicting folk tales and satirical subject matter in clear forms and bright, expressive colours, had been a staple of national consciousness and communication - especially in the huge hinterland outside the major cities and towns. Icons, depicting stylised images of religious figures, were typically painted on limewood bases and placed not only in churches, but in public buildings and on roadsides in small makeshift shelters. In houses which observed the Russian Orthodox religion, it was also customary to hang icons across the corner of the room - the so-called 'red corner' - in part to symbolise the protective presence of divinity. Although also religious in origin, the *lubok* was later used to communicate secular subjects - political satire, songs and folk stories. Much later in the nineteenth century, and subject to regular censorship, the form became increasingly commercialised with designs sold and circulated on paper - Moscow became one of the centres for this flourishing trade during the upswing of interest in national cultural forms such as painting, literature and music.[6] Despite the Academy and Salon traditions of painting and sculpture originally imported from Europe by Catherine II and Peter the Great, Russia had a vibrant, native visual culture which remained both popular and socially accessible.

Even before the events of 1917, members of the avant-garde had been drawn to these native art forms, not just for their directness and simplicity, but because of the visceral sense of national identity which they conveyed. Although the Russian Orthodox Church was subdued and its churches closed or requisitioned in the aftermath of the October Revolution, the legacy of its devotional forms continued to inform the avant-garde modernism of artists such as Natalya Ghoncharova, Mikhail Larionov and Kasimir Malevich. The bright colours and the shallow pictorial space of the *lubok* and the linear forms of the icon were used to fashion styles such as 'Neo-Primitivism' and 'Cubo-Futurism'. Although western critics saw in these depictions a synthesis and an appropriation of modernist ideas, they were perceived by their makers as principally Russian in inspiration and content. This national legacy, together with the commercial advertising graphics of the pre-Revolutionary era and a tradition of satirical cartoons and newspaper graphics, was to prove no less influential on the iconography of the political posters which were produced in the aftermath of 1917.[7]

"TO HORSE, WORKERS AND PEASANTS - THE RED CAVALRY IS THE BEST GUARANTEE OF VICTORY!"

Instantly recognisable in their tall, peaked and winged 'Budenovka' caps - named after Marshal Budyonny - the Red Cavalry were synonymous with the Civil War and the spectacular victories won by Tukhachevsky, Budyonny, and Chapayev against the Whites.

In the early years of the Revolution, there was a conscious decision by the Red Army command to move away from the symbols of Tsarist militarism. Epaulettes, braiding and other symbols of command were abandoned and uniforms remodelled - sometimes with theatrical effect - on much earlier lines, taking inspiration from the conical helmets and padded armour worn by Alexander Nevsky's soldiers in the 13th Century.

For a time, even the practice of awarding medals was replaced by other forms of honour. Thus, Trotsky chose to award Chapayev with a pocket watch after a successful offensive and made sure that the cameras were there to capture both the event and his arrival at the front in an armoured train.

This contrasted strongly with the return to the ranks of General and Marshal in the 1930s, and the increasing appeal to the military legacy and uniforms of the Russian Army of 1812 during the Great Patriotic War.

НА КОНЯ РАБОЧИЙ И СЕЛЯНИН!
КРАСНАЯ КАВАЛЕРИЯ—
ЗАЛОГ ПОБЕДЫ!

"THE CHILDREN OF LENIN"

The Revolution was synonymous with youth, but education had virtually come to a standstill as a result of the Civil War and foreign intervention. Thousands of orphans were displaced, street gangs roamed many towns, and the Scouting Movement – created in Russia on Baden Powell's model – had been hopelessly compromised by its partisanship of the White cause.

While Felix Dzerzhinsky and his Cheka took over the running of children's homes, a new youth organisation, the Young Pioneers – that owed much to the inspiration of Lenin's wife, Krupskaya – was founded in 1922.

This striking poster, from 1924, celebrates the seventh anniversary of the October Revolution. Resplendent in his red scarf – proudly worn by each and every member from 1922 to 1991 – this Pioneer doubtless beats out the timbre to such popular tunes as 'The Eaglet', 'Chapayev walked the Urals' and 'May there always be sunshine'.

Because Lenin had no children of his own, Soviet educationalists were keen to stress that every boy and girl in the USSR was under his care.

Members of the Russian artistic avant-garde - including Ghoncharova, Gustav Klutsis, Larionov, El Lissitzky, Malevich, Liubov Popova, Olga Rozanova and Vladimir Tatlin were instinctively drawn to the ideals of the Revolution. Between 1917 and 1921 Moscow and Leningrad became major crucibles of avant-garde modernism, arguably eclipsing in artistic and design innovation, the western capitals of Berlin, Paris and London. In particular Malevich and Tatlin were to play prominent organisational roles in the new cultural and artistic institutions established to direct and manage both artistic education and cultural policy. Like many of their peers, they perceived in the political aspirations of Socialist Revolution a reflection of the iconography and innovation of their own avant-garde practice. In the words of the Soviet poet and playwright, Vladimir Mayakovsky: 'We do not need a dead mausoleum of art where dead works are worshipped, but a living factory of the human spirit - in the streets, in the tramways, in the factories, workshops and workers' home'.[8]

The 1st May celebrations and the annual commemoration of the October Revolution provided the opportunity for huge street pageants and festivals, decorated with brightly coloured hoardings and canvases. For the initial anniversary of the Revolution in 1918 Nathan Altman choreographed the erection of large Futurist designs and sculptures in Petrograd (previously St Petersburg), the ambition of which echoed Lenin's own plans for a nationwide scheme of 'monumental propaganda' comprising over forty large scale sculptures celebrating the heroes of the Revolution. Ironically, in the years fol-

lowing his death in 1924, Lenin was himself to become, on Stalin's instigation, the subject of a personality cult, duly embalmed and installed in Aleksei Shchusev's modernist mausoleum in Red Square. The visual corollary of this process is already apparent in a poster design, one of 10,000, by Yakov Moiseevich Guminer (page 25) simply titled *The apotheosis of Lenin*. The magnified 'V' for Vladimir and for the numeral '5' frames a photomontage flanked by Bolshevik banners, which appear no less imperial for their colour and symbolism. The diagonals of the 'V' coincidentally suggest the Constructivist motif of angled typography, used to signify the powerful vectors of Soviet technological progress, motifs habitually used in the photomontages of Aleksander Rodchenko,

ПРОЛЕТАРИИ ВСЕХ СТРАН, СОЕДИНЯЙТЕСЬ

ПОД ЗНАМЕНЕМ КОМИНТЕРНА

НА ЗАЩИТУ СССР

ОГИЗ — ИЗОГИЗ

"WORKERS OF ALL COUNTRIES UNITE, UNDER THE BANNER OF THE COMMUNIST INTERNATIONAL, IN HONOUR OF THE USSR!"

The October Revolution was at once both a national and an international event. This poster by Kochergin, published in Moscow and Leningrad in 1933, sought to highlight the role of the Comintern (the Third Communist International, founded in 1920) in bringing revolution to the working class across the world; while stressing the guiding role of the USSR, as the first workers' state, in realising that goal.

The image of British tanks at the head of White Guard armies and interventionist forces was burned deep into the Soviet consciousness. The mechanised tracks, multiple gun turrets and iron shells are reworked here to symbolise Capitalism, itself. Intent upon driving up profits through warfare and imperialism, the lumbering Capitalist – resplendent in his top hat – disgorges poison gas clouds as he advances towards the Soviet frontier.

However, his moment is passed and his death knell is at hand. The figure of the Red Guard – symbolising here both the international and Soviet working class – is about to despatch him with a blow to his back.

Up until the outbreak of the Second World War, the imagery born out of the Civil War would still dominate the revolutionary poster. The problem, both artistically and politically, was that the organised working class came to be viewed increasingly in terms of the appearance and needs of the Soviet worker.

Lissitsky and Klutsis.

Although documentary photography and cinema were to emerge as the favoured mediums of the Revolution, the distinctive genre of the revolutionary propaganda poster became a hugely influential cultural form. Although advertising posters had existed in Russia before 1917, the acute material shortages which characterised the immediate aftermath of the Revolution and the period of Civil War which followed (c.1918-1921), made this comparatively cheap form of mass communication especially attractive. Despite the difficult conditions of the period, the disruptions to paper supplies from the Baltic, unreliable fuel supplies and transport, the damage to printing presses and a frequent dearth of skilled labour, Stephen White has estimated that between 1918 and 1921, over 3,600 poster designs were reproduced in varying multiples.[9] The difficulty of sustaining consistent newspaper or journal production and distribution, also caused by the continually moving fronts of the Civil War being waged between Bolshevik and 'White' or monarchist forces, made the poster a cheap and potentially far more effective and flexible means of communication.

As design and cultural historians have noted, early Soviet poster campaigns addressed issues of ideology; illustrating threats to the survival of the state, emphasising the importance of literacy, health and the importance of collective labour in the pursuit of social and political goals. The technique of photomontage, associated with Rodchenko and Klutsis which combined text and superimposed photography, was to prove especially effective in creating direct and emotive images - from pictures of the new Dnieper Dam to dramatising the latest production figures and quotas from heavy industry or agriculture. Photomontage was later to develop into single-frame still photography or 'factography' which was widely deployed by artists such as Lissitsky for the images used for the propaganda journal *USSR in Construction* (1930-41).[10] Both the techniques of photomontage and the incorporation of complete single frame photographs within posters were to become recurrent iconographical features of poster designs from the 1920s onwards.

The legacy of the *lubok* in the bright colour contrasts and that of the icon with the dominance of a single figure to dramatise meaning, is especially apparent in Luke Martyanovich Emelianov's poster, *Fight the pests!* (page 8). Similarly dramatic iconography is employed in *Vote Communist!*, (page 16) an unattributed pro-Comintern image - no designer is listed, which is encouraging a turnout for the German Communist Party (KPD). The starkly stylised and polarised figure groupings recall the linear forms and motifs of the icon as does Nikolai Kogout's *We defeated the enemy with weapons* (page 10). Against a panorama of industrialised production symbolised by a train silhouette, teams of factory workers, telegraph wires, cranes and smokestacks, a blacksmith and his female assistant, forge armaments, symbolised by the pyramid of completed rifles with bayonets, depicted on the left middleground of the composition.

The use of the blacksmith or *kuznets* became an established part of the repertoire within Soviet political posters, although the iconography of its use changed through time.[11] Widely deployed until 1930, and extensively featured on stamps, fabrics and official seals, the heroic 'worker icon' of the blacksmith was felt to have a resonance for both the industrialised and agricultural worker alike; the hammer and anvil symbolising the forging of the new Soviet future and the constructive role of the skilled worker in achieving such.

Used from 1918 onwards, the symbols of the hammer and sickle soon became synonymous with the Soviet state. Although women were not to be found in village or industrial forges, the counterpart of the female worker dramatises the collaborative union of gender integral to Socialist labour. Kogout's poster of 1920 was among the first to depict the new iconography of women as co-workers rather than as abstract revolutionary symbols - pervasive in contemporary representations of the French Revolution and the Paris Commune.

"THE APOTHEOSIS OF LENIN"

This photomontage by Yakov Guminer was published to commemorate the fifth anniversary of Lenin's death, in 1929. As the inspiration and driving force behind the Bolshevik Revolution, Lenin could not easily be replaced.

His premature death, in January 1924, left a gaping hole at the heart of the international working class movement and left many of the questions surrounding the development of the Communist Party – most notably its transformation from an underground organisation into a party of government – unresolved.

Concerned to protect his memory, his colleagues passed a series of edicts within weeks of his death aimed at channeling and controlling the use of his image. He appeared in everything from posters and postcards, magazines and academic tracts, to childrens' toys and games. However, his face was not used on cigarette packets and sweet wrappers which were quickly discarded and likely to be trampled underfoot.

Making a design feature of the letter 'V', in his name, the artist devotes the central portion of the poster to Vladimir Ilyich Lenin's time in government: whether at a Red Square Parade, listening to speeches by the Comintern or Komsomol, or at an unveiling of a statue of Marx; an essential dynamism is seen to be the essence of his character. His changing appearance, from infant, to school boy, to exile, to leader of the Soviet state, is charted in the upper panel; while at the bottom his lying in state and mausoleum are shown alongside crowd scenes witnessing the spontaneous outpouring of grief that greeted the news of his passing.

Significantly, the text is limited to his name and the relevant dates – those of his life and anniversary – everything else is held to be superfluous. His record and the images say it all.

The iconography of the Soviet worker underwent a series of changes, from the iconic *kuznets* to depictions within an increasingly industrialised context - *homo Sovieticus* - depicted either in schematic outline, through greater specificity or choreographed collectively. Nikolai Mikhailovich Kochergin (page 22) returns to the iconic device of the schematic, red figure attacking the forces of capitalist aggression which are depicted as a mechanised cypher, part armoured tank and part human. Reproduced in a print run of 30,000 copies, it is titled *Workers of all countries unite under the banner of the Communist International in honour of the USSR.*

Some of the posters reproduced here reference Communist Party activities in countries outside the Soviet Union where the Comintern continued an active policy of political agitation and protest. For example, one poster distributed by the Communist Party of Denmark (page 90) dating from the 1920s, invites workers, women and young people to take part in an anti-imperialist war demonstration which is to converge upon the Southern Danish town of Sonderborg. The CPGB commissioned the recruitment poster (page 15) *The Menin Road or the Lenin Road?* which puns off the title of Leo Tolstoy's epic novel, *War and Peace* and the horror of the trenches (Menin Road). The poster is a reminder of the rapprochement which existed between the Communist Party of the Soviet Union (CPSU) and the cadres of the CPGB, even before the highpoint of allied Soviet détente during the Great Patriotic War 1941-1945.

The dual division of the picture space recalls similar devices used in Soviet posters such as Viktor Nikolayevich Deni's *Crossed out by the October Revolution* (page 12) in which defeated opponents including the Tsar Nicholas II and the Tsarina, Rasputin, assorted court advisers and Counter-Revolutionary generals have been symbolically 'erased' from history. The Romanov flag and the emblem of the two-headed eagle are inverted in defeat with the repeated device of money bags used as both a decadent frame and as a signifier of the demonised capitalist figure which dominates the right side of the composition.

In recent years the genre of the Soviet political poster has attracted increasing levels of collecting and curatorial interest. This has been driven by the increasingly globalised and commodified nature of the art market, changing fashions and, in no small part, by a generation of Russian and émigré buyers with a nostalgic, if often conflicted, interest in the history of the USSR.

As a medium of critical engagement, the Soviet political poster was as defined by Marxist-Leninist ideology as it was by a profound and continuous sense of national and collective identity. Although conceived as an entirely ephemeral cultural form, the history of the Soviet political poster marks out the continuum of Soviet power and nationhood, from the Bolshevik Revolution of 1917 through to the Civil War of 1919-21, the Great Patriotic War, the Cold War and the decades which followed. Noting the tumultuous contexts of its initial production, Stephen White has suggested that it was at 'times of transcendent national need' – particularly of the Civil War period, that Soviet poster art attained a pinnacle of 'achievement'.[12] The selection of examples which have been reproduced here, now fully catalogued and archived with the generous support of the GMB and Leverhulme Trust, are testaments to that conviction.

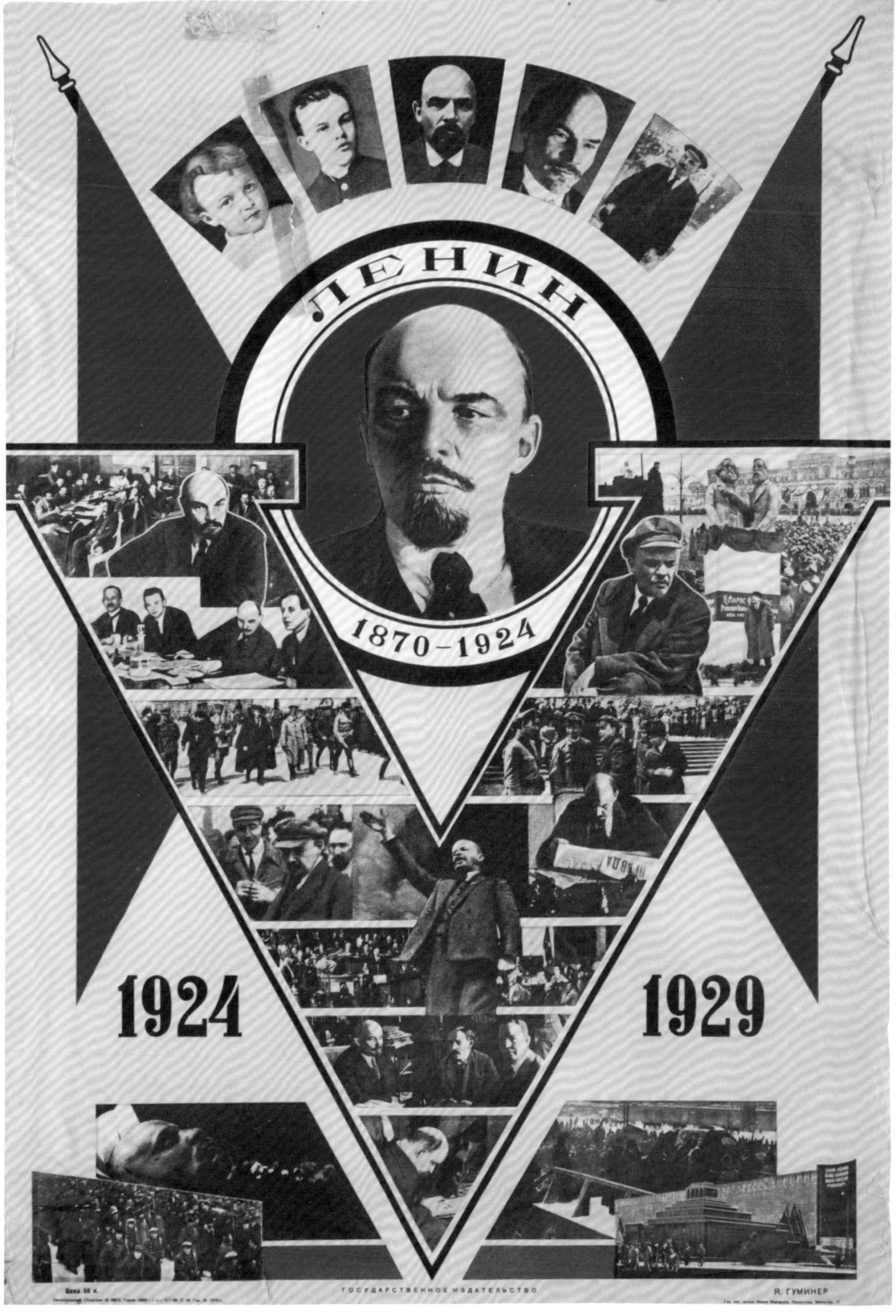
ЛЕНИН
1870–1924
1924
1929
ГОСУДАРСТВЕННОЕ ИЗДАТЕЛЬСТВО
Я. ГУМИНЕР

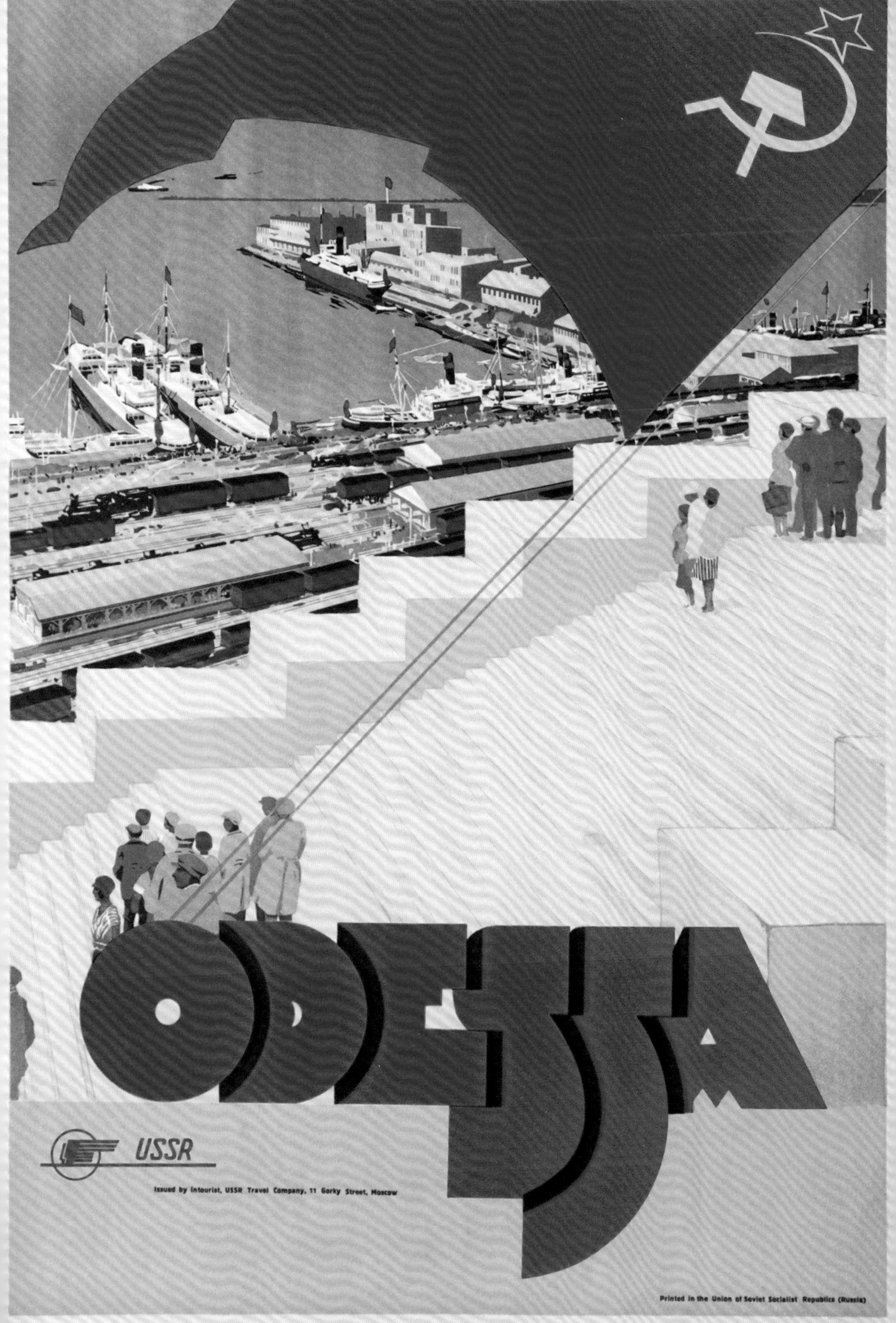
ODESSA
USSR
Issued by Intourist, USSR Travel Company, 11 Gorky Street, Moscow
Printed in the Union of Soviet Socialist Republics (Russia)

EXPERIENCE

'I was sixteen years old when I learnt that the hour was divided into minutes... In all other countries, the peasants had one or two hundred years to develop the habit of industrial precision and of the handling of machines. Here they only had ten years'.

(Gletkin's speech, from the Third Hearing in Arthur Koestler's *Darkness at Noon*)

In the space of half a century Russia changed from being a principally agrarian and feudal country in which serfdom was an accepted way of life and Tsarist autocracy the norm, to a highly centralised and industrialised economy which, for a time, led the space race and competed with the United States for global supremacy.[1] Such vying for political and military supremacy not only determined the outcome of World War Two, but also shaped the Cold War which followed, irrevocably changing the course of twentieth century history. These epochal shifts were witnessed by a single generation, prompting the ringing declaration of Vladimir Mayakovsky's *Poem of a Soviet Passport* (1929): 'You now: read this and envy, I'm a citizen of the Soviet Socialist Union!' Years later such a tangible sense of national pride and achievement remains as evident in the iconography of, for example, an Intourist poster introducing the attractions of Odessa for Soviet citizens and overseas visitors alike.

"ODESSA: A TOURIST'S PARADISE"

Issued in 1935, by the Intourist holiday firm, this bright vision of the Black Sea port stressed its role as a magnet for travellers and a hub of trade and communication.

The Odessa Steps, the scene of a Tsarist massacre of peaceful protesters in 1905 – made famous by Eisenstein in his film *Battleship Potemkin* – are shown glistening in the light cast by a peaceful Soviet Union. Once the scene of division, they are re-imagined by the artist as somewhere where the people and foreign visitors can mingle, take in the views and pass the time of day.

Founded in 1929, Intourist was the state owned travel agency of the USSR until its privatisation in 1992. Offering unrivalled service and value, it was the way that most visitors experienced the Soviet Union.

"MAY DAY GREETINGS TO THE HEROES AND HEROINES OF SOCIALIST TOIL!"

Published in time for May Day, 1941, with the obligatory quotation from Stalin – proclaiming that: 'Friendship among the nations of the USSR is the greatest and biggest conquest. Because when there is friendship, the nations of our fatherland will be free and invincible' – the poster emphasises both the positive role of women in Soviet society and the equality enjoyed by all ethnic groups under the Constitution.

Though cotton is picked in the Central Asian Republics and the cotton mills lie far to the west, production is overseen by Moscow, and all women are sisters in the unified Soviet state. Though the mill worker is differenced from the traditional costume and lifestyle of the woman who works out in the cotton fields – by her modish dress and short hair – they are united by their gender, their politics, and their productive work.

Together they have harnessed raw materials and the power of nationalised industry to create beautiful cloth for the benefit of all.

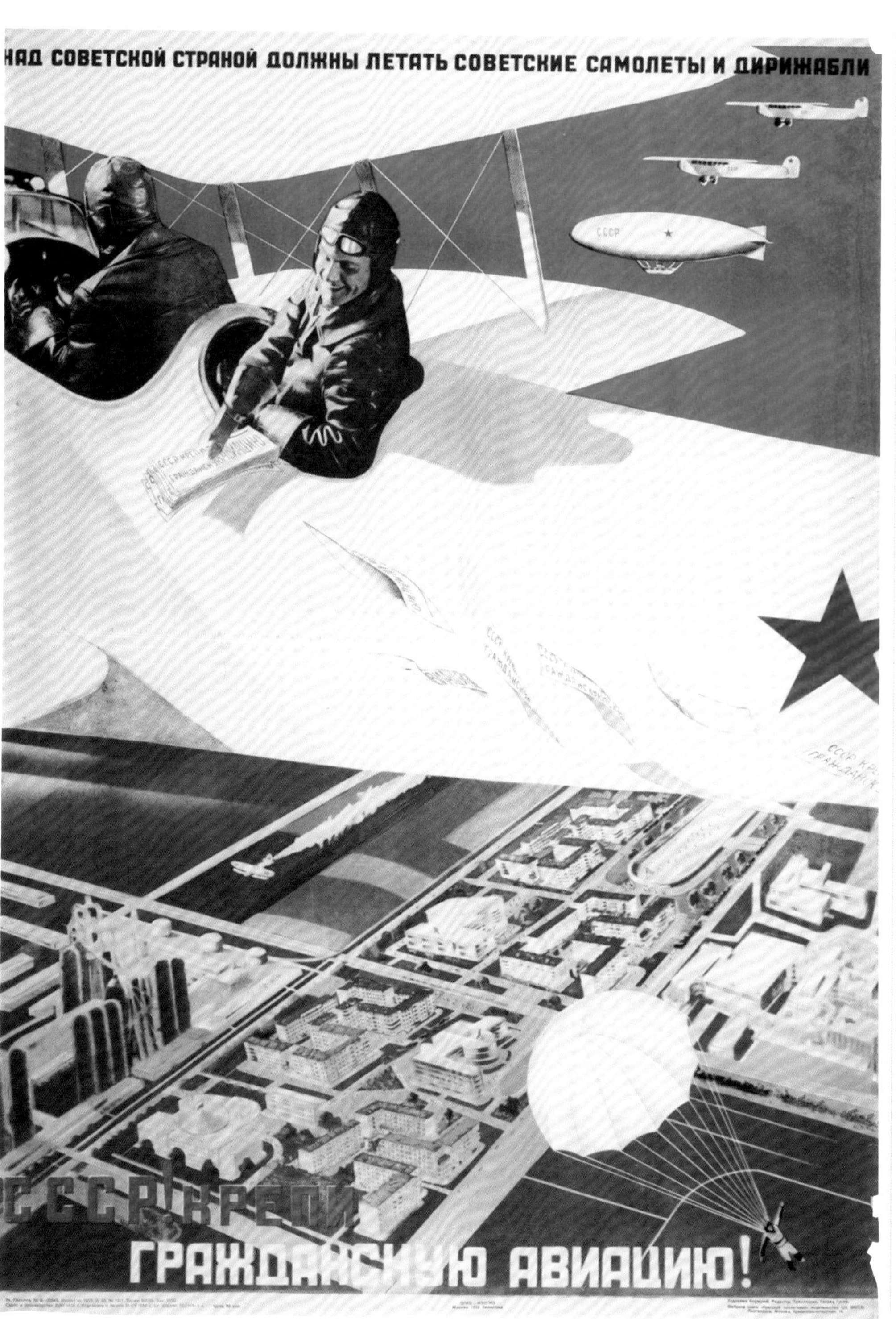

"USSR! STRENGTHEN THE NATION'S AVIATION!"

At the end of the Civil War, the young Soviet state was in possession of a handful of aircraft – mainly captured from foreign interventionist forces – of very different manner, utility and model. Over the next decade, Soviet aviation expanded rapidly and was honed, through designers such as Mikoyan, Yakolev and Ilyushin, to encompass both civil and military air fleets.

Zeppelins, airliners, and mail planes are all showcased here, though as the additional text spells out this was still often more of an aspiration than a reality.

This photomontage was the work of Koretsky and Povolovskaya, and was published by the Red Proletarian Book Factory, Moscow, in April 1933.

But the breakneck pace of Soviet industrialisation was achieved at a high human cost. After the ravages of Civil War and famine, the Bolsheviks re-introduced a measure of private enterprise and private ownership, allowing small businesses to operate under the auspices of the New Economic Policy (NEP) which continued through 1921-28. But it was Josef Stalin who, as General Secretary, succeeded Lenin as leader of the Communist Party of the Soviet Union (CPSU) and who drove the country's industrialisation programme and the collectivisation of agriculture which followed. By the end of the decade, the NEP programme had been reversed – a policy change made explicit in the tenor of Kalmykov's poster (page 35) which castigates 'private entrepreneurs' and 'corrupt speculators'.

КОМСОМОЛЬЦЫ
НА УДАРНЫЙ
СЕВ

"THE KOMSOMOL - SOWS THE GROUND!"

As Gustav Klutsis shows in this photomontage, from 1931, the Komsomol – Young Communist League – were at the forefront of the campaign to collectivise agriculture.

Though today this image may appear to be no more than a pastiche of all things Soviet – evoking a Marina Lewycka novel or a *Leningrad Cowboys* movie – at the time, the political theatre of young political activists leaving the towns to help bring in the harvest was both inspirational and an endeavour of vital significance for the Soviet economy.

With his vivid colours, streaming banners and bold modernist typography designed by the Red Proletarian workshop, Klutsis succeeds in evoking the passionate commitment and political will of the age.

The first Five-Year Plan (1928-32) inaugurated a series of huge infrastructure projects such as the Dnieper Dam (1927-32), designed to supply hydro-electricity to the new and burgeoning cities and towns, followed by the construction of the White Sea-Baltic Canal (1931-33), a manually dug canal of some 227km in length which connected the White Sea in the north to Lake Onega and the Baltic in the west of the country. The railway infrastructure was extended to allow the shipping of raw materials and new industrial cities were created from scratch in the Volga, the Kuzbas and at Magnitogorsk in the Urals. The Moscow metro, the stations of which were faced with marble and lit by chandeliers, became operational in May 1935 and was showcased as one of the great architectural and subterranean engineering projects of the time. Such achievement is the direct focus of Mikhail Taranov's stylised portrayal of the metro system in *Metropolis!* (see below). In a vista reminiscent of the futuristic laboratory paintings of Alexander Deineka, the metro disgorges citizens into the newly re-designed spaces of Soviet modernity.

"METROPOLIS!"

This is a stunning modernist vision of: 'Outstanding transportation for the proletarian capital', in 1932, before the Moscow metro had actually opened. Indeed, several of the lines envisaged, here, were not actually built until the close of the decade.

To contemporary eyes, his vision of Moscow is far more evocative of the Fordist consumerism of the USA rather than Stalin's USSR. Yet, at the time, the Soviet Union sought to be judged on the breakneck speed of its technological advance. This poster finds its echo in *New Moscow* by Yuri Pimenov, wherein an emancipated young woman speeds carefree through a wide city boulevard in the latest model automobile. For a while, it seemed as if you could be a Communist and have it all.

The Moscow metro was designed not only as a means of alleviating congestion on Moscow's ring-roads, but also as a showcase for the Soviet system. No expense was spared on the vast subterranean halls that gleamed like peoples' palaces. Overseen by Lazar Kaganovitch - then viewed as Stalin's possible successor, but an individual who actually outlived the Soviet Union – the metro was partly modelled on the London Underground and was opened in May 1935.

ПРОЛЕТАРСКОЙ СТОЛИЦЕ–ОБРАЗЦОВЫЙ ТРАНСПОРТ

МЕТРО

МЕТРОПОЛИТЕН

"UNDER THE BANNER OF LENIN"

Printed in both Moscow and Leningrad, in 1934, this image marked Stalin's appropriation of Lenin's political legitimacy and his ascendancy as the unchallenged leader of the Communist Party. It would also serve as the model for much of the subsequent official Communist iconography across the globe, with Mao at the time of the Cultural Revolution being particularly in its debt.

However, at this point, Stalin's personal imagery was still fluid. He is shown in his informal revolutionary fatigues rather than in his later guise as war leader, in full dress uniform bedecked with medals. Furthermore, it was usual to see the figure of Lenin depicted in motion – arguing, gesticulating, exhorting – whereas Stalin, by way of contrast, tended to be portrayed in more static poses. The key to the change in Stalin's imagery, here, is the statue of Lenin pointing over the new industrial plants in the background. Stalin is mirroring the actions of his

Several of the posters reproduced here date from the first Five-Year Plan and evoke a tangible sense of dynamism and possibility which arose from the headlong drive to modernisation. The recognition of the transformative power of labour underpins the counter-intuitive equation of *2 + 2 = 5!* – 'the arithmetic of financial planning – plus the enthusiasm of workers' by Yakov Moiseevich Guminer (page 36). Indirectly, the poster also anticipates the cult of the Stakhanovite 'shock worker' – named after Aleksei Stakhanov – who in a single shift mined many tonnes of coal over his quota. During the second Five-Year Plan in the mid 1930s, the cult of the shock worker and the Taylorist efficiency measures with which it became associated, spread throughout the heavy industry, textile and agricultural sectors as a means of boosting over production and increasing morale.

Valentina Kulagina's poster with the strapline *Comrades coal miners!* (page 34) depicts a miner with hydraulic drill and oilskins working away at a sheer coal face. The composition succeeds in suggesting the spatial confinement and harsh conditions of working underground whilst the poster text records new methods of industrial management and the employment of highly trained engineering personnel. The subject of agricultural production (textile swatches and cotton are depicted in the centre of the composition), is the subject of another poster design (page 28) which records fraternal *May Day greetings to the heroes and heroines of socialist toil.*

illustrious predecessor and their will is, according to this poster, one and the same.

Not only is the future dynamic, prosperous, and shaped by new industrial technologies, it is also – as we are shown – subject to a historical logic that finds its fullest expression in Stalin's account of *The Foundations of Leninism* published in 1924, and in the resolutions on agriculture and heavy industry promulgated by the XVII Congress of the Communist Party of the Soviet Union, in 1934.

Produced in time for the Congress, the poster picks out the 'chain of victories' won by Leninism that have made such rapid advances possible in the USSR. These are depicted, in the three images on the side of Stalin's podium, as 'the storming of the Perekop Heights, the victory over chaos' (i.e. the battle won by Frunze over the White forces that effectively ended the Russian Civil War); the creation of new industrial giants, and the collectivisation of 'Socialist agriculture'.

"COMRADES COAL MINERS!"

Signed by the artist Kulagina, printed in the summer of 1933, and distributed in 10,000 copies from Moscow and Leningrad, this poster pre-empted the Stakhanovite movement of 'shock workers' which would claim and greatly enlarge upon this same imagery.

The text of the poster stresses the progress being made by the Party to 'lead the coal industry to Bolshevik victory' through educating the workers in better technique, industrial management and to acquire specialised engineering and technical skills.

"WE WILL SWEEP FROM THE MARKET PLACE THE SPECULATORS AND THE CORRUPT!"

This poster by Kalmykov was published in Moscow and Leningrad, in July 1932, at the climax of the first Five-Year Plan. The struggle against the kulaks from 1929-32 had practically amounted to the declaration of a new civil war in the countryside. Assassinations, grain hoarding, cattle maiming and full-scale peasant risings had all failed to stop the process of collectivisation, as Komsomols, NKVD and army units, from the cities, forced the pace of change.

Under the NEP, there had been approximately 25,000,000 private farms. By the time this poster rolled off the presses, there were only 25,000 (1%) of those remaining.

For Party activists this escalation of class struggle seemed to be another decisive break with the past and a milestone in the building of Communism. The poster contrasts the muscular worker, and doughty collective farm woman, confronting their polar opposites: the speculator, and the greedy kulak's wife. Like the gopher and the caterpillar, in the image from 1924, they start up from out of the ground and threaten to carry off the produce created by others.

The text hammers home the message to collective farmers: 'Do not open any shops to private entrepreneurs or private speculators, who try to make money out of workers and peasants!' This was taken from a resolution passed by the Council of People's Commissars 'On the Production of Goods in the Collective Farms'.

The collective farm, imagined here, is a place of plenty and order, where clothes shops, canteens, and the market stalls, themselves, are all run by co-operatives: by and for the people.

The necessity of increasing agricultural production is a recurrent subject from this period. One of the most iconic posters from the Marx Memorial Library's collection is the design by Gustav Klutsis *The Komsomol - sows the ground!* (page 30). In a characteristic adaption of other photomontage designs of the time, the diminishing perspectival scale of the tractor motif and the angle of its presentation slices through the picture plane, suggesting a ploughed furrow or the powerful vectors of industrial production. The effective colour juxtaposition of red (the iconic colour symbolising divinity) and green with its connotations of the organic and the natural, conveys in a simple and direct way the association of harvest and food production with Bolshevik economy and technological know-how. Other poster designs of the period look to the perceived threats to agricultural production such as Viktor Ivanovich Govorkov's design, *Guard the socialist harvest with vigilance* (page 39) in which the central figure of the farmworker scanning the steppe horizon is flanked by a watch tower and (right) a figure on horseback.

"2 + 2 = 5!"

Stalin's plan for 'Socialism in One Country' was built upon the twin tracks of rapid industrialisation in the towns, and the collectivisation of agriculture in the countryside. If the industrial might of Germany was not to fire the forges of world revolution, and the small Russian proletariat had all but been destroyed in the Civil War: then the working class would have to be fashioned anew in the Soviet Union through these measures.

Every other consideration was subordinated to the fulfilment of the first Five-Year Plan. Progress was so rapid that it was completed a year earlier than planned: in 1932 as opposed to 1933. This was, the poster boldly claims, as the result of: 'The arithmetic of financial planning, plus the enthusiasm of the workers' which enabled the fulfilment in record time.

The Plan was intended to establish the USSR as a major power that could no longer be pushed around, or considered backward. The Party demanded a 110% rise in productivity, but as Stalin argued, in 1931: 'To lower the tempo means to lag behind. And laggards are beaten! ... we don't want to be beaten!'

New cities appeared in Soviet Central Asia and the Urals. The Soviet Union now possessed a tractor building industry. Oil flowed once more from Baku, new railways linked Siberia to the centre, and Lenin's dream of electrification had been fulfilled.

The immediate human cost was never factored in to the picture. Alongside the enthusiasm of the workers who created these wonders, there was also Yagoda's growing army of common criminals and political prisoners, who needed no wages and whose directed labour was also crucial to the achievement of the Five-Year Plan.

For them '2 + 2' really did equal 5.

"WAR PROGRAMMES ON PIG IRON AND STEEL ARE THE ACHIEVEMENT OF WORKERS OF ALL COUNTRIES!"

Produced by the Red Proletarian book factory, in Moscow, in 1932, this poster combines Socialist internationalism with more than a nod to the days of 'War Communism' during the Civil War, The first Five-Year Plan, characterised by enormous construction projects – such as the Magnitogorsk steel plant in the Urals and the Dnieper dam – came to an early close at this time and, in contrast to later plans, largely succeeded in raising industrial output.

Construction was the order of the day, shock workers were celebrated, and through a decree of July 1930, 200 artists were despatched for periods of two months at a time to research and draw inspiration from collective farms and factories.

Stalin's belief in 'Socialism in One Country' - holding the bastion rather than exporting international revolution overseas, necessitated a strong and technologically developed military infrastructure. The iconography of some of the other posters reproduced here look to the overhaul of the armed forces which Stalin believed essential in holding and defending the Soviet bastion - against both internal civil war and external threat. A second poster by Klutsis, *Long live our happy socialist motherland. Long live our beloved great Stalin!* (page 44) deploys his familiar motif of a plunging perspective line with Stalin himself taking the salute from the Kremlin as formations of Soviet aviation pass overhead. Each of the planes is named (in descending size) after leaders of the Revolution - starting with Lenin and Stalin - and then through the various members of the politburo and the Party elite, including Gorky, Voroshilov, Molotov and Mikoyan, with the concluding name that of the Leningrad Party leader, Sergei Kirov. Other posters underline technological and weapons-based innovations e.g. *Investors strengthen the battle forces of the Red Army* (page 42) and the efforts made to professionalise the Soviet military.

ВЫПОЛНЕНИЕ ПРОГРАММЫ ПО ЧУГУНУ, СТАЛИ И ПРОКАТУ —

ДЕЛО ТРУДЯЩИХСЯ ВСЕЙ СТРАНЫ

НАТАЛИЯ ПИНУС 32

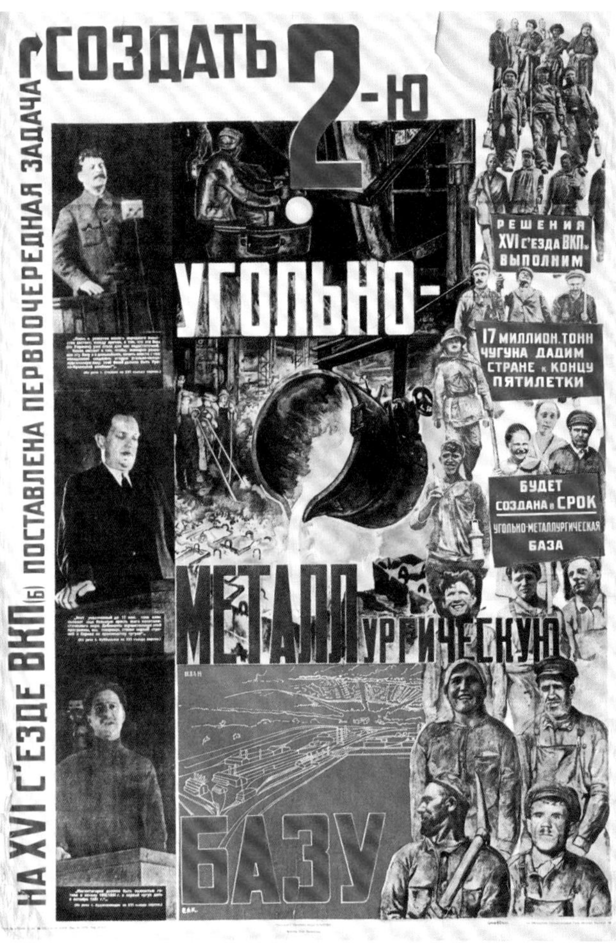

ALL-OUT FOR PRODUCTION:

"THE NATIONAL METALLURGICAL CENTRES"

This poster, published in Moscow and Leningrad, in 1930, is a riot of colour, figures and laden with text. Printed in order to encourage the steel industry, edging it towards the attainment of output quotas for the first Five-Year Plan, it frames the actual process of production with, on the left side, pictures and quotations from the Party leadership, and with pronouncements of the workers, themselves, on the right.

A text snakes round, from the bottom left of the poster, setting the scene from the Congress of the Communist Party: 'Resolutions about priorities on the production of pig-iron'.

Stalin, at the top, proclaims from the rostrum of the 16th Party Congress – held in June to July 1930 – that the 'fact is that this existing centre [of production in the Ukraine] has become insufficient for our national economy. To start with, we have to develop this centre in every possible way and, in a further perspective, to start simultaneously building another centre of metallurgy. These two centres will become the Uralo-Kuznieckiy plant'.

In the middle, Valerian Kuibyshev is quoted as proclaiming at the same Congress that: 'The plan for a 17 million ton increase in production will cause even greater fury in the Capitalist world. Once we have achieved this programme, we will be, comrades, European leaders in the production of pig-iron'.

At the bottom of the poster, Sergo Ordzhonikidze – one of the original Bolshevik leaders, who had seen considerable service in the Civil War – informed Party members that the plant at 'Magnitogorsk should be ready for use around 1932-33 and we should produce the first pig-iron in October 1931'.

On the other side of the poster, the banners born aloft by the workers bear testament that these edicts are being carried out: 'The decisive Congress of the Communist Party came to these conclusions; 17 million tons of pig-iron will be given to the country by the end of the Five-Year Plan; and the metallurgical centre will be built on time'.

In 1930, Kuibyshev was in charge of GOSPLAN – the central planning of the economy – and Ordzhonikidze was the Commissar for Heavy Industry. Worn out through over-work, Kuibyshev would die of a heart attack in January 1935. Laid low by accusations of 'industrial wrecking' – because of his opposition to the Show Trials, Ordzhonikidze shot himself, in 1937.

The cities of Samara and Vladikavkaz were, respectively, re-named in their honour.

But despite these immense and irrevocable changes, there were powerful continuities which linked the pre- and post-Revolutionary eras. From being owned by the Tsar and administered through an extensive court of nobles and civil servants, all land, labour and production was effectively nationalised and passed to the Party and the Soviet State. Although forms of religious worship were proscribed, the highly centralised and elaborate power structures of the Communist Party of the Soviet Union (CPSU) emulated in no small measure the gradations of an imperial power which had also stretched the length and breadth of the Russian land mass. The expected adherence of the political cadres and Party members was no less exacting than the compliance and deference exacted by the Tsars. What Martin Amis has described as the 'violent chaos' of forced collectivisation and famine arising, in part, from the forced repatriation of kulak livestock and food, demonstrated another form of post-imperial hegemony, although executed for different reasons.

The secret police, the Tsarist Okhrana before 1917; the Cheka after the Revolution through to 1922, was successively re-constituted and underwent several name changes in the period explored within this chapter – the GPU (1922-23); OGPU (1923-34) and the NKVD (1934-43), although its core responsibility of State security and surveillance remained unchanged throughout. Lenin's dismantling of the Constituent Assembly and the 'Reign of Terror' must have been seen by many as arbitrary as the punishment meted out by the Okhrana before 1917. Similarly, the cult of personality which started with Lenin and which shaped representations of Stalin within Soviet culture was, in origin, a distortion of the Tsar's patrilineal role as the 'little father' of his people and God's appointed representative on Earth.

"GUARD THE SOCIALIST HARVEST WITH VIGILANCE"

This poster, created by an artist by the name of Govorkov, was part of a print-run of 80,000 published simultaneously in Moscow and Leningrad in April 1935.

Many of the themes current at the time of the Civil War were reworked during the collectivisation of agriculture, with the kulaks becoming synonymous with the White Guards and saboteurs of the earlier era. The very fact that the harvest needed to be under armed guard, in a state which had been at peace for more than a decade, demonstrates just how unpopular collectivisation was with large sections of the peasantry.

As the poster makes clear, the whole of village society – from the elderly, to men serving in the militia and Komsomol, right down to the boys and girls of the Young Pioneers – needed to be mobilised in order protect vital food supplies and ward off insurrection in the countryside.

ЗОРКО ОХРАНЯЙ СОЦИАЛИСТИЧЕСКИЙ УРОЖАЙ

MIKHAIL TUKHACHEVSKY (1893-1937)

Mikhail Tukhachevsky graduated top of his class at the Alexander Military Academy and was commissioned as a lieutenant in the Semenovsky Guards Regiment, on the eve of the First World War. Decorated for bravery under fire, he was captured by the Germans, in 1914, and distinguished himself by the frequency and audacity of his escape attempts.

Finally managing to escape successfully, in 1917, he returned to Russia and immediately rallied to the Bolshevik Revolution. Appointed as one of Trotsky's 'military specialists' - former Tsarist officers who had gone over to join the Red Army - he took charge of the defence of Moscow against the White Guards, in 1918.

Thereafter, his rise was meteoric. He re-organised the 1st Red Army, re-taking Simbirsk - Lenin's birthplace - on 9 September 1918; and liberating Samara from the Czech Legion, on 8 October 1918. On Frunze's initiative, he took command of the 5th Red Army, in the spring of 1919, shattering General Khanzin's Cossacks, in May, and taking Perm and Ufa in quick succession. After defeating General Dutov's White 'Army of the West', in a protracted fire-fight which raged across great expanses of forest, his men liberated Omsk on 15 November 1919.

Further victories followed, with Tukhachevsky defeating Denikin on the heights of Bataisk and sweeping the Whites out of Ekaterinodar, their last stronghold in the mountains of the Caucasus.

Assigned overall command of the war against Poland, in 1920, he led a lightning campaign that saw the Ukraine freed and Red units in the outskirts of Warsaw, by August. However, Budyonny, Stalin and Voroshilov failed to support his advance and, with over-extended supply lines, a Polish counter-attack spelled unexpected disaster for his forces on the Vistula.

He had staked everything on the belief that the presence of Red troops would be enough to spark risings of the Polish working class, in their support. When this did not happen, the conflict took on a patriotic, rather than internationalist, perspective that had major long-term significance for the Red Army. Henceforth, it would begin to think of itself as an increasingly Russian and regular formation, as opposed to a nation-less spearhead of world revolution.

The defeat spurred Tukhachevsky on to make a full study of military science. Though he would break the Kronstadt rebellion, which threatened Soviet power in March 1921, and put down a series of risings by kulaks in the Tambov region; the rest of his career would be spent working on the evolution of new military doctrines, many of which are still taught to this day.

In 1931, he began his re-organisation of the Soviet military, with the support of his friends Ordzhonikidze, Kuibyshev and Kirov. While they endured, he could hope to counterbalance the hatred and professional jealousy of the plodding Budyonny and the vainglorious Voroshilov. When they had disappeared from the scene, the climate would suddenly turn chill upon the most accomplished Soviet commander of the age.

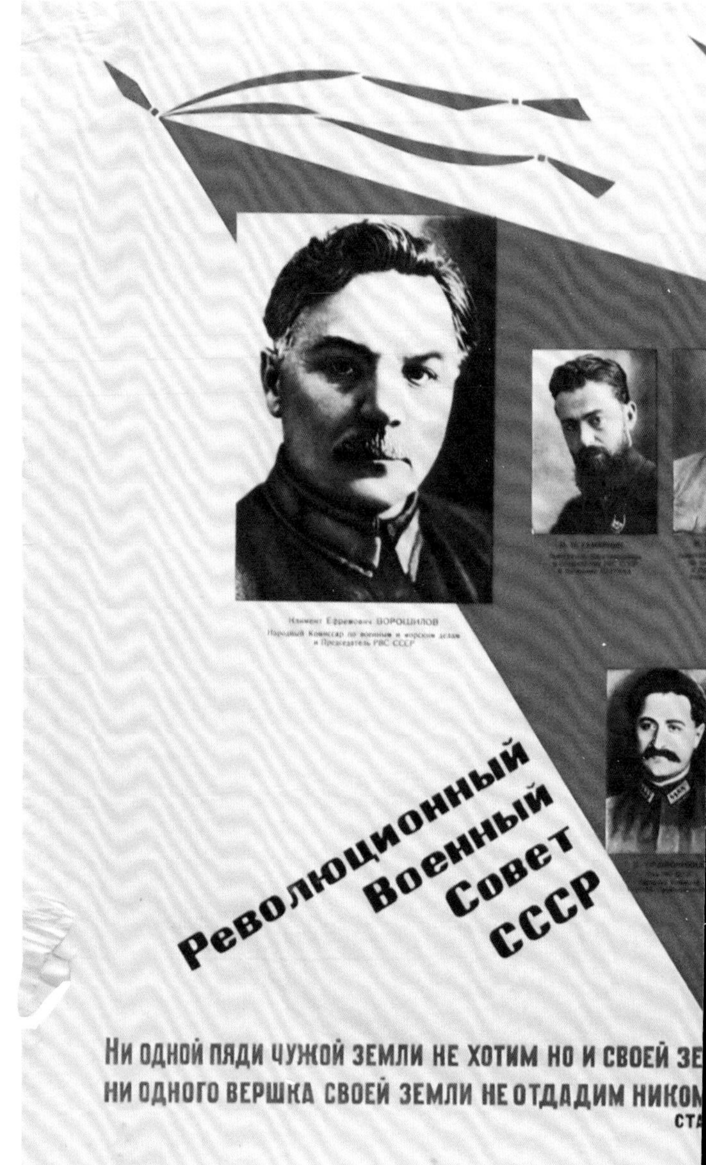

"THE REVOLUTIONARY WAR COUNCIL OF THE USSR"

Published in November 1933 in both Moscow and Leningrad, this photomontage shows the old Soviet High Command – who had all risen to prominence during the Civil War – at the apogee of their power and self-confidence. Indeed, the quote from Stalin proclaims their pledge that while: 'We do not want even a hands breadth of a foreign land, we will not give away even a finger-tip of our own land to anyone'.

Though Klement Voroshilov, as National Commissar of War, is given prominence at the head of the group, it was Mikhail Tukhachevsky (pictured on the top row, third from the left) who provided the inspiration and dynamism for the Red Army. He created a modern mechanised force, with armoured divisions and airborne support that was equal to any in the world. Unfortunately he also

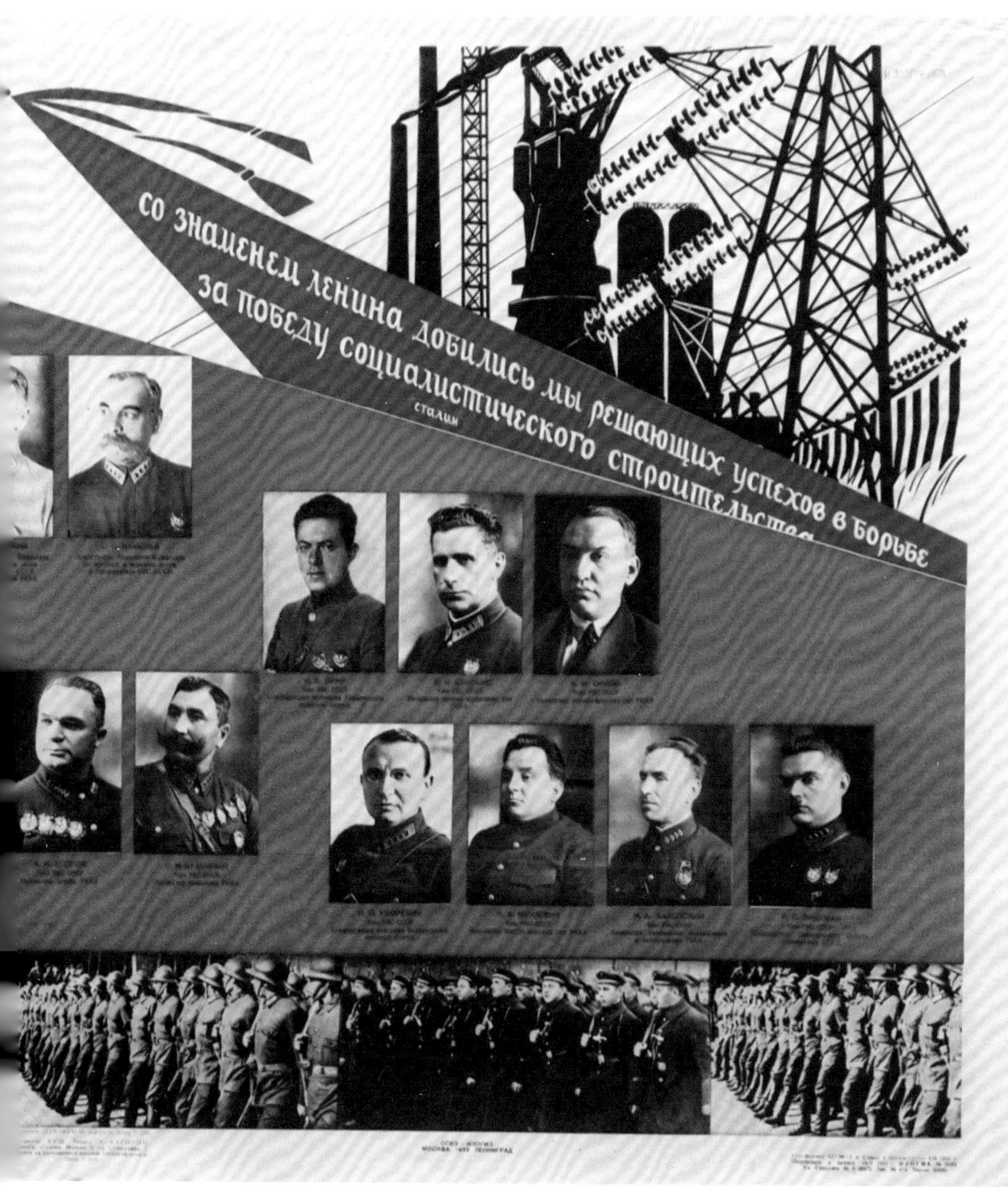

demanded by Germany were high. The signing of the Brest-Litovsk Treaty in March 1918 ceded over one third of Soviet territory to Germany - including much of the Ukraine - one of the central food producing regions of the former Russian Empire.

со знаменем ленина добились мы решающих успехов в борьбе за победу социалистического строительства
сталин

As Brandon Taylor has noted, the programme for monumental propaganda (discussed in chapter one), fell between the signing of the treaty with Germany and the full mobilisation of 'War Communism' in the face of internal civil conflict. By the Autumn of 1918, the Bolsheviks faced the biggest threat to the survival of the Revolution.[2] In April of that year, the Western powers had intervened on the side of the Counter-Revolutionary forces, motivated by the pressing need to keep Russia on side in the war against Germany. In the absence of a second, Eastern front, the Western allies faced an even more protracted war of attrition with soldiers dug in along a static line of defence on both sides. Both the refusal of the Western powers to recognise the leaders of the Revolution and their subsequent active opposition to the regime's actual survival ensured that the initial years of the Soviet Union were those of embattled and hostile isolation - conditions which determined not just the collective psychological outlook of successive Soviet leaders but which also delineated the pragmatic and instrumental approach to all cultural planning and policy issues.

aroused the jealousy of Voroshilov and Semyon Budyonny (third row, third from the left) who believed in the supremacy of cavalry over tanks and connived to bring about his fall during the great purges.

Of the fourteen senior commanders shown here, in 1933, only two – Voroshilov and Budyonny – would survive the decade. The Red Army would be left without leadership, experience and intellect at the very point when it was most needed. Yet, as Dmitri Shostakovich went to work digging tank traps outside Leningrad, in the winter of 1941, he recalled his friend Tukhachevsky who had modernised the city's defenses just prior to his arrest. The young composer had no doubt that it was this foresight which had saved the city and paused on his shovel, for a moment, in order to give thanks.

The new Bolshevik order faced major pre-occupations between 1919-21, not least internal Civil War, famine and the western expeditionary forces which had been landed in Murmansk and Archangel. One of the first executive orders taken by the new Bolshevik leaders was to extricate Russia as it was then, from what was perceived to be the dynastic conflict of the First World War. The concessions

ИЗОБРЕТАТЕЛЬ, КРЕПИ БОЕВ
„В ЦЕЛЯХ НАДЛЕЖАЩЕЙ ПОСТАНОВКИ МАССОВОГО ИЗОБРЕТАТЕЛЬСКОГО ДВИЖЕНИЯ СОЗДАТЬ В ЧАСТЯХ И СОЕДИНЕНИЯХ РККА ЯЧЕЙКИ ИЗОБРЕТАТЕЛЕЙ РККА".
(Из приказа Реввоенсовета СССР, № 13, от 25 января 1932 г.)
КРАСНОАРМЕЙЦ
ИЗОБРЕТАТЕЛЬСКИ
ВСЕСОЮЗНО
Цена 40 коп.

The cultural sphere was recognised as a crucial weapon in the nascent state's battles for hearts and minds. An initial steer was given in the essay *Art & Revolution* (1924) in which Leon Trotsky, Commissar for Military and Naval Affairs (1918-1925) and a highly respected veteran of the October Revolution and the Civil War, mapped out the Party's expectations of the Soviet avant-garde; art was to have relative autonomy and independence - enabling its practitioners to find their way to the international workers' cause through willing adherence and visual experimentation rather than central diktat. In retrospect, Trotsky can be seen as mediating the highly pluralistic environment of the mid-NEP period in which many artistic persuasions and orientations - from complete abstraction to forms of figuration, and a range of intermediate stylistic practices in between, competed for the attention of the Party and the engagement of the state - effectively the principal commissioning and employing organisations, regardless of the small scale private enterprise permitted by the NEP.

But the pattern for the future politicisation of cultural practice can be traced to the collection of works, *V.I. Lenin on Literature and Art* and Lenin's *Party Organisation and Party Literature* (1905). Although the overarching pattern in mind was realist literature (Lenin was a great admirer of Charles Dickens), the implications for other forms of artistic practice and the need for their subservience to the political objectives of the state are clear enough in Lenin's formulations.

"INVENTORS STRENGTHEN THE BATTLE FORCES OF THE RED ARMY!"

Designed by Suryaninov, Usynin and Yakovlyev, and issued by the Military Revolutionary Council, at the beginning of 1933, this poster spells out the need – forced home again and again by Tukhachevsky – for specialist units within the Red Army.

In particular, while a group of young soldiers is taking instruction in stripping down a machine gun, the call is being made through the text for: 'Red Army soldiers and ... navy members, who develop innovative solutions, to join the All-Union Society of Inventors!'

ю мощь красной армии!

„...Из страны слабой и не подготовленной к обороне Советский Союз превратился в страну, могучую в смысле обороноспособности, в страну, готовую ко всяким случайностям, в страну, способную производить в массовом масштабе все современные орудия обороны и снабдить ими свою армию в случае нападения извне“.

(И. СТАЛИН)

КРАСНОФЛОТЦЫ, ВНОСИТЕ СВОИ
ЕДЛОЖЕНИЯ, ВСТУПАЙТЕ В ЧЛЕНЫ
БЩЕСТВА ИЗОБРЕТАТЕЛЕЙ!

ИЗОГИЗ
З Ленинград

Худ. Сурвиннов. Редактор Усыкин. Техред А. А. Яковлев.

This was not just talk. The decisive defeat of the Japanese army at Khalkhin Gol, in 1939, showed precisely how effective the Red Army could be when well led and well armed. Tragically, these lessons would have to be relearned after the military catastrophes of 1941.

ВЛАДИМИР ЛЕНИН
ИОСИФ СТАЛИН
МАКСИМ ГОРЬКИЙ
МИХАИЛ КАЛИНИН
ВЯЧЕСЛАВ
КЛУЦИС 35
ДА ЗДРАВСТВУЕТ НАША СЧАСТЛИВАЯ СОЦИАЛИСТИЧЕСКАЯ РОДИНА.
ДА ЗДРАВСТВУЕТ НАШ ЛЮБИМЫЙ ВЕЛИКИЙ СТАЛИН!

"LONG LIVE OUR HAPPY SOCIALIST MOTHERLAND. LONG LIVE OUR BELOVED, GREAT STALIN!"

Gustav Klutsis produced this photomontage poster, showing a highly stylised vision of a May Day parade, in November 1935. Stalin and Voroshilov take the salute on Red Square and acknowledge both the crowd and the waves of aircraft passing overhead.

The text exhorts the whole of the 'Soviet nation to build the air fleet', while the wings of the aircraft – loosely based upon the ill-fated prototype of the 'Maxim Gorky' airliner – bear the names of Soviet heroes, past and present. The names of Lenin and Stalin come first and are followed interestingly enough by Gorky, himself, then – in descending order of type face – Kalinin, Molotov, Voroshilov, Ordzhonikidze, Kaganovich, Kosior, Chubar, Mikoyan, Andreyev and, finally, the late Sergei Kirov. While Ordzhonikidze, Kosior and Chubar would all fall during the purges, the rest of the grouping around Stalin would enjoy long careers at the heart of the Soviet government.

This snapshot of official opinion shows their relative standing in the hierarchy during the mid-1930s, though Voroshilov's relatively modest ranking in the fly past is not reflected by his prominence, beside Stalin, on the mausoleum.

Although the 1920s was largely characterised by relative cultural pluralism with various artistic groupings and interests vying for the ear of the Soviet State and the Party - the principal sources of patronage and effective employment, the trend which gradually emerged favoured the realist academic and figurative forms of painting and sculpture. The so-called 'Wanderers' or 'Itinerant' artists of the later nineteenth century - such as Ilya Repin (1844-1930), Vasili Perov (1833-1882) and Vasili Surikov (1848-1916) who had broken away from the Imperial Academy of St Petersburg to pursue painting with a contemporary narrative comment, famous examples of which included Repin's *Barge Haulers of the Volga* (1873), provided the preferred model for emulation by the Soviet avant-garde. The work of the Itinerants had also been supported by the critic and revolutionary Nikolai Chernyshevsky (1828-1889) whose critical writings on art and aesthetics such as *What Is To Be Done* (1863) was a significant influence on Lenin's pragmatic approach to directing artistic policy.[3]

Realism was judged the most effective means of communicating the values of the nascent Soviet state to both the industrial proletariat and agricultural workers alike. Central to the Party's approach to such art were the ideas of '*partiinost*' - adherence to the directions of the Party and '*narodnost*' - which can be understood as the promotion of ideas and values which reflect the interests of the people.[4] These principles increasingly steered both the formation of cultural policy and influenced those organisations which were concerned to gain Party and state favour in commissions and in securing influence. Artistic practice which deviated from this tendency - either through abstraction or through more subjective forms of individual expression, was seen as symptomatic of 'bourgeois formalism' and its practitioners discouraged - although more severe sanctions were to follow in the years ahead.

"ALL SOVIET NATIONS WILL VOTE FOR FURTHER STRENGTHENING OF OUR BRAVE RED ARMY AND THE WAR NAVY!"

Under the streaming banners of the Red Army, Airforce, and Navy, the Soviet soldier and sailor steel their gaze towards a confident future. The sailor's capband identifies him as a crewman aboard the battleship 'October Revolution'.

Illustrated by V. Stenberg and published in vast numbers – the second edition of the poster ran to 200,000 copies – this poster extolling patriotic and military virtue was published in April 1938.

Commissioned as the 'Gangut', in 1911, the battleship was renamed, in 1918, after it had participated in the mutiny of the Baltic fleet and rallied to the Bolshevik cause. Thereafter, it saw desperate service during the siege of Leningrad, in 1941-43, before being converted to a training ship in 1954.

Contrary to appearances, the Soviet military was experiencing a profound crisis in 1938. Its best commanders had been arrested, armoured units laid up, and specialist training departments disbanded. Up to 80% of colonels had disappeared and the services fully subordinated to the will of the Party.

While this may have made good sense to Stalin and Voroshilov in the Kremlin, the reliance upon youthful enthusiasm over leadership and technology – as evidenced by this poster – would soon bear bitter fruit during the disastrous Winter War with Finland. In 1939-40, the Finnish proletariat – largely broken in Mannerheim's concentration camps – failed to rise and Voroshilov's badly led and poorly equipped conscripts were cut to pieces on the Karelian Isthmus.

20
ЛЕТ
ВЛКСМ
КИМ
МАРАТ
ДА ЗДРАВСТВУЕТ ЛЕНИНСКО-СТАЛИНСКИЙ КОМСОМОЛ–
ШЕФ ВОЕННО-МОРСКОГО ФЛОТА
И ВОЕННО-ВОЗДУШНОГО ФЛОТА!

However, as Brandon Taylor has noted, the Soviet Union was not exceptional in the sponsoring of figuration *per se*. Realism in painting and sculpture had been widespread throughout Europe in the early 1920s and 1930s.[5] In the aftermath of the 1914-1918 'Great War' one academic has described the political appetite for a 'call to order' within cultural practice as a form of chastened response to the economic and social legacy of the protracted conflict which had re-drawn the map of the Western powers. In France, the United States, Great Britain and Italy for example, variations of figurative and academic painting and sculptural styles were widespread, co-existing with more avant-garde and abstract practice. But the Soviet Union was to become exceptional in the efforts taken both to direct and codify cultural practice and in the awareness of the political and social purposes that it could serve. What Cullerne Bown has described as a 'comprehensive Bolshevik policy towards the arts' took shape gradually, culminating in the 1932 edict which established Soviet Socialist Realism as the prescribed artistic style of Soviet Russia. But indications were already apparent as to the future drift of cultural policy with the founding in 1922 of the Association of Artists of Revolutionary Russia (AKhRR) whose members were committed to depicting '...the present day: the life of the Red Army, the workers, the peasants, the revolutionaries, and the heroes of labour'.[6] Other organisations such as the Society of Easel Painters (OSt) explored contemporary subject matter (life in the cities and the factories) through a combination of figuration and techniques taken from modernism. Whilst earlier, principally modernist, accounts of Soviet art have given emphasis to the avant-garde artists who favoured abstraction in this period, they were by no means in the majority, and irrespective of Party intervention, forms of figurative painting and sculpture remained the norm - even without any explicit steer from state or Party.

In 1932 the Central Committee centralised its oversight in respect of all Soviet cultural and literary groups. Two years later the First Congress of the Writers' Union formalised the principles of Socialist Realism which was to become the mandated style for all artistic practice within Soviet controlled and administered territory. Although variations in practice evolved after Stalin's death in 1953, Soviet Socialist Realism remained as the officially sanctioned cultural style until the fall of the Berlin Wall in 1989. Artists either complied with it, or they ceased to practice - choosing in the words of one contemporary - 'the genre of silence'.

But in one of the ironies of the system, the codification of so much artistic practice, although achieved at a high cost, especially in terms of the constraint on artistic imagination and the punitive action taken against many, at least conceded art's crucial social and civic role within modernity. Such a proposition was never acknowledged in the West, despite the alleged value placed on artistic and cultural expression.

What happened in the USSR also underlined the extent to which both Russian and Soviet cultural norms had evolved in distinct disaffinity with those of the West. Cold War accounts, such as Camilla Gray's *The Russian Experiment in Art 1863-1922* (first published in 1962), reflected the preconceptions of looking at Soviet culture and its Russian antecedents through a distorting Western - and modernist - lens.

THE YOUNG COMMUNIST LEAGUE IN ACTION:
"TWENTY YEARS OF THE KOMSOMOL"

With a policy of national service established by the new Socialist state, the Young Communist League quickly became a significant organisation within the armed forces.

In this poster by N. Denisov and N. Vatolina, the navy – represented by a sailor from the newly refurbished battleship 'Marat' – and the airforce – showcasing the new Yak fighters and more generic sketches of planned Ilyushin bombers – are shown at the forefront of the nation's defences.

Published by the Iskusstvo plant, in July 1938, the image boldly proclaims: 'Long Live the Leninist-Stalinist Komsomol – the leader of the War Navy and the War Air forces!'

ВПЕРЕД! ПОБЕДА БЛИЗКА!

ГВАРДИЯ

THE GREAT PATRIOTIC WAR

TASS WINDOWS AT THE FRONT 1941-45

The political poster went into battle on the very first day of the Great Patriotic War (1941–1945), just as it had during WWI, the Revolution and ensuing Civil War

In the days, weeks and months following Vyacheslav Molotov's highly charged radio broadcast announcing the German invasion of the USSR four men would gather around a table, curtains drawn, to begin their evening's work.[1]

Mikhail Kupriyanov (1903-1991), Porfiry Krylov (1902-1990) and Nikolai Sokolov (1903-2000), in whose Moscow apartment they met, were artists collectively known as Kukryniksy – a pseudonym derived from the first syllable of each of their names. The fourth man, Samuil Marshak (1887-1964), was a poet. Together they worked in their makeshift studio designing posters that would be hand stencilled and used to spread the latest news about the war. Their work was often interrupted by air-raid sirens requiring them to leave Sokolov's flat and assemble outside to work as temporary firemen to further assist the war effort.[2]

The posters they produced became known as TASS Windows (*Okna TASS*) – so called because they were displayed in shop windows (*okna*), in town squares, and on walls all over the city. News about the war was relayed from the front by TASS, the official Soviet telegraph agency, whereupon the three members of Kukryniksy would sketch out their ideas – giving visual expression to the last-minute communiqués – whilst Marshak translated them into humorous verse. The immediacy of this method of disseminating information meant that the first Kukryniksy poster was completed, and displayed all over Moscow, within 24 hours of the start of the war.[3] This scenario was repeated for the duration of the war by other teams of artists and writers, not just in Moscow, but also in towns and cities throughout the Soviet Union.

"FORWARD! VICTORY IS NEAR!"
This poster, published by the State Publishing House Iskusstvo in Moscow and by the Red Proletarian works in Moscow, in 1944, was used by Robin Page Arnot to publicise the war effort in Britain, for the 'Aid Russia Campaign'.

The skies are filled by Yakolevs and Stormoviks, while the new T-34 tanks roll on inexorably towards Berlin, and banners stream in the wind. The leading soldier is a veteran of several campaigns and has been decorated with the Order of the Red Banner.

By summer 1944, Soviet propaganda was keeping pace with reality. The poster was distributed in time for the general offensive launched on 21st June 1944, which would see Bucharest and the Western Ukraine liberated by the end of August, and the Baltic republics freed by the end of October.

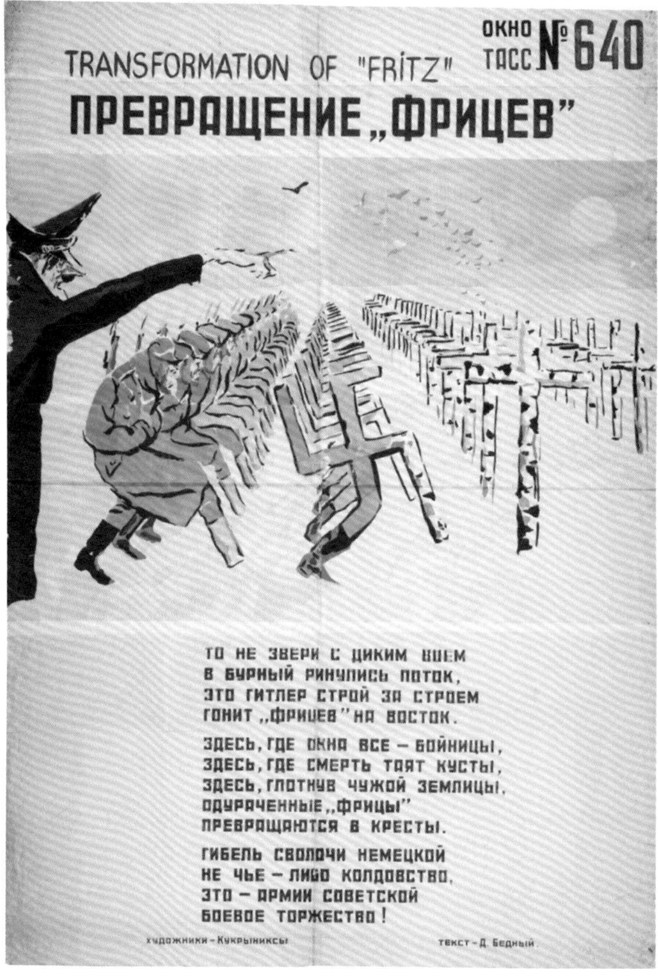

"THE TRANSFORMATION OF FRITZ"

Beneath a flock of vultures, lines of goose-stepping German soldiers – pejoratively referred to in the title and text as 'Fritz' – are depicted in this TASS Windows poster cowering under Hitler's command as he sends them eastwards to their deaths. The first row of men, red-nosed and hunched in submission, begins to transform into swastikas. The second row sees them partially converted into burial crosses of white birch – the national tree of Russia – a transformation that is complete in the final rows. The poster was designed by the collaborative trio, the Kukryniksy, who frequently caricatured Hitler with the exaggerated facial features of a long, thin, pointed nose and chin along with a flat, black, 'comb-over' hairstyle – partially obscured in this rendering by his equally exaggerated cap. He is typically shown, as is evident here, with long arms and thin, bony, claw-like hands. The poster, produced in 1942, with a text by the poet Demian Bednyi, is an affirmation of the strengthened Soviet confidence in a possible triumph brought about by the Red Army's successful counteroffensive in the Battle of Moscow, during which the Wehrmacht was forced to retreat.

The Great Patriotic War was the name given to Soviet involvement in World War Two between 22nd June 1941 and 9th May 1945. That the war was deemed particularly patriotic stems from Molotov's radio address of 22nd June 1941, during which he made comparisons to both the Russian defeat of Napoleon in 1812 and the Russian involvement in WWI, each of which had been described as *otechestvennaia voina* (a patriotic war): the Latin word *patria* means 'the fatherland'.[4] In his announcement Molotov set the tone of the war by calling for the Soviet people to 'wage a victorious war for our Fatherland' and to respond to the German invasion in a manner 'worthy of real Soviet patriots'.[5] The injustice felt by the Soviet people over the events leading up to the war, as well as the invasion itself, had a polarising effect – friends and enemies; heroes and villains; the brave and the cowardly were all readily demarcated. Posters helped to affirm the legitimacy of the Soviet position.

A powerful and effective weapon the propaganda poster was used, not only during specific conflicts, but also more generally in the fight against fascism during the 1930s: a role that it continued to play throughout the Great Patriotic War. Artistic controls, though, had led to a decline into uniformity following the Civil War.[6] The onset of the Great Patriotic War, however, with its culture of polarity, reinvigorated the tradition whilst at the same time bringing a resurgence of the symbolism that had characterised the visual arts in the Bolshevik era. With high levels of illiteracy across the country, the striking and anarchic Bolshevik poster was reliant upon simple and familiar imagery – with a minimum of text – to effectively convey its message: that poster art needed to be accessible to the masses.[7] Nevertheless, by the beginning of the war literacy rates had still not increased substantially[8] and so the visual message continued to be paramount: poster designs still needed to be concise and expressive. Posters of this period abound with images that were intended to rally the population against the enemy.

Пьём воду родного Днепра,
будем пить из Прута, Немана и Буга!
очистим советскую землю
от фашистской нечисти!
ВИКТОР ИВАНОВ -43

"WE DRINK THE WATERS OF OUR DNIEPER, WE WILL DRINK FROM THE PRUT, NIEMEN AND BUG TOO! WE WILL CLEAN OUR SOVIET LAND FROM THE FASCIST DIRT!"

Illustrated by V. Ivanov, with typography by the Gosplanizdata workshop, this poster was printed in December 1943, and captures just one representative moment on the road towards victory. With the Germans routed, a young soldier quenches his thirst – symbolically reclaiming his homeland from his foes – before rejoining the advance and crossing the bridgehead.

ОКНО ТАСС №1079
„НОВЕЙШАЯ“ ЕВРОПА
„Молодые силы всей Европы: теперь собраны у нас“, говорят берлинские дикторы. Под „молодыми силами“ подразумеваются кроме Симы и Цанкова, Петэн со слюнявкой, беглый дуче и финны явно нефинского выпуска. Что же, пусть собираются: легче будет их ловить.
ХУДОЖНИКИ – КУКРЫНИКСЫ
„КРАСНАЯ ЗВЕЗДА“

"NEWEST EUROPE"

Employing their own particular style of biting caricature in this TASS Windows poster, the Kukryniksy have depicted fascists – represented by the 'new Europe' of Benito Mussolini, Marshal Philippe Pétain, Horia Sima and Alexander Cankov – as cowardly, weak and powerless, seen here cowering under the dubious protection of a symbolically shell-damaged Nazi helmet. A potent weapon of propaganda, caricature was used to good effect, as in this example, to mock the enemy thereby making him an object of fun rather than of fear.

The Soviet military newspaper *Red Star* reports, according to the poster's text, that far from gaining strength and protection by assembling in one place they will, instead, be easier to catch.

The poster was one of 650 copies, each hand stencilled in Moscow in October 1944.

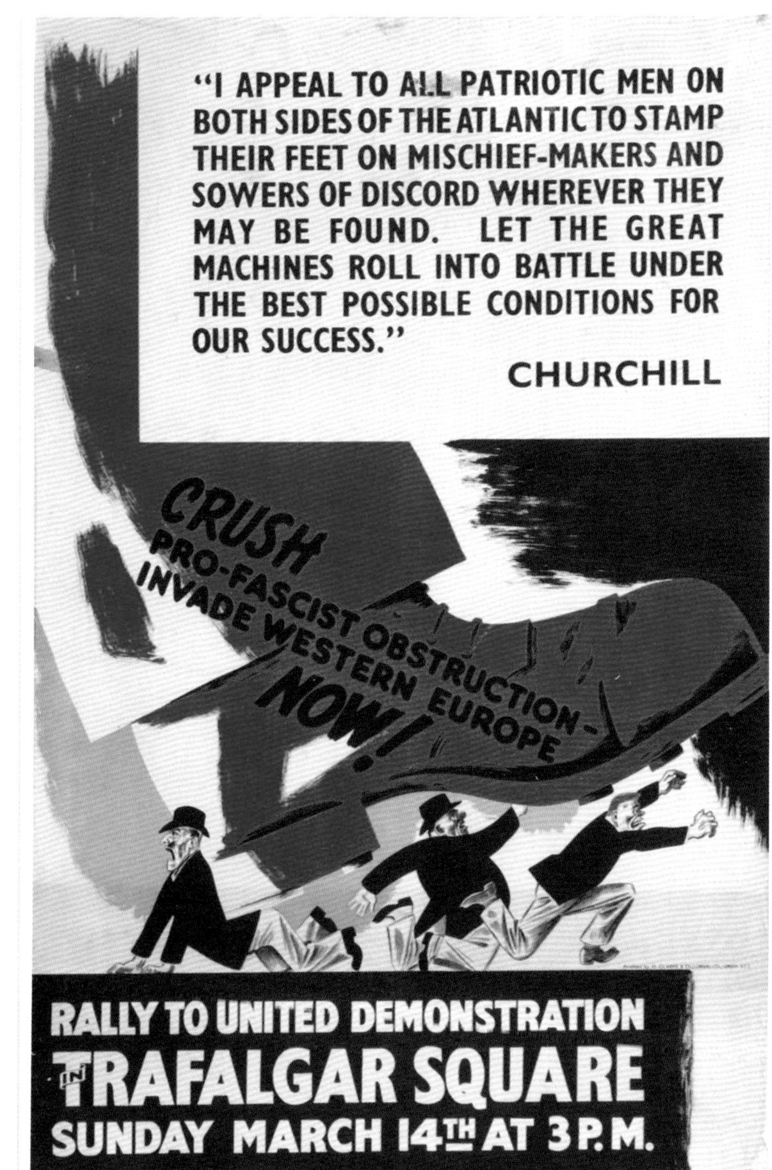

CHURCHILL'S CALL TO:
"INVADE WESTERN EUROPE NOW!"
At the climax of the campaign to open a Second Front in Europe, the Communist Party organised a series of demonstrations in Trafalgar Square that mobilised tens of thousands of protesters. Support was strong in the services and, in a move that was unthinkable at the time of the Russian Civil War, Churchill and Pollitt worked towards the same ends.

This particular poster was printed just a few doors down from the Marx Memorial Library, in Clerkenwell Green, in March 1943.

The demonising or ridiculing of the enemy, through the use of caricature and satire, is a common device in political imagery, although not a novel one: even the old Russian world was characterised by a culture of 'us' and 'them' wherein everyone was either friend or enemy.[9] Self-evidently, the wartime enemy was often foreign,[10] marking a departure from Bolshevik iconography in which enemies were more often domestic – the Tsarist, priest, kulak or capitalist, for example, and others representing the old regime. The exaggeration embodied in caricature ensured that the enemy was easily recognisable whilst also lessening his capacity to induce fear by representing him as an object of pity or fun. The effectiveness of caricature derives from its forensic ability to ruthlessly pinpoint the essence of its subject, whether a natural physical appearance, an acquired characteristic or a small conceit such as clothing or a hairstyle. Its success relies on its capacity for rendering its subject with great accuracy. Hitler's vanity and physical characteristics, for example, were a gift to caricaturists who parodied him mercilessly by depicting him as puny, thin and scrawny, with his idiosyncratic hairstyle and moustache, and long, bony, clawed hands. In the tradition of negative propaganda Germans in general, and Hitler in particular, were represented as weak, bumbling and inept. Images of the invader also focused on his bestial nature, perpetuating older depictions of fascists as wild beasts, wolves and vultures. As a de-humanising device, Soviet propagandists also represented Nazism as a disease, drawing on the influence of Lenin, who used the terminology of parasites to describe class enemies as 'bloodsuckers', 'spiders and 'leeches' and who had defined the most important objective of the Revolution as the cleansing of Russian soil of such harmful creatures.[11] Similarly emotive language is used in the text of the poster by Victor Ivanov (1909-1968) titled *We drink the waters of our Dnieper, we will drink from the Prut, Niemen and Bug too* (page 51), which exhorts the Soviet people to cleanse their native land of 'Nazi vermin'.[12] Nevertheless, effective and successful political imagery does not rely only on the negative propaganda of caricature and satire. The Socialist Realist mode of picture making, which had been state policy since 1932, was well suited to the practice of positive propaganda, which elevates its subject, making every soldier a hero and every man aspire to be one.

ОКНО ТАСС №

ЧТО ПОСЕЕШЬ, ТО ПОЖНЁШЬ

ФАШИСТСКОГО ЗЛОДЕЯ
БРОСАЕТ В ЖАР И В ДРОЖЬ:—
КОЛХОЗНИК БУДЕТ СЕЯТЬ
ОВЕС, ПШЕНИЦУ, РОЖЬ.

В ПОЛЯХ ПОД СОЛНЦЕМ ЗНОЙНЫМ
НАШ УРОЖАЙ ВЗОЙДЕТ.
А ГИТЛЕР СЕЯЛ ВОЙНЫ
И СМЕРТЬ СВОЮ ПОЖНЕТ.

ХУДОЖНИК—П. СОКОЛОВ-СКАЛЯ

И. ПЕТРОВА

"YOU WILL REAP WHAT YOU SOW!"

In this TASS Windows poster from 1944 a determined and heroic Red Army soldier takes centre stage to protect the Kolkhoznik (collective farmer) from a wild-eyed, demonic Hitler. The allegorical inference is that the strength of socialism – seen here in the form of collective farming – will grow and harvest crops to sustain the community whilst the seeds of fascism will reap only death. The poster was designed by Pavel P. Sokolov-Skalya, a well-known painter, and one of many such artists who were quick to respond to the war by designing propaganda posters.

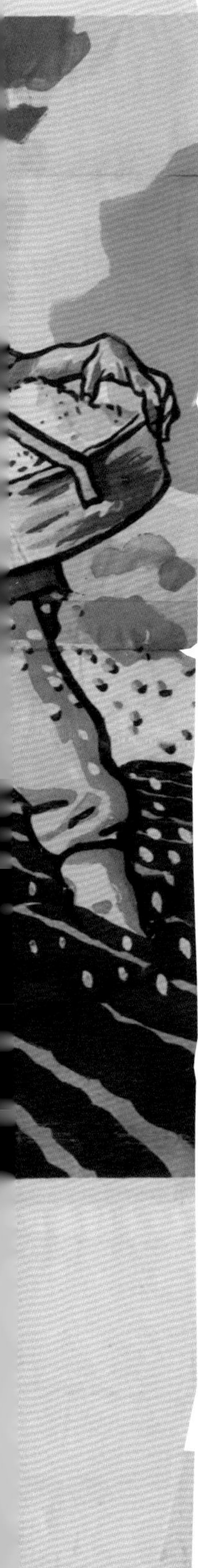

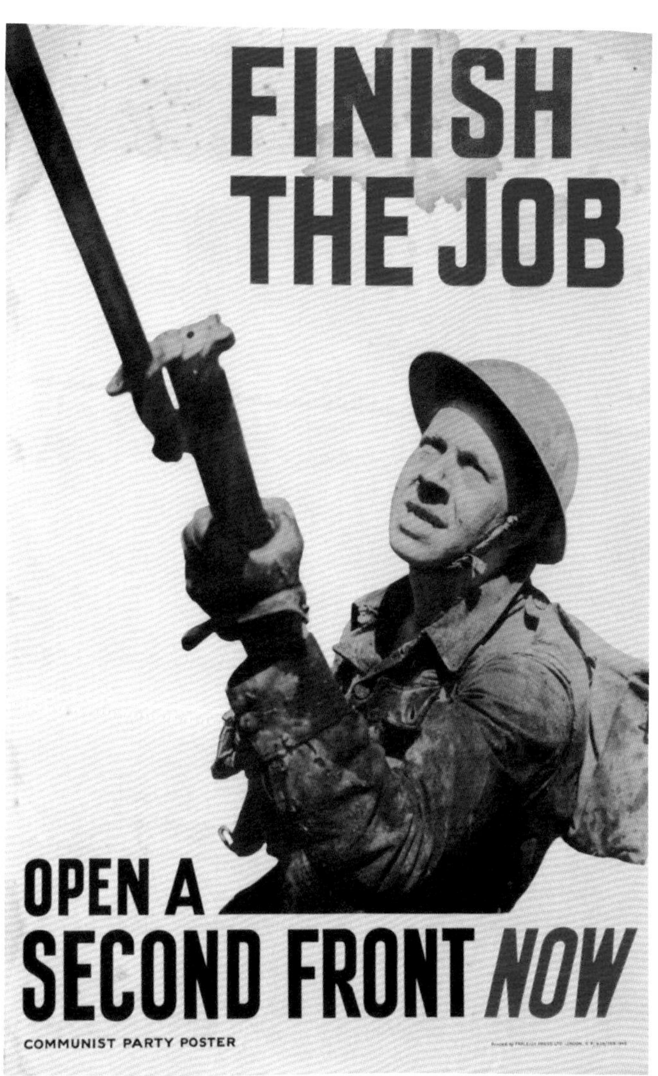

FINISH THE JOB
OPEN A SECOND FRONT NOW
COMMUNIST PARTY POSTER

Although many new, young poster designers contributed to the political imagery of the Great Patriotic War, several of the most prominent artists from the Civil War period were still active at this time. Viktor Deni, Dmitri Moor, Boris Efimov and the members of Kukryniksy, for example, all continued to design posters for this latest conflict. Designers of all ages borrowed from the political art of earlier times whilst re-fashioning its iconography for a new generation. As Victoria Bonnell notes, the fascist depicted during the Great Patriotic War was virtually indistinguishable from the fat capitalist of Bolshevik posters, except for some differences in apparel.[13] The traditional Russian *lubok* (pl. *lubki*) – a type of broadsheet originating as a simple satirical or religious woodcut – was the ancestor of much wartime poster art.[14] Characterised by simple images with an accompanying narrative, and often produced in series, *lubki* resemble the modern day comic strip. The allegorical *lubok*, deeply rooted in Russian culture, was the perfect vehicle for posters aimed at a largely illiterate society because it combined bold and familiar imagery with brief, often witty and satirical captions. The style had been recycled several times, most notably during the Civil War, when the artist Mikhail Cheremnykh (1890-1962) initiated ROSTA Windows posters – a predecessor of the TASS Windows of the 1940s.

"FINISH THE JOB!"

Churchill's war-time pronouncement that it was 'the Russian Army that tore the guts out of the German military machine', had a deep resonance with the British people. Though Britain had taken the lead and endured heroically for the sake of all humanity, in 1940, it now appeared that the Soviet Union was shouldering a disproportionate share of the fight.

Always at its best as a campaigning body, the British Communist Party had swung fully behind the war effort and led the campaign for a Second Front in Europe. Untainted by appeasement and strengthened by its leading role in opposing fascism in the 1930s, its membership rose from approximately 17,000 members in 1939 to more than 45,000 in 1945.

Published by the Farleigh Press, a Party owned business, in February 1943, the poster harnesses the image of the ordinary British Tommy – brave, brusque and businesslike – with a strong and well-honed message. Pulling no punches, it worked to great effect. Soon the slogan would be chalked on walls, and would spring up like wildfire across factories, mines, and freight depots the length and breadth of the land.

ОКНО ТАСС №878
ВСЕНАРОДНАЯ ПОМОЩЬ ФРОНТУ
На всём протяжении войны врагу не удалось превзойти нашу армию по качеству вооружения. В то же время наша промышленность давала фронту всё большее и большее количество боевой техники.
(Из доклада товарища И. В. Сталина 6 ноября 1943 г.)
художник – В. ЛАДЯГИН

ROSTA, the state news agency between 1918 and 1935, produced posters in order to muster support for the new Soviet state. In Moscow alone, over two million ROSTA posters were made.[15] Brought out of storage and dusted off again at the beginning of the Great Patriotic War, the *lubok* aesthetic was appropriated and re-imagined, as both news and propaganda, for a broad viewership.[16] In the making of Windows posters the emphasis was on co-operation and collaboration, and the decision to re-launch them for the war effort was made at a meeting of the Union of Artists within 48 hours of Hitler's invasion.[17] The contribution that TASS posters made was so significant that when President Kalinin made a visit to one of the collectives in December 1941, at the height of the Battle of Moscow, he commented that 'just as historians of the October Revolution have not passed over the ROSTA Windows, so historians of the Patriotic War will not forget the TASS Windows...'[18]

ОКНО ТАСС № 969

НАШ КРЫМ

СОВЕТСКИЙ ВОИН-БОГАТЫРЬ СЕМИМИЛЬНЫМИ ШАГАМИ ПРОХОДИТ ПО БЛАГОДАТНОМУ СОВЕТСКОМУ КРЫМУ, СМЕТАЯ В МОРЕ ОСТАТКИ ПРЕЗРЕННЫХ ГЕРМАНО-РУМЫНСКИХ РАЗБОЙНИЧЬИХ БАНД.

(Газета „Правда“)

ДОЖНИК – П. СОКОЛОВ-СКАЛЯ

"ALL NATIONS HELP OUT AT THE FRONT"

Designed by Vladimir Ladyagin and hand painted in the winter of 1943, this TASS Windows poster acknowledges the help given to the army by the Soviet people. The title, *All nations help out at the Front* and the warm handshake between the two men – representing the military and industry – says it all. The decisive victory of the Red Army in the Battle of Kursk would have been impossible without the support of the Soviet people working in the mines, factories and farms. At the beginning of the war industrial production was slow to adapt to military needs but the Soviet people rose to the challenge and kept their military forces supplied with the weapons, food and equipment needed for victory. The text is taken from a report given by Stalin on 6th November 1943.

"OUR CRIMEA!"

The possessive 'our' in this poster entitled *Our Crimea!*, along with its date of May 1944, tells us that the subject represented here is the Soviet victory over the Wehrmacht in the so-called Crimean Offensive – in fact a series of offensives – fought between 8th April and 12th May 1944. The Red Army's liberation of the Crimea from German occupation, following the fall of Sevastopol on 9th May, led to the mass evacuation of German and Romanian soldiers across the Black Sea. The evacuation was badly mishandled and tens of thousands of men perished, many of whom drowned at sea.

In this TASS Windows poster, number 969, the artist, Pavel P. Sokolov-Skalya, has employed distortion of scale to elevate the soldier and symbolise the Red Army's 'ownership' of the Crimea. The Soviet soldier stands, confident and victorious, astride the peninsula aiming his rifle at the unfortunate enemy drowning in the Black Sea. The poster's text is taken from a report in the Soviet newspaper *Pravda* which refers to the German and Romanian troops as 'pirates'.

ОКНО ТАСС № 793

ОДИН НА ТРОИХ

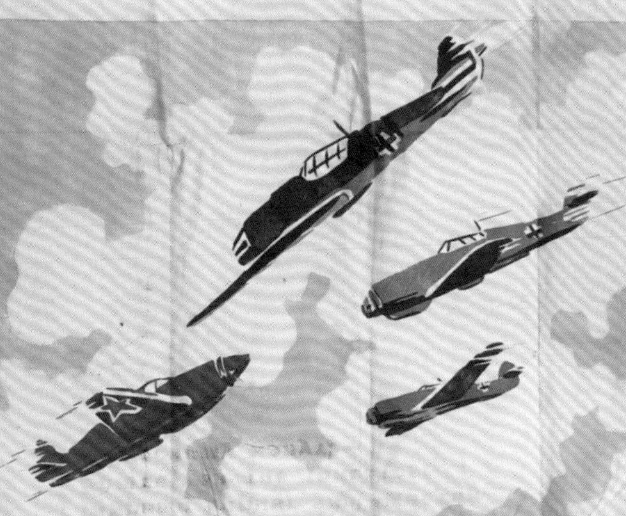

„Мессершмиттов" тройка вьется.
Русский сокол с тройкой бьется.
Геринг крякнул: — гут! —
Жирный Геринг зло смеется,
Брюхо толстое трясется:
— Русскому капут! —

Что случилося? Гляди ты!
Герингу сюрприз:
„Мессершмитты" русским сбиты!
Немцы пламенем обвиты,
Полетели вниз!

художник — П. Саркисян текст — ДЕМЬЯН БЕДНЫЙ

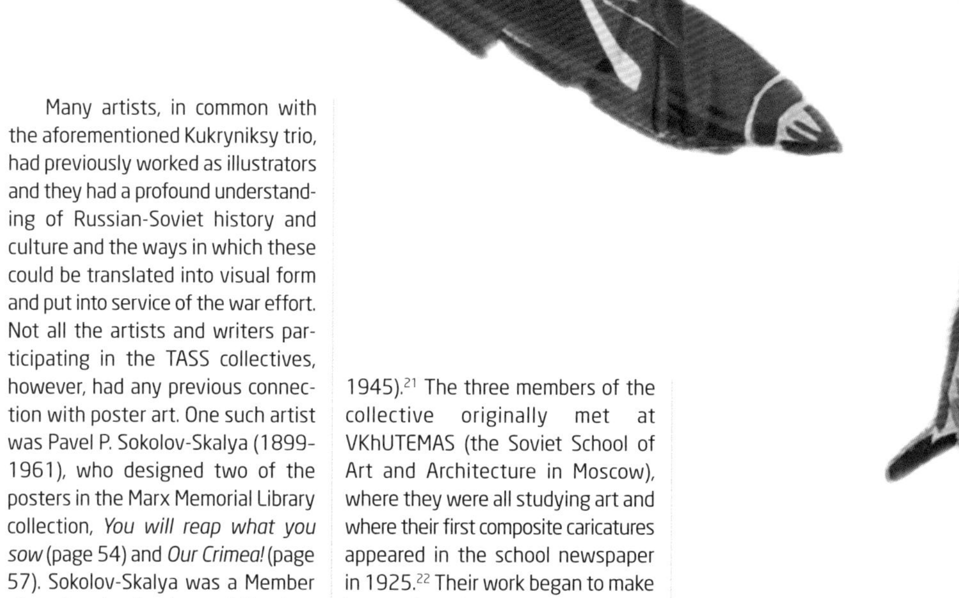

Many artists, in common with the aforementioned Kukryniksy trio, had previously worked as illustrators and they had a profound understanding of Russian-Soviet history and culture and the ways in which these could be translated into visual form and put into service of the war effort. Not all the artists and writers participating in the TASS collectives, however, had any previous connection with poster art. One such artist was Pavel P. Sokolov-Skalya (1899-1961), who designed two of the posters in the Marx Memorial Library collection, *You will reap what you sow* (page 54) and *Our Crimea!* (page 57). Sokolov-Skalya was a Member of the Russian Academy of Fine Arts and had, up until the war, been a painter.[19] By the war's end, though, he had become the leading designer of TASS Windows and one of its most prolific artists, producing a total of 176 posters.[20]

Striking an early blow against fascism, the first TASS Windows poster was designed, as we have seen, by the Kukryniksy. It was a biting caricature depicting a Red Army soldier bayoneting Hitler and was titled *We shall mercilessly crush and destroy the enemy*. During the course of the war the Kukryniksy designed over 200 posters, working in many cases with poets such as Marshak and Demian Bednyi (1881-1945).[21] The three members of the collective originally met at VKhUTEMAS (the Soviet School of Art and Architecture in Moscow), where they were all studying art and where their first composite caricatures appeared in the school newspaper in 1925.[22] Their work began to make its way from the pages of the newspaper to the wider press and in 1930 they began to design posters.[23] Preparatory drawings for each poster – sketched from life and using each other as models – were undertaken individually, and then collectively discussed and critiqued so that the best and most appropriate version was chosen for subsequent production.[24]

Although some TASS Windows posters were reproduced lithographically, most were hand painted using cardboard stencils. After the final design had been chosen, and the accompanying text or caption written, the outline would be copied onto card and then cut out to provide a template for each section of the final poster. Artists worked in relays over a 24-hour period to paint a section of poster from each stencil. The American photographer, Margaret Bourke-White, who documented the war in her book, *Shooting the Russian War*, recalls visiting a TASS Windows 'poster factory', which she describes as a 'twenty-four-hour beehive of many of the best writers, poets, artists and caricaturists in the country'.[25] When the paint was finally dry, the posters were glued together – in four to eight sections – to form the finished product.[26] Given the circumstances of their production, colour variations often occurred across sections of the same poster and on many examples it is possible to see individual brush marks. The completed posters were often huge and could exceed 170 x 120 centimetres: a necessary requirement for viewing from a distance. The posters were painted with poor quality, water-based paint onto cheap, mass-produced, paper made from acidic wood pulp.[27] As many as 24 new posters were designed and produced every month during the course of the war – many of which were reproduced in up to 1,000 copies.[28] Once the Moscow TASS collective had completed the required number of posters, the stencils were sent to other cities for re-use by other collectives throughout the Soviet Union.[29] Each poster was folded several times for transportation and this, along with the poor quality of paint and paper, meant that many literally came apart along the lines of adhesion or substantially disintegrated.

"ONE AGAINST THREE!"

In true propagandist tradition, this TASS Windows poster uses caricature to turn a figure of terror to one of ridicule. Hermann Goering, the Commander of the Luftwaffe, is depicted as thoroughly debauched, fat and conceited – bloated and weakened by his addiction to morphine and bearing a 'beauty spot' in the form of a swastika. The painter, Petr Sarkisian, uses a sequence of images in the style of a comic-strip to tell how, against the odds, one Russian 'Falcon' has shot down three German Messerschmitts. Demian Bednyi, who wrote the text, pokes fun at Goering by describing how his 'fat belly' wobbles when he laughs. Although he was designated Hitler's successor in 1939 and promoted to the rank of Reichsmarschall in 1940, by the time this poster was produced some three years later, Goering's star had begun to wane. Found guilty of war crimes at the Nuremberg Trials, he evaded the hangman's noose by swallowing cyanide.

"FORWARD! TO THE WEST!"

The Soviet Navy had always provided an elite corps to fight alongside the regular army, and had distinguished itself in every action from the storming of the Winter Palace to the battles of the Civil War and the desperate defence of Sevastopol from May to July 1942.

Though this sailor has a generic cap band, rather than one identifying his own ship, he is symbolic of the tens of thousands of young men – such as Ivan Sivkov, Victor Kuskov and Caesar Kunikov – who served from the Barents Sea to the Baltic, and the Black Sea to the Pacific Ocean, in order to free their country from the terror of fascism.

The work of V. Ivanov, this poster was published in both Moscow and Leningrad, in 1942, as the battle for Sevastopol was raging.

The six complete TASS posters in the Marx Memorial Library collection – all of which are reproduced in this catalogue – exhibit varying degrees of fragility. One is in a very good state of preservation, but the remaining five are damaged due to their friability. By definition posters are ephemeral and not designed for durability. It is surprising, therefore, that so many have survived, especially when the uses to which they were often put during wartime is taken into account.

As well as designing posters, the Kukryniksy also devoted time to making propaganda leaflets that were distributed behind enemy lines. They worked for the Red Army, often making visits to the front line during which they saw roadside hoardings displaying their drawings, which had been copied and enlarged by a skillful soldier.[30] In a short article, published in the *Soviet War News* in 1945, which provides a fascinating first-hand account of their practice, they recount how Red Army artists sometimes enlarged their caricatures of Hitler, which were then hoisted aloft in the trenches to inflame the German troops. Soviet snipers then picked the Germans off one by one when, furious at their ridiculing of Hitler, they tried to shoot down the caricatures.[31] Clearly, wit and humour were just as important at the front as armaments. The Kukryniksy provided both, having joined forces with some of the TASS Windows poets and bought a tank for use by the Red Army, which they presented in person.[32]

The extent of the contribution by writers and poets to the war effort is often eclipsed by their more visible, and visually expressive, counterparts. The model and major influence for the TASS Windows poetic texts was the Futurist artist, poet and playwright Vladimir Mayakovsky (1893-1930) who, along with the artist Mikhail Cheremnykh, was one of the organisers of the ROSTA Windows posters of the Civil War era and who wrote the text for more than 600 of those posters. Mayakovksy's inspiration, which had a direct influence on Bednyi and Marshak, is exemplified in his essay *How Verses are Made* in which he explains his rationale for writing poetry thus: 'Example: social demand – song lyrics for the Red Army soldiers off to the Petrograd front. Target – to smash Yudenich. Material – army slang. Tool of production – a chewed pencil stub. Method – rhyming *chastushki*' (folk ditties).[33] Mayakovsky's method underscores the importance of tailoring the text to both the cause for which is intended and to a specific audience – a practice also implemented by poster artists.

Виктор Иванов -42 г.

ВПЕРЕД! НА ЗАПАД!

„Пусть вдохновляет вас в этой войне мужественный образ наших великих предков“
Сталин
Основные даты жизни и деятельности М. И. Кутузова
Основные даты жизни и деятельности М. И. Кутузова
Фельдмаршал
Михаил Илларионович
Кутузов
1745–1813
Сражение при Кагуле
В сражении при Кагуле (1770 год) 27-тысячное войско П. А. Румянцева разгромило 150-тысячную армию противника, занимавшего укрепленный лагерь. В то же время выделенный в тыл 11-тысячный отряд сдерживал натиск вражеской 80-тысячной конницы. В сражении при Кагуле особо отличился М. И. Кутузов.
Взятие Измаила
Под командованием Суворова Кутузов сыграл важную роль во взятии Измаила (1790 год).
„На такой штурм можно решиться только раз в жизни,“—говорил после победы Суворов, а о Кутузове написал в своем донесении: „Он шел на моем левом крыле, но был моей правой рукой“.
Памятник М. И. Кутузову в Ленинграде
Бородино
В Бородинском сражении русские нанесли противнику огромный урон и обескровили его. Бородино явилось переломным этапом в Отечественной войне 1812 года.
Слава Кутузова неразрывно связана со славою России, с памятью о величайшем событии новейшей истории. Его титло: спаситель России; его памятник: скала святой Елены. Имя его не только священно для нас, но не должны ли мы еще радоваться, мы, русские, что оно звучит русским звуком.
А. С. Пушкин
Трудно себе представить историческое лицо, деятельность которого так неизменно постоянно была бы направлена к одной и той же цели. Трудно вообразить себе цель более достойную и более совпадающую с волей всего народа. Еще труднее найти другой пример в истории, где бы цель, которую себе поставило историческое лицо, была бы так совершенно достигнута, как та цель, к достижению которой была направлена вся деятельность Кутузова в 12 году.
Л. Н. Толстой
Бой под Малоярославцем
Вынужденный оставить Москву, Наполеон сделал попытку прорваться на юг к Калуге. В сражении при Малоярославце Кутузов отбросил противника и заставил его отступать по уже разоренной им смоленской дороге.
„Прибытие Кутузова совсем переменило положение дел.“

Whilst the pictorial component of a poster often has primacy over the text – because it is instantly seen and understood from a distance – the words that accompany the image add another layer of meaning. To be effective the poster's image is necessarily simplified for instant appeal. The text, however, often provides a more nuanced approach to the subject, perhaps accentuating elements of the message that cannot be represented in the image. Like their artistic colleagues, the ROSTA and TASS Windows writers also turned to the past for inspiration. Two of the most well-known and prolific TASS windows writers were proletarian poet Demian Bednyi and the aforementioned children's author and poet Samuil Marshak, who worked closely with the Kukryniksy. A master of anti-fascist satire, Bednyi, a long-standing contributor to the Soviet newspaper *Pravda*,[34] modelled his satirical writing on old Russian fables and *raeshnik* – theatrical performances that ridiculed class enemies.[35] Bednyi's poetic condemnations of capitalism, the aristocracy and the bourgeoisie during the Bolshevik era evolved into the denunciation of fascism that we see in his TASS Windows poster titled *The transformation of Fritz* (page 50)[36] which pillories German troops for putting their faith in Hitler, who ultimately sends them to their deaths. Although in poor health Bednyi contributed to 113 TASS Windows posters before his death, barely two weeks after the end of the war.[37]

Although the TASS posters were made in large numbers, they form only a small proportion of propaganda poster output during the war. The majority of Soviet war posters were reproduced in printed form at Iskusstvo, the State Printing Works, in Leningrad and Moscow, many in print runs of 100-200,000.[38] Despite the repeated use of Russian symbolism that harked back to earlier times, the iconography of Soviet posters had much in common with mainstream European poster art.[39] Gestures such as clawed hands, raised fists, salutes and pointing fingers were recurrent symbols in European and American war posters. The sailor depicted in Victor Ivanov's poster, *Forward! To the West!*, (page 61) for example, raises his rifle in an instantly recognisable rallying gesture. His direct forward gaze, making eye contact with the viewer, is a motif also found in posters produced in other countries. Although the specifically Soviet symbols of the red star and red banner, for example, were still evident in military posters, there is a dilution of socialist and communist imagery with little reference to motifs like the hammer and sickle.[40] In the early days of the war, posters featuring specifically communist motifs and slogans began to give way to those whose iconography appealed to a more general patriotism. Whilst posters of the 1920s and 1930s abound with images of Lenin and Stalin, these references too begin to appear less frequently. Rather than being present through his image, Stalin is more often represented indirectly, for example through his speeches, whilst Lenin was rendered a little more explicitly through depictions of medals on which his portrait was engraved.[41]

"FIELD MARSHAL KUTUZOV (1745-1813)"

At the outset of the Great Patriotic War, the USSR had appealed to the military traditions of the young Red Army – and to figures such as Budyonny and Voroshilov from the Civil War – for inspiration. Crushing early defeats, the discrediting of those two Marshals – as the tank replaced the horse as battle winner – and the need to unite the broadest base of the Russian people against the Nazi invader, soon prompted a dramatic rethink.

Popular military heroes from Tsarist times, such as Suvorov and Prince Bagration, came to take their place alongside successful Bolshevik commanders, of the stamp of Chapayev and Frunze, in the pantheon as the Communist Party attempted to fuse ideology with patriotism.

Among Tsarist generals, there was none to rival the popularity or the explicit lessons to be drawn from the individual's biography, as Kutuzov.

As one of the heroes of Tolstoy's *War and Peace* and celebrated by Pushkin, he was renowned for drawing Napoleon's invading army onwards into the heart of Russia, fighting stubborn rearguard actions, denying the Emperor a supply base through his burning of Moscow, and finally destroying it piecemeal as winter provoked a calamitous retreat. In the darkest days of 1941-42, Kutuzov's example of tenacity and fighting spirit were remembered and put to good effect.

Part poster, part history lesson, this sheet was illustrated by P.A. Alyakrinsky and written by N.M. Korobkov for the Committee of Cultural Education. 70,000 copies were printed in Moscow, in 1945, for distribution at the front which then lay in the very same German territories that he had liberated before his death in 1813.

A quote from Stalin, at the top of the poster, urges the modern Soviet soldier to: 'Let the images of our heroic ancestors inspire you in this war'; while Tolstoy and Pushkin are both cited in his praise. For Tolstoy, 'It is difficult to present to present a historical personage whose activity is so immutably and determinedly dedicated to one aim. It is difficult to imagine such an aim that is more worthy and more convergent with the will of the whole nation. And it is even more difficult to find another such example in history, where a historically conditioned aim is as perfect as the one that led Kutuzov to committing great deeds within the space of just 12 years'.

More prosaically, Pushkin concluded that: 'Kutuzov's glory is inseparably joined with the glory of Russia and with the memory of the great events of contemporary history; his name – the saviour of Russia; his monument – the rock of St. Helena [upon which Napoleon was imprisoned]. His name is sacred not only for us ... but his glory will be carried with the sound of the Russian language'.

"ALL HOPE IS IN YOU, SOLDIER OF THE RED ARMY"

The work of V. Ivanov, this poster was published by the state Iskusstvo plant in Moscow and Leningrad in 1943. The Nazi regime and war effort were built upon slave labour. Millions of Soviet citizens were deported to concentration camps in the West with more than seven million of them perishing there. In Belarus alone, out of a pre-war population of 8.8 million, more than 380,000 men, women and children were driven into Germany to work as slaves, while 2.2 million were murdered over the course of the war. Of approximately 270 urban areas, in this one Soviet Republic, more than 200 were rased to the ground. Consequently, it takes little empathy to understand the message of this poster to sons, fathers and husbands serving in the Red Army. Their loved ones were truly calling to them from behind the wire and only military success and the ultimate fall of Berlin, could hope to achieve their freedom.

ВСЯ НАДЕЖДА НА
Художник В. Иванов
Редактор Поволоцкая
А30158 от 5/IV 1943 г. Изд. № 6069. Объем ½ п. л. Тир. 40000. Цена 60 коп.

The emotional temperature of Soviet poster symbolism fluctuated throughout the war years as it reflected the sequence of the conflict. The imagery that dominated visual propaganda typically consisted of representations of the enemy, expressions of suffering, and depictions of heroism. In the early months of the war, posters appealed to Soviet citizens to rally round and support the military, often by taking practical steps such as increasing the production of armaments. Poster designers also aimed to bolster the morale of soldiers at the front by representing them as masculine and heroic symbols of courage. Nina Vatolina's (1915-2002) Red Army soldier in her poster captioned *Forward! Victory is near* (page 48) has an expression of conviction and determination which conveys confidence in the possibility of victory. Her use of exaggerated perspective foregrounds the soldier whilst the composition, with its multiple figures carrying red flags, emphasises the notion of nationwide resistance to the enemy. More recruits were needed at the front, and so to encourage volunteers to come forward, the Red Army soldier always appears, in true propagandist style, as handsome, young and fresh faced – in truth, of course, the antithesis of

wartime reality. Although the young soldier in Ivanov's previously mentioned poster of the Dnieper River (page 51) must have been thirsty and tired, he is represented as looking clean, fresh and rested, despite having probably just returned from battle. As the tide of war began to turn in 1942-3 posters began to encourage the westward advancement of Soviet forces, an injunction explicitly expressed in both the gesture and caption of another of Ivanov's posters, *Forward! To the West!* (page 61).

Early Soviet propaganda often represented women as schemers and liars[42] but by the start of the Great Patriotic War they were depicted as strong, determined and invincible, as exemplified in a much-reproduced poster by Iraklii Toidze (1902-1985) titled *The Motherland is Calling* in which Mother Russia is symbolically represented as a fierce, even confrontational, mature woman. Nevertheless, as war progressed more prominence began to be given to representations of women either as munitions workers or as defenceless victims of fascist aggression. In a 1943 poster jointly designed by Victor Ivanov and Olga Burova (b.1911) (see above) German soldiers are aiming their rifles at several figures held captive in a compound enclosed by fencing made from barbed wire and white birch posts. Her face framed by barbed wire, an anxious young, blonde woman looks out imploringly and beseeches, according to the slogan: *All hope is in you, soldier of the Red Army* (see left).The poster is stripped of anything that might clutter the image and detract from the pathos of the victim's direct emotional appeal. The desire to save women and children is a potent propaganda imperative – an effective device that plays on feelings of loyalty and protection and one that was utilised to induce Soviet men to fulfill their patriotic duty. Unsurprisingly, the Soviet woman calling on the Red Army soldier to save her was also a recurring theme in Soviet films of the period such as *She Defends the Motherland*, made in 1943 by Fridrikh Ermler.[43] These themes and motifs address the general issues that might concern any nation in times of conflict. But because of the speed with which they could be produced, specific events of the war were more likely to be depicted in stencilled, rather than printed, posters. Sokolov-Skalya's response was swift when, following a botched evacuation of German troops in the Crimea, thousands of soldiers drowned in the Black Sea. His TASS Windows poster No. 969, titled *Our Crimea!* (page 57) was produced within days of the incident in May 1944.

"HOIST THE BANNER OF VICTORY OVER BERLIN!"

The road to victory over fascism had been a hard one. More than 11 million Soviet soldiers had been killed in action and 4 million more perished in Nazi prison camps. In addition, at least 16 million Soviet civilians had been murdered by Hitler's forces, or had perished from hunger or bad treatment in German slave labour camps. More than 7 million died in the concentration camps.

Yet, on the morning of May Day 1945, sergeants Yegorov and Kantaria broke from cover to run the Red Flag up over the shattered dome of the Reichstag. Its tattered crimson folds served as the apotheosis of the whole Soviet Army; not just Zhukov's victorious divisions but all those who had fallen on the way, from the blackened walls of the Brest Fortress, and the ruined factories and rubble of Stalingrad, to the banks of the Vistula, the Oder and the Spree.

It was their triumph, and their day.

Published simultaneously in Moscow and Leningrad, in an edition of 50,000 copies, this poster from 1945 by V. Ivanov sold for 2 rubles a time. It shows the victory parade of the Red Army in Berlin, with the Brandenberg Gate draped in the colours of the three great wartime allies: the United States, the Soviet Union and Great Britain. In the moment of triumph, the Stars and Stripes, the Union Jack and the Hammer and Sickle are caught by the same wind and intertwine.

In the final year of the war the Soviet Union began to acknowledge the possibility of triumph over the invaders, and villages and small towns began to celebrate victories. This confidence found expression in posters that depicted, smiling, gleeful and triumphant Red Army soldiers. *Hoist the banner of victory over Berlin!*, (see right) another poster by Victor Ivanov produced in 1945, sees victorious, flag-waving Red Army troops in front of the Brandenburg Gate – Berlin's arch of triumph and a national symbol of Germany and, by extension, of fascism itself although ironically originally a symbol of peace – just before the gate was heavily damaged and Berlin was divided. By the end of the war the Soviet Union had honoured over 10,000 individuals as heroes. And heroes, of course, function as examples of dedication and courage, embodying not only individual sacrifice, but also the collective strength of the nation, and from whom lessons can be learned. The words of Stalin: 'Let the images of our heroic ancestors inspire you in this war' form the caption for a poster, (page 62) produced in 1945 and printed, unusually, by the Public Opinion Publishing Office. It celebrates the achievements of Russian Field Marshal Mikhail Kutuzov, as an exemplary hero. Kutuzov participated in the Russo-Turkish War of 1787-91 and repelled Napoleon's invasion of Russia in 1812. During the Great Patriotic War the Soviet government established the Order of Kutuzov – one of the highest military decorations – in honour of his achievements.

Whilst not every Soviet citizen was able to fight at the front line, the work of those who stayed behind, such as the artists and writers whose posters influenced the course of the Great Patriotic War were every bit as crucial to victory as those engaged in physical combat. Many were honoured by the state for their contribution to the war effort – the Kukryniksy were awarded five Orders of Lenin between them and Sokolov-Skalya received two Stalin Prizes.[44] Although Vladimir Mayakovsky's oft-quoted declaration that: 'I want the pen to be mightier than the bayonet'[45] might not be an original sentiment, it is one that is often expressed because it has an inherent truth. Those who were responsible for the war posters often worked in difficult conditions and with little sleep but they were aware that they were an important factor in the fight against fascism. 'Could there be anything more agonising for a Soviet man or for an artist,' wrote Sokolov-Skalya, 'than the realisation that he is cut off from his people? Is there anything more fulfilling however, than the realisation that you are fighting together with the rest of your country? I am fighting the war and my weapon is three hundred posters. I see my posters in the streets of Moscow on the walls and in shop windows.'[46]

ВОДРУЗИМ НАД БЕРЛИНОМ ЗНАМЯ ПОБЕДЫ!

VÝSTAVA 30 LET KSČ

PRAHA - PAMÁTNÍK OSVOBOZENÍ

VYDAL SEKRETARIÁT ÚSTŘEDNÍHO VÝBORU KSČ

VYTISKLY GRAFICKÉ TISKÁRNY N. P. ZÁK. ZÁVOD VELKÝ ŠENOV

FROM OCTOBER TO FEBRUARY

The snow had drifted across the Old Town Square in Prague all morning, dappling the bronze of Jan Hus' statue and turning to mush on the cobbles, under the tramp of a hundred thousand pairs of boots

Trade Unionists, co-operative farmers, townsfolk and members of the factory militias gathered under a bewildering variety of flags and homemade banners. The flag of Czechoslovakia predominated but there were also trade union emblems, the hammer and sickle and even one Yugoslav standard. Swamped by the sudden onrush of humanity, a stage set up to commemorate the Czech contribution to the 1914-18 war lay forlorn and forgotten huddling up against the building site of the old town hall. Rubble was everywhere, the legacy of another war that had ended, in Prague, not three years before. Renovation and renewal were the orders of the day; as Nazi bullet holes were plastered over and the shells of gutted medieval buildings painstakingly restored.

It was in this spirit that Klement Gottwald stepped on to the balcony above the crowds, snowflakes dusting the fur peak of his cap, sheaves of handwritten notes in hand, voice crackling into the forest of microphones that carried news of the national emergency out to the rest of Czechoslovakia and to the world. The revolution that he had always hoped and planned for had finally arrived, though not in the form that anyone could have expected the day before. His partners in the coalition, the right wing National Socialist, People's and Slovak Democratic Parties had all resigned, hoping to bring down the government and to halt the process of land reform and nationalisation, wresting away control of the police and armed forces from the Communists and their Social Democrat allies.

The resulting constitutional crisis, transformed by Gottwald into the February Revolution of 1948 would confirm the power of the Communist Party in Czechoslovakia for the next fifty years but it would also throw up as many questions as answers for the Movement that had inspired it. Since 1917, the October Revolution and Lenin's thesis on the nature of the party - in *What is to be Done?* - had served as the blueprints for revolutionaries across the globe. However, Czechoslovakia was very different. Prosperous, despite the depredations of the Nazis, technologically advanced, and having experienced a Western style parliamentary democracy, between 1918 and 1938, the post-war republic did not resemble Russia, China, Vietnam, or even Yugoslavia, where armed insurrection and the support of the peasantry had been decisive factors. By way of contrast, the Czech Communist Party had come to power through the ballot box[1].

"30 YEARS OF THE COMMUNIST PARTY OF CZECHOSLOVAKIA"
Issued by the Communist Party of Czechoslovakia (KSC), in 1951, the poster advertised an exhibition held in the National Memorial atop Zizkov Hill, Prague.

Founded in May 1921, as the result of a split in the ranks of the Social Democrats between Left and Right wings, the KSC had championed those dispossessed by the depression of the late '20s and led the struggle against fascism in the '30s. It had a proud record of struggle and sacrifice during the Nazi occupation and had played a leading role in the resistance, culminating in the Slovak national uprising in 1944 and the liberation of Prague in 1945.

Post war elections and the February Revolution had transformed it from a party of protest to a party of government. The celebration of its history, as envisaged in this poster, was one of optimism and progress. Wild flowers sit well with heavy industry, and the palms of victory garnered from the Liberation and the subsequent revolution. Inspiring every step along the way is Gottwald's political vision witnessed here by the heavily thumbed edition of his collected works.

Benefitting from the leading role, taken by Communists in the Liberation of Czechoslovakia and the Germans, the party had emerged as the largest single party in government. In the elections of May 1946, the Party had won over 40% of the vote in Czech lands and 38% nationwide, making it by far the strongest political force in the Second Republic. Moreover, while Plzen and Western portions of the country had been freed by the Americans, it had fallen to Marshal Konev and the Red Army to take Prague. Liberation came to the city on the very last day of the war and was achieved only as a result of a fearsome struggle against SS divisions and a motley collection of Vlasov's nationalists, pro-fascists, White Guards and war criminals. Having saved the city from total destruction at their hands, it was not altogether surprising that the Red Army and the Soviet Union that inspired it should be held in high regard by ordinary Czech citizens. Indeed, one schoolmaster interviewed by an American journalist in 1947, hinted at the disenchantment felt with bourgeois democracy and the role of the West. Before 1938, he explained, 'we were an independent country. We played an important role in the League of Nations. Benes was a popular figure in Geneva. And what did it get us?... Munich and six years of enslavement'.[2]

The trouble was that the Communist Party had taken the brunt of the struggle against the invaders. Twenty five thousand of its pre-war members had been executed or died in the concentration camps, its leadership had lost some of its most important and attractive figures: Honza Zika and Julius Fucik had died leading the resistance, while Jan Sverma had perished leading the Slovak national uprising. This left Gottwald who had escaped to Moscow after the Munich betrayal as the undisputed leader of Communism in Czechoslovakia.

A professional revolutionary, he had been apprenticed as a carpenter in Vienna and worked for a time as a lamplighter in the Imperial capital. He had fought in the First World War and experienced the Russian Revolution as it unfolded. A worker through and through, he instinctively understood the needs and aspirations of his class and alongside Harry Pollitt and Wilhelm Pieck, gave the leadership of the Comintern a distinctively proletarian edge.

FROM OUT OF THE ABYSS, PROGRESSIVE GERMANY SENT ITS:

"VERY BEST GREETINGS FOR A MERRY CHRISTMAS"

Even in the darkest of times, humanity has a way of re-asserting itself. Consequently, amid the ruins and horrors of the Third Reich, the German Communist Party sought to picture a return to family life and to envisage a better future for all.

With its few remaining members returning from concentration camps, from exile, or with the forward units of the advancing Red Army, the KPD still found the strength to issue this profoundly optimistic vision of a new

KOMMUNISTISCHE PARTEI DEUTSCHLANDS

FROHE WEIHNACHT NUR DURCH AUFBAU

Germany in time for Christmas 1945.

At that point, the future of Germany was still largely undecided and its partition between the Eastern and Western powers was far from inevitable. Indeed, it was not until 1948 that the DDR was founded as a separate state.

Unsurprisingly, the KPD fared differently in the division of East and West Germany. It was outlawed in the Western Federal Republic following the Karlsruhe trial in 1956, with many of its activists jailed or forbidden from following their professions even as former Nazis were permitted office in both the state and the military. By way of contrast, in the Eastern German Democratic Republic, the KPD merged with the Left wing of the Social Democrats, on 21-22 April 1946, to form the SED (the Socialist Unity Party). This move was symbolised by the handshake between Wilhelm Pieck, on behalf of the KPD, and Otto Grotewohl, for the Social Democrats, on the floor of the Berlin Congress.

Yet, within the conditions of the day, he was also surprisingly independent and subtle; characteristics which are entirely forgotten by his modern detractors. His speeches resonate with a sense of Czech history - of the loss of nationhood after the battles of Lipany and the White Mountain - while at the height of the February crisis; he turned down Stalin's offer of Soviet military intervention point-blank.[3]

Flying into Kosice, at the end of the war, he had laid the foundation - together with the other democratic party leaders - for the peacetime governance of Czechoslovakia. The National Committees would become the basis for the administration of the new state, which would be both democratic and explicitly anti-fascist. The existence, individuality and equality of the Slovak nation would be respected by its Czech partners; and foreign policy would be orientated towards a security alliance with the Soviet Union. German and Hungarian finance capital would be nationalised,

"5 YEAR PLAN IN 4 YEARS – WE CAN DO IT!"
Even in 1948, the Stakhanovite ideal of the model worker was still potent. This poster of a foundryman by V. Ivanov was enormously influential in Czech political art and provided the inspiration for countless examples after the February Revolution.

Statistics, once again, were everything, with the drive for exponential increases in output often masking poor quality, waste, bad working conditions and damage to the natural environment.

as part of war reparations, and there would be a ban on the restoration of fascist parties. The army – under the command of the war hero – General Svoboda – would be purged of pro-fascist officers and the security apparatus would be put under the control of a Communist minister. Crucially, there could be no equation of the restoration of free market capitalism with the restoration of democracy. Land reform was a priority, with all banks, insurance companies, mines and key industries nationalised in October 1945. This was the first example of the major redistribution of wealth anywhere in Western Europe.

Gottwald was quick to declare that the 'dictatorship of the Proletariat and the Soviets are not the only road to Socialism', while the editor of his speeches and writings felt that 'in May 1945 there had been a fundamental turn in the history of Czechoslovakia, which then embarked upon the ... gradual transition to Socialism'. The posters marking the VIII Congress of the Czechoslovak Party, in March 1946, though utilising the imagery of the alliance between the factory workers and the peasantry evoked a feeling for the richness of the countryside, of a rural – as opposed to an urban ideal – and employed the nation's flag rather than overt Communist imagery. Indeed, every effort was made to celebrate national heroes and heroines – such as Jan Hus, Jan Komensky, and Bozena Nemcova – rather than imported icons, such as Lenin and Stalin.

There was a sense that the future belonged to Communism, as the Devetsil futurist group of the 1920s-30s had been explicitly Marxist, and the most outstanding poets and literary figures of recent times - Jiri Wolker, Julius Fucik and Vitezslav Nezval - had all been prominent Communists. In its Czech setting, Communism needed to equate to a level of consumerist plenty and democratic freedom, greater not less than that enjoyed in the West. It is precisely within this context of rising expectations that the trade union poster *The mountains belong to the workers!* (see right) was pitched.

Gottwald made clear that there was a distinction between 'dogmatic and creative Marxism, and that we Czech Communists are no dogmatists. Secondly, in our country, at this stage of our development (in 1947), class and national interests coincide'. To his critics on the ultra-Left, who alleged that the Party had dispensed with class struggle, he asked 'what do you suppose the nationalisation decree means? We had to fight for it, and it was not easy to advance it as far as we have. Removing control of big industry and finance from private ownership is class struggle'. Then came the rub, as he reminded his audience that: 'Of course, if reaction were to lift its head and subvert or sabotage the decree we should be neither silent nor idle'.[4]

This is precisely what came to pass within barely a twelve months. 1947 had seen the crops fail, and the dividing lines between the Communists and Social Democrats, on one side, and the National Socialists, and the People's and Democratic parties, on the other, widen from fissures, to cracks, to an unbridgeable divide. The Left-wing of the government had attempted to win over the small farmers, tradesmen and civil servants through imposing a tax upon the super-rich, intended to compensate the drought-stricken small farmers and successfully championing increased wage claims for state employees. Plans were outlined for further land reform, including the nationalisation of all land over 50 hectares, for the complete nationalisation of all foreign trade, and for the nationalisation of all businesses and factories employing more than 30 people.

"THE MOUNTAINS BELONG TO THE WORKERS!"

Issued by the trade unions – under the umbrella of the ROH, the Revolutionary Trade Union Movement – this undated poster, issued c.1949-51, celebrates the sweeping programme of nationalisation that followed the February Revolution. Ordinary factory workers now had greater leisure, access to healthcare and education and were able to take vacations in previously exclusive, privately owned, hotels that were now run by the state for the enjoyment of all.

ROH
REKREACE

HORY PATŘÍ PRACUJÍCÍM

PRÁCE 5

VYBUDUJEME OSTRAVSKO-OCEĽOVÝ ZÁKLAD VÝSTAVBY SOCIALIZMU

Despite the signs that the Communists would lose seats, if not power, in the election scheduled for 1948; it was the right-wing of the ruling coalition that struck first, handing in their resignations en mass to President Benes, in the belief that it would collapse the government. In the event, they badly miscalculated. They had not attempted to carry with them either the President, or Jan Masaryk - the son of the popular founder of the First Republic - about whom a genuine opposition might have crystallised. They believed solely in the efficacy of parliamentary, as opposed to extra-parliamentary action to break the deadlock of constitutional crisis; put too much reliance upon the USA to rally international opinion to their aid; and orchestrated their attempted *coup d'etat* at precisely the moment when the ROH - the Czechoslovak trade union movement - and the Workers' Councils (both natural supporters of the Communists) were holding their congresses in Prague.

In the event, they did not even carry with them the majority of cabinet ministers and Gottwald, holding his nerve, simply maintained the business of the government as normal. From the rooftop above the Old Town Square, on 21 February 1948, he called upon 'all good Czechs and Slovaks, all of you - workers, peasants, tradesmen and intellectuals - to unity and unanimity. Set up Action Committees ... in communities, districts and regions composed of democratic and progressive representatives of all parties and of all national organizations ... Be united and decisive - and your truth will prevail!'[5]

"KLEMENT GOTTWALD (1896-1953), PRESIDENT OF CZECHOSLOVAKIA (1948-53)"

The caption proclaims that: 'We shall build the steel industry in Ostrava and develop Socialism'. The poster was issued by the Ministry of Information and Education and published by the newly-nationalised Orbis press agency in 1949-50. Gottwald, the architect of the February Revolution, appears here as the father of the nation. A kindly, patriarchal figure, he is seemingly more at home in a fashionably well-cut suit than in a revolutionary's customary battle dress. Indeed, you might be forgiven for thinking that he was a technocrat or engineer, as opposed to a head of state and consummate politician. A copy of the Party's newspaper, *Rude Pravo* (Red Truth), sits neatly folded on his desk, underneath a bound volume recording the proceedings of the IX Party Congress. Held in Prague, between 25-29 May 1949, the Congress initiated a series of enormous new industrial projects, ranging from dams, railways and power stations to factories and steel works. The plant at Ostrava, named after Gottwald, himself, was the showcase for all these developments and is shown here both as a picture on the president's wall and as the front page of the daily newspaper. Theory has met with practice, and the will of the Party expressed through its plans to develop heavy industry is shown as being synonymous with progress and prosperity.

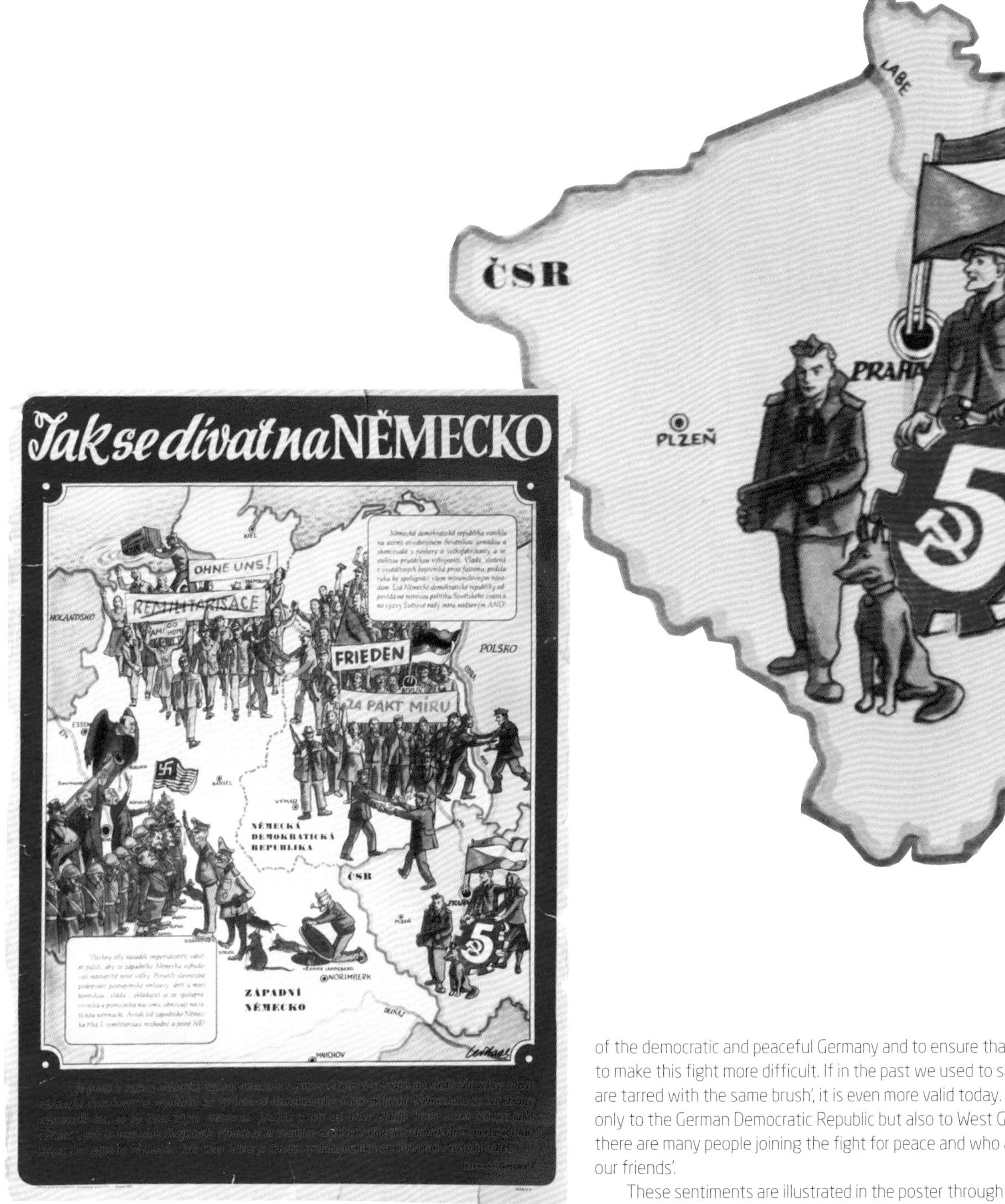

ANOTHER VIEW OF DIVIDED EUROPE:

"HOW TO VIEW GERMANY"

Issued by the Ministry of Education & Information, and published by Orbis in April 1951, this is an image that is a million miles away from the Western propaganda that followed on from Churchill's 'Iron Curtain' speech.

Large blocks of text, drawn from the speeches of President Gottwald, punctuate lively cartoon images of a Europe divided between the United States military, together with its new – and formerly Nazi – allies in Bonn; and the progressive peoples' of the new Socialist democracies.

Against a background of the rearmament of the West German military and the establishment of the DDR, in the East, Gottwald writes from a Czech perspective, that: 'It is therefore in our interest to watch, understand and support the great fight of the German Democratic Republic for unification of the democratic and peaceful Germany and to ensure that we do nothing to make this fight more difficult. If in the past we used to say 'not all Germans are tarred with the same brush', it is even more valid today. This relates not only to the German Democratic Republic but also to West Germany, where there are many people joining the fight for peace and who are, therefore, our friends'.

These sentiments are illustrated in the poster through the West German people demonstrating for unification and against the re-militarisation of their country; while across the divide East Germans embrace Czech and Polish workers in the spirit of friendship and unity. All that seems to be preventing the embrace of East and West Germans is the presence of the American army and its allies among the Prussian junkers. General Eisenhower snaps out a Nazi salute, which is returned by the leaders of the Bonn government, while – with far greater historical accuracy – a US serviceman releases Nazi rats and war criminals from the sewer of Landsberg jail.

A loving Czechoslovak couple cradle the symbol of the first Five-Year Plan, which has become synonymous with their nationhood, while a border guard and his dog guard the frontier. The border patrols had paid a heavy price in the fight against so-called 'Werewolf' gangs of pro-Nazi partisans in the immediate aftermath of the Second World War. It was, therefore, unsurprising that Socialist Czechoslovakia should seek to officially celebrate their heroism and vigilance in this manner.

"FARMERS – CO-OPERATIVE WORKERS: STRIVE FOR HIGHER YIELDS!"

Unlike the majority of Socialist countries in Eastern Europe, Czechoslovakia was not primarily an agrarian nation. This said, Slovakia – in contrast to its Czech partner – was still overly reliant upon agricultural production and the drive towards collectivisation of both small and large farms was central to the Two-Year Plan (1947-48) and the first Five-Year Plan (1949-53).

A general strike was called for 24 February and effectively paralysed the country, closing down factories, shops and offices, bringing commerce and the transport network to a standstill. Print workers pulled the plug on right-wing newspapers and armed militias were established in Prague, Bratislava and other major cities which rallied to the government. In Slovakia, units of former partisans were swiftly re-established in the border districts, while the police and the army – under Svoboda – declared their loyalty to Gottwald and the people. With the Factory Committees exercising the functions of parliament and the workers' militias patrolling the streets, on 25 February, President Benes confirmed the resignations of the right-wing ministers and approved the list of replacements recommended by the Communist Prime Minister. The news was transmitted swiftly to the tens of thousands of protesters gathered, that afternoon, to hear Gottwald speak at a mass rally in Wenceslas Square.

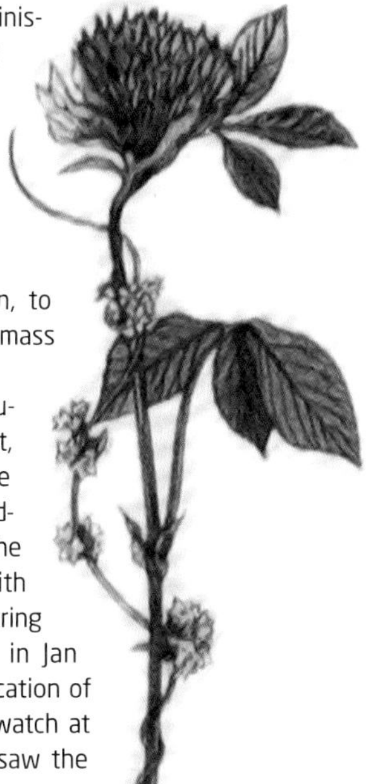

The February Revolution had swept all before it, with a minimum of force and little in the way of bloodshed. It also refashioned the imagery of the Party – with the workers' militias appearing as new Red Guards, as in Jan Cumpelik's masterful evocation of a tense night, spent on watch at the factory gates – and saw the Czechoslovak Party and its propagandists drawn closer, both politically and stylistically, into the Soviet orbit. Artists like Max Svabinsky, who had already enjoyed an enormously long and rich career, painting in the National Romantic and Art Nouveau styles, switched to Socialist Realism. But Socialist Realism, itself, was experiencing a crisis.[6]

However, while the government took its inspiration from the Soviet Union, it attempted to adapt its policies to suit local conditions. In particular, the Co-operative Movement had a strong appeal. The Central Co-operative Council was established in May 1945 and was enshrined in law, as part of the new constitution of 9 May 1948. Within a decade almost 80% of villages had become part of the co-operative system.

This poster concludes with the injunction to 'Destroy the Weeds!' and fulfills a purely practical purpose in depicting the most common types, namely wild spinach, persicaria, creeping thistle, white mustard, couch grass, wild radish, white campion and greater dodder.

MÍR MUSÍ BÝT VYBOJOVÁN!

RUCE PRYČ OD KOREJE!

SVOBODU KOREJSKÉMU LIDU!

NOVÝMI VÝROBNÍMI ÚSPĚCHY

POSÍLÍME REPUBLIKU, POMŮŽEME VĚCI MÍRU NA CELÉM SVĚTĚ!

"PEACE MUST BE FOUGHT FOR! HANDS OFF KOREA!"

The Cold War suddenly turned hot in Korea from 1950-53 and Czechoslovakia offered what support it could to its brothers and sisters engaged in struggle against American military might. There is no room for doubt in this poster, issued by Orbis c.1951, that US aggression is at the root of the problem. While a Korean fighter, supported by a Chinese soldier, stamp out their diminutive enemies – who are portrayed as little more than vermin – a blood stained General MacArthur scuttles away into the shadows.

The progressive forces in the world – Poles, Czechs, the French and Italians, both white and blue collar workers – are grouped together under the folds of the banner of the Soviet Union. The factories, hydro-electric plants and foundries in the background suggest the economic fruits of Socialism made synonymous with peace.

This said, the slogan exhorting the idea that peace can only be bought at the price of renewed war will jar the senses of modern readers. The final declaration, urging 'Freedom to all Korean people! We shall strengthen the [Czechoslovak] Republic by new industrial achievements. We shall support peace in the whole world!', brings together national economic policy with international security concerns.

The struggle for peace and national determination are hereby tied to support for Sino-Soviet military intervention in the peninsula and the drive for industrialisation at home.

The premature death of Andrei Zhdanov, in 1948, removed its foremost theorist and champion from the scene, at the very time when Czechoslovakia was holding its own Congress of National Culture, while the diminishing returns to be garnered from fresh Five-Year Plans seemed increasingly at odds with the cheery declarations of the propaganda poster. More worryingly still, their necessarily simplistic arguments attuned to a society where illiteracy was still widespread, worked less assuredly in Czechoslovakia, where even the youngest child knew its letters. In a similar fashion, despite the best attempts of the propagandists, the robust Stakhanovite shock-workers and rosy-cheeked collective farm girls of official Soviet art, did not easily find their counterparts in Czechoslovakia, with its small proletariat, high skills base, and no tradition of vast semi-feudal estates.

Furthermore, the appalling losses suffered by the Soviet Union in the Great Patriotic War, coupled with the knowledge that the USA had been prepared to drop the atom bomb on Hiroshima and Nagasaki, shifted the genre from celebrating revolution, and revolutionary war, to peace. Indeed, so associated did the dove become with the Soviet sponsored World Peace Movement - largely through Picasso's work - that it was regularly denounced in Washington as a 'Communistic device'.

With the USA allocating a federal budget of more than $100 million, in October 1951, to fund anti-Communist agitation - and the infamous *Radio Free Europe* - in order to wage the Cold War more effectively, it was perhaps unsurprising that the new Socialist states felt under threat. The rearmament of Western Germany, under the direction of many former Nazi officers, and the outbreak of the Korean War, in June 1950, generated a new series of subjects for the poster artist, which were respectively treated with humour and pathos.

However, the Show Trials formed another - and far less welcome - importation from the Soviet Union, which were handled uncritically in the governmental posters. The root cause of the trials, aside from the animosity of North America, was the refusal of Marshal Tito to let Yugoslavia become entirely subordinated to Stalin's will and the needs of the Soviet economy. The edifice of Communist unity, so tenaciously upheld since 1917, suddenly threatened to crumble as the Yugoslavs attempted to chart their own path to Socialism.

Initially, Gottwald - despite an inflammatory phone call from Mathias Rakosi, Stalin's prime henchman in Hungary - tried to shrug the whole matter off. Tito had, after all, been rapturously received in Prague, in 1946, and enjoyed enormous prestige in the international Communist movement for his wartime heroism. Furthermore, Gottwald presided over one of the only two European Communist parties - the other was the British Party under Pollitt - which lacked a history of vicious sectarianism; and he intended to keep it that way.

This became increasingly difficult once Tito decisively split away from the Soviet camp - becoming, in the process, a prime target for satirical propaganda - and Rakosi initiated, at Stalin's behest, a blistering series of show trials that tore apart his own government, at every level. In a vicious, though rarely noticed, historical irony, it was the General Secretary of the Czechoslovak Party, Rudolf Slansky - who would become the most prominent victim of the purges - who first countenanced the use of the Show Trials and the terror in his own land.

"PEACE TO THE CHILDREN OF THE WHOLE WORLD!"

Issued by the Ministry of Information & Education, and published by the Orbis Agency, this photomontage poster was timed to coincide with the 1951 May Day festivities held across Czechoslovakia.

A Young Pioneer holds a poster showing the aftermath of a US bombing raid on Korea. The apparent stability and joyfulness of childhood in Socialist Czechoslovakia is contrasted by the destruction of innocence by the military actions of the Western alliance.

MÍR

dětem
celého
světa

VYDALO MINISTERSTVO INFORMACÍ A OSVĚTY · KVĚTEN

Peace to children of all the world

"CZECHOSLOVAKIA AT THE OUTSET OF THE COLD WAR"
Printed by the Czechoslovak-Soviet Friendship Society, in 1949-51, the poster contrasts the power of the Czech working classes, once allied to the Soviet Union, with the intellectually and morally bankrupt statesmen of the bourgeois Western powers. The slogan, at the bottom, reads: 'The forces of Peace led by the Soviet Union cannot be conquered!'

Gottwald, unwilling to be their victim, was able to outmanoeuvre and to finally destroy his rival; but at a terrible cost to his own Party and to the legitimacy of the movement he had inspired for so long. One of the reasons for the crisis lay in the changing nature of the Party in Czechoslovakia. Its participation in the democratic process after the end of the war had seen its membership grow exponentially, a trend further accelerated after the victory of the February Revolution, when many felt – for the first time in its history – that Party membership was a sound route to a good job and a stake in the new system. The Party certainly aided this process, publicly stating that its aim was 2 million members in time for the elections of 1948. In the five months that followed the revolution, membership rose by 856,657 in the Czech lands and by 196,928 in Slovakia, leading the target figure to be surpassed by more than half a million. This was all a far cry from Lenin's conception of the Party as a small nucleus of professional revolutionaries, and inevitably the composition of the cadres altered. In 1947, 49.1% of the Party were workers by trade but, by 1949, this proportion had fallen to only 39.3%: a worrying trend for the pre-war membership, who recalled the days of illegality, and a potentially lethal statistic in the hands of those who were prepared to turn witch hunter.[7]

On one side of the scales, marked 'In the name of New War', Churchill clings to Uncle Sam, while their allies – Bevin, De Gaulle, Blum and Schumacher – scrabble to keep hold. Uncle Sam carries a copy of the NATO Treaty, signed in May 1949, while clenching a missile between his teeth. Yet the cast of 'villains', backing US power, are not just limited to old reactionaries. Bevin, by then one of the most hawkish and anti-communist foreign secretaries is targeted for particular censure, as is Marshal Tito – until recently the hero of the anti-fascist resistance – who is rendered ridiculous, here, through his penchant for comic opera uniforms.

Upsetting the balance of these malign forces 'In the name of a lasting peace' is the power of the organised working class, standing for 'Peace and Democracy'.

"PEACE!"

The Russian word 'Mir' has a double meaning, of 'Peace' and also to signify the earth or world. It is entirely appropriate here, as a loving mother proudly cradles her child and looks out expectantly towards us. It is up to all of us to compel our governments to ensure that the future is free from the threat of nuclear war.

Designed by N. Vatolina and published in Moscow, in 1965, in a huge print-run of 245,000 copies, this is an image that serves to redefine the priorities of the Soviet Union and which also has an immediate and universal relevance.

Real incidents of sabotage and civil unrest, manifesting themselves at the time of President Benes' funeral and in the attempts by university students to break up the Sokol festival in 1948, seemed to give credence to the atmosphere of fear and suspicion which suddenly descended upon the state. The optimism, spontaneity and heady enthusiasm, born of revolution, that fired revolutionary art found it hard to flourish amid mutual suspicion and a climate of fear. It could not hope to flourish through the purges, in war-blasted economies attempting to make good the damage wrought by Hitler's armies, and in the space left by the increasing distance between the ideal and the reality of day-to-day life under Socialism. When the impulse no longer matched the statement, both the art form and the polity that inspired it could not help but be debased.

Gottwald was to drag himself through the entire process of the Show Trials, as former friends accused one another of the most incredible and heinous crimes, and as even the previously irreproachable widow of Jan Sverma, a national hero, was convicted of anti-party activities. Yet, the inspiration for the trials and for the whole edifice of Socialist Realism failed with a single heartbeat. Stalin's death, from a stroke on 5 March 1953, began the end for them both.

Gottwald attended the funeral but interminable hours spent atop Lenin's mausoleum, in sub-zero temperatures, chilled him to the bone and brought on the sudden onset of pneumonia. The rolling gun salutes that accompanied Stalin's last journey, reverberated through his own frame. One can only speculate if he sought to justify his own record, as the fever gripped him, and to balance his attainment of social and economic justice for the Czech working class, and his bravery in confronting fascism, with the suffering wrought upon his own friends and comrades on account of a master, newly departed and now being consigned to the tomb. His revolution, which had burst upon the fault-line of divided Europe, had compelled artists and designers - no less than the politicians who commanded them - to re-think and re-imagine the possibilities offered by Marxism just at the point when the Cold War threatened nuclear holocaust. Yet, it was clear that, in its European setting, the process set in motion by the shots from the quarter-deck of the cruiser, 'Aurora', in October 1917 had found their coda in the events of February 1948.

Alongside Gottwald stood Khrushchev, bulky and inscrutable, already planning for the future. Snowfall seemed to accompany the defining moments of the President's life. It whirled about him, as it had on the balcony above the Old Town Square, clinging to the red flags and black drapes that brought mourning to Moscow, blanching the catafalque and wiping the canvas, turning all about to a void.

DOPADLI
JSME
NEBEZPEČNOU
ŠKODNOU
KAPITALISMUS
SVERMOVA
SLING
CLEMENTIS

"WE HAVE CAPTURED THE DANGEROUS VERMIN"
This poster, calculated to whip up popular support for the Show Trials of 1952, identifies three prominent party members with capitalism's attempt to destroy socialism in Czechoslovakia. Once again, it is the industrial working class which will smash the threat.

In reality, it was an internal power struggle within the ruling power which led to the fall of the Foreign Minister, Vladimir Clementis; the Brno party secretary, Otto Sling; and the politburo member, Marie Svermova. Shown here as snakes, Sling had fought in Spain with the International Brigades, Clementis had done much to promote Slovak culture, and Svermova was the widow of one of Gottwald's closest comrades; Jan Sverma, who had perished leading the Slovak National Uprising against the Nazis.

Clementis – later the subject of a short story by Milan Kundera – is shown as the first of the snakes to be decapitated, having been forced to resign from the government in 1950. All three were decried as 'bourgeois nationalists' and tried together alongside Rudolf Slansky, the former General Secretary of the Party. It is interesting that Slansky, the main defendant in the trials, is not depicted here as the fourth snake or even as the hand of capitalism, itself. This probably reflects the continuing uncertainty of the government over the form, content and identities of the individuals to be tried.

Sling was executed, alongside Clementis and Slansky, on the 3 December 1952, proclaiming his innocence and devotion to the Party until the last. Marie Svermova was sentenced to 20 years' imprisonment.

All three were rehabilitated by the Czechoslovak Communist Party in 1963.

ENDNOTES

CHAPTER 1

[1] See: Marx Memorial Library, *Minute Books*, (8 February 1996; 21 March 1996; 12 February 1998)

There are frequent mentions of the 'difficult', 'dirty' and 'cold' conditions at the warehouse (12 November 1998; 21 January 1999; and 11 March 1999).

The photographs on page 9, from 2004, reveal something of the chaos.

The situation necessitated a report by one of the present authors to the, then, Library Chair which – with hindsight – is as direct as it is graphic in its call for immediate action: 'The work last summer cleared the aisles, permitted unobstructed movement through two-thirds of the warehouse ... and considerably reduced the chances of a serious accident occurring through the removal of crates piled up some 7-8 feet high ... The picture is further complicated by the fact that an old warehouse is far from the ideal place to store paper and delicate materials (such as the posters, which are still languishing somewhere under the crates brought back from the T&G). The damage to the roof done by past flooding has never been repaired. Indeed, it could not be repaired as the crates effectively prevented access by workmen to the site. This means that dust and other detritus constantly blows down from the upper floors, further degrading our stock.' (J. Callow to M. Rosser, *Report on the Shacklewell Lane Store*, January 2005, p.1).

The Finance Committee reported that the warehouse 'roof was leaking again' and that a 'vast quantity of books' were stored there (18 October 2001). Perhaps most worrying of all was the suggestion, by the then librarian, of 'the possibility of selling Soviet posters to a collector, at sums in the region of eg.£1,500' (9 December 1993). Fortunately, this was not acted upon by the Committee.

[2] L. Phelan, 'Polemical Provenance', *Morning Star*, (13 September 2010), p.35.

[3] M. Tupitsyn, *Gustav Klutsis and Valentina Kulagina: Photography and Montage after Constructivism*, (Steidl, Goettingen, 2004), p.208.

[4] Tupitsyn, *Gustav Klutsis*, p.210.

[5] Peter Kenez, *The Birth of the Propaganda State: Soviet Methods of Mass Mobilization*, (CUP, Cambridge, 1985), p.73.

[6] See: Orlando Figes, *Natasha's Dance: A Cultural History of Russia*, (Penguin Books, London, 2003), pp.171-2.

[7] For a more detailed discussion of the influences on the genesis of the Soviet political poster, see: Stephen White's *The Bolshevik Poster*, (Yale University Press, New Haven and London, 1988), pp.1-17.

[8] Quoted in Camilla Gray, *The Russian Experiment in Art 1863-1922*,(Thames & Hudson, London,1986), p.219.

[9] Stephen White, *The Bolshevik Poster*, (Yale University Press, New Haven and London, 1988), p.91.

[10] For a detailed discussion of Soviet photomontage and factographic practices see: Benjamin Buchloh's 'From Factura to Factography', in *October*, vol. 30 (Autumn), published by MIT Press, 1984, pp.82-119.

[11] Victoria Bonnell, *Iconography of Power*, (University of California Press, Berkeley and Los Angeles, 1999), pp.23-34.

[12] White, p.130.

CHAPTER 2

[1] For one readable and incisive account of aspects of this transformation, see: 'Russia Through the Soviet Lens', in Orlando Figes, *Natasha's Dance: A Cultural History of Russia*, (Penguin Books, London, 2003), pp.434-521.

[2] Brandon Taylor, *Art and Literature Under the Bolsheviks: The Crisis of Renewal 1917-1924*, (vol.1) (Pluto Press, London, 1991), p.57.

[3] Chernishevsky was also an influential critic whose ideas, along with those of Nikolai Nekrasov and Mikhail Dobrolyubov, supported the Slavophile or nationalist movement in Russia in the 1860s. The realist artists such as Repin who he commended where among those favoured by Lenin and Stalin. See: Camilla Gray, *The Russian Experiment in Art 1863-1922*, (Thames & Hudson, London, 1986), p.10.

[4] Matthew Cullerne Bown, *Art Under Stalin*, Phaidon, (Oxford, 1991), pp.25-6.

[5] Brandon Taylor, *Art and Literature Under the Bolsheviks: Authority and Revolution 1924-1932* (vol. 2), (Pluto Press, London, 1992), pp.x-xi.

[6] Bown, *Art Under Stalin*, p.33.

CHAPTER 3

[1] Kukryniksy, 'Ourselves and Our Work', *Making Hitler Look Silly: Posters and Cartoons by Kukryniksy the Famous Russian Trio* (London, *Soviet War News*) 1945, p.5.

[2] Kukryniksy, p.5.

[3] Kukryniksy, p.5.

[4] Billie Melman, *Borderlines: Genders and Identities in War and Peace, 1870-1930* (Routledge, London, 1998), p.99.

[5] Vyacheslav Molotov quoted in Graeme Gill, *Symbols and Legitimacy in Soviet Politics* (CUP, Cambridge, 2011), p.148.

[6] Professor D. W. Spring, *Soviet Posters from the Great Patriotic War 1941-5, The TASS Poster Series from the Hallward Library*, University of Nottingham (Adam Matthew Publications), online at: http://www.ampltd.co.uk/collections_az/ [accessed 3rd March 2010]. Some of the changes in the iconography of posters were explored more fully in Jane Powell's paper, *The Changing Iconography of Cold War Posters at the Marx Memorial Library*, which was presented at the conference 'Art Histories, Cultural Studies and the Cold War' held at the IGRS, University of London in September 2010.

[7] Victoria E. Bonnell, *Iconography of Power: Soviet Political Posters under Lenin and Stalin* (University of California Press, Berkeley and Los Angeles, 1997), p.4.

[8] Spring, [accessed 3rd March 2010].

[9] Abbott Gleason, *Views and Re-Views: Soviet Political Posters and Cartoons, Then and Now*, an essay to accompany the exhibition of the same name at Brown University Library, online at: http://dl.lib.brown.edu/Views_and_Reviews/essay.html [accessed 3rd April 2011].

[10] Domestic enemies were still considered a threat. In the iconography of Great Patriotic War posters, fascist sympathisers replaced the bourgeoisie of earlier times.

[11] Lenin quoted in Michael Mann, *The Dark Side of Democracy: Explaining Ethnic Cleansing* (CUP, Cambridge, 2005), p.322.

[12] This is one translation of the poster's text. Alternative translations might be, for example, 'fascist scum' or 'fascist filth'. The overall sentiment is the same, however, demanding the 'cleansing' of Soviet soil or land.

[13] Bonnell p.223.

[14] Hubertus Jahn, *Patriotic Culture in Russia During World War I* (Cornell University Press, New York, 1995), p.12.

[15] Bonnell, p.5.

[16] Melman, p.98.

[17] The Victoria and Albert Museum, online at: http://collections.vam.ac.uk/item/O101261/poster-warrior-dont-retreat/ [accessed 21st April 2011].

[18] Spring, [accessed 3rd March 2010].

[19] Maria Lafont, *Soviet Posters: The Sergo Grigorian Collection* (Prestel, Munich, Berlin, London, New York, 2007), p.284.

[20] Spring, [accessed 3rd March 2010].

[21] Kukryniksy, pp.5-6.

[22] Gleason, [accessed 3rd April 2011].

[23] Elena Kuznetsova, 'Who Are the Kukryniksi?', *Making Hitler Look Silly: Posters and Cartoons by Kukryniksy the Famous Russian Trio* (London, *Soviet War News*, 1945), p.3.

[24] Kuznetsova, p.3.

[25] Margaret Bourke-White, *Shooting the Russian War* (Simon and Schuster, New York, 1942), p.171.

[26] Harriet K. Stratis and Peter Zegers, 'Under a Watchful Eye: The Conservation of Soviet TASS-Window Posters', *Art Institute of Chicago Museum Studies*, Vol. 31, No. 2, p.93.

[27] Stratis and Zegers, p.93.

[28] The Victoria and Albert Museum, http://collections.vam.ac.uk/item/O101257/poster-fascist-reports/ [accessed 21st April 2011].

[29] Special Collections Research Centre, George Washington University, Washington, D.C., online at: http://www.gwu.edu/gelman/spec/ead/ms2276.xml [accessed 24th April 2011].

[30] Kuznetsova, p.4.

[31] Kukryniksy, p.5.

[32] Kuznetsova, p.4.

[33] Reprinted in Maxim Gorky, Vladimir Mayakovsky, Alexei Tolstoy, Konstantin Fedin, *The Art and Craft of Writing*, tr. Alex Miller (University Press of the Pacific, Honolulu, Hawaii, 2000), p.130.

[34] Katerina Clark, Evgeni Aleksandrovich Dobrenko, Andre Artizov, and Oleg V. Naumov, *Soviet Culture and Power: a History in Documents, 1917-1953* (Yale University Press, New Haven,2007), p.147.

[35] The Great Soviet Encyclopedia. "*Raeshnik*", online at: http://smartdefine.org/raeshnik/definitions/694788 [accessed 23 April 2011].

[36] This poster features in the exhibition, *Windows on the War: Soviet TASS Posters at Home and Abroad, 1941-1945*, which is on display between 31 July and 23 October 2011, at the Art Institute of Chicago. The authors would like to acknowledge the help given by the exhibition's Research Associate, Jill Bugajski, who kindly provided alternative translations for some of the posters' texts.

[37] Spring, [accessed 3rd March 2010].

[38] Spring, [accessed 3rd March 2010].

[39] Jahn, p.70.

[40] Gill, p.147.

[41] Gill, p.147.

[42] Bonnell, p.72.

[43] Denise J. Youngblood, '*A War Remembered: Soviet Films of the: Great Patriotic War*,' The American Historical Review, June 2001, online at: http://www.historycooperative.org/journals/ahr/106.3/ah000839.html [accessed 5 Apr. 2011].

[44] For more on the members of the Kukryniksy see: N. I. Baburina, *The Soviet political poster 1917-1980 from the USSR Lenin Library Collection*, (Penguin Books, Harmondsworth, England, 1985).

[45] Mayakovsky quoted in the text of TASS Windows poster No. 1000 titled '*Our Thousandth Blow*', The Art Institute of Chicago website, online at: http://www.artic.edu/aic/collections/artwork/192373 [accessed 24th April 2011].

[46] Quoted in N. I. Baburina, *The Soviet political poster 1917-1980 from the USSR Lenin Library Collection*, (Penguin Books, Harmondsworth, England, 1985), p.5.

CHAPTER 4

[1] K. Gottwald, *Selected Speeches and Articles, 1929-53*, (Orbis, Prague, 1954), pp.152-157; V. Kun (ed.), Vitezny Unor ve Fotografii, (Culture & Propaganda Secretariat of the KSČ, Prague, 1949), pp.8-9 and 18-26; M. Myant, *Socialism and Democracy in Czechoslovakia, 1945-1948*, (Cambridge University Press, Cambridge, 1981), pp.140-141; M. Tejchman, *February 1948 and Today*, (The Orbis Press Agency, Prague, 1978), pp.16-18; and P.E. Zinner, *Communist Strategy and Tactics in Czechoslovakia, 1918-48*, (Pall Mall Press, London and Dunmow, 1963), pp.183-186.

[2] M. Hindus, *The Bright Passage*, (Doubleday & Company, New York, 1947), p.277.

[3] Gottwald, *Selected Speeches*, p.98; K. Kaplan, *The Short March. The Communist Takeover in Czechoslovakia, 1945-1948*, (C. Hurst & Company, London, 1981 rpt. 1987), p.175; and F. Necasek, *Klement Gottwald, Communist Premier of Czechoslovakia*, (CPGB, London, 1947), pp.6-9.

[4] Hindus, *Bright Passage*, pp.219, and 223-224; Z. Kratochvilova (ed.), *Klement Gottwald, Selected Writings, 1944-1949*, (Orbis Press Agency, Prague, 1981), pp.12 and 19; V. Nezval, *Song of Peace*, trans. J. Lindsay and S. Jolly, (Fore Publications Ltd., London, 1950), pp.3-4 and *passim*; M. Otruba and Z. Pesat (eds.), *The Linden Tree. An Anthology of Czech and Slovak Literature, 1890-1960*, (Artia, Prague, 1962), p.82; and D. Sayer, *The Coasts of Bohemia. A Czech History*, (Princeton University Press, Princeton, New Jersey, 1998), pp.209-210, 212-213 and 215-216.

[5] Gottwald, *Selected Speeches*, p.157; and Kaplan, *Short March*, pp.176-181 and 183.

[6] T. Petiskova, *Ceswkoslovensky Socialisticky Realismus, 1948-1958*, (Gallery, Prague, 2002), pp.24-25 and 34-35.

[7] Institute of Marxism-Leninism of the CP Czechoslovakia and CP Slovakia (eds), *An Outline of the History of the CPCz*, (Orbis Press Agency, Prague, 1980), p.247.

"THE INTERNATIONAL KNOWS NO FRONTIERS"

Organised jointly by the Danish and German communist parties in the fortress town of Sonderborg, this mass – cross border – aimed to rally 'workers, women and the youth' to a call for 'War against imperialist wars'.

Seized by Germany in the Second Schleswig war of 1864, Sonderborg was returned to Denmark as a result of Germany's defeat in 1918 and the resulting plebiscite of 1920. However, the town had a substantial German population and strong ties of kinship and culture ensured that both Communist parties operated freely within the region, during the 1920s.

The foreign interventionists, wearing French issued helmets and backed by British Mark IV tanks, are dwarfed by the power of the Red Guardsman and his supporters among the international working class movement.

The 'Red cross-border' rallies, such as this, emphasised the shared values and interests of workers, who refused to put their nation before their class.

Rotes Grenztreffen

in Sonderborg am 3. August

Arbeiter, Frauen, Jugend beteiligt euch in Massen

Aufmarsch aller Teilnehmer morgens 10 Uhr in Kollund, von dort geschl. Abfahrt nach Sonderborg

Massen-Kundgebung in Sonderborg
Mittags 2 Uhr

Krieg dem imperialistischen Kriege

KPD, Bez. Wasserkante • KP Dänemark

BIBLIOGRAPHY

Ades, D.; Benton, T.; Elliott, D; and Boyd Whyte, I., (eds), *Art and Power. Europe under the Dictators, 1930-45*, (Hayward Gallery, London, 1995).

Bonnell, V.E., *Iconography of Power: Soviet Political Posters under Lenin and Stalin*, (University of California Press, Berkeley, 1999).

Cullerne Brown, M., *Art under Stalin*, (Phaidon, Oxford, 1991).

Cullerne Brown, M., *Soviet Socialist Realist Painting, 1930s-1960s*, (Oxford Museum of Modern Art, Oxford, 1992).

Elliot, D., (et al), Art into Production. *Soviet Textiles, Fashion and Ceramics, 1917-1935*, (Museum of Modern Art, Oxford, 1984).

Elliott, D., *New Worlds. Russian Art and Society, 1900-1937*, (Thames & Hudson, London, 1986).

Gorky, M.; Radek, K.; Bukharin, N.; Zhdanov, A.; et al, *Soviet Writers' Congress, 1934. The Debate on Socialist Realism and Modernism in the Soviet Union*, ed. H.G. Scott, (Lawrence & Wishart, London, 1935 rpt. 1977).

Gray, C., *The Russian Experiment in Art, 1863-1922*, (Thames & Hudson, London, 1971 revised edition 1996).

Guerman, M., *Art of the October Revolution*, (Aurora Art Publishers, Leningrad, 1979 rpt. 1986).

Petiskova, T., *Ceskoslovensky Socialisticky Realismus, 1948-1958*, (Gallery, Prague, 2002).

Phelan, L., *'Polemical Provenance'*, *Morning Star*, (Monday 13 September 2010), p.35.

Prokhorov, G., *Art under Socialist Realism. Soviet Painting, 1930-1950*, (Craftsman House, Roseville East, New South Wales, 1995).

Taylor, B., *Art and Literature under the Bolsheviks: Vol.1 The Crisis of Renewal, 1917-1924*, (Pluto Press, London, 1991).

Taylor, B., *Art and Literature under the Bolsheviks: Vol.2 Authority and Revolution, 1924-1932*, (Pluto Press, London, 1992).

Tolstoy, V.; Bibikova, I.; and Cooke, C., (eds), *Street Art of the Revolution. Festivals and Celebrations in Russia, 1918-33*, (The Vendome Press, Thames & Hudson, London; and Iskusstvo, Moscow, 1984 rpt. 1990).

Tupitsyn, M., *The Soviet Photograph, 1924-1937*, (Yale University Press, New Haven and London, 1996).

Tupitsyn, M., *Gustav Klutsis and Valentina Kulagina. Photography and Montage after Constructivism*, (Steidl, Goettingen, 2004).

White, S., *The Bolshevik Poster*, (Yale University Press, New Haven and London, 1988).

Zhdanov, A.A., *On Literature, Music and Philosophy*, (Lawrence & Wishart, London, 1950).

слава героям советского союза!
УСИЛИЯМИ
ПАРТИИ И
ПРАВИТЕЛЬСТВА
ВСЕ
ЧЕЛЮСКИНЦЫ
СПАСЕНЫ!

"GLORY TO THE HEROES OF THE SOVIET UNION!"

This poster, by G. Leonov, was produced by the wonderfully evocative Whistle artists' collective and published in both Moscow and Leningrad in November 1934. It celebrates the successful rescue of Otto Schmidt's expedition from an ice-flow, near the Bering Strait, in April 1934, and the subsequent award of the title "Hero of the Soviet Union" to many of the leading participants.

The SS 'Chelyuskin' had attempted to chart a Northern Sea route from Murmansk to the Pacific, in a single season. However, the ice closed in around it and eventually crushed it to pieces. As the crew and the members of the expedition escaped onto the ice, the Soviet Government mounted an enormous air sea rescue which saw all but one of Schmidt's men saved.

The site of the makeshift airfield, hacked out of the ice by the expedition – known as 'Chelyuskinites' due to the name of the ship – is marked by a giant red banner. The rescuers' hastily converted aircraft, airship, steamers together with the icebreaker, the 'Krasin', are shown hurrying to the aid of the marooned men.

As a triumph of man over nature, the epic saga of the Chelyuskin could not be bettered and formed the basis of many subsequent novels, television programmes and feature films in many Socialist countries.

INDEX

"FOR THE BUILDERS OF SOCIALIST INDUSTRY - CULTURALLY SOCIALIST CITIES!"

Appropriately enough for the context of this book, the poster by Daniil Cherkes – published in October 1932 by the Agitmass Department – combines the theme of cultural progress with manufacture and industry. Sports stadia, green public spaces, wide avenues and municipal buildings sit side-by-side with electric pylons and well-regulated factories. The Soviet city, we are told, is to be centrally planned and will owe nothing to the capitalist past.

SOWJET UNION
10 Jahre
UdSSR

'TEN YEARS OF THE SOVIET UNION!'

What the revolutionaries knew all too well, and later generations forgot, was that there was nothing pre-ordained about the survival of the first workers' state. Lenin made a note on his office wall of the number of days that the Paris Commune of 1871 had held out. When the Bolsheviks remained in power for three months, he felt validated.
A decade later, the Russian Revolution appeared to many as a miraculous success. Everything had been hurled at it by the Western powers - armies, blockades, attempts at sabotage and diplomatic isolation – yet still it survived.
The trouble was that the revolution had failed to ignite a pan-European insurrection as had been expected. Germany, always seen as the potential powerhouse of a Communist revolution, but the movement had been crushed by the unexpected rise of Nazism.
This said, the German Communist Party under Ernst Thaelmann and Wilhelm Pieck had developed into a capable and confident mass party, that held seats in the Reichstag and believed itself to be on the threshold of power. In 1927, it looked for inspiration to the Soviet Union and saw a future of friendship between the two nations, whereby the German worker could strech out his hand to embrace the Red Guard.

It would take the imposition of the disastrous 'Class against Class' policy of the Comintern to pitch Communist against Social Democrat, and to turn this vision to dust. Within six short years the party would be outlawed by Hitler, who came - in Pastor Niemoller's words – 'first for the Communists', and Thaelmann would be jailed, without trial, until his murder in Buchenwald Concentration Camp in August 1944.

LIST OF ILLUSTRATIONS

Under the banner of Lenin [1934]
Aleksandr Mizin, **p.32**

Comrades coal miners! [1933]
Valentina Kulagina, **p.34**

We will sweep from the market place the speculators and corrupt! [1932]
Kalmykov (attr.), **p.35**

2 + 2 = 5! [1931]
Yakov Guminer, **p.36**

War programmes on pig iron and steel [1932]
Natalia Pinus, **p.37**

The national metallurgical centres [1930]
Artist unknown, **p.38**

Guard the socialist harvest with vigilance [1935]
Viktor Govorkov, **p.39**

The revolutionary war council of the USSR [1933]
Nikolai Dolgorukov, **p.40**

Inventors strengthen the battle forces of the Red Army! [1933]
Vassily Suryaninov, **p.42**

Long live our happy socialist motherland. Long live our beloved, great Stalin! [1935]
Gustav Klutsis, **p.44**

All Soviet nations will vote! [1938]
Vladimir Stenberg (attr.), **p.45**

Twenty years of the Komsomol [1938]
Nikolai Denisov and Nina Vatolina, **p.46**

Forward! Victory is near! [1944]
Viktor Ivanov, **p.48**

The transformation of Fritz [1943]
Kukryniksy, **p.50**

We drink the waters of our Dnieper! 1943]
Viktor Ivanov, **p.51**

Newest Europe [1944]
Kukryniksy, **p.52**

Invade Western Europe now! [1943]
Artist unknown, **p.53**

You will reap what you sow! [1944]
Pavel P. Sokolov-Skalya, **p.54**

Finish the job! [1943]
Artist unknown, **p.55**

All nations help out at the Front! [1943]
Kukryniksy, **p.56**

Our Crimea! [1944]
Pavel P. Sokolov-Skalya, **p.57**

One against three! [c. 1943]
Petr Sarkisian, **p.58**

Forward! To the West! [1942]
Viktor Ivanov, **p.61**

Field Marshal Kutuzov (1745-1813) [1945]
Petr Alyakrinsky, **p.62**

All hope is in you, soldier of the Red Army [1943]
Viktor Ivanov and Olga Burova, **p.64**

Hoist the banner of victory over Berlin! [1945]
Viktor Ivanov, **p.67 (and front cover)**

30 years of the Communist Party of Czechoslovakia [1951]
J. Herman, **p.68**

Very best greetings for a Merry Christmas [1945]
Heinz Voelkel, **p.71**

5 year plan in 4 years - we can do it! [1948]
Viktor Ivanov, **p.72**

The mountains belong to the workers! [1949-51]
Otcenasek, **p.75**

Klement Gottwald [1949-50]
K. Skela, **p.76**

How to view Germany [1951]
Artist unknown, **p.77**

Farmers - co-operative workers: strive for higher yields! [c. 1951]
Artist unknown, **p.78**

Peace must be fought for! Hands off Korea! [c. 1951]
Artist unknown, **p.80**

Peace to the children of the whole world! [1951]
Artist unknown, **p.83**

Czechoslovakia at the outset of the Cold War [1949-51]
Artist unknown, **p.84**

Peace! [1965]
Nina Vatolina, **p.86**

We have captured the dangerous vermin [1952]
Artist unknown, **p.88**

The International knows no frontiers [n.d.]
Artist unknown, **p.90**

Glory to the heroes of the Soviet Union [1934]
G. Leonov, **p.92**

For the builders of socialist history - culturally socialist cities [1932]
Daniil Cherkes, **p.93**

Ten years of the Soviet Union [1927]
Artist unknown, **p.94**

СЛАВА
НАШЕЙ
РОДИНЕ
ЛЮБИМОЙ

NewStatesman
John Carpenter House
7 Carmelite Street
London EC4Y 0AN
Tel 020 7936 6400
Fax 020 7305 7304
Subscription enquiries, reprints and syndication rights:
Stephen Brasher
sbrasher@newstatesman.co.uk
0800 731 8496

Editor
Jason Cowley
Editorial Research
Philip Maughan
Art Director
Anja Wohlstrom
Photography Editor
Rebecca McClelland
Chief Sub-Editor
Nana Yaa Mensah
Production Editors
Jill Chisholm
Angela Derbyshire
Editors
Caroline Crampton
Jonathan Derbyshire
Sophie Elmhirst
Dan Hancox
Helen Lewis
Michael Prodger
Charlotte Simmonds
Becky Slack
Deputy Photography Editor
Catherine Hyland
Sub-Editors
Sarah Bancroft
Prudence Hone
Graphic Design
Emily Foster
Dan Murrell
Interns
Kamila Kociałkowska
Jonathan Socrates
Nicola Tilley
Laura Vanweydeveld
Laura Williams

Commercial Director
Peter Coombs
020 7336 5296
Senior Account Manager
Yeaisn Ahmed
020 7936 6462
Account Manager
Alexandra Dorling
Advertising Production
Leon Parks
020 7936 6461
Partnerships and Events Manager
Rosalind Goates

Contents

Free thinking since 1913

How to make a revolution: H G Wells interviews Joseph Stalin 48

A Woolf among rabbits: the world of Lewis Carroll 148

The World at War

Dreams and Delusions

A Radical Century

Voices from Elsewhere

▶

Contents

Free thinking since 1913

Last words from a contrarian: Hitch's final interview 168

Under western eyes: a letter from Joseph Conrad 223

Cover artwork *Martina Flor/ Handsome Frank*

Lives and Letters

The Critical Condition

The Rest of Life

Jason Cowley Editor's Note

The New Statesman century: political commitment, radical causes, literary style

On 23 November 1957 the philosopher and pacifist Bertrand Russell published in the *New Statesman* an open letter to two "Most Potent Sirs", the US president, Dwight Eisenhower, and the first secretary of the Soviet Communist Party, Nikita Khrushchev, in which he wrote passionately about the dangers nuclear weapons posed to the world. The Campaign for Nuclear Disarmament (CND) was launched as a result of a slightly earlier *NS* article, "Britain and the Nuclear Bombs", by J B Priestley, which is republished on page 84. Kingsley Martin, the editor of the *NS* from 1931-60, chaired the first meeting of CND, at which Russell and Priestley were present.

Unilateral nuclear disarmament – eventually adopted as official policy by the Labour Party in 1982, a decision it ultimately regretted – was one of the great radical causes Martin championed during his long and successful editorship. The paper became the pulpit from which this son of a Nonconformist minister and his allies addressed the world.

Russell's letter would have a powerful effect. Shortly before Christmas 1957, a letter from the Soviet embassy arrived at the *NS* offices in Great Turnstile Street, London. It was opened and, because it was written in Russian, swiftly discarded in a wastepaper basket, from where it was rescued only later, by either Norman Mackenzie or Paul Johnson, then staff editors. I spoke to both men about the letter and each claimed to have retrieved it. Whoever did so, the letter turned out to be from Khrushchev, and enclosed with it was an article by him, an unsolicited reply to Russell, which the *NS* promptly published. Early in 1958, the US secretary of state, John Foster Dulles, writing on behalf of Eisenhower, responded to both Khrushchev and Russell.

That cold war nuclear diplomacy was being played out in the *New Statesman* was testament to its extraordinary influence in the immediate postwar years, when it succeeded in articulating the hopes and aspirations of a generation of progressives who believed that history was moving in their direction, and became essential reading for anyone seriously interested in politics and culture, irrespective of their ideological allegiances.

*

The first issue of the *New Statesman* was published on 12 April 1913. The paper was founded in a spirit of optimism by Beatrice and Sidney Webb with £5,000-worth of donations, including £1,000 from George Bernard Shaw, an early influence on the paper. Beatrice was not hopeful. "If I were forced to wager, I should not back our success," she wrote in a diary entry. The Webbs wanted their own weekly paper to serve as a forum for their ideas and to help promote and argue for what they hoped would be a scientific socialist transformation of society – the lead editorial published in the first issue spoke of the "world movement towards collectivism". Through their research – they co-founded the London School of Economics and the Fabian Society and William Beveridge worked for them as a young researcher – the Webbs helped to lay the foundations of the welfare state.

Yet they were a curious couple with some odd opinions, even for their time. Resolute statists rather than liberals, they were not much interested in personal freedom. They were imperialists. They showed an alarming interest in eugenics. And they were fellow-travellers of the Soviet Union, publishing a much-derided book titled *Soviet Communism: an Ideal Civilisation?* (1935). A later, revised edition dropped the question mark.

Quite early on, the *New Statesman*, edited in its early years by Clifford Sharp, a Fabian who became a keen supporter of the Asquithian Liberals, began to slip free from their influence. In 1931, and now under the editorship of Kingsley Martin, who had worked previously as a leader writer on the *Manchester Guardian*, the *New Statesman* merged with the *Nation*, the old weekly voice of social Liberalism. John Maynard Keynes, as chairman of the *Nation*, joined the board of the renamed *New Statesman and Nation*. So these were the forces that defined the *NS*: the Fabians, Keynes, Whig radicalism and the Bloomsbury literary and arts crowd.

> The NS has always been at its best when at its boldest

The *NS* was conceived as a weekly "review of politics and literature". Note those two words, "politics" and "literature". H G Wells and Shaw were among the literary artists who wrote regularly for the paper on political matters. Later, in the early 1920s, the novelist Arnold Bennett served as chairman and became one of the chief benefactors. From the beginning, it published poetry and fiction as well as political and economic commentary.

Yet there was a decisive separation between the politics and the literature, between what was published in the so-called front and back halves of the paper. Over time the *NS* became known as a "pantomime horse", with the "political" front and "cultural" back characterised by differing sensibilities and aspirations. There seemed to be no bridge

DAN MURRELL

between the two "halves", or worlds, of the paper. The understanding was that the front half was rigidly political in mission and intent while the back was more plural, unpredictable and ecumenical. It was as if the demands of politics and literature were in some way antagonistic; that to concentrate too much on the political would be to neglect the literary and to be too literary would be to misunderstand or to be insufficiently serious about politics.

When Martin Amis worked at the *Statesman* as literary editor in the late 1970s, he was amused by the political commitment of his friends and fellow staffers Christopher Hitchens and James Fenton, both then on the hard Trotskyite left. He has written of how Hitchens improved as a writer, his prose gaining in "burnish and authority", only after the fall of the Berlin Wall in 1989, as if before then he had been constrained by a self-imposed demand to hold a fixed ideological line and this had affected his literary style.

*

The *New Statesman* has been, I think, at its best when it has been at its boldest: when it has aspired to be much more than a magazine obsessed with the machinations and personalities of the Westminster power game; when it has campaigned (CND, Charter 88, against appeasement and colonialism, for women's and gay rights) as well as reported and denounced; and when it has been as interested in good literary style as in exposing the injustices of the world. Above all, even in the leanest years, when it came close to bankruptcy, the *NS*, as the pieces collected here remind us, has always known what it was against: subordination, privation, unaccountable power, the mystique of hierarchy, social and economic inequalities, racial and sexual discrimination.

Today, no longer on life support, the *NS* has returned to something like robust health. We are published on paper and in several digital formats, and we have a vibrant and ever-growing website. And the division between the front and back halves has been abolished – it is a weekly review of politics and literature, as originally intended.

This centenary volume is a celebration of and a showcase for the richness and breadth of the *NS*'s archive, and we have used it as an opportunity to republish some of our favourite articles and writers. We have organised the magazine into seven sections: The World at War, Dreams and Delusions, A Radical Century, Voices from Elsewhere, Lives and Letters, The Critical Condition and The Rest of Life. I wrote or spoke to many previous *NS* editors to ask for their recommendations for this volume. Some of the articles have been edited or slightly truncated. Some, such as the article that launched Charter 88 or the letter that led to the creation of Mass Observation, have been included because they are of consequential importance. Others have been chosen because of their prescience or the insights they offer into world-historic figures, such as Hitler and Stalin. And others have been chosen because of their intrinsic literary value, such as Virginia Woolf's short piece on Lewis Carroll, in which she writes wonderfully of the mystery and ruthlessness of childhood, or the academic and critic Frank Kermode's reflection on the death of T S Eliot. And we chose several others simply because they made us laugh – such as Gore Vidal's magisterial taking down of Lord Longford, the actor Hugh Grant's undercover investigation into phone-hacking, or Paul Johnson's attack on James Bond. It's an eclectic selection and, I hope, also a valuable and entertaining one.

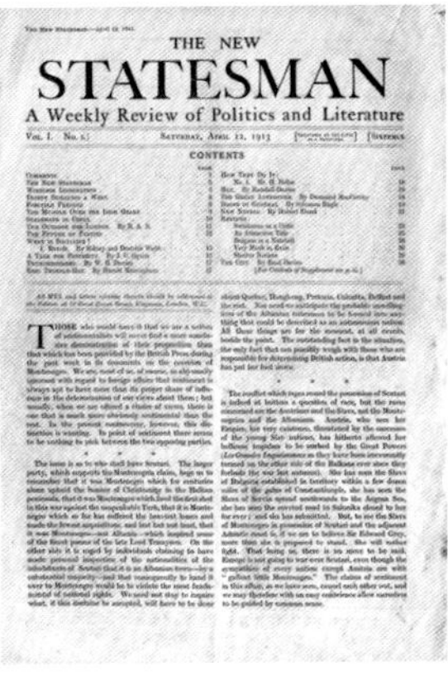

THE NEW
STATESMAN
A Weekly Review of Politics and Literature

Vol. I. No. 1.] Saturday, April 12, 1913 [Sixpence

CONTENTS

*

In the closing paragraph of *Homage to Catalonia* (1938), George Orwell, who had a troubled and unhappy relationship with the *New Statesman*, writes of returning to England from the Spanish civil war, in which he fought, was shot in the throat and almost died. He finds England reassuringly unchanged, at once becalmed and complacent:

> And then England – southern England, probably the sleekest landscape in the world. It is difficult when you pass that way, especially when you are peacefully recovering from sea-sickness with the plush cushions of a boat-train carriage under your bum, to believe that anything is really happening anywhere. Earthquakes in Japan, famines in China, revolutions in Mexico? Don't worry, the milk will be on the doorstep tomorrow morning, the *New Statesman* will come out on Friday . . .

All these years later, the *New Statesman* is still coming out at the end of each week, even though the world has changed in ways that even the far-seeing Orwell could never have imagined and at a time when so many other print titles have been devoured by the internet.

I hope you enjoy this special centenary edition. A second volume will be published later in the year. ●

The World at War

FOX PHOTOS/HULTON ARCHIVE/GETTY IMAGES

In January 1941, firemen on the roof of Cannon Street Station in London look out towards St Paul's Cathedral and the ruins of buildings around it

12 JULY 1913

A Note on Irish Nationalism

By George Bernard Shaw

One of the best-known early contributors to the New Statesman was the playwright and Fabian activist George Bernard Shaw. His fame helped gain early publicity for Beatrice and Sidney Webb's new weekly review of politics and literature. He also contributed £1,000 of the £5,000 in donations that funded its launch. Shaw's style was theatrical and pugnacious and invariably favoured satire and exaggeration over fact. Here he ridicules his countrymen and women, attempting to offend both Irish nationalists and Ulster loyalists.

The world seems just now to have made up its mind that self-consciousness is a very undesirable thing and Nationalism a very fine thing. This is not a very intelligent conclusion; for, obviously, Nationalism is nothing but a mode of self-consciousness, and a very aggressive one at that. It is, I think, altogether to Ireland's credit that she is extremely tired of the subject of herself. Even patriotism, which in England is a drunken jollity when it is not a Jewish rhapsody, is in Ireland like the genius of Jeremiah, a burning fire shut up in the bones, a pain, a protest against shame and defeat, a morbid condition which a healthy man must shake off if he is to keep sane. If you want to bore an Irishman, play him an Irish melody, or introduce him to another Irishman.

Abroad, however, it is a distinction to be an Irishman; and accordingly the Irish in England flaunt their nationality. An Englishman who had married an Irishwoman once came and asked me could I give him the name of any Englishman who had ever done anything. He explained that his wife declared that all England's statesmen, all her warriors, all her musical composers, all her notables of every degree were Irishmen, and that the English could not write their names until the Irish taught them. I suggested Gladstone. "She says he was an Irishman," was the reply. After this, it was clear that the man's case was desperate; so I left him to his fate.

From this you may gather that the reaction against the Nationalist variety of self-consciousness does not mean a reaction against conceit, against ignorance, against insular contempt for foreigners, against bad manners and the other common human weaknesses which sometimes masquerade as patriotism. Ireland produces virulent varieties of all of them; for it is, on the whole, a mistake to suppose that we are a nation of angels. You can always find something better than a good Englishman and something worse than a bad one; but this is not so in Ireland: a bad Irishman is the vilest thing on earth, and a good one is a saint. Thackeray's *Barry Lyndon* is a very accurate sketch of the sort of thorough-paced scoundrel Ireland can produce, not when she is put to it, but quite wantonly, merely for the fun of being mischievous.

In point of conceit, Ireland, especially northern Ireland, can stagger humanity. The Ulster Unionist is not a shrewd calculator who, on

If you want to bore an Irishman, introduce him to another Irishman

a careful estimate of the pressure of public opinion on any Government which should try to coerce Belfast into submission to a Dublin Parliament, concludes that he can safely bluff Home Rule out of Ulster: he really believes that he can fight and conquer the British Empire, or any other empire that is not Ulster and Protestant. If there were nothing else to be considered except the salvation of the Ulsterman's soul, it would be a positive duty for the British Empire to blow him sky high to convince him that even a Unionist God (and he believes in no other, and therefore does not really believe in God at all) has occasionally to look beyond Down and Antrim.

But these military moral lessons cost more than the souls of the regenerated are worth; and it would, I think, be more sensible to make Ulster an autonomous political lunatic asylum with an expensive fleet and a heavily fortified frontier to hold against the Pope, than to thwart its inclinations in any way. The alternative, if England would stand it, would be to make Ulster a province of England, and have the Education Acts and the Factory Acts applied in the English manner; but I doubt if Ulster would tamely submit to be identified with a country where men touch their hats to a Roman Catholic Duke of Norfolk, and meet him at dinner as if he were their equal.

What will finally settle the Ulster question is just the old-fashioned romantic Nationalism of which the South is so deadly tired. It is clear, as the world is now constituted, that prudent young men should aim at being as unlike Orangemen and as like human beings as possible, even as in the South the young men are discovering that in point of insufferableness there is not a halfpenny to choose between a Nationalist and an Orangeman. Thus, though the Protestant boys will still carry the drum, they will carry it under the green flag, and realise that the harp, the hound, and the round tower are more satisfactory to the imagination than that stupidest of decorative designs, the Union Jack. And the change can be effected without treachery to England; for, if my personal recollection does not deceive me, the Gaelic League began in Bedford Park, London, after a prolonged incubation in Somerset House.

It is not very long since I stood on the coast of Donegal and asked two boys how many languages they had. They had three. One was English, which they spoke much better than it is ever spoken in England. The second was Irish, which they spoke with their parents. The third was the language invented by the Gaelic League, which I cannot speak (being an Irishman), but which I understand to be in its qualities comparable to a blend of Esperanto with fifth-century Latin. Why should not Ulster adopt this strange tongue?

The truth is that all the Nationalist inventions that catch on now are not Irish at all. For instance, the admirable comedies of Synge, who, having escaped from Ireland to France, drew mankind in the manner of Molière, and discreetly assured the public that this was merely the human nature of the Blasket Islands, and that, of course, civilised people never admired boastful criminals nor esteemed them according to the atrocities they pretended to commit. The Playboy's real name was Synge; and the famous libel on Ireland (and who is Ireland that she should not be libelled as other countries are by their great comedians?) was the truth about the world. ●

Why the Germans Are Not Loved

By Havelock Ellis

It may seem a futile question to discuss. "*Circumspice*", one may be told, is the answer; you have only to look around Europe. Yet there is a certain interest in discussing this attitude of the world towards Germans when we realise that it is 2,000 years old. To seek to exacerbate passions that are already acute would be an unworthy task. The Germans are a great factor in the world's life; they will not be exterminated, whatever happens; they even have a large part—as they like to remind us—in our own blood. We shall still have to live in the world with them, and may as well try to understand them. If the world has not loved them, that is scarcely matter for exultation.

In Germany itself this attitude of the world is not unrealised; indeed, it is often morbidly exaggerated. Thoughtful Germans have from time to time anxiously pondered over the problem. One such attempt to elucidate the matter, made a few years ago, seems worth bringing forward, because the events of today serve to put it in a new light. Professor Georg Steinhausen speaks with high authority. He is at the very centre of that "*Kultur*" we now hear so much about. He is, indeed, its historian as well as the editor of the *Archiv für Kultur-Geschichte*. Moreover, Steinhausen, even in discussing so delicate a topic as the world's estimate of Germans, is reasonable and fair-minded. He desires for his country a civilisation of finer quality, for Germany still lacks, he remarks, what the French, the English, even the Dutch, have achieved—an evolved spirit of civilisation, an independent art of living, a high *Lebensstil*. What such a man has to say is better worth hearing than the fanatical and less typical utterances of extremists, so wearisomely dinned into our ears of late.

"There is no people so unloved as we are. Why is it?" he asks. (He is writing, it must be remembered, five years ago.) Germany's position in the world reminds him of England's a century ago when she attacked unprotected Denmark, though he hastens to qualify this remark by adding that Germany has no such crime on her conscience; "Germany's policy is the most peaceful and well-meaning in the world." Steinhausen finds a partial answer to his question in the reflection that the reputation of nations is chiefly founded on their exterior qualities, and the good qualities of the German are interior. Even Tacitus, he remarks, who admired the courage and chastity of the Germans, regarded them as drunken and violent barbarians. Their cunning also impressed the Romans, and their aptitude for lying, as Velleius Paterculus records. In the fifth century the Goths were for Salvianus "*Gothorum gens perfida*". Their frenzy of drunkenness has been specially noted from the first and all through, often with gluttony in addition. Gregory of Tours gave a disgusting picture of their drinking habits, so also Venantius Fortunatus and a long succession of writers, down, it may be said, to the present. Their uncleanliness also impressed Salvianus and others, while Sidonius complained that their women reeked of onions.

> "Alas! I know well," said Luther, "that we Germans are beasts and mad brutes"

Steinhausen is not, however, inclined to rely exclusively on the mere exteriority of the Germans' bad traits. He finds another explanation, which had, indeed, already been put forward by Nietzsche: Europeans are the legatees of the ancient Roman Empire, and have thus inherited its profound horror of the Teutonic barbarians who in successive waves rolled over their civilisation. The Goths from Prussia who sacked Rome in 410, but spared the sacred places, were far outdone in the perpetration of horrors by their descendants who accompanied Charles of Bourbon to the later sack of Rome in 1527; and still later, in the Thirty Years War, the troops of Mansfeld, which were a terror to their enemies, were a still greater terror to their friends.

It is natural, therefore, that the Latin races of today, who are still closer to ancient civilisation, should grow impatient when they hear Gobineau and Houston Chamberlain declare that the German is the salt of the earth and European civilisation a Teutonic creation, declaring on their side that civilisation is a Mediterranean product, and that the Germans have merely been a destructive element. Such a criticism, the fair-minded Steinhausen admits, is in part not unjust. The Germans had their own sources of culture, and the modern world owes to the Germans (in the wide sense, including the English) much that it possesses. (It must always be remembered that to the Teutonic mind the English, though not "*Deutsch*", are "German". Hence the resentment felt in Germany at our "treachery" in turning against a race regarded as being of our own stock. They overlook the fact that "England", and even "*Deutschland*", are really inhabited by races of highly mixed composition, and neither exclusively "Germanic", even in the widest sense.)

But this debt to Germany only began in the middle of the 18th century. It has proceeded rapidly, and "today world-civilisation is no more Latin, but a great part Germanic"—that is, as we should express it, Anglo-Saxon and Germanic.

Whatever the explanation of the world's opinion of the Teuton, Professor Steinhausen admits and even emphasises that opinion; few of its more notable expressions seem to have escaped him. "*Teutonici, nullius amici*", was the Latin saying of the thirteenth century. "The friend of none!" comments the Professor. "A sad saying, but very significant. It corresponds to the judgment of many peoples concerning the medieval Germans." A haughty self-consciousness was noted of them and embodied in fifteenth-

L'OGRE
Nous verrons bien c'qu'il a dans l'ventre!

***"Grossiers et communs"*: a 1914 French cartoon shows patriots climbing into the mouth of the "Ogre" Bismarck to find out if he's got any guts**

century proverbs, as was their clownishness. They were not loved by their fellow-crusaders in the Holy Land: "*grossiers et communs*", wrote the Troubadour Peire Vidal. The Germans, on their part, passed this attitude on, and in their turn have always called the Slavs "barbarians". Petrarch continued the tradition, but in his hands it becomes a more refined and discriminating criticism; he admired Cologne, but he could only find signs of material prosperity, none of spiritual exultation. It was, Steinhausen points out, mainly "the coarse atmosphere of drunkenness and gluttony" which made Germany seem barbarous, so that, in 1471, Giantonio Campano said that it made him sick even to hear the word "Germany".

The Germans themselves admitted the truth of the foreigners' charges. "Alas! I know well," said Luther, "that we Germans are, and always will be, beasts and mad brutes, as the peoples around call us, and as we well deserve." "*Porco tedesco*", said the Italian proverb; "*Allemands ivrognes*", the French, though at the same time their prowess was admitted: "Let him who wants to be hacked in pieces quarrel with the Germans." Even the English, though they had the least right of all to make fun of "other Germans" on these grounds, joined in the general chorus. He quotes Shakespeare's Portia on the German, the observations of the judicious Fynes Moryson—whose *Itinerary*, it may be added, was the Baedeker for Europe of the 17th century—and the epigram of John Owen that if in wine there is truth, certainly it will sooner or later be discovered by the Germans.

In the middle of the 18th century there was indeed a sudden fashion of admiration for the German poetry of the time, its sentiment and its naïveté; but this fashion had almost passed by 1790. It was not until Madame de Staël's revelation of the "German soul" in 1813, in *De l'Allemagne*, that Germany became really a fashion in France. The new industrial development has not made Germany more loved, says Steinhausen, though it has increased respect and admiration. Notwithstanding all the military and industrial and economic activities of Germany, there remains the feeling, he confesses, that the Germans are barbarous, more especially in the developments of Prussian militarism. (It may be noted that Steinhausen, probably because he himself belongs to Prussia, deliberately omits to consider the Prussianisation of modern Germany as a factor in the European attitude.) "All Prussians," says Maurice Barrès, "are under the operation of beer, which lulls, without changing, their brutal souls;" and René Bazin remarks: "I do not hate the Germans—I even admire them—but the more I learn to know them the more I feel that they are different, that I belong to another race, and that I cherish an ideal which they cannot understand." This feeling of superiority on the part of the Latins, as the judicial Steinhausen observes, is not without justification; it is based on their ancient civilisation, and on the possession of a cultivated art of living which, he admits, the Germans, for all their efforts, still lack.

"The Englishman, also, has a definite culture of life, and a civilisational style of living, without which life is unthinkable to him, and which no one denies. He, too, feels himself in consequence to be superior to the noisy and ill-bred German, unskilfully stiff, or formlessly jovial, or socially incorrect." Such feelings, Steinhausen concludes, together with hatred of the feudal-military system, affect all peoples outside Germany, especially those proud of their "freedom" (it is the Professor who places that word in inverted commas). So it is that Ferrero in *L'Europa Giovane* calls Bismarck a barbaric genius only fit for Huns. Behind this exposition one detects a certain sadness. Steinhausen is on the side of that idealistic individualism which he evidently regards as the finest and deepest Germanic trait.

To Germany's other defects is to be added her extreme self-consciousness of superiority, and Steinhausen quotes a Serb as to the Germans "always crying aloud their own good qualities and running down foreigners whom at the same time they are ridiculously imitating". This attitude has accompanied Germany's sudden rise to prosperity, which again arouses, especially among the English, "envy and jealousy".

In the end Steinhausen consoles himself with the thought that other nations are beginning to regard Germany as a model. The Russians are in science and in economics the pupils of the Germans. So also are the Balkan peoples. Germany's friends are growing in Italy. The French are beginning to be just to Germany. The Belgian Maeterlinck has declared that "Germany is the moral conscience of the world". The Americans recognise the blessings which Germany has brought. The Japanese appreciate and imitate Germany. "So we Germans need not take tragically the world's lack of love for us. Politically it may today be dangerous. But against that danger our might will protect us."

Doubtless there are some who will smile gleefully to observe how even that place of refuge which Professor Steinhausen imagines that Germany holds in the world's heart has today fallen down at every single point like a house of cards. But it is matter for tragedy more than comedy. Whatever the might of Germany may prove to be worth, it remains a tragedy for itself and all mankind that one of the youngest and most vigorous of great nations—eagerly striving to snatch at that culture which is the mature growth of centuries—should seek to thrust its gifts on the world by brute force, while yet dimly realising that one of the greatest of national assets is love. ●

BAUME & MERCIER

MAISON D'HORLOGERIE GENEVE 1830

Republican fighters are marched downhill from a post on the Somosierra, northern Spain, as they surrender to nationalists in 1936

3 OCTOBER 1936

On the Spanish Front

By Claud Cockburn

When it comes to coverage of the Spanish civil war, the New Statesman is better known for whom and what it failed to publish – George Orwell – than what it did. Orwell called Kingsley Martin, the editor of the NS from 1931-60, the "corrupt face" of censorship, although this should not obscure the importance of all that Martin did publish about that conflict. As Orwell writes in "Homage to Catalonia", Claud Cockburn's analysis is skewed by his pro-communist sympathies; but his eyewitness accounts were among the finest to emerge from the war.

At the offices of the Cultural Commission they were reading the first leaflets dropped over Madrid by the German planes, threatening "ruthless bombardment".

José Bergamín, a member of the Commission, said to me: "Today is probably our last chance for a long time to come and see some of the finest pictures in the world." In those first weeks of the war, the picture galleries at least had bloomed. The Cultural Commission of the People's Front, composed of the leading artists, art critics and writers of Spain, had been busy unearthing from steel vaults in the Bank of Spain pictures which for years had lain hidden there serving as bonds, deposited or hoarded by grandee owners.

The list of the newly discovered pictures—now hung in the Prado—by itself reads like the catalogue of some splendid new gallery. The Prado was packed all day with people going to see the new-found treasures. "This afternoon," Bergamín went on, "we shall have to start putting them back in the dark again. They may bomb tonight. Fortunately the Prado is bomb-proof."

In the small hours, sirens mounted on motor cars screamed through the darkened streets. Militiamen hammered on bedroom doors, warning everyone to get downstairs. In the lounge of the Hotel Florida people drifted uncertainly about, stumbling over chairs and divans in the darkness. Someone lit a cigarette, and a voice like a pistol shot from the street outside ordered us to be careful with the lights. There was an argument as to whether we should go to the cellar or stay in the lounge. "I have observed," said a French lady, "that Mr So-and-So is staying in this hotel." She mentioned the agent of a notorious American financial magnate. Mr So-and-So was known to maintain the closest relations with the German Embassy. "If he goes to ▶

▸ the cellar I think we may assume that the raid is intended to be serious." Presently we saw him picking his way towards the cellar. Someone asked him why he did not go to the Germany Embassy and really be safe. "The German Embassy," he said sadly, "left by plane today for Alicante." We went to the cellar.

The planes were not clearly heard. A bomb screamed through the air and the crash merged abruptly into the agonised screaming of women's voices somewhere far off.

*

Under the garden trees at the British Embassy, the militia guard played cards. Inside, impoverished gentlewomen, escaping enemy agents who wanted to get British passports, and an assortment of crooks, hung about, most of them insisting on seeing the Chargé d'Affaires immediately.

"And so," I said to the diplomat, "when my Spanish friends ask me why the British Government is going on in this way, I don't really know what explanation to give."

"Well," he said, "we shall have to maintain an attitude of reserve, of course. We shall hope to arrange things with the rebels in a more or less satisfactory manner. As for me," he said, beaming and pumping my hand vigorously, "I have an absolutely clear conscience, I am absolutely neutral. You can assure your Spanish friends of that."

*

Morning, afternoon and evening, the recruits gathered round the sergeant instructors asking when the rifles would come. "Tomorrow perhaps." On the fourth day they gave us dummy rifles. A middle-aged lieutenant, who had fought in the old army in Africa and been cashiered the previous year as a suspected Socialist, explained to me why he thought the newspapers must be making a mistake about the attitude of the British Government on the "neutrality" question.

"Apart from anything else," he said, "it is quite clear to me that the British Government cannot have such an attitude, for I think that it will not be possible for the British to agree to the Germans controlling the mid-Atlantic from here, and Portugal, and the Moroccos. It is impossible."

"You forget," I said, "that you have not a monopoly of traitors in your country. Your General Franco is prepared to give away bits of Spain to foreign powers to help him beat the people of Spain. Our Government is full of similar people who are prepared to open any gate to the enemies of England rather than support a democratic Government in Spain or lead a joint action of the democratic Powers."

"And the patriots in your country, the democrats and so on. How strong do you estimate them to be?"

"Strong but split," I said.

"That's bad."

*

"One dead, four wounded." The Sergeant handed to the Captain his report on the accident we had just suffered on the winding road to the front. The lorry in which our platoon was packed and racing had gone fast round a hairpin bend and overturned.

"He was driving too fast," said the Sergeant.

"He was not," said the Captain. "You have to understand, and all the comrades have to understand, that nowadays we can't drive any slower on this road. Before they had all the new planes, yes. Now, you drive slowly along this road and the next thing you know their planes have spotted you. If we lose men in accidents, that isn't the driver's fault."

"What about our planes?" someone asked. "Can't they drive them away?'

"Well, Englishman," said the Captain, laughing and turning to me, "what about our planes? Are they going to send us a present from Portugal for a change?"

The dead man and the four wounded men lay on the roadside in a line together, waiting for a lorry back.

*

We moved into position on the Sierra. The men we had relieved told us it was a quiet spot. Then, somewhere over on the left, our people took some prisoners whose story indicated the quiet would not last long. The prisoners said that the big attack was scheduled for the thirteenth of September, but was being held up until the new German planes arrived.

It began, sure enough, on the sixteenth. The Junkers, with first-class German pilots and machine gunners aboard, and sometimes—so prisoners told us—a couple of Spaniards for "look see", flew low in squadrons, bombing and machine-gunning the line of our riflemen on the hill-tops.

Morning and evening we lay under the rocks, helpless, and trying to keep ready to jump out to meet a wave of infantry attack the moment the planes were gone. Our water supply was under machine-gun fire, rifle bullets kept coming on to the rock shelter we used as a kitchen, so the eating and drinking was on a limited scale. Sometimes we were on guard for as much as 15 hours of the 24. It was uncomfortable because you could neither sit nor stand. You could not sit because you could not see to fire, nor stand because if you stood up you got a bullet in the head. We perched uncomfortably among the rocks, looking across the Guadarrama plain.

*

One night three men were reported to have slept on duty.

The Captain called a meeting of the platoon, and explained the circumstances. He sat cross-legged in the middle of a circle of men, huddled in thin blankets against the terrible wind of the Sierras, pressed close under the parapets and rocks, with bullets whining intermittently above them.

"You all understand," he said, "the gravity of the offence. You are here of your own free will, holding a point which is not simply of significance for us, although we may well die here, nor yet for Madrid and for Spain, but also for civilisation in all the world." He went on to speak more particularly of the perils brought upon others by a guard who sleeps on duty.

The question was then thrown open to discussion, the words of the speakers being occasionally inaudible as a big shell howled overhead and burst on the hillside behind.

It was proposed that those who had slept and the Sergeant responsible for making the rounds of the guards should be shot. The Sergeant, a former butcher's boy, who had joined three weeks before and been elected Sergeant only ten days ago, spoke haltingly but with terrible earnest in favour of his own execution. When he had finished he squatted silent, nervously fingering his rifle.

The three guards who had slept—one of them was only sixteen years old and had been a delivery boy in Valencia—spoke against execution, declaring they would never do it again, and suggesting some alternative penalty.

The difficulty was that whenever a "fatigue" was proposed it was found to be something which everyone was compelled to do anyway. One of those who had slept—whom I had already threatened to shoot on the previous night—proposed that "the Englishman" should be put in charge of all these hard cases. "We can rely on him to shoot them if necessary." In the end they went unpunished, and that was the last occasion when there was any sleeping on guard in our platoon.

The battle developed, day in and day out, into a bloody game wherein the poorly armed forces of the democrats sought, by desperate assaults and reckless endeavours, to even out the difference between them and the German air force on the other side. One day we were told that now, indeed, it must be frankly said that the position was hopeless, but that nevertheless retreat could not be contemplated, for it might roll up the whole Sierra front.

"We can only die once," said the Captain. "And we have the satisfaction of knowing that we are dying for ourselves and for all free peoples of the world, too. Isn't that so, Englishman?" There was discussion of the situation. One man said to me: "Do you believe that if we resist bravely here, fighting until we are every one of us killed, that the time we gain will be of use to the democratic Powers in preparing to come to the help of Spain?" I told them that every hour we gained there would be an hour more gained for these people in England who were fighting day and night with us against the "neutrality" pact and on behalf of the people of Spain.

'That," said one of the Assault Guards who was with us, "is very satisfactory." ●

PROVIDING A TALENTED WORKFORCE TO MEET THE NEEDS OF INDUSTRY

David Duffy, Managing Director of the Career Transition Partnership (CTP) highlights how the MOD funded organisation is fast becoming a key resourcing partner for leading companies.

In the changing world of work, the one constant is the need for employers to access exceptional talent to enhance their workforce.

The CTP is a partnering agreement between the Ministry of Defence and Right Management who is a global leader in talent and career management workforce solutions. The CTP has been the official provider of the MOD resettlement provision since 1998 and in that time, has helped over 180,000 Service personnel make the transition from the Armed Forces. This is achieved through a series of career transition workshops, vocational training and job finding support including events, both physical and virtual; employment consultants and a job site called RightJob.

For employers we offer a high quality, no cost recruitment service. We provide a personalised service based on your recruitment needs. Our Account Managers can discuss your particular requirements and advise you on how best to use the services of the CTP. We have provided the route for hundreds of organisations to secure highly skilled employees, whilst making significant savings on their recruitment spend.

Employers recognise the investment made by the Armed Forces in the high quality training of its military personnel in a range of trades such as engineers, technicians, aviation and IT specialists, logisticians, drivers, chefs, administrators, and experienced managers up to board room level. The CTP has now become a key resourcing partner for leading organisations, such as Openreach, who over the last 24 months have recruited over 1,000 Service leavers.

Liv Garfield, Chief Executive of Openreach, says *"For us, as an employer, it's fantastic that we've been able to recruit so many ex-Armed Forces personnel through the CTP. They are highly skilled, motivated and disciplined and have experience of complex engineering tasks in challenging environments, whilst having a disciplined approach and a very positive attitude."*

To find out more about how to access the high quality, no-cost solution offered by the CTP, call our Central Employment Team on 0121 236 0058.

career **transition** partnership

The Ministry of Defence working with Right Management

www.ctp.org.uk/employers

10 JULY 1937

Should We Intervene?

By John Maynard Keynes

WH Auden's poem *Spain* is fit to stand beside great predecessors in its moving yet serene expression of feeling towards the heart-rending events of the political world. The theme of the poem lies in the comparison between the secular achievements of the past and the hope which is possible for the future with the horrors of the present and the sacrifices which perhaps it demands from those of this generation who think and feel rightly. Yesterday, all the past. To-morrow, perhaps the future. "But to-day the struggle", his refrain runs.

I view with revulsion the growing tendency to make of the struggle between the two ideologies another War of Religion, to believe that the issue can or will be settled by force of arms, and to feel that it is our duty to hasten to any quarter of the world where those of our faith are oppressed. Assume that the war occurs, and let us suppose, for the sake of argument, that we win. What then? Shall we ourselves be the better for it and for what it will have brought with it? What are we going to do with the defeated? Are we to impose our favourite ideology on them in an up-to-date Peace Treaty, or do we assume that they will adopt it with spontaneous enthusiasm? At best we should be back exactly where we were. Defeat is complete disaster. Victory would be useless, and probably pernicious.

Therefore I maintain that the claims of Peace are paramount. It is our duty to prolong peace, hour by hour, day by day, for as long as we can. We do not know what the future will bring, except that it will be quite different from anything we could predict. I have said in another context that it is a disadvantage of "the long run" that in the long run we are all dead. But I could have said equally well that it is a great advantage of "the short run" that in the short run we are still alive. Life and history are made up of short runs. If we are at peace in the short run, that is something. The best we can do is to put off disaster, if only in the hope that something will turn up. While there is peace, there is peace. It is silly and presumptuous to say that war is inevitable; for no one can possibly know. The only conclusion which is certain is that we cannot avoid war by bringing it on. If, thinking of Spain, someone urges that self-interest does not entitle us to abandon others, I answer that for Spain peace—peace on any terms—is her greatest interest. Spain will work out her future in due course. It is not the outcome of the civil war which will settle it. It would be much more plausible to argue that British imperial interests or French security require the defeat of Franco than that the interests of Spaniards require it.

I do not claim that war can always be avoided. I do not need to answer the question whether war is even defensible. Our knowledge of human nature tells us that in practice there are circumstances when war on our part, whether defensible or not, is unavoidable. We are brought, therefore, to the second aspect of foreign policy. The first duty of foreign policy is to avoid war. Its second duty is to ensure that, if it occurs, the circumstances shall be the most favourable possible for our cause.

By postponement we gain peace to-day. Have we anything to lose by it? Our capacity for cunctation is one of our most powerful and characteristic national weapons. It has been our age-long instrument against dictators. Since Fabius Maximus there has scarcely been a stronger case for cunctation than there is to-day. It is maddening and humiliating to have to take so much lip. We may, conceivably, have to submit to greater humiliations and worse betrayals than any yet. Those who applaud war and believe they have something to gain from it have an inevitable advantage in a game of bluff and in the preliminary manoeuvres. But we have to look farther ahead; believing that time and chance are with us, and taking precautions that, *if* we are forced to act, we can make quite sure. This seems cold and shifty to the poet. Yet I claim the benefit of the first part of one of Auden's stanzas:

> What's your proposal? To build
> the just city? I will.
> I agree.

leaving to him the second part:

> Or is it the suicide pact, the romantic
> Death? Very well, I accept.

For consider the immediate political factors staring us in the face. At the moment Russia is disorganised and France at a disadvantage. Each is at a low ebb but each needs mainly time. Before long we ourselves will possess the most predominant sea-power in European waters that we have ever enjoyed in our history. Meanwhile what is happening to the brigand powers? One of them is busily engaged in outraging every creed in turn. Both of them are spending a lot of money on an intensive propaganda to persuade the rest of the world that they are the enemies of the human race. It is having the desired result, not least in the United States. No one trusts or respects their word. I doubt if even Japan thrills greatly to their croonings. Yet even so, all this needs time to sink in, at home as well as elsewhere.

These tactics are not characteristic of great statesmen and conquerors. They appear to be morbid, pathological, diseased. I gravely doubt their technical efficiency and expect that every sort of idiocy is going on behind the scenes. It is unlikely that those who talk so much nonsense will act quite differently. It is very probable that, given time, they will over-play their hands, overreach themselves and make a major blunder. It is in the nature of their type of behaviour that this should happen. And if, indeed, the thieves were to have a little more success, nothing is likelier than that they would fall out amongst themselves.

Near the beginning of the Abyssinian affair our Foreign Office was guilty of the most disastrous error of policy in recent history. It is natural, therefore, to distrust them. But though it has been hateful in its immediate consequences and cruel in some of its details, I am not inclined to criticise the broad outline of Mr [Anthony] Eden's Spanish policy. I should have been afraid if his critics had had a chance to take over from him. The task of a cunctator is always a thankless one. To be for ever allowing the brigands yet a little more rope, to be holding up the cup for them to fill yet fuller is not a distinguished office. It is never possible, unfortunately, to estimate a statesman by his results, since we never have for comparison the consequences of the alternative course.

I bid Auden, therefore, to pass by on the other side. If he will be patient and unheroic, in due course, perhaps, he will be shown (in his own words):

> History the operator, the
> Organiser, Time the refreshing river. ●

FOX PHOTOS/HULTON ARCHIVE/GETTY IMAGES

"My long struggle to win peace has failed." On 3 September 1939 Prime Minister Neville Chamberlain announced that Britain was at war with Germany

9 SEPTEMBER 1939

The First Week of War

Leader Column

To have begun the war by dropping leaflets instead of bombs on the towns of Germany is a right and imaginative stroke, of good augury for the future. We have been forced into this war; its object must be the overthrow of the Nazi rulers of Germany and the construction of a Europe in which the German people can live under common institutions with those of Britain and France and other countries. Therefore, to enlighten the German people about the behaviour of their rulers is the most important of all the tasks before us. The public has not been given enough information about these splendid exploits by which 12,000,000 leaflets appear to have been dropped in Germany without the loss of a British aeroplane. During the first days of the war, indeed, news of all sorts has been withheld to an unnecessary and unwise extent. The morale of this country depends on the knowledge of the common people, just as the morale of the German people depends on their ignorance.

Hitler's object is clearly to overwhelm the Poles before attempting battle on the Western Front. German operations against Poland have proceeded according to obvious (and presumably foreseen) plan, though with somewhat less than the clockwork precision achieved by the incomparable army which [Alexander] von Kluck commanded in August 1914. The German boast that Warsaw lay three days' march from the Reich frontier has not been realised; but, timetable apart, the war has been conducted by the aggressor on lines which were to be expected. The resistance put up by the Polish troops has been stubborn; but Poland is as incapable as Belgium in 1914 of prolonged resistance on her frontiers against German invasion. The evacuation of the Government from Warsaw to Lublin indicates that the threat to the capital is regarded as serious; but it must not be supposed that Poland has no reserves with which to fight on a shortened, straighter line. The German claims in the matter of prisoners are relatively small.

Diplomatic Preparation

The chronicle of the immediate steps that led our country into war with Nazi Germany covers only two weeks, and includes little that is doubtful or liable to subsequent correction in essentials, though the future historian will be able to amplify it. It opens with the correspondence between Mr Chamberlain and Herr Hitler, for which in an atmosphere of growing tension Sir Nevile Henderson acted as courier and go-between. The first despatch, dated August 22nd, is one of the clearest and straightest documents ever launched from Downing Street. After a significant reference to the German military movements on the Polish frontier, the conclusion of the Russo-German treaty of neutrality and our own partial naval mobilisation, Mr Chamberlain delivered his warning. This time there shall be no misunderstanding as there may have been in 1914: Great Britain without delay, if the case arises, will employ all her forces to fulfil her obligation to Poland. Nor, if war once starts, will it come to an early end—a remark designed presumably to remove the illusion that the Western Powers would be willing to make peace, once Poland had been overrun. But, Mr Chamberlain insists, the differences between Poland and Germany can be resolved without the use of force. The first step must be to restore confidence. There should be a period of truce to all incitements and polemics, during which complaints might be investigated. Thereafter negotiations could start, either directly or through a neutral intermediary. But the result would have to be guaranteed by other Powers.

Hitler and the Empire

Hitler's replies were a subject as much for the psychologist as the historian. They were defiant, boastful, but so far friendly that they offered to take the British Empire under the Führer's wing. He began, in a despatch of August 23rd, by reminding the British Government of his previous attempts to win British friendship. But before this could be achieved the Polish question must be settled. He had, he suggested, approached Poland with unparalleled magnanimity, and after she had rebuffed him he had had to face a wave of appalling terrorism and atrocities, intolerable for a Great Power. Like Mr Chamberlain, Hitler anticipated that a struggle with England would be a long war, but Germany could sacrifice neither her national interests nor her honour. But since the British military preparations were a menace to Germany, she would reply with the immediate mobilisation of her forces. The failure to keep the peace would lie at the door of those who refused to revise the "Diktat" of Versailles. His verbal communication of August 25th to our Ambassador was more constructive and more revealing. On the main point it was uncompromising. Poland, he declared, continued her provocations: he must abolish these Macedonian conditions. In short, the problem of Danzig and the Corridor must be solved. If this meant a bloody and incalculable war with England, at least it would not be, like the last, a war on two fronts. The Russian pact would last a long time, and ▶

▶ would render Germany "secure economically for the longest period of war". In other words, Hitler had lost his fear of a British blockade. Thus assured of victory, he then went on to patronise the British Empire, if it would come to terms. He is "a man of great decisions", and would even be prepared to give the Empire "an assurance of German assistance" in any part of the world—in other words, to take us under his protection. He would even agree to "a reasonable limitation of armaments". His colonial demands would have to be satisfied, however, and his treaties with Russia and Italy must remain intact. Finally, he would be pleased to regard his Western frontiers as final, with their fortifications.

Wasted Moderation

The British reply of August 28th was an admirable document, cool, sensible and firm. It would be pleasant to talk about the conditions of a lasting Anglo-German friendship, disarmament and a return (a characteristic Chamberlain touch) to "the normal activities of peaceful trade". But, first of all, the Polish question must be settled by direct negotiation, and the result must be guaranteed by other Powers. The German reply of August 29th was a rambling document, which continued the complaints of Polish "barbaric actions", and suggested that the Polish Government had lost control of its populations. None the less, Germany did intend to respect Poland's vital interests, while insisting on the return of Danzig and the Corridor to the Reich. Though sceptical of the result, she would negotiate: if there were to be guarantors, Russia must be one of them. The despatch ended with the abrupt demand that a Polish plenipotentiary must reach Berlin by August 30th. To this in a series of brief, urgent telegrams the British Government (after mentioning German provocations and acts of sabotage) replied that the suggested procedure was "wholly unreasonable". The German suggestions for a settlement should first be transmitted to Warsaw, which should then be invited to make its own suggestions for further negotiation. The British Government would consider using its good offices in Warsaw, but it must see the draft of the proposed settlement first. Speed was desirable, but to expect a Polish plenipotentiary to arrive that same day in Berlin was impossible. These counsels of moderation were unheeded.

The Sixteen Points

The German Government had meanwhile drafted in sixteen points its plan for a settlement. This was read rapidly over in German to Sir N Henderson at midnight on August 30th by Herr von Ribbentrop, who gave him no copy, on the grounds that it was too late, since no Polish plenipotentiary had reached Berlin by the hour fixed by the Führer. The Polish Ambassador in Berlin sought an interview next morning, which was refused on the ground that he was an ambassador only, and not a plenipotentiary. Late that evening he was at last received, but found thereafter that all communications with Warsaw had been cut. The German Government late that night broadcast its proposals. Save in that form, across the air, they never reached Warsaw. Next morning, between 5 and 6am, the German armies began the invasion of Poland. In a final verbal communication the German Government did at last transmit a copy of the plan to the British Government. The preface is a curiously twisted narrative of events, packed with complaints of Polish "subterfuges" and of their mobilisation. The sixteen points, intended obviously for German consumption, have only a retrospective interest. Danzig was to be handed over unconditionally. The Poles were to withdraw from the Corridor, where on the Saar model a plebiscite would be conducted by Britain, France, Italy and Russia twelve months hence. In any event, Poland might keep a demilitarised Gdynia, and Germany a corridor across the Corridor. Damage suffered by minorities since 1918 was to be compensated. The tone of this document was that of a "Diktat". The last word in the correspondence was a telegram from London, dated 11pm on August 31st, assuring Berlin that the Poles were trying to "establish contact" with it.

The Leaders' Speeches

When on Friday, September 1st, Mr Chamberlain faced the Commons, Germany's armies were already on Polish soil, and several Polish towns had been bombed. The House adopted a Conscription Act applying to the ages 18 to 41, and voted a credit for £500,000,000. The Prime Minister's speech was in his usual style, quiet, and unrhetorical. But it reviewed the events that led up to the war on the Poles in terms that came near vehemence. Germany had deliberately refused to negotiate with Poland. The responsibility for a terrible disaster would lie on the shoulders of one man, who had plunged the world into misery to serve his own senseless ambition. He then told the House that the British and French Ambassadors were informing the German Government that unless it promptly withdrew its forces from Polish soil the two Governments would fulfil their obligations to Poland. His peroration, while declaring that we had no quarrel with the German people, was morally a declaration of war for the destruction of the Nazi government. So long as it existed there would be no peace in Europe.

In the Reichstag, meanwhile, a few hours earlier, Danzig was incorporated in the Reich. The Führer abused the Poles in his more full-blooded style, and mutilated history till it was unrecognisable. His pretence was that the Polish Government, which never in fact received his proposals, had refused to negotiate. He thanked Italy but would not call on her to fight. He dwelt with peculiar emphasis on the Russian Pact, which he treated as a pledge of peace "for ever". Once more, as in his despatch to London, he dwelt on the value of Russia's "economic co-operation". Finally, as he proposed to go to the front in his favourite corporal's uniform, he named first Göring and then Hess as his successors. He said, that he had ordered his air force to attack military objectives only.

The Interval of Delay

On Saturday, September 2nd, the House and the listening nation lived through an interval of bewilderment—an interval of wondering whether at the last moment the reluctance of the Great Powers to begin war upon each other might after all lead to a truce and negotiations. The House of Commons expected an announcement that we were fighting on the side of the Poles. Mr Chamberlain explained that Mussolini had proposed an immediate cessation of hostilities and a conference between Great Britain, France, Poland, Germany and Italy, and that the British Government was "in communication with the French Government as to the limit of time within which it would be necessary for the British and French Governments to know whether the German Government were prepared to effect such a withdrawal". If Hitler would withdraw his troops, conversations were still possible "on the understanding that the settlement arrived at was one that safeguarded the vital interests of Poland and was secured by an international guarantee". The House was restive; Mr [Arthur] Greenwood, Sir Archibald Sinclair and others urged that we were in honour bound to fulfil our pledge without delay. The Poles had already been fighting for 38 hours. Mr [James] Maxton pleaded that we should not lose any possibility of peace; even postponement would be something gained. Mr Chamberlain explained that for himself he had little hope of a favourable reply from the Führer, but that he must wait for the views of the French Cabinet which was in session at that moment. When the House met on Sunday a state of war already existed between Britain and Germany. At 9am the British Ambassador had delivered a final ultimatum which expired at 11am and Mr Chamberlain had spoken to the nation on the wireless at 11.15. The corresponding French Note gave Hitler until 5pm. The Prime Minister's announcement of war was made in words of complete and moving simplicity. He said that everything he had hoped for had crashed into ruins. He hoped to live "to see the day when Hitlerism has been destroyed and a liberated Europe has been re-established". And so, after more dramatic speeches from Mr Greenwood, Sir Archibald Sinclair and Mr Churchill, we entered the war. ●

Standing in front of the wreckage of her house, London, Valentine's Day 1941

25 JANUARY 1941

The Blitz

By John Strachey

At five minutes to seven on a Friday evening Ford was getting into his overalls when the Blitz began, noisily. He put on his tin hat and went to the door to have a look out, wondering if he ought to go along to the post without eating his dinner, which was ready.

As he put his head out, a man said "Warden", out of the dark. "Warden," went on the voice irritably. "Come and see these dreadful lights. Don't you think you ought to put them out at once?" Ford went down the street a few yards and found a man in a trilby hat pointing towards the trees in Bedford Court. There were the lights all right, two of them behind the trees and, as they watched, three more came slowly drifting and dropping through the higher sky, red, white and orange. "I'm afraid I can't put *those* lights out," Ford said. "You see, those are flares dropped from German aeroplanes." "Oh, are they?" said the man; his voice was still censorious. The plane droned lower and lower. The guns thumped, spat and crashed. "Don't you think it rather unwise to stand about without a tin hat just . . ." Ford said. But he failed to complete his sentence. A swish had begun. He dropped like a stone full length into the gutter.

The man in the trilby hat took no notice whatever, either of the swish or of the disappearance of his interlocutor. He began explaining how he had always said that the "best way to deal with them 'Uns . . ." Ford, however, listening, his ear very much to the ground, heard the swish end in a thud without a bang. So the war plans of the man in the trilby hat passed, literally, over his head. Ford picked himself up; another swish began. Something in its note seemed to him menacing. He flung open the area gate and had crashed down the steps by the time this swish ended, with what then seemed a loud bang (although a little later he was to think of it as having been an almost incredibly small bang). Emerging from the area—he hoped with dignity—he found the man in the trilby hat still explaining his own method of bombing Berlin. He had apparently again not noticed that he had been speaking to the black-out alone. Ford heard, not very loud, but unmistakably, the tinkle of falling glass and the cracking of broken masonry. The man, it may be at length disgusted at this Warden's inattention, remarked, "Well, I must be going on now," and passed into the night.

Ford began to run. He ran in what he thought was the direction of the noises, along Marlow Square, past the Sub-post, deciding (probably wrongly) not to go in and report first, but to go straight for the incident. It did not cross his mind that there could be any difficulty in ▶

finding it. Nor did there seem to be. He ran into Gage Street, crossed Royal Walk and the top of James Street, which he glanced down. It touched his consciousness that the outline of its houses—a quarter seen in the blackness—looked unfamiliar. But he thought nothing of that. Now he saw a masked torch, switched on at the far end of Gage Street. In a moment he found Ivy Rawlings standing over a very small crater, just where the street joined the pavement. They used their torches and saw that a couple of cellars were broken in, but the houses seemed undamaged.

"It was quite a small one, then," Ford said.

A white hat came up—Mr Strong on his bicycle. "Come with me to Royal Walk."

"Is there another incident there?" Ford asked as they walked.

Strong said, "Considerable damage reported in Royal Walk, but no crater found yet."

Just then a car came up. Strong said, "Stay and stop the traffic." They were just back to the top of James Street. Ford stood about for a bit.

There was no traffic. He began to sense that they were on the fringe of something. He looked down James Street. He could see nothing at all. Surely even tonight one should be able to see the outline of the rows of houses? The darkness down James Street was, he now realised, something yet again. Thick, like rough woollen curtains. You looked into, or on to, total blankness. He felt that something wasn't there. (Nor was it.)

He began to walk down James Street. Immediately he was in another world. People were moving about and coming up. He saw that the houses opposite him were very considerably shattered. He looked farther down the street and saw that there were no houses. He became conscious of the smell. The unmistakable, indescribable, incident smell flooded into his nostrils. It is more than a smell, it is an acute irritation of the nasal passages from the powdered rubble of dissolved houses; it is a raw, brutal smell. He realised that the particular darkness which hung over James Street was due, not to the moonless night, but to the fact that the whole of this area was still covered by an unsettled dust cloud. Here's the incident all right, he thought.

Before he had got opposite to the part of James Street that did not appear to be there, he met Miss Sterling. She pointed at the shattered-looking but still standing houses and said, "There's a good many people in there." Mrs Morley came up, smooth and undisturbed. She said, "The mobile unit" (a sort of medical advance guard consisting of doctor, nurse and stretcher bearers) "has just gone in there," pointing to No 50.

Ford went into this house. The ground- and first-floor rooms were more or less all right—nothing more than blown-out window frames and shattered plaster. But up from the first floor the stairs were ankle deep in rubble. He went up, passing the second-floor rooms. The two top-floor rooms and the top landing were deeply encumbered with debris, rubble, slates and roof timber. He looked up; there was no roof overhead. There were dark clouds, picked out with momentary sparkles of shell bursts, reflected gun flashes and an uneasy searchlight waving its futility.

A warden inspects damage in the vicinity of St Paul's, May 1941

CORBIS

> A swish had begun. He dropped like a stone full length into the gutter

In the first room two men of a stretcher party, a nurse and another man were bending over a figure lying on a heap of the plaster rubble. Ford saw that it was an injured man. His breathing was violent and laboured. They seemed to be trying to get something down his throat through some sort of tube. One of the stretcher bearers saw Ford. Pointing to the back room he said, "There are two more in there." Ford looked in, cautiously using his torch, supplementing its metal hood with his hand. This room was wrecked. One side of it was heaped halfway up to the ceiling with debris. Several roof timbers lay across it. Ford began to clamber his way into it. He saw something dark lying at his feet. He put the beam of his torch on it and saw that it was a girl. She lay partly in, partly out of, the heaped-up debris of plaster and brick, her body perhaps a third buried, like a high bas-relief. She lay in a pleasant attitude, one hand curved behind her head, her legs a little pulled up, to form, with her body, a gentle S shape. He had seen that attitude once before, in the little Museum of Prehistory in the Dordogne; a skeleton of a prehistoric girl of the Mousterian age, from one of the abris (they had their abri too). Celia had said, "I never knew that a skeleton could be attractive and elegant; that one's bones may be chic after twenty thousand years." Here in the top-floor back of James Street was the same charming position.

Ford hadn't much doubt that she was dead. She looked so small for one thing; and there was a severe head wound. But he wondered what could have caused fatal injuries. The roof timbers were fairly light and had had only a few feet to fall. With a feeling of intimacy, he took up her unresisting hand and felt for a pulse. To his surprise he felt, or thought he felt, a very feeble beat. He went back to the front room and said, "Is there a doctor here?" One of the stretcher party said, "He's a doctor, but he's busy." He pointed to an oldish man bending over the other casualty. Ford said, "I think the girl in here is alive. Will you come and see?" The doctor gave no sign of having heard. But after a time he came. He ran a hypodermic into the grey, debris-encrusted flesh of her arm—"just in case", he said. He felt for the pulse, but said, "Very improbable."—"Where's the injury?" said the doctor. Ford said, "Her head, I think." "The *head*?" said the doctor, as if astonished. Then he ran his fingers over her skull, under her blood- and rubble-matted hair. But he said nothing. Ford said, "Shall I take her downstairs?" The doctor said, "No."

So they left her, lying easily on the debris, looking through the roof at the sky. ●

The Little Man: an Obituary of Adolf Hitler

By Leonard Woolf

Reading the obituaries of Adolf Hitler which have appeared since his reported death, one sees that about him personally there is nothing to be said except that he was the modern Little Man, inflated into a world force and then apotheosised. There is some quality of greatness which can be detected in all the "great men" of action who hitherto had left their mark on history, even though the mark was almost always a curse and the immense evil that they did lived after them and the little, if any, good was interred with their bones. But in the diseased, perverted egotism of the Führer's personality there was not a shred of greatness; there were only exaggerations of littleness, of meanness, vindictiveness, envy, malice, cunning and cruelty. The dreary desert of *Mein Kampf* and of the two volumes of Hitler's speeches reveals a mind remarkable only for its colourless insignificance and its crazy fanaticism; ignorant, stupid and cunning, the author appears to be a kind of depersonalised caricature of all the most despicable qualities of the Little Man.

How did this sub-human, stunted product of the European slum obtain his enormous power in Germany and Europe and become an object of worship in his own country and of admiration and adulation elsewhere? That is one of the most important and puzzling questions which the end of the war and of Hitler raises, for, unless we can answer it correctly, we cannot know what is at the root of the breakdown in our civilisation. To pretend that the answer is to be found in the obsessions of Vansittartism and a double dose of sin in all Germans is to shirk the issue and to comfort oneself with the illusion that, thank God, we are not as other sinners are.

The inter-war years were years when dictators sprouted all over Europe, and they were all Little Men, caricatures of human silliness and viciousness. There was the tawdry braggart Mussolini, flattered and courted by British Tory Ministers; there were a bunch of Balkan princelets or kinglets; there was the Greek Metaxas; and the rat-like Caudillo is still with us. They have all been worshipped and hated in their own countries and their power bolstered up by their admirers in the old democracies. Even in England we had the sinister spectacle of the posturing Mosley and his Blackshirt toughs finding followers among "respectable" people.

The Germans are more thorough and carry the logic of stupidity and savagery farther than other European peoples, but the seeds of Hitlerism and its abominations were in the soil of every European nation, and in many besides Germany they flowered and set their poisonous fruit. The flower is the dictatorship of the Little Man and the gangster; the fruit is the rule of everything which is most vile in the slum ideals of capitalist society.

It is not Hitler who has made the bloody desert of our age; it is the desert of our age which made Hitler; and if Adolf Hitler had not come to power in Germany, some other stunted Little Man or crude gangster would have seized power and provided the abominations. There are periods in history when power is so unstable, when the forces and beliefs in civilised society become so disorientated that the winds of chance and force may blow almost anyone, who is ruthless and savage enough, into the dictatorship over a people or even over the world.

One side of civilisation consists in the communal control of power. The Roman Republic, when it disintegrated into the Roman Empire, failed to provide this control, and within a hundred years the civilisation of Julius Caesar and Virgil was disappearing in the anarchy and barbarism of the Caracallas and Galluses. There was the same failure in the capitalist, middle-class civilisation of Europe in the nineteenth century. We failed to establish communal control of economic power, and that produced the anarchy of the capitalist gangster and the class war; we failed—and are failing once more at San Francisco—to establish communal control of national power, and that produced the international anarchy which made the world wars of 1914 and 1939 inevitable. It is in these periods of anarchy that the Caracallas and Hiders, the gangsters and the Little Men, find their opportunity and are transformed by the Legions or the *Wehrmacht*, by the Hugenbergs and Neville Chamberlains, into war lords and world rulers.

Double your threat. By Vicky (Victor Weisz), *NS*, 1954

Another side of civilisation consists in civilised beliefs. In the economic class war of the nineteenth century and in the international war of 1914 beliefs and standards which form the basis of civilisation disintegrated. Democracy, liberty and equality, law, justice and humanity are not just words or "machinery"; they are the essential framework of civilised life. From 1914 onwards the statesmen, writers and ruling classes in the democracies, upon whom depended the upholding of these standards, and therefore of civilisation, again and again betrayed them and compromised with barbarism. Religion and the Churches had long since done the same.

In such circumstances it is not surprising that Hitler, the depersonalised Little Man, could use the machinery of modern democracy to appeal to the hatred, the envy, all the littlenesses of all the other thwarted Little Men. The result can be seen in Dachau and Buchenwald. And on Thursday, May 3rd, 1945 (not 225AD, but 1945AD), the *Times* reported that Mr de Valera called on the German Minister in Dublin to express his condolence of Hitler's death. Mr de Valera in the previous week must have seen the photographs of Dachau and Buchenwald. He is a Roman Catholic and the head of a State which purports to base its whole policy and actions upon the Christian religion and the Catholic Church. In Mr de Valera's condolences we can see the degradation of civilised beliefs and standards which made Hitler and his Nazi regime possible. ●

Open Letter to Eisenhower and Khrushchev

By Bertrand Russell

This remarkable correspondence was initiated by the philosopher and pacifist Bertrand Russell. His "Open Letter" appeared in the New Statesman in November 1957, and although he may not have expected a reply, two weeks before Christmas the first secretary of the Communist Party, Nikita Khrushchev, sent an unsolicited response, which the NS published on 21 December. Early in 1958 the US secretary of state, John Foster Dulles, wrote in on President Eisenhower's behalf, and nuclear diplomacy was played out in the pages of the NS at the height of the cold war.

Most Potent Sirs,

I am addressing you as the respective heads of the two most powerful countries in the world. Those who direct the policies of these countries have a power for good or evil exceeding anything ever possessed before by any man or group of men. Public opinion in your respective countries has been focused upon the points in which your national interests are thought to diverge, but I am convinced that you, as far-seeing and intelligent men, must be aware that the matters in which the interests of Russia and America coincide are much more important than the matters in which they are thought to diverge. I believe that if you two eminent men were jointly to proclaim this fact and to bend the policies of your great countries to agreement with such a proclamation, there would be throughout the world, and not least in your own countries, a shout of joyful agreement which would raise you both to a pinnacle of fame surpassing anything achieved by other statesmen of the past or present. Although you are, of course, both well aware of the points in which the interests of Russia and America are identical, I will, for the sake of explicitness, enumerate some of them.

(1) The supreme concern of men of all ways of thought at the present time must be to ensure the continued existence of the human race. This is already in jeopardy from the hostility between East and West and will, if many minor nations acquire nuclear weapons, be in very much greater jeopardy within a few years from the possibility of irresponsible action by thoughtless fanatics.

Some ignorant militarists, both in the East and in the West, have apparently thought that the danger could be averted by a world war giving victory to their own side. The progress of science and technology has made this an idle dream. A world war would not result in the victory of either side, but in the extermination of both.

The hope of world dominion, either military or ideological, is one which has hovered before many men in the past and has led invariably to disaster. Philip II of Spain made the attempt and reduced his country to the status of a minor power. Louis XIV of France made the attempt and, by exhausting his country, led the way to the French Revolution, which he would have profoundly deplored. Hitler, in our own day, fought for the world-wide supremacy of the Nazi philosophy, and perished miserably. Two great men propounded ideologies which have not yet run their course: I mean the authors of the Declaration of Independence and the Communist Manifesto. There is no reason to expect that either of these ideologies will be more successful in conquering the world than their predecessors, Buddhist, Christian, Moslem, or Nazi. What is new in the present situation is not the impossibility of success, but the magnitude of the disaster which must result from the attempt. We must, therefore, hope that each side will abandon the futile strife and agree to allow to each a sphere proportionate to its present power.

(2) The international anarchy which will inevitably result from the unrestricted diffusion of nuclear weapons is not to the interest of either Russia or America. There was a time when only America had nuclear weapons. This was followed by a time when only Russia and America had such weapons. And now only Russia, America and Britain possess them. It is obvious that, unless steps are taken, France and Germany will shortly manufacture these weapons. It is not likely that China will lag far behind. We must expect that the manufacture of engines of mass destruction will become cheaper and easier. No doubt Egypt and Israel will then be able to follow the example set by the great powers. So will the states of South America. There is no end to this process until every sovereign state is in a position to say to the whole world: "You must yield to my demands or you shall die." If all sovereign states were governed by rulers possessed of even the rudiments of sanity, they would be restrained from such blackmail by the fear that their citizens also would perish. But experience shows that from time to time power in this or that country falls into the hands of ▶

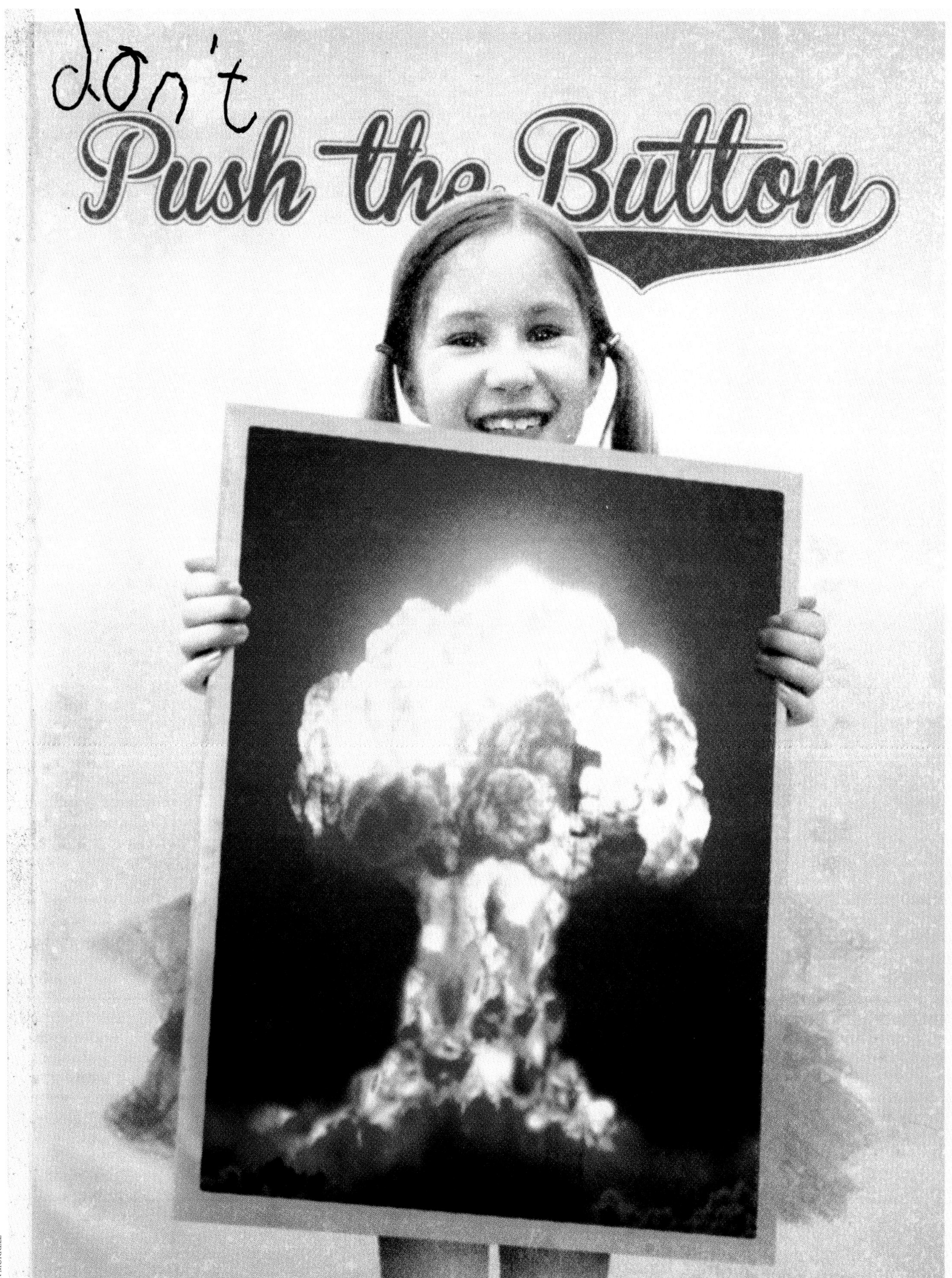

©DAN MURRELL

▶ rulers who are not sane. Can anyone doubt that Hitler, if he had been able to do so, would have chosen to involve all mankind in his own ruin? For such reasons, it is imperative to put a stop to the diffusion of nuclear weapons. This can easily be done by agreement between Russia and America, since they can jointly refuse military or economic assistance to any country which persists in the manufacture of such weapons. But it cannot be achieved without agreement between the two dominant powers, for, without such agreement, each new force of nuclear weapons will be welcomed by one side or the other as an increase to its own strength.

(3) So long as the fear of world war dominates policy and the only deterrent is the threat of universal death, so long there can be no limit to the diversion of expenditure of funds and human energy into channels of destruction. It is clear that both Russia and America could save nine-tenths of their present expenditure if they concluded an alliance and devoted themselves jointly to the preservation of peace throughout the world. If they do not find means of lessening their present hostility, reciprocal fear will drive them further and further, until, apart from immense armaments, nothing beyond a bare subsistence will be left to the populations of either country. In order to promote efficiency in the preparation of death, education will have to be distorted and stunted. Everything in human achievement that is not inspired by hatred and fear will be squeezed out of the curriculum in schools and universities. Any attempt to preserve the vision of Man as the triumph (so far) of the long ages of evolution, will come to be viewed as treachery, since it will be thought not to minister to the victory of this group or that. Such a prospect is death to the hopes of all who share the aspirations which have inspired human progress since the dawn of history.

(4) I cannot but think that you would both rejoice if a way could be found to disperse the pall of fear which at present dims the hopes of mankind. Never before, since our remote ancestors descended from the trees, has there been valid reason for such fear. Never before has such a sense of futility blighted the visions of youth. Never before has there been reason to feel that the human race was travelling along a road ending only in a bottomless precipice. Individual death we must all face, but collective death has never, hitherto, been a grim possibility.

And all this fear, all this despair, all this waste is utterly unnecessary. One thing only is required to dispel the darkness and enable the world to live again in a noon-day brightness of hope. The one thing necessary is that East and West should recognise their respective rights, admit that each must learn to live with the other and substitute argument for force in the attempt to spread their respective ideologies. It is not necessary that either side should abandon belief in its own creed. It is only necessary that it should abandon the attempt to spread its own creed by force of arms.

I suggest, Sirs, that you should meet in a frank discussion of the conditions of co-existence, endeavouring no longer to secure this or that more or less surreptitious advantage for your own side, but seeking rather for such agreements and such adjustments in the world as will diminish future occasions of strife. I believe that if you were to do this the world would acclaim your action, and the forces of sanity, released from their long bondage, would ensure for the years to come a life of vigour and achievement and joy surpassing anything known in even the happiest eras of the past.

Bertrand Russell

Nikita Khrushchev replies to Bertrand Russell

Nikita Khrushchev

Dear Lord Russell,

I was extremely interested to read your open letter addressed to the President of the United States and to myself. We, the Soviet people, understand and hold dear the main idea expressed in your letter – to protect mankind from the threat of a war which would be waged with the most terrible weapons of destruction ever known to the world; to safeguard universal peace and prosperity, on the basis of peaceful co-existence between states; and, above all, through the normalisation of relations between the Soviet Union and the United States.

Everyone is agreed that if a new world war should break out, it would bring untold suffering to the people. For this reason the chief concern of all people, whatsoever their way of thinking, should be to prevent such a tragic turn of events. Man's reason and conscience cannot be reconciled to such a danger, cannot but rise up against the propaganda churned out day after day, propaganda which is accustoming the nations to the idea of the inevitability of atomic war.

The government and Communist Party of the Soviet Union, expressing the wishes of the people of our country, are doing and will do everything possible to prevent the outbreak of a new war. We are convinced that, in the present situation, war is not fatally inevitable, that war can be prevented, if everyone who wants to preserve peace will struggle for it actively and in an organised way.

We were pleased to notice that you support the ending of the arms race which only brings nearer the catastrophe of war. You appeal for an end to the distribution of nuclear weapons, so that the armies of those states which at the present time do not yet possess such weapons will not receive them. Of course, this would be a step forward, especially if you take into account the fact that plans exist for handing over nuclear weapons to – for example – Western Germany, whose government openly stakes its territorial claims in Europe; and the fact that nuclear weapons, brought in from across the ocean, are deployed on the territories of West European member states of NATO. These weapons are imposed on these states under the guise of defence against aggression. In reality, the deployment of nuclear weapons on the territories of those countries is a mortal blow to their security, since, if an aggressor breaks the peace, then, in accordance with the inexorable logic of war, shattering retaliatory attacks on the territories, those countries in which atomic weapon bases are situated, will be inevitable.

You certainly know that the Soviet Union has frequently come out with a proposal that nuclear weapons should not be deployed beyond the state frontiers of those countries which possess them already; and that, in particular, it has also proposed that the US, Britain and the USSR, should reach agreement not to deploy their nuclear weapons in either Western or Eastern Germany. For its part, the government of the German Democratic Republic has proposed to the government of the Federal Republic of Germany that they act together so that there shall be neither German nor foreign nuclear weapons on German territory. The Polish and Czechoslovak governments have announced that if agreement is reached between the Federal Republic of Germany and the German Democratic Republic, then, similarly, neither Poland nor Czechoslovakia would produce nuclear weapons or deploy them on their territory. As you can see, the Socialist states are doing everything in their power to prevent further distribution of nuclear weapons. Unfortunately, this has not yet met with a response from the western powers.

However, even if we succeeded in preventing the further distribution of nuclear weapons in the world, all this would by no means remove the danger of nuclear war. For, even now this danger is very great. The Soviet Union considers that the danger of atomic war will only be removed finally and completely when the manufacture and use of atomic and hydrogen weapons will have been completely prohibited and the stockpiles destroyed. For almost 12 years now the Soviet government has been demanding such a solution of this question and has made quite a few concrete proposals in the UN in support of these aims. If the western powers would express a sincere desire to end the danger of atomic war, then it would be possible – tomorrow, even – to advance along this path, taking, for a start, such steps as the immediate ending of nuclear weapon tests and renunciation of the use of such weapons. But it must be said straight out that, up to the present, unfortunately, we have not had evidence of any such desire by the American, British or French governments. The fact is that those quarters which formulate the policies of those countries wish to preserve war in their arsenal as a means of securing the aims of their foreign policy.

We, the Soviet people, engaged in building Communist society – a social system in which, alongside the achievement of material abundance for all, there will for the first time be the free development of man's spiritual wealth, in all its diversity – understand particularly well your concern over the criminal policy of militarism, which absurdly wastes society's material resources, which corrupts man morally and which leads to people being brought up in the spirit of fear and hate. It is impossible to be reconciled to such a prospect – all the more so when today the wonderful discoveries of science have given man such immense power over the forces of Nature.

As a philosopher and humanist, deeply concerned at the abnormality of the present international situation, you understand very well along what lines solution of the present situation must be sought. "The one thing necessary," you write, "is that East and West should recognise their respective rights, admit that each must learn to live with the other and substitute argument for force in the attempt to spread their respective ideologies. It is not necessary that either side should abandon belief in its own creed. It is only necessary that it should abandon the attempt to spread its own creed by force of arms."

I am ready to lend my name to those words, since they correspond fully to the conception of peaceful co-existence between states with different social systems, upon which our state has based its foreign policy since the first day of the establishment of Soviet power. There is no need to say how glad I would be to hear that your words had met with similar support from the US government.

In order to "live with the other" both sides must recognise what politicians call the status quo. The right of each country to develop as the people of that country desire must be recognised. The conduct of "cold war", engaging in threats, aiming at changing state frontiers and interfering in other countries' domestic affairs with the aim of changing their social structure – these things must not be permitted. "Cold war" and the arms drive will lead to a new and very bloody war.

You are completely right, of course, when you say that one of the chief reasons for the present state of tension in international relations, and for all that is meant by "cold war", is the abnormal character of the relations between the Soviet Union and the United States of America. The normalisation of these relations would beyond a doubt lead to a general improvement in the international situation. The Soviet Union has always tried for just such a normalisation of relations with the United States, and it will continue to do so. We have taken quite a few definite steps in this direction. You will probably remember, for example, that in January 1956 the Soviet government proposed to the government of the USA that a treaty of friendship and co-operation be concluded between our two countries. Our proposal still holds. We have tried and will continue to try to re-establish Soviet-American trade relations, which were broken off by the government of the US, and we want to open up cultural, scientific and technical exchanges with the United States.

The Soviet leaders have always believed that personal contacts with government leaders of other countries are of very great importance, as one of the most effective ways of improving international relations. We readily took part in the Geneva four-power conference of heads of government, and, as you are no doubt aware, we have also met the government leaders of many other countries.

I fully support your proposal, Lord Russell, that the leaders of the Soviet Union and the United States should meet and frankly discuss conditions of co-existence. Like you, we are convinced that there are far more questions on which the interests of the Soviet Union and the United States coincide than there are questions on which our interests differ. This, precisely, is why on the Soviet side the opinion has been repeatedly expressed that a high-level meeting between representatives of the USSR and the United States would be most useful for both our countries, as well as for peace among all nations.

N Krushchev
Moscow, 7 December 1957

Bull's-eye for hawks. Ralph Steadman (*NS*, 1983)

Mr Dulles replies to Russell and Khrushchev

John Foster Dulles

SIR – On behalf of the President I am replying to Lord Russell's letter to him and to Mr Krushchev published in the 23 November issue of the *New Statesman*. I have also read Mr Krushchev's reply thereto.

Surely if we lived in a world of words, we could relax to the melody of Mr Krushchev's lullaby. The world in which we live is, however, made of stuff sterner than mere words. It is necessary now, as it has always been necessary, to look behind the words of individuals to find from their actions what their true purpose is.

I note that Mr Krushchev directs himself to Lord Russell's statement that as between the East and West, "It is not necessary that either side should abandon belief in its own creed. It is only necessary that it should abandon the attempt to spread its own creed by the force of arms." The creed of the United States is based on the tenets of moral law. That creed, as well as the universal conviction of the United States, rejects war except in self-defence. This abhorrence of war, this determination to substitute peaceful negotiation for force in the settlement of international disputes, is founded on the religious convictions that guided our forefathers in writing the documents that marked the birth of America's independence. I do not think that it is possible to find in the history of the United States any occasion when an effort has been made to spread its creed by force of arms. There is, therefore, no need on our side to "abandon" what Lord Russell condemns. On the contrary, it would be abhorrent that there should be introduced into our creed the concept of its maintenance or extension by methods of violence and compulsion.

Unhappily, it is otherwise with the creed of Communism, or at least that variety of Communism which is espoused by the Soviet Communist Party. Marx, Lenin, and Stalin have all consistently taught the use of force and violence. Marx said "the proletariat, by means of revolution, makes itself the ruling class". Lenin taught that the dictatorship of the proletariat means "unlimited power based on force and not on law"; and Stalin said that the ruling bourgeois classes can "only be removed by the conscious action of the new classes, by forcible acts of these classes by revolution". These teachings have never been disavowed by the Soviet Communist Party of which Mr Krushchev is now the First Secretary. On the contrary, as recently as 16 November last, the Communist Parties rededicated themselves ▶

in the Moscow declaration to the cause of world revolution directed by the Soviet Communist Party. There are indeed multiple examples of the continuing use of force by the Soviet Communist Party and by other Communists of the same school. A recent illustration is Hungary where, at the behest of the Hungarian Communist Party, the Soviet Communist Party requested the Soviet government to invade with massive military force to repress the people and to assure that they would continue to be subject to a rule dictated by the Hungarian Communist Party.

It is quite improbable that the Soviet Communist Party should now abjure the use of force and violence to maintain the supremacy of its creed where that party, directly or through satellite Communist Parties, is today dominant. The Soviet Communist Party seized power by violence of an intensity and extent that shocked the civilised world. It has extended its power by violence, absorbing one nation after another by force or the threat of force. Within the Soviet Union it has perpetuated its power only by force and violence, the nature of which is usually kept hidden but which is occasionally revealed, as when Mr Krushchev in his speech to the 20th Congress – a speech sought to be kept secret – portrayed the cruel practices employed by Stalin through Beria to maintain his despotism.

Nowhere in the world today does the Communist Party maintain its rule except by forcibly imposing that rule upon the great majority of the people as against their wishes. Although Communist Parties today rule nearly 1,000 million people, comprising what at one time were nearly 20 independent nations, never anywhere have these Communist Parties been willing to have free elections or to limit their rule to peoples whom they persuade by peaceful means. The fact of the matter is that the Communist Parties depend upon force and violence and could not exercise power anywhere in the world today if they should relinquish that. It is equally true that they could not achieve ultimately their announced goal of world domination without involving the same forcible methods which they have consistently used to gain and retain rule where they have it.

That, I feel, is the heart of the problem. That is why those who have freedom must be organised to preserve it. If, indeed, Lord Russell could persuade the Communist Parties of the world to renounce dependence upon force and violence and to exercise power only when this reflected the freely given consent of the governed, then indeed the world would become a happier and safer place in which to live. I earnestly hope that the idealism and persuasiveness of Lord Russell may move the Communist Parties in this direction.

Mr Krushchev's letter deals primarily with a world war which would be a nuclear war. I do not doubt that the Soviet rulers, like all other people who want to go on living, reject that concept. The United States not only rejects that concept, but strives earnestly to do something to remove the danger of nuclear war.

A decade ago, when the United States had a monopoly of atomic weapons and of the knowledge of how to make them, we proposed that we and all others should forgo such destructive weapons and assure that the power of the atom should be used for peaceful purposes. We proposed an international agency to control all use of atomic energy. That proposal was rejected by the Soviet Union, with the consequence that nuclear weapons today exist in vast and growing quantities.

In a further effort to stem the increase of nuclear weapons and their irresponsible spread throughout the world, the United States joined in proposals that fissionable material should no longer be produced for weapons purposes and that existing nuclear weapons stockpiles should be steadily diminished by agreed contributions to peaceful purposes internationally controlled. This proposal, too, has been rejected by the Soviet Union.

> The hope of world domination has hovered before many men

Now a new source of danger to humanity looms in the use of outer space for weapons purposes. Both the Soviet Union and the United States are beginning to make such use of outer space. But the United States, in pursuance of its peaceful purposes, proposed that we should not repeat the mistake of ten years ago but should quickly take steps to assure that outer space shall be used only for peaceful purposes. President Eisenhower eloquently pleaded for this peaceful step in his letter of 12 January to Chairman Bulganin. Thus, the Soviet is afforded, now for the third time, a chance to demonstrate that its words of peace mean something more than a mere effort to lull the non-Communist world into a mood of illusory security.

At the moment its propaganda efforts are primarily directed, as was Mr Krushchev's letter, to trying to assure that Western Europe shall be armed only with weapons of the pre-atomic age, while the Soviet Union uninterruptedly develops the most modern weapons of the nuclear age and of the age of outer space. At the recent North Atlantic Council meeting, the heads of the 15 member governments had this to say:

> The Soviet leaders, while preventing a general disarmament agreement, have made it clear that the most modern and destructive weapons, including missiles of all kinds, are being introduced in the Soviet armed forces. In the Soviet view, all European nations except the USSR should, without waiting for general disarmament, renounce nuclear weapons and missiles and rely on arms of the pre-atomic age.
>
> As long as the Soviet Union persists in this attitude, we have no alternative but to remain vigilant and to look to our defences.

But also they said:

> We are also prepared to examine any Proposal, from whatever source, for general or partial disarmament, and any proposal enabling agreement to be reached on the controlled reduction of armaments of all types.

While of course nuclear war is the form of war most to be dreaded, particularly if, to nuclear power, is added the use of outer space, it is essential to avoid war of any kind, and to renounce all use of force as a means of subjecting human beings to a ruler to which they do not freely consent. That, I take it, is the heart of what Lord Russell seeks. I can assure you it is also what is sought by the government of the United States and also by all of our people who adhere to the creed of America as it is expressed in the words of the American Declaration of Independence: "We hold these truths to be self-evident, that all men are created equal, that they are endowed by their Creator with certain inalienable rights, that among these are life, liberty and the pursuit of happiness; that to secure these rights governments are instituted among men, deriving their just powers from the consent of the governed."

That, I assure you, is the creed of America. It is the creed by which we live and in defence of which many Americans have laid down their lives in a supreme act of fellowship with those of other lands who believe in the dignity of men and men's rights to have governments not imposed upon them but chosen by them. Such a creed cannot be imposed by force because to use force to impose a creed would of itself be a violation of our creed.

I revert again to Lord Russell's statement that "it is not necessary that either side should abandon belief in its own creed". Certainly that is true of the United States, whose creed comprehends the renunciation of violence and force to spread its creed. The same, unfortunately, cannot be said of Soviet Communism, whose creed comprehends the use of force and violence. Therefore I believe that it is necessary that at least that part of the Soviet Communist creed should be abandoned in order to achieve the peaceful result which is sought by Lord Russell and all other peace-loving people.

It is the steadfast determination of the United States – you may call it creed – to work in a spirit of conciliation for peaceful solutions based on freedom and justice and the great problems facing the world today.

John Foster Dulles
(Published in the NS of 8 February 1958)

No Chance of Peace in Chicago

By Nora Sayre

The film critic Nora Sayre wrote Around New York columns for the NS in the 1960s. Here, she reports from Chicago during the Democratic National Convention as police brutalised young anti-Vietnam and social activists.

Such blood: released from bruised and broken veins, from foreheads, scalps and mouths, from eyesockets, shattered wrists and skulls. Broad bloodstreaks on the pavements showed where bodies had been dragged. We all bleed inwardly from the particular atrocities we witnessed. I saw seven policemen clubbing one girl – long after she had fallen; a row of sitting singers whose heads were cracked open by a charge of running cops; a photographer's camera smashed thoroughly into his eyes. Each day, scores staggered bleeding through the streets and parks, reeling or dropping, their faces glistening with Vaseline – for Mace. Gas rinses your lungs with the lash of iodine and vinegar: your own breath burns your throat. Outside the Hilton, a nice little old lady patted a rebel on the chest, murmuring, "Knock the socks off them." Then she and I were suddenly hurled against the wall when a hundred policemen seized their blue wooden barricades to ram the crowd (mainly onlookers and press) against the building with such force that many next to me, including the old lady, were thrust through plate-glass windows. People sobbed with pain as their ribs snapped. (I still have ribs, thanks to an unknown man's magnificently fat, soft back.) Voiceless from gas, I feebly waved my credentials, and the warrior who was about to hit me said: "Oops, press." He let me limp into the hotel, where people were being pummelled into the red carpet, while free Pepsi was offered on the sidelines.

Since delegates, McCarthy workers, newsmen and spectators were thrashed along with the demonstrators, many learned what blacks have always known: that the democracy of savagery makes no distinctions – everyone is guilty for his mere presence or existence. The Chicago police made niggers of us all: rubble with no protection or defence. In future, we can easily share the ghettos' fate, without uncoiling any imagination. I watched beatings and gassings from a second-floor McCarthy room. Twelve policemen surged in, slammed the windows, drew the curtains and told us to turn away and watch the TV set, where [Hubert] Humphrey was starting to speak – "and that's an order". The Chicago cops, whose trucks advise "Reach out and grab the greatest summer ever", direct traffic as though they were flogging bodies. Seasoned Chicago reporters said that they're extremely afraid of the local blacks. Hence they took a special revenge on the marchers, primarily because the police failed to subdue last April's ghetto riots. Yet a recent poll suggests that 71.4 per cent of queried citizens "find police actions justified".

Thus it's delicate to determine what the protest accomplished. As James Reston noted, the young, the poor, the black and the intelligent "have the fewest votes", and the demonstrations were probably deplored by the voting majority. Still, "voting with bodies" wasn't bootless. Tom Hayden: "We are coming to Chicago to vomit on 'the politics of joy'." Indeed they did. The motto is: "There can be no peace in the US until there is peace in Vietnam" – and there won't be. At a Black Panther rally, young white revolutionaries vowed "to join the blacks – by putting ourselves in the same crisis that blacks are in". And certainly a whole new collaboration is accelerating. A black militant replied: "The strongest weapon we have is all of us. United black-white opposition." Undoubtedly new militants were created; some liberals became radicals, some dissenters became revolutionaries. The most triumphant moral point came from Dick Gregory: "Had there been a bunch of young people who challenged Hitler the way you challenged Mayor Daley, there might be a whole lot of Jews alive today."

After that statement, one's pride in the throng kept dilating. The aims are so simple: peace, liberation for blacks, a radically new America. These goals must be repeated, because the tactics confuse older (often sympathetic) people. The movement seethes with such contradictions about method and leadership that, when Humphrey said it was "programmed", one wished that he were right.

A few leaders are lavishly irresponsible: they excite the most naive – hippies and teenagers – who don't know that the mild term "personal risk" can mean getting killed or maimed. These gentle waifs, plus a few glittering hysterics, usually rush to the front; at moments, one feared that they would be used as fodder. Different leaders springing to the microphones instructed the crowd to be cool, to get hot, that they were helpless, that they were powerful, to go home, to gather, to disperse in small groups, to mass for a huge non-violent march – in which other leaders warned that they'd be trapped. (And they were.) Many marchers were too inexperienced to choose clearly. Obviously, the need for organisation is as desperate as the ache for peace.

One comes lurching out of these vast flesh-packs with a reeking dilemma about "violence" – which is now a suitcase-word for assassinations, student protests, ghetto riots, mugging, and nut crimes. For the Right, these are indistinguishable. For SDS [Students for a Democratic Society], violence means wrecking Selective Services files or bombing a draft board – at night, when no one's there to be hurt. Yet how do you draw a dotted line between street fights and killing, between "good" and "bad" violence? Any brand of violence is contagious, as this land of assassination knows. However, since madness now seems to be the country's most pungent odour, more people may become violent merely to get attention, merely to be heard. Many of us are wrestling with evaluations of the fact of force. If violence in the US could result in peace in Vietnam, then I would support it – with a ravaging disgust at a society which forces one to make such a choice.

I haven't the physical courage to fight in the streets, but I bless those who do. A Chicago clergyman was sympathetic; he said that the church hasn't yet decided its own position: "since no social change occurs without violence". Certainly, the new revolutionaries cannot remould America on their own. (And, at moments, some sound like the general who said that he had to destroy a Vietnamese village in order to save it.) But their power could be a partial fuel for change – if a right-wing renaissance doesn't stifle us all. That possibility hums in every wire of the mind. Chicago taught us what law and order can mean. After all, these protesters were not violent. The streets were dangerous because of the police.

The Day Saigon Fell

By James Fenton

Last Tuesday morning I was woken by the doorman, who came into the bedroom carrying one loaf of French bread, two cubes of local sugar and some Coca-Cola. He returned a little later with ice, and insisted I get up and eat. Next came a young man looking for an American who had promised to get him out. I told him he should not leave, since this was his country, and if he went now he would never get back. He said, misunderstanding: "I like going to the country. My family always goes to the country for holidays. We go to Rach Gia and Ha Tien." I said that Ha Tien was now in the hands of the Vietcong. He said: "Do you think people are happy in Ha Tien?" I said I thought so.

The 24-hour curfew seemed not very strict so I set out to find the other journalists. Saigon looks beautiful when the streets are deserted. Families were standing in their doorways, smiling. A group of soldiers passed, smiling. A beggar girl with a tattered white silk blouse runs laughing along beside me. She is young, with a slightly idiot look and no teeth. There is a Sunday morning atmosphere. I meet one of the Popular Defence Force who tells me that the airport was attacked during the night. I appear to have slept through everything.

All the journalists were talking about the previous night's fighting at the airport. They had seen planes shot down by Strela missiles and it was clear that the American evacuation was about to begin. As it turned out, many of those who had airily said they would stay decided to leave, whereas some who had been reluctant to stay finally did so.

I drove to the airport with a colleague. Many families were being turned away. Beside us was a hole made by the artillery of the night before. In the distance, a column of black smoke. But there was no sign of a ground attack. There was no small arms fire, excepting the shots fired over the heads of those, like us, who were trying to enter the airport.

Back in central Saigon the streets were quiet, with soldiers lounging at crossings and no one actually enforcing the curfew. One small restaurant was open, in which a group of lieutenants were drinking Scotch and eating Chinese chicken. They asked me to join them.

One, called Minh, insisted that they would all be killed. I tried to say that I thought they were wrong but when I explained why there was a certain degree of hostility. "How long did you spend with the Communists?" they asked. I said I hadn't been with the Communists. We began talking in French. They were amused, they said, that when I started speaking in French I began to tremble.

PHILIP JONES GRIFFITHS/MAGNUM PHOTOS

A casualty caught up in the Tet Offensive, 1968

I moved to the Continental Hotel, but then there was pressure from the journalistic community to cross the square to the Caravelle. The American evacuation had begun and the foreigners and accomplices of the war were assembling. The new Prime Minister had officially told the Americans to leave Vietnam in the next 24 hours. Everybody assumed that the majority of them had already gone when, in mid-afternoon, it became clear that there had been a tremendous hitch in the plans.

In the American Embassy even the diplomats were worried about the fact that the big helicopter had not yet arrived. People began to wonder whether the North Vietnamese would start shelling the embassy. But outside the gates the crowd had not yet grown to alarming proportions. There were shady Koreans, a few stranded Americans and a few hundred Vietnamese waiting around. There was a sound of automatic fire nearby, and around the embassy the police would occasionally fire into the air when some angry man became too importunate.

The ice was finally broken when one of the officers asked in Cambodian whether I spoke Khmer. A little, I said. Then we were able to begin. I asked them why they were afraid of a Communist takeover. They were well aware that in Phnom Penh the people had greeted the Khmer Rouge with open arms. But they said that that was only a kind of presentation. Afterwards, there would be a settling of accounts. They insisted they were going to die. I asked what they were going to do now. They said they were going to sit there all day, until they died.

But as the evening progressed, and the helicopters began arriving, the mood of the city suffered a terrible change. Everything accelerated at the same pace. The helicopters circled round and round in the sky. The sky began to darken. It began to rain, looting began. People looted the most extraordinary things. Bed-heads, wardrobes, mattresses, part of this, bits of that – and then the sensible things like canned beer from the Brinks Building, the oldest centre of American operations in South Vietnam.

It became at this point rather frightening; for the first time I found that the youths on motor-bikes were shouting "Go back to your country" and other slogans indicating that they presumed all white faces were American. What people are afraid of here, as they were in Phnom Penh, is a pogrom by the "friendlies". Even if Saigon had not been falling, even if crowds and crowds were not trying to get out, it would have been enough to see the helicopters. The evacuation was so public, so noisy, so inaccessible, and took such a very long time.

At about seven in the evening the panic, however, was partially curbed when the electricity failed and everyone began to go home. Returning to the hotel, I noticed that there were very few soldiers left on the street corners. By ten, however, the police had got things under control. The pace of the war seemed to have slacked off. I came with a plainclothed police escort to the Reuters office to file this, and we did not encounter any danger. We walked down the middle of the road, hand in hand; we were rather like the butcher and the baker in "The Hunting of the Snark".

It is now 11 o'clock and the sound of the war has begun once again. We know that Hanoi has demanded an unconditional surrender and we know that must come soon. ●

The bloody battle for pacifism

By Mark Urban

Britain's appetite for conflict has been in decline since the First World War but that doesn't mean that force is always futile

Britain in 1913 was a nation yearning for war, straining like a tethered bulldog ready to be let loose on the Hun. Today its appetite for conflict has almost disappeared – and it is this plunging arc of warlike sentiment that shapes almost everything that has happened in defence policy in the past few decades.

Ideologues might have explained the First World War in terms of the conspiracy of international capital or the machinations of an evil kaiser, but the popular enthusiasm for it was breathtaking. Inspired by Kitchener's iconic recruiting poster and an atmosphere of patriotic frenzy, millions volunteered.

In one day in September 1914, the army enlisted as many recruits (roughly 30,000) as it had signed up during the whole of 1913. By the end of the war, 5.7 million men, almost a quarter of all the adult males in Britain, had served, though by 1916 that early enthusiasm had dissipated and the state was obliged to introduce conscription.

The zenith of Britain's imperial enthusiasm was short-lived, stretching for 60 or 70 years through the late-Victorian and Edwardian periods up to the eve of the Great War. During this time, an insult demanded avenging by a gunboat and people supported overwhelming other countries in order to produce prosperity at home, an idea which now, despite the recession, seems distinctly unclean.

Today the British army needs to find only 4,000 or so infantry soldiers each year but often has problems doing so. The population has grown in the meantime beyond 60 million.

While millions may sit at home shooting at "terrorists" on their computer or gaming console, the desire to experience combat for real in Afghanistan is limited to a tiny proportion of the population. Societal tolerance for the use of force, in terms of political opinion, appetite for risk, or application of the law, has deteriorated so sharply that academics have written about the "criminalisation of the warrior".

A big part of this change took place in the early 20th century, between 1913 and 1916. In the horror of the fighting in Ypres and on the Somme, pals battalions – friends who had volunteered together from pit towns or pastures – were killed en masse. *"Dulce et decorum"*, the notion that it was sweet and fitting to die for your country, was spat out with bitter irony by the war poet Wilfred Owen.

> The despatch of troops in a muddled way can be worse than doing nothing

The resulting pacifism and a reluctance to rearm in the 1930s produced a crisis in 1940 that Britain was lucky to survive. The earlier scarring of the national psyche shaped the way that we made war or structured our forces, too.

Many of those who volunteered for the tank forces in the 1930s, or after the outbreak of the Second World War, did so because fathers or other relatives who had experienced the trenches told them to avoid the infantry at all costs. "If I was going into action," one of those volunteers, now in his 97th year, told me, "it was going to be in a tank." Throughout the war, British generals sought to use manoeuvre and firepower to limit casualties.

Just 16 per cent of the British 2nd Army fighting in Normandy in 1944 came from the infantry. When things got bogged down in the battle to get out of the hedgerows and the foot soldiers started taking heavy casualties, the troops used massive firepower to break the stalemate. The British emerged from Normandy with lower casualties, proportionately, than the Germans or Americans, yet even this price caused rumblings in parliament and very nearly cost Bernard Montgomery his job as commander of the forces.

In the decades after 1945, the existence of nuclear weapons and the UN charter principle that territorial disputes should not be resolved by force reduced the chances of interstate warfare and undermined the strategists' axiom embodied in Carl von Clausewitz's formulation "moderation in war is a logical absurdity". The risks of nuclear war might have limited all-out conflict but British leaders still sent the armed forces into action many times; however, the national willingness to accept loss of life continued to erode.

The justness of the cause or the issues at stake may play an important part at the outset but the will to continue seems to ebb away with sustained losses. Afghanistan may have seemed a more just war than Iraq to many (although polls showed a majority supported even that action during its early days), yet after hundreds of fatalities public faith has been lost and people want the troops home.

Since Britain lacks the means or will to conduct large-scale operations on its own, it acts as part of international coalitions. That makes it even harder to agree war aims or to sustain losses. It is easy to blame these doubts on Tony Blair for fighting in support of a manifestly unpopular US president and his policies, but other examples hardly show Britain, or western democracies more generally (the US is an exception), to be any more confident in their willingness to use force.

Thousands of foreign troops were deployed in the 1990s to the former Yugoslavia with

PETER MACDIARMID/GETTY IMAGES

little idea of the purpose of their presence. General Rupert Smith, who at one stage commanded the UN force in Bosnia-Herzegovina, highlighted the muddled thinking that led to the creation by UN Security Council fiat of "safe havens" in places such as Srebrenica when he commented that their wording was designed "to appear strong and decisive, while at the same time avoid exposing their own national troops to risk". As the massacre in Srebrenica subsequently showed, the despatch of troops in a tentative or muddled way, giving false hope to desperate people, can be even worse than doing nothing.

The natural desire to avoid glorifying war – or to build a world in which it has no place – has produced a political atmosphere in which the aspiration that force, like crime, ought not to pay has been transformed in the minds of many into a certainty that it does not and can never work. Yet there is too much recent history that disproves this notion: from the Falklands to Nato's air strikes in Bosnia to Sierra Leone, Britain has been involved in operations where force has proved useful and effective.

It is a measure of how widespread the rejection of force has become that it is quite common to hear even commanders of the armed forces use such formulations as "No counter-insurgency was ever won by force alone" or "You always end up negotiating". Granted, most insurgencies have had to be addressed by political and economic action as well as military measures, but from the crushing of the Scottish Jacobites in 1745 to the 2009 Sri Lankan offensive against the Tamil Tigers, there have been campaigns where a security problem (as opposed to core separatist yearnings) has been dealt with by brute force.

Many are so convinced of the futility of war that the commentary surrounding modern conflict often fixes upon killing of civilians or friendly forces, or questions surrounding the legality of force. That war is a horrendous business in which life is often snuffed out in the most arbitrary way is clear to anyone who has experienced it: but, objectively, civilian loss of life or casualties of "friendly fire" today are of an order of magnitude less than those in the Second World War, which many still consider as the ultimate just use of force.

Although most people would accept the theory that state violence can be used in self-defence, few in western democracies are willing to support wars of choice. That small proportion of the British force in Helmand Province that actually goes outside its bases now does so in such a ponderous way, laden with body armour, crawling along because of the threat of improvised bombs, and knowing that it might be subject to UK law for actions committed in the wilds of Afghanistan, that it is questionable what it can achieve.

Certain British leaders, most obviously Tony Blair, have tried to swim against the public tide, but the consequence of committing troops into a situation where public support soon waned was a withdrawal from southern Iraq that left US generals questioning the usefulness of British soldiers. In Afghanistan one hears the logic of "We can't have another Basra" as one of the reasons for not leaving as quickly as possible, yet in Helmand, too, it could be argued that this country's reputation for military effectiveness has suffered with the US allies we sought to impress.

In this atmosphere, with ever fewer of us experiencing military life, it is hardly surprising that the forces are vulnerable to further cuts. Today the operational fighter force of the RAF can be measured in the scores rather than hundreds, the "submarine service" sometimes has only two boats available for patrol and the army is reduced to being able to maintain just 6,500 troops for sustained operations.

It might be argued that this is the logical outcome of the growing rejection of military force in British society, of the long road travelled since 1913. Not all countries, though, are subject to the same process. There are those that are still raising their defence spending and millions who still believe it is a sweet thing to die for their nation or faith. The implications of what might happen if Britain ends up confronting a society intent on using this power are sobering. ●

Mark Urban is a broadcaster and historian. His latest book, "The Tank War", is newly published by Little, Brown (£17.99)

17 SEPTEMBER 2001

In Buildings Thought Indestructible

Leader Column

Peter Wilby edited the New Statesman between 1998 and 2005. He was widely censured – but also celebrated in some quarters – for suggesting in this leading article that the United States may have played some part in provoking the horrific attacks of 11 September 2001.

The connection between the dreadful attacks on New York and Washington and the other big news story of the month – the attempts by refugees to enter Britain and Australia – may not be immediately obvious. But they are intimately related: both bring the wretched of the earth dramatically and disruptively into the minds of the prosperous West. In most of Africa, and in much of Latin America, Asia and the Middle East, war, disease and extreme poverty are endemic. Trapped in such conditions, what can people do? The rulers of the rich countries tap their blackboards: pull your socks up, get wired up to Microsoft, start a small business, instal a better system of government, follow the example of those good children in South Korea, listen to your IMF nanny. These lessons may seem tedious and impracticable to the very poor. Instead, they strive to live in the west, where people (if the television shows are any guide) seem to enjoy prosperity without visible effort. Alternatively, they can strike out in rage. That, after all, is what America has often done against those who dare to cross it.

Look at the pictures showing Americans running in terror from the New York explosions and then ask yourself how often in the past (particularly in Vietnam and more recently in Iraq) you have seen people running in terror from American firepower. American bond traders, you may say, are as innocent and as undeserving of terror as Vietnamese or Iraqi peasants. Well, yes and no. Yes, because such large-scale carnage is beyond justification, since it can never distinguish between the innocent and the guilty. No, because Americans, unlike Iraqis and many others in poor countries, at least have the privileges of democracy and freedom that allow them to vote and speak in favour of a different order. If the United States often seems a greedy and overweening power, that is partly because its people have willed it. They preferred George Bush to Al Gore and both to Ralph Nader.

These are harsh judgements, but we live in harsh times. Since the communist bloc began to weaken in the 1980s capitalism has reverted to type, though with most of the misery exported from the industrialised nations. A world in which there is only one superpower deprives poor countries of the best lever for improving themselves that they ever had: if one side wouldn't provide aid, in cash or kind, they could go straight to the other. True, this kind of blackmail allowed many cruel and corrupt dictators to retain power. But you may be sure that, if the Soviet Union were still a reality and a threat, the debt crisis would not exist. There was no debt crisis in Germany after the Second World War, for the simple reason that both America and the Soviet Union wanted to make a success of their own halves of the defeated nation, and cancelled most of the war debt. Western Europe recovered after 1945 thanks to the Marshall aid programme, introduced by a US government that feared more countries going communist.

The death of the Soviet Union also deprived the global poor of something more intangible: not exactly hope, perhaps, but the sense of an alternative, of possibility. Precisely because the awfulness of life under eastern European tyrannies was largely hidden, communism offered inspiration and idealism, distant goals of justice and equality that (however grotesque it might seem) the dispossessed aspired to. Now, all that seems on offer is another can of Coca-Cola or another episode of *Dynasty*. Americans would do well to ask themselves why, despite beaming their way of life to every corner of the globe, their ideals and values have failed to inspire the Third World young in the way that Marxism did and Islam now does. (Indeed, it often seems that the only people truly inspired by the US are a small band of disciples in London, with Gordon Brown and Tony Blair at their centre.) The answer, surely, is that American values too easily come over as shallow and hypocritical.

GRIZELDA

"What did you tweet?" Wry comment in the *NS*, 2012

Americans and their supporters may reasonably argue that the attacks on New York and Washington have more to do with the labyrinthine conflicts and hatreds of the Middle East than with the plight of poor people; moreover, they may say, the most likely culprits are members of a group led by an exiled Saudi millionaire. Nevertheless, terrorism on this scale – greeted with enthusiasm on the streets of many poor countries – needs a sympathetic climate, a sea in which it can swim. And the US government and media (along with their British cheerleaders) themselves raise the ideological stakes when they claim that we have seen attacks on freedom and democracy. That is one way of putting it: another is to say that these attacks, using deeply symbolic targets, have hit a civilisation that has grown complacent, selfish and, in some respects, decadent. Bertolt Brecht, in his early poem "Vom armen B B", provides as apt a commentary as any on an extraordinary day:

We have lived, a careless people
In buildings we thought indestructible
(Thus we erected the skyscrapers of Manhattan
And the thin antennae that cross the Atlantic)
My generation has made itself homeless
In mad pursuit of a vague ideal
(Thus we dabbled in drugs and religion
Trod the thin line between the real and unreal)
Of these cities all that will remain is what passes through them: the wind!
The house makes the feaster merry: now it has been emptied.
We know now that we are only temporary
And after us will come: nothing . . . ●

17 MAY 2004

America's Gulag

By Stephen Grey

This startling report by the award-winning investigative journalist Stephen Grey, which exposed the George W Bush administration's use of "extraordinary rendition" – the extrajudicial transfer of terrorism suspects to countries known to employ torture – was a world exclusive and its impact echoed around the world.

8 October 2002.

Over the Atlantic, at 30,000 feet, on board a Gulfstream jet, Maher Arar looked out through the portholes at the clouds beneath and the red glow of dawn. Stretching out on the wide, upholstered leather seat, he glanced across at the large video screen on which was displayed the path of the plane from its departure point near New York, onwards to Washington, DC, and then to its final refuelling point at Portland, Maine, before heading across the ocean. A telecommunications engineer in Ottawa, Canada, Maher was used to air travel – but not to such luxury. His companions – specialists attached to the CIA – were preparing to switch on another in-flight film, an action movie.

Maher could think only of what fate lay ahead of him when he reached the country the United States was now sending him to for interrogation and from which his family had once fled – Syria. He recalls: "I knew that Syria was a country that tortured its prisoners. I was silent and submissive; just asking myself over and over again: 'How did I end up in this situation? What is going to happen to me now?'" Maher had been arrested at New York's JFK Airport at 2pm on 26 September, after a holiday in Tunisia. He was accused of membership of al-Qaeda and of knowing two other Syrian-Canadians who were said to be terrorists. Maher was baffled; he hardly knew the pair. They both seemed ordinary Muslims like him. Although Maher was a Canadian citizen, after interrogation in New York he was told he would be deported to Syria. It petrified him. One of the CIA agents, who called himself Mr Khoury, had explained that he, too, was originally from Syria. Khoury was wearing a grey lounge suit; Maher was still wearing an orange boilersuit and was shackled with steel handcuffs and chains. During the flight, Khoury lent him a turquoise polo shirt. Maher would be wearing that shirt for the next three months. He would be wearing it as his arms, his palms and the soles of his feet were beaten with electric cables.

After the plane landed in Jordan, he was taken to a Damascus jail. He was not alone: from the cells around him, he heard the screams of those under torture. One prisoner was from Spain, another from Germany. All had been flown in to help America's war on terrorism. There was no daylight in his cell, just a dim glow through a hole in the reinforced concrete of his ceiling. Maher wanted to pray towards Mecca, but no guard would tell him which direction that was. And anyway, he could bend only one way – forwards, towards the metal door. He couldn't keep track of the days, but knew that about once a week he would be brought out to wash himself.

Maher was inside a secret system. His flight was on a jet operated for the CIA by the US Special Collection Service. It runs a fleet of luxury planes, as well as regular military transports, that has moved thousands of prisoners around the world since 11 September 2001. Some of the prisoners have gone to Guantanamo, hundreds more have been transferred from one Middle Eastern or Asian country to another – countries where the prisoners can be more easily interrogated. The operations of this airline – and the prisoners that it transports – have been shrouded in total secrecy. The airline's operations are embarrassing because they highlight intense co-operation with the regimes of countries such as Egypt, Syria and Pakistan, which are criticised for their human rights record. The movements of these planes expose a vast archipelago of prison camps and centres where America can carry out torture by proxy. The operations are illegal – they violate the anti-torture convention promoted by George W Bush which prohibits the transfer of suspects abroad for torture.

When Alexander Solzhenitsyn wrote *The Gulag Archipelago*, he described a physical chain of island prisons clustered in Soviet Russia's northern seas and Siberia. But the description was also metaphorical: the archipelago was a chain of prisons around which swirled the sea of normal society. The American archipelago also operates as a secret network that remains largely unseen by the world. Although a few of the prisons have become well known – Guantanamo, in Cuba; the CIA interrogation centre at the US airbase in Bagram, just north of Kabul; the airbase on British Diego Garcia – there are others, hidden from view: the floating interrogation centre located on board a US naval vessel in the Indian Ocean; an unknown jail referred to only as Hotel California by the CIA. Of those operated by America's allies, the worst prisons include the Scorpion jail and the Lazoghly Square secret police headquarters in Cairo, and the Far' Falastin interrogation centre in Damascus, Syria.

The transfer to these prisons, unregulated by any law, has become known as "rendition", a term used as an alternative to lawful "extradition". Rendition was invented by Sandy Berger, Bill Clinton's national security adviser, who described it as a "new art form". After 9/11, a trickle of renditions became a flow, and became the foundation of a whole system to tackle world terrorism. J Cofer Black, former head of the CIA's counterterrorism centre, testified in 2002 that there were at least 3,000 terrorist prisoners being held worldwide.

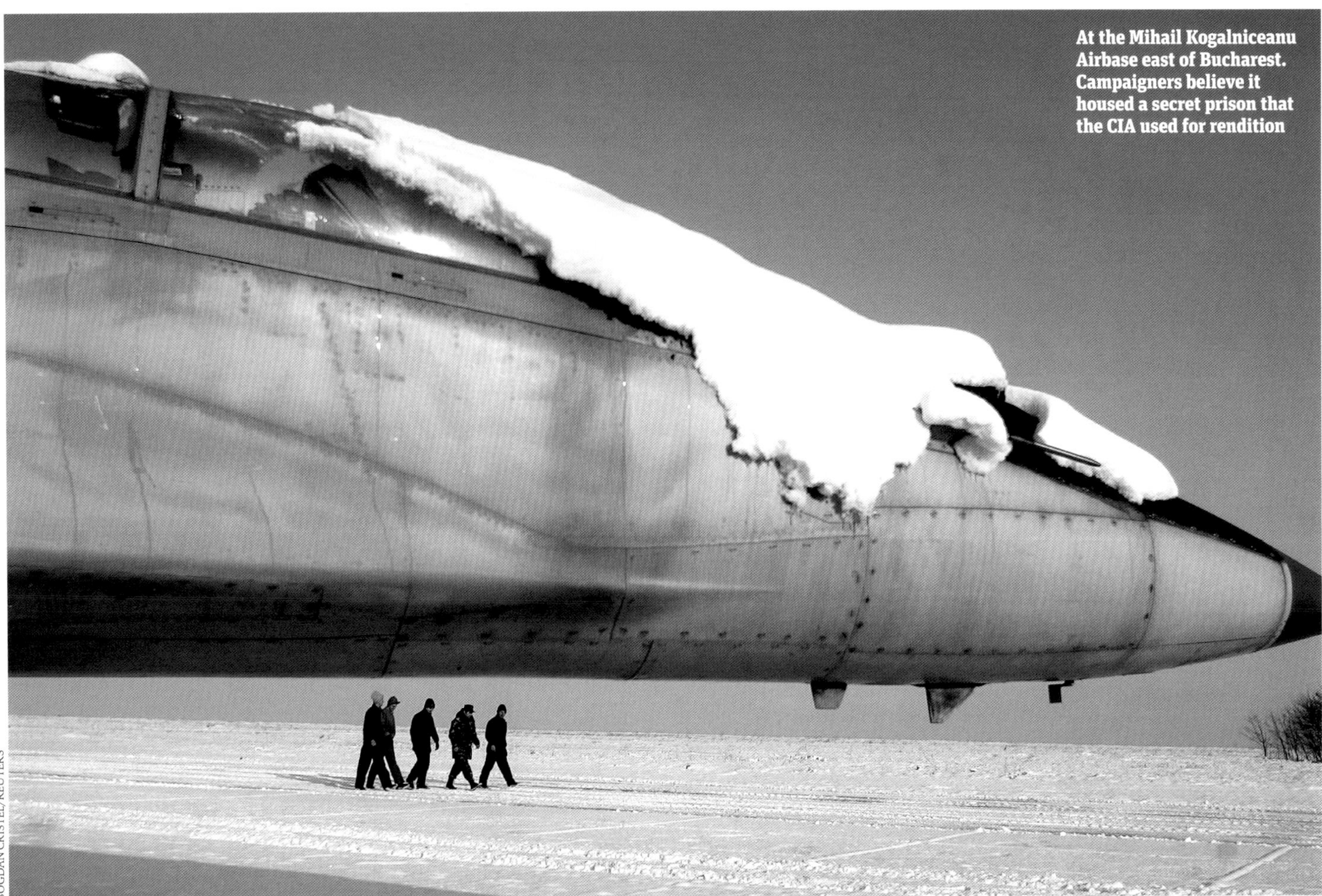

At the Mihail Kogalniceanu Airbase east of Bucharest. Campaigners believe it housed a secret prison that the CIA used for rendition

BOGDAN CRISTEL/REUTERS

Intelligence documents show the scale may be even greater. In the two years following 9/11, the Sudanese intelligence service alone claimed to have sent more than 200 captured prisoners into US custody. Of the terrorist suspects seized by America in the same period, only US citizens such as John Walker Lindh, the Californian found fighting with the Taliban, or those arrested within the US, such as Zacarias Moussaoui, accused of being a would-be hijacker in the 9/11 attack, would make it to court.

Tora Bora, Afghanistan, early December 2001.

Up in the foothills of the Spin Ghar Mountains on the border between Afghanistan and Pakistan, a British special forces soldier reaches into his pocket to find his tangle of plastic handcuffs. Grabbing his prisoner's arms, he locks them tight around the wrists.

Daylight reveals the detritus of a four-hour night fight. On the churned-up slopes of rough grass and patches of snow, blankets, personal belongings, empty shell-casings and the bodies of 38 Islamic warriors lie abandoned. Another 22 fighters, the survivors, are kneeling on the ground. The prisoners, from across Arabia, from Pakistan and even from Chechnya, are dressed in brown and grey shalwar kameez and thin sandals. Their hands are tied behind their backs, held taut with plasticuffs. Their heads are covered with canvas bags. These arrests provided the entry point into the American archipelago. Although Britain and other allies would later criticise America's tactics and its treatment of terror prisoners (the British high court would call it "monstrous"), this operation proved how UK soldiers were involved with US activities from the beginning.

> In 2002 there were at least 3,000 terrorist prisoners being held worldwide

As a "combat zone", Afghanistan provided some legal cover for the arrests. But Britain and America also seized many others across the border in Pakistan. Operating outside the law, the CIA has established snatch squads around the world. They have allowed the arrests of suspects, including Britons, which would be illegal if they took place on home soil. For instance, Wahab al-Rawi, a Briton, was questioned, but never arrested or held by MI5 in the UK. He came to be arrested only following a tip-off from MI5 to the CIA when he visited Gambia, in West Africa.

Al-Rawi is Iraqi-born, but a British citizen. He is enormous, and cannot walk too far without running out of breath. Wahab sits in a jail cell in the Gambian capital, Banjul. His questioner is an American, Lee, "from the embassy". Wahab has been answering questions about his supposed membership of al-Qaeda. He has been in jail for the past four days. A businessman whose family fled persecution from Saddam Hussein in Iraq, he had invested £300,000 after mortgaging his house to back his latest business venture: a mobile factory to process Gambian peanuts. His brother Bisher, who is handy with anything technical, had come out to help fix up the equipment. Wahab and Bisher got into trouble after surveillance information was passed to the US by MI5. Both Wahab and Bisher are friends with a Jordanian Islamic preacher in London called Abu Qatada who is accused of having links to terrorists. Abu Qatada is eventually locked up by the British, but there is insufficient (or no) evidence to arrest or hold Wahab or Bisher. Instead, their details are passed on to the US as part of an "intelligence exchange" in the post-11 September world.

"When I asked Lee whether I could see the British consul to protest at my arrest, he laughed," recalls Wahab. "'Why do you think you're here?' he asked me. 'It's your government that tipped us off in the first place.'" The CIA official was thereby breaching the Vienna Convention, which requires foreign detainees to get access to their nation's consulate. ▶

▶ Across the world, the involvement of the CIA in the arrest of suspects, typically bypassing local laws, has become routine. Rendition arrests probably began in earnest in Tirana, Albania, in July 1998 when a team of CIA operatives ran an operation with Albania's secret police. They tailed a group of five Egyptian Islamist militants, foiling their plan to destroy the US embassy with a truck bomb. They were captured and taken to police headquarters where, as the CIA waited outside, they were tortured. They were then bundled into an unmarked US Gulfstream jet waiting at the airport and flown to Cairo.

After being handed over to the Egyptian government, Ahmed Osman Saleh was suspended from the ceiling and given electric shocks; he was later hanged after a trial *in absentia*. Mohamed Hassan Tita was hung by his wrists and given electric shocks to his feet and back. Shawki Attiya was given electric shocks to his genitals, suspended by his limbs and made to stand for hours in filthy water up to his knees. Ahmad Ibrahim al-Naggar was kept in a room with water up to his knees for 35 days; had electric shocks to his nipples and penis; and was hanged without trial in 2000.

December 2002, downtown Damascus, Syria.

In a bustling street, taxis are honking their horns. Pedestrians hurry by. They hurry because no one on this road likes to linger too long. The office building beside the road has a certain reputation. It is the headquarters of the Mukhabarat, foreign intelligence. Elsewhere in the city, the atmosphere is relaxed. The president, the young British-educated former eye doctor Bashar al-Assad, is in London with his English wife, Asma, on a state visit to see Tony Blair and the Queen. Blair welcomes al-Assad with lunch at Downing Street and the Syrian president enthuses about "the warm personal relations I enjoy with Mr Blair".

Maher Arar has no access to radio or television to hear news of the rapprochement between the two countries. He is still in his cell, barely wider than his torso and about two inches longer than his height. As Blair sits down to chat to al-Assad about progress on the war on terror and the need to support the US/UK plan to invade Iraq, Arar is reaching the end of his tether. For days he has endured beatings, constant questioning and demands that he confess. He is, in fact, ready to confess to anything. He signs a false statement saying that he went for training in Afghanistan. But what he cannot do – because he knows nothing – is provide useful information that the Syrians can pass back to US intelligence.

In the depths of Far' Falastin jail, Arar has no contact with other prisoners. All he can hear, during the ten months of his imprisonment, is the sound of them screaming. In the beginning, the jailers take him upstairs regularly to be questioned and beaten. Before sessions he is placed in a waiting room where he gets to hear the torture of other prisoners. They call out: "*Allah-u-allah*" – "God, oh, God," they cry. Once he hears the sound of someone's head being slammed repeatedly against the metal interrogation table...

The former CIA agent Bob Baer, who worked covertly for the US across the Middle East until the mid-1990s, describes how each Middle Eastern country has a purpose in the archipelago. He says: "If you want a serious interrogation, you send a prisoner to Jordan. If you want them to be tortured, you send them to Syria. If you want someone to disappear – never to see them again – you send them to Egypt."

Cairo, 2003. Each night before sunset, a flotilla of feluccas is untied from jetties in the city centre and sails up against the current on a cool Nile breeze. The boats, filled with tourists, move silently in the calm water. As it grows dark, the tourists may notice a handful of floodlit watchtowers and the silhouettes of guards standing on their turrets. Just yards from where they are enjoying the sunset is the entrance to what for many is a version of hell.

> Just yards from the tourists is what for many is a version of hell

Behind the walls and watchtowers that announce Tora Prison is an inner complex, a 320-cell annexe shaped like the letter "H", known as *el-Aqrab*, or the Scorpion. Some of America's most secret prisoners are held in solitary confinement here. And here, too some of the most infamous names in Islamist extremism have been confined, from the Cairo-born doctor Ayman al-Zawahiri, who became Osama Bin Laden's right-hand man, to Sayyid Qutb, the intellectual who defined the philosophy that has inspired two generations of Islamist terrorists. Many argue that Tora's harsh conditions have helped to breed this extremism. The Scorpion annexe is something else again. No outsider knows who is being held within its walls. Since its construction was completed in 1993, no visitor – no family member, no lawyer – has been allowed inside.

Egyptian officials speak proudly of what they are doing to help the war on terror. It is the latest phase in a long line of covert US co-operation with the Egyptian government stretching back many years. Egypt still receives about $2bn a year in aid from America, of which $1.3bn is military aid. Nowadays, the co-operation is geared towards helping Egypt ward off Islamist extremism, and also to escape criticism for its repressive measures.

Normally, all prisoners of Britain, the US and its allies would have the protection of the law of *habeas corpus*. But US federal judges have argued that enemy aliens do not have these rights. After 9/11, Congress authorised the American president to "use all necessary and appropriate force against those nations, organisations or persons [whom] he determines planned, authorised, committed or aided" the attacks. It further recognised presidential authority to decide on any other actions "to respond to, deter or prevent acts of international terrorism".

Counterterrorism Centre, CIA headquarters, Langley, Virginia. 6 November 2002.

An eye in the sky at 10,000 feet shows live pictures of a convoy of cars moving down a desert highway 12,000 miles away. The picture is being captured by an unmanned Predator spy plane and conveyed by satellite from the Hadramaut region of Yemen. Although it is 4am at the Counterterrorism Centre, the little operations control booth is crowded, as it always is these days. The technology is the product of billions of dollars of spending. At the back of the room stand the CIA's lawyers – always present when life-or-death decisions are to be made. But they have already signed up to what will happen next. At the centre of the screen are some black cross-hairs. They are locked on to the car in front. It only remains for Cofer Black, the long-time head of the Counterterrorism Centre, to give the order. A key turns, a button is pressed, and the aptly named "Hellfire" missile streaks home. An explosion fills the screen. The target that night is a wanted terrorist named Abu Ali, aka Qaed Salim Sinan al-Harethi. A few hours later, when his death is confirmed, the agents celebrate their success. However, bystanders are also killed, including a US citizen named Kamal Derwish, from Buffalo, New York State.

Assassination of America's enemies seemed a clever tactic after 9/11. The CIA's political masters ordered it to kill terrorist leaders when it was possible to do so with minimum "collateral damage". But it often went wrong.

In the post-9/11 debate on tactics and policy there has been very little effort to address the roots of terrorism. Rather like the cowboy song – "Don't try to understand 'em/Just rope, throw and brand 'em" – Bush's response to the crisis has been too focused on retaliation. The military has defended the use of terror tactics. A former US army colonel, Alex Sands, declared: "The whole point of using special operations is to fight terror with terror. Our guys are trained to do the things that traditionally the other guys have done: kidnap, hijack, infiltrate." Yet as the world gains glimpses of George W Bush's archipelago, revulsion at the Americans' modus operandi – and support for the suspects they deliver into the torturers' hands – will grow. Rope, throw and brand 'em may no longer prove a suitable containment policy. ●

Dreams and Delusions

Flight of fancy: swinging on a lamp-post in the West End of Newcastle, 1975

6 SEPTEMBER 1924

English Socialism

By G D H Cole

Nothing is more significant in the world of to-day than the collapse of Socialistic doctrines. Only a decade ago the outlines of the Socialist policy seemed well-defined, and Socialism itself a body of doctrines and a programme as clear as the sun at noon-day. When a man said he was a Socialist, you could tell within narrow limits what he stood for and what he believed. There were differences as to method and rapidity of change. Some Socialists thought of Socialism as a product of revolution, and some—the greater number—as the result of a prolonged course of evolutionary change. But as to the end itself they were substantially agreed. The State, democratised by the extension of the franchise and the growth in popular education, would take upon itself the full burden of conducting the national affairs. Industry and commerce would become departments of State action; we should all become Civil Servants and work for the State in a spirit of mutual service. Such an outcome was in line with the actual tendency of political affairs. It was in line also with the development of industry. The trust was the forerunner of nationalisation.

To-day, all that structure of Socialist ideas lies in ruins. Men still call themselves Socialists, probably in greater numbers than ever before. But now, when a man calls himself a Socialist, he conveys by the name little information about his ideas and beliefs. A few—perhaps all the younger converts, regard the State and its works with an aloof and critical hostility. Socialism is still no doubt a faith; but it is, like the faith of some modern Churchmen, a faith that has discarded all its doctrines —a disembodied faith in the soul of a dead idea.

All this has come out very clearly in the proceedings of the past fortnight at the Summer School conducted by the Independent Labour Party. The ILP is, or is reputed to be, the pioneering propagandist body of Socialism, as well as the tail that wags the dog of political Labour. It is supposed to supply the ideas which the great Trade Unions then accept and finance. What the ILP thinks to-day the Labour Party will think to-morrow. But the puzzle is to discover what the ILP is thinking to-day. The discussions at the Cloughton Summer School leave us with the impression, not that the ILP has a policy which it is endeavouring to press upon the Government, but that, having recognised the inadequacy of the old Socialist policy, it is seeking feverishly everywhere for a new policy to take its place.

In one sense, this is a healthy sign; for it means that the leaders of the ILP are trying to take stock of their position in the light of present realities. There was a notable tendency to concentrate discussion at Cloughton on actual problems of to-day and to-morrow, and to propound and argue positive remedies meant for early application. There was much said about next steps in agricultural policy, in the control of banking, and in industrial legislation, and little about plans to be realised on the morrow of the Revolution. The talkers were really trying to face things as they saw them in the world of fact. But—and this is the really significant thing—they were facing the facts in a strictly empirical and particularist spirit, as if each problem stood by itself and had to be judged on its merits. There was no indication of a clear unifying principle in the light of which all problems could be seen in their true aspect. In short, in this representative gathering of Socialists, there appeared no common basis of Socialist doctrine.

> There is upon us a time of transition in ideas when party labels mean ever less

Much that was said at Cloughton was excellent. Especially on the agricultural question, the ILP with its plan for collective control of imports and marketing is, we believe, working along sound lines. But the disappearance of the old State Socialist faith is manifest here also. Gone are the days when the Socialist, confronted by the rural problem, could declare for nationalisation of the land, and look round triumphantly, as if that settled the whole matter. The ILP proposes, indeed, State control of the industry; but the distance it has gone from the old faith is measured by the form which the proposed control is to take. No longer is the Civil Servant to be the agent of Socialism; State control is to be administered through the farmers and rural workers organised into a representative authority for agricultural affairs. Guild Socialism, if it has not secured acceptance for its own schemes, has at any rate made short work of State Socialism in its traditional forms.

It is evident that the members of the Socialist bodies have an uneasy sense that the old dogmas of Socialism are melting away. This appears plainly in their attitude to the Labour Government. Those who defend the Government most warmly say that it is not Socialist, and is not pursuing a Socialist policy. Now it is the mission of the ILP to make the Government Socialist and to ensure that it shall launch a Socialist programme. But what is this programme to be? In discussing the Government, the Cloughton Summer School spoke with two voices. One voice commended the Government's practicality in facing immediate issues; the other blamed it for wandering from the straight path of Socialism. Speaker after speaker urged that, while it should continue to deal with the problems of the day much as it has been, it should also make a plain declaration of its Socialist faith by introducing into Parliament really Socialist measures and challenging defeat on this fundamental issue. So much was easily said; but on what issue was the fundamental challenge to be made? Nationalisation of mines and railways, or even banks? All these are challenges. They would arouse the necessary opposition; but would they evoke the no less necessary enthusiasm on the Socialist side? There were not wanting at Cloughton speakers who held that these things are not Socialism. Perhaps they are not; but, if they are not, what is?

Socialism lives as an idea; it is no longer living as a programme. And, even as an idea, can it live long in its disembodied state? Communism has arisen to challenge it, and to beat it at its own game of bourgeois-scaring. Socialism, now that Communism is in the field, has no longer the attraction of seeming to be on

James Jarché's portrait for the *Daily Herald* of a miner with his family in the Rhondda Valley, South Wales, June 1931

the extreme left. It has still, no doubt, a faint aroma of human brotherhood, and this is its remaining source of strength. It still appeals to men's pacific and friendly impulses and emotions, whereas Communism has stolen its old appeal to their fighting instinct. But a political creed cannot live on moral impulses, however generous. It must include a policy as well as a moral rule of life, or it will cease to be a gospel for the workaday world and become even as the Musical Banks in *Erewhon*.

The ILP leaders, understanding this, are trying hard to find for the old soul of Socialism a new bodily habitation. They may succeed in devising a new policy and a good one suited for the needs of the day. But we doubt if it will be recognisably a Socialist policy, unified by any principle reasonably to be called "Socialist". It will pick and choose, as the Labour Government has picked and chosen, among proposals drawn from many schools of thought. It will bring forward plans not vitally different from those which might be drafted by clever businessmen, or clever Liberals, or clever Conservatives. There will be indeed this difference, that the new Socialism, more regardful of the claims of the wage-earner, will be less regardful of vested interests in property. But, as the plain declarations against confiscation made at Cloughton show, this divergence is less deep than on the surface it appears. The new Socialism makes to property concessions of expediency which differ little in practice from admissions of right.

The new evolutionary Socialism of the ILP—if we are still to call it Socialism—is already in conflict and will before long be in violent conflict with the revolutionary doctrines of Communism. Communism is as definite as Socialism is now eclectic and accommodating, except in Russia, where, having achieved power, it has also had to face the realities of government. Communism in England or France can be a faith, because it has no need to be really a policy. It lives on its possession of just that simplification of issues which is no longer possible for the ILP. It stands where Socialism stood forty years ago. If it succeeds, it will dissolve, as Socialism has dissolved, in the deep waters of its own success.

But there is this difference. The old Socialism was not merely a faith, but a scheme. It wanted this and that—definite things to be done, the sum of which was Socialism. In urging these things, it has left its mark everywhere. No party, no body of political or economic opinion, but has been deeply influenced by the Socialist ideas whose full application it has rejected. This power to influence diverse streams of thought was the strength of Socialism. Communism, on the other hand, is a "take it or leave it" sort of doctrine. It is not a programme in the same sense; it does not admit of eclecticism and partial applications. Communism is all or nothing.

And, as in this country with its living tradition of accommodation and adjustment Communism cannot be all, it is doomed, we believe, to be nothing. The virtue which has passed out of Socialism has not passed into Communism. It has passed to no definite group of men, or body of doctrine. It has diffused itself through men of many different groups. In a sense this is a weakness, for only defined groups have the cohesion necessary for effective action. But this is only to say that, while the old groups are in dissolution, the new are yet unformed. The new principle of unification is yet undiscovered.

It is groped for, not only by the ILP, but wherever men of goodwill are gathered together for the discussion of public affairs. When it is found, it will group men anew—to their surprise often and mortification at their strange new companionships. Till it is found men will grope on, trying to find in old faiths firm anchorage for changing opinions. There is upon us a time of transition in ideas, when party labels mean ever less, and men uneasy in old faiths cling to them only in default of new. "Lord, I believe," says the Socialist of to-day. But he adds, "Help thou mine unbelief." ●

The then chancellor of the exchequer, Winston Churchill (seated right), accepts mock-honours from students at Queen's University, Belfast, in rag week, 1926

TOPICAL PRESS AGENCY/HULTON ARCHIVE/GETTY IMAGES

22 MAY 1926

Should We Hang Mr Churchill or Not?

By Clifford Sharp

By the spirit and manner in which Mr Baldwin ended the great strike he almost atoned for the way in which he precipitated it. For there is no longer any doubt that it was precipitated by the action of the Government, and, what is more, quite deliberately precipitated. It is, of course, a matter of common knowledge now that the strike need not have occurred, that is to say that at the very moment of the breaking off of negotiations the Prime Minister had come to an understanding with the Trade Union leaders, which, though it would not have solved the problem of the mines, would have prevented the other Unions from coming out. The inexplicable abandonment of negotiations—which was condemned by all independent critics, including those who habitually support the Conservative Government—at such a stage has been generally attributed to a sudden panic in the Cabinet created by the action of the *Daily Mail* machinists. Let us quote the account of the negotiations given by the Attorney-General, Sir Douglas Hogg, in the *British Gazette* of May 11th:

> While the Cabinet was discussing the document [ie, the peace formula which had been drawn up by Lord Birkenhead, the Prime Minister and the Trade Union leaders] news arrived that the Natsopas [*Editor*: members of the National Society of Operative Printers and Assistants] had declined to allow the *Daily Mail* to appear with a leading article entitled "For King and Country" . . . It was thus clear that a General Strike had not only been threatened but had actually begun.

The action of the Natsopas had nothing to do with the threatened General Strike. It was an act of mutiny which the Trade Union leaders would instantly have condemned and repudiated, since they were still hoping that there would be no strike at all. They were offered no opportunity, however, either of repudiation or of explanation. They had heard nothing of the events in the *Daily Mail* office, and when they returned to the conference room with the agreed formula they found it dark and locked. The Cabinet had declared war and gone to bed.

These facts are not disputed. All that remains uncertain is their explanation. We, like most people, attributed the Government's critical decision to momentary panic which would have been dissipated if they had listened to explanations or waited until the morning. The truth, however, appears to be even more discreditable to them. What actually happened, it seems, was this. The Prime Minister, Lord Birkenhead and Sir Arthur Steel-Maitland were fighting desperately for peace, whilst a section of the Cabinet, led by Mr Winston Churchill, Mr Neville Chamberlain and Mr Bridgeman, were itching for a fight. The peace party succeeded in arranging terms based on the Royal Commission's Report, upon which the strike would be called off and the miners left, if they would not agree, to fight alone. With these terms they returned in triumph to the Cabinet room only to find Messrs Churchill and Chamberlain in charge and a clear majority in favour of war at all costs. When the Prime Minister proposed nevertheless to go forward with the negotiations and avert the strike, he was faced with the immediate resignation of seven of his colleagues—Churchill, Neville Chamberlain, Bridgeman, Amery, "Jix", Cunliffe-Lister, and one other of whose identity we are not sure. So he gave way. He ought not to have given way, of course, but excuses may perhaps be found for an utterly exhausted man who, having fought the Trade Unions for days and nights, found himself called upon at the last moment to fight his own colleagues. Mr Churchill was the villain of the piece. He is reported to have remarked that he thought "a little blood-letting" would be all to the good. Whether he actually used this phrase or not there is no doubt about his tireless efforts to seize the providential opportunity for a fight.

So much for the way the strike began. When it ended Mr Baldwin had regained control of his Cabinet and had acquired so enormous a personal popularity in the country that he could afford to let all his colleagues resign if they wanted to. He took charge of affairs without consulting anybody, and without any Cabinet authorisation—which would certainly not have been forthcoming from the fight-to-a-finish section—he insisted upon peace. Thereby he atoned for his previous surrender. "Victimisation" was being attempted in almost every industry. Men were being asked to return to work as new hands, at much lower wages, under humiliating conditions, and so on. The Prime Minister stopped all that within twenty-four hours, by his insistence upon the necessity of forgetting the past and looking only to the future. Some of his colleagues and many of his supporters railed at him for his "weakness"; but this time he stood firm—and gave us peace. His atonement, we think, should be accepted. He blundered on that Sunday night in agreeing to war, but ever since then he has fought for peace, and fought with an extraordinary measure of success.

We do not know whether there is anybody left who still honestly believes that the strike

Resistance: students volunteered to work in special services groups during the strike

was a "revolutionary" attempt to subvert the British Constitution. Its real nature, at any rate, was shown clearly enough by the actual course of events. It was a strike "in furtherance of a trade dispute", and nothing more; and in so far as it secured for the miners—if they would but have seized the chance—a better hearing than they would otherwise have had, it may not unreasonably be claimed to have been a successful strike, despite the inevitable, and in our view timely, "surrender". Not only was it not a strike against the Constitution, it was not even a strike against the Government; that was only because the Government had intervened—and rightly, though very ineffectively, intervened—in the struggle between the miners and the mineowners. If it had not intervened the strike would have taken place just the same; but then the truth would have been clear to everybody—namely, that it was a strike against the inefficiency and grasping obstinacy of the mineowners—nothing more and nothing less. The Constitution was never threatened either by word or by deed.

> A General Strike without violence can't succeed: it is a contradiction in terms

The result of the strike is not unsatisfactory. It has shown that an industrial upheaval can take place, in this country at any rate, without the loss of a single life. But what is far more important, it has shown that the weapon of the General Strike is worthless in the hands of those who are not prepared to go to all lengths of revolutionary violence. It is a weapon which revolutionaries (being a tiny minority) could never wield; yet unless it is they who wield it, it is blunt and ineffective. And so from henceforth we may hope that it will be discarded by the Trade Union movement. It has been tested and broken, and we all know where we are far more clearly than we did a month ago. The Trade Unions of Britain stood by their comrades in the mines, and perhaps by their wonderful solidarity they achieved something for them; but certainly the majority of them will never again wish to resort to so desperate a measure. The currency of the phrase, a "General Strike", has been so depreciated that we are not likely to hear it again save from the mouths of that minority which never has, and never can, learn anything from experience. The TUC decreed its own failure when it ordered its men to avoid conflicts with the police or the volunteers.

For a General Strike without violence cannot succeed; it is almost a contradiction in terms. With violence, on the other hand, it amounts to a revolution—which the Trade Union world does not want nor seems ever likely to want. Everybody understands this now, and that is why the strike was perhaps worthwhile. We have bought experience at a pretty high price; but we have got it; and no section of the community, we suppose, is more satisfied with the bargain than the "constitutional" leaders of the Labour movement. The irrepressible left-wingers are silenced; their dreams are dissolved; they must set about the Sisyphean task of converting the Trade Unions of Great Britain to revolutionary ideas, or admit failure. For having so notably helped to teach us all this, ought we to thank Mr Churchill or ought we to hang him on a lamp-post for the incorrigible "blood-letter" that he is? We are really not quite sure what is the proper answer to that question; but probably—to be on the safe side—it would be best that he should be hanged. ●

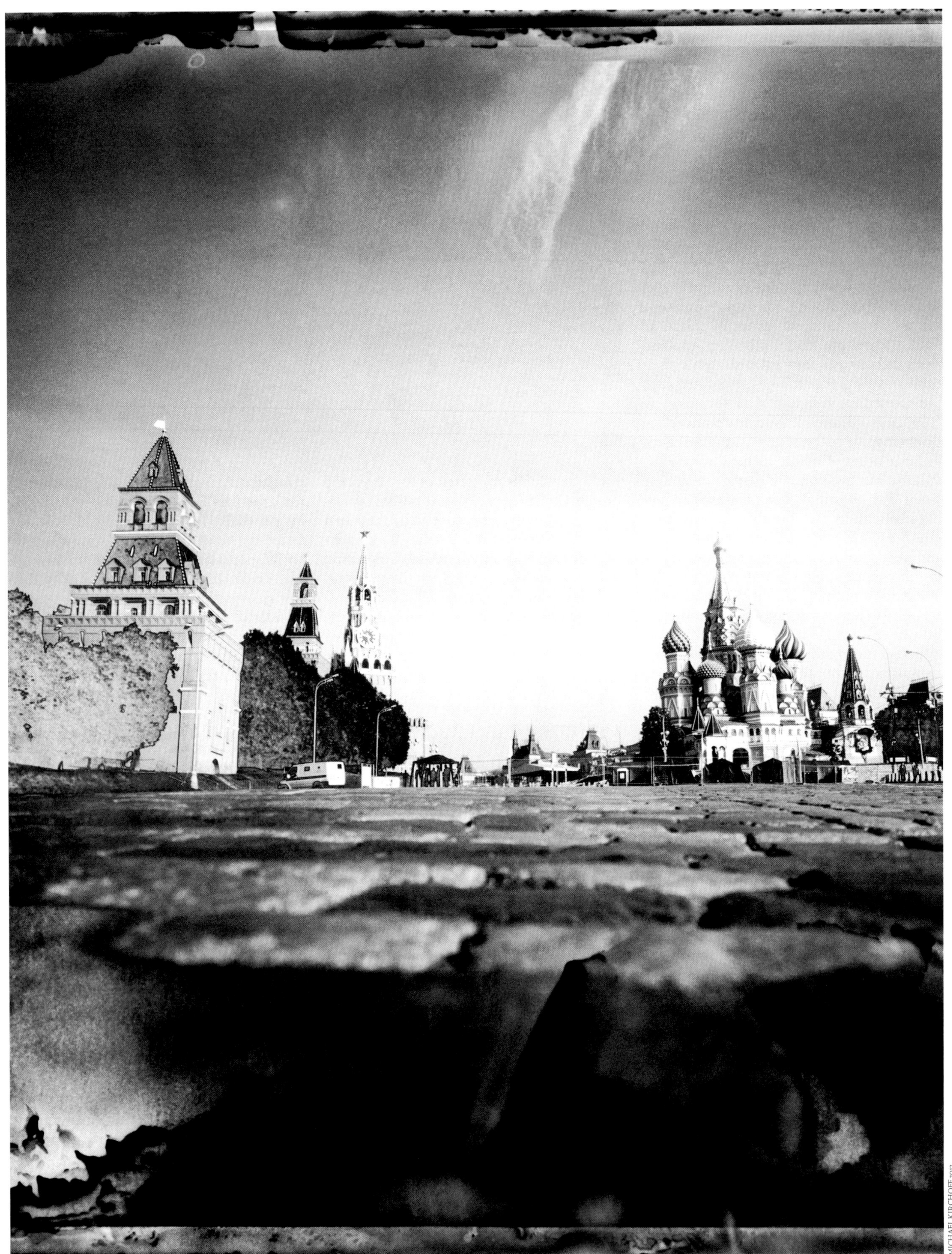

MICHAEL KIRCHOFF 2013

Virgin cobbles upturned: the common people of Moscow would never have been liberated, Stalin argued, without violence

17 NOVEMBER 1934

"It seems to me that I am more to the Left than you, Mr Stalin"

By H G Wells

In 1934, H G Wells arrived in Moscow to meet Soviet writers interested in joining the international PEN Club, of which he was then president. While there, Joseph Stalin granted him an interview. His deferential conversation was criticised by John Maynard Keynes and George Bernard Shaw, among others, in the New Statesman.

Wells I am very much obliged to you, Mr Stalin, for agreeing to see me. I was in the United States recently. I had a long conversation with President Roosevelt and tried to ascertain what his leading ideas were. Now I have come to ask you what you are doing to change the world...

Stalin Not so very much.

Wells I wander around the world as a common man and, as a common man, observe what is going on around me.

Stalin Important public men like yourself are not "common men". Of course, history alone can show how important this or that public man has been; at all events, you do not look at the world as a "common man".

Wells I am not pretending humility. What I mean is that I try to see the world through the eyes of the common man, and not as a party politician or a responsible administrator. My visit to the United States excited my mind. The old financial world is collapsing; the economic life of the country is being reorganised on new lines. Lenin said: "We must learn to do business," learn this from the capitalists. Today the capitalists have to learn from you, to grasp the spirit of Socialism. It seems to me that what is taking place in the United States is a profound reorganisation, the creation of planned, that is, Socialist, economy. You and Roosevelt begin from two different starting points. But is there not a relation in ideas, a kinship of ideas, between Moscow and Washington? In Washington I was struck by the same thing I see going on here; they are building offices, they are creating a number of state regulation bodies, they are organising a long-needed civil service. Their need, like yours, is directive ability.

America and Russia

Stalin The United States is pursuing a different aim from that which we are pursuing in the USSR. The aim which the Americans are pursuing arose out of the economic troubles, out of the economic crisis. The Americans want to rid themselves of the crisis on the basis of private capitalist activity, without changing the economic basis. They are trying to reduce to a minimum the ruin, the losses caused by the existing economic system.

Here, however, as you know, in place of the old, destroyed economic basis, an entirely different, a new economic basis has been created. Even if the Americans you mention partly achieve their aim, ie, reduce these losses to a minimum, they will not destroy the roots of the anarchy which is inherent in the existing capitalist system. They are preserving the economic system which must inevitably lead, and cannot but lead, to anarchy in production. Thus, at best, it will be a matter, not of the reorganisation of society, not of abolishing the old social system which gives rise to anarchy and crises, but of restricting certain of its excesses. Subjectively, perhaps, these Americans think they are reorganising society; objectively, however, they are preserving the present basis of society. That is why, objectively, there will be no reorganisation of society.

Nor will there be planned economy. What is planned economy? What are some of its attributes? Planned economy tries to abolish unemployment. Let us suppose it is possible, while preserving the capitalist system, to reduce unemployment to a certain minimum. But surely, no capitalist would ever agree to the complete abolition of unemployment, to the abolition of the reserve army of unemployed, the purpose of which is to bring pressure on the labour market, to ensure a supply of cheap labour. You will never compel a capitalist to incur loss to himself and agree to a lower rate of profit for the sake of satisfying the needs of the people.

Without getting rid of the capitalists, without abolishing the principle of private property in the means of production, it is impossible to create planned economy.

Wells I agree with much of what you have said. But I would like to stress the point that if a country as a whole adopts the principle of planned economy, if the government, gradually, step by step, begins consistently to apply this principle, the financial oligarchy will at last be abolished and Socialism, in the Anglo-Saxon meaning of the word, will be brought about. The effect of the ideas of Roosevelt's "New Deal" is most powerful, and in my opinion they are Socialist ideas. It seems to me that instead of stressing the antagonism between the two worlds, we should, in the present circumstances, strive to establish a common tongue for all the constructive forces.

Stalin In speaking of the impossibility of realising the principles of planned economy while preserving the economic basis of capitalism, I do not in the least desire to belittle the outstanding personal qualities of Roosevelt, his initiative, courage and determination. Undoubtedly Roosevelt stands out as one of the strongest figures among all the captains of the contemporary capitalist world. That is why I would like once again to emphasise the point that my conviction that planned economy is impossible under the conditions of ▶

capitalism does not mean that I have any doubts about the personal abilities, talent and courage of President Roosevelt. But if the circumstances are unfavourable, the most talented captain cannot reach the goal you refer to. Theoretically, of course, the possibility of marching gradually, step by step, under the conditions of capitalism, towards the goal which you call Socialism in the Anglo-Saxon meaning of the word, is not precluded. But what will this "Socialism" be? At best, bridling to some extent the most unbridled of individual representatives of capitalist profit, some increase in the application of the principle of regulation in national economy. That is all very well. But as soon as Roosevelt, or any other captain in the contemporary bourgeois world, proceeds to undertake something serious against the foundation of capitalism, he will inevitably suffer utter defeat. The banks, the industries, the large enterprises, the large farms are not in Roosevelt's hands. All these are private property. The railroads, the mercantile fleet, all these belong to private owners. And, finally, the army of skilled workers, the engineers, the technicians, these too are not at Roosevelt's command, they are at the command of the private owners; they all work for the private owners. We must not forget the functions of the State in the bourgeois world. The State is an institution that organises the defence of the country, organises the maintenance of "order"; it is an apparatus for collecting taxes. The capitalist State does not deal much with economy in the strict sense of the word; the latter is not in the hands of the State. On the contrary, the State is in the hands of capitalist economy. That is why I fear that in spite of all his energies and abilities, Roosevelt will not achieve the goal you mention, if indeed that is his goal. Perhaps in the course of several generations it will be possible to approach this goal somewhat; but I personally think that even this is not very probable.

Socialism and Individualism

Wells Perhaps I believe more strongly in the economic interpretation of politics than you do. Huge forces striving for better organisation, for the better functioning of the community, that is, for Socialism, have been brought into action by invention and modern science. Organisation, and the regulation of individual action, have become mechanical necessities, irrespective of social theories. If we begin with the State control of the banks and then follow with the control of the heavy industries, of industry in general, of commerce, etc, such an all-embracing control will be equivalent to the State ownership of all branches of national economy. Socialism and Individualism are not opposites like black and white. There are many intermediate stages between them. There is Individualism that borders on brigandage, and there is discipline and organisation that are the equivalent of Socialism. The introduction of planned economy depends, to a large degree, upon the organisers of economy, upon the skilled technical intelligentsia who, step by step, can be converted to the Socialist principles of organisation. And this is the most important thing, because organisation comes before Socialism. It is the more important fact. Without organisation the Socialist idea is a mere idea.

Stalin There is no, nor should there be, irreconcilable contrast between the individual and the collective, between the interests of the individual person and the interests of the collective. There should be no such contrast, because collectivism, Socialism, does not deny, but combines individual interests with the interests of the collective. Socialism cannot abstract itself from individual interests.

> "Revolution has always been a struggle, a painful and a cruel struggle"

Socialist society alone can most fully satisfy these personal interests. More than that, Socialist society alone can firmly safeguard the interests of the individual. In this sense there is no irreconcilable contrast between Individualism and Socialism. But can we deny the contrast between classes, between the propertied class, the capitalist class, and the toiling class, the proletarian class? On the one hand we have the propertied class which owns the banks, the factories, the mines, transport, the plantations in colonies. These people see nothing but their own interests, their striving after profits. They do not submit to the will of the collective; they strive to subordinate every collective to their will. On the other hand we have the class of the poor, the exploited class, which owns neither factories nor works, nor banks, which is compelled to live by selling its labour power to the capitalists and which lacks the opportunity to satisfy its most elementary requirements. How can such opposite interests and strivings be reconciled? As far as I know, Roosevelt has not succeeded in finding the path of conciliation between these interests. And it is impossible, as experience has shown. Incidentally, you know the situation in the United States better than I do, as I have never been there and I watch American affairs mainly from literature. But I have some experience in fighting for Socialism, and this experience tells me that if Roosevelt makes a real attempt to satisfy the interests of the proletarian class at the expense of the capitalist class, the latter will put another President in his place. The capitalists will say: Presidents come and Presidents go, but we go on for ever; if this or that President does not protect our interests, we shall find another. What can the President oppose to the will of the capitalist class?

Wells I object to this simplified classification of mankind into poor and rich. Of course there is a category of people which strive only for profit. But are not these people regarded as nuisances in the West just as much as here? Are there not plenty of people in the West for whom profit is not an end, who own a certain amount of wealth, who want to invest and obtain a profit from this investment, but who do not regard this as the main object? They regard investment as an inconvenient necessity. Are there not plenty of capable and devoted engineers, organisers of economy, whose activities are stimulated by something other than profit? In my opinion there is a numerous class of capable people who admit that the present system is unsatisfactory and who are destined to play a great role in future capitalist society. During the past few years I have been much engaged in and have thought of the need for conducting propaganda in favour of Socialism and cosmopolitanism among wide circles of engineers, airmen, military technical people, etc. It is useless to approach these circles with two-track class-war propaganda. These people understand the condition of the world. They understand that it is a bloody muddle, but they regard your simple class-war antagonism as nonsense.

The class war

Stalin You object to the simplified classification of mankind into rich and poor. Of course there is a middle stratum, there is the technical intelligentsia that you have mentioned and among which there are very good and very honest people. Among them there are also dishonest and wicked people; there are all sorts of people among them. But first of all mankind is divided into rich and poor, into property owners and exploited; and to abstract oneself from this fundamental division and from the antagonism between poor and rich means abstracting oneself from the fundamental fact. I do not deny the existence of intermediate middle strata, which either take the side of one or the other of these two conflicting classes, or else take up a neutral or semi-neutral position in the struggle. But, I repeat, to abstract oneself from this fundamental division in society and from the fundamental struggle between the two main classes means ignoring facts. The struggle is going on and will continue. The outcome will be determined by the proletarian class – the working class.

Wells But are there not many people who are not poor, but who work and work productively?

Stalin Of course, there are small landowners, artisans, small traders, but it is not these people who decide the fate of a country, but the toiling masses, who produce all the things society requires.

Wells But there are very different kinds of capitalists. There are capitalists who only think about profit, about getting rich; but there are also those who are prepared to make sacrifices. Take old [J P] Morgan, for example. He only thought about profit; he was a parasite on society, simply, he merely accumulated wealth. But take [John D] Rockefeller. He is a brilliant organiser; he has set an example of how to organise the delivery of oil that is worthy of emulation. Or take [Henry] Ford. Of course Ford is selfish. But is he not a passionate organiser of rationalised production from whom you take lessons? I would like to emphasise the fact that recently an important change in opinion towards the USSR has taken place in English-speaking countries. The reason for this, first of all, is the position of Japan, and the events in Germany. But there are other reasons besides those arising from international politics. There is a more profound reason, namely, the recognition by many people of the fact that the system based on private profit is breaking down. Under these circumstances, it seems to me, we must not bring to the forefront the antagonism between the two worlds, but should strive to combine all the constructive movements, all the constructive forces in one line as much as possible. It seems to me that I am more to the Left than you, Mr Stalin; I think the old system is nearer to its end than you think.

The technician class

Stalin In speaking of the capitalists who strive only for profit, only to get rich, I do not want to say that these are the most worthless people, capable of nothing else. Many of them undoubtedly possess great organising talent, which I do not dream of denying. We Soviet people learn a great deal from the capitalists. And Morgan, whom you characterise so unfavourably, was undoubtedly a good, capable organiser. But if you mean people who are prepared to reconstruct the world, of course, you will not be able to find them in the ranks of those who faithfully serve the cause of profit. We and they stand at opposite poles. You mentioned Ford. Of course, he is a capable organiser of production. But don't you know his attitude towards the working class? Don't you know how many workers he throws on the street? The capitalist is riveted to profit; and no power on earth can tear him away from it. Capitalism will be abolished, not by "organisers" of production, not by the technical intelligentsia, but by the working class, because the aforementioned strata do not play an independent role. The engineer, the organiser of production does not work as he would like to, but as he is ordered, in such a way as to serve the interests of his employers. There are exceptions of course; there are people in this stratum who have awakened from the intoxication of capitalism. The technical intelligentsia can, under certain conditions, perform miracles and greatly benefit mankind. But it can also cause great harm. We Soviet people have not a little experience of the technical intelligentsia. After the October Revolution, a certain section of the technical intelligentsia refused to take part in the work of constructing the new society; they opposed this work of construction and sabotaged it. We did all we possibly could to bring the technical intelligentsia into this work of construction; we tried this way and that. Not a little time passed before our technical intelligentsia agreed actively to assist the new system. Today the best section of this technical intelligentsia is in the front rank of the builders of Socialist society. Having this experience, we are far from underestimating the good and the bad sides of the technical intelligentsia, and we know that on the one hand it can do harm, and on the other hand it can perform "miracles". Of course, things would be different if it were possible, at one stroke, spiritually to tear the technical intelligentsia away from the capitalist world. But that is Utopia. Are there many of the technical intelligentsia who would dare break away from the bourgeois world and set to work reconstructing society? Do you think there are many people of this kind, say, in England or in France? No; there are few who would be willing to break away from their employers and begin reconstructing the world.

Achievement of political power

Stalin Besides, can we lose sight of the fact that in order to transform the world it is necessary to have political power? It seems to me, Mr Wells, that you greatly underestimate the question of political power, that it entirely drops out of your conception. What can those, even with the best intentions in the world, do if they are unable to raise the question of seizing power, and do not possess power? At best they can help the class which takes power, but they cannot change the world themselves. This can only be done by a great class which will take the place of the capitalist class and become the sovereign master as the latter was before. This class is the working class. Of course, the assistance of the technical intelligentsia must be accepted; and the latter, in turn, must be assisted. But it must not be thought that the technical intelligentsia can play an independent historical role. The transformation of the world is a great, complicated and painful process. For this task a great class is required. Big ships go on long voyages.

Wells Yes, but for long voyages a captain and navigator are required.

Stalin That is true; but what is first required for a long voyage is a big ship. What is a navigator without a ship? An idle man.

Wells The big ship is humanity, not a class.

Stalin You, Mr Wells, evidently start out with the assumption that all men are good. I, however, do not forget that there are many wicked men. I do not believe in the goodness of the bourgeoisie.

Wells I remember the situation with regard to the technical intelligentsia several decades ago. At that time the technical intelligentsia was numerically small, but there was much to do and every engineer, technician and intellectual found his opportunity. That is why the technical intelligentsia was the least revolutionary class. Now, however, there is a superabundance of technical intellectuals, and their mentality has changed very sharply. The skilled man, who would formerly never listen to revolutionary talk, is now greatly interested in it. Recently I was dining with the Royal Society, our great English scientific society. The President's speech was a speech for social planning and scientific control. Thirty years ago, they would not have listened to what I say to them now. Today, the man at the head of the Royal Society holds revolutionary views, and insists on the scientific reorganisation of human society. Your class-war propaganda has not kept pace with these facts. Mentality changes.

Stalin Yes, I know this, and this is to be explained by the fact that capitalist society is now in a cul-de sac. The capitalists are seeking, but cannot find a way out of this cul-de-sac that would be compatible with the dignity of this class, compatible with the interests of this class. They could, to some extent, crawl out of the crisis on their hands and knees, but they cannot find an exit that would enable them to walk out of it with head raised high, a way out that would not fundamentally disturb the interests of capitalism. This, of course, is realised by wide circles of the technical intelligentsia. A large section of it is beginning to realise the community of its interests with those of the class which is capable of pointing the way out of the cul-de-sac.

Wells You of all people know something about revolutions, Mr Stalin, from the practical side. Do the masses ever rise? Is it not an established truth that all revolutions are made by a minority? ▶

Michael Cummings's caricature of the new left, 1951

Stalin To bring about a revolution a leading revolutionary minority is required; but the most talented, devoted and energetic minority would be helpless if it did not rely upon the at least passive support of millions.
Wells At least passive? Perhaps subconscious?
Stalin Partly also the semi-instinctive and semi-conscious, but without the support of millions, the best minority is impotent.

The place of violence

Wells I watch Communist propaganda in the West, and it seems to me that in modern conditions this propaganda sounds very old-fashioned, because it is insurrectionary propaganda. Propaganda in favour of the violent overthrow of the social system was all very well when it was directed against tyranny. But under modern conditions, when the system is collapsing anyhow, stress should be laid on efficiency, on competence, on productiveness, and not on insurrection. It seems to me that the insurrectionary note is obsolete. The Communist propaganda in the West is a nuisance to constructive-minded people.
Stalin Of course the old system is breaking down, decaying. That is true. But it is also true that new efforts are being made by other methods, by every means, to protect, to save this dying system. You draw a wrong conclusion from a correct postulate. You rightly state that the old world is breaking down. But you are wrong in thinking that it is breaking down of its own accord. No; the substitution of one social system for another is a complicated and long revolutionary process. It is not simply a spontaneous process, but a struggle; it is a process connected with the clash of classes. Capitalism is decaying, but it must not be compared simply with a tree which has decayed to such an extent that it must fall to the ground of its own accord. No, revolution, the substitution of one social system for another, has always been a struggle, a painful and a cruel struggle, a life-and-death struggle. And every time the people of the new world came into power they had to defend themselves against the attempts of the old world to restore the old power by force; these people of the new world always had to be on the alert, always had to be ready to repel the attacks of the old world upon the new system.

Yes, you are right when you say that the old social system is breaking down; but it is not breaking down of its own accord. Take Fascism for example. Fascism is a reactionary force which is trying to preserve the old system by means of violence. What will you do with the Fascists? Argue with them? Try to convince them? But this will have no effect upon them at all. Communists do not in the least idealise methods of violence. But they, the Communists, do not want to be taken by surprise; they cannot count on the old world voluntarily departing from the stage; they see that the old system is violently defending

Champion of the intelligentsia: H G Wells

itself, and that is why the Communists say to the working class: Answer violence with violence; do all you can to prevent the old dying order from crushing you, do not permit it to put manacles on your hands, on the hands with which you will overthrow the old system.

As you see, the Communists regard the substitution of one social system for another, not simply as a spontaneous and peaceful process, but as a complicated, long and violent process. Communists cannot ignore facts.
Wells But look at what is now going on in the capitalist world. The collapse is not a simple one; it is the outbreak of reactionary violence which is degenerating to gangsterism. And it seems to me that when it comes to a conflict with reactionary and unintelligent violence, Socialists can appeal to the law, and instead of regarding the police as the enemy they should support them in the fight against the reactionaries. I think that it is useless operating with the methods of the old insurrectionary Socialism.

The lessons of history

Stalin The Communists base themselves on rich historical experience which teaches that obsolete classes do not voluntarily abandon the stage of history. Recall the history of England in the seventeenth century. Did not many say that the old social system had decayed? But did it not, nevertheless, require a Cromwell to crush it by force?
Wells Cromwell acted on the basis of the constitution and in the name of constitutional order.
Stalin In the name of the constitution he resorted to violence, beheaded the king, dispersed Parliament, arrested some and beheaded others!

Or take an example from our history. Was it not clear for a long time that the Tsarist system was decaying, was breaking down? But how much blood had to be shed in order to overthrow it?

And what about the October Revolution? Were there not plenty of people who knew that we alone, the Bolsheviks, were indicating the only correct way out? Was it not clear that Russian capitalism had decayed? But you know how great was the resistance, how much blood had to be shed in order to defend the October Revolution from all its enemies, internal and external.

Or take France at the end of the eighteenth century. Long before 1789 it was clear to many how rotten the royal power, the feudal system, was. But a popular insurrection, a clash of classes was not, could not be avoided. Why? Because the classes which must abandon the stage of history are the last to become convinced that their role is ended. It is impossible to convince them of this. They think that the fissures in the decaying edifice of the old order can be repaired and saved.

That is why dying classes take to arms and resort to every means to save their existence as a ruling class.
Wells But were there not a few lawyers at the head of the great French Revolution?
Stalin I do not deny the role of the intelligentsia in revolutionary movements. Was the great French Revolution a lawyers' revolution and not a popular revolution, which achieved victory by rousing vast masses of the people against feudalism and championed the interests of the Third Estate? And did the lawyers among the leaders of the great French Revolution act in accordance with the laws of the old order? Did they not introduce new, bourgeois-revolutionary law?

The rich experience of history teaches that up to now not a single class has voluntarily made way for another class. There is no such precedent in world history. The Communists have learned this lesson of history. Communists would welcome the voluntary departure of the bourgeoisie. But such a turn of affairs is improbable, that is what experience teaches. That is why the Communists want to be prepared for the worst and call upon the working class to be vigilant, to be prepared for battle.

Who wants a captain who lulls the vigilance of his army, a captain who does not understand that the enemy will not surrender, that he must be crushed? To be such a captain means deceiving, betraying the working class. That is why I think that what seems to you to be old-fashioned is in fact a measure of revolutionary expediency for the working class.

How to make a revolution

Wells I do not deny that force has to be used, but I think the forms of the struggle should fit as closely as possible to the opportunities presented by the existing laws, which must be defended against reactionary attacks. There is no need to disorganise the old system because it is disorganising itself enough as it is. That is why it seems to me insurrection against the old order, against the law, is obsolete; old-fashioned. Incidentally, I deliberately exaggerate in order to bring the truth out more ▶

▶ clearly. I can formulate my point of view in the following way: first, I am for order; second, I attack the present system in so far as it cannot assure order; third, I think that class war propaganda may detach from Socialism just those educated people whom Socialism needs.

Stalin In order to achieve a great object, an important social object, there must be a main force, a bulwark, a revolutionary class. Next it is necessary to organise the assistance of an auxiliary force for this main force; in this case this auxiliary force is the party, to which the best forces of the intelligentsia belong. Just now you spoke about "educated people". But what educated people did you have in mind? Were there not plenty of educated people on the side of the old order in England in the seventeenth century, in France at the end of the eighteenth century, and in Russia in the epoch of the October Revolution? The old order had in its service many highly educated people who defended the old order, who opposed the new order.

Education is a weapon the effect of which is determined by the hands which wield it, by who is to be struck down. Of course, the proletariat, Socialism, needs highly educated people. Clearly, simpletons cannot help the proletariat to fight for Socialism, to build a new society.

I do not underestimate the role of the intelligentsia; on the contrary, I emphasise it. The question is, however, which intelligentsia are we discussing? Because there are different kinds of intelligentsia.

Wells There can be no revolution without a radical change in the educational system. It is sufficient to quote two examples – the example of the German Republic, which did not touch the old educational system, and therefore never became a republic; and the example of the British Labour Party, which lacks the determination to insist on a radical change in the educational system.

Stalin That is a correct observation. Permit me now to reply to your three points. First, the main thing for the revolution is the existence of a social bulwark. This bulwark of the revolution is the working class.

Second, an auxiliary force is required, that which the Communists call a Party. To the Party belong the intelligent workers and those elements of the technical intelligentsia which are closely connected with the working class. The intelligentsia can be strong only if it combines with the working class. If it opposes the working class it becomes a cipher.

Third, political power is required as a lever for change. The new political power creates the new laws, the new order, which is revolutionary order.

I do not stand for any kind of order. I stand for order that corresponds to the interests of the working class. If, however, any of the laws of the old order can be utilised in the interests of the struggle for the new order, the old laws should be utilised. I cannot object to your postulate that the present system should be attacked in so far as it does not ensure the necessary order for the people.

And, finally, you are wrong if you think that the Communists are enamoured of violence. They would be very pleased to drop violent methods if the ruling class agreed to give way to the working class. But the experience of history speaks against such an assumption.

Wells There was a case in the history of England, however, of a class voluntarily handing over power to another class. In the period between 1830 and 1870, the aristocracy, whose influence was still very considerable at the end of the eighteenth century, voluntarily, without a severe struggle, surrendered power to the bourgeoisie, which serves as a sentimental support of the monarchy. Subsequently, this transference of power led to the establishment of the rule of the financial oligarchy.

Stalin But you have imperceptibly passed from questions of revolution to questions of reform. This is not the same thing. Don't you think that the Chartist movement played a great role in the reforms in England in the nineteenth century?

"Obsolete classes do not voluntarily abandon the stage of history"

Wells The Chartists did little and disappeared without leaving a trace.

Stalin I do not agree with you. The Chartists, and the strike movement which they organised, played a great role; they compelled the ruling class to make a number of concessions in regard to the franchise, in regard to abolishing the so-called "rotten boroughs", and in regard to some of the points of the "Charter". Chartism played a not unimportant historical role and compelled a section of the ruling classes to make certain concessions, reforms, in order to avert great shocks. Generally speaking, it must be said that of all the ruling classes, the ruling classes of England, both the aristocracy and the bourgeoisie, proved to be the cleverest, most flexible from the point of view of their class interests, from the point of view of maintaining their power.

Take as an example, say, from modern history, the General Strike in England in 1926. The first thing any other bourgeoisie would have done in the face of such an event, when the General Council of Trade Unions called for a strike, would have been to arrest the trade union leaders. The British bourgeoisie did not do that, and it acted cleverly from the point of view of its own interests. I cannot conceive of such a flexible strategy being employed by the bourgeoisie in the United States, Germany or France. In order to maintain their rule, the ruling classes of Great Britain have never forsworn small concessions, reforms. But it would be a mistake to think that these reforms were revolutionary.

Wells You have a higher opinion of the ruling classes of my country than I have. But is there a great difference between a small revolution and a great reform?

Is not a reform a small revolution?

Stalin Owing to pressure from below, the pressure of the masses, the bourgeoisie may sometimes concede certain partial reforms while remaining on the basis of the existing social-economic system. Acting in this way, it calculates that these concessions are necessary in order to preserve its class rule. This is the essence of reform. Revolution, however, means the transference of power from one class to another. That is why it is impossible to describe any reform as revolution.

What Russia is doing wrong

Wells I am very grateful to you for this talk which has meant a great deal to me. In explaining things to me you probably called to mind how you had to explain the fundamentals of Socialism in the illegal circles before the revolution. At the present time there are only two persons to whose opinion, to whose every word, millions are listening – you and Roosevelt. Others may preach as much as they like; what they say will never be printed or heeded.

I cannot yet appreciate what has been done in your country; I only arrived yesterday. But I have already seen the happy faces of healthy men and women and I know that something very considerable is being done here. The contrast with 1920 is astounding.

Stalin Much more could have been done had we Bolsheviks been cleverer.

Wells No, if human beings were cleverer. It would be a good thing to invent a five-year plan for the reconstruction of the human brain, which obviously lacks many things needed for a perfect social order. *[Laughter]*

Stalin Don't you intend to stay for the Congress of the Soviet Writers' Union?

Wells Unfortunately, I have various engagements to fulfil and I can stay in the USSR only for a week. I came to see you and I am very satisfied by our talk. But I intend to discuss with such Soviet writers as I can meet the possibility of their affiliating to the PEN Club. The organisation is still weak, but it has branches in many countries, and what is more important, the speeches of the members are widely reported in the press. It insists upon this free expression of opinion – even of opposition opinion. I hope to discuss this point with Gorky. I do not know if you are prepared yet for that much freedom here.

Stalin We Bolsheviks call it "self-criticism". It is widely used in the USSR.

If there is anything I can do to help you I shall be glad to do so. ●

30 JANUARY 1937

Will Stalin Explain?

By Kingsley Martin

New Statesman attitudes to the Soviet Union were in flux for many years. As fascism spread in the 1930s, many NS writers (and readers) wanted to see Stalin as an ally in the international resistance. But this did not entirely cloud editorial vision on the purges, as shown in this piece by Kingsley Martin (NS editor from 1931-60), which explores the peculiar tone of the victims' confessions.

According to their confessions, Radek, Sokolnikov and the other Old Bolsheviks now on trial for their lives in Moscow have for years been plotting with Trotsky and with Japanese and German Fascists to overthrow the revolutionary regime which they have spent their lives in establishing. Their plan, they tell us, was to seize power for themselves by murdering Stalin and Molotoff; and at the same time to surrender part of Russia's Eastern territory to Japan and the Ukraine to the Germans. Holding that a war with Japan and Germany was inevitable, Radek declares that he and his accomplices arranged to weaken Russia as much as possible. Thousands of railway breakdowns were arranged. Disease germs were to be spread among the populace and acts of sabotage to take place in factories and workshops all over the USSR.

This is a curious story. The various parts of the plot do not seem to hold together, nor is any adequate motive suggested for such a monstrously perverted enterprise. That the remnant of the old Bolshevik guard should have become critical of Stalin and have wished to supersede him is credible enough. That in a dictatorship they may have been driven to underground intrigues is perfectly possible. But no one acquainted with the personalities and the records of Radek and Sokolnikov will readily believe, on the uncorroborated evidence of these confessions alone, that these men have entered into negotiations with Fascists for the destruction of Socialist Russia. Radek, a master of vituperation and brilliant analyst of foreign affairs, has been the most influential journalist of the regime. We can imagine him capable of many kinds of trickery, but that he should plot to hand over his country to foreign Fascism puts a heavy strain on credulity. Equally difficult is it to cast Sokolnikov for such a role. An unusually able and apparently devoted servant of the USSR, he has been acknowledged as one of the principal architects of Russia's financial stability, and perhaps more than any other Russian, he paved the way, as Ambassador in London, for that improved relationship with the Western democracies which has been the pivot of Stalin's foreign policy.

> The confessions are mysterious whether we accept them as true or not

Supposing we accept the whole of this story as true. Even so, the present trials in Moscow remain incomprehensible. There are two mysteries: the mystery of the confessions, which are equally mysterious whether we accept them as true or not, and the even greater mystery why such trials should now be publicly staged and such confessions broadcast.

None of the explanations given for the confessions seem even plausible. It is unconvincing to ascribe them to the process of cross-examination in which the confessions or anticipated confessions of one conspirator are used to extort confessions from another. Even supposing that, as a result of this process, all the accused men found it impossible to hide their guilt, how astonishing that no one of them should have followed the example of Dimitroff in Berlin and boldly stood up for himself and defended the conspiracy on the ground of patriotism? In the last trial, when the prisoners grovelled in the dirt and declared themselves miserable sinners, we were told that this strange behaviour was the product of Russian masochistic psychology. We were referred to passages in Dostoevsky and Turgenev for similar examples of self-abasement. On this occasion, however, the prisoners do not grovel nor do they boast. Most of them confess almost with a smile. Radek even goes so far as to joke about his coming execution. Such an attitude in the witness box is equally unexplained by allegations of past torture or threats of future torture. There is no sign of anything of the sort. The prisoners are in good health; they speak freely in court and, with the world listening, declare that no pressure has been brought to bear upon them. Confessions, extorted by torture, would certainly be repudiated in open court by one or other of the prisoners; threats to the families of the accused or of torture at a later stage, which might cow the weaker among them, would certainly not succeed in every case where the accused are as experienced and tough a set of men as these. It is no

Stalin with his inner circle in 1934, including Abel Yenukidze (far left) who Stalin had expelled from the Communist Party and finally shot in 1937

S/W/CAMERA PRESS

wonder in these circumstances that some quite intelligent people fall back on almost fantastic speculations. Some have suggested that Kameneff and those who were condemned with him are now living incognito and in comfort at a Russian watering place and that the present prisoners anticipate a like fate if they make the right confessions. In this case their trial is merely the Russian equivalent of applying for the Chiltern Hundreds. Others talk of a drug which is supposed so to reduce the resistance power of the victim, that after he has been hypnotised under its influence he remains convinced of what he has been told, even after the immediate effects of the drug have worn off. We want far more evidence than we at present possess of any drug with such terrible potentialities. The mystery of the confessions is still unsolved.

The second and politically more important mystery is why Stalin should have permitted a trial so damaging to the interests of his country. What can be the motive for announcing to Japan and Germany that Russian factories have been honeycombed with saboteurs? Are such declarations calculated to bring Russia support from the Western democracies? The effect inside Russia must surely be equally damaging. We can imagine nothing more likely to undermine confidence inside the USSR than publicly to proclaim that Radek, whose articles have hounded other men to their death, has all the time been a traitor plotting its destruction. Who will now believe in the utterances of Radek's successor? One of the most certain and terrible results of such trials is that it undermines all trust. In whom are the public to have confidence in future? And what must be the effect on public servants waiting in the atmosphere of terror and suspicion engendered by a series of such trials?

We wish that Stalin would explain his reason for putting such a priceless propagandist weapon at the disposal of his enemies in foreign countries. One common assumption is that he is animated by hatred of the other old associates of Lenin, and in the circumstances comparison is inevitable between events in Russia and other revolutions where groups have gone on struggling for power long after the revolution was over. But the present trials have more political significance than this. It is clear that we are witnessing the climax of the long struggle between those who supported Stalin's doctrine of "Socialism in one country" and those who have continued to believe that Trotsky was right in advocating the policy of fomenting world revolution. This struggle reached a new phase at the Seventh Congress where the new policy of the "united front" and co-operation with democratic forces in foreign countries was decided upon. We may regard this trial as a final effort to eliminate opposition on this fundamental issue before the new constitution is put into operation. If this is the root of the matter it remains curious that Stalin should not realise the damaging effect of such a spectacular method of removing his opponents.

It has always been a central part of Communist theory that the time would come when the bourgeoisie would be so far liquidated and the country so far unified under the happier organisation of Communism that conspiracy, espionage and violence would disappear. Russia has advanced economically beyond the hopes of the most enthusiastic Socialist. It seemed as if the time for relaxation of the political dictatorship had arrived. There were signs of a freer atmosphere as well as an improved standard of life. These trials do not encourage any such optimistic view. To doubt the truth of the confessions is to accuse the Soviet Government of a disregard for the most elementary principles of justice. But to accept them as they stand is to draw a picture of a regime divided against itself, a regime in which the leaders are at a deadly feud with each other, a regime in which the only way to express discontent is in conspiracy and the only way to suppress conspiracy mass execution. If there is an escape from this dilemma Stalin should tell us what it is. ●

17 OCTOBER 1942

Between Democracy and the Crank

By Arthur Koestler

The one entirely self-revealing sentence he wrote has never been exactly translated. The original says: *In der Groesse der Luege liegt immer ein Faktor des Geglaubtwerdens.* An exact rendering is difficult because the sentence has no logical structure; it is a mystic's proposition in his own grammar. The nearest approximation would be: "The Greatness of a lie always contains an element of being believed." Note that the verb "contains" is related not to "lie" but to "greatness". "Greatness" here has a mystical double meaning: it stands both for quantity (a big lie) and for grandeur, majesty. Now this majestic lie, the apotheosis of the Absolute Untruth, is said to contain the quality of being believed. In other words, the lie is not laboriously constructed so as to be believed; it is born by intuition and its very greatness automatically compels adoration. This is one of the keys to the Crank's mysticism; actually the one which opened for him the door to power. Obviously, if the key was strange, the lock must have been even stranger.

But the lock is a problem for the historian; we are concerned only with the key. The Crank in his unhappy youth knocked at many doors, and was always refused. He tried his hand as an artist, but his sunsets in aquarelle did not sell. He worked on a building site, but was refused the fraternity of his fellow workers because he drank milk instead of beer, and made crankish speeches. He joined the Army, but never got further than his first stripe. He lived in Salvation Army shelters, under bridge-vaults, and in casual wards; he mixed with the *Lumpen-proletariat*, the nomadic outcasts in the no-man's-land of society. This period lasted for several years; it was a unique experience for a future statesman. Here the master-key began to take its first rough shape, the shape of a sovereign contempt for the people. True, he mistook the refuse for the substance, but this mistake proved to be an asset not a liability. He divined that the mentality of the crowd is not the sum total of the mentality of the individuals which form it, but their lowest common denominator; that their intellectual powers are not integrated by contact but bewildered by the interference of their minds—light plus light resulting in darkness; that their emotional vibrations, however, increase by induction and self-induction like the current in a wire coil. By descending into the bottom strata of society the Crank made the discovery of his life: the discovery of the lowest common denominator. The master key was found.

Its magic worked first on its owner. The frustrated Crank became the inspired Crank. His face in those early years, an unshaped pudding with a black horizontal dot, came to life as the lights of obsession were switched on behind the eyeballs. The features of it retained their crankish ridiculousness, with the black dot under the upturned nose and the second black dot pasted on the forefront, but it now assumed the grotesque horror of a totem-mask worn at ritual dances where human sacrifices are performed. His shrill voice became even shriller, an entranced incantation, while the catchwords it conveyed were simple in their ever-repeated monotony, like the rhythmical beating of the tom-tom in the bush. He knew it and in those early days called himself the Drummer.

He first spoke at small meetings and tried the formula: disintegration of the intellect by interference, increase of the crowd-emotion by induction. It worked. Now those were the days after his nation's defeat, when certain powers were on the search for useful cranks to divert the energies of the embittered populace, and they discovered that this was a very useful crank. Though its effect became visible only later this was a historic event: the key had met the lock.

History is always written in terms of keys and locks; the keys are shaped by subjective individual factors, the locks by objective constellations in the structure of society. If the course of history is determined in its broad outlines, there is always a margin left for undetermined. It is the margin of chance in all probability calculations; the chance of a given lock constellation meeting a key which fits, and vice versa. How many potential Wellingtons died as retired Colonels in Cheltenham we cannot know. And vice versa: if the Gracchi had been a little less dilettanti, Rome might have survived; and if this Crank had been killed in time, Weimar might have survived and the present war postponed or even avoided. As it is, men must die with open eyes to fill in the blind margin of chance; and the danger that this may happen again, that another future Crank may discover the master-key to the masses, will persist—until the lowest common denominator of men has gradually been lifted to a level beyond his reach. This, perhaps, is the basic issue between Democracy and the Crank. ●

Slow, slow, quick, quick, slow

By Christian Wolmar

Changes in transport have affected every aspect of our lives, from where we live and work to where we go on holiday, but will the next 100 years see travel speed up or slow down?

There are few areas where change over the past century has been as great as in transport. It is not just that the distances covered in today's frenetic world would have been unthinkable in 1913, but that whole new means of mass transport, such as aeroplanes and high-speed trains, have been developed. Moreover, it is transport that has been the biggest driver of the way people's lives have changed – both through their own increased mobility and through a far greater access to a variety of goods.

It is instructive to consider these changes from the standpoint of the period just before the First World War. This was the heyday of the railways, a golden age in the eyes of some. The two other modes of travel that came to dominate the 20th century, motoring and flying, depended on new inventions whose potential had barely begun to be understood.

In contrast, the railways had been around for more than 80 years and were a mature industry, characterised by a multitude of private companies often in competition with one another. The railways went everywhere. They had to, as there was no other realistic way of travelling long distances. When Sherlock Holmes needed to dash off to some godforsaken place to ascertain the culprit of some misdeed, his first request to Watson was to consult *Bradshaw's*, the comprehensive guide to train schedules, and then to call a hansom cab to the appropriate London terminus.

Britain's railway network was completed in 1899, in effect, with the opening of the Great Central, the last main line to be built until the opening of the first section of the Channel Tunnel Rail Link in 2003. No significant railways were built during the whole of the 20th century, but a few branch and relief lines were laid down in the Edwardian era, bringing the network to its all-time peak of 20,000 miles when war broke out. By then, it was reckoned, every village in Britain was within 20 miles of the railway and every town had a station.

Trains were for all the classes. Cheap workmen's trains brought vast numbers of daily commuters into the big cities in the early morning, and the middle classes travelled to their offices later. The bosses made the journey in style. The Metropolitan Railway even had a first-class carriage where breakfast was served to the bankers, who did not need to arrive at the office before 10am.

> Rocket-propelled shoes are unlikely to be seen in 2113

Holidays were invariably taken by rail, again with a neat class distinction. Hoi polloi would pop over to Ramsgate or Blackpool for a day's outing on a bank holiday special while Cook's Tours organised personalised trips around Britain taking in Cornwall, Wales and the Highlands in three weeks, with comfortable accommodation on the train. It was largely safe though not always so, with half a dozen fatal crashes annually and a death toll of more than 100 in a bad year, in contrast to today: there has been just one passenger fatality in a crash caused by a railway since 2002.

Yet there was little alternative. With few roads tarmacked, cars were still unreliable; a chauffeur prepared to get under the bonnet was pretty much de rigueur – and expensive. The car industry consisted of dozens of small firms that were still struggling with basic design problems and had not yet begun producing in mass numbers, unlike in the US where the Model T Ford first hit the streets in 1908.

As for planes, the Wright brothers started messing about with their biplanes a decade or so before 1913 and Louis Blériot had made the first Channel crossing by air in 1909. However, the first regular commercial flights would not take place until after the First World War and flying remained a rather hazardous activity until after the Second World War.

Railways provided virtually all the logistics for fighting in the First World War. Lorries could not be used daily for long journeys because they required constant attention and repair, and the roads, especially in the remote areas where the trenches had been laid, quickly turned into quagmires. After the Great War, the 200 or so companies that ran the railways were consolidated into just four, an arrangement that led almost inevitably to their full nationalisation 25 years later following the Second World War.

It is in the postwar period, however, that the change in transport has been greatest. Between the wars, trains remained dominant. The rich and the relatively affluent made use of cars, wreaking havoc incidentally on less mobile people. By 1930, road deaths had reached a staggering 7,300 on barely a tenth of the traffic (compared to less than 2,000 annually today), but the main form of transport remained the railways and, increasingly in the run-up to renewed war, buses and coaches.

But it was after the Second World War that travel expanded most rapidly, due to greater affluence and motorisation. The number of private cars leapt from three million in 1950 to 20 million in 1990, a growth rate of 3.7 per cent annually. In 1950 the average Briton still travelled only five miles a day; that has now risen to more than 30 miles and it is forecast to exceed 60 miles by 2025 unless firm measures are taken to address global warming, or costs rise dramatically. It is almost impossible to exaggerate the effect of all this mobility.

Housing, work, leisure and our social relations are all determined by our ability to move

SSPL VIA/GETTY IMAGES

rapidly and cheaply across the world. The locations of hospitals, council buildings, shops and all kinds of other facilities can be further away from those they serve because of this assumed increase in mobility. Cities have been planned around the available transport, businesses are located near airports or motorways, and suburban life is feasible thanks only to the car and, sometimes, the train.

There is only one mode of transport (other than walking) that has remained largely unaffected by modernisation. Glance at a bicycle of 1913 and it is virtually identical to today's models, apart from the use of modern alloys. Oddly, the humble bike is also enjoying a renaissance as people seek to keep fit and be green – and because, as in 1913, when urban traffic moved at the same pace as today, it is often the quickest way to get around. *Plus ça change.*

Therefore, one must be careful of extrapolating linear projections for British transport. Car growth has slowed remarkably since 2008 and actual mileage travelled has fallen since 1998. Rail passenger numbers were supposed to be in terminal decline in the postwar period when cars were becoming ubiquitous, and even the London Underground looked as if its days were numbered.

The Beeching cuts of the 1960s and 1970s looked like the first of many that would go even deeper but, in fact, the railways are enjoying a remarkable revival due to a combination of road congestion and improved carriage comfort and convenience. This will inevitably result in a further boost if plans to build a set of high-speed lines are realised. Aviation, too, has at times had a bumpy ride. Recessions and oil-price shocks dent the ever-rising line on a graph and information technology presents a lingering threat to the industry.

The most significant change to transport in the next hundred years is likely to be driverless cars. Not only will it have huge implications for land use – will people care where they live if they can be driven around in their bubble? – but it will blur the distinction between personal and public transport. Imagine being driven to your office and then telling the car or pod to go away and park itself. It will also be bad news for those struggling against obesity.

The restraining factor, of course, will be cost. If fuel prices become prohibitive, driving long distances will become too expensive. The other potential dampener on demand is technology. Why travel for a meeting if you can have a 3D conversation with your business associate as if he was sitting in front of you? On the other hand, sun, sand and sex will remain big drivers of travel.

The same considerations apply to air travel. If it remains cheap, expect continued growth, but given its intensive use of fuel and the little scope for alternatives, demand is likely to be constrained. Do not, however, expect all those promised inventions that were characteristic of predictions of the future in the 1950s to materialise. Individual rocket-propelled shoes and personal mini-helicopters are as unlikely to be seen in 2113 as they are now. Nor will it be worthwhile travelling to Australia by rocket – except, perhaps for the odd Richard Branson-type billionaire. Naturally, by then the effects of global warming, caused in part by all this hypermobility, may have wrecked our 21st-century transport systems.

There are, in fact, signs that people are beginning to realise that this increase in mobility does not equate with greater freedom. Living centrally or in places where having a car is not essential has become more desirable to many people. Access rather than mobility is seen as the key. Indeed, all these predictions could be utterly wrong, just as no Edwardian would have guessed that hordes of drunken twentysomethings would be taking to the air in flying machines that travel at 500 miles an hour to go to stag parties in Riga with cheap beer and naked, gyrating women as the main attraction, on tickets that cost them barely a couple of days' wages. ●

Christian Wolmar is seeking the Labour nomination for the 2016 London mayoral election. His latest book is "The Great Railway Revolution: the Epic Story of the American Railroad" (Atlantic Books, £9.99). He tweets at: @christianwolmar

HS2 WHAT YOU SHOULD KNOW

GROWTH

Experts say London gains most. Even HS2 Ltd say 73% of jobs from Phase 1 will be in London not the West Midlands.

FUNDING

HS2 needs a £26bn subsidy, yet the 51m alternative solution that sweats existing assets needs none – and more than meets DfT's long distance demand forecast.

RAIL CUTS

HS2 Ltd's latest business case contains £7.7bn of cuts to existing rail services which help pay for the new line.

COSTS

You could build a new Millennium Dome every 6 miles between London and Birmingham for the same cost of constructing Phase1 of HS2.

BUSINESS

0.0095%

HS2 was so important to British business that just 429 out of 4.5 million of them responded to the 2011 national consultation on HS2.

CONNECTIVITY

Studies show the UK already has shorter rail journey times between the capital and its five largest cities than other major Western European countries.

BENEFITS

Over 55% of HS2's claimed benefits come from journey time savings and assume people don't work on trains.

SWITCHING

CO_2 CO_2 CO_2 CO_2 CO_2 CO_2 CO_2

89% of HS2's passengers will transfer from less polluting alternatives to high speed rail (65%) or be new trips (24%)

CAPACITY

Virgin trains are only 52% full in the peak and intercity standard class capacity can be tripled – by longer trains, less 1st class and solving pinchpoints on the line.

Produced by HS2 Action Alliance www.hs2aa.org

10 NOVEMBER 1956

Eden's Fall

By J P W Mallalieu

At the height of the Suez crisis in November 1956, Anthony Eden's premiership was nearly at an end. On 6 November British forces had stormed the beaches at Port Said, Egypt, while the ailing prime minister continued to struggle to justify the invasion. He finally resigned for health reasons on 9 January 1957. Here, Mallalieu documents the physical, as well as the political, strain that Eden was under.

The Prime Minister sprawled on the front bench, head thrown back and mouth agape. His eyes, inflamed with sleeplessness, stared into vacancies beyond the roof except when they switched with meaningless intensity to the face of the clock. His hands twitched at his horn-rimmed spectacles or mopped themselves in a white handkerchief, but were never still. The face was grey except where black-ringed caverns surrounded the dying embers of his eyes. The whole personality, if not prostrated, seemed completely withdrawn.

Meanwhile, over his head, there raged an Opposition storm. Selwyn Lloyd was being cross-examined mainly about leaflets dropped on Egypt by British planes and which purported to describe Britain's war aims. He had not seen their content nor authorised their publication. Like one of those citizens who must so infuriate Dr Gallup, he stood at the box and did not know. The Prime Minister looked as though he did not care. By now Mr Antony Head, a sheaf of papers in his hand, had moved along the bench to the Prime Minister's side. The Prime Minister shot another penetrating glance at the face of the clock and then reverted to the rafters, ignoring his Minister of Defence. Mr Head nudged him, pointing down to the papers in his hand. The Prime Minister put on his spectacles, focused and became alert. Within the minute he was at the despatch box for the first time that afternoon, reading the report that Port Said was negotiating for a surrender and for a cease-fire. The Tory benches exploded behind him and the Prime Minister left the chamber all aglow. It seemed that, against the odds, he had found his faery child.

Next day was different. The surrender was not a surrender and the cease-fire was not a cease-fire. Further, there was Mr Bulganin. The Prime Minister was nowhere to be seen. He was on the phone to the Americans, to the United Nations, to the French. He would make a statement at six o'clock. Meanwhile, the corridors were filled with little groups of Conservatives, arguing in whispers. In the chamber, Mr Gaitskell, whose brilliant leadership in this crisis had been as brilliantly supported by Mr Bevan, Mr Griffiths and others, quietly but firmly put question after question at the empty space reserved for the Prime Minister. Mr Butler took notes and then, with that flair of his for getting it all ways without at the same time appearing blatantly dishonest, conveyed the impression that he stood shoulder to shoulder with the Prime Minister, that as Leader of the House he was above all this party mess, and that he entirely agreed with everything Gaitskell had said. There the matter rested until six o'clock, when the Prime Minister entered the chamber, slumped on to the front bench and began his habitual exploration of the ceiling. By now it was generally believed that he would announce a cease-fire in accordance with the United Nations request. That is what he did; and once again the Conservatives, except for some half-dozen members of the Suez group who sat in flushed silence, rose from their seats and cheered; and once again the Prime Minister left the chamber all aglow with his faery child.

> Contrary to popular belief he has never been a man of strong principle

The Conservatives had wildly cheered what looked like the success of their Prime Minister's policy. They had also wildly cheered what looked like its certain failure. The Prime Minister looked equally gratified on both occasions. This needs some explanation. It seems that since the crisis broke, the Conservative Party in the House of Commons have been like spectators in the casino at Monte Carlo, taking no part in the play and having no say in the stakes, but just watching someone else gamble with their money. The Prime Minister seems to have taken all the decisions without more than perfunctory consultation even with his Cabinet. All who watched him knew that this was a gigantic gamble. About half believed that it would succeed and about half that it would fail; but in the mounting anxiety there were no set groups, urging this course or that. There was only feverishness; and when on Monday it looked as though the gamble might have come off, even those who had been doubtful of its success and, when they had calm moments to think about it, were least enthusiastic about its morality, were overwhelmed with relief. When this relief proved groundless, and they could hear the mounting roar from outside of the middle-class revolt which the gamble had provoked, all except the most extreme Suez group longed for the whole thing to be called off.

But the Prime Minister's performance can only be explained in terms of delusion. Contrary to popular belief he has never been a man of strong principle. He is supposed to have been a leading opponent of Munich and appeasement. Yet, though he was Minister for League of Nations Affairs when the Hoare-Laval Pact was signed, he sat silent throughout, accepting what was the negation of a League of Nations principle. Having succeeded to the Foreign Secretaryship as a result of this silence, he held on to it, not until disagreement on a great issue forced him to resign, but until Chamberlain's interference in the Foreign Office had reduced him to the position of office boy. It was his pride rather than his principles which provoked his resignation. Since the war he has been continuously under the shadow of the great personality. Over and over again he must have overheard the invidious comparisons made between Sir Winston and himself. When at last he became Prime Minister, he determined to show the world that he, too, was a strong man. He took his chance during the past month. He has probably failed; but the overwhelming burden of taking, on his own account, decisions which have come near to breaking the Anglo-American alliance and the Commonwealth has now made him as incapable of distinguishing between success and failure as it has made him incapable of distinguishing between truth and lies. Eden may be pitied; but he will not be forgiven. ●

The Rise of the Know-Nothing Left

By Paul Johnson

The historian and journalist Paul Johnson made his name writing for and then editing (1965-70) the New Statesman. He gave up on socialism in the 1970s and became an ardent Thatcherite. Here he expresses derision at a Labour movement in hock to the "fascist" anti-intellectualism of trade unionism. After Margaret Thatcher's landslide victory in 1979, he became a leading adviser on trade union policy and a powerful pro-Tory polemicist.

The biggest change that has overcome the British socialist movement in my time has been the disintegration of Labour's intellectual Left. The outstanding personalities who epitomised, galvanised and led it are dead and have never been replaced. I am thinking, for instance, of G D H Cole, whose activities covered the whole spectrum of working-class activism and whose voluminous writings constituted a *summa theologica* of left-wing theory and practice; of R H Tawney, who placed the modern Left firmly in a long historical context and who endowed its philosophising with enormous intellectual and literary distinction; of R H S Crossman, who brought the bracing austerities of reason into the grossest skulduggeries of practical politics; and, above all, of Aneurin Bevan. The majesty of Bevan's contribution lay in the fact that he transcended classes and categories – a working man with the instincts and capacities of a philosopher-king, a man of action with a passion for reflection, a romantic devoted to the pursuit of pure reason, and an egalitarian obsessed by excellence. Around these, and other, great planets swam many scores of satellites, collectively constituting a huge left-wing galaxy of talent and intelligence.

And where do we find the left wing of the party today? Without a struggle, with complacency, almost with eagerness, it has delivered itself, body, mind and soul, into the arms of the trade union movement. There is a savage irony in this unprecedented betrayal, this unthinking *trahison des clercs*. For Labour's intellectual Left had always, and with justice, feared the arrogant bosses of the TUC, with their faith in the big battalions and the zombie-weight of collective numbers, their contempt for the individual conscience, their invincible materialism, their blind and exclusive class-consciousness, their rejection of theory for pragmatism, their intolerance and their envious loathing of outstanding intellects. The whole of Cole's life was devoted to demonstrating, among other propositions, that trade union organisation was not enough, that there was a salient place for the middle-class intelligentsia in the socialist movement, and an essential role for didacticism. What Labour lacked, argued Tawney, was what he termed "the hegemonic way of thinking": it concentrated on the base trade union aim of sectional gains for its own members instead of trying to create a new moral world.

> "Elitist" has become the prime term of abuse on the syndicalist Left

Bevan, though a trade unionist, never regarded trade unionism as a substitute for socialism – in some ways he thought it an enemy, indeed a part of the capitalist system. He fought bitterly against the attempts by the TUC to determine Labour policy in conference and to usurp the political role in government. He believed passionately that Parliament was the instrument of strategic change, and its control the political object of social democracy – he would have resisted at all costs the brutal threat of a syndicalist takeover. Crossman put the anti-union case a little more crudely: what invalidated the TUC claim to control Labour was its sheer lack of brains and talent. Hence his notorious article pointing out that only five trade union MPs were fit to participate in a Labour ministry. For this heinous heresy he was dragged before the inquisition and, just as Galileo was forced to recant his heliocentric theory, Dick was made to pay public homage to the dazzling genius of his trade union "friends". Afterwards, he said to me: "There was only one thing wrong with my article – I should have written three, not five."

In those days, it was a dismally common event to see a left-winger stretched on the rack of trade union power. Intellectuals from Stafford Cripps to Bertrand Russell were the victims of drumhead courts-martial conducted by the union satraps. Yet today the leaders of what is hilariously termed the Left look to the unions as the fountain-head of all wisdom and socialist virtue. Mr Michael Foot, a Minister of the Crown, will not stir an inch unless he has the previous approval of the TUC General Council. Mr Eric Heffer, Foot's *doppelgänger* and cheerleader on the back benches, regards any criticism of British trade unionism as a compound of high treason and the Sin Against the Holy Syndicalist Ghost. Did this gigantic U-turn come about because the trade union bosses have undergone a cataclysmic change of heart and transformed their whole philosophy of life and politics? Not a bit of it. It is true that the general secretaries of the biggest unions no longer, as in [Arthur] Deakin's day, pull the strings from behind a curtain, but prefer to strut upon the stage of power themselves. It is true, also, that they inspire more genuine fear than they did 20 years ago, as their crazy juggernaut lurches over the crushed bodies of political opponents. In other respects, however, their metaphysic has not altered: it is still a relentless drive to power by the use of force and threats.

The union leaders still regard money as the sole criterion of success and social progress. They are prime victims of what Tawney, in *Equality*, called "the reverence for riches, the *lues Anglicana*, the hereditary disease of the English nation". Blind to the long term, to the complexities of the economic process, to the well-being and rights of other human beings – blind, in fact, to what Tawney called "fellowship", to him the very core of the socialist ethic – they see the whole of the political struggle in immediate cash terms. The other day one of them said he would not hesitate to bring the entire publicly owned steel industry to a halt, and throw perhaps hundreds of thousands of his "comrades" out of work, unless he was offered "more money on the table", as he put it. Asked if he would heed the activities of the government conciliation service, he said he was not going to take advice from those he contemptuously referred to as "college boys".

Indeed, one of the startling characteristics of modern British trade union activists is their systematic dislike for intellectual and cultural eminence and their hostility towards higher education. Here a great and deplorable shift in attitudes has taken place since the 19th century. To me, the saddest newspaper report of recent years was a survey of the miners' clubs of South Wales, which revealed that their libraries had been sold off to dealers in order to clear space for juke-boxes, pin-tables and strip shows. Part of the price the left wing of the Labour Party has paid for its alliance with the trade union bosses has been the enforced adoption of a resolutely anti-intellectual stance. If miners prefer strip-shows to self-education, the argument runs, then so be it: the fact that the collective working masses express such a preference *in itself* invests the choice with moral worth. Anyone who argues the contrary is "an elitist".

"Elitist", in fact, has become the prime term of abuse on the syndicalist Left. It is a useful bit of verbiage to be hurled at those who, by any stretch of the imagination, can be accused of criticising wage-inflation, strikes, aggressive picketing, the Shrewsbury jailbirds, the divinity of Hugh Scanlon, "free collective bargaining", differentials, overmanning and other central articles of syndicalist theology. And equally, anyone who pays attention to quality, who insists on the paramountcy of reason, who does not believe the masses are always right or that the lowest common denominator is the best, and who considers there are more things in heaven and earth than are dreamt of in the philosophy of a Mick McGahey or an Arthur Scargill – well, he or she can be dismissed as an elitist too. Crossman, Tawney, Cole, above all Bevan, would have been given short shrift today – elitists, the lot of them.

It says a great deal for the power of the syndicalist Left in the councils of the Government, and even in the immediate entourage of Harold Wilson (who, secretly, is one of the outstanding elitists of our time), that anti-elitism has, to some extent, become official government policy, at any rate in the sphere of higher education. Our universities used to be autonomous, and for all practical purposes exempt from state control or guidance – a very elitist and reprehensible state of affairs! But all this is now being changed as the financial cuts begin to bite and the University Grants Committee progressively takes up its role as the Government's instrument of supervision. Earlier this year, Reg Prentice, one of Harold's innumerable Education Ministers, sneeringly told the universities to "live off their fat" and, if necessary, "sell their art treasures". Direction of the anti-elitist policy has now devolved on the Prime Minister's personal academic henchman, Lord Crowther-Hunt. In an earlier incarnation he

Tony Benn leads a march in London, May Day 1975

was Dr Norman Hunt, an assiduous gatherer of Westminster anecdotage with a fashionable prole accent, who made himself useful to Harold Wilson and other Labour magnificos.

The new anti-elitist spirit in the realms of higher education both complements and echoes the alliance between the trade unions and Labour's know-nothing Left. Away with the ivory towers! To hell with expensive research which ordinary people can't understand, and will probably come to nothing anyway. The job of a university is to turn out field-grey regiments of "socially relevant" people, with the right egalitarian ideas, the capacity to learn by heart the latest fashionable slogans, and to march, shout, scream, howl and picket as and when required. Degradation of the universities, of course, would fit in neatly with the syndicalisation of the Labour Party, since the ideal student – according to the anti-elitists – is one who conforms as closely as possible, mentally, emotionally and culturally, to a trade union militant. The operation is part of an uncoordinated but nevertheless impressive effort to proletarianise the educated classes, and to smash to bits what are venomously referred to as "middle-class values" (such as honesty, truthfulness, respect for reason, dislike of lawbreaking, hatred of violence and so forth).

It is by no means confined to students. At a recent conference of local authority education officials, a former headmaster and university vice-chancellor had the temerity to attempt a half-hearted defence of elitism and was promptly denounced, by a yobbo from Glamorgan, as "an educational fascist". But students are the prime targets of the anti-elitists because they can be so easily organised into rent-a-mobs by Labour's syndicalists and their allies (and future masters) even further to the Left. As all totalitarian rulers have discovered, once you have hacked away the logical and rational foundations on which the edifice of civilisation rests, it is comparatively easy to invert the process of ratiocination, dress up the results in verbiage, and sell them to thousands of apparently well-educated people.

A typical example of anti-elitist Newspeak is a dissenting minority report of a Yale Committee on Freedom of Expression, appointed after left-wing students smashed up a meeting addressed by William Shockley in 1974. The overwhelming majority of the Yale academics concluded that disruption of a speech should be regarded as an offence against the university, and one which could lead to expulsion. The dissentient, speaking for the Left, argued that free speech was both undesirable and impossible until there had been "liberation from, and increased self-consciousness of, the social and irrational factors that condition knowledge and pre-form the means and structures of language". Hidden in this ugly gobbet of verbiage is the thoroughly totalitarian idea that the meanings not merely of words but of moral concepts must be recast to conform to political expediency – the very essence of Newspeak. The example is American; but there are plenty of parallels over here, not always expressed quite so naively as by the Essex student leaders who refused even to discuss an "independent report" on their activities, for which they had clamoured, on the grounds that "reason is an ideological weapon with which bourgeois academics are especially well armed"!

When reason ceases to be the objective means by which civilised men settle their differences and becomes a mere class "weapon", then clearly the anti-elitists are making considerable progress. How long will it be before the books are burning again, and the triumph of the "Common Man", that figment of violent and irrational imaginations, is celebrated by another *Kristallnacht*? Already, at the extreme fringe of the syndicalist Left, the aggrosocialists are taking over public meetings, with their ideological flick knives and their doctrinaire coshes. Not long ago, hearing and seeing a group of students and trade unionists giving the Nazi salute, and shout *"Sieg heil!"* at some very stolid-looking policemen, I shut my eyes for a few seconds, and tried to detect the redeeming note of irony in their chanting. For the life of me, I could not find it. What differentiated these mindless and violent youths from Hitler's well-drilled thugs? Merely, I fear, the chance of time and place, a turn of the fickle wheel of fortune.

Unreason and thuggery are always the enemies, whatever labels they carry; for labels are so easily removed and changed. I remember Adlai Stevenson – an elitist if ever there was one – saying wearily: "Eggheads of the world unite, you have nothing to lose but your yokes." Perhaps it is time for the elitists to stand up for themselves – there may not be so few of us, either – and start the long business of rescuing the Labour Left from the know-nothings and the half-wits. ●

Setting the tone: Bill Clinton

12 FEBRUARY 1999

Thatcherism With a Human Face

By Anthony Giddens

In its review of 1998 a few weeks ago, *Newsweek* chose, as "European of the Year", not an individual but a movement: the Third Way. The term has come to stand for the revival of social democracy. For the first time, the centre left holds power simultaneously in the UK, Germany, France and Italy, as well as in nine of the other 11 European Union countries.

Yet the first current political leader to talk about a "Third Way" wasn't a European, but President Bill Clinton. In his 1996 State of the Union address, Clinton claimed to have found a new way in politics. Further, the Third Way has become a subject of global interest. One of its most prominent expositors is the Brazilian president and former sociologist, Fernando Henrique Cardoso. The notion has also attracted the attention of political leaders in Mexico, Argentina and Colombia. I recently lectured at the Chinese Academy of Social Sciences. I was surprised by the informed nature of the discussion, and by the consensus that the Third Way might be relevant to China. A similar lecture provoked even more interest in Korea.

Yet many European social democrats remain suspicious of the Third Way. They associate the term with Clinton and Tony Blair, whom they see as too closely connected with neoliberal policies.

For such critics, the Third Way is little more than Thatcherism with a human face. It is a betrayal of social democratic ideals of collective provision for the poor and the needy. The theme has become commonplace among Blair's opponents in the UK. Stuart Hall and Martin Jacques pursued it stridently in a one-off reissue of *Marxism Today*, entitled simply "Wrong!". Roy Hattersley has produced a string of eloquent articles along the same lines, the latest of which appeared in the *New Statesman*.

Right-wing authors, on the other hand, see the concept of the Third Way as an empty one. A recent article in the *Economist*, for example, called it "Goldilocks politics", offering the voters warmed-over porridge, a vague mish-mash of ideas without anything substantial to chew on. Changing his imagery, the author argued that trying to give an exact meaning to the Third Way is like wrestling with an inflatable man. If you get a grip on one limb, all the hot air rushes to another.

I don't believe either of these criticisms is accurate. Third Way politics, as I understand it, stands in the traditions of social democracy. Indeed, it is social democracy, revived and modernised. And it is far from an empty notion. On the contrary, the Third Way is a serious attempt to confront some of the main political dilemmas of the age. The Third Way seeks to go beyond the two dominant political philosophies of the postwar period. One is old-style social democracy, which held prime place for a quarter of a century or so after the war. It was rooted in Keynesian demand-management, interventionist government, the welfare state and egalitarianism.

The other is neoliberalism or market fundamentalism. The neoliberals believe that markets are always cleverer than governments, and that therefore the scope of government and the state should be reduced to a bare minimum. Neoliberals are hostile to the welfare state, which they see as crippling productivity through stifling individual initiative.

Each of these positions – corresponding to the old left on the one hand and the new right on the other – still has its adherents. Yet it is plain that each is out of touch with the demands of the moment. Few people – certainly not the bulk of the electorate in the developed countries – want to go back to top-down, bureaucratic government. But it has become equally obvious that society cannot be run as if it were a gigantic marketplace. People have voted for centre-left parties in such large numbers in Europe, and have continued to support President Clinton in the US, because they want something different.

The Third Way is that something. It is not yet a fully fledged political philosophy, but it is well on its way to becoming one. The old left would like to cling to the policies that seemed to work so well during the early postwar years. It isn't possible. The changes since then have been far too thoroughgoing. The most important are those involved with globalisation, which has gathered pace since the collapse of Soviet communism.

Reactions to, and interpretations of, globalisation mark some of the new fault-lines in politics. Those on the more traditional left usually take one of two views. The first denies that much has actually changed in the world over the past 30 years. The second treats globalisation as a destructive force which must be resisted by all means possible.

Third Way politics, by contrast, accepts the reality of globalisation and recognises that it brings benefits as well as problems. To put it differently, the Third Way is a positive social democratic response to globalisation. In contrast to neoliberals, Third Way thinkers argue that globalisation needs collective management. It calls for active government on all levels – global, national and local.

It has become commonplace to argue that, as globalisation advances, government becomes increasingly redundant. The Japanese business guru Kenichi Ohmae is one among many who argue that political power has become exhausted. Politicians, he argues, strut on an empty stage. The nation state has become a mere "fiction".

The Third Way sees a greater role for government in a globalising world, rather than a diminished one. But "government" is no longer to be identified only with national government. This is not to say that the nation state becomes obsolete – indeed, a prime goal of Third Way politics is to reassert national identity and purpose against a global backdrop. Globalisation, however, does push us, on the one hand, towards decentralisation and devolution of power and, on the other, towards the emergence of transnational forms of governance.

That is one reason why Third Way politics is so developed in Europe, where we have the European Union. The EU is not a nation state writ large, nor is it an international association, like the UN. In the EU, nations have voluntarily given up some of their sovereignty, pooling their resources so that all can gain.

Third Way politics no longer equates "public" with the state

Third Way politics looks for dynamic government rather than big government. It places a strong emphasis upon reviving public institutions, but no longer equates the "public" with the sphere of the state. Public institutions are often best defended, or reconstructed, by a combination of agencies, of which the state is only one. For example, in regions where external competition or technological change have destroyed local industries, old-fashioned government interventionism is of little use. But acting in combination with business and local community organisations, government can help kick-start renewed economic development.

Rosabeth Moss Kanter of Harvard Business School has documented how effective some of these endeavours have been in the US. Her work helps to dispel the myth that the high levels of employment in the US have been achieved only through the creation of poorly paid jobs in deregulated labour markets. One of the many examples she gives is of industrial regeneration in the greater Denver area. In the late 1980s, the petroleum-dependent Denver economy was in recession. A new regional coalition, the Greater Denver Corporation, successfully led a drive to restructure the local economy. One of Kanter's points is that not-for-profit and community groups were vital to this achievement – and that they acted in conjunction with business and government.

That still leaves the question of the modernising left's attitudes towards the welfare state and social justice. We should be sceptical of the idea that there was a golden age for the welfare state. Old-left writers and politicians like to look back to a time when all was well with the world – when the welfare state protected citizens from cradle to grave and full employment was the order of the day. The reality was a lot more mixed. Welfare systems have often been bureaucratic and inefficient; they have often failed those whose needs have been greatest. Full employment was only achieved against the backdrop of the traditional family, in which many women were excluded from the labour market.

Third Way thinkers insist that the welfare state stands in need of radical reform, but they don't want to reduce it to a safety net. Rather, as with other aspects of the Third Way programme, the key concern is modernisation. A modernised welfare state would be one that is both internally reformed and brought into line with the demands of the global marketplace. It would, among other things, emphasise education, employability, the dissolution of poverty traps and the creation of pensions systems that take account of increased worker mobility and the decline of traditional corporate employment.

So does the Third Way mean that we should abandon the classic concern of social democracy: with social justice and the battle against inequality? It does not and must not. But here we see the beginnings of a possible division between Third Way politicians, prefigured in disagreements between the French premier, Lionel Jospin, and Tony Blair. Blair's version of Third Way politics seems to see inequality mainly as a question of barriers to individual opportunity. Many other social democrats, like Jospin, believe that social justice involves reducing inequality of outcome, too. I think they are right. If it is to live up to its billing as modernised social democracy, Third Way politics needs to sustain this classic concern. But it must also recognise that existing welfare systems have not actually been very effective in redistributing income and wealth between rich and poor. We have to look for other solutions. Third Way politics must embody a redistributional programme, but one compatible with individual initiative and freedom.

I don't think this aspiration should be confined to affluent countries. As with other aspects of Third Way politics, it applies much more generally. It is an essential component of the global dialogue now under way. Whatever the outcome, Third Way thinking is likely to be at the core of political debates over the next decade or two, just as neoliberalism was for the previous 20 years and old-style social democracy the 20 years before that. ●

Instageddon: portrait of Tony Blair by kennardphillipps from their 2011 photo essay @earth

5 MAY 2003

The Defeat of the Left

By Nick Cohen

Has the left – by which I mean the left that opposes New Labour – begun to grasp the magnitude of its defeat? Only six weeks ago it wasn't hyperbolic to imagine that Iraq would destroy Tony Blair's government. A host of superlatives attached themselves to the anti-war movement. The revolt of 139 Labour MPs against the motion authorising war against Iraq was the greatest Commons rebellion by members of a governing party. Robin Cook's resignation speech was met by the first round of applause in the Commons.

The anti-war demonstration of 15 February had a fair claim to be the largest demonstration in British history. According to the pollsters, between half and two-thirds of the population opposed war without UN approval. The intellectual leaders of the liberal left were united in disgust. BBC presenters battled unsuccessfully to contain their outrage. The letters pages of the *Guardian* and *Independent* became wailing walls for despairing Labour Party members. Catholic and Anglican bishops, and the best playwrights, poets and novelists, were all against the Prime Minister. There had been nothing like it before.

It was reasonable to predict that the roar of fury would humble Blair. No prime minister had survived unscathed when large sections of his power base turned on him. The common sense of politics dictated that his wings would be clipped and his power confined. He would be forced to bend before a renaissance of the British left – no, the world left! – based on the inspiring principle of... Aye, there was the rub. What principle?

The old order has restored itself with insolent ease. Blair is as secure in Downing Street as he has ever been. His approval ratings have shot back up. Sixty-three per cent of the population decided, once the war had been won, that they supported it after all. Blair hasn't been forced to placate his critics by moving to the left. His excited aides are chattering about increasing the cost of tuition fees, dismantling the NHS, disciplining the Labour back benches, sacking Clare Short and sidelining Gordon Brown – the last of which would be an act of base ingratitude, as Brown helped save Blair's bacon. In other words, demonstrations and rebellions without parallel have led to a resurgence of the right.

Then we must add the sad news that Iraq has destroyed a derisive caricature of Blair which had been sapping his authority. In the popular mind, he was becoming established as an oily flatterer who told people what they wanted to hear rather than what they needed to hear. But Rory Bremner may now have to drop the gags about how Alastair Campbell and the focus groups run Downing Street. Blair took a risk and he won. The British left threw everything it had at him and failed to get one shot on target.

The left is used to fighting and losing honourably. To be on the left is to lose, almost by definition. But this is different.

This time, the left deserved to lose. It defeated itself by abandoning its fraternal obligations to the opposition in Iraq. It failed to stick by its comrades in a moment of crisis. The interests of opposing George Bush or Tony Blair or the oil corporations were put ahead of the interests of an oppressed people. However honourable the motives of some (if not all) of the anti-war protesters were, they ran into the problem that the only way to bring down Ba'athist tyranny was foreign invasion. To oppose the war was to agree that the Iraqis should continue to live in a prison state.

I cannot begin to prove this, but I suspect a reason for what the forlorn editor of the anti-war *Daily Mirror* said was the fastest switch in opinion he'd seen was the switch from complex questions to a simple one. Before the war, the questions were about the nature of the international order and about the existence or otherwise of weapons of mass destruction. Once the war started, it was a matter of who you wanted to win. British soldiers who risked their lives to prevent civilian casualties? Or the Iraqi secret policemen who earned their medals by killing civilians?

Where did the left go wrong? It wasn't anti-Americanism; it was wider than that. It was part of a critique, adopted by left-wing intellectuals, which expresses absolute scepticism about everything from the west – except themselves.

"The language of priorities is the religion of socialism," said Nye Bevan. On that test, it was reasonable for socialists to ask if Taliban Afghanistan was worse than Bush's America and if Tony Blair was superior to Saddam Hussein because he didn't order chemical weapons attacks on Glaswegians. But the leftist critique forbids comparison. Opposition must be total.

It is easy enough to get that way. You hate your country and the reigning global order of which it is part. Words such as "democracy" and "freedom" sound, on the lips of its leaders, like "love" on the lips of a whore. When the time for war comes, those leaders demonise enemies who seem almost to have been picked at random from a world heaving with suffering. Dictators half the public has never heard of, and with whom the west once did business, are turned into monsters overnight by the state and the corporate media. Suddenly, they are "tyrants" or "terrorists"; suddenly, they are "evil". Then you look at Britain, at the spin and the corporate influence and the base appeal to chauvinistic instincts. How dare Blair force other countries to change their governments when his own is so debased! What arrogance! But sophisticates know that Blair does not have the independence to be truly arrogant. He is the poodle of the White House. And when you hear Bush's America claim to be the land of the free, you can't keep your breakfast down.

You can justify every step in your argument with libraries full of supporting evidence. But to focus on hypocrisy is to give tyrants carte blanche. Underlying your thought is the parochial belief that the capitalist west is at the root of all oppression – a belief that means you can't oppose all the oppressors from China to the Congo via Syria whose crimes have little to do with the west. You lose a sense of universal standards, and you forget the fraternal obligation to give the victims of oppression a fair hearing. You are caught in a looking-glass world where you match the hypocrisies of the powerful with your own equal hypocrisies in the opposite direction.

Consistency might place you briefly on the same side as Bush and Blair

Central to the left's opposition to the war was the charge that it was inconsistent for the west to support and arm Saddam in the 1980s (though it should be said that the Soviet Union and some Arab regimes also played a role) and then to resort to violence to overthrow him many years later. Yet there is an equal and opposite inconsistency in the left's opposing what it considered a fascist regime in the 1980s and then later campaigning against an attempt to overthrow it. When Saddam was America's ally, the left campaigned for the Iraqi Kurds. When he invaded Kuwait and became America's enemy, the Kurds were dropped. And just before the start of the second Gulf war, when the Kurdish leaders said there was no other way to end the tyranny, the left slandered them as stooges of the CIA in a shocking betrayal of the principles of fraternity.

Why can't you be consistent? Because consistency might place you briefly on the same side as Bush and Blair. It would force you to talk the language of priorities. For you to support them as they overthrew Saddam, but oppose them in other spheres, was as inconceivable as a football fan supporting Manchester United for the first half of a match and Arsenal for the second. You begin to hint, as did George Galloway, that perhaps your enemies' enemies might not be so bad. Even if most Afghans don't actually like the Taliban and most Iraqis don't support Saddam, what guarantee is there that they would prefer foreign intervention from countries as maggot-eaten as your own? Surely they will fight the imperialists and create a second Vietnam? Anti-racism used to mean freeing people from oppression. But, you ask, what if imposing human rights on societies that have found their own ways of coping is in itself a type of racism? Isn't it, you wonder, elitist to assert that one form of government is "better" than another?

Pure opposition is more of a cultural than a political phenomenon. It is the force behind much radio and TV journalism. Broadcasters change the subject whenever they are proved wrong. They show irresponsibility in its purest form because they are not required to defend the stands they take. Nor should they. It is actionable to suggest that the work of broadcasters is influenced by their principled beliefs. Their job is to find the hardest question imaginable – "Won't Baghdad be the second Stalingrad?"; "How can you convince us there won't be a Shia theocracy by Tuesday teatime?" – and deliver it with a sneer. In the search for the killer blow, they shift between wildly contradictory positions in the blink of an eye.

What works well at the BBC, however, is fatal for the politically committed. They cannot imitate Jeremy Paxman and assert with clairvoyant confidence that the Arab street will rise up; or that hundreds of thousands will die; or that there will be millions of refugees; or that Israel will ethnically cleanse the West Bank; or that attacks by Saddam's fascistic militia will begin a popular uprising against the Americans; or that Baghdad will be a second Stalingrad (or was it Grozny?). The politically committed are meant to be able to understand the world and show how their principles could improve it. When they make false prediction after false prediction – as right- and left-wing opponents of the war did – they appear shameless or stupid. When they are proved wrong, Blair wins and deserves to win. ●

"More equal than ever". Ralph Steadman (*NS*, 1997)

BRITISH CARTOON ARCHIVE, UNIVERSITY OF KENT WWW.CARTOONS.AC.UK

God and The Big Bang

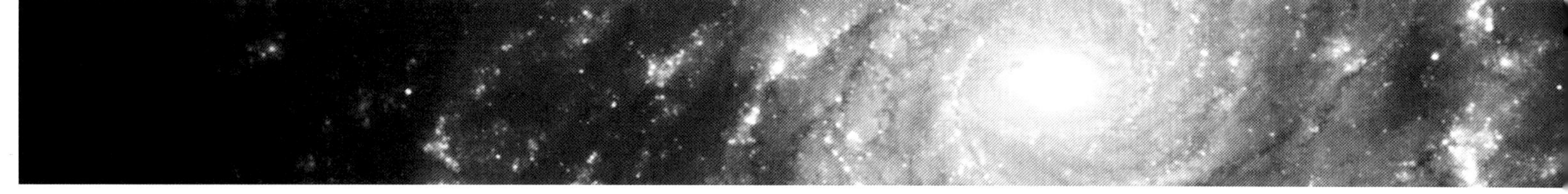

"Have those who disbelieved not considered that the heavens and the earth were united [in a single state] **and We tore them apart; and We made from water every living thing. Then will they not believe?"** [21:30]

The enormously vast universe has been the object of curiosity since time immemorial. Greek philosophers, including Aristotle, believed that the universe had always existed and would continue to do so eternally. This was also the mainstream view in scientific circles at the beginning of the 20th century, aptly known as the 'steady state theory'.

An eternal state of the universe meant that there was no inherit need for a Creator – for what does not have a beginning does not necessitate a need for a cause. However, advancements in science would shatter this view and fundamentally prove that the universe had a beginning.

In 1922, physicist Alexander Friedmann, produced computations showing that the structure of the universe was not static and that even a tiny impulse might be sufficient to cause the whole structure to expand or contract according to Einstein's 'Theory of General Relativity'. George Lemaitre was the first to recognise the implications of what Friedmann concluded. Based on these computations, Lemaitre declared that the universe must have had a beginning and that it was expanding as a result of something that triggered it. He also stated that the rate of radiation could be used as a measure of the aftermath of that 'something'.

The theoretical musings of these two scientists did not attract much attention and probably would have gone ignored except for new observational evidence that rocked the scientific world in 1929. That year, American astronomer Edwin Hubble, made one of the most important discoveries in the history of astronomy. He discovered that galaxies were moving away from us at speeds directly relative to their distance from us and from each other.

A universe where everything constantly moves away from everything else implied a constantly expanding universe. Stephen Hawking writes, 'The expansion of the universe was one of the most important intellectual discoveries of the 20th century, or of any century.'

Since the universe is constantly expanding, were we to rewind a film of its history, then necessarily we would find the entire universe was in a joint state, referred to by some as the 'Primordial Atom'. Many scientists and philosophers resisted the idea of a beginning to the universe because of the many questions that it raised – primarily what or who caused it. However, Penzias and Wilson's discovery of microwave radiation emanating from all directions, possessing the same physical characteristics [namely petrified light which came from a huge explosion during the first seconds after the birth of the universe], left little doubt about the fact that the universe had a beginning.

For fourteen hundred years, since the revelation of the Qur'an, Muslims have had trouble understanding the verses **'The heavens and the earth were united** [**in a single state**] **and We tore them apart.'** [21:30] and a related verse, **'...the heaven We constructed with strength, and indeed, We are its expander.'** [51:47]

However, with the assistance of scientific advancements, we can now understand these verses in a new light. The miraculous nature of the Qur'an lies in the diverse knowledge it contains. Its verification of scientific facts shows that its message is as applicable to the scientist in his laboratory today as it was to the Bedouin in the desert.

The Government Needs to Know How Afraid People Are

By Rowan Williams

Not since Robert Runcie's 1985 report "Faith in the City" has an archbishop of Canterbury clashed so publicly with an incumbent government. Rowan Williams's lead article, published in the issue of the NS that he guest-edited, became a media sensation and led to a rift between Downing Street and Lambeth Palace. Williams questioned the morality of the coalition government's austerity policies and their democratic legitimacy.

The political debate in the UK at the moment feels pretty stuck. An idea whose roots are firmly in a particular strand of associational socialism has been adopted enthusiastically by the Conservatives. The widespread suspicion that this has been done for opportunistic or money-saving reasons allows many to dismiss "big society" initiatives; the term has fast become painfully stale. But we are still waiting for a full account of what a left-inspired version of localism might look like.

Digging a bit deeper, there are a good many on the left and right who sense that the tectonic plates of British – European? – politics are shifting. Managerial politics, attempting with shrinking success to negotiate life in the shadow of big finance, is not an attractive rallying point, whether it labels itself (New) Labour or Conservative. There is, in the middle of a lot of confusion, an increasingly audible plea for some basic thinking about democracy itself – and the urgency of this is underlined by what is happening in the Middle East and North Africa.

This casts some light on the bafflement and indignation that the present government is facing over its proposals for reform in health and education. With remarkable speed, we are being committed to radical, long-term policies for which no one voted. At the very least, there is an understandable anxiety about what democracy means in such a context. Not many people want government by plebiscite, certainly. But, for example, the comprehensive reworking of the Education Act 1944 might well be regarded as a matter for probing in the context of election debates. The anxiety and anger have to do with the feeling that not enough has been exposed to proper public argument.

I don't think that the government's commitment to localism and devolved power is simply a cynical walking-away from the problem. But I do think that there is confusion about the means that have to be willed in order to achieve the end. If civil-society organisations are going to have to pick up responsibilities shed by government, the crucial questions are these. First, what services must have cast-iron guarantees of nationwide standards, parity and continuity? (Look at what is happening to youth services, surely a strategic priority.) Second, how, therefore, does national government underwrite these strategic "absolutes" so as to make sure that, even in a straitened financial climate, there is a continuing investment in the long term, a continuing response to what most would see as root issues: child poverty, poor literacy, the deficit in access to educational excellence, sustainable infrastructure in poorer communities and so on? What is too important to be left to even the most resourceful localism?

> We are being committed to radical policies for which no one voted

Government badly needs to hear just how much plain fear there is around such questions at present. It isn't enough to respond with what sounds like a mixture of "This is the last government's legacy" and "We'd like to do more, but just wait until the economy recovers a bit". To acknowledge the reality of fear is not necessarily to collude with it. But not to recognise how pervasive it is risks making it worse. Equally, the task of opposition is not to collude in it, either, but to define some achievable alternatives. And, for that to happen, we need sharp-edged statements of where the disagreements lie.

The uncomfortable truth is that, while grass-roots initiatives and local mutualism are to be found flourishing in a great many places, they have been weakened by several decades of cultural fragmentation. The old syndicalist and co-operative traditions cannot be reinvented overnight and, in some areas, they have to be invented for the first time. This is not helped by a quiet resurgence of the seductive language of "deserving" and "undeserving" poor, nor by the steady pressure to increase what look like punitive responses to alleged abuses of the system. If what is in view – as Iain Duncan Smith argues passionately [elsewhere in the *NS*] – is real empowerment for communities of marginal people, we need better communication about strategic imperatives, more positive messages about what cannot and will not be left to chance and – surely one of the most important things of all – a long-term education policy at every level that will deliver the critical tools for democratic involvement, not simply skills that serve the economy.

For someone like myself, there is an ironic satisfaction in the way several political thinkers today are quarrying theological traditions for ways forward. True, religious perspectives on these issues have often got bogged down in varieties of paternalism. But there is another theological strand to be retrieved that is not about "the poor" as objects of kindness but about the nature of sustainable community, seeing it as one in which what circulates – like the flow of blood – is the mutual creation of capacity, building the ability of the other person or group to become, in turn, a giver of life and responsibility. Perhaps surprisingly, this is what is at the heart of St Paul's ideas about community at its fullest; community, in his terms, as God wants to see it.

A democracy that would measure up to this sort of ideal – religious in its roots but not exclusive or confessional – would be one in which the central question about any policy would be: how far does it equip a person or group to engage generously and for the long term in building the resourcefulness and well-being of any other person or group, with the state seen as a "community of communities", to use a phrase popular among syndicalists of an earlier generation?

A democracy going beyond populism or majoritarianism but also beyond a Balkanised focus on the local that fixed in stone a variety of postcode lotteries; a democracy capable of real argument about shared needs and hopes and real generosity: any takers? ●

A Radical Century

MICHAEL WARD/HULTON ARCHIVE/GETTY IMAGES

The poet Benjamin Zephaniah, pictured here scrutinising a CND badge in 1982, was among the many artists who campaigned against nuclear weapons

Embracing Genetically Modified (GM) crops — or not: Could this become one of the most defining decisions of our era?

By Robert Verkerk PhD, Founder, Alliance for Natural Health International *(www.anhinternational.org)*

Human interdependence with the natural world

Sometimes we need to be reminded that our existence and on-going survival is inextricably linked to the natural world around us. Our own genes, as well as those of the plants, animals and microorganisms with which we share our world, reflect the experiences of our biological predecessors over many millions of years. Our own genome echoes not the environment of today, but rather those to which we were exposed over 20,000 years ago, even before the Neolithic agricultural and population boom of around 10,000 years ago.

GM crop adoption in the face of uncertainty

It was 30 years ago almost exactly that evidence of successful insertion of foreign genes into plant genes was first published. Commercialisation of genetically modified (GM) crops followed 13 years later. Today, 170 million hectares, over 10% of the global agricultural land area, are cultivated with GM crops. Nearly all of this represents just two traits: Roundup® herbicide tolerance, resistance to specific insect pests, or a combination of both. Of the 28 countries that planted GM crops in 2012, only 8 were industrialised.

The Human Genome Project has revealed how little, not how much, we understand about the genetic control of life. Recent studies show that most of the 98% of the DNA within the human genome that is non-coding — until very recently commonly referred to as 'junk DNA' — has vital functions. These may include regulation of gene expression, organisation of chromosome architecture and signals controlling epigenetic inheritance.

Scientists have known for over 50 years that horizontal gene flow occurs between microorganisms, being a major mechanism of antibiotic resistance. A similar finding was discovered in plants much more recently. However, such gene flows appear to occur over evolutionary time scales. Human tampering with gene flow, and specifically the insertion of genes from unrelated species or ones made synthetically, in a manner that overrides the rules of genetic exchange in nature, could have dire, unexpected and unpredictable, multigenerational effects on life on our planet — human life included. This has of course been the prevailing concern among the world's most prominent ecologists who are opposed to GM crop cultivation.

Over-simplification: a tool to sway public opinion?

Pro-GM arguments issued by governments and the biotech industry have generally greatly over-simplified highly complex issues, many of which, contrary to what is suggested, remain highly uncertain. The impression often given is that all scientists are supportive of the technology, while non-scientists who are resistant to it are either uninformed or unprepared to accept modern, industry-driven technologies. The public is not told that the majority of ecologists — the group of scientists whose professional background should provide the greatest insights over the implications of the technology — have deep reservations about the wide-scale adoption of the technology in agriculture. Rarely are politicians or the public told that GM crops have yet to demonstrate their potential to alleviate poverty or that they do not consistently offer improved yields or reduced agricultural inputs. Nor are they informed that nearly all major crop developments that have improved yields, drought resistance, insect or pathogen resistance, even in recent years, have been the result of non-GM plant breeding techniques.

Furthermore, the suggestion made by Professor Anne Glover, chief scientific advisor to the President of the European Commission, that GM crops are proven safe because Americans have been exposed to them for nearly 20 years is naïve at best. Most of this exposure has occurred recently given the 100-fold increase in GM crop area between 1996 and 2012. Moreover, epidemiological evidence of human health effects is likely to be, at least during these early years of exposure, lost as 'noise' within the growing epidemics of inflammatory diseases such as allergies and the big four chronic, killer diseases; cancer, heart disease, diabetes and obesity.

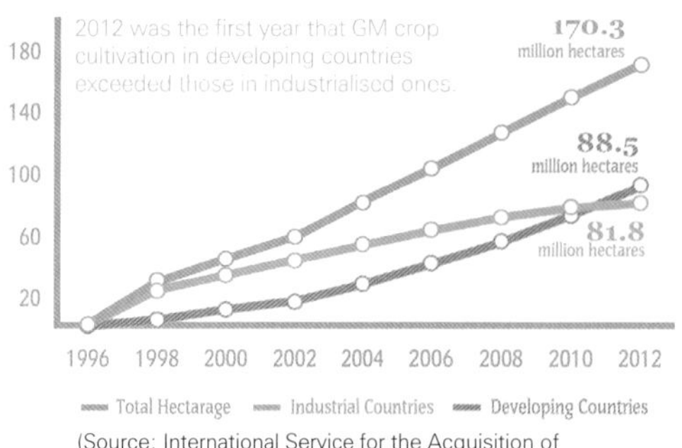

(Source: International Service for the Acquisition of Agri-Biotech Applications, 2013; www.isaaa.org)

There are only four major GM crops that dominate the market: soybean, cotton, maize and oil seed rape. GM soybean is by far the most widely cultivated GM crop, representing around 80% of the world's soybean hectarage.

The need for genuine scientific, social and political debate

While pro-GM governments continue to try their damnedest to turn around public objection to GM technology, the reality is that rational debates, scientific or otherwise, are very few and far between. Protagonists on each side of the debate appear to speak different languages, have markedly differing values, and will often profess a thorough understanding of risks and benefits when nearly all of the issues are plagued with uncertainty.

We need also to bear in mind that public objection to the consumption of GM foods is maintained in part because pro-GM protagonists have yet to unequivocally demonstrate either the absence of significant long-term risks or indeed benefits that are unique to GM crop technologies. Other major concerns are intellectual property issues and the concentration of the world's agricultural resource into the hands of a few corporations.

The precautionary principle

Owing to the level of uncertainty that exists around GM, the 'precautionary principle' should be invoked. The stakes are exceedingly high — potentially implicating all manner of life on Earth. Accordingly, the decision to embrace (or otherwise) GM technology as tried, tested and proven safe, may become one of the most defining decisions of humanity.

We therefore owe it to future generations to exercise our right of choice with utmost care.

1 NOVEMBER 1913

Women's Hidden Discontent

By Christabel Pankhurst

Militancy is, as it were, the flowering of the woman's movement for equality. Women's long-existing, hidden discontent with their condition of inferiority, and the patient and law-abiding Woman Suffrage campaign of the last century, were the preparation for militancy.

The non-militant suffrage agitation was of the nineteenth century; the militant agitation is of the twentieth. The anti-militant Suffragism of the present day is, in the opinion of the militant women, an anachronism. Militancy is a political weapon used by women as the only discoverable substitute for the vote. But it is more than that. It is a means of breaking up the false relation of inferior to superior that has existed between men and women, and it is a means of correcting the great faults that have been produced in either sex by the subjection of women.

Subjection had made women unnaturally diffident and unnaturally submissive. Their dominion over women has made men overbearing and vainglorious. Militancy is a sign and an expression of the fact that women have shaken off their diffidence and their servility. Women's militancy is an education to men, because it shows them women not any longer appealing to them—"coaxing them", as Mr Lloyd George has put it—but, instead, denying their title to withhold the vote.

Anti-militancy involved an admission that men ought to be obeyed and their laws obeyed by women in spite of the disfranchisement of women. Anti-militancy is therefore perilously near to anti-Suffragism. It is, in fact, indistinguishable from the policy of patient Griselda. For Suffragists to be law-abiding at any and every cost is an evil, because this flatters the self-importance of men and disinclines them to concede a demand so meekly made of them. Militancy has not only educated men by proving that there is a limit to women's endurance, but it has roused the best in them. Never since the days of John Stuart Mill, who, with other men of a most exceptional quality, made the Woman Suffrage cause his own, have men so greatly served this cause as during the days of militancy. The spectacle of women fighting for liberty and literally facing death for its sake has more power to rouse men's sense of justice than have any words, however wise and eloquent.

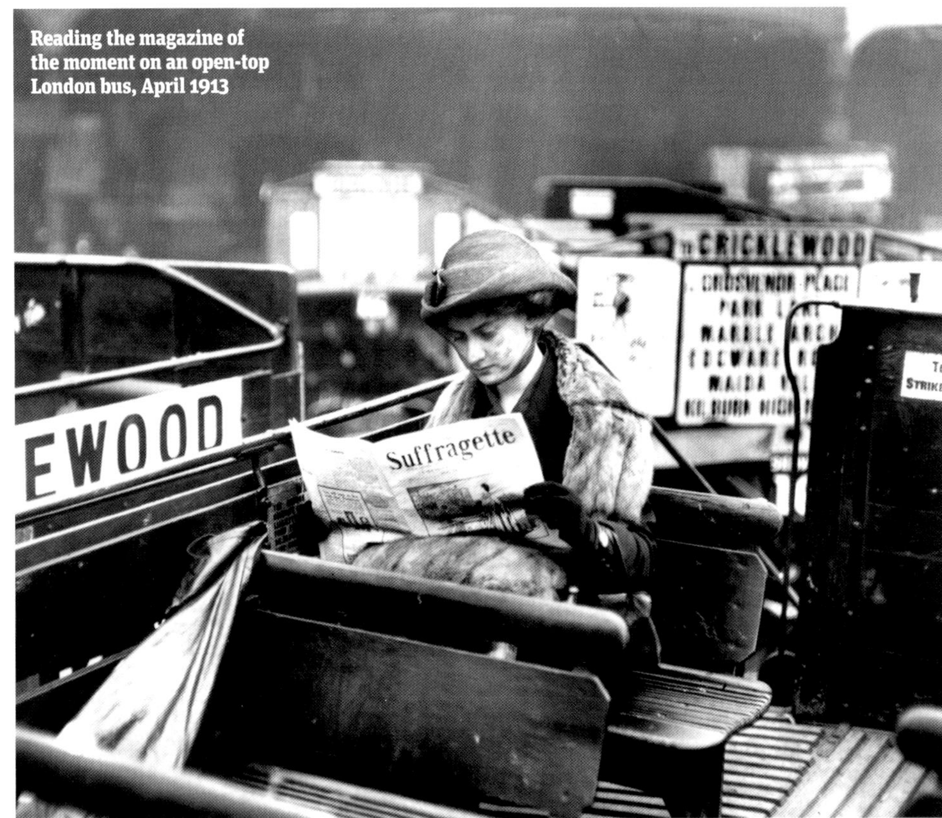

Reading the magazine of the moment on an open-top London bus, April 1913

There has been much vague denunciation of militancy, but not a single valid argument has been brought against its use. As a political method it holds the field to the exclusion of every other, save that of voting. It is idle to point to other countries in which women have won the vote by peaceful means. These other countries are not Britain. Politics and political activity do not in any other country hold the same high place in the interest of men as they hold in Britain. Ours is an old country. Prejudice and conservatism in the ugliest sense of the term are entrenched here as they are entrenched nowhere else, unless it be in Turkey. The British man's attitude towards women—above all the British politician's attitude towards women—is a matter of contempt and derision in our Colonies, in America, and in all those enlightened countries where women have the vote. Comparisons between Suffrage conditions in Britain and Suffrage conditions elsewhere are in the highest degree misleading. Besides, it is impossible to ignore the fact that it is since the beginning of British militancy, which has called to attention the whole civilised world, that the greater number of Suffrage victories have occurred. Nothing can be more unprofitable than for a British Suffragist to be daydreaming about the victories won by peaceful methods in countries more enlightened than her own. There is for her no wisdom save in reflection upon the past political history of her own country, in observation of the conditions now existing there, and in the invention of a policy based upon historical knowledge and upon a knowledge of the temperament of her countrymen and the political conditions of her own land. For the British Suffragist militancy is the only way. Militancy will succeed where all other policies will fail.

The virtue of militancy proceeds from the fact that government rests upon the consent ▶

of the governed. When the unenfranchised become ungovernable, then is enfranchisement given to them. The only reason why militancy has not long ago resulted in the conquest of votes for women is that not enough women have been militant. The number of militants required to create a situation from which the Government will be driven to escape by granting votes for women is a matter which experiment alone can determine. To those who still doubt the necessity of militancy, the final answer is this. Consider the men who now are at the head of the political parties, consider the men not yet advanced to leadership who are likely to succeed them, and then say whether you believe that the Asquiths, the Lloyd Georges, or the F E Smiths, of the present or of the future, are likely to be moved to give votes to women by reasoned and patient appeal—by anything save sheer compulsion!

The case for militancy as a political method is unassailable. Attacks upon militancy have, however, been made chiefly on the score of morality. Militancy, we are told, is wrong, and lawlessness and violence are wrong. The breach of a law, as John Hampden and others have taught by word and by example, is right or wrong according to the nature of the law and the authority possessed by the lawgiver. Bad laws made without due authority ought not to be obeyed, but ought to be resisted by every honest man and woman. It is such laws that militant Suffragists have broken. By marching to Parliament Square they have broken laws which seek to prevent them as voteless citizens from using the only means available to them of claiming the redress of their grievances. But apart from that, all the laws on the Statute book are, as they affect women, bad for want of lawful authority in those who have made them. Women's claim to the vote implies a denial of the validity of any law to which their consent has not been obtained.

Violence is wrong, say the anti-militants. Nothing could be more untrue. Violence has no moral complexion whatsoever. In itself it is neither right nor wrong. Its rightness or wrongness depends entirely upon the circumstances under which it is used. If violence is wrong in itself, then it is wrong to break a breakfast egg, it is wrong to hammer in a nail, it is wrong to pierce a tunnel through the rock, it is wrong to break into a burning house to save the life of a child. Yet, as we know, all these actions are entirely moral. This is because, though violent, they, like militancy, are justified by the motive of those who do them and the object with which they are done. If there are any who still condemn militancy, then they must condemn Nature herself, the Arch-Militant, who to achieve her purposes works so much violence.

Police arrest Emmeline Pankhurst on the Mall, 1914

The strange fact is that many fervent anti-militants are themselves in favour of militancy—when it is the militancy of men. Some of the foremost amongst them vigorously upheld the South African war, with all its accompaniments of farm-burning and concentration camps. Their souls were thrilled to sympathetic approval when men were militant in Turkey at the time of the revolution, when men were militant during the Chinese revolution, and when men were militant in the Balkan States. Approval of all this militancy was publicly expressed by the leaders of anti-militant Suffragism. Even women they will allow to be militant provided they are not militant in the cause of votes for women. Thus in the official organ of the law-abiding movement we read these words:

> "If you don't like militancy give us the vote, and that quickly!"

> The world is governed by ideas, and force is helpless against them. Not the arms of France, but the faith of Joan of Arc turned the tide of fortune against the English in the Hundred Years' war. Not the arms of William of Orange, but his spirit and the spirit of his people, their patriotism, their religion, wore down the innumerable hosts of Spain.

These words represent precisely the view held by the militants, though they come strangely from the pen of women who condemn militancy. It is the conviction of the militants that their lesser force will overcome the greater force directed against them by the Government. This will happen because of the faith that is in the militants, and because of the spirit of which militancy is the expression. But that does not mean that Suffragists can win without the use of force. If Joan of Arc had relied upon faith without force it is not unlikely that the English would have been in possession of France at the present day. If William of Orange had trusted to spirit, patriotism and religion and nothing more to win his battles, his military successes would have been inconspicuous indeed! The truth is that violence in such cases is itself the expression of the faith, spirit, patriotism and religion of those who employ it. It is then that we have militancy. Violence that is not inspired by spirit and illuminated by faith is not militancy, it is brutality. It is the Suffragettes who are militant, while the Government seek to overcome them by brutality.

People have said as an argument against militancy that it "rouses the beast in men"—the beast that, as they say, civilisation has put to sleep. If there are men possessed by a familiar spirit so unpleasant as to deserve this name, it is time that that spirit were driven out of them. Better far that well-fed, self-reliant, happy women should undertake the task of luring forth the beast and slaying it than that its victims should be, as now they are, white slaves and other unhappy, exploited women. It would seem that the anti-militants take a less favourable view of the nature of the opposite sex than do the Suffragettes. The Suffragettes pay men the compliment of believing that the brutal is not an essential and unchangeable part of them to be drugged into quiescence, but never to be eradicated.

There are people, again, whose objections to militancy seem to be based on the fact that it involves destruction of property. They would appear to forget that human liberty may, after all, be worth some broken windows or a blaze or two. Whatever may happen, militancy done for the sake of votes for women is not likely to be so destructive to the material interests of the country as was the South African war, waged for the sake of votes for men.

In answering objections to militancy, the Suffragettes have regard to the objections raised by the women rather than to those raised by men. To men critics a sufficient reply is this: "If you don't like militancy give us the vote, and that quickly!" It ill becomes men to prate of mere property and the Suffragettes' destruction of it, while the nation is being ravaged by venereal disease and innocent women in thousands are being infected by such disease.

The opposition to women's militancy is founded upon prejudice, and upon nothing else. For the very same acts of militancy that militant women commit would, if they were committed by voteless men, be applauded. The moral law which the Suffragettes have defied is not the moral law accepted for themselves by men. It is slave morality that the militant women have denied and defied—slave morality according to which active resistance to tyranny is the greatest crime that a subject class or a subject sex can commit. ●

The Alliance for Intellectual Property offers many congratulations to the New Statesman on its 100th Anniversary. However, many readers may not know that the intellectual property which underpins this publication is even older. The first UK Trade Mark Registry was set up in 1875 and copyright protection for journalists, authors, musicians, and artists, amongst others, dates back to the Statute of Anne in 1710, so Britain has long realised the importance to consumers, businesses, entrepreneurs and innovators of valuing innovation and creativity.

IP rights form the bedrock of British iconic design, culture and intellectual creativity. From the Mini and the Burberry check, to Mr Kipling and the Dyson vacuum cleaner; from The Beatles and the BBC to Harry Potter and the Premier League, it is hard to think of a service, product or activity which doesn't depend on IP – providing us with work, entertainment and education. Internationally these brands project an iconic and positive picture of our country. In the UK it's difficult to imagine life without the UK film industry; our music industry; world renowned British authors and publications; business software and computer gaming; sporting events, iconic design; our vibrant art scene; fashion and globally recognisable brands. All of these industries are entirely dependent on intellectual capital but they are also vulnerable to theft.

The protection of intellectual property is not a 'nice to have' it is an absolute essential. It protects investment in innovation and income generated by IP rights which is so crucial in enabling creators and investors to dedicate time and resources to new projects.

However, this protection is under threat from those who seek to use other people's rights without permission for their own commercial end, and without having contributed to any development costs. Worryingly, the myth is growing that intellectual property somehow stifles innovation and locks up creativity. The reality could not be more different. The UK is a world leader in IP and the rest of the world clamours for our original content and innovative products. As the global economic focus shifts from manufacturing and assembly to the development of products and services which require highly skilled employees, the UK's dependency on IP can only increase.

Valuing IP is not about left or right ideologies: it's about people from all backgrounds being able to earn a living from their creativity; about businesses being able to invest with clarity allowing us, as consumers, to enjoy the brands, music, books, films and sport we love. If we don't champion its central and positive role in delivering growth and investment to businesses and the economy, and choice and certainty for consumers, we will all be the poorer.

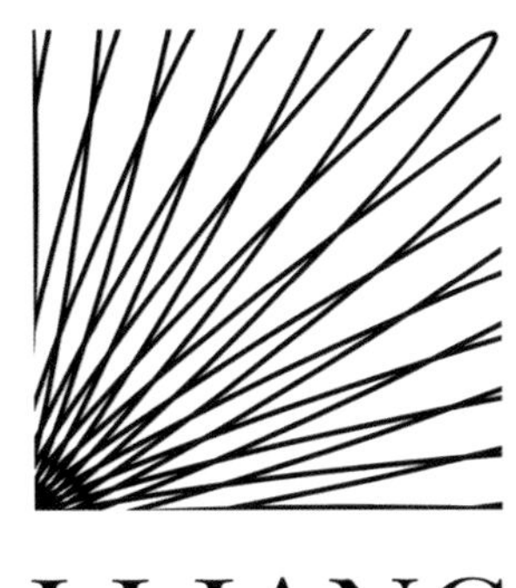

ALLIANCE

FOR INTELLECTUAL PROPERTY

For more information about the Alliance contact lucy@allianceforip.co.uk or call 020 7803 1319

Follow us on Twitter @AllianceIP

Alliance members and supporters:
Anti-Copying in Design,
Anti-Counterfeiting Group,
Association of Learned and Professional Society Publishers,
Authors' Licensing and Collecting Society,
British Brands Group, British Jewellery,
Giftware & Finishing Federation,
BPI (British Recorded Music Industry),
British Video Association,
Business Software Alliance,
Cinema Exhibitors Association,
Copyright Licensing Agency,
Design and Artists Copyright Society,
Educational Recording Agency,
Entertainment Retailers Association,
Federation Against Copyright Theft,
Film Distributors Association,
Motion Picture Association,
Premier League, PRS for Music,
Publishers Association,
Publishers Licensing Society,
UK Interactive Entertainment,
UK Music, Video Standards Council

THE ALLIANCE FOR INTELLECTUAL PROPERTY

The Alliance for Intellectual Property campaigns for intellectual property to be valued, for its contribution to the UK's economy, society and culture to be recognised and for a robust, efficient legislative and regulatory regime which enables maximum benefit to be derived from IP rights.

Our members include representatives of the audiovisual, music, games and business software industries, branded manufactured goods, publishers, authors, sports broadcasters, retailers and designers.

Using the experience gained over nearly 15 years of representing associations with IP interests, we pride ourselves on the increased profile for, and changing attitudes towards, IP in the wider public policy debate.

THE ECONOMIC CONTRIBUTION OF INTELLECTUAL PROPERTY

- The creative industries employ 1.5m people, contribute over £36bn to the UK economy and account for over 10% of the UK's exports
- The UK design industry employs 350,000 people and UK businesses spend around £35.5bn on design each year
- IP is the basis for the £16bn which companies invest annually in the UK economy by building brands
- UK brand-building industries generate around £1bn in GVA though exports alone
- Film & television-related tourism is worth an estimated £1bn a year to the UK
- The UK is the second largest exporter of television in the world by hours behind the US
- The UK music industry generates around £4 billion globally and employs 130,000 people every year
- The UK music and publishing industries each contribute nearly £5bn annually to the UK
- The UK is home to some of the world's biggest publishing companies with the publishing industry estimated to be worth £19 billion
- The UK games development sector is the largest in Europe
- The Premier League is the one of the most successful sporting leagues in the world, with a global television audience of 4.7 billion

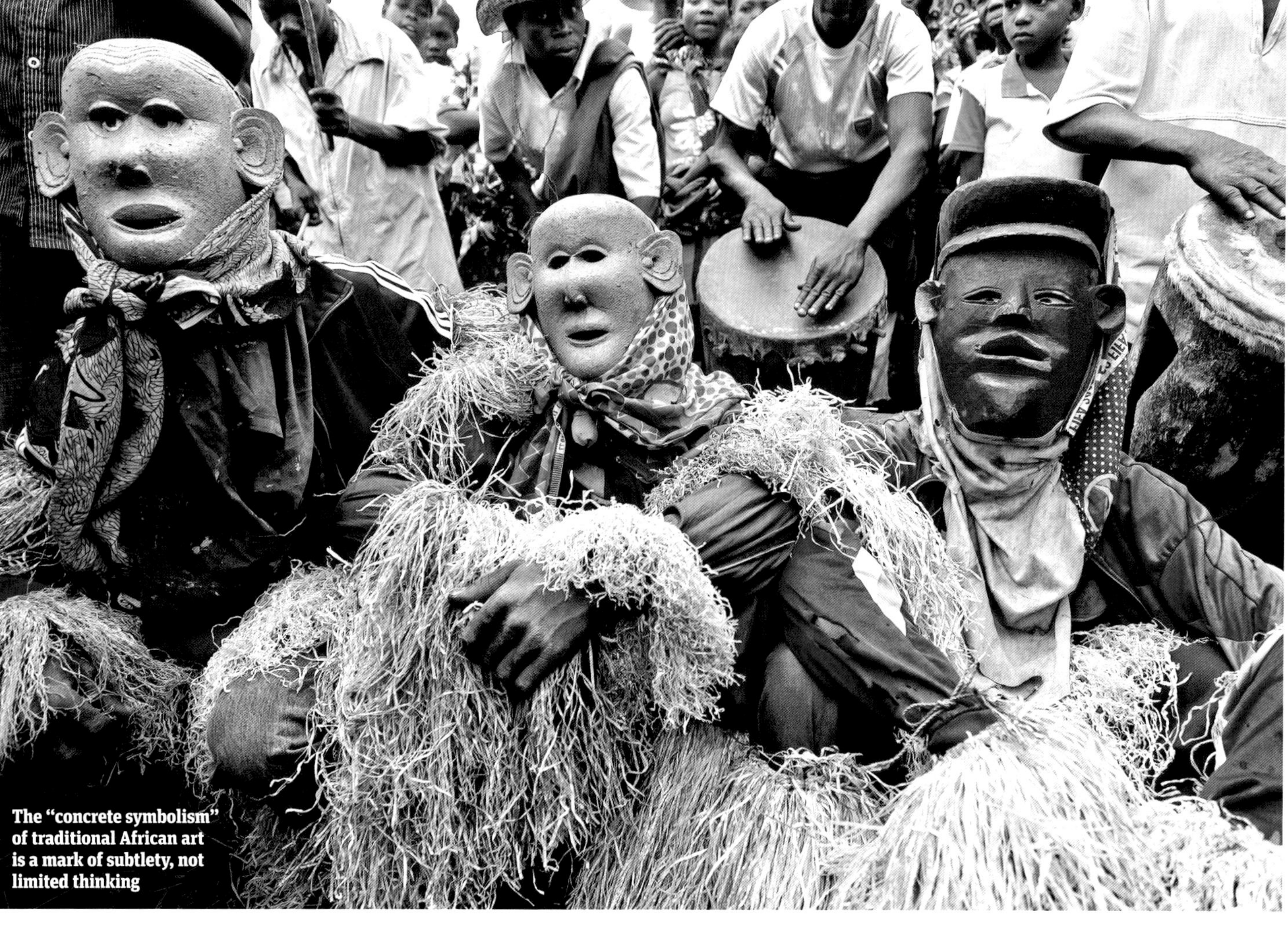

The "concrete symbolism" of traditional African art is a mark of subtlety, not limited thinking

8 AUGUST 1936

"Primitives"

By Paul Robeson

When discriminating racially, popular opinion lays emphasis on the Negro's colour. Science, however, goes deeper than that and bases its arguments on the workings of the Negro mind.

Man, say certain of the scientists, is divided into two varieties—the variety which thinks in concrete symbols, and the variety which thinks in abstract concepts. The Negro belongs to the former and Western man to the latter.

Now the man who thinks in concrete symbols has no abstract conception of such words as "good", "brave", "clever". They are represented in his mind by symbolic pictures. For instance, "good" in a concrete mind is often represented as a picture of a woman with a child. The drawing of this picture would be the way of conveying an idea of goodness to a person of the same mentality. Such pictures become conventionalised into a kind of written language. Now to the Western mind this may seem a clumsy way of going about things, but it is a method which has given the world some of the most delicate and richest art, and some of the profoundest and most subtle philosophy that man has ever known.

For it is not only the African Negro, and so-called primitive people, who think in concrete symbols—all the great civilisations of the East (with possibly the exception of India) have been built by people with this type of mind. It is a mentality that has given us giants like Confucius, Mencius, and Lao-tze. More than likely it was this kind of thinking that gave us the understanding and wisdom of a person like Jesus Christ. It has, in fact, given us the full flower of all the highest possibilities in man—with the single exception of applied science. That was left to Western man to achieve and on that he bases his assertion of superiority.

Now I am not going to try to belittle the achievements of science. Only a fool would deny that the man who holds the secrets of those holds the key position in the world. I am simply going to ask—having found the key, has Western man—Western bourgeois man

VLAD SOKHIN / AGENTUR FOCUS/EYEVINE

(the reason for the distinction is made clear later)—sufficient strength left to turn it in the lock? Or is he going to find that in the search he has so exhausted his vitality that he will have to call in the co-operation of his more virile "inferiors" before he can open the door and enter into his heritage? For the cost of developing the kind of mind by which the discoveries of science were made has been one which now threatens the discoverer's very life.

The reason for this lies in the fact that Western man seems to have gained more and more power of abstraction at the expense of his creative faculties. There is not much doubt that the artistic achievements of Europe have steadily declined. It is true that this decline is partly obscured by an output of self-conscious, uninspired productions, which have a certain artificial grace; but discriminating people have little difficulty in distinguishing these lifeless imitations from the living pulsing thing.

It may be argued that preference for live art over dead imitation may be simply a question of taste and is of no fundamental importance. Neither would it be if the change was something confined to that small minority usually described as artists, but unfortunately what shows amongst these is only a symptom of a sickness that to some extent is affecting almost every stratum of the Western world. The whole problem of living can never be understood until the world recognises that artists are not a race apart. Every man has some element of the artist in him, and if this is pulled up by the roots he becomes suicidal and dies.

In the East this quality has never been damaged—to that is traceable the virility of most Eastern peoples. In the West it remains healthy and active only amongst those sections of the community which have never fully subscribed to Western values—that is, the exploited sections, plus some rebels from the bourgeoisie. The result is, that as Western civilisation advances, its members find themselves in the paradoxical position of being more and more in control of their environment, yet more and more at the mercy of it. The man who accepts Western values absolutely, finds his creative faculties becoming so warped and stunted that he is almost completely dependent on external satisfactions; and the moment he becomes frustrated in his search for these, he begins to develop neurotic symptoms, to feel that life is not worth living, and, in chronic cases, to take his own life.

This is a severe price to pay even for such achievements as those of Western science. Though European thought, in its blind worship of the intellect, has tried to reduce life to a mechanical formula, it has never quite succeeded. Its entire peasantry, large masses of its proletariat, and even a percentage of its middle class have never been really touched. These sections have thrown up a series of rebels who have felt rather than analysed the danger and cried out loudly against it.

Many of these have probably been obscure people but others have been sufficiently articulate to rise above the shoulders of their fellows and voice their protest in forms that have commanded world-wide attention. Of such persons one can mention Blake and D H Lawrence. In fact one could say that all the live art which Europe has produced since the Renaissance has been in spite of, and not because of, the new trends of Western thought.

I do not stand alone in this criticism of the Western intellect. Famous critics support me. Walter Raleigh, when discussing Blake, writes: "The gifts with which he is so plentifully dowered for all they are looked at askance as abnormal and portentous, are the common stuff of human nature, without which life would flag and cease. No man destitute of genius could live for a day. Genius is spontaneity—the life of the soul asserting itself triumphantly in the midst of dead things."

> There are more Negros of the first rank than the world cares to recognise

In the face of all this can anyone echo the once-common cry that the way of progress is the way of the intellectual? If we all took this turning should we not be freeing ourselves from our earthy origins by the too-simple expedient of pulling ourselves up by the roots?

But because one does not want to follow Western thought into this dilemma, one none the less recognises the value of its achievements. It is simply that one recoils from the Western intellectual's idea that, having got himself on to this peak overhanging an abyss, he should want to drag all other people up after him into the same precarious position. That, in a sentence, is my case against Western values. It is not a matter of whether the Negro and other so-called "primitive" people are incapable of becoming pure intellectuals (actually, in America, many have), it is a matter of whether they are going to be unwise enough to be led down this dangerous by-way.

A reconstructed "statue of Apollo", Vicky (*NS*, 1956)

Perhaps the recognised fact that over-intellectualism tends towards impotence and sterility will result in the natural extinction of that flower of the West that has given us our scientific achievements, and to the rise of the more virile, better-balanced European, till now derided and submerged. Some people think that in the European proletariat this new Western man is already coming to birth. We, however, who are not Europeans, may be forgiven for hoping that the new age will be one in which the teeming "inferiors" of the East will be permitted to share.

Naturally one does not claim that the Negro must come to the front more than another. One does, however, realise that in the Negro one has a virile people of many millions. That, when he is given a chance, he is capable of holding his own with the best Western Europe can produce is proved by the quality of his folk music both in Africa and the Americas—also by the works of Pushkin, the Russo-African poet; or by Ira Aldrich—the actor who enslaved artistic Europe in the last century. Even a writer like Dumas, though not in the first rank, is a person who could hardly have been fathered by a member of an inferior race. Today there are in existence more Negroes of the first rank than the world cares to recognise.

In reply, it will of course be argued that these are isolated instances. "It may be true," people will say, "that the African thinks as Confucius thought, or as the Aztecs thought; that his language is constructed in the same way as that language which gave us the wonder of Chinese poetry; that he works along the same lines as the Chinese artist; but where are his philosophers, his poets, his artists?"

Even if this were unanswerable, it would not prove that the African's golden age might not lie ahead. It is not unanswerable, however. Africa has produced far more than Western people realise. More than one scientist has been struck by the similarity between certain works by long-dead West African artists and exquisite examples of Chinese, Mexican and Javanese art. Leading European sculptors have found inspiration in the work of the West African. It is now recognised that African music has subtleties of rhythm far finer than anything achieved by a Western composer.

Such achievements can hardly be the work of a fundamentally inferior people. When the African realises this and builds on his own traditions, borrowing mainly the Westerner's technology, he may develop into a people regarding whom the adjective "inferior" would be ludicrous rather than appropriate. ●

Observing Britain

Fiona Courage, Curator of the Mass Observation Archive, University of Sussex

In December 1936 the New Statesman reported on the unfolding drama surrounding Edward VIII's relationship with Mrs Simpson and his impending abdication. These events sparked several letters to the correspondence pages, including one from Geoffrey Pike commenting in the December 12 issue that the situation could provide "material for that anthropological study of our own civilisation". This letter provoked surrealist poet Charles Madge and documentary film maker Humphrey Jennings to respond on January 2, 1937 detailing their proposal to recruit voluntary observers from around the UK to participate in an 'anthropology of ourselves'. On the same page was a poem written by ornithologist-anthropologist Tom Harrisson, who was at that time engaged in an observational-ethnographic project based in Bolton. This coincidence of publication brought the two projects together to form Mass Observation, an independent and idiosyncratic survey project that aimed to recruit everyday people in Britain to become "the cameras with which we are trying to photograph contemporary life".

Mass Observation collected an unparalleled amount of information in the form of observational fieldwork, questionnaires, diary writing and ephemera recording all aspects of everyday life in Britain between 1937 and the mid-1950s. Its social survey was particularly rich on life on the Home Front during World War II. It details the most intimate aspects of individual lives alongside opinions on national and international events. You can get a taste of its methods and findings by imagining an investigator standing on a street corner counting hat wearers in Bolton, reading through the war jokes, reporting on the price of carrots and looking through dream diaries kept through the worst days of the Blitz.

The material collected by these original investigators was used in several contemporary publications and broadcasts but such was the volume collected that much lay undisturbed until the archive of papers was transferred to the University of Sussex in the early 1970s at the invitation of Vice Chancellor Lord Asa Briggs. As a charitable trust in the care of the University, the Mass Observation Archive has been used by a multitude of researchers and students from historians studying the everyday of the Home Front to linguists looking at changing speech patterns in regional dialects. The Archive has also served as inspiration for writers and artists over the years, including Simon Garfield's bestselling diary anthologies and Victoria Wood's Bafta award winning portrayal of 'Housewife 49' based on the diaries of Mass Observation's longest serving volunteer writer, Nella Last.

The arrival of the Mass Observation Archive at the University of Sussex initiated a new phase in the organisation's activity. Sussex anthropologist, Professor David Pocock was inspired to revive some of Mass Observation's methods to capture a picture of contemporary Britain in the late 1970s. In 1977 an open call was placed in the national press inviting readers to send in observations and experiences of the Queen's Silver Jubilee. Its success inspired the establishment of the Mass Observation Project (MOP) in 1981 which has collected views, opinions and experiences of contemporary Britain from volunteer writers for the last 32 years. The Panel submit qualitative, in depth responses to themed questionnaires sent out three times

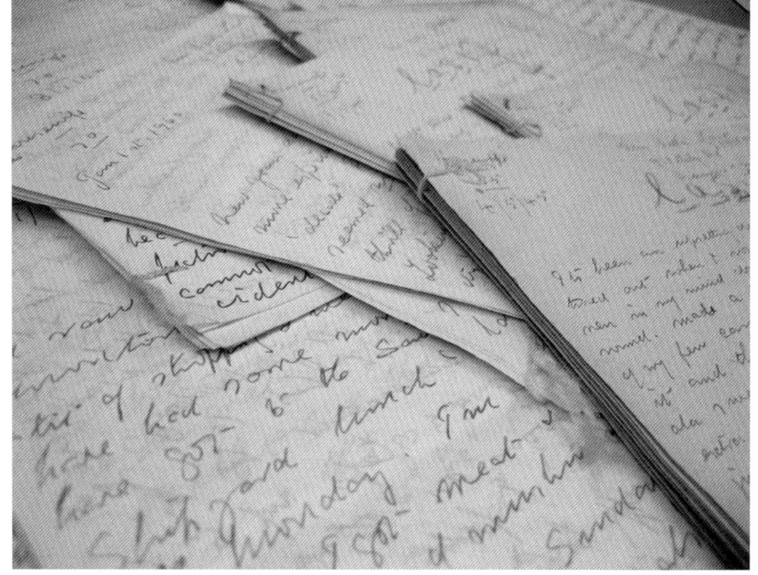

a year. Some are quietly reflective; some are robustly opinionated. Over 4500 people have contributed since 1981, and over 100 writers have written continuously since the start of the project.

The MOP was moulded into a long term life writing project under the direction of Professor Dorothy Sheridan who worked with researchers from a variety of backgrounds to create this unique record of daily life. In recent years Mass Observation has experimented utilising new technology both to record and to provide access to its data. A project with the British Library used blogs to capture reactions to the 2012 Diamond Jubilee celebrations and we use Twitter to elicit responses to our annual call for 12 May day diaries. Our recent Observing the 1980s project has made digitised extracts from our 1980s writings freely available on the internet alongside recordings from the British Library Sound Archive and ephemera from the era.

The materials generated by the original organisation and more recent projects are also being used to work with new audiences, bringing Mass Observation out of the archive and into the via a programme of creative learning activities. The Mass Observation Charitable Trust has recently appointed an Education Officer who is working with schools and community groups to use Mass Observation documents and methods to inspire learning and creativity. Recent initiatives include creative writing in prisons, local community learning, and a Heritage Lottery funded project that will enable us to work with schools, community groups and families, encouraging them to get involved in documenting their everyday lives in exciting and innovative ways.

For more information about the Mass Observation Archive and its activities, visit us at **www.massobs.org.uk**

30 JANUARY 1937

Anthropology at Home

By Tom Harrisson, Humphrey Jennings and Charles Madge

The following letter launched the social research project Mass Observation, aimed at producing an "anthropology of ourselves".

Sir—Man is the last subject of scientific investigation. A century ago Darwin focused the camera of thought on to man as a sort of animal whose behaviour and history would be explained by science. In 1847, Marx formulated a scientific study of economic man. In 1865, Tylor defined the new science of anthropology which was to be applied to the "primitive" and the "savage". In 1893, Freud and Breuer published their first paper on hysteria; they began to drag into daylight the unconscious elements in individual "civilised" man. But neither anthropology nor psychology has yet become more than an instrument in the hands of any individual, which he applies (according to his individuality) to primitives and abnormals.

By 1936 chaos was such that the latent elements were crystallised into a new compound. As so often happens, an idea was being worked out in many separate brains. A letter in the *New Statesman and Nation* from Geoffrey Pyke, arising out of the Simpson crisis, explicitly mentioned the need for an "anthropology of our own people". A fortnight later a letter called attention to a group centred in London for the purpose of developing a science of Mass Observation, and this group effected contact with other individuals and with a group working in industrial Lancashire, which had so far concentrated on field work rather than formulation of theory. These interests are now united in the first, necessarily tentative, efforts of Mass Observation.

Mass Observation develops out of anthropology, psychology, and the sciences which study man—but it plans to work with a mass of observers. Already we have fifty observers at work on two sample problems. We are further working out a complete plan of campaign, which will be possible when we have not fifty but 5,000 observers. The following are a few examples of problems that will arise:

- Behaviour of people at war memorials.
- Shouts and gestures of motorists.
- The aspidistra cult.
- Anthropology of football pools.
- Bathroom behaviour.

E.PHILLIPS/HULTON ARCHIVE/GETTY IMAGES

- Beards, armpits, eyebrows.
- Anti-Semitism.
- Distribution, diffusion and significance of the dirty joke.
- Funerals and undertakers.
- Female taboos about eating.
- The private lives of midwives.

In these examples the anthropological angle is obvious, and the description is primarily of physical behaviour. Other inquiries involve mental phenomena which are unconscious or repressed, so that they can only be traced through mass-fantasy and symbolism as developed and exploited, for example, in the daily press. The outbreak of parturition-images in the press last October may have been seasonal, or may have been caused by some public stimulus: continuous watch on the shifting popular images can only be kept by a multitude of watchers. The observers will also provide the points from which can be plotted weather-maps of public feeling in a crisis.

The subject demands the minimum of prejudice, bias and assumption; the maximum of objectivity. It does not presuppose that there are any inexplicable things. Since it aims at collecting data before interpreting them, it must be allowed to doubt and re-examine the completeness of every existing idea about "humanity", while it cannot afford to neglect any of them. Equally, all human types can and must assist in this work. The artist and the scientist are at last joining forces and turning back towards the mass from which they had detached themselves.

It does not set out in quest of truth or facts for their own sake but aims at exposing them in simple terms to all observers, so that their environment may be understood, and thus constantly transformed. Whatever the political methods called upon to effect the transformation, the knowledge of what has to be transformed is indispensable. The foisting on the mass of ideals or ideas developed by men apart from it, irrespective of its capacities, causes mass misery, intellectual despair and an international shambles. We hope shortly to produce a pamphlet outlining a programme of action. We welcome criticism and co-operation. ●

31 OCTOBER 1953

A Magistrate's Figures

By E M Forster

E M Forster was 74 when he published this plea for the decriminalisation of homosexuality. Not only did he feel unable to write openly about his sexuality, he was forced to make the case in stark and violent terms. He was right in sensing a shift in public opinion, however. The Wolfenden report followed four years later and became law in 1967. Forster died in 1970.

From time to time one sees a reference in the newspapers to a homosexual case. Two or three cases may be reported in a week, another week may pass without any mention and one is left with the vaguest idea as to how frequent such cases are.

That vagueness has now been dispersed. Last week a Police Court magistrate, a man of wide experience, was dealing with a case of importuning male persons, and he is reported as saying that in his court alone there were over six hundred such cases every year. The figure is so staggering that one suspects a press error, and quotes it subject to correction. But it was evidently large, for the magistrate was greatly concerned, and even expressed the wish that he could send all such offenders to prison. His figure seems to exclude graver charges; they have doubtless come before him, too, and they would further increase the total. And he does not say how many of the charges were brought as a result of a complaint to the police by the person importuned, and how many were the result of police observation. Here, also, figures would be interesting.

If six hundred cases, or a large number of cases, pass through a single police court in a year, what can the figures be for all England? Imagination fails and one is overwhelmed by disgust or by pity. It is terrifying to think of thousands of people—for they must run into thousands—going into the streets for a purpose which they know to be criminal, risking detection and punishment, endangering reputations and incomes and jobs—not to mention the dangers of blackmail. What on earth do they do it for? Some critics will denounce them as infamous. Others will jeer at them for being so daft. Neither criticism goes deep enough. They are impelled by something illogical, by an unusual but existent element in the human make-up. They constitute an

Young men at a bohemian nightclub in Soho, 1955

extremely small item in society, but an item larger than has been hitherto supposed.

Suggestions for dealing with them, and with the problem generally, are propounded from time to time. Occasionally there is a purity campaign in the press, and a clean-up is eloquently demanded. But where are these people to be cleaned to? Difficulties always arise when we regard human beings as dirt. They can be pushed about from one place to

Difficulties always arise when we regard human beings as dirt

another, but that is all. Prison—that facile solution—is not a remote magical enclave, as it is sometimes supposed. Prison is a place, it is part of society, even when society ignores it, and people who are pushed into it exist just as much as if they had been pushed into the next parish or over the frontier. They can, of course, be pushed right out of the world. That certainly would clean them up, and that has in the past been tried. It is, however, unlikely that the death penalty for homosexuality will be re-established. Civilisation has in this direction become milder. Moreover, holocausts would have to be repeated for each generation periodically.

There is, of course, the remedy of medical treatment, the scope and the methods of which are still controversial. More satisfactory (if it could be achieved) would be an immediate change in the law. If homosexuality between men ceased to be per se criminal—it is not criminal between women—and if homosexual crimes were equated with heterosexual crimes and punished with equal but not with additional severity, much confusion and misery would be averted; there would be less public importuning and less blackmail. But it is unlikely that the law will be changed. Reformers are too optimistic here. In their zeal they do not consider the position of the average MP, through whom the reform must take place. An MP may be sympathetic personally, but he has to face his constituency and justify his vote, and experience has shown how hostile an electorate can be to anything it considers sexually unusual. His enemies will denounce him, his friends will be afraid to defend him, and he may endanger his seat. Change in the law is unlikely until there is a change in public opinion; and this must happen very slowly, for the great majority of people are naturally repelled by the subject and do not want to have to think about it. Even when it does not revolt them it bores them.

Less social stigma under the existing law—that is all that can be hoped for at present, and there are some grounds for hope. Violent and vulgar denunciations do not work as they did, and are apt to recoil on the denouncer. There is more discussion, less emotion, fewer preconceptions. More laymen read modern psychology, which even when it does not satisfy raises salutary doubts. The stigma attaching to the homosexual is becoming more proportioned to the particular facts of each case. Some courts make increasing use of probation.

As a contrast to the magistrate referred to above, one may quote the remarks of a judge, Mr Justice Hallett. Speaking at about the same time as the magistrate, and dealing with an offence far more serious than importuning, the judge is reported as saying: "It will be a great joy to me and to other judges when some humane method for dealing with homosexual cases is devised, and when something more can be done than simply locking up the offenders." In such indications as these there is certainly ground for hope. ●

2 NOVEMBER 1957

Britain and the Nuclear Bombs

By J B Priestley

J B Priestley's "Britain and the Nuclear Bombs" was the essay that led to the creation of the Campaign for Nuclear Disarmament (CND). Not only did Priestley drop his usually comic style, he articulated the fears of a generation and helped to launch a mass movement. The first CND meeting was chaired by the NS editor, Kingsley Martin, at the end of November 1957.

Two events of this autumn should compel us to reconsider the question of Britain and the nuclear bombs. The first of these events was Mr Aneurin Bevan's speech at the Labour Party conference, which seemed to many of us to slam a door in our faces. It was not dishonest but it was very much a party conference speech, and its use of terms like "unilateral" and "polarisation" lent it a suggestion of the "Foreign Office spokesman". Delegates asked not to confuse "an emotional spasm" with "statesmanship" might have retorted that the statesmanship of the last ten years has produced little else but emotional spasms. And though it is true, as Mr Bevan argued, that independent action by this country, to ban nuclear bombs, would involve our foreign minister in many difficulties, most of us would rather have a bewildered and overworked Foreign Office than a country about to be turned into a radioactive cemetery. Getting out of the water may be difficult, but it's better than drowning.

The second event was the successful launching of the Soviet satellite, followed by an immediate outbreak of what may fairly be called satellitis, producing a rise in temperature and delirium. In the poker game, where Britain still sits, nervously fingering a few remaining chips, the stakes have been doubled again. Disarmament talks must now take place in an atmosphere properly belonging to boys' papers and science fiction, though already charged with far more hysterical competitiveness. If statesmanship is to see us through, it will have to break the familiar and dubious pattern of the last few years. Perhaps what we need now, before it is too late, is not statesmanship but lifemanship.

One "ultimate weapon", the final deterrent, succeeds another. After the bombs, the intercontinental rockets; and after the rockets, according to the First Lord of the Admiralty, the guided-missile submarine, which will "carry a guided missile with a nuclear warhead and appear off the coasts of any country in the world with a capability of penetrating to the centre of any continent". The prospect now is not one of countries without navies but navies without countries. And we have arrived at an insane regress of ultimate weapons that are not ultimate.

> Perhaps what we need now is not statesmanship but lifemanship

But all this is to the good; and we cannot have too much of it, we are told, because no men in their right minds would let loose such powers of destruction. Here is the realistic view. Any criticism of it is presumed to be based on wild idealism. But surely it is the wildest idealism, at the furthest remove from a sober realism, to assume that men will always behave reasonably and in line with their best interests? Yet this is precisely what we are asked to believe, and to stake our all on it.

For that matter, why should it be assumed that the men who create and control such monstrous devices are in their right minds? They live in an unhealthy mental climate, an atmosphere dangerous to sanity. They are responsible to no large body of ordinary sensible men and women, who pay for these weapons without ever having ordered them, who have never been asked anywhere yet if they wanted them. When and where have these preparations for public warfare ever been put to the test of public opinion? The whole proceedings take place in the stifling secrecy of an expensive lunatic asylum. And as one ultimate weapon after another is added to the pile, the mental climate deteriorates, the atmosphere thickens, and the tension is such that soon something may snap.

The more elaborately involved and hair-triggered the machinery of destruction, the more likely it is that this machinery will be set in motion, if only by accident. Three glasses too many of vodka or bourbon-on-the-rocks, and the wrong button may be pushed. Combine this stock-piling of nuclear weapons with a crazy competitiveness, boastful confidence in public and a mounting fear in private, and what was unthinkable a few years ago now only seems unlikely and very soon may seem inevitable. Then western impatience cries "Let's get the damned thing over!" and eastern fatalism mutters "If this has to be, then we must accept it". And people in general are in a worse position every year, further away ▶

STOP NUCLEAR SUICIDE CAMPAIGN FOR NUCLEAR DISARMAMENT 2 CARTHUSIAN ST LONDON EC1

COURTESY OF THE ADVERTISING ARCHIVES

The grin reaper: an early CND poster lays out a vision of the future and exhorts the British public to "Stop nuclear suicide"

▶ from intervention; they have less and less freedom of action; they are deafened and blinded by propaganda and giant headlines; they are robbed of decisions by fear or apathy.

It is possible, as some thinkers hold, that our civilisation is bent on self-destruction, hurriedly planning its own doomsday. This may explain the curious and sinister air of somnambulism there is about our major international affairs; the steady drift from bad to worse, the speeches that begin to sound meaningless, the conferences that achieve nothing, all the persons of great consequence who somehow feel like puppets. We have all seen people in whom was sown the final seed of self-destruction. Our individual civilisation, behaving in a similar fashion, may be under the same kind of spell, hell-bent on murdering itself. But it is possible that the spell can be broken. If it can, then it will only be by an immensely decisive gesture, a clear act of will. Instead of endless bargaining for a little of this in exchange for a little of that, while all the time the bargainers are hurried down a road that gets steeper and narrower, somebody will have to say "I'm through with all of this".

In plain words: now that Britain has told the world she has the H-bomb she should announce as early as possible that she has done with it, that she proposes to reject, in all circumstances, nuclear warfare. This is not pacifism. There is no suggestion here of abandoning the immediate defence of the island. Indeed, it might be considerably strengthened, reducing the threat of actual invasion, which is the root fear in people's minds, a fear often artfully manipulated for purposes far removed from any defence of hearth and home. No, what should be abandoned is the idea of deterrence by the threat of retaliation. There is no real security in it, no faith, hope, nor charity in it.

But let us take a look at our present policy entirely on its own level. There is no standing still, no stalemates, in this idiot game; one "ultimate weapon" succeeds another. To stay in the race at all we risk bankruptcy, the disappearance of the Welfare State, a standard of living that might begin to make Communist propaganda sound more attractive than it does at present. We could in fact be so busy defending ourselves against Communism somewhere else, a long way off, that we would wake up one morning to hear it knocking on the back door. Indeed, this is Moscow's old *heads-I-win-tails-you-lose* policy.

Here we might do well to consider western world strategy, first grandiloquently proclaimed by Sir Winston in those speeches he made in America just after the war. The Soviet Union was to be held in leash by nuclear power. We had the bomb and they hadn't. The race would be on but the West had a flying start. But Russia was not without physicists, and some German scientists and highly trained technicians had disappeared somewhere in eastern Europe. For the immediate defence of West Germany, the atom bomb threat no doubt served its turn. But was this really sound long-term strategy? It created the poisonous atmosphere of our present time. It set the Russians galloping in the nuclear race. It freed them from the immense logistic options that must be solved if large armies are to be moved everywhere, and from some very tricky problems of morale that would soon appear once the Red Army was a long way from home. It encouraged the support of so-called peoples' and nationalistic and anti-colonial wars, not big enough to be settled by nuclear weapons. In spite of America's ring of advanced air bases, the race had only to be run a little longer to offer Russia at least an equally good set-up, and, in comparison with Britain alone, clearly an enormously better set-up.

> It is possible that our civilisation is bent on self-destruction

We are like a man in a poker game who never dare cry "I'll see you". The Soviet Union came through the last war because it had vast spaces and a large population and a ruthless disregard of losses, human and material. It still has them. If there is one country that should never have gambled in this game, it is Britain. Once the table stakes were being raised, the chips piling up, we were out. And though we may have been fooling ourselves, we have not been fooling anyone else.

This answers any gobbling cries about losing our national prestige. We have none in terms of power. We ended the war high in the world's regard. We could have taken over its moral leadership, spoken and acted for what remained of its conscience; but we chose to act otherwise – with obvious and melancholy consequences both abroad, where in power politics we cut a shabby figure, and at home, where we shrug it all away or go to the theatre to applaud the latest jeers and sneers at Britannia. It has been said we cannot send our ministers naked to the conference table. But the sight of a naked minister might bring to the conference some sense of our human situation. What we do is something much worse: we send them there half-dressed, half-smart, half-tough, half-apologetic, figures inviting contempt. That is why we are so excited and happy when we can send abroad a good-looking young woman in a pretty new dress to represent us, playing the only card we feel can take a trick – the Queen.

It is argued, as it was most vehemently by Mr Bevan at Brighton, that if we walked out of the nuclear arms race then the world would be "polarised" between America and the Soviet Union, without any hope of mediation between the two fixed and bristling camps. "Just consider for a moment," he cried, "all the little nations running, one here and one there, one running to Russia, one to the US, all once more clustering under the castle wall . . ." But surely this is one of those "realistic" arguments that are not based on reality. The idea of the Third Force was rejected by the very party Mr Bevan was addressing. The world was polarised when, without a single protest from all the guardians of our national pride, parts of East Anglia ceased to be under our control and became an American air base. We cannot at one and the same time be an independent power, bargaining on equal terms, and a minor ally or satellite. If there are little nations that do not run for shelter to the walls of the White House or the Kremlin because they are happy to accept Britain as their nuclear umbrella, we hear very little about them. If it is a question of brute power, this argument is unreal.

It is not entirely stupid, however, because something more than brute power is involved. There is nothing unreal in the idea of a third nation, especially one like ours, old and experienced in world affairs, to which other and smaller nations could look while the two new giants mutter and glare at each other. But it all depends what the nation is doing. If it is still in the nuclear gamble, without being able to control or put an end to the game, then that nation is useless to others. And if it is, then we must ask ourselves what course of action on our part might have some hope of changing the world situation. To continue doing what we are doing will not change it. Even during the few weeks since Mr Bevan made his speech the world is becoming more rigidly and dangerously polarised than ever, just because the Russians have sent a metal football circling the globe. What then can Britain do to de-polarise the world?

The only move left that can mean anything is to go into reverse, decisively rejecting nuclear warfare. This gives the world something quite different from the polarised powers: there is now a country that can make H-bombs but decides against them. Had Britain taken this decision years ago the world would be a safer and saner place than it is today. But it is still not too late. And such a move will have to be "unilateral"; doomsday may arrive before the nuclear powers reach any agreement; and it is only a decisive "unilateral" move that can achieve the moral force it needs to be effective.

It will be a hard decision to take because all habit is against it. Many persons of consequence and their entourages of experts would have to think fresh thoughts. They would have to risk losing friends and not influencing people. For example, so far as they involve nuclear warfare, our commitments to Nato, Seato and the rest, and our obligations to the Commonwealth, would have to be sharply adjusted. Anywhere from Brussels to Brisbane, reproaches would be hurled, backs would be turned. But what else have these countries to suggest, what way out, what hope for man? And if, to save our souls and this planet, we are willing to remain here and take certain risks, why should we falter because we might have complaints from Rhodesia and reproaches from Christchurch, NZ?

American official and service opinion would be dead against us, naturally. The unsinkable (but expendable) aircraft carrier would have gone. Certain Soviet bases allotted to British nuclear attack would have to be included among the targets of the American Strategic Air Service. And so on and so forth. But though service chiefs and their staff go on examining and marketing their maps and planning their logistics, having no alternative but resignation, they are as fantastic and unreal in their way as their political and diplomatic colleagues are in theirs. What is fantastic and unreal is their assumption that they are traditionally occupied with their professional duties, attending in advance to the next war, Number Three in the world series. But what will happen – and one wrong report by a sleepy observer may start if off – will not be anything recognisable as war, an affair of victories and defeats, something that one side can win or that you can all call off when you have had enough. It will be universal catastrophe and apocalypse, the crack of doom into which Communism, western democracy, their way of life and our way of life, may disappear for ever. And it is not hard to believe that this is what some of our contemporaries really desire, that behind the photogenic smiles and cheerful patter nothing exists but the death wish.

> Alone, we defied Hitler; and alone we can defy this nuclear madness

We live in the thought of this prospect as if we existed in a permanent smog. All sensible men and women – and this excludes most who are in the *VIP-Highest-Security-Top-Secret-Top-People Class*, men now so conditioned by this atmosphere of power politics, intrigue, secrecy, insane invention, that they are more than half-barmy – have no illusions about what is happening to us, and know that those responsible have made two bad miscalculations. First, they have prostituted so much science in their preparations for war and they have completely changed the character of what they are doing, without any equivalent change in the politics of and relations between states. Foreign affairs, still conducted as if the mobilisation of a few divisions might settle something, are now backed with push-button arrangements to let loose earthquakes and pestilences and pronounce the death sentences of continents. This leaves us all in a worse dilemma than the sorcerer's apprentice. The second miscalculation assumed that if the odds were multiplied fast enough, your side would break through because the other side would break down. And because this has not happened, a third illusion is being welcomed, namely, that now, with everything piling up, poker chips flung on the table by the handful, the tension obviously increasing, now at last we are arriving at an acknowledged drawn game, a not-too-stale stalemate, a cosy old balance of power. This could well be the last of our illusions.

The risk of our rejecting nuclear warfare, totally and in all circumstances, is quite clear, all too easy to understand. We lose such bargaining power as we now possess. We have no deterrent to a nuclear threat. We deliberately exchange "security" for insecurity. (And the fact that some such exchange is recommended by the major religions, in their earlier and non-establishment phases, need not detain us here.) But the risk is clear and the arguments against running it irrefutable, only if we refuse, as from the first too many of us here have refused, to take anything but short-term conventional views, only if we will not follow any thought to its conclusion. Our "hard-headed realism" is neither hard-headed nor realistic just because it insists on our behaving in a new world as if we were living in an old world.

Britain runs the greatest risk by just mumbling and muddling along, never speaking out, avoiding any decisive creative act. For a world in which our deliberate "insecurity" would prove to be our undoing is not a world in which real security could be found. As the game gets faster, the competition keener, the unthinkable will turn into the inevitable, the weapons will take command, and the deterrents will not deter. Our bargaining power is slight; the force of our example might be great. The catastrophic antics of our time have behind them men hag-ridden by fear, which explains the irrationality of it all, the crazy disproportion between means and ends. If we openly challenge this fear, then we might break this wicked spell that all but a few uncertified lunatics desperately wish to see broken, we could begin to restore the world to sanity and lift this nation from its recent ignominy to its former grandeur. Alone, we defied Hitler; and alone we can defy this nuclear madness into which the spirit of Hitler seems to have passed, to poison the world. There may be other chain-reactions besides those leading to destruction; and we might start one.

The British of these times, so frequently hiding their decent, kind faces behind masks of sullen apathy or sour, cheap cynicism, often seem to be waiting for something better than party squabbles and appeals to the narrowest self-interest, something great and noble in its intention that would make them feel good again. And this might well be a declaration to the world that after a certain date one power able to engage in nuclear warfare will reject the evil thing for ever. ●

Russell addresses a rally to support nuclear disarmament, Trafalgar Square, London, February 1961

17 FEBRUARY 1961

Civil Disobedience

By Bertrand Russell

In February 1961, the NS announced that Bertrand Russell and others who considered civil disobedience a valid form of protest would take part in an unlawful demonstration against Polaris and Britain's nuclear policy. As the editors stressed, "We do not believe that either [Russell's] assumptions or the tactics he advocates are correct in present circumstances, but we believe that he should have a full opportunity to explain his position."

There are two different kinds of conscientious civil disobedience. There is disobedience to a law specifically commanding an action which some people profoundly believe to be wicked. The most important example of this case in our time is conscientious objection. This, however, is not the kind of civil disobedience which is now in question.

The second kind of civil disobedience, which is the one that I wish to consider, is its employment with a view to causing a change in the law or in public policy. In this aspect, it is a means of propaganda, and there are those who consider that it is an undesirable kind. Many, however, of whom I am one, think it to be now necessary.

Many people hold that law-breaking can never be justified in a democracy, though they concede that under any other form of government it may be a duty. The victorious governments, after the Second World War, reprobated, and even punished, Germans for not breaking the law when the law commanded atrocious actions. I do not see any logic which will prove either that a democratic government cannot command atrocious actions or that, if it does, it is wrong to disobey its commands.

Democratic citizens are for the most part busy with their own affairs and cannot study difficult questions with any thoroughness. Their opinions are formed upon such information as is easily accessible, and the Authorities can, and too often do, see to it that such information is misleading. When I speak of the Authorities, I do not think only of the politicians, whether in office or in opposition, but equally their technical advisers, the popular press, broadcasting and television and, in the last resort, the police. These forces are, at present, being used to prevent the democracies of Western countries from knowing the truth about nuclear weapons. The examples are so numerous that a small selection must suffice.

I should advise optimists to study the report of the committee of experts appointed by the Ohio State University to consider the likelihood of accidental war, and also the papers by distinguished scientists in the proceedings of the Pugwash Conferences. Mr Oskar Morgenstern, a politically orthodox American defence expert, in an article reprinted in *Survival*, says: "The probability of thermonuclear war's occurring appears to be significantly larger than the probability of its not occurring." Sir Charles Snow says: "Speaking as responsibly as I can, within, at the most, ten years from now, some of those bombs are going off. That is the certainty." (The *Times*, 28 December 1960.) The last two include intended as well as accidental wars.

The causes of unintended war are numerous and have already on several occasions very nearly resulted in disaster. The moon and flights of geese have been mistaken for Russian missiles. Nevertheless, not long ago, the Prime Minister, with pontifical dogmatism, announced that there will be no war by accident. Whether he believed what he said, I do not know. If he did, he is ignorant of things which it is his duty to know. If he did not believe what he said, he was guilty of the abominable crime of luring mankind to its extinction by promoting groundless hopes.

Take, again, the question of British unilateralism. There is an entirely sober case to be made for this policy, but the misrepresentations of opponents, who command the main organs of publicity, have made it very difficult to cause this case to be known. For example, the labour correspondent of one of the supposedly most liberal of the daily papers wrote an article speaking of opposition to unilateralism as "the voice of sanity". I wrote a letter in reply, arguing that, on the contrary, sanity was on the side of the unilateralists and hysteria on the side of their opponents. This the newspaper refused to print. Other unilateralists have had similar experiences.

Or consider the question of American bases in Britain. Who knows that within each of them there is a hard kernel consisting of the airmen who can respond to an alert and are so highly trained that they can be in the air within a minute or two? This kernel is kept entirely isolated from the rest of the camp, which is not admitted to it. It has its own mess, dormitories, libraries, cinemas, etc, and there are armed guards to prevent other Americans in the base camp from having access to it. Every month or two, everybody in it, including the Commander, is flown back to America and replaced by a new group. The men in this inner kernel are allowed almost no contact with the other Americans in the base camp and no contact whatever with any of the inhabitants of the neighbourhood.

It seems clear that the whole purpose is to keep the British ignorant and to preserve, among the personnel of the kernel, that purely mechanical response to orders and propaganda for which the whole of their training is designed. Moreover, orders to this group do not come from the Commandant, but direct from Washington. To suppose that at a crisis the British government can have any control over the orders sent from Washington is pure fantasy. It is obvious that at any moment orders might be sent from Washington which would lead to reprisals by the Soviet forces and to the extermination of the population of Britain within an hour.

> The moon and flights of geese have been mistaken for Russian missiles

The situation of these kernel camps seems analogous to that of the Polaris submarines. It will be remembered that the Prime Minister said that there would be consultation between the US and the UK governments before a Polaris missile is fired, and that the truth of his statement was denied by the US government. All this, however, is unknown to the non-political public.

To make known the facts which show that the life of every inhabitant of Britain, old and young, man, woman and child, is at every moment in imminent danger and that this danger is caused by what is misnamed defence and immensely aggravated by every measure which governments pretend will diminish it – to make this known has seemed to some of us an imperative duty which we must pursue with whatever means are at our command. The Campaign for Nuclear Disarmament has done and is doing valuable and very successful work in this direction, but the press is becoming used to its doings and beginning to doubt their news value. It has therefore seemed to some of us necessary to supplement its campaign by such actions as the press is sure to report.

SALLY GREENHILL/ALAMY

We shall not be moved: Russell and CND supporters

There is another, and perhaps even more important reason, for the practice of civil disobedience in this time of utmost peril. There is a very widespread feeling that the individual is impotent against governments, and that, however bad their policies may be, there is nothing effective that private people can do about it. This is a complete mistake. If all those who disapprove of government policy were to join in massive demonstrations of civil disobedience, they could render governmental folly impossible and compel the so-called statesmen to acquiesce in measures that would make human survival possible. Such a vast movement, inspired by outraged public opinion, is possible; perhaps it is imminent. If you join it, you will be doing something important to preserve your family, friends, compatriots, and the world.

An extraordinarily interesting case which illustrates the power of the Establishment, at any rate in America, is that of Claude Eatherly, who dropped the bomb on Hiroshima. His case also illustrates that in the modern world it often happens that only by breaking the law can a man escape from committing atrocious crimes. He was not told what the bomb would do and was utterly horrified when he discovered the consequences of his act. He has devoted himself throughout many years to various kinds of civil disobedience with a view to calling attention to the atrocity of nuclear weapons and to expiating the sense of guilt which, if he did not act, would weigh him down. The Authorities have decided that he is to be considered mad, and a board of remarkably conformist psychiatrists has endorsed that official view.

Eatherly is repentant and certified: Truman is unrepentant and uncertified. I have seen a number of Eatherly's statements explaining his motives. These statements are entirely sane. But such is the power of mendacious publicity that almost everyone, including myself, believed that he had become a lunatic.

In our topsy-turvy world those who have power of life and death over the whole human species are able to persuade almost the whole population of the countries which nominally enjoy freedom of the press that any man who considers the preservation of human life a thing of value must be mad. I shall not be surprised if my last years are spent in a lunatic asylum – where I shall enjoy the company of all who are capable of feelings of humanity. ●

30 NOVEMBER 1984

Greenham Common

By Lynne Jones

The peace activist Lynne Jones wonders whether the fear of nuclear devastation is the best basis for a peace movement: "There's something paradoxical about terrifying people and then expecting them to challenge a government armed with that kind of might."

We are lying ten yards from the silos. An owl swoops over us, wings caught in the headlights of a passing car. We have crawled, run, walked across the runway and through woods to get here and are now waiting for the evening rush of traffic to diminish before running through the last brightly lit area, in an attempt to get over the inner fence. Groups of women have been doing this every night. On one occasion 21 hijacked an airforce bus, drove up to the inner silo fence and started cutting before being arrested. The actions continue in spite of the fact that the camp is under the worst pressure for months. Evictions occur sometimes twice a day – they aren't pleasant. The bailiffs on one accession emptied the Elsan on the ground before taking it. The water standpipe has been taken and the Water Board, having decided we are "illegal", has refused to replace it.

I am soaked to the skin and covered in mud; my coat was lost crawling through the first lot of wire. There are three rabbits hopping about in front of my nose. The traffic seems endless. Why am I doing this? The media aren't interested, haven't been for months. Am I wasting my time?

***

But how do we define effective action? Greenham has long stopped being a publicity exercise. The actions of the last year – that occupation of the air traffic control tower, the perpetual incursions and blockades, the removal of sections of fence and documents from inside the base – have changed from mass symbolic set pieces to a form of perpetual resistance; the nearest non-violence can get to guerrilla warfare.

They have not lost their symbolic value. On Nagasaki Day the women stripped naked, covered the ground and themselves with ashes and then blockaded. But they have far more to do with preventing those who run the base operation efficiently than with publicity seeking. In this it would appear that we are being effective. A friend visiting the USAF Commander recently remarked that his desk was covered in newspaper cuttings about the camp. The Defence Committee Hearing at Greenham on physical security last May was entirely preoccupied with the camp.

Not that their discussion showed much understanding of our psychology. Defence Minister Keith Speed suggested that an extremely dull 10ft-high wall with TV surveillance on top should be built. Having nothing to watch we would get bored and go away. Mr Ward (head of SI) did point out that this would appear to be "walling in the Americans and thus provide the peace camp with a sort of victory. So far as is possible we would like Greenham not to become so much like a prison camp that it resembled no other American Airforce base in this country."

> For many women, it is their first contact with organised violence

Meanwhile the tracking of the cruise convoy has become increasingly efficient. So far there has been no secret dispersal at all, while on the last exercise five peace activists in a van actually joined the convoy for a period. Wing Commander March admitted that the convoys had to travel at "indecent haste" whereas "under normal circumstances" (!) this would not be necessary.

***

The MoD spent £8¾ million on overtime last year – £6 million of that on demonstrations. Far from occupying a few troublemakers the ten-day action in September demonstrated the power of the camp to attract thousands of new women from as far away as New Zealand and the USA, and as Liz pointed out, "Women who live here any length of time simply don't go back to being housewives." Greenham for many is their first contact with organised violence in the form of dogs, army, police, soldiers and barbed wire – it is unforgettable. "They see women being arrested on trivial charges while significant laws such as the Genocide Act are ignored. It completely changes your attitude to authority."

Few women pass through the camp without deciding that cruise missiles are just one particular and frightening manifestation of our lack of self-determination. So that it seems completely natural to move from here to campaigns against Violence against Women; support for Nicaragua, Namibia, or miners' picket lines. Some sections of the peace movement see all this diversity as diluting the real issue of nuclear weapons. And it can't be denied that, while we find it easy to see and explain the connections between these issues, working in more than one place at once is difficult.

Sarah Hipperson, writing in a recent issue of *Women for Life on Earth*, described her disappointment that thousands of women don't come to the camp to obstruct the cruise convoys on their return. "I remember raging bitterly that Greenham women may be everywhere but they certainly aren't on Greenham Common while this 'beast' is out travelling through our country preparing for mass murder . . . If 1,000 women came to Greenham to picket think how stretched the police would be looking after all the pickets in the country. Indeed if this was done once a week that would be a practical as well as political promotion of non-violence to strengthen and solidify it." However, connections work both ways and making them has brought other women to Greenham – black women, miners' wives.

***

The strangest thing is that I am not scared. Gathering with other women outside the fence in the dusk I was terrified: images of myself shot, caught on barbed wire, beaten up by soldiers or bitten by Alsatian dogs, flickering on the edge of my mind. They have cleared now and lying in the mud beside Hera and Skipper, women I love and trust, I feel quite safe, intent only on how we might get over that fence, and what has happened to the other women. Those who worry that the camp has lost its sense of direction by using its energy to maintain a women's community, rather than challenge cruise, miss the point that the only possibility of an effective challenge comes out of creating that community.

***

That's not to say we have Utopia. I can't think of a more insane place to try and create it than

Camp life: for many protesters the campaign was an opening into broader political awareness

HULTON ARCHIVE/GETTY IMAGES

on a public highway outside a barbed wire fence with no shelter to its name. We have had bitter quarrels over the use of money, the ability to act as we choose without limiting others' freedom to do likewise. We have seen women come here mad with distress, and have failed utterly to help them, and then ourselves left in disgust . . . and come back again, because somehow the centre holds – a shared belief that even if we can't live up to our own ideals the effort is worth it.

Sometimes it works – over the ten days' action, workshops were held, shit pits dug, litter collected and countless actions taken with no sense of a central leadership. When the evictions began again, women appeared miraculously with hot food; water is dropped off by total strangers twice a day. If getting rid of cruise means abandoning the attempt to look after each other it isn't worth doing.

***

The traffic has lessened, it seems quiet. We get up and start to run towards the wire. A soldier appears from behind an observation box. Another appears 100 yards away down the fence. "Stop running," he yells. We put our hands up, smiling, and walk towards him. He looks incredibly young and scared. Fifteen soldiers anxiously gather around seven women and push us into a Land Rover. We're driven to the administration block and searched. Cathy, plump and blonde in silky blue bomber jacket (USAF), is acting tough with Skippy – "Siddown or I'll sidya down." Sarah is pacing up and down while a nervous RAF man follows her with an exasperated expression. "Sit down!" he says in desperation. "You're working for death," she replies, "and I'm not doing anything you say!"

Cathy calls for help and a large MoD policeman arrives. "Look Miss Green, you know the form, sit down, please." (There are no chairs and the only reason I am sitting on a very cold floor is to write notes.)

"You know the form – You're preparing for murder! Why have you made that woman sit alone?"

"Because I fancy her and I don't fancy you!"

Another MoD officer arrives, glances at her and at the series of open doors. "Can I have those doors locked please!" Last time Sarah was here she removed lecture notes discussing the operational deficiencies in the running of the base and its preparedness for chemical and biological warfare.

"Didn't I tell ya it was goin' to be one of those nights?" Cathy remarks. "It will be 'one of those nights' every night until you get rid of cruise," Sarah retorts.

***

There's much discussion in the peace movement on the need for new ways of thinking; a growing realisation that fear of the effects of nuclear weapons is not the best basis for action. Indeed there's something paradoxical about first terrifying people and then expecting them to be brave enough to challenge a government armed with that kind of might.

So we are discussing realistic alternatives. Many of the new alternatives seem remarkably like the old. I am no less terrified by the prospect of conventional warfare, however defensive. While we remain in a society whose organising principles are violence and exploitation, the lesser of two evils is still evil.

Yet pacifism is not discussed; it is seen as a form of "weakness" and everyone is still frightened. If Greenham stands for anything it is to challenge that. "Non-violent action," Liz remarked to me one day, "is simply a way of overcoming fear of one sort or another." I see the continuing existence of the peace camp as a constant reminder of the possibility of non-violence as a creative struggle that doesn't have to end in defeat. For three years a small bunch of women have successfully held on to a patch of land in the face of a government with all the coercive powers of the State at its disposal and at the same time they have created a network and philosophy of personal responsibility that stretches across the world.

***

They haven't charged us and we are released in twos, walking past the security box and through a gate that divides two realities – ours which says that conflicts can be resolved without violence and theirs, where the presence of violence prevents anything being resolved at all. ●

Rebooting the City

By Alex Brummer

Some of our financial history lessons have been learnt and we are better placed to recover from the Great Recession of 2009-2010 than we were from the equivalent crisis of 1913-14

In the midst of the credit crunch of 2007, the precursor to the Great Recession of 2009-2010, the governor of the Bank of England, Sir Mervyn King, a fierce intellectual economist, came up with a big idea. If Britain was ever to pull itself out of the biggest financial crisis of his lifetime, it needed to learn the lessons of the past.

King decided to host an elite book club at his home in Notting Hill Gate, west London, where leading economists and economic historians could read, discuss and acquire knowledge from the crises of an earlier age. It was from this esoteric club that King discovered a theme that would pepper his speeches to City bigwigs at the Mansion House as the recession unfolded.

The UK, he would argue, was living through its most destructive financial and banking crisis since 1913-1914 – the period immediately leading up to the First World War – when a series of runs on banks had destroyed confidence in the British economy.

At that time, amid huge withdrawals of gold reserves from the City of London, the Bank of England raised interest rates from 8 per cent to the emergency rate of 10 per cent. The impact on City trading was so severe that the London Stock Exchange, with a history dating back to the coffee houses of the 17th century, was forced to close its doors. It required intervention on a vast scale by the government of Prime Minister Herbert Asquith, the Bank of England, and by the bankers and the financiers to prevent the country and its commercial system tipping into an abyss.

In exchange for a moratorium on paying debt and government injections of cash and capital, the City set about reorganising itself. The great merchant banks N M Rothschild, Hambros, Barings, Morgan Grenfell, Lazard's and others eventually came together to form what became known as the Accepting Houses Committee. Together, it promised to guarantee "bills of exchange", used by the banks and commercial enterprises to settle debts.

This mystique-laden and privileged group – with special access to the Bank of England – would remain at the heart of Britain's financial system until the last decades of the 20th century. With reforms ushered in by Margaret Thatcher's laissez-faire government of the 1980s and warmly embraced by its New Labour successors, existing City structures were swept away and the seeds were sown for the credit crunch and the great panic of 2007-2008.

> The First World War left the City's pre-eminence all but destroyed

Britain's best-known economist, John Maynard Keynes, wrote in the immediate aftermath of the August 1914 financial crisis: "We cannot yet reckon up losses . . . I do not believe that anything has occurred to derogate from the international position of London."

He could not have been more wrong. The loss of gold reserves, the wreckage of the banking system and the need to liquidate huge overseas investments to fund the First World War left the City's pre-eminence as a financial centre – like that of Amsterdam before it – all but destroyed.

New York then became the world's leading financial centre until the latter part of the 20th century, when London's geography, openness and easygoing regulation, encouraged by Chancellor Gordon Brown from 1997 onwards, allowed it to re-establish itself as the world's leading financial entrepôt.

The lessons of the pre-Great War crisis were well learned in the City and the system of "accepting houses", with the ear of the Bank of England, was able to maintain a surprising degree of stability for the financial system.

By the early 1920s a degree of certainty had been restored and sterling was trading reasonably soundly on the foreign exchange markets. The then governor of the Bank of England, Montagu Norman, came to believe that a return to the "gold standard" would help restore stability to the UK economy and the City's prestige internationally. He set about persuading the Treasury and the politicians, and in his April Budget of 1925 the chancellor, Winston Churchill, announced its return.

But what proved a source of celebration in the City was a disaster for the rest of the country as the linking of the exchange rate to gold destroyed the nation's competitiveness, leading to mass unemployment and a general strike. Large-scale deflation and economic hardship, followed by a run on Britain's gold reserves, forced the nation off the gold standard in 1931.

It proved a blessing in disguise. Amid the stock-market crash of 1929 and then the Great Depression, Britain's economic policymakers had the flexibility to operate a loose monetary policy that protected the country from the financial collapse afflicting the United States and parts of Europe.

The early half of the 20th century was one of continuous crisis for Britain's financial system as the cost of two world wars drained the national reserves, turned the country into a large-scale debtor nation and helped dismantle its dominance of world trade, built on em-

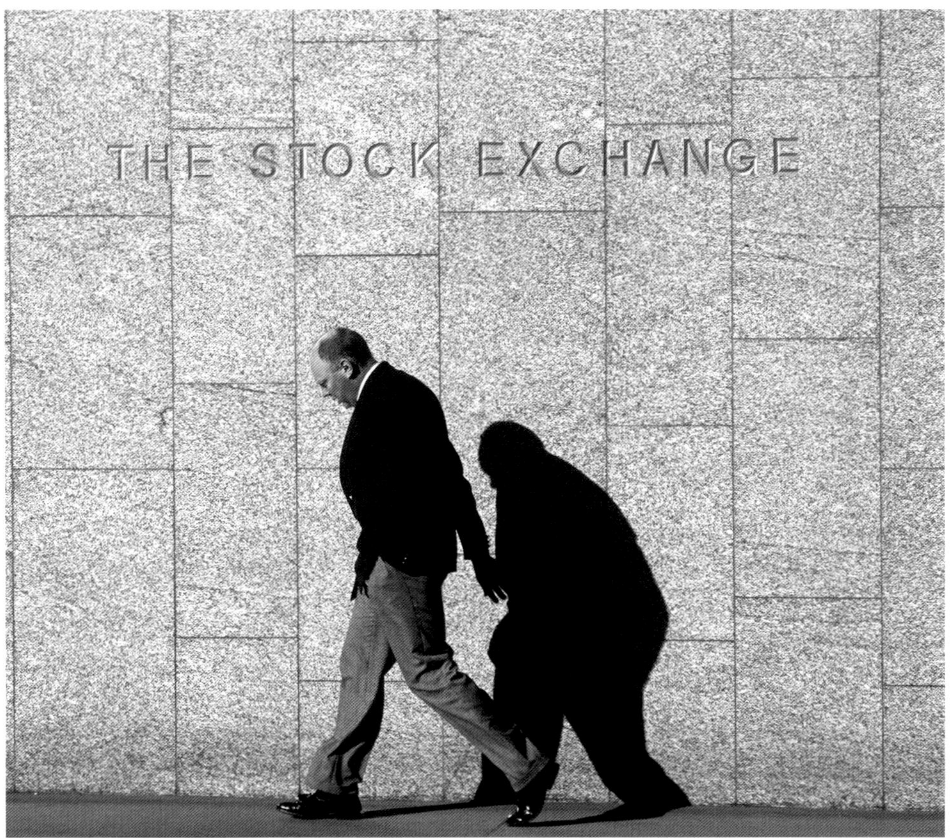

CORBIS

pire. Yet amid all the uncertainty, the City of London began to rebuild itself as a financial centre serving the rest of the globe.

It was assisted by a new generation of financial refugees from Nazi Germany, most notably Siegmund Warburg, the founder of S G Warburg, who saw the opportunity to restore London to the eminence it had enjoyed before 1914. Before long his house and the other City firms moved beyond trade finance and support of British industry and became experts in capital raising and bids and deals.

They were handed an enormous gift by the American authorities when it froze Egyptian dollar assets overseas during the 1956 Suez crisis and imposed taxes and regulations on dollar fundraisings for overseas enterprises and countries in the US.

The result was an explosion of what became known as eurodollar business in London. By the early 1980s roughly $180bn a year of fundraising was being done in London and the great UK financial houses were benefiting.

Success did not come easily. Britain and the City had to navigate through the Labour prime minister Harold Wilson's devaluation of the pound in 1967. There followed the market disruption caused of the breakdown of the Bretton Woods system of fixed exchange rates in 1973 and the sterling crisis of 1976, which led Britain into the arms of the International Monetary Fund.

The Thatcher government opened the floodgates to overseas investment in the 1980s, first by removing exchange controls and then through "Big Bang", which freed the City from its archaic rules and history. In the ensuing explosion of business, London became the biggest foreign exchange market and the best place to raise money and organise takeovers in the world.

New Labour under Gordon Brown would contribute to the financial boom by embracing "soft-touch" regulation and tearing up the old rulebook. In 1997, regulation was removed from the Bank of England to a new and, as it turned out, ineffectual regulator – the Financial Services Authority.

The Americans and Europeans sought to get in on the action, buying up the old accepting houses. Warburg fell to UBS of Switzerland, the merchant banking arm of Schroders to Citibank of New York and Rothschild's trading arm Smith New Court became part of Merrill Lynch.

Britain's established and staid clearing banks, such as Barclays and the Royal Bank of Scotland, went on merger sprees in the 1990s and established their own huge "casino" banking activities to rival those of the overseas incomers. The bonus culture and a determination to make easy money led the whole UK financial system into exotic products based around US sub-prime mortgages. When these products began to implode in 2007-2008, it brought a booming City of London to its knees. Brown's promise to end "boom and bust" was in tatters.

Downing Street and Threadneedle Street soon recalled the events of the early 20th century, and with the cash machines about to dry up at two leading houses, Halifax and Bank of Scotland (HBOS) and RBS, the government and the Bank of England stepped in with huge capital injections and monetary assistance totalling almost £1trn.

The City and British finance were saved again, as they had been saved just before the Great War. The names of those bankers who had brought the nation to its knees – men such as Fred Goodwin (stripped of his knighthood) and Sir James Crosby of HBOS (who renounced his title) – became infamous.

The rebuilding of Britain's financial system after the Great Recession will be a laborious process. Reform in the shape of new regulatory structure is under way. The Bank of England, which lost prudential supervision of the banks in 1997, has been restored to pre-eminence. The Canadian central banker Mark Carney was recruited by Chancellor George Osborne in 2012 with the aim of turning finance around. In the Budget of March 2013, he was granted a mandate to restore growth and with it the reputation of the financial market.

Slowly but surely, the system is rebooting. The City of London remains the leading global centre for foreign-exchange, interest-rate and derivatives trading, much to the annoyance of the bureaucrats at the heart of the European Union in Brussels.

The big American houses such as Goldman Sachs remain as entrenched in the City as before the crash, seeing it as best placed for global trading activities. The London Stock Exchange has become a magnet for initial public offerings of shares from the new wealth-creating economies, from Russia and Kazakhstan to Indonesia and Brazil.

Recovery from the Great Recession has been slow and stuttering as Britain has struggled with it budget deficits and debt, the legacies of the Great Recession. Output in the first half of 2013 was still below where it was at the peaks achieved in 2007, when the financial sector was at full tilt.

Yet there are signs of life coming back. The services sector, which now constitutes more than 70 per cent of the British economy and includes everything from financial services such as banking and insurance to information technology and legal services, is expanding. The depth of Britain's financial trading infrastructure, with a history of 350 years, gives it a huge lead over rival centres.

It has, however, suffered a shock on a par with that of a hundred years ago. That crisis held back the City for half a century. The early indications are that the steps taken to correct the system this time will work more rapidly, eventually restoring stability and prosperity. But it is going to be a long road to recovery from the biggest bust in several generations. ●

Alex Brummer is City editor of the Daily Mail

POOL PHOTOGRAPH/CORBIS

2 DECEMBER 1988

Charter 88

By Stuart Weir, Anthony Barnett and Jolyon Jenkins

Charter 88 was launched in a special edition of the New Statesman in response to the Conservative victory in the 1987 general election. Echoing the US Declaration of Independence, the document called for broad constitutional and electoral changes. As the list of signatories grew and donations poured in, the organisation set up its base at the NS offices, then in Shoreditch, east London.

We have been brought up in Britain to believe that we are free: that our Parliament is the mother of democracy; that our liberty is the envy of the world; that our system of justice is always fair; that the guardians of our safety, the police and security services, are subject to democratic, legal control; that our civil service is impartial; that our cities and communities maintain a proud identity; that our press is brave and honest.

Today such beliefs are increasingly implausible. The gap between reality and the received ideas of Britain's "unwritten constitution" has widened to a degree that many find hard to endure. Yet this year we are invited to celebrate the third centenary of the "Glorious Revolution" of 1688, which established what was to become the United Kingdom's sovereign formula. In the name of freedom, our political, human and social rights are being curtailed while the powers of the executive have increased, are increasing and ought to be diminished.

A process is under way which endangers many of the freedoms we have had. Only in part deliberate, it began before 1979 and is now gathering momentum. Scotland is governed like a province from Whitehall. More generally, the government has eroded a number of important civil freedoms: for example, the universal rights to habeas corpus, to peaceful assembly, to freedom of information, to freedom of expression, to membership of a trade union, to local ▶

Our Master Watchmaker never loses his concentration

With his legendary concentration and 45 years of experience our Master Watchmaker and renowned craftsman, Gilbert O. Gudjonsson, inspects every single timepiece before it leaves our workshop.

All the watches are designed and assembled by hand in Iceland. Only highest quality movements and materials are used to produce the watches and every single detail has been given the time needed for perfection.

The JS Watch co. Reykjavik Atelier and exclusive retail shop located at Laugavegur 62, in the trendy "101" area of Reykjavik is often refered to as "Probably the world's smallest watch manufacturer".

The quantity of watches produced is limited, giving them an exclusive and truly personal feel.

www.jswatch.com

government, to freedom of movement, even to the birth-right itself. By taking these rights from some, the government puts them at risk for all.

A traditional British belief in the benign nature of the country's institutions encourages an unsystematic perception of these grave matters; each becomes an "issue" considered in isolation from the rest. Being unwritten the constitution also encourages a piecemeal approach to politics; an approach that gives little protection against a determined, authoritarian state. For the events of 1688 only shifted the absolute power of the monarch into the hands of the parliamentary oligarchy.

The current administration is not an un-English interruption in the country's way of life. But while the government calls upon aspirations for liberty, it also exploits the dark side of a constitutional settlement which was always deficient in democracy.

The 1688 settlement had a positive side. In its time the Glorious Revolution was a historic victory over Royal tyranny. Britain was spared the rigours of dictatorship. A working compromise between many different interests was made possible at home, even if, from Ireland to India, quite different standards were imposed by Empire abroad. No criticism of contemporary developments in Britain should deny the significance of past democratic achievements, most dramatically illuminated in May 1940 when Britain defied the fascist domination of Europe.

But the eventual victory that liberated Western Europe preserved the paternalist attitudes and institutions of the United Kingdom. These incorporated the popular desire for work and welfare into a post-war national consensus. Now this has broken down. So, too, have its conventions of compromise and tolerance: essential components of a free society. Instead, the inbuilt powers of the 1688 settlement have enabled the government to discipline British society to its ends: to impose its values on the civil service; to menace the independence of broadcasting; to threaten academic freedom in universities and schools; to tolerate abuses committed in the name of national security. The break with the immediate past shows how vulnerable Britain has always been to elective dictatorship. The consequence is that today the British have fewer legal rights and less democracy than many other West Europeans.

The intensification of authoritarian rule in the United Kingdom has only recently begun. The time to reverse the process is now, but it cannot be reversed by an appeal to the past. Three hundred years of unwritten rule from above are enough. Britain needs a democratic programme that will end unfettered control by the executive of the day. It needs to reform a Parliament in which domination of the lower house can be decided by fewer than 40 per cent of the population; a Parliament in which a majority of the upper house is still determined by inheritance.

We have had less freedom than we believed. That which we have enjoyed has been too dependent on the benevolence of our rulers. Our freedoms have remained their possession, rationed out to us as subjects rather than being our own inalienable possession as citizens. To make real the freedoms we once took for granted means for the first time to take them for ourselves.

The time has come to demand political, civil and human rights in the United Kingdom. The first step is to establish them in constitutional form, so that they are no longer subject to the arbitrary diktat of Westminster and Whitehall.

> The time has come to demand political, civil and human rights in the UK

We call, therefore, for a new constitutional settlement which would:

- Enshrine, by means of a Bill of Rights, such civil liberties as the right to peaceful assembly, to freedom of association, to freedom from discrimination, to freedom from detention without trial, to trial by jury, to privacy and to freedom of expression.
- Subject executive powers and prerogatives, by whomsoever exercised, to the rule of law.
- Establish freedom of information and open government.
- Create a fair electoral system of proportional representation.
- Reform the upper house to establish a democratic, non-hereditary second chamber.
- Place the executive under the power of a democratically renewed parliament and all agencies of the state under the rule of law.
- Ensure the independence of a reformed judiciary.
- Provide legal remedies for all abuses of power by the state and the officials of central and local government.
- Guarantee an equitable distribution of power between local, regional and national government.
- Draw up a written constitution, anchored in the idea of universal citizenship, that incorporates these reforms.

Chris Riddell on the shaming of Liberty (*NS*, 2001)

Our central concern is the law. No country can be considered free in which the government is above the law. No democracy can be considered safe whose freedoms are not encoded in a basic constitution.

We, the undersigned, have called this document Charter 88. First, to mark our rejection of the complacency with which the tercentenary of the Revolution of 1688 has been celebrated. Second, to reassert a tradition of demands for constitutional rights in Britain, which stretches from the barons who forced Magna Carta on King John, to the working men who drew up the People's Charter in 1838, to the women at the beginning of this century who demanded universal suffrage. Third, to salute the courage of those in Eastern Europe who still fight for their fundamental freedoms.

Like the Czech and Slovak signatories of Charter 77, we are an informal, open community of people of different opinions, faiths and professions, united by the will to strive, individually and collectively, for the respect of civil and human rights in our own country and throughout the world. Charter 77 welcomed the ratification by Czechoslovakia of the UN International Covenant on Political and Civil Rights, but noted that it "serves as a reminder of the extent to which basic human rights in our country exist, regrettably, on paper only".

Conditions here are so much better than in Eastern Europe as to bear no comparison. But our rights in the United Kingdom remain unformulated, conditional upon the goodwill of the government and the compassion of bureaucrats. To create a democratic constitution at the end of the 20th century, however, may extend the concept of liberty, especially with respect to the rights of women and the place of minorities. It will not be a simple matter: part of British sovereignty is shared with Europe; and the extension of social rights in a modern economy is a matter of debate everywhere. We are united in one opinion only, that British society stands in need of a constitution which protects individual rights and of the institutions of a modern and pluralist democracy.

The inscription of laws does not guarantee their realisation. Only people themselves can ensure freedom, democracy and equality before the law. Nonetheless, such ends can be far better demanded, and more effectively obtained and guarded, once they *belong to everyone by inalienable right.* ●

FRED THORNHILL/REUTERS

A fielder runs head-on into an outfield wall advertising banner at a Major League Baseball game in Toronto

The Tyranny of the Brands

By Naomi Klein

What are we to make of the extraordinary scenes in Seattle that brought the 20th century to a close? A *New York Times* reporter observed that this vibrant mass movement opposed to unregulated globalisation had materialised "seemingly overnight". On television, the reliable experts who explain everything couldn't sort out whether the protesters were right-wing nationalists or Marxist globalists. Even the American left seemed surprised to learn that, contrary to previous reports, it did, in fact, still exist.

Despite the seemingly unconnected causes that converged in Seattle that week, there was a common target: the multinational corporation in general and McDonald's, Gap, Microsoft and Starbucks in particular. And what has given the movement against them a new energy and a new urgency is a profound shift in corporate priorities. That shift centres on the idea of corporate branding and the quest to build the most powerful brand image. It will, I believe, be one of the issues that shapes the first decade of the 21st century.

Branding seems like a fairly innocuous idea. It is slapping a logo on a product and saying it's the best. And when brands first emerged, that was all it was. At the start of the Industrial Revolution, the market was flooded with nearly identical mass-produced products. Along came Aunt Jemima and Quaker Oats with their happy comforting logos to say: our mass-produced product is of the highest quality.

But the role of branding has been changing, particularly in the past 15 years: rather than serving as a guarantee of value on a product, the brand itself has increasingly become the product – a free-standing idea pasted on to innumerable surfaces. The actual product bearing the brand name has become a medium, like radio or a billboard, to transmit the real message. The message is: It's Nike. It's Disney. It's Microsoft. It's Diesel. It's Caterpillar. The late graphic designer Tibor Kalman said that a brand used to be a mark of quality; now, it is "a stylistic badge of courage".

This shift in the role of the brand is related to a new corporate consensus, which emerged in the late 1980s. It held that corporations were too bloated: they were oversized, they owned too much, they employed too many people, they were weighed down with too many things. Where once the primary concern of every corporation was the production of goods, now production itself began to seem like a clunky liability.

The Nikes and Microsofts, and later the Tommy Hilfigers and Intels, made the bold claim that production was only an incidental part of their operations. What these companies produced primarily were not things, they said, but ideas and images, and their real work lay not in manufacturing, but in building up their brands. Savvy ad agencies began to think of themselves as brand factories, hammering out what is of true value: the idea, the lifestyle, the attitude. Out of this heady time, we learnt that Nike was about "Sport", not shoes; Microsoft about "Communications", not software; Starbucks about "Community", not coffee; Virgin about a "Fun-loving Attitude", not an airline, a record label, a cola, a bridal gown line, a train – or any of the other brand extensions the company has launched. My favourite is Diesel, whose chief executive says he has "created a movement", not a line of clothes.

> The brand itself has become the product – a free-standing idea

The formula for these brand-driven companies is pretty much the same: get rid of your unionised factories in the West and buy your products from Asian or central American contractors and subcontractors. Then, take the money you save and spend it on branding, on advertising, superstores, sponsorships. Based on the success of this formula, virtue in the corporate world has become a sort of race towards weightlessness: the companies which own the least, keep the fewest employees on the payroll and produce the coolest ideas (as opposed to products) win the race.

I have come to think of such companies as transcendent brands because their goal is to escape almost all that is earthbound and to become pure idea, like a spirit ascending. This is a goal that is available not only to companies, but also to people. We have human brands as well as company brands. Bill Gates has quit as chief executive of Microsoft so that he can tend to his true mission: being Bill Gates. Michael Jordan has stopped playing basketball and has become a pure brand-identity machine. And not only does he now have his own "Jordan" superstores, he is the first celebrity endorser to get other celebrities endorsing his label. Michael Jordan is no longer an athlete, he is an attitude.

It wasn't until the internet stock explosion that the extent of this shift became apparent. It marks the complete triumph of branding: the ascent of companies, most of which have yet to make a profit, that exist almost purely as ideas of themselves, leaving no real-world trace at all.

This shift to branding explains many of the most fundamental economic and cultural shifts of the past decade. Power, for a brand-driven company, is attained not by collecting assets but by projecting one's brand idea on to as many surfaces of the culture as possible: the wall of a college, a billboard the size of a skyscraper, an ad campaign that waxes philosophic about the future of our global village. Where a previous generation of corporate giants used drills, hammers and cranes to build their empires, these companies need an endless parade of new ideas for brand extensions, continuously rejuvenated imagery for marketing and, most of all, fresh new spaces to disseminate their brand's idea of itself.

In this way, these corporate phantoms become real. If we think of a brand-driven company as an ever-expanding balloon, then public space, new political ideas and avant-garde imagery are the gases that inflate it: it needs to consume cultural space in order to stave off its own deflation. This is a major change. Marketing, in the classic sense, is about association: beautiful girl drinks soda, uses shampoo, drives car; soda/shampoo/car become associated with our aspiration to be beautiful like her.

Branding mania has changed all that: association is no longer good enough. The goal now is for the brands to become real-world, living manifestations of their myths. Brands ▶

are about "meaning", not product attributes. So companies provide their consumers with opportunities not merely to shop but to experience fully the meaning of their brand. The brand-name superstore, for instance, stands as a full expression of the brand's lifestyle in miniature. Many of these stores are so palatial, so interactive, so hi-tech that they lose money hand over fist. But that doesn't mean they aren't working. Their real goal is to act as a 3D manifestation of the brand, so grand that their rather mundane products will carry that grandeur with them like a homing device.

SAEED KHAN/AFP/GETTYIMAGES

But this is only the beginning. Nike, which used just to sponsor athletes, has taken to buying sporting events outright. Disney, which through its movies and theme parks has sold a bygone version of small-town America, now owns and operates its very own small town, Celebration Florida.

In these branded creations, we see the building blocks of a fully privatised social and cultural infrastructure. These companies are stretching the fabric of their brands in so many directions that they are transformed into enclosures large enough to house any number of core activities, from shopping to entertainment to holidays. The companies are no longer satisfied with having a fling with their consumers, they want to move in together.

These companies are forever on the prowl for new ways to build and strengthen their images. This thirsty quest for meaning and virgin space takes its toll on public institutions such as schools, where, in North America, corporate interests are transforming education, seeking not only to advertise in cafeterias and washrooms but to make brands the uncritical subjects of study. Maths textbooks urge students to calculate the circumference of an Oreo cookie, Channel One broadcasts Burger King ads into 12,000 US schools and a student from Georgia was suspended last year for wearing a Pepsi T-shirt on his school's official "Coke Day".

Another effect is to restrict choice. Brands are selfish creatures, driven by the need to eliminate competitors. So Reebok, once it lands a deal to sponsor campus athletics, wants to exclude not only competing brands but also, as was the case at the University of Wisconsin, all disparaging remarks made about Reebok by officials of the university. Such "non-disparagement" clauses are standard in campus sponsorship deals. Disney, after it bought ABC, decided that it would rather ABC News no longer covered Disney's scandals, and focused instead on promoting its movies in various feats of "synergy".

There is another, more tangible, effect of the shift from products to brands: the devaluation of production itself. The belief that economic success lies in branding – production is a distant second – is changing the face of global employment. Building a superbrand is extraordinarily costly: it needs constant managing, tending, replenishing, stretching. The necessity for lavish spending on marketing creates intense resistance to investment in production facilities and labour. Companies that were traditionally satisfied with a 100 per cent mark-up from the cost of factory production to the retail price have spent the decade scouring the globe for factories that can make their products so inexpensively that the mark-up is closer to 400 per cent.

That's where the developing world's "free-trade zones" (free, that is, of taxes and wage or other labour regulations) come in. In Indonesia, China, Mexico, Vietnam, the Philippines and elsewhere, the export-processing zones (as these areas are also called) are emerging as leading producers of garments, toys, shoes, electronics and cars. There are almost 1,000 zones around the world, spread through 70 countries and employing approximately 27 million workers.

Inside the zones, workers assemble the finished products of our branded world: Nike running shoes, Gap pyjamas, IBM computer screens, Old Navy jeans, or VW Bugs. Yet the zones appear to be the only places left on earth where the superbrands actually keep a low profile. Their names and logos aren't splashed on the façades of the factories. In fact, where a particular branded product is made is often kept secret. And unlike in the brand-segregated superstores, competing labels are often produced side by side in the same factories; glued by the same workers, stitched and soldered on the same machines.

Regardless of where the zones are located, the hours will be long – 14-hour days in Sri Lanka, 12 in Indonesia, 16 in southern China, 12 in the Philippines. The workers are mostly young women; the management, military-style; the wages, sub-subsistence; the work, low-skill and tedious. The factories are owned by contractors or subcontractors from Korea, Taiwan or Hong Kong; the contractors meet orders for companies based in the US, Britain, Japan, Germany and Canada.

These pockets of pure industry are cloaked in a haze of transience: the contracts come and go with little notice (in Guatemala the factories are called "swallows" because they might take flight at any time); the workers are predominantly migrants; the work itself is short-term, often not renewed. Many factory workers in the Philippines are hired through an employment agency inside the zone walls which collects their cheques and takes a cut.

We tend to think that globalisation moves jobs from one country to another. But in a brand-based economy, the value of the work itself moves to a drastically degraded rung of the corporate hierarchy. What is being abandoned in the relentless quest to reduce the costs of production is the Fordist principle: that labour not only creates products but, by paying workers a decent wage, creates the consumer market for that product and others like it. In Indonesia, the young women factory workers making Nike shoes and Gap jeans live a notch above famine victims and landless peasants.

And so we are left with an odd duality: brands have never been more omnipresent, nor have they ever generated as much wealth. All around us we see these new creations replacing our cultural institutions and our public spaces. And yet, at the same time, these same companies are oddly absent from our lives in the most immediate of ways: as steady employers. Multinationals that once identified strongly with their role as engines of job growth now prefer to identify themselves as engines of "economic growth".

The extent of this shift cannot be overstated. Among the total number of working-age adults in the USA, Canada and the UK, those with full-time, permanent jobs working for someone other than themselves are in the minority. Temps, part-timers, the unemployed and those who have opted out of the labour force entirely now make up more than half of the working-age population.

We know that this formula reaps record profits in the short term. It may, however, prove to be a strategic miscalculation. When corporations are perceived as functioning vehicles of wealth distribution – trickling down jobs and tax revenue – they get deep civic loyalty in return. In exchange for steady pay cheques and stable communities, citizens attach themselves to the priorities of the local corporate sector and don't ask too many questions about, say, water pollution. In other words, dependable job creation served as a kind of corporate suit of armour. Only now, without realising it, brand-driven multinationals have been shedding that armour: first came their inability to respect public space, next came their betrayal of the central promise of the information age – the promise of increased choice – and, finally, they severed the bond between employer and employee. They may be big and rich, but suddenly there is nothing to protect them from public rage.

And that is the true significance of Seattle. All around us we are witnessing the early expressions of this anger, of the first, often crudely constructed lines of defence against the rule of the brands. We have, for example, the growth of "culture-jamming", which adapts a corporation's own advertising to send a message starkly at odds with the one that was intended. So, Apple Computers' "Think Different" campaign acquires a photograph of Stalin with the slogan "Think Really Different". The process forces the company to foot the bill for its own subversion.

The principles of culture-jamming – using the power of brand names against themselves in a kind of brand boomerang – are being imported to much more direct and immediate political struggles. People are beginning to fight the big global economic battles by focusing on one or two brand-name corporations and turning them into large-scale political metaphors.

Think of the campaigns that trace the journeys of brand-name goods back to their unbranded points of origin: Nike sneakers back to the sweatshops of Vietnam; Starbucks lattes back to the sun-scorched coffee fields of Guatemala and now East Timor; and virtually every ingredient of a McDonald's hamburger dissected into its bio-engineered beginnings.

There is a clear difference between these campaigns and the corporate boycotts of the past, whether against Nestlé for its baby formula, or against Union Carbide for its infamous toxic accident in Bhopal, India. In those cases, activists had targeted a specific corporation engaged in an anomalously harmful practice. Today's anti-corporate campaigns simply piggyback on the high profile of their brand-name targets as a tactical means of highlighting difficult, even arcane issues. The companies being targeted – Disney, Mattel, Gap and so on – may not always be the worst offenders, but they do tend to be the ones who flash their logos in bright lights on the global marquee. It may seem unfair to single such companies out for their "success", as some have argued, but it is precisely this success which is becoming an odd sort of liability.

> Of the top 100 economies, 51 are multinationals and only 49 are countries

Take McDonald's. In opening more than 23,000 outlets worldwide, the company has done more than spread the gospel of fast, uniform food. It has also, inadvertently, become equated in the public imagination with the "McJob", "McDonaldisation" and "McWorld". So when activists build a movement around McDonald's, as they did around the McLibel Trial, they are not really going after a fast-food chain, but harnessing the branding might behind the chain as a way to crack open a discussion on the otherwise impenetrable global economy: about labour, the environment and cultural imperialism.

Many superbrands are feeling the backlash. With typical understatement, Shell Oil's chief executive, Mark Moody, states: "Previously, if you went to your golf club or church and said, 'I work for Shell', you'd get a warm glow. In some parts of the world, that has changed a bit." That change flowed directly from the anti-corporate campaign launched against Shell after the hanging of the Nigerian author and activist Ken Saro-Wiwa, who was fighting to get Shell to clean up the environmental devastation left behind when it pumped oil out of the Niger Delta. Had the campaigners focused on the dictatorship alone, the death of the activist could well have been yet another anonymous atrocity in Africa. But because they dared to name names – to name Shell as the economic interest behind the violence – it became an instantly globalised campaign, with protests at petrol stations around the world. The brand was the campaign's best asset.

At the heart of this shift in focus is the recognition that corporations are much more than purveyors of the products we all want; they are also the most powerful political forces of our time, the driving forces behind bodies such as the World Trade Organisation. We've all heard the statistics: how corporations such as Shell and Wal-Mart bask in budgets bigger than the gross domestic products of most nations; how, of the top 100 economies, 51 are multinationals and only 49 are countries. So, although the media often describe campaigns like the one against Nike as "consumer boycotts", that tells only part of the story. It is more accurate to describe them as political campaigns that use consumer goods as readily accessible targets, as public-relations levers and as popular education tools.

I doubt this current surge of anti-corporate activism would have been possible without the mania for branding. Branding, as we have seen, has taken a fairly straightforward relationship between buyer and seller and – through the quest to turn brands into media providers, art producers, town squares and social philosophers – transformed it into something much more intimate. But the more successful this project is, the more vulnerable these companies become to the brand boomerang. If brands are indeed intimately entangled with our culture, then, when they do wrong, their crimes are not easily dismissed. Instead, many of the people who inhabit these branded worlds feel complicit in their wrongs. And this connection is a volatile one, akin to the relationship of fan and celebrity: emotionally intense but shallow enough to turn on a dime.

Branding, as I have stated, is a balloon economy: it inflates with astonishing rapidity but it is full of hot air. It shouldn't be surprising that this formula has bred armies of pin-wielding critics, anxious to pop the corporate balloon and watch it fall to the ground.

Behind the protests outside Nike Town, behind the pie in Bill Gates's face, behind the shattering of a McDonald's window in Paris, behind the protests in Seattle, there is something too visceral for most conventional measures to track – a bad mood rising. And the corporate hijacking of political power is as responsible for this mood as the brands' cultural looting of public and mental spaces.

All around the world, activists are making liberal use of the tool that has so thoroughly captured the imagination of the corporate world: branding. Brand image, the source of so much corporate wealth, is also, it turns out, the corporate Achilles heel. ●

Voices from Elsewhere

© IAN BERRY/MAGNUM PHOTOS

The divide: in Ian Berry's 1969 photograph, a young black woman looks after a white child in South Africa

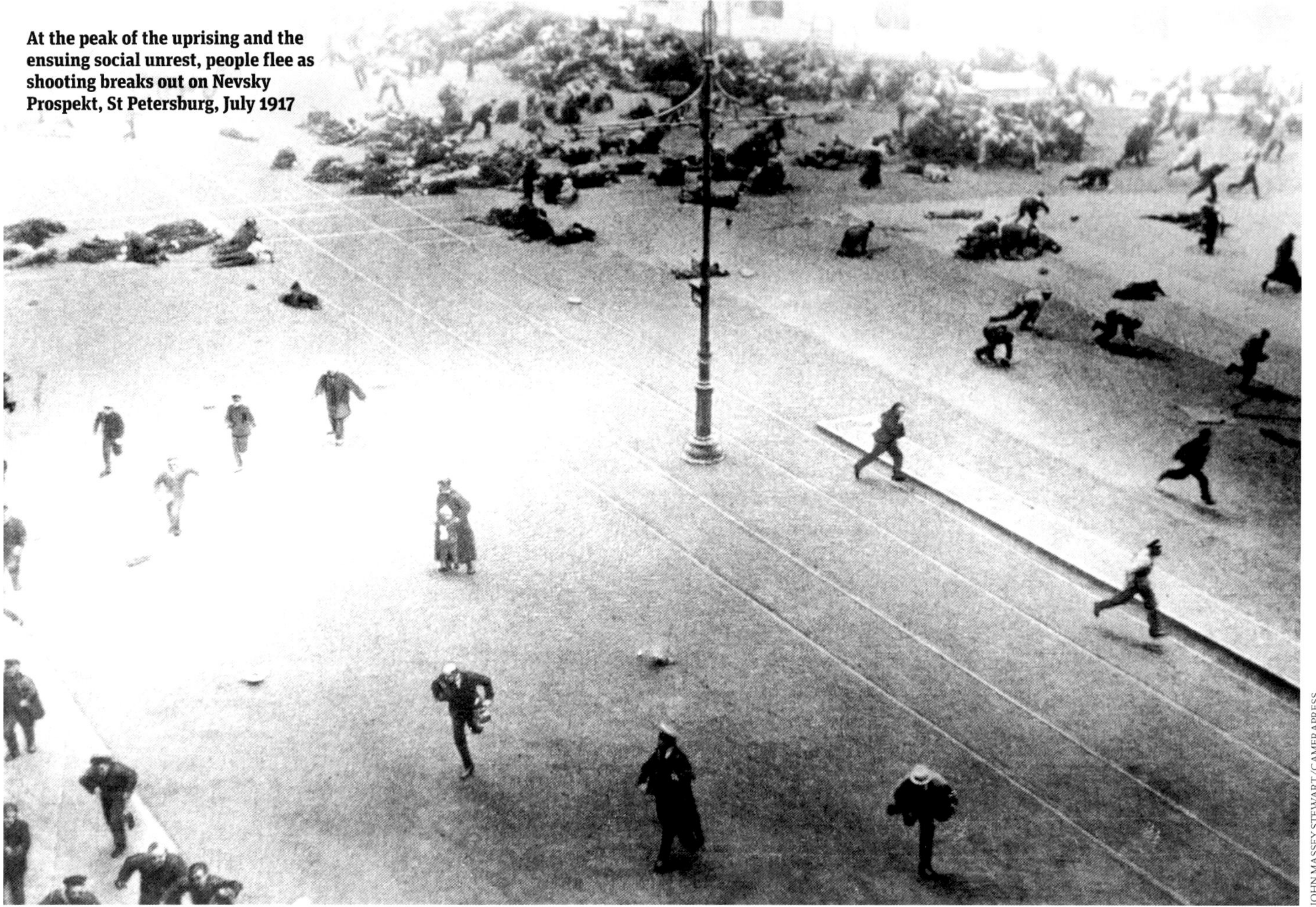

At the peak of the uprising and the ensuing social unrest, people flee as shooting breaks out on Nevsky Prospekt, St Petersburg, July 1917

JOHN MASSEY STEWART/CAMERAPRESS

15 DECEMBER 1917

The Bolshevik Revolution

By Julius West

A week's continuous contemplation of Petrograd makes one feel sorry for its future historians, unless, indeed, they happen to be classical scholars. Classical study, I think, generally includes a course of M Maurice Baring's works, which contain some extracts alleged to have come out of the diary of an English governess in Paris during the French Revolution. Read those extracts, and you get the sensations of the bourgeois resident in the Petrograd of to-day. He is on his dignity; he is vaguely aware that his city is in the hands of a crowd with whom he has no connection; and he stays at home as much as he can. If he meets a friend he generally asks him how it is all going to finish. And where the devil is the Provisional Government's army?

The resident, in fact, knows extremely little. For a week Petrograd has been very nearly cut off from the rest of Russia, and entirely separated from the outside world. The train service is casual; the telephones can only be used for official business; the telegraph, apparently, no longer exists. All the non-Socialist papers have been stopped, and the Socialist papers which do not support the Bolsheviks are coming out under great difficulties, succumbing one after another. The news published is highly coloured, and there is very little of it, anyway. The public is frankly unable to make head or tail of the whole business. Remember that four armies are supposed to be marching on Petrograd. First of all there is the Provisional Government, somewhere in the outer suburbs; we can hear its guns occasionally. This is being chased by Bolsheviks coming to help the Lenin Government. This army consists of detachments from the Northern Front and parts of the garrisons of Reval and Narva. Then there are the Germans who, according to current rumour, are landing indiscriminately all over the place. And some time after they all get here, the Cossacks will arrive from the south, under General Kaledin. And we shall all have the time of our lives.

The soldiers one meets all express the same sentiment: "Wish we could catch Kerensky —we'd soon drop him into the Neva." The Soviet, having placed him in office, now looks on him as a traitor — it has gone to the left, he has gone to the right. The bourgeois always disapproved of his Socialism, and the fact that he was a compromise. And the rest of the population is filled with the perfectly natural desire to hit a man because he is down.

Petrograd, all things considered, is extraordinarily quiet. There have been siege and murder and massacre; but the promiscuous "joy-firing" which was a feature of the July outbreak has lost most of its attractions. The Bolsheviks' plan of campaign was essentially sound. They had a list of the buildings to be occupied, and they occupied them. First on the list was the government bank—that needed very few men. The Winter Palace required larger numbers, but as soon as it was taken some hundreds of soldiers and "Red Guards" (armed factory workers and mostly young fellows of about twenty, very slightly disciplined) were set free for the next job. The Government offices were merely policed by Red Guards. An enormous number of these youths were put on to preventing outrages by professional criminals.

When the seats of the Government had been captured, the only part of the garrison remaining loyal to the Provisional Government was dealt with. Here the atrocities occurred. One officers' training school after another was surrounded, fired at with rifles, machine-guns, and, in one case at least, artillery, and captured. Wherever the Cadets ("Junkers") had put up an obstinate resistance, something in the nature of a massacre occurred; otherwise they might hope for decent treatment. At one officers' training school, the Red Guards and the mob, irritated by a resistance of several hours, which had made a street appear as if an exceptionally competent Zeppelin had been at work, at the end rushed into the ruined building and looted wildly and viciously. Boots were torn off corpses, and I heard men outside the school yelling at those inside to hand out more boots through the windows, and receive the reply: "There aren't any more dead here."

In spite of this and similar affairs, in spite of intermittent gunfire and the very occasional cracking of rifles, the town is quiet. On Sunday 4 November, when Petrograd was expecting an outbreak, and none occurred, the principal streets were deserted. On Sunday 11 November, when the firing was still taking place, the Nevsky swarmed with well-dressed people. Large crowds got as near as they could to the Telephone Station in the Morskaya, hoping to see its capture. And here it may not be out of place to notice the wonderfully prompt way in which the population has adapted itself to the present state of siege. A week ago Petrograd was the most nervous city on earth. A friend suddenly remarked with emphasis, as he nearly twisted his ankle, "*Bozhe moy!*" (My God). And a panic or something very much like it at once spread down the street for some hundreds of yards. But now! I was in the Nevsky when a sailor lifted up his rifle and fired, apparently for no other reason than *épater le bourgeois*. And a few people ran, and a good many stopped, but there was nothing in the nature of a panic.

The revolution has had a peculiar and immediate effect on oratory, both of the Soviet and the Municipal Duma. Up to a week ago long speeches were the rule, and they were seldom regarded as successful unless they contained at least due reference to the "*categoritchesky imperativ*". This has now gone. Short speeches are now all the fashion. Lenin abolished the present land system in a twenty minutes' speech, while speeches at the Municipal Duma, where the anti-Bolshevik movement flies a neutral flag, seldom exceed the length of a respectable interruption. But what posterity will chiefly miss seeing will be the posters. Posters always were a feature

Where the devil is the Provisional Government's army?

of the Revolution, but during the last few days they have attained their apotheosis. The walls scream with the names of the Council of National Commissars, as Lenin's Government calls itself. The Edict on Peace yells at one. The Land "Decret" is all over the place. Other posters tell one what is alleged to be happening in Moscow (entirely misleading news, between ourselves), that shops which obstinately remain shut will have their stocks confiscated, that the "counter-revolution" is at it again, and that more Red Guards are wanted. And among and between them all is a pathetically inopportune little poster for which British propaganda must be responsible; it is headed "How the British Soldier regards Discipline", and is signed "Tomi Atkins".

The shortage of Red Guards is really the whole Bolshevik position in a nutshell. The Provisional Government has not the power to remain in office; the Bolsheviks have not quite enough force to turn it out. They completely underestimated the number of men needed to run the country. This is the sort of thing which has been happening in consequence:

(Scene: The Ministry of Labour. Enter one SHLIAPNIKOV.)

SHLIAPNIKOV (*in the entrance hall*).—I am the new Minister of Labour.

THE HALL PORTER (*dispassionately*).—Really? First floor, along the hall, last door on the left.

(*Exit SHLIAPNIKOV accordingly. HALL PORTER puts on his coat and goloshes and goes home.*)

SHLIAPNIKOV (*in his cabinet*).—Porter... Porter... PORTER! (*After much delay an attendant enters.*) Tell the heads of the Departments I want to talk to them. Send them all in here. I am the new Minister.

(*Attendant goes out and returns after about ten minutes.*)

ATTENDANT—I'm sorry, but I can't find any.

SHLIAPNIKOV—What! Not here at twelve o'clock! Tell them to come to me as soon as they get here. I'll make an example of 'em.

ATTENDANT—Well, the fact is they've all just gone home. We're all going home. All except a chauffeur. I'm going home. Good bye. (*Exit.*)

SHLIAPNIKOV (*rushes out of his cabinet and finds building deserted. In the yard a chauffeur, tinkering with a car*).—Get that thing ready at once to take me to the Smolny.

CHAUFFEUR (*severely*).—AND WHERE AM I TO GET MY BENZINE FROM?

CURTAIN.

Every Government office, in fact, has gone on strike. A great many shops are still shut, or else doing business in a furtive sort of way. All motors have been requisitioned by the Soviet, even the ambulances belonging to the Municipal Council. The railway workers are understood to have gone on strike with the object of preventing bloodshed; starvation will make everybody more reasonable, apparently. Soldiers behave as if under hypnotism, or just awaking from it. I heard a soldier catch at the word "heroes" in a tramcar and repeat sleepily: "They are all heroes. Lenin is a hero, Trotsky is a hero, Kamenev is a hero. But, I tell you, the other people have got some heroes too. Rodzianko is a hero, Miliukov is a hero."

But we go to bed early, and that, no doubt, is very good for us. Because the Governments of Russia during the last month or two have been so busy suppressing one another that they haven't had the time to put the clock back, and we are still in mid-November, enjoying the blessings of the Daylight Saving Act. ●

JOHN MASSEY STEWART/CAMERAPRESS

After the looting of the Winter Palace, 1917

Malaria control and elimination: learning from the past

By **Alex Hulme**, Malaria Consortium

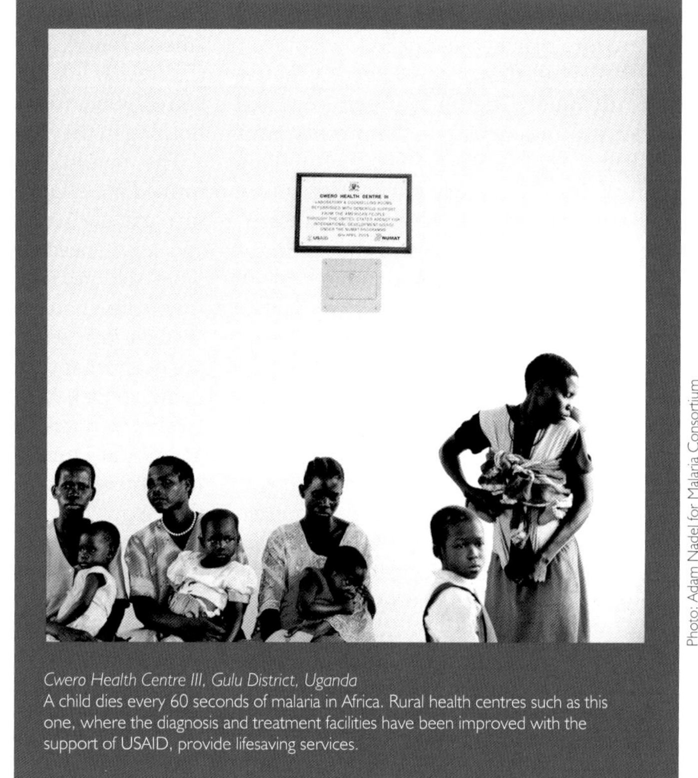

Cwero Health Centre III, Gulu District, Uganda
A child dies every 60 seconds of malaria in Africa. Rural health centres such as this one, where the diagnosis and treatment facilities have been improved with the support of USAID, provide lifesaving services.

Photo: Adam Nadel for Malaria Consortium

The New Statesman was born just 16 years after a British doctor discovered that malaria is transmitted by mosquitoes, an extremely important finding. But the fight against malaria is one that far predates this discovery. It has killed millions of people since before we were aware it even existed. Even today, the death toll wrought by this disease continues to shock, although it has been both preventable and treatable for over a century.

With well over half a million people – mostly children – still dying from malaria, global attention has undergone a 'revival' since 2000 with the introduction of dedicated global funding such as The Global Fund to fight AIDS, Tuberculosis and Malaria, and the US President's Malaria Initiative, and with likes of Bill Gates vowing to see it wiped out - with support from the Bill & Melinda Gates Foundation.

Efforts to support this aim have been many and varied, from the simple mosquito net to chemical spraying, smelly socks to laser technology and, we hope, soon a vaccine. But underestimating a disease which continues to survive and evolve even now could lead to devastating consequences.

Increased Investment

Since the turn of the century, investments in malaria control have created unprecedented momentum and yielded remarkable returns.

In Africa, malaria deaths have been cut by one third within the last decade and globally 50 countries are on track to reduce malaria cases by 75% by 2015. In countries where access to malaria control interventions has improved most significantly, the number of child deaths overall has fallen by approximately a fifth.

The fight against malaria is going beyond control to elimination; four countries have been certified malaria-free in the last 10 years, and 34 additional countries are working towards malaria elimination targets.

As mentioned, these successes have been achieved through a significant increase in financing from global donors and the development of new technologies to control malaria, as well as greater domestic and international political commitment to beat this disease.

Learning from the Past

Since 2010, however, malaria funding has begun to slow down, leaving a critical funding gap. The World Health Organisation estimates that there is an annual shortfall of around US$3.6 billion for malaria control, and addressing the gap is crucial if we are ever going to defeat this disease.

History has shown that the consequences of failing to address this funding gap would be catastrophic. Over the past century, shortfalls in the funding of malaria control programmes have led to massive resurgences of the disease, even compared with what was present before. Other causes that undermined elimination efforts in the past also included over-reliance on a single tool, fall-off in quality and interest, inadequate long-term planning and limited attention to ownership by the people.

Setting an Example: Sri Lanka

The consequences of any reduction of commitment for malaria control programmes are perhaps best demonstrated through Sri Lanka's experiences.

During the 1960s, following a decade of malaria control efforts, Sri Lanka came close to malaria elimination with near zero cases in 1963. But over-confidence meant funding for continued control dropped and as a result, the country saw a huge resurgence of the disease, with an estimated 1.5 million cases during the two-year period 1967–1968. These levels were far greater than at any time in the 20 years previously, showing the potential damage that a loss of financial focus can bring about.

Sri Lanka is only today getting back to the low levels of malaria achieved in the 1960s, with only 684 cases being reported in 2010 and no deaths over the last 10 years. But this remains an important example of how resurgence remains a real threat and the consequences of relaxing any commitment to elimination can take decades to remedy.

Investing in the Future

The implications for today are similarly worrying. Experts have estimated that a decline in malaria control now could allow global mortality numbers to return to pre-2000 levels, when 1.3 million people died from malaria a year. It is also a race against time, as resistance to current drugs and insecticides increases.

Therefore, 2013 is the time to renew the global and national commitment to fight malaria. The malaria focused community, including the Roll Back Malaria Partnership, has been and will continue to be instrumental in raising awareness of the burden of malaria.

Financing institutions such as The Global Fund, the world's largest external source of finance and provider of three quarters of all international financing for malaria, must be supported and replenished by the international community. Without this, achievement of the goals for malaria control, elimination and eventual eradication will almost certainly be put at risk.

Huge progress has been made against malaria over the past decade, driven by simple scientific advances like mosquito nets treated with insecticide, quicker diagnostic tests and more effective antimalarial drugs. We are saving more lives than ever before and cases of malaria continue to decrease.

To continue these achievements sufficient funding must be found so that the endemic countries have the resources and technical support they need. Only then will it be possible to finish the job and see that malaria is eliminated worldwide.

www.malariaconsortium.org

Malaria Consortium is the one of the world's leading NGOs dedicated to the comprehensive control of malaria and other infectious tropical diseases, particularly those affecting young children. We work directly with the people most affected, as well as governments and the private sector, helping to bring an end to deaths from treatable and preventable diseases.

3 SEPTEMBER 1932

Common Lodging Houses

By Eric Blair (George Orwell)

Common lodging houses, of which there are several hundred in London, are night-shelters specially licensed by the LCC. They are intended for people who cannot afford regular lodgings, and in effect they are extremely cheap hotels. It is hard to estimate the lodging house population, which varies continually, but it always runs into tens of thousands, and in the winter months probably approaches fifty thousand. Considering that they house so many people and that most of them are in an extraordinarily bad state, common lodging houses do not get the attention they deserve.

The average lodging house ("doss-house", it used to be called) consists of a number of dormitories, and a kitchen, always subterranean, which also serves as a sitting-room. The conditions in these places, especially in southern quarters such as Southwark or Bermondsey, are disgusting. The dormitories are horrible fetid dens, packed with anything up to a hundred men, and furnished with beds a good deal inferior to those in a London casual ward. Normally these beds are about 5ft 6in long by 2ft 6in wide, with a hard convex mattress and a cylindrical pillow like a block of wood; sometimes, in the cheaper houses, not even a pillow. The bed-clothes consist of two raw umber-coloured sheets, supposed to be changed once a week, but actually, in many cases, left on for a month, and a cotton counterpane; in winter there may be blankets, but never enough. As often as not the beds are verminous, and the kitchens invariably swarm with cockroaches or black beetles. There are no baths, of course, and no room where any privacy is attainable. The charges paid for this kind of accommodation vary between 7d and 1s 1d a night. It should be added that, low as these charges sound, the average common lodging house brings in something like £40 net profit a week to its owner.

Besides the ordinary dirty lodging houses, there are a few score, such as the Rowton Houses and the Salvation Army hostels, that are clean and decent. Unfortunately, all of these places set off their advantages by a discipline so rigid and tiresome that to stay in them is rather like being in jail. In London the common lodging house where one gets both liberty and a decent bed does not exist.

The curious thing about the squalor and discomfort of the ordinary lodging house is that these exist in places subject to constant inspection by the LCC. When one first sees the murky, troglodytic cave of a common lodging house kitchen, one takes it for a corner of the early nineteenth century which has somehow been missed by the reformers; it is a surprise to find that common lodging houses are governed by a set of minute and (in intention) exceedingly tyrannical rules. According to the regulations, practically everything is against the law in a common lodging house. Gambling, drunkenness, or even the introduction of liquor, swearing, spitting on the floor, keeping tame animals, fighting—in short, the whole social life of these places—are all forbidden. Of course, the law is habitually broken, but some of the rules are enforceable, and they illustrate the dismal uselessness of this kind of legislation.

Lodging house keepers charge 1s for a bed less restful than a heap of straw

To take an instance: some time ago the LCC became concerned about the closeness together of beds in common lodging houses, and enacted that these must be at least 3ft apart. This is the kind of law that is enforceable, and the beds were duly moved. Now, to a lodger in an already overcrowded dormitory it hardly matters whether the beds are 3ft apart or 1ft; but it does matter to the proprietor, whose income depends upon his floor space. The sole real result of this law, therefore, was a general rise in the price of beds. Please notice that though the space between the beds is strictly regulated, nothing is about the beds themselves—nothing, for instance, about their being fit to sleep in. The lodging house keepers can, and do, charge 1s for a bed less restful than a heap of straw.

Another example of LCC regulations. From nearly all common lodging houses women are strictly excluded; there are a few houses specially for women, and a very small number to which both men and women are admitted. It follows that any homeless man who lives regularly in a lodging house is entirely cut off from female society—indeed, cases even happen of man and wife being separated owing to the impossibility of getting accommodation in the same house. And yet a common lodging house is only a hotel at which one pays 8d a night instead of 10s 6d. This kind of petty tyranny can, in fact, only be defended on the theory that a man poor enough to live in a common lodging house thereby forfeits some of his rights as a citizen.

One cannot help feeling that this theory lies behind the LCC rules. All these rules are in the nature of interference-legislation—that is, they interfere, but not for the benefit of the lodgers. Their emphasis is on hygiene and morals, and the question of comfort is left to the lodging house proprietor, who, of course, either shirks it or solves it in the spirit of organised charity. As to cleanliness, no law will ever enforce that, but the sleeping accommodation could easily be brought up to a decent standard. Common lodging houses are places in which one pays to sleep, and most of them fail in their essential purpose, for no one can sleep well in a packed dormitory on a bed as hard as bricks. The LCC would be doing an immense service if they compelled lodging house keepers to divide their dormitories into cubicles and, above all, to provide comfortable beds.

There seems no sense in the principle of licensing all houses for "men only" or "women only", as though men and women were sodium and water and must be kept apart for fear of an explosion; the houses should be licensed for both sexes alike, as they are in some provincial towns. And the lodgers should be protected by law against various swindles which the proprietors and managers are now able to practise on them. Given these conditions, common lodging houses would serve their purpose, which is an important one, far better than they do now. After all, tens of thousands of unemployed and partially employed men have literally no other place in which they can live. It is absurd that they should be compelled to choose, as they are at present, between an easy-going pigsty and a hygienic prison. ●

A photographic portrait of Lawrence by Edward Weston, 1924

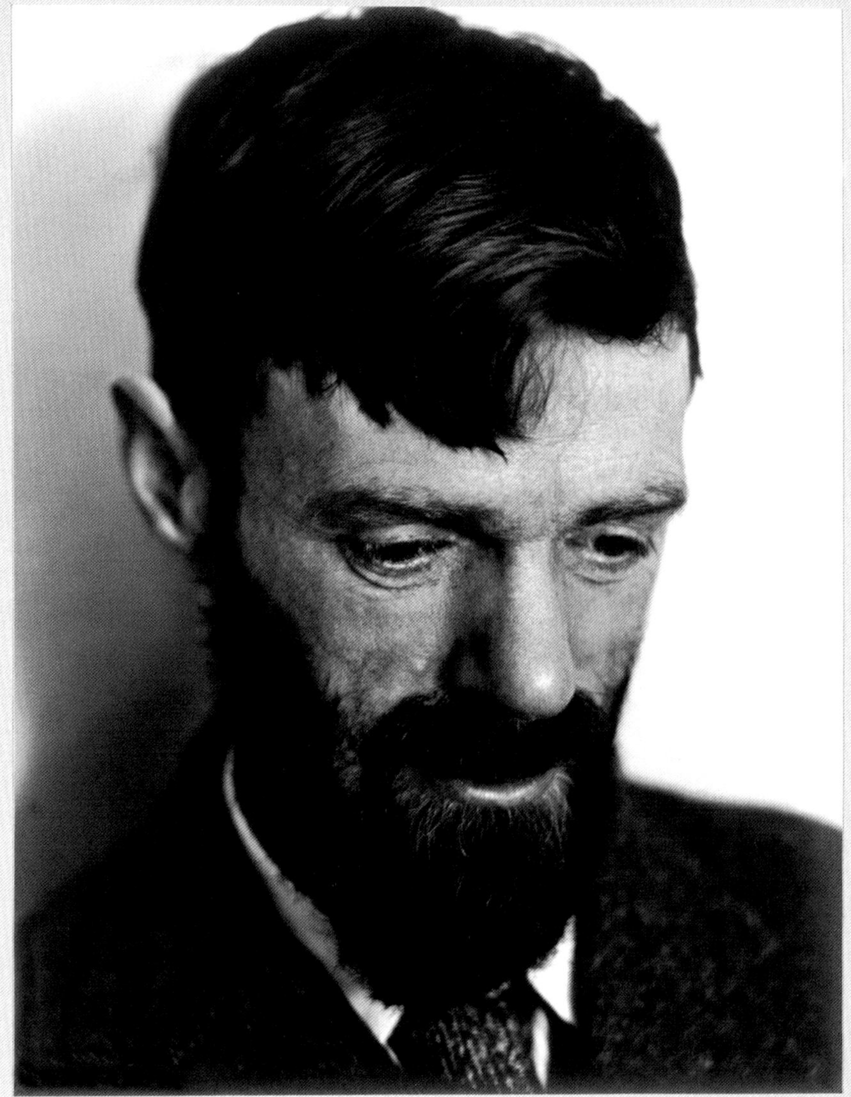

D. H. Lawrence

Edward Weston
Mexico 1924

PUBLISHED 13 OCTOBER 1934, WRITTEN 1928

A Letter from Germany

By D H Lawrence

We are going back to Paris tomorrow, so this is the last moment to write a letter from Germany. Only from the fringe of Germany, too.

It is a miserable journey from Paris to Nancy, through that Marne country, where the country still seems to have had the soul blasted out of it, though the dreary fields are ploughed and level, and the pale wire trees stand up. But it is all void and null. And in the villages, the smashed houses in the street rows, like rotten teeth between good teeth. You come to Strasbourg, and the people still talk Alsatian German, as ever, in spite of French shop-signs. The place feels dead. And full of cotton goods, white goods, from Mülhausen, from the factories that once were German. Such cheap white cotton goods, in a glut.

The cathedral front rearing up high and flat and fanciful, a sort of darkness in the dark, with round rose windows and long, long prisons of stone. Queer that men should have ever wanted to put stone upon faithful stone to such a height without having it fall down. The gothic! I was always glad when my card-castle fell but these goths and alemans seemed to have a craze for peaky heights.

The Rhine is still the Rhine, the great divider. You feel it as you cross. The flat, frozen, watery places. Then the cold and curving river. Then the other side, seeming so forsaken. The train stands and steams fiercely. Then it draws through the flat Rhine plain, past frozen pools of flood-water, and frozen fields, in the emptiness of this bit of occupied territory.

Immediately you are over the Rhine, the spirit of place has changed. There is no more attempt at the bluff of geniality. The marshy places are frozen. The fields are vacant. There seems nobody in the world.

It is as if the life had retreated eastwards. As if the Germanic life were slowly ebbing away from contact with western Europe, ebbing to the deserts of the east. And there stand the heavy, ponderous round hills of the Black Forest, black with an inky blackness of Germanic trees, and patched with a whiteness of snow. They are like a series of huge, involved black mounds, obstructing the vision eastwards. You look at them from the Rhine plain, and you know that you stand on an actual border, up against something.

The moment you are in Germany, you know. It feels empty, and, somehow, menacing. So must the Roman soldiers have watched those black, massive round hills: with a certain fear, and with the knowledge that they were at their own limit. A fear of the invisible natives. A fear of the invisible life lurking among the woods. A fear of their own opposite.

> Out of the very air comes a queer, bristling feeling of uncanny danger

So it is with the French: this almost mystic fear. But one should not insult even one's fears. Germany, this bit of Germany, is very different from what it was two and a half years ago, when I was here. Then it was still open to Europe. Then it still looked to western Europe for a reunion, for a sort of reconciliation. Now that is over. The inevitable, mysterious barrier has fallen again, and the great leaning of the Germanic spirit is once more eastwards towards Russia, towards Tartary. The strange vortex of Tartary has become the positive centre again, the positivity of western Europe is broken. The positivity of our civilisation has broken. The influences that come, come invisibly out of Tartary. So that all Germany reads *Men, Beasts and Gods* with a kind of fascination. Returning again to the fascination of the destructive East, that produced Attila.

So it is at night. Baden-Baden is a quiet place. No more Turgenevs or Dostoevskys or Grand Dukes or King Edwards coming to drink the waters. All the outward effect of a world-famous watering-place. But empty now, a mere Black Forest village with the wagon-loads of timber going through, to the French.

The Rentenmark, the new gold Mark of Germany, is abominably dear. Prices are high in England, but English money buys less in Baden than it buys in London, by a long chalk. And there is no work—consequently no money. Nobody buys anything, except absolute necessities. The shopkeepers are in despair. And there is less and less work.

Everybody gives up the telephone—can't afford it. The tramcars don't run, except about three times a day to the station. Up to the Annaberg, the suburb, the lines are rusty, no trams ever go. The people can't afford the ten Pfennigs for the fare. Ten Pfennigs is an important sum now: one penny. It is really a hundred Milliards of Marks.

Money becomes insane, and people with it.

At night the place is almost dark, economising light. Economy, economy, economy—that, too, becomes an insanity. Luckily the government keeps bread fairly cheap.

But at night you feel strange things stirring in the darkness, strange feelings stirring out of this still-unconquered Black Forest. You stiffen your backbone and you listen to the night. There is a sense of danger. It is not the people. They don't seem dangerous. Out of the very air comes a sense of danger, a queer, *bristling* feeling of uncanny danger.

Something has happened. Something has happened which has not yet eventuated. The old spell of the old world has broken, and the old, bristling, savage spirit has set in. The war did not break the old peace-and-production hope of the world, though it gave it a severe wrench. Yet the old peace-and-production hope still governs, at least the consciousness. Even in Germany it has not quite gone.

But it feels as if, virtually, it were gone. The last two years have done it. The hope in peace-and-production is broken. The old flow, the old adherence is ruptured. And a still older flow has set in. Back, back to the savage ▶

The bristling Black Forest. From *Transitions: the Dresden Project* by Fredrik Marsh

polarity of Tartary, and away from the polarity of civilised Christian Europe. This, it seems to me, has already happened. And it is a happening of far more profound import than any actual *event*. It is the father of the next phase of events.

And the feeling never relaxes. As you travel up the Rhine valley, still the same latent sense of danger, of silence, of suspension. Not that the people are actually planning or plotting or preparing. I don't believe it for a minute. But something has happened to the human soul, beyond all help. The human soul recoiling now from unison, and making itself strong elsewhere. The ancient spirit of prehistoric Germany coming back, at the end of history.

The same in Heidelberg. Heidelberg full, full, full of people. Students the same, youths with rucksacks the same, boys and maidens in gangs come down from the hills. The same, and not the same. These queer gangs of *Young Socialists*, youths and girls, with their non-materialistic professions, their half-mystic assertions, they strike one as strange. Something primitive, like loose, roving gangs of broken, scattered tribes, so they affect one. And the swarms of people somehow produce an impression of silence, of secrecy, of stealth. It is as if everything and everybody recoiled away from the old unison, as barbarians lurking in a wood recoil out of sight. The old habits remain. But the bulk of the people have no money. And the whole stream of feeling is reversed.

So you stand in the woods about the town and see the Neckar flowing green and swift and slippery out of the gulf of Germany, to the Rhine. And the sun sets slow and scarlet into the haze of the Rhine valley. And the old, pinkish stone of the ruined castle across looks sultry, the marshalry is in shadow below, the peaked roofs of old, tight Heidelberg compressed in its river gateway glimmer and glimmer out. There is a blue haze.

Time seems to be whirling with mysterious swiftness to a sort of death

And it all looks as if the years were wheeling swiftly backwards, no more onwards. Like a spring that is broken and whirls swiftly back, so time seems to be whirling with mysterious swiftness to a sort of death. Whirling to the ghost of the old Middle Ages of Germany, then to the Roman days, then to the days of the silent forest and the dangerous, lurking barbarians.

Something about the Germanic races is unalterable. White-skinned, elemental, and dangerous. Our civilisation has come from the fusion of the dark-eyed with the blue. The meeting and mixing and mingling of the two races has been the joy of our ages. And the Celt has been there, alien, but necessary as some chemical reagent to the fusion. So the civilisation of Europe rose up. So these cathedrals and these thoughts.

But now the Celt is the disintegrating agent. And the Latin and southern races are falling out of association with the northern races, the northern Germanic impulse is recoiling towards Tartary, the destructive vortex of Tartary.

It is a fate; nobody now can alter it. It is a fate. The very blood changes. Within the last three years, the very constituency of the blood has changed, in European veins. But particularly in Germanic veins.

At the same time, we have brought it about ourselves—by a Ruhr occupation, by an English nullity, and by a German false will. We have done it ourselves. But apparently it was not to be helped.

Quos vult perdere Deus, dementat prius.

Il Duce emerges on a balcony in this picture from 1931, thought to have been taken by Lady Ottoline Morrell

20 APRIL 1935

The Ministry of Emotion

By Stephen Potter

Even from train windows, it is easy to see real signs of the new, accelerated, martial Italy. Even in the train itself, with its timetable, and the freedom of its staff from such major tricks as the stealing of luggage, or such minor tricks, common three years ago, as selling you pillows at one station, and waking you up at the next to remove them forcibly as "soiled" in the hope that you will buy new ones. Inside and outside the railways are efficient and clean: the foreign coal-dust has all been licked up by the new electric engines.

Beyond, the fields really are cultivated to the margins. Only near Rome does waste grass appear, and one is told of this, that part is the area recently reclaimed from a three-thousand-year-old dynasty of swampy malarial mosquitoes, and part has been ceded to the State because its owners had failed to improve it. On the Appian way, in Rome itself, no rubbish is allowed to collect in the corners of ancient monuments. And there are certainly soldiers, and an atmosphere of uniforms. The guard of this train has a holster at his hip. Not only officers seem able to wear cloaks with the experienced grace of Shakespearean actors, nor can these be all of them mountain troops who add 5 per cent to their height by the tremendous nailiness of their boot-soles. Ranks and uniforms are so numerous that porters, postmen and black-shirts merge into one overwhelming soldierish majority.

"Soldierish" rather than "militarist", if there is such a distinction. For once in Italy, walking about in Rome, it is easy to observe, from these very soldiers, that there is little alteration in the Italians themselves. That there is something here which must be absolutely distinguished from the boring, inhuman, German militarism. Watch them marching. No detachment, however small, marches without a band. Often it is a band and nothing else. And there is no correct playing, elbows stiff, of toneless march music, but a gay comic opera tune, with bugles waving from left to right to balance the marcher, heads bowing in exaggerated time to the music, exactly like children playing. It is true that foreign correspondents sometimes give a different picture. I observed on blank walls the sign "W DUCE", which they have told us about, and knew that it meant "Long Live the Duce". Or "W Fascismo", I saw. And I moralised on the fact that in this country a "W RAMSAY" would not live five minutes without some rude addition, whereas in Italy the signs

receive no such defacement. But my respectful interest was suddenly turned to righteous indignation when I saw next to a "W Duce" a "W GUERRA" and other sinister words which I could not translate.

It was only by chance that I found out that "GUERRA " did not stand for WAR, but was the name of a champion bicyclist. The Italians are still too gay, and their climate is still too sunny, for them to be fanatical very long, or very exclusively. All the more wonder, that on this unteachable race, least susceptible to logic, whose national characteristic for fifteen hundred years has been an inability to be loyal to anything larger than a town, a race incapable of acting to rule (whether *Thou shalt not kill*, or *Thou shalt use hand signals when driving a car*), should have been imposed a new Italy logical, obedient, and unified.

The world's answer to this problem—"Mussolini"—needs some elaboration. Mussolini himself, it seems, is the most scientific of men. Critics are misled by his face, an intensification of a well-known Italian type which happens to follow rhetorical "strong man" lines. But he is not at all above being amused at himself, and at the fantastic extent of his power. Ministers, ambassadors, etc, are given to understand that Mussolini prefers a good joke to salaams at the end of an interview. His personal life is much more domestic than imperial. He seems to have no thoughts of money, taking a small, unspecified, and variable allowance from the State when he wants it. His working time is beautifully organised down to five hours a day.

Italian soldiers of the 1914 generation get drafted into the new national army, April 1935

GAMMA-KEYSTONE VIA GETTY IMAGES

But one of Mussolini's specialities, indeed his most notable gift, is certainly a talent for rhetoric. As an orator, he must not be judged by English standards. In Italy, the emotional sequence follows classical lines. It is a rhetoric of *onward . . . idealism . . . forward ye peoples*. Of this kind of speech, Mussolini is an academic master. However rational he may be as an explainer of policy in speeches when rhetoric is not pertinent, it is by his emotive oratory that he is known. He himself has seen to that. For Mussolini has added another to his many portfolios. He is minister of emotion. The ramifications of this office are wide, and extend far beyond speech making. In Rome, its works are ever present. Towering above all is the Emotion headquarters, the Victor Emmanuele monument, which last week seemed to be in better form than ever, floodlit, and lined with hundreds of flickering lamps for an anniversary. In the Rome beneath, the subordinates of the department are at work. The news placard announces an Italian football victory over Austria as NEW TRIUMPH FOR FASCIST SPORT. In the movie of *Cleopatra* (Cecil B de Mille), which I had seen in London, it was noticeable that Caesar's rapid, dictatorish walk was popular with an amused Roman audience. Would there be any special reaction to the assassination *et tu Brute* scene? It was cut out. The department will not allow the possibility of such an act to be even suggested.

But most obvious in Rome last week were the bookshops. Photographs of the Duce were obscured by maps, filling half the window. Each map showed North-East Africa, and on each the Italian possessions were painted green, looking strangely large against the uncoloured remainder. Even from the other side of the street one could see, in the Ethiopean corner, green Italian land bearing down on the pale, colourless Abyssinia.

The Italians are still too gay for them to be fanatical very long

In this kind of organisation, surely, is to be found one explanation of Mussolini's power. It certainly seems to be the explanation of his mysterious aggressiveness in Abyssinia. Mussolini, so careful to keep his relations with big powers cordial; Mussolini, whose kind of dictatorship has begun lately to seem so admirable a contrast to Hitler's, appears to be about to perform an act of blatantly Nazi bellicosity. Common-sense reasons for such a war, whatever penetrations of Africa Germany or Japan may be contemplating, seem such as must appear to the Duce, even if his Achilles heel is a Roman mania for expansion, negligible. But for a director of public feeling, such a war would have much to recommend it. United Italy has never, till now, been united. Difficult as we find it to imagine a time when its big-gum-boot shape was not part of the map, it is one of Europe's most recent additions. Nor, so far, has Italy ever won a war, however many times the Italian children are made to recite "Italy won the war at the battle of Vittorio Veneto". More pertinently still, even the children know that at Adowa, in Abyssinia, the Italians suffered a disgraceful reverse. Now can Adowa be avenged—indeed the department have been preparing for this line of thought by maintaining that Adowa was a disaster, but not a defeat: a setback in the gradual "civilisation" of a barbaric race now at last about to be completed. One small victory is all that is required, and in the course of winning it the sending off of troop-trains, the effective use of beautiful Italian engines in the mechanised divisions, and the triumphant return of not too badly wounded war heroes, will bind the bound *fascisti* closer than ever.

Mussolini will know how to build triumphal arches over the measliest strip of semi-desert acquisition. It is all part of his daily round. For it is by giving the governing to the governors, and emotions to the people, that he has succeeded in setting up the world's least democratic, most scientific rule (bar Russia) in the country least likely to submit to it. ●

We create
chemistry

2 OCTOBER 1943

Famine in India

By An Anonymous Soldier

"There's a famine down there," they told me. Probably people dying and so forth.

I knew that, of course—had read about it in the paper—but on the eve of my move I pigeonholed and forgot the information. Anyway, poverty is so ever present in India that forgetting is a protective armour.

On the journey I had too much to do to think of the people or the country. This was a Company move, and I was responsible for 150 Indian troops from the hills, in land as foreign to them as it was to me.

After a couple of days of slow journeying, we changed trains at a fair-sized junction. Fires were started and food prepared on the platform. I had to make some arrangements, and when I returned the men were all eating. This was the first time I saw the beggars. They were not like other Indian beggars, calling for an anna from a passing train. These people did not ask for money. They wanted food, and they stood there watching the men of their own nation cooking and eating. I counted about 30 of these beggars as they clustered on the railway line between the two platforms; they were of all ages and in one condition; the majority were women; some were blind and all were ill. One old man, tall, with a fine head and straggly beard was being led by a woman; his sightless eyes looked up high over the heads of those squatting on the platform. Some of the beggars were silent and a very few were still; most were watching closely, for occasionally, as a man finished his food, he would walk to the edge and sweep the scraps on to the line. The watchers, who had drawn closer, rushed forward then and scraped in the dirt for the few grains of rice, until they were driven back by a couple of railwaymen.

The blind old man, at these times, hearing the movement and the shouts, made a low noise rather like a whine, perhaps an echo of days when he had been a prosperous beggar. For the more romantic of my readers I say with reluctance that this old man had no more dignity than the others. His head was lifted and twisted on a scraggy neck; he was very dirty and his rags revealed no suspicion of former beauty. He was hungry. Like the other beggars he had a small cloth and a tin which he held out for scraps. The men of my Company were rather embarrassed and when I arrived were giving the remains of their food in a hurried way, as though the giving were distasteful.

We left that place with few regrets and soon after approached our destination. All along the line we met these train beggars—railway stations seem to be the hope of those who can walk from their village. The children were the most pitiful; naked boys and girls with no flesh or large pot-bellies lined the train.

One day I went into a stationmaster's office to borrow his timetable. I sat facing him, my back to the door, when I heard someone come in and stand beside me. I looked up. He was a tall Indian, not very well dressed, rather the ordinary type of matriculate in the middle twenties that abounds in India. But he spoke excellent English. He stood still and straight and over my shoulder spoke to the stationmaster. "Excuse me, there is a man on the platform out there in a dying condition. Is there anything you can do? I will gladly pay the cost."

The stationmaster did not appear to have heard. The other waited. After about a minute the stationmaster finished writing, blotted the last words and reached for a small scrap of paper. Without turning his head he shouted: "Oh, Chowkidar!"—An old man appeared. "Take this," the stationmaster said in his language, "and give it to the policeman on duty."

Then he turned to the stranger. "The police know what to do," he said shortly. The tall Indian, obviously dubious, left the room.

The poor man's burden: cartoon by Vicky (*NS*, 1962)

"Do you get many of them?" I asked the stationmaster.

"Two or three a day," he answered in the same tone. "We can do nothing."

About ten minutes later I left and had lunch in the station refreshment room—a plate heaped high with eggs, fish, bread, bacon and beans, costing Rs1.8. An hour later, I strolled on to the platform to look for my train.

The dead man was still there. He was lying half in a pool of water, near the edge of the platform on his back, his face uncovered, except for the flies. He was not old, in rags, the skin stretched over his bones. What movement his discoverer had seen had most certainly ceased. I spoke to a naked little boy on the platform—which was full, though no one was paying attention to the body.

"Is he dead?" I asked.

The child's face lit up and he smiled.

"Oh, yes," he said, "he's dead."

Two days later I came through the same station and stopped again to change trains. About five yards from where the dead man had lain was another body—this time the face was covered. I went to see the stationmaster.

"There's another dead man there," I told him.

"I know," he answered as before, "the sweepers will take it away." I suppose I looked what I felt, for suddenly his reserve went and he talked rapidly, his English suffering a little.

"What can we do?" he said. "We can do nothing. Every day they come here and die. Two and three of them. For us there is nothing to do. They get no food in the village that used to support them. Mostly they are people with no land and no family. They suffer the first. The other day, let me tell you something. I was there, sitting in my office when an old man and a little girl came right inside, the little girl begging for food. I was about to turn them out, when the old man dropped dead at my feet. Right at my feet. Just dropped dead. What could I do? I gave the little girl some money for food. Before night she was dead also.

"And I will tell you something," he added, "that little girl was the same age as my little girl. That's what I thought. She's the same age as my little girl." ●

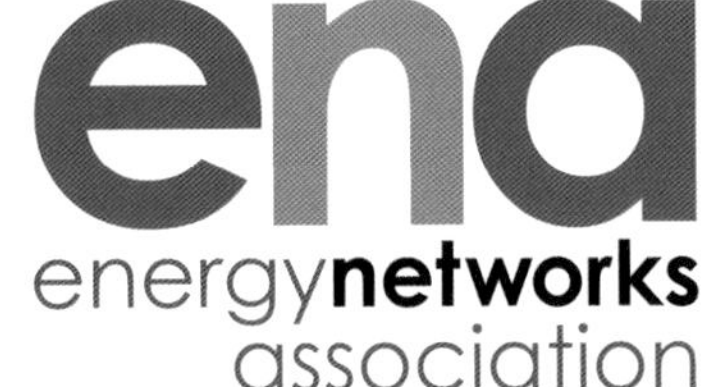

The Voice of the Networks

Shaping a smarter future

by David Smith CEO

Picture the scene. It's a rainy rush hour in a busy metropolis. The tubes are packed, the roads are busy and everyone is miserable, wet, and wants to get home. Then the power goes off. Everything powered by electricity stops. Stations go dark, traffic lights are blank and equipment and appliances fall silent. That was the scene in South London and North West Kent in August 2003. This was a failure in that vital component of the energy system – the transmission and distribution networks – 'the Grid'. It lasted barely half an hour but happens so rarely, especially on that scale, that it was dramatic.

As one of the most reliable electricity grids in the world we take it for granted. It's been around for over 70 years. But challenges lie ahead of us that will see it change beyond recognition. As we embark on a new low carbon world, the problem for the energy industry is that our consumers, who in the long run hold the key to our energy future, have no sense of personal responsibility as far as energy is concerned – and who can blame them. Energy is one of the constants in our lives. We switch it on and switch it off with as little thought as we draw the curtains or open our front door. If we think about it at all we are only interested in keeping the lights on and the bills down. So how do we meet these expectations and deliver carbon reductions at the same time? The key to the solution are those very energy networks that ensure the lights stay on.

The energy networks are the hub that will facilitate the necessary change. Our homes were built with only a certain amount of electricity capacity in mind and the copper was put in the ground to provide it. With the greater use of renewables, solar panels on homes and electric vehicles there will need to be a smarter approach to managing our demand than just more expensive copper. The development of a smarter network and in time a fully integrated smart grid are critical to achieving this.

Put simply it is about getting more from our existing assets. It is about showing people that we can deliver a low carbon world without sending bills sky high. And this is happening now. In the Orkney's using a smarter network to integrate new wind generation cost only £500,000 rather than the £30m of conventional network investment that would have been needed. That is what a smarter network means in reality; delivering low carbon secure energy at a low cost.

To deliver real energy change will need the active participation of the public. Now we have a major opportunity as we embark on the smart meter roll-out, the largest consumer engagement programme ever, to educate everyone about how they can help themselves. Without everyone doing their little bit, the challenge of meeting capacity at peak times will continue to grow. A collaborative approach is needed.

Network companies are delivering projects like that in the Orkneys across the UK through the Low Carbon Networks Fund (LCN Fund). The hugely successful annual LCN Fund Conference, hosted by ENA, has offered a glimpse of our energy future. Now we are sharing this learning globally through the Smarter Networks Portal, the first of its kind. Through this we hope to be able to inspire even more.

So the clear message from the networks is we are the enablers of our sustainable, secure and affordable energy future. We've come a long way since Faraday and the creation of the national grid over 70 years ago, but the developments so far will be dwarfed by what will come next. We welcome the changes ahead as a time of great opportunity. A revitalised industry, a boost to introduce innovation and all while delivering on a reliable and cost-effective network for the future. It's a major challenge too, but we're preparing for tomorrow's networks today.

www.energynetworks.org 

10 NOVEMBER 1956

Hungary's Feast of the Dead

By Bruce Renton

There was a smell of mouldering corpses outside the Hungarian parliament. It was dusk, and the great bridges linking Buda and Pest over the Danube, catching the last rays of an autumn sun, were all one could recognise of the Budapest that was. The population hurried over the rubble in Rakosi Street. They crowded round the cars of the western journalists. For the moment they paid no attention to the youths nearby engaged in tommy-gun battles with the last of the AVO secret police troops in the houses. The revolution seemed to have been won. The trophy of an Italian colleague brought home to me the fact that this had been a revolution in the real and full sense of the word: it was the blue-banded hat of an AVO officer. The previous owner was hanging by his feet from the yellow-leaved branches of the trees outside the AVO central barracks on the Pest bank of the Danube.

A strange silence, broken by the whine of stray bullets, fell over the stricken city as the news got around that 200 Russian tanks were moving into positions around the city. At the Hotel Duna a babble of western journalists tried vainly to get through to their capitals. Embassies were burning documents. Columns of rebels responded to Russian tanks by moving to the outskirts of the city. One suddenly realised that they could no longer be called "rebels"; they were Hungarians.

Budapest that night was a city of candles. From afar it had at times a Scandinavian Christmas air. Candles in the windows of the houses, candles in the cemeteries, candles over the corpses of freedom fighters stretched out and draped in green, red and white flags in Republic Square, in a great feast of the dead. Boys, solemn and determined, tearless, lit candles on the spot where their fathers had fallen. But the faces of the AVO troops whose bodies were heaped in the square had been crushed and spat on. Scores of cigarette ends had burned them beyond recognition. Parliament Square was silent, save for a few weeping women who crossed themselves before the candles under the walls of Parliament.

It seems hopeless to continue this correspondence. As we raced madly back to the Italian legation, shooting in the squares helped us lose ourselves in the now deserted, dark and rubble-covered streets. There was a row with an embassy employee whose baby Fiat 600 we had smashed that day. Several hundred dollars changed hands—almost as if dollars were no longer worth anything. It was a nightmare dash for the road to Vienna. At one point the freedom fighters, with the aid of guns, only just prevented us from driving into the Russian tanks. A youth in a military raincoat, two pistols in his pockets, waved the direction of Vienna with one of them, and shouted after us in the darkness, "*Danke, danke, danke fur alles.*" It was a forlorn cry that I took away from Hungary. The freedom fighters jumped out at every corner, poking barrels through the car windows, looking for escaping AVO troops. Their hands shook and they were ready to die or kill. The Russian troops guarding the marshalling yards at Komaron were out in battle array, as we raced along the bank of the Danube with the Czech border on the other side. In the morning those same Russians, who would soon be busy with slaughter, had smiled and waved at us. Not until then had I fully understood the significance of the "smile policy".

> The Russians were bringing down the curtain with a bang and a massacre

The Russians were bringing down the curtain with a bang and a massacre. I remembered that when I had first arrived at the Hungarian frontier a week before, and we had all jumped on to a Hungarian lorry which had loaded up with Austrian newspapers at Vienna, it had seemed utterly incredible that this brave, enthusiastic people had freed itself. There had to be a catch somewhere. It was the sight of the red flags burning underneath the walls of the Györ town hall that frightened me. It was the sight of the Hungarian girls carrying away the remains of massive red stars. It was the complete, spontaneous and violent destruction of the Communist regime. It did not make sense. The Russians were bound to react by massing an entire panzer army—and not for Hungary alone. We were all convinced that the tanks which were moving towards the Austrian border from the Pressburg bridge on the Czech frontier were not intended merely for Hungary. In Györ, the first large town inside Hungary, the people had trampled on each other to snatch the western newspapers from our hands. They had yelled in a wild enthusiasm.

Now in Györ there was black grief. There was not much time—one could feel it in the air. But we stopped to say goodbye to our new friends. I went into the house of a young doctor who was a member of the Györ freedom committee. His family slept on mattresses on the floor, his armchairs were in an advanced state of decomposition.

"The British and the French betrayed us," he said. "To attack Egypt now was to make a dirty bargain of the Hungarian people. The panzers came in from the Ukraine, crossed the frontier after Suez." I gave him fruit and chocolate. "If the Russians attack," he said, "we shall all die." He pointed to the round, close-cropped head of his baby boy, who was eating the first and probably the last banana of his life. "We can never go back to what we were," said the doctor. "He will die, too."

And as I write, Russian tanks are attacking Györ. ●

How to change the balance of power

By Catherine Mitchell

The only way to counter fuel poverty and rising prices is to switch on a new, broad-based energy policy

Energy and its uses over the past century can be linked to differing policy frameworks: the one in place before the Second World War; the statism that came in after the war; the one developed by Thatcher at the end of the 1980s; and – as yet unfulfilled – the framework we need to adopt in this age of climate change and resource concerns. Each paradigm has been (or will be) based on different technologies and fuels, different economic growth models and different drivers, as well as different views of stakeholder rights and ways of making decisions.

The current energy policy is to reduce carbon emissions by 80 per cent – compared to 1990 levels – by 2050, in order to have a chance of staying within a 2° global warming limit. The energy system we will need in order to meet our targets will be nothing like the one in place today. Moreover, the rate of change required is unprecedented and we will need to devise a system capable of adapting.

However, we have inherited six key challenges that raise concerns over our ability to undertake the transition successfully:

- Our centralised energy system;
- The dominance of a few large companies that expect to make money selling energy;
- The laissez-faire, market-oriented policy paradigm, including our system of regulation, which undermines a strategic approach.

Together, these result in:

- the inflexible way we operate the system;
- the lack of headway made in renewables and in improving energy efficiency;
- the difficulties of innovating, whether it be with technologies, new entrants, new business models, new modes of operating or new relationships with energy, such as local authority or customer involvement.

Centralisation

The great bulk of energy used in Britain between 1913 and 1956 came from coal. It served as solid fuel for heating homes and for industry; it was the fuel for electricity, for railways, and even the basis for "town gas", distributed through a pipe network.

The remainder came mainly from hydro and wind stations. At that time, the suppliers of energy were either small private companies (for example, a privately owned coal mine or group of mines or electricity-producing power plant) or municipally owned electricity and gas providers.

> Energy policy needs to be meshed with the needs of society

It was the Second World War that altered this model under the Attlee government. Coal, electricity and gas were brought into national ownership: the National Coal Board, the British Electricity Authority (which became the Central Electricity Generation Board in 1957) and 12 regional gas boards. One critical reason behind the co-ordination of assets into state hands was to ensure security, safety and standards (including costs to customers) across the various industries and geographical locations.

With the advent of nuclear weapons, nuclear power became an important new source of energy. The United Kingdom Atomic Energy Authority was set up in 1954 to oversee the development of civil nuclear power in Britain, and Calder Hall opened in 1956 as the country's first provider of nuclear energy. This development has tied Britain, first, into a powerful and mutually supportive civil and military nuclear relationship and, second, into a centralised electricity system, because nuclear power is a large and inflexible technology that requires all other electricity technologies to fit around it.

The 1973 oil shock

The use of oil for transport and as a fuel for electricity was minimal up until the Second World War. Afterwards, when manufacturing took off and automobiles became affordable for a bigger percentage of the population, oil use began to rise sharply. There was little domestic onshore production in the petroleum industries (though oil had been found in Britain from the mid-1800s) and most of the oil we used was imported from the Middle East. However, the 1973 "oil shock" – the Arab embargo imposed as punishment for US intervention in Israel – was a fundamental driver of new attitudes to energy. The rapid understanding of the extent to which western countries had become dependent on cheap Middle Eastern oil fundamentally altered energy policy around the world, though in very different ways depending on the country.

Britain's reaction to the oil shock was to speed up its exploration and development of the North Sea for both oil and gas – thereby merely swapping Middle Eastern oil for a closer neighbour. We did not take the opportunity to diversify from oil or gas, or even husband what we had. As a result, while Britain rapidly became almost self-sufficient in those energy sources, North Sea oil peaked in 2001. Natural gas peaked a few years later.

Market ideology and corporate dominance

The energy privatisations (gas in 1986, coal in 1987, electricity in 1990 and nuclear in 1996) were intended to depoliticise energy policy

GLOBAL WARMING IMAGES/REX FEATURES

and improve the efficiency of each sector. The effects of privatisation have varied across these industries, but in post-privatisation electricity the business continued to be dominated by large companies (rather than state-owned institutions), centralised technologies and practices, and continued to lock out new entrants, new business models, decentralised technologies and any serious attempts to reduce energy use.

The "independent" regulators established a clear procedural process for change dominated by incumbent interests. The rules and incentives set up at privatisation "fit" the technologies and structures in place, and were meant to ensure that the early investors (called "Sids" after British Gas advertisements urged consumers to "tell Sid" about applying for shares) would not lose money. Each decade brings another attempt to shape energy more to the needs of society. However, no government so far has been prepared to take on the might of the conventional, centralised energy system; each change further entrenches the incumbents, as we are experiencing now under electricity-market reform.

The demands of climate change

There have been numerous studies investigating the technological pathways we could take to meet our greenhouse-gas and carbon-emissions targets. The choice of pathways has enormous effect on society, as costs are spent at different times and in different areas. While the total costs of either pathway might be similar, the indirect and distributional impacts are far from homogeneous.

As such, energy policy must mesh with the vision of what we want as a society. Britain, with its market-based economy, is neither used to thinking in these terms nor capable of implementing such a vision, even if it had one. As is becoming clear from the efforts of Denmark and Germany, long-term structural change requires a more managed strategy. This is not turning our backs on markets: rather, it is being open-minded about the possible ways for us to reach our desired outcomes.

Affordability in a multipolar world

The rapid development of the emerging economies over the past decade has altered global markets. These economies suck resources and energy, causing fossil-fuel and resource prices to rise, raising costs of goods and food around the world, and also affecting long-standing relationships between energy producer and consumer countries.

The present expense of moving towards sustainability (by developing nuclear power, renewable energy, infrastructure upgrades, energy efficiency measures, and so on) is an added cost to the system. Yet by far the biggest cost has resulted from global fossil-fuel price rises and spikes, which can only get worse. Britain's notion of energy security is having to adapt to this new, multipolar reality but, more immediately, the political issue of affordability has become ever more critical.

Fuel poverty is dependent on quality of housing, on incomes and on the cost of energy, and is generally defined as when more than 10 per cent of one's net income is spent on energy. Britain has always had a high number of fuel-poor because of the poor quality of our buildings. This last is not unique to Britain, but what has been unique is our inability (or lack of will) to upgrade. However, the rising costs of fossil fuels, coupled with the costs of energy transition, have widened the political focus of affordability from the fuel-poor to society at large. It is risky to predict where oil and gas prices are going, but the long-term structural demand based on rising use in the emerging economies points to higher prices.

The only way for people to lower their bills or keep them stable is to use less energy, so that even though prices may rise, bills stay stagnant. Efficiency is therefore central to addressing fuel poverty and affordability issues in wider society. It is also beneficial, improving comfort in the home and energy security and helping to reduce climate change. Why, then, have our efforts on this score been so paltry? Success will occur only when the large companies find their ability to sell limitless energy capped, or explore new areas for profit. The rules of access to the energy system, the costs and the means of making money, are all under the influence of the regulator. Until these rules and incentives are geared towards a sustainable economy and opened up to new practices, we will make little headway.

How well is Britain set?

Global energy systems have entered a phase of efficiency, flexibility and resilience based on "smart" communication technologies. This is not necessarily entirely decentralised – there might be some large hydro, wind or gas power plants involved – but its momentum runs opposite to that of the British system.

Energy policy needs to be meshed with society's needs. In other words, it needs to become part of a sustainable growth strategy.

The essential requirement is to make energy policy understandable and relevant to life: not only to ensure that our children and grandchildren don't live in a world negatively and materially affected by climate change but also to introduce energy systems that offer opportunities for prosperity to society.

Thatcherism had resonance with a swath of Britain because Margaret Thatcher created an aura of opportunity. From a Labour perspective, green social democracy in a multipolar world needs to provide that same sense of opportunity, and it could – not least as a buffer from world fossil-fuel prices, spiralling costs of nuclear power and nuclear waste. But this will not happen under the present electricity-market reform, which serves as just one more entrenchment on behalf of an inflexible, centralised system. The Labour Party will have to bite the bullet and stand clearly behind a more managed energy transition. ●

Catherine Mitchell is Professor of Energy Policy at the University of Exeter

Critical thinking at the critical time™

The UK will explore shale gas, and so it should

By **Kerstin Duhme,**
Managing Director, Head of the Brussels Energy Practice, FTI Consulting

The prospect of shale gas has been approaching Europe for a few years now. People in the UK have increasingly found the words hydraulic fracturing, fracking and shale gas entering their vocabulary. We have also been hearing of the benefits and the potential risks based on the US experience.

However, with growing public attention to the issue in the UK, alongside academic studies and political scrutiny, the facts about shale gas development are becoming clearer and, as a result, support for shale gas is increasing. The UK has therefore set a course to embark on exploratory drilling of its shale gas resources, and it is right to do so.

All media articles about shale gas begin with looking at the US experience, and there is clearly no doubt that shale's impact has revolutionised the US energy sector. The price of gas in the US has plummeted and led to increased investment in gas-fired power stations. This has secured lower energy prices for industry and consumers alike and has also contributed - alongside a growing renewable energy sector - to the US cutting its carbon dioxide emissions by more than any other country in the last five years. Due to the extent of gas available, the US is now looking to become one of the world's main suppliers of natural gas.

Shale gas development is also fostering new jobs in the oil and gas industry in addition to other sectors of the economy able to benefit from improved access to cheap natural gas. Given this, there is little surprise that the last European Council Summit focussed on how Europe could put its own indigenous energy resources to use, in order to introduce a similar boost to its economic competitiveness.

The UK in particular is currently behind the stage of shale gas development in the US (the UK has only performed a partial hydraulic fracture of one shale gas well so far). Yet, the nascent shale gas industry in the UK has openly engaged with years of scrutiny and is set to restart exploration in 2014. Cuadrilla, who have been active in the Bowland Shale in Lancashire, recently joined forces with Centrica who invested heavily in the company's concession, giving greater industry drive and experience to the UK's exploration efforts. Cuadrilla estimates there could be 200 trillion cubic feet of gas in Lancashire, and if a fraction of this can be produced it will have a considerable effect on the UK's gas supply and economy. Indeed, a recent study from the Institute of Directors estimated that potential production phase investment in the UK could peak at £3.7 billion a year and support 74,000 jobs.

In addition, the UK government has moved to endorse the exploration for shale gas, with the Chancellor of the Exchequer championing the resource's potential effect on the economy. This decision has been made in a responsible manner, with the Secretary of State for Energy and Climate Change making clear that the interests of the environment and community groups will always be taken into account in the UK, whilst not standing in the way of exploring the opportunity.

The academic community has also responded to these developments. Many universities are engaged in studying and explaining the effects of shale gas production in Europe. In particular, Durham University is running a leading European research programme on the issue and the British Geological Survey is investigating the UK's shale gas. The strong engagement of the UK's academic institutions in this debate will continue to foster a more fact-based discussion of shale gas in the UK's media and an avoidance of the misinformation which has plagued the debate in other European states.

Similarly, the role of FTI Consulting in Europe's move to explore shale gas is to ensure that any current lack of information is addressed and to bring clarity on industry's activities through media, academic and government sources. FTI Consulting has been working for many years with the major, global shale gas companies in the US, Canada and Europe to assist them in these efforts. The situation remains the same in each region we work in: people want more reputable information on the industry and industry is reacting to these calls.

In the UK in particular, the position of the different sections of society – industry, government, academia and media – means that the country has the potential to take a leading position in Europe to successfully and responsibly begin developing shale gas; based on a good public understanding of what shale gas development is and what it means for the UK. Indeed, recent research by the University of Nottingham, published in March, showed that public understanding and acceptance of shale gas had slightly improved over the past year in the UK, with the percentage of people responding that shale gas extraction should be allowed in the UK rising to 55%.

Overall, it appears the UK will start to explore its shale gas resources in some form, however the extent and pace at which this happens remains to be seen. What is clear is that the UK is in a good position to take these next steps.

Email:
Kerstin.Duhme@fticonsulting.com

Under a Misapprehension

By James Fenton

A man called Kolley Kibber goes down to Brighton and becomes convinced he is about to be murdered? Ridiculous. I gave up the book after a few pages and began to go over my code of conduct on arrival in Belfast. Above all, be vigilant, circumspect and discreet. Do not, if you value your life, be found talking to children. At some point, I told myself, you will find yourself in an impossible hole. Don't panic, and don't try to be clever.

The first time I visited Belfast, for instance, I set out to find my IRA contacts and walked straight into trouble. I was going down a desolated street early on a Sunday morning when I became aware of an army barricade at the other end. Halfway along the street, deciding to try a different route, I turned round and, in a slight access of nerves, lit a cigarette. Immediately I was challenged by the armed soldier at the post. I explained that I was looking for a street adjacent to my actual destination. What I did not know was that it had been levelled to the ground months before. There was no possible reason, on a cold November morning, to be visiting it, and the Protestant vigilante who was with the soldier found my explanations, shouted down the empty road, most unsatisfactory. Immediately afterwards I learnt to my cost about not talking to children.

On this occasion, however, I was determined not to do or say anything silly. One afternoon I took a two-shilling taxi up to Andersonstown, in order to join one of the prongs of the PD [People's Democracy] march. I arrived a little early, nobody was around, and in order to while away the time I entered a local pub. Within a couple of minutes I was joined by three youths of about 17, who as they sat down appeared to be mumbling something for me to hear. I think I indicated in my polite way that, yes, the table was free and they were welcome to join me. Then I noticed that they all appeared to be carrying something bulky under their coats. Finally I caught what they were saying, which was: "Put your hands on the table, and don't try anything clever."

We all sat there terrified out of our wits and before I could say "You are the Provisional IRA and I claim my five pounds" one of them whispered: "We are the Provisional IRA and watch out because we've got a gun on you."

Rebels without a cause: a Provo mural in Belfast

PETER TURNLEY/CORBIS

I didn't, on reflection, believe them about the gun, but that wasn't really the main point. What worried me, when they were unconvinced by my press card, was the fact that my pockets were full of documents relating to arms searches. This was difficult to explain away. "Look," I said, "if I was an army or RUC spy, as you claim, would I have come in here with so little identification but carrying all these figures?" They replied that they had seen much worse cases than this. So we sat there, and during the half-hour that followed, while someone went to check what they should do, they bought me drinks and gave me cigarettes like a man about to be shot.

> Their main concern was to avoid appearing like bandits

The irony of the situation was that when I told the truth about my general attitude to the IRA nobody believed me. Gradually therefore, as garrulousness and stout began to tell, I began questioning them and criticising the politics of the Provisionals. They in turn asked me about life in England, and I must say the Catholic Church should congratulate itself on having produced such a set of high-minded bigots. Our first clash came over the question of drugs. "You must admit," they said, "that in Ireland the working people have put an end to all that." Later, after I had been taken by car to another part of Andersonstown and made to sit in an upstairs room (on the floor, for fear of the ubiquitous army surveillance), I asked them about their ultimate political aims. Suppose, I said, the IRA won tomorrow, and a United Irish state under their political domination was set up, what would they do with their success? How would they change society? The most articulate of the youths thought for a moment and simply replied: "I suppose we would just clean up the dirt."

Is it right to judge a movement by its young recruits? Clearly not, though the complete lack of political direction in my captors' minds was to a large extent a reflection of their leadership. Their main concern was to avoid appearing like bandits: after the initial histrionics, as I was passed from hand to hand to more senior officers, and as the contents of my pockets were scrutinised with blank incomprehension, every propriety was observed.

My money for instance was carefully counted out and returned to me in full. I was given continual assurances that there was no connection between the IRA and the recent spate of assassinations, and that I was not about to become another statistic. It was very comforting, and built up into a picture of an organisation desperately striving for some kind of respectability. When I was finally identified and independently vouched for, three hours after the original incident, we shook hands and parted on the best of terms.

But I kicked myself all the way back to the hotel for having behaved like a carefree man in a quite embattled town. And I had forgotten to ask what would have happened to me had I in fact been a spy. To calm myself, I ran a hot bath and settled down with a book. A man called Kolley Kibber had gone down to Brighton and became convinced that he was about to be murdered. Somehow I knew I was not going to get very far with this one. ●

14 DECEMBER 1973

The Greek Lesson

By Christopher Hitchens

The following report is as remarkable for what it does not say as what it does. In December 1973, a 24-year-old Christopher Hitchens flew to Athens to identify his mother's body after she killed herself in a suicide pact with her lover. Despite the "lacerating howling moment", as he called it in his memoir "Hitch-22", he wrote about the deteriorating political situation in Greece as institutions collapsed around him.

Athens Polytechnic, November 1973

When young students and workers drove back the police around Athens Polytechnic and broadcast their appeal to the nation over a pirate radio, they put an end to nearly seven years of suspended animation in Greek politics. The departure of [Colonel Georgios] Papadopoulos has not gone any way towards solving the resulting crisis, and more cracks appear daily in the ranks of army, church and state.

In the office of Captain Nicolas Balaskas, of the First District Athens Police Station in Lekkas Street, I saw three objects on the walls. The first was the symbol of military rule – a phoenix framing a soldier with a bayonet and the legend "21 April, 1967", date of the first coup. The second was a cabinet with the words "ITT Greece", and the third was a sentimental picture of Jesus Christ. These three tokens, and their setting, are a fair representation of the unholy trinity that runs Greece today, which now ponders how to reproduce itself after the total discrediting of Papadopoulos. Things which a year ago were described as foreign-inspired propaganda are now said openly by tame hacks – that the old regime was corrupt, despotic and incompetent. The Greeks notice this change of tone, and could be forgiven for expecting some changes to be made. But none is forthcoming; if anything the lid is clamped down even more tightly than before. *Vradyni*, the paper which had been most critical, was closed by the military police last week.

Fresh reports come in daily of arrests and disappearances, with the usual tales of horror from the barracks at the city's edge where hundreds of people are still held at the regime's pleasure. Literally nobody believes that the real figure for deaths is less than 50, and I met one man who had his bullet wound treated privately because he knew that the hospitals were death traps.

The effect of all this has been to produce an enormous cynicism and contempt in the minds of ordinary Greeks. "We are making progress," they say; "it is now 22 April 1967." And they are well aware that power is held by a man whose face nobody has really ever seen – Brigadier Ioannides, head of ESA, the military police whose HQ opposite the American Embassy was the only organ of the old regime which could inspire terror as well as dislike.

A striking feature of the new situation created by the street rebellion is that the initiative has passed, perhaps for good, from the old politicians like [Konstantinos] Karamanlis, [Panagiotis] Kanellopoulos *et al.* As long as political life remained frozen, their exile courts and statements could be taken seriously. But now even Andreas Papandreou must look to his laurels. A few days before the latest coup, the magazine *Politika Thema* produced a suggested Left-Right coalition cabinet, headed by Kanellopoulos, which could restore "normality". Quite apart from the fact that the edition was rapidly withdrawn from sale, the whole idea seems more stale and remote today.

It was, however, John Zighdis, formerly prominent in the Centre Union Party, who gave me the best profile of the "class of '67", and their internal divisions: I reproduce it here.

First, the gangsters. Men like Papadopoulos and [Stylianos] Pattakos who were personally corrupt and intellectually destitute; only really interested in power.

Second, the Puritans. Men like Ioannides and Colonel Ladas, leader of the 4 August Nazi revival group. Fanatical believers in martial virtue and social discipline, often veterans of the anti-communist crusade after the civil war.

Third, the ineptly named Quadafis. Lower-rank officers with a populist and nationalist streak who are for the independence of Greece above all. They have no oil to bargain with, and very few men of any quality.

Fourth, the professional officers. The new President Ghizikis is the classic example; not very political, though very anti-communist.

KEYSTONE/HULTON ARCHIVE/GETTY IMAGES

Mainly concerned about law and order.

The recent coup was the work of groups two and four, who are obviously the strongest. But because of a truly grotesque shortage of talent in the ranks, they have had to draw upon groups one and three already. The three new ministers appointed last week were all old Papadopoulos hands, and many of the lower echelons are likewise peopled with familiar time-servers. Such major changes as there have been are for the worse. The new head of Athens police is Vassili Lambrou, notorious for his personal involvement in the torture of prisoners.

I spoke to one man who had been interrogated by him, but because of his eminence fell into the category of "non-torturable", as Graham Greene's Captain Segura regretfully dubbed the elite. Lambrou attempted to be subtle, and said: "Look, join us, we have more than 50 per cent of Greeks on our side." "So hold an election," replied my courageous friend. Lambrou smashed a chair and walked out – a colourful variant of the "hard man/soft man" routine. The appointment of such a man shows how little the feeble lobbies of "world opinion" are feared and one must concede the commonsense of the regime in ignoring them.

CIA Preferences

It worries the Americans, however. They want Greece as a base as well as a base in Greece, and the evidence is that while the CIA favour Ioannides, United States policy generally prefers a "Turkish solution" where the armed forces simply guarantee a right-wing majority in parliament without themselves shouldering power. Significantly General Ghizikis was visited only a few days before the coup by Lieutenant General Wilson, Nato air force commander for southern Europe. Nato is anxious for a cosmetic agreement to be reached in Greece whereby the Sixth Fleet still have Piraeus as their home port, the internal "stability" of the country is maintained, but the smear of totalitarianism does not disfigure the picture. The trouble is that they know as well as anybody that free elections would lead to a Left majority, and the unleashing through it of even more revolutionary impulses. A "Greek spring" would therefore be as welcome to them as a hole in the head. So they regretfully soil their hands with Ioannides as the enforcer of Western democracy.

It is not only old politicians and bureaucrats who are taking their distance from the new order. Other forces have been brought into play by the courage of the young, and one of the most important of these is the church. Many of its clergy and laity were revolted at the way in which Papadopoulos was able to suborn the hierarchy into a nakedly pro-junta stance. The worst of these was undoubtedly Archbishop Ieronymous, Patriarch of Athens, but even he made an attempt to leap off the sinking ship last Sunday. In a live sermon on the radio, he had begun an attack on the "dark forces" in the new regime when a sudden click deprived listeners of further enlightenment.

The previous night, ESA men had shut down the offices of *Christinaiki*, the largest religious paper in Greece. Its final leading article had begun "The tyrant has fallen, now let the tyranny fall too", and had attacked "the fact that the clergy have abandoned their mission and become part of the state machinery, a class whose mission became a trade". On the one occasion I could verify, a single copy of that edition was read by 120 people in a café and on the pavement outside, which makes ironic nonsense of the old Papadopoulos slogan "A Greece for Christian Greeks". The ideological confusion of the regime is now complete. The day after the Polytechnic massacre, the then Press Minister was reduced to reading out an article on student subversion by Professor Max Beloff from the *Daily Telegraph*.

A Chilean Echo

The state of the opposition in the country is not such, however, as to enable it to take full opportunity of the critical divisions among the oligarchy. The Left has never fully recovered from the disaster of 1967, and its failure to learn the lessons of 1965, when the elder Papandreou funked the chance to sack Papadopoulos from the army after revelations of politically motivated sabotage. Hysterical pressure from the right-wing press and the Palace caused him to retreat. It did him no good, as the Palace dismissed his Administration anyway a short time afterwards. There is a definite Chilean echo to that episode, and it was noticeable that Polytechnic students were eager for news from Santiago when I spoke to them. They were, quite rightly, exultant about the support they had attracted from workers but, equally rightly, pessimistic about the lack of continuing contact between their spokesmen and the workers' unofficial leaders. Finally, the scars of the civil war are far from fully healed and the regime is not slow to exploit the fact.

NICHOLAS TSIKOURIAS/HULTON ARCHIVE/GETTY IMAGES

Bus barricades: protesters block a street in Athens

But it may be that popular feeling has outstripped the orthodox Left. In particular, the Communist Party has been very hard hit by the combination of historical hangovers and contemporary repression. It is split into two factions, one run from Moscow and the other directed from Greece itself. The latter group is proclaimed as more "flexible" but presents a much less ideological face. Theodorakis has left them, as has the famous wartime resistance hero Manolis Glezos, and they face a growing challenge from the Left in the shape Trotskyist and other groups.

Popular Discontents

One of the main grievances among militants generally, as also among other pre-1967 groups like the Lambrakis youth, is that they were left unprepared for the original coup, and saw the cream of their leaders snatched from bed without a fight; Chile again. At present the policy of the Greek internal faction is the construction of a broadly based national government and according to one of their leaders in an interview with me they are prepared to drop the demand for a withdrawal from Nato if it is necessary to get an agreement with Kanellopoulos.

But while the Left remains divided and defeated, popular opposition grows. The economy is stagnant, unemployment is rising and it will take more than the new regime's pledge to "activate free enterprise" before the downward trend is reversed. I spoke through a neutral interpreter with a group of building workers who had been among the crowd outside the Polytechnic and they told me about minimal welfare benefits, cretinous trade unions, low wages and widespread redundancy, as well as the widespread resentment against the regime and its uniformed agents. They said they would be prepared to support a guerrilla war, but were afraid that the population in the countryside might not be with them. The rural areas, though, have been denuded of many thousands of peasants in past years, as young men flock to France and West Germany to form a sub-proletariat in the Common Market and cushion the unemployment problem of the colonels. Franco [in Spain] and [Marcello] Caetano [in Portugal] use the same safety valve, but as the more advanced nations put up the shutters against migrant workers this year, they will face the same problem as the Greeks, which is the return of many workers who no longer accept the old political and economic conditions as a natural law.

They, and countless other Greeks, have learnt the most important lesson of all in the last few weeks – that the seemingly all-powerful dictatorship can be thwarted and made to retreat. In Greek, the word "Syntagma" means both "constitution" and "regiment". After a seven-year sleep, it now seems to more and more people that the two words need no longer be interchangeable. ●

MICHAEL MAUNEY/TIME & LIFE PICTURES/GETTY IMAGES

Chessmen: President Allende (on right) confers with a colleague in a hallway at La Moneda, Santiago, 1971

Why Allende Had to Die

By Gabriel García Márquez

Forty years have passed since the Chilean president Salvador Allende died at La Moneda Palace in Santiago, attempting to defend himself with an AK-47 he had been given by Fidel Castro. Here, in a piece from the New Statesman published in 1974, the Nobel Prize-winning novelist Gabriel García Márquez explores Allende's record in Chile, his rivals' dealings with the United States and the rise of his successor – the army general Augusto Pinochet.

It was towards the end of 1969 that three generals from the Pentagon dined with five Chilean military officers in a house in the suburbs of Washington. The host was Lieutenant Colonel Gerardo López Angulo, assistant air attaché of the Chilean Military Mission to the United States, and the Chilean guests were his colleagues from the other branches of service. The dinner was in honour of the new director of the Chilean Air Force Academy, General Carlos Toro Mazote, who had arrived the day before on a study mission. The eight officers dined on fruit salad, roast veal and peas and drank the warm-hearted wines of their distant homeland to the south, where birds glittered on the beaches while Washington wallowed in snow, and they talked mostly in English about the only thing that seemed to interest Chileans in those days: the approaching presidential elections of the following September. Over dessert, one of the Pentagon generals asked what the Chilean army would do if the candidate of the left, someone like Salvador Allende, were elected. General Toro Mazote replied: "We'll take Moneda Palace in half an hour, even if we have to burn it down."

One of the guests was General Ernesto Baeza, now director of national security in Chile, the one who led the attack on the presidential palace during the coup last September and gave the order to burn it. Two of his subordinates in those earlier days were to become famous in the same operation: General Augusto Pinochet, president of the military junta, and General Javier Palacios. Also at the table was Air Force Brigadier General Sergio Figueroa Gutiérrez, now minister of public works and the intimate friend of another member of the military junta, Air Force General Gustavo Leigh, who ordered the rocket bombing of the presidential palace. The last guest was Admiral Arturo Troncoso, now naval governor of Valparaíso, who carried out the bloody purge of progressive naval officers and was one of those who launched the military uprising of September 11.

That dinner proved to be a historic meeting between the Pentagon and high-ranking officers of the Chilean military services. On other successive meetings, in Washington and Santiago, a contingency plan was agreed upon, according to which those Chilean military men who were bound most closely, heart and soul, to US interests would seize power in the event of Allende's Popular Unity coalition victory in the elections.

The plan was conceived cold-bloodedly, as a simple military operation, and was not a consequence of pressure brought to bear by International Telephone and Telegraph. It was spawned by much deeper reasons of world politics. On the North American side, the organisation set in motion was the Defence Intelligence Agency of the Pentagon but the one in actual charge was the naval intelligence agency, under the higher political direction of the CIA, and the National Security Council. It was quite the normal thing to put the navy and not the army in charge of the project, for the Chilean coup was to coincide with Operation Unitas, which was the name given to the joint manoeuvres of American and Chilean naval units in the Pacific. Those manoeuvres were held at the end of each September, the same month as the elections, and the appearance on land and in the skies of Chile of all manner of war equipment and men well trained in the arts and sciences of death was natural.

During that period, Henry Kissinger had said in private to a group of Chileans: "I am not interested in, nor do I know anything about, the southern portion of the world from the Pyrenees on down." By that time, the contingency plan had been completed to its smallest details and it is impossible to suppose that Kissinger or President Nixon himself was not aware of it.

Chile is a narrow country, some 2,660 miles long and an average of 119 wide, and with ten million exuberant inhabitants, almost three million of whom live in the metropolitan area of Santiago, the capital. The country's greatness is derived not from the number of virtues it possesses but, rather, from its many singularities. The only thing it produces with any absolute seriousness is copper ore but that ore is the best in the world and its volume of production is surpassed only by that of the United States and the Soviet Union. It also produces wine as good as the European varieties but not much of it is exported. Its per capita income of $650 ranks among the highest in Latin America but, traditionally, almost half the gross national product has been accounted for by fewer than 300,000 people.

In 1932, Chile became the first socialist republic in the Americas and, with the enthusiastic support of the workers, the government ▶

attempted the nationalisation of copper and coal. The experiment lasted only for 13 days. Chile has an earth tremor on average once every two days and a devastating earthquake every presidential term. The least apocalyptic of geologists think of Chile not as a country of the mainland but as a cornice of the Andes in a misty sea and believe that the whole of its national territory is condemned to disappear in some future cataclysm.

Chileans are very much like their country in a certain way. They are the most pleasant people on the continent, they like being alive and they know how to live in the best way possible and even a little more; but they have a dangerous tendency toward scepticism and intellectual speculation. A Chilean once told me on a Monday, "No Chilean believes tomorrow is Tuesday," and he didn't believe it, either. Still, even with that deep-seated incredulity – or thanks to it, perhaps – the Chileans have attained a degree of natural civilisation, a political maturity and a level of culture, that sets them apart from the rest of the region. Of the three Nobel Prizes in Literature that Latin America has won, two have gone to Chileans, one of whom, Pablo Neruda, was the greatest poet of this century.

Kissinger may have known this when he said that he knew nothing about the southern part of the world. In any case, US intelligence agencies knew a great deal more. In 1965, without Chile's permission, the nation became the staging centre and a recruiting locale for a fantastic social and political espionage operation: Project Camelot. This was to have been a secret investigation that would have precise questionnaires put to people of all social levels, all professions and trades, even in the furthest reaches of a number of Latin American nations, in order to establish in a scientific way the degree of political development and the social tendencies of various social groups. The questionnaire destined for the military contained the same question that the Chilean officers would hear again at the dinner in Washington: what will their position be if communism comes to power? It was a wild query.

Chile had long been a favoured area for research by North American social scientists. The age and strength of its popular movement, the tenacity and intelligence of its leaders and the economic and social conditions themselves afforded a glimpse of the country's destiny. One didn't require the findings of a Project Camelot to venture the belief that Chile was a prime candidate to be the second socialist republic in Latin America after Cuba. The aim of the United States, therefore, was not simply to prevent the government of Allende from coming to power in order to protect American investments. The larger aim was to repeat the most fruitful operation that imperialism has ever helped bring off in Latin America: Brazil.

The last photograph: inspecting La Moneda under guard, 1 April 1973

GAMMA-KEYSTONE VIA GETTY IMAGES

On 4 September 1970, as had been foreseen, the socialist and Freemason physician Allende was elected president of the republic. The contingency plan was not put into effect, however. The most widespread explanation is also the most ludicrous: someone made a mistake in the Pentagon and requested 200 visas for a purported navy chorus, which, in reality, was to be made up of specialists in government overthrow; however, there were several admirals among them who couldn't sing a single note. That gaffe, it is to be supposed, determined the postponement of the adventure. The truth is that the project had been evaluated in depth: other American agencies, particularly the CIA, and the American ambassador to Chile felt that the contingency plan was too strictly a military operation and did not take current political and social conditions in Chile into account.

> The jolly ladies of the bourgeoisie took to the streets beating empty pots

Indeed, the Popular Unity victory did not bring on the social panic US intelligence had expected. On the contrary, the new government's independence in international affairs and its decisiveness in economic matters immediately created an atmosphere of social celebration.

During the first year, 47 industrial firms were nationalised, along with most of the banking system. Agrarian reform saw the expropriation and incorporation into communal property of six million acres of land formerly held by the large landowners. The inflationary process was slowed, full employment was attained and wages received a cash rise of 30 per cent.

All Copper Nationalised

The previous government, headed by the Christian Democrat Eduardo Frei, had begun steps towards nationalising copper, though he called it "Chileanisation". All the plan did was to buy up 51 per cent of US-held mining properties and for the mine of El Teniente alone it paid a sum greater than the total book value of that facility.

Popular Unity, with a single legal act supported in Congress by all of the nation's popular parties, recovered for the nation all copper deposits worked by the subsidiaries of the American companies Anaconda and Kennecott. Without indemnification: the government having calculated that the two companies had made a profit in excess of $800m over 15 years.

The petite bourgeoisie and the middle class, the two great social forces that might have supported a military coup at that moment, were beginning to enjoy unforeseen advantages and not at the expense of the proletariat, as had always been the case, but, rather, at the expense of the financial oligarchy and foreign capital. The armed forces, as a social group, have the same origins and ambitions as the middle class, so they had no motive, not even an alibi, to back the tiny group of coup-minded officers. Aware of that reality, the Christian Democrats not only did not support the barracks plot at that time but resolutely opposed it, for they knew it was unpopular among their own rank and file.

Their objective was something else again: to use any means possible to impair the good health of the government so as to win two-thirds of the seats in Congress in the March 1973 elections. With such a majority, they could vote for the constitutional removal of the president of the republic.

The Christian Democrats make up a huge organisation cutting across class lines, with an authentic popular base among the modern industrial proletariat, the small and middle-sized rural landowners and the petite bourgeoisie and middle class of the cities. Popular Unity, while also inter-class in its make-up, was the expression of workers of the less-favoured proletariat – the agricultural proletariat – and the lower middle class of the cities.

The Christian Democrats, allied with the extreme right-wing National Party, controlled the Congress and the courts; Popular Unity controlled the executive. The polarisation of these two parties was to be, in effect, the polarisation of the country. Curiously, the Catholic Frei, who doesn't believe in Marxism, was the one who took the best advantage of the class struggle, the one who stimulated it and brought it to a head, with an aim to unhinge the government and plunge the country into the abyss of demoralisation and economic disaster.

The economic blockade by the United States, because of expropriation without indemnification, did the rest. All kinds of goods are manufactured in Chile, from automobiles to toothpaste, but this industrial base has a false identity: in the 160 most important firms, 60 per cent of the capital was foreign and 80 per cent of the basic materials came from abroad. In addition, the country needed $300m a year in order to import consumer goods and another $450m to pay the interest on its foreign debt.

But Chile's urgent needs were extraordinary and went much deeper. The jolly ladies of the bourgeoisie, under the pretext of protesting rationing, galloping inflation and the demands made by the poor, took to the streets, beating their empty pots and pans.

It wasn't by chance, quite the contrary; it was very significant that that street spectacle of silver foxes and flowered hats took place on the same afternoon that Fidel Castro was ending a 30-day visit that had brought an earthquake of social mobilisation of government supporters.

Seed of Destruction

President Allende understood then – and he said so – that the people held the government but they did not hold the power. The phrase was more bitter than it seemed and also more alarming, for inside himself Allende carried a legalist germ that held the seed of his own destruction: a man who fought to the death in defence of legality, he would have been capable of walking out of La Moneda Palace with his head held high if the Congress had removed him from office within the bounds of the constitution.

The Italian journalist and politician Rossana Rossanda, who visited Allende during that period, found him aged, tense and full of gloomy premonitions as he talked to her from the yellow cretonne couch where, seven months later, his riddled body was to lie, the face crushed in by a rifle butt. Then, on the eve of the March 1973 elections, in which his destiny was at stake, he would have been content with 36 per cent of the vote for Popular Unity. And yet, in spite of runaway inflation, stern rationing and the pot-and-pan concert of the merry wives of the upper-class districts, he received 44 per cent. It was such a spectacular and decisive victory that when Allende was alone in his office with his friend and confidant, the journalist Augusto Olivares, he closed the door and danced a *cueca* all by himself.

> Allende carried a legalist germ that held the seed of his own destruction

For the Christian Democrats, it was proof that the process of social justice set in motion by the Popular Unity coalition could not be turned back by legal means but they lacked the vision to measure the consequences of the actions they then undertook. For the United States, the election was a much more serious warning and went beyond the simple interests of expropriated firms. It was an inadmissible precedent for peaceful progress and social change for the peoples of the world, particularly those in France and Italy, where present conditions make an attempt at an experiment along the lines of Chile possible. All forces of internal and external reaction came together to form a compact bloc.

CIA Financed Final Blow

The truck owners' strike was the final blow. Because of the wild geography of the country, the Chilean economy is at the mercy of its transport. To paralyse trucking is to paralyse the country. It was easy for the opposition to co-ordinate the strike, for the truckers' guild was one of the groups most affected by the scarcity of replacement parts and, in addition, it found itself threatened by the government's small pilot programme for providing adequate state trucking services in the extreme south of the nation. The stoppage lasted until the very end without a single moment of relief because it was financed with cash from outside. "The CIA flooded the country with dollars to support the strike by the bosses and ... foreign capital found its way down into the formation of a black market," Pablo Neruda wrote to a friend in Europe. One week before the coup, oil, milk and bread had run out.

During the last days of Popular Unity, with the economy unhinged and the country on the verge of civil war, the manoeuvring of the government and the opposition centred on the hope of changing the balance of power in the armed forces in favour of one or the other. The final move was hallucinatory in its perfection: 48 hours before the coup, the opposition managed to disqualify all high-ranking officers supporting Allende and to promote in their places, one by one, in a series of inconceivable gambits, all of the officers who had been present at the dinner in Washington.

At that moment, however, the political chess game had got out of the control of its players. Dragged along by an irreversible dialectic, they themselves ended up as pawns in a much larger game of chess, one much more complex and politically more important than any mere scheme hatched in conjunction by imperialism and the reaction against the government of the people. It was a terrifying class confrontation that was slipping out of the hands of the very people who had provoked it, a cruel and fierce scramble by counterpoised interests, and the final outcome had to be a social cataclysm without precedent in the history of the Americas.

A military coup under those conditions would not be bloodless. Allende knew it.

The Chilean armed forces, contrary to what we have been led to believe, have intervened in politics every time that their class interests have seemed threatened and they have done so with an inordinately repressive ferocity. The two constitutions that the country has had in the past 100 years were imposed by force of arms and the recent military coup has been the sixth uprising in a period of 50 years.

The bloodlust of the Chilean army is part of its birthright, coming from that terrible school of hand-to-hand combat against the Araucanian Indians, a struggle that lasted 300 years. One of its forerunners boasted in 1620 of having killed more than 2,000 people with his own hands in a single action. Joaquín Edwards Bello relates in his chronicles that during an epidemic of exanthematic typhus the army dragged sick people out of their houses and killed them in a poison bath in order to put an end to the plague. During a seven-month civil war in 1891, 10,000 died in a series of gory encounters. The Peruvians assert that during the occupation of Lima in the war of the Pacific, Chilean soldiers sacked the library of Don Ricardo Palma, taking the books not for reading but for wiping their backsides.

History of Brutality

Popular movements have been suppressed with the same brutality. After the Valparaíso earthquake of 1906, naval forces wiped out the longshoremen's organisation of 8,000 ▶

workers. In Iquique, at the beginning of the century, demonstrating strikers tried to take refuge from the troops and were machine-gunned: within ten minutes, there were 2,000 dead. On 2 April 1957, the army broke up a civil disturbance in the commercial area of Santiago and the number of victims was never established because the government sneaked the bodies away. During a strike at the El Salvador mine during the government of Eduardo Frei, a military patrol opened fire on a demonstration to break it up and killed six people, among them some children and a pregnant woman. The post commander was an obscure 52-year-old general, the father of five children, a geography teacher and the author of several books on military subjects: Augusto Pinochet.

The myth of the legalism and the gentleness of that brutal army was invented by the Chilean bourgeoisie in their own interest. Popular Unity kept it alive with the hope of changing the class make-up of the higher cadres in its favour. But Allende felt more secure among the Carabineros, an armed force that was popular and peasant in its origins and that was under the direct command of the president of the republic. Indeed, the junta had to go six places down the seniority list of the force before it found a senior officer who would support the coup. The younger officers dug themselves in at the junior officers' school in Santiago and held out for four days until they were wiped out.

That was the best-known battle of the secret war that broke out inside military posts on the eve of the coup. Officers who refused to support the coup and those who failed to carry out the orders for repression were murdered without pity by the instigators. Entire regiments mutinied, both in

Santiago and in the provinces, and they were suppressed without mercy, with their leaders massacred as a lesson for the troops.

The commandant of the armoured units in Viña del Mar, Colonel Cantuarias, was machine-gunned by his subordinates. A long time will pass before the number of victims of that internal butchery will ever be known, for the bodies were removed from military posts in garbage trucks and buried secretly. All in all, only some 50 senior officers could be trusted to head troops that had been purged beforehand.

Foreign Agents' Role

The story of the intrigue has to be pasted together from many sources, some reliable, some not. Any number of foreign agents seem to have taken part in the coup. Clandestine sources in Chile tell us that the bombing of La Moneda Palace – the technical precision of which startled the experts – was actually carried out by a team of American aerial acrobats who had entered the country under the screen of Operation Unitas to perform in a flying circus on the coming 18 September, Chile's national independence day. There is also evidence that numerous members of secret police forces from neighbouring countries were infiltrated across the Bolivian border and remained in hiding until the day of the coup, when they unleashed their bloody persecution of political refugees from other countries of Latin America.

Brazil, the homeland of the head gorillas, had taken charge of those services. Two years earlier, she had brought off the reactionary coup in Bolivia, which meant the loss of substantial support for Chile and facilitated the infiltration of all manner and means of subversion. Part of the loans made to Brazil by the United States was secretly transferred to Bolivia to finance subversion in Chile. In 1972, a US military advisory group made a trip to La Paz, the aim of which has not been revealed. Perhaps it was only coincidental, however, that a short time after that visit, movements of troops and equipment took place on the frontier with Chile, giving the Chilean military yet another opportunity to bolster their internal position and carry out transfer of personnel and promotions in the chain of command that were favourable to the imminent coup.

> Allende shouted at Palacios: "Traitor!" and shot him in the hand

Finally, on September 11, while Operation Unitas was going forward, the original plan drawn up at the dinner in Washington was carried out, three years behind schedule but precisely as it had been conceived: not as a conventional barracks coup but as a devastating operation of war.

It had to be that way, for it was not simply a matter of overthrowing a regime but one of implanting the Hell-dark seeds brought from Brazil, until in Chile there would be no trace of the political and social structure that had made Popular Unity possible. The harshest phase, unfortunately, had only just begun.

In that final battle, with the country at the mercy of uncontrolled and unforeseen forces of subversion, Allende was still bound by legality. The most dramatic contradiction of his life was being at the same time the congenital foe of violence and a passionate revolutionary. He believed that he had resolved the contradiction with the hypothesis that conditions in Chile would permit a peaceful evolution toward socialism under bourgeois legality. Experience taught him too late that a system cannot be changed by a government without power.

That belated disillusionment must have been the force that impelled him to resist to the death, defending the flaming ruins of a house that was not his own, a sombre mansion that an Italian architect had built to be a mint and that ended up as a refuge for presidents without power. He resisted for six hours with a sub-machine gun that Castro had given him and was the first weapon that Allende had ever fired.

Around four o'clock in the afternoon, Major General Javier Palacios managed to reach the second floor with his adjutant, Captain Gallardo, and a group of officers. There, in the midst of the fake Louis XV chairs, the Chinese dragon vases and the Rugendas paintings in the red parlour, Allende was waiting for them. He was in shirtsleeves, wearing a miner's helmet and no tie, his clothing stained with blood. He was holding the sub-machine gun but he had run low on ammunition.

Allende knew General Palacios well. A few days before, he had told Augusto Olivares that this was a dangerous man with close connections to the American embassy. As soon as he saw him appear on the stairs, Allende shouted at him: "Traitor!" and shot him in the hand.

Fought to the End

According to the story of a witness who asked me not to give his name, the president died in an exchange of shots with that gang. Then all the other officers, in a caste-bound ritual, fired on the body. Finally, a non-commissioned officer smashed in his face with the butt of his rifle.

A photograph exists: Juan Enrique Lira, a photographer for the newspaper *El Mercurio* took it. He was the only one allowed to photograph the body. It was so disfigured that when they showed the body in its coffin to Señora Hortensia Allende, his wife, they would not let her uncover the face.

He would have been 64 years old next July. His greatest virtue was following through but fate could grant him only that rare and tragic greatness of dying in armed defence of an anachronistic booby of bourgeois law, defending a Supreme Court of Justice that had repudiated him but would legitimise his murderers, defending a miserable Congress that had declared him illegitimate but which was to bend complacently before the will of the usurpers, defending the freedom of opposition parties that had sold their souls to fascism, defending the whole moth-eaten paraphernalia of a shitty system that he had proposed abolishing but without a shot being fired.

The drama took place in Chile, to the greater woe of the Chileans, but it will pass into history as something that has happened to us all, children of this age, and it will remain in our lives for ever. ●

Gabriel García Márquez worked as a journalist in Colombia before his debut novella, "Leaf Storm", was published in 1955. He is now suffering from dementia and can no longer write

Ex-Spies I've Known in the Commons

By Andrew Roth

In the face of the government's ludicrous inconsistencies in handling blabbing former MI5 agents, it is barely possible that Mrs Thatcher may retreat into conceding a select committee on the security services. If she does, ask mischievous MPs, will she name to it curmudgeonly Cranley Onslow, whom she sacked as a Foreign Office minister but who is now chairman of the Tory backbenchers' 1922 Committee? He is the latest of a long line of ex-spooks on Tory benches.

Former MI6 men in Parliament are a dead giveaway through the places they worked previously and the unimaginatively clumsy way in which they try to disguise those former jobs. Cranley Onslow joined MI6 and the Foreign Office after serving in the 7th Hussars. He was posted, nominally as consul, to Maymyo, near the Burma-China border, in 1955-56. He then transferred back to the office of the Foreign Office's permanent under secretary, who controls foreign intelligence operations. When I pointed out in *Parliamentary Profiles* proofs that he was an ex-MI6 man, he refused to confirm or deny, simply threatening a libel action.

The first spook I knew in the Commons was the handsome, blond and genial Neil ("Billy") McLean, who came in for Inverness in the 1954 by-election. I had previously known him in South Asia where he "happened" to turn up in all the hotspots I was covering as a foreign correspondent. He also managed to get into and get expelled from a few places like Sinjiang, the Northwest China rubbing point with Russia, that I could not penetrate.

He was involved in a 1949 attempt to win Albania back to Western sympathies in the wake of Tito's defection from Stalinism. But the effort, according to last week's obituary in the *Times*, was foiled by Philby's treason. Although a splendid mixer, McLean naturally found the Commons a relatively dull place. In his pursuit of imperial interests he actually called for the assassination of the Communist-backed Congolese leader Patrice Lumumba. What cost him his seat in 1964 in Inverness was one of the least-known rearguard imperial actions of modern times.

In September 1962 republican rebels attacked the Sana'a palace of the Imam of Yemen, with the promised support of President Nasser's Egyptian troops already sailing up the Red Sea. The CIA persuaded President Kennedy to back Nasser and the republicans. In December 1962 the Tory MP for Inverness flew to the Yemen. For the next five years McLean served as the Imam's principal military adviser in fighting the republicans and Nasser's troops in an unofficial British interlude between the American intervention in Vietnam and the Russians' in Afghanistan.

McLean naturally found the Commons a relatively dull place

A contemporary ex-MI6 man who outlasted McLean was the tall, bald, rubber-faced Henry ("Bob") Kerby, the MP for Arundel and Shoreham from the 1954 by-election until his death in 1971. He was a fascinating example of a radical reactionary who had moved from the right wing of the Liberals, where he was a pal of Edward Martell, to the imperial right wing of the Tories.

But privately he was radical in his detestation of the Establishment and particularly its corrupting honours system. Apart from his friends in the imperial right wing, he found it easier to mix with the Labour left than with Establishment "snobs" or with the pro-European "Bow Group queers" as he dismissed the Heathmen. It was one of the greatest ironies that when the Soviet leaders Khrushchev and Bulganin visited Britain in 1956, his old enemy Ted Heath called on Kerby to introduce him and interpret for him.

He was an oddball in his Russophilism. Although his mother came from a wealthy Scots family, he was an outsider partly because he was born in Russia in 1914. When the family were forced out by Revolution, they took with them Bob's nanny, with whom he spoke Russian for the rest of her long life. After he joined the regular Army in 1933, his facility with Russian made him a natural for transfer into intelligence. While the Soviet-Nazi pact was in place he was posted to Riga as an embassy attaché, and then to Malmö, Sweden.

When the Russians were attacked, he was switched to operations with resistance movements behind the Nazi lines, particularly in Denmark (where he was jailed briefly), Poland and Yugoslavia. Although I knew which government decorated him, I was never able to get anything directly out of him about his MI6 exploits because, he repeatedly insisted, he would lose his pension if he blabbed. He was a deeply serious and patriotic intelligence man in his political operations, which were sometimes misunderstood. He was one of my sources for my "scoop" on the Profumo affair. Like George (later Lord) Wigg, he was scandalised that a millionaire War Secretary from the Establishment "kissing ring" should make himself so vulnerable through a "tart".

Other former spooks men have passed through the Commons more quietly, like dry, uptight Lieutenant Colonel John Cordeaux, a former Royal Marine who made virtually no impact as MP for Nottingham Central 1955-64. He hid his transfer into MI6 beneath the typical disguise of "seconded to Foreign Office 1942-46". His decorations by the Dutch, the Danes and the Norwegians immediately after the war showed where he had operated.

The older generation of spooks did not have the recently granted discretion of blabbing to Chapman Pincher and Nigel West (alias Rupert Allason, the Tory candidate for Torbay) with selective impunity. ●

"But they were telling us he'd turned vegetarian"

Instant recognition: Yasser Arafat leaves the residence of the PLO ambassador to Tunisia, 1988

ABBAS/MAGNUM PHOTOS

2 DECEMBER 1988

Arafat's Agenda

By Edward Said

The 19th session of the Palestine National Council, formally titled the "*Intifada* Meeting", was momentous and, in many great and small ways, unprecedented. There were fewer hangers-on, groupies and "observers" than ever before. Security was tighter and more unpleasant than during the 1978 PNC session, also held in Algiers.

Algiers had just had its own brutally suppressed *intifada*, so the presence of several hundred Palestinians and at least 1,200 members of the press was not especially welcomed by the Benjedid government, which paradoxically needed the event to restore some of its revolutionary lustre. The three-and-a-half-day conclave also accomplished more than any Palestinian meeting in the post-1948 period. Above all, it secured for Yasser Arafat the certainty of his place in Palestinian and world history.

None of the approximately 380 members came to Algiers with any illusion that Palestinians could again get away simply with creative ambiguity or affirmations of the need to struggle. The *intifada*'s momentum and its ability to have created a clear civil alternative to the Israeli-occupation regime necessitated a definitive statement by the PNC. This required an unambiguous claim for sovereignty over whatever Palestinian territories were to be vacated by the occupation. There also had to be an equally unambiguous statement on peaceful resolution of the conflict between Palestinian Arabs and Israeli Jews, based on UN Resolutions 181 (partition), 242 and 338. In short the PNC was asking of itself nothing less than an emphatic transformation: from liberation movement to independence movement. Jordan's recent withdrawal of claims for the West Bank made the need for transformation urgent and compelling.

Everyone gathering in Algiers knew that this profound step was Arafat's: first to define, then to persuade us to take, then finally to choreograph politically. When I arrived, he handed me the Arabic draft of the declaration of statehood and asked me to render it into English. It had been written by committee, then rewritten by the Palestinian poet and PNC member Mahmoud Darwish, then, alas, covered with often ludicrously clumsy insertions and inexplicable deletions. Darwish later told me that the Old Man had struck the phrase "collective memory" because, we opined, he took it as poetic. "Tell him it has a serious and even scientific meaning," Darwish implored me: "Maybe he'll listen to you." He didn't, and I didn't listen when Arafat wanted phrases from other such declarations inserted.

Perhaps the oddest thing about this PNC – with its obvious postmodern rhetorical anxieties – was that we discussed the two main documents (the declaration of statehood and the political resolutions) in public debates for hours on end without a piece of paper before us. After the opening ceremonies on Saturday, the council divided itself into two committees, the political and the *intifada*. Arafat had the texts memorised, and Nabil Shaath, chair of the political committee, had them before him. All discussion took place in the riveting atmosphere of that committee, with speaker after speaker sounding off on what, after all, was the most significant political moment in Palestinian life since 1948.

By about 9.30pm on Monday 14 November the political programme had been passed. George Habash and supporters fought each sentence almost word by word on the crucial 242/338 paragraph, which was voted on in different forms half a dozen times. The ungainly paragraph that resulted shows the effect of those battles, although the substance remains unmistakable. At one point, Arafat stood up and recited the entire programme from memory, indicating where the clause, sentence and paragraph breaks occurred, so that there could be no mistake about meaning, emphasis, conclusion.

For the first time in PNC history, voting by acclamation wasn't going to be enough; Habash had insisted on precise tallies, which emerged to his disadvantage: 253 for, 46 against, and ten abstentions. There was a sad nostalgia for what he represented, since in effect by voting against him we were taking leave of the past as embodied in his defiant gestures. The declaration ceremonies that closed the meetings were jubilant, yet somehow melancholy.

About this break with the past there could be no doubt whatever. To declare statehood on the basis of Resolution 181 was first of all to say unequivocally that an Arab Palestine and an Israeli state should coexist in a partitioned Palestine. Self-determination would thus be for two peoples, not just for one. Most of us there had grown up with the reality (lived and remembered) of Palestine as an Arab country, refusing to concede anything more than the exigency of a Jewish state, one at our expense in the loss of our land, our society and uncountable thousands of lives. As we met, a million and a half of our compatriots were under brutal military occupation, fighting tanks and fully armed soldiers with rocks and an unbending will. For the first time also, we implicitly recognised a state that offered us nothing but the empty formulas of Camp David or the openly racist threats of "transfer". The declaration of statehood spelled out principles of equality, mutuality and social justice far in advance of anything in the region. Then too the *principle* of partition was asserted, not the territories specified in the 1947 UN resolution. All of us felt that since Israel has *never* declared its boundaries, we could not declare ours now; better to negotiate the question of boundaries with Israel and a confederal relationship with Jordan directly. There was no doubt, however, that we were discussing the territories occupied by Israel in 1967.

Second, there was absolute clarity in speaking of a peaceful settlement to the conflict. "Armed struggle" does not appear in the binding resolutions to the political programme. Central to those resolutions is a long and awkward sentence endorsing an international peace conference based on 242 and 338. The language surrounding acceptance of the UN resolutions raises no reservations about that acceptance but simply states the obvious. Representation by the PLO on an equal footing with other parties, the aegis of the Security Council, the *implementation* of 242 and 338, the centrality of the Palestinian-Israeli conflict, the inalienable rights of the Palestinian people – all these are mentioned as the *context*, the history, the Palestinian interpretation, of what we are accepting. This was especially necessary because 242 and 338 say nothing about the political actuality of the Palestinian people, which in 1967 seemed scarcely evident.

Third, the rejection of terrorism (also affirmed in the declaration) emphatically distinguishes between resistance to occupation, to which Palestinians are entitled according to the UN Charter and international law, and indiscriminate violence against civilians by states or by individuals and groups. Note that there exists no all-purpose definition of terrorism, one that has international validity and impartiality of application. Also note that Israel has always arrogated to itself the right to attack civilians in the name of its security.

Finally and most important, all the resolutions clearly intend willingness to negotiate directly. There are no disclaimers about the "Zionist entity", or about the legitimacy of Israeli representatives. All the relevant passages about peace, partition and statehood in the 1964 Palestinian National Covenant are flatly contradicted by the 1988 PNC resolutions. All the refusals, attacks and insults heaped on the council's results, both by Israel and the usual array of US "experts", signify consternation. Clearly, the more Palestinians take responsible and realistic positions, the less acceptable we become, not just because Palestinians want peace but because Israelis don't know what to do when peace is offered to them. There is a dispiriting continuity here between the early days of Israel's existence, when Ben-Gurion refused peace with the Arabs, and the all-out rejection trundled out today by Likud and Labor alike.

The point is not that the council's documents are perfect and complete but that they must be interpreted as everyone in Algiers intended – as a beginning that signals a distinct break with the past, as an assertion of willingness to make sacrifices in the interests of peace, as a definitive statement of the Palestinian acceptance of the international consensus. A few days before the Algiers meeting Ariel Sharon appeared on Italian television vociferating about the need to kill Arafat. That no comparable sentiment was expressed about an Israeli leader at any time in Algiers is a fact that furnishes its own eloquent comment on the real difference now between Israeli and Palestinian leaders.

These are dangerous times for Palestinians; the occupation will get worse, and assassinations and full-scale political war will intensify. For once, however, the record is unmistakable as to who is for peace, who for bloodshed and suffering. But our campaign for peace must be joined.

Why is Israel not asked whether it is willing to coexist with a Palestinian state, or negotiate, or accept 242, or renounce violence, or recognise the PLO, or accept demilitarisation, or allay Palestinian fears, or stop killing civilians, or end the occupation, or answer any questions at all? ●

A Diplomatic History

UN resolutions accepted by PNC as basis for a peace settlement:

181 Passed by the General Assembly in 1947. Plan of partition with economic union of Palestine at the end of British Mandate. It establishes two independent states for the territory, one Jewish, the other Arab. Rejected by the Palestinian side and superseded by the war of 1947-48 when Israel established its pre-1967 borders.

242 Passed by the Security Council in 1967. Calling for withdrawal of Israeli troops from territories occupied in that year's conflict (West Bank and Gaza Strip); and for "respect for and acknowledgement of the sovereignty, territorial integrity and political independence of every state in the area".

338 Passed by Security Council in 1973. Calling for an end to the Arab-Israeli conflict of that year, for an immediate truce and for the implementation of Resolution 242. ●

8 SEPTEMBER 1989

Terror in the Townships

By R W Johnson

In July 1989 the outgoing South African president, P W Botha, met Nelson Mandela in secret, an important point on the journey towards freedom for Mandela – who was still in prison – and the new South Africa. But as R W Johnson's hyperbolic reporting shows, even as the last election under apartheid approached, ingrained poverty and violence in the townships continued to tear lives apart.

"Do you see," said Monica, the hitcher I'd picked up on the road out of Durban, "These comrades, they come to my friend and me and they say, why are you in school? You must not be in school. And then they do this to me with tear gas" – she pointed to scars, white against her black skin, on her face and inside her mouth, but I still couldn't understand quite what they'd done. "I was ugly, all burnt, for long time. My friend, they pushed this wire in one of her eyes and out the other one. Right through. One eye is come right out. She no see nothing now. *Ikona!* [No way!] These comrades, they are no good."

I agree they don't sound too good. "So I run away. Cannot stay at that school, I'm 19, I must get Matric – I'm Standard 9 now. I mus' still get money. But I watch out for comrades. They are not good people."

I asked Monica how she managed to "get money", though I didn't really have too many doubts. She grinned so broadly that I couldn't help laughing. This made her somewhat indignant. "But I mus' have go with guys for money. What else I do? Many girls do that. Too much. In my class, ten girls do that. Is no good business. The headmaster very angry, he catch me in a car with a white guy. Two times. Next time he say he make me leave school, but I mus' need money."

Monica looked at me hopefully. "You on, guy? Twenty Rand." I say, well no. Monica suddenly looks a lot less young and shoots me a bargaining glance. "Ten Rand?" (£2.30). I say, look, I don't want to sleep with you but here's five Rand. "You crazy guy or what?" says Monica, but honour is satisfied. She goes off shaking her head, but happy. As with so many black girls using prostitution to put themselves through school, you wonder how long she's going to live.

Monica lives in Kwa Mashu, just outside Durban. As townships go, it's not too bad. That is, although there are occasional flare-ups of UDF *vs* Inkatha fighting – and there is a great deal of house-burning going on this week because of comrade activity over the elections – the death-toll is very moderate compared to a place like Mpumalanga, twenty miles out of Durban, where ten or 12 people die due to political causes every week – usually hacked to death with *pangas* as they try to escape from their petrol-bombed houses. A lot get burned to death – but the AK-47 is, so to speak, writing more and more death certificates round here. (You only ever used to see AK-47s at night, they say, but now you can sometimes even see them in daytime. Mind you, the AK is still a luxury: the crude pipe-guns manufactured by illicit township gun factories are far more common.)

> Soweto has seen the rise of "jackrolling", car-borne gangs cruising the streets

The violence is deep-seated and beyond too much rational analysis. At Mpumalanga, for example, one ward is Inkatha, so everyone wears khaki trousers, but in the next ward you wear yellow vests to show you're UDF. The khaki trousers and yellow vests will kill one another on sight – I heard of one unfortunate who came from out of town, innocently wearing khaki trousers. He was dragged out of his taxi by the yellow vests. Of course, it might sound easy to have both the right trousers and the right vest in your wardrobe, but the trouble is that you'll get taken out on a raiding party with one gang or the other and have to kill someone to prove yourself. And then their relatives will want to kill you, so your only security lies in sticking with the gang you've "joined".

Most Africans living in places like Mpumalanga (and there are quite a few such places here in Natal) are simply terrified and, on getting home from the office, the factory or the white home in the suburbs, just barricade themselves in. No one's too sure any more how much politics has to do with the killings. You don't ask, you just hide and you absolutely don't want to join anything. Militant radicals or Inkatha supporters will try to tell you how the masses support them, but don't believe it. Most of the masses are like Monica: they don't really care, they just want to be left alone. The adults, anyway. The young students are more committed, which makes them the target of whatever the opposing group is.

The thing that Kwa Mashu people are really frightened of is the Senoras, a sort of vigilante super-gang which has come to dominate the township in the last few months. The Senoras are in the habit, inter alia, of descending on schools – 50 to 100 toughs with *pangas* – to "sort out" the students (ie, presumed radicals). It's assumed the Senoras get paid by someone for doing this, but nobody knows by whom. The headmasters are terrified – one I talked to said he simply closed down the school and hid when he heard the Senoras were coming. Unless you're willing to spend the school budget on AK-47s, this is logical enough.

Across the way in Lindelani, the alarming Mr Tshabalala ("Mr T") holds sway – his fighters being (of course, nature imitateth not art but television) the "A-Team". But Mr T – by profession a squatter shacklord and warlord – has just been on trial for murder again, so the A-Team has been fairly quiet. Now that Mr T's been found not guilty again various aggrieved parties are bound to try to kill him, so the A-Team will doubtless be getting ready for some pre-emptive mayhem to show that trying to kill Mr T would be a thoroughly bad idea.

In addition, of course, there is now a general assumption of a life expectancy of nil for those brave souls who gave evidence against Mr T in court. Under his not altogether benign rule, Lindelani has its own "people's courts", with often extremely brutal sentences being carried out on the spot – one punishment, for

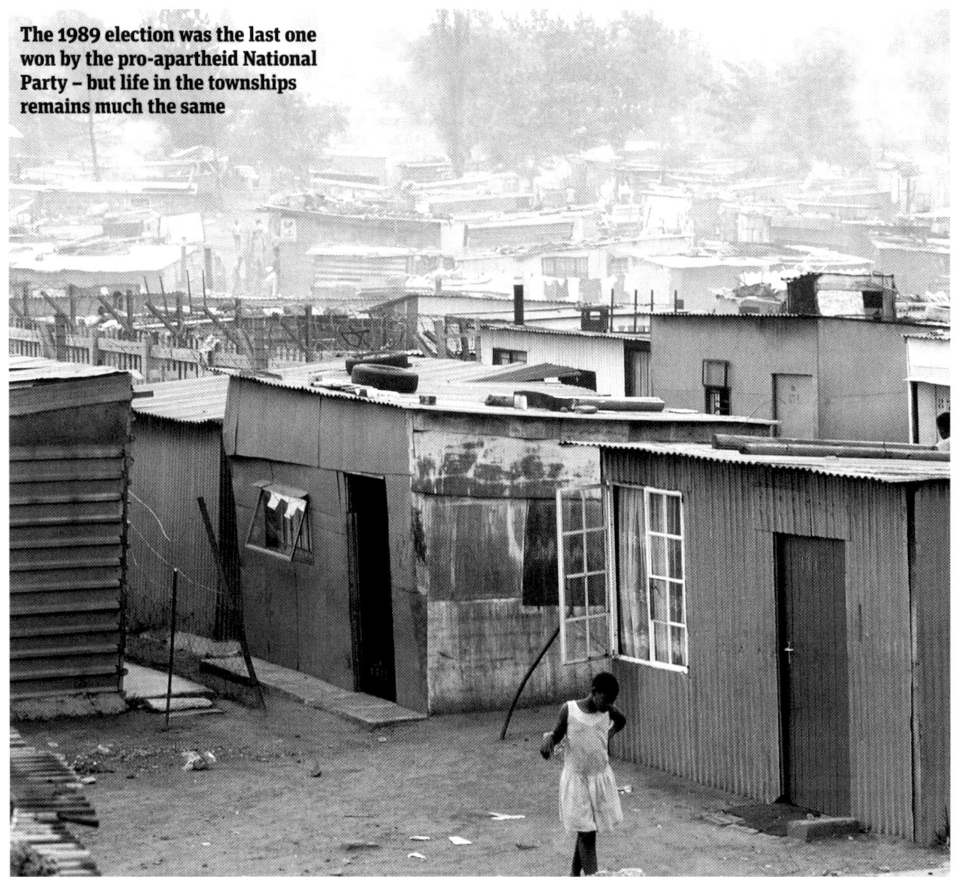

The 1989 election was the last one won by the pro-apartheid National Party – but life in the townships remains much the same

LILY FRANEY/GAMMA-RAPHO VIA GETTY IMAGES

example, being to gouge out someone's eye and then make them eat it. Both Mr T's little feudal state and the people's court phenomenon should really be understood as simply the most structured forms of gang rule; the basic reality, beyond and alongside politics and everything else, is the gang.

It's not always very structured. In the 54 miles separating Durban and Pietermaritzburg, there are perhaps a thousand African children living wild in the bush, having been driven out there by squatter-camp gang wars. These kids – often likened to pirates or flocks of wild birds – are skilled fighters and have become violence-entrepreneurs, operating protection rackets and hiring themselves out as fighters in various community conflicts. They've found a growing market all right.

Doubtless, even such groups develop a leadership structure in time with the emergence of strong men or, at least, strong children. But reality here is often two-faced. A pharmacist friend told me how, driving through a township to deliver some medical supplies the other day, he was cheerfully greeted by a crocodile of uniformed schoolchildren marching unaccountably down the road in the middle of the school day. Later, he found that an intruder into their school had attempted to rape one of the schoolgirls and, when she had resisted, had knifed her. Her classmates voted to suspend classes while they went off to burn the intruder's house down and kill him if they could. It was while they were on their way to do this errand that they had encountered my pharmacist friend and shown such good humour.

Rape, especially gang-rape, has become a growing problem in the townships. Soweto, in particular, has seen the rise of "jackrolling" – car-borne gangs cruising the streets, alighting on women of their choice. Some gangs have now taken to bursting into houses to gang-rape young girls, and then threatening the terrified parents with a particularly painful death if they fail to ensure that their daughters are there and available next time the jackrollers decide to pay a call.

But horror stories about gangs are really a dime a dozen. Nobody doubts that in both Coloured and African townships gang activity has increased to a record intensity and rapacity, nor that rising unemployment is the fundamental cause.

The terrible and worsening violence in the black townships and squatter camps of South Africa – both political and gang-related – poses insuperable problems for the self-designated Mass Democratic Movement (ie, the pro-ANC left) here. The MDM furiously rejects the term "black-on-black violence", saying that this term leaves out apartheid's responsibility in creating the framework for violence. Moreover, says the MDM, the term reinforces the government propaganda image of white rule holding the ring for law and order in the face of a black population eager only to set about killing one another.

In fact, the MDM has no alternative to offer instead of "black-on-black" (which, privately everyone uses), and such a response is almost frivolous. With communities living in terror and people being raped, robbed and killed in large numbers, to waste energy on the mere question of terminology seems odd for a movement which insists, above all, on its community-mindedness.

And, of course, the embarrassment goes deeper than that. For example, it is a basic ANC demand that the army (the SADF) must be withdrawn from the townships. But in the face of the escalating internal violence there, many blacks are often only too glad to see the police and the SADF in their midst, hated though they are. Quite often it is terrified blacks who appeal to the police and SADF to come in to their areas to restore order.

Or again, the MDM leadership appeals insistently for increased sanctions against South Africa – but everyone knows that economic sanctions have already contributed heavily to black unemployment and that the worse unemployment gets, the worse the violence will get. Similarly, the work stay-away is one of the MDM's favourite weapons – there is another stay-away going on this election week – but every stay-away kills more black jobs as employers respond with more automation or by switching employment to Indians and Coloureds. And more job losses mean more unemployment, more violence, more gangs.

Some radicals still hanker after the ANC slogan of 1983-86, "Make the townships (and thus South Africa) ungovernable", but the fact is that they are close to ungovernability right now and this simply increases black suffering to no particular political effect.

This week's election will make no difference to all this. All else apart, the realities of township life are just not amenable to a political quick-fix, whoever is in power. One day a black government is going to have to face up to the fact that even majority rule is not going to make the townships and their problems go away, that the left needs an urban policy and a security policy as much as anyone else. Perhaps we'll find troops and armoured cars in the townships even then.

At present, the black middle classes have built themselves palatial homes in select little class enclaves within the townships – this is how a Winnie Mandela or a Desmond Tutu lives now. This class currently provides most of the country's black political leadership, but when apartheid ends much of that class is clearly going to flee into the relative peace and security of the white suburbs. That leadership will then find itself having to deal with the seething world of the townships from exactly the same vantage point now enjoyed by the whites. Despite all the rhetoric now, how different their approach then will really be is hard to know. For Monica's sake – and thousands like her – one has to live in hope. ●

No Limits to the Law in New Orleans

By James Fox

Something terrible lies at the heart of New Orleans – a rampant, widespread and apparently uncontrollable brutality on the part of its police force and its prison service. The horrors of its criminal justice system from decades before Hurricane Katrina and up to now lie somewhere between, with little exaggeration, *Candide* and Stalin's Gulags.

Spit on the sidewalk here, and you may be arrested – New Orleans has the highest incarceration rate of any city in the United States – and if you're poor and black and can't pay bail, you will enter a place where any protection under the American constitution and the Bill of Rights is stripped away. You will wait weeks or months to be charged, whether innocent or not, and in the meantime you will be subjected to foul, overcrowded jail conditions, prisoner-to-prisoner violence and the brutality of the deputies who guard you. God help you if you have a medical condition, or a mental-health problem, or if you're pregnant (you may deliver in leg chains – it has happened). "A minor offence in New Orleans," one civil rights attorney told me, "can get you into a hellish place."

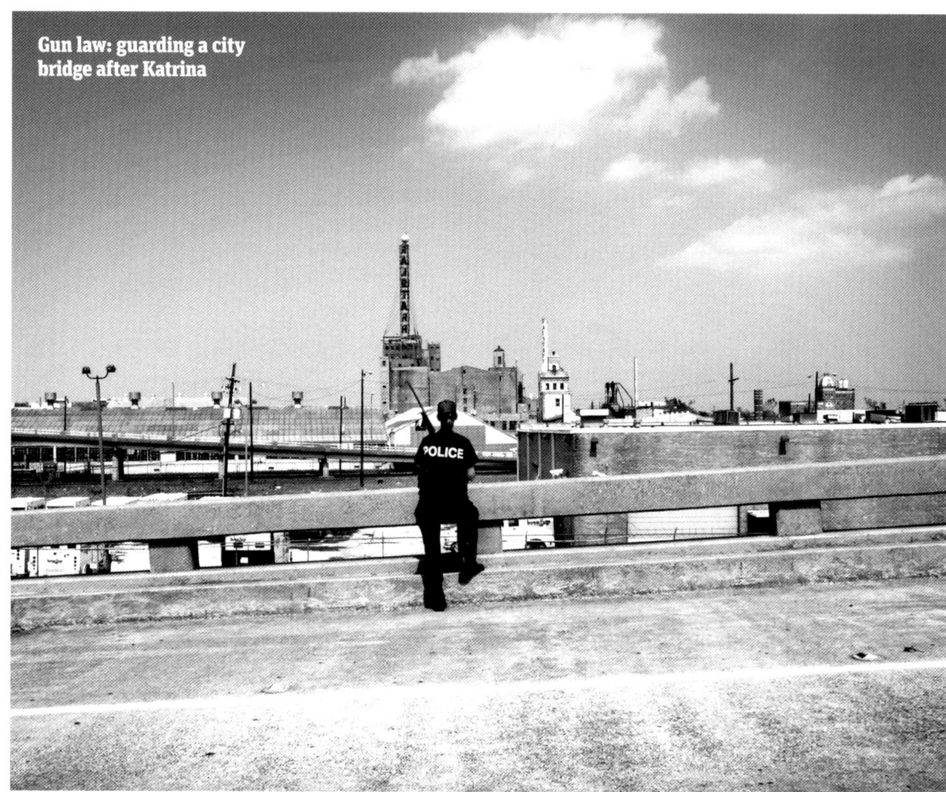

Gun law: guarding a city bridge after Katrina

On 17 March this year, the federal department of justice (DoJ) decided enough was enough and made moves to have the New Orleans Police Department (NOPD) placed under the supervision of a federal judge. The New Orleans jail system will likely follow.

The department released a report covering only the past two years and ignoring several current federal investigations of police officers for murder. It says, more or less, that the NOPD is incapable on any level; that it is racist; that it systemically violates civil rights, routinely using "unnecessary and unreasonable force"; that it is "largely indifferent to widespread violations of law and policy by its police officers" and appears to have gone to great lengths to cover up its shootings of civilians. "NOPD's mishandling of officer-involved shooting investigations," the report says, "was so blatant and egregious that it appeared intentional in some respects."

The department can't even handle its sniffer dogs: "We found that NOPD's canines were uncontrollable to the point where they repeatedly attacked their own handlers."

This month, two policemen were up in court, one accused of the killing and both of its cover-up in July 2005, a month before the flood, of Raymond Robair, a 48-year-old handyman. He was, it is alleged, viciously beaten and dropped off by both of them in a wheelchair in front of Charity Hospital. He died there of a ruptured spleen from the beating he took.

Civil rights lawyer Mary Howell told me: "I tried at the time to get the justice department to investigate the Robair case and to no avail. Essentially, after 11 September 2001, certainly here in New Orleans, virtually all federal government civil rights enforcement stopped and everybody was diverted into anti-terrorism. Only in the summer of 2008 did they start investigating.

"Without [the work of a print journalist, A C Thompson] and without Obama being elected, none of this would be happening. The last time I looked there were 11 different investigations that the feds were conducting here and at least 20 different police officers who were either indicted or found guilty of a variety of federal offences coming out of Katrina and the immediate pre-Katrina period."

Henry Glover, a 31-year-old African American, was shot by a police sniper as he picked up goods behind a shopping mall during Katrina. He was taken by his brother, a friend and a passer-by to a nearby school that police were using as a special operations centre. There a Swat team let Glover bleed to death and beat his rescuers. Another policeman took the body in the rescuer's car to the levee and torched it, putting two shots into the body (he later called that "a very bad decision"). The incinerated car with Glover's remains inside it lay a block from the police station for weeks.

Last December, three policemen were convicted for the crime: one of manslaughter, one of burning the body and one of falsifying evidence. Eleven other officers who admitted they had lied in testimony or withheld knowledge were reassigned to desk duty or suspended.

That the police force in New Orleans is "a significant threat to the safety of the public", as the DoJ says, is obvious. But the same problems can be seen all over the South, from Miami to Mississippi to Alabama; and the same nationwide, according to Paul Craig Roberts, a former editor of the *Wall Street Journal* and former assistant secretary to the treasury under Ronald Reagan, who wrote recently: "Police in the US now rival criminals, and exceed terrorists as the greatest threat to the American public."

In New Orleans the culture of systemic brutality is old and deep. In 1970 a producer friend went to sign the great pianist James Booker, then in Orleans Parish Prison. He came into the warden's office shackled, walking on his knees. In the mid-1990s what Howell calls "a series of horrific events" culminated in roughly 20 police officers being prosecuted for major felonies: rape, arson, kidnapping, bank robbery. "We had a cop who was doing bank robberies in his lunch hour," she says. "We have two now on death row, one of whom is there – a first for the US – for having a citizen murdered for filing a complaint against him for misconduct."

Howell adds: "Going into Katrina, our police department was a train wreck – in terms of the police, in terms of the jail, in terms of what was going on in the courts. It was just a deeply dysfunctional system. Katrina didn't cause the dysfunction in the system, it just exposed it."

A young civil rights lawyer, Chloe Cockburn, who has worked for criminal justice reform in New Orleans, recently wrote a term paper on the subject of the return of corporal punishment to American prisons.

The movement towards rational punishment – from a time when segregation from society was considered punishment enough – has been abandoned in favour of retribution, Cockburn argues. "There's evidence across the culture of people accepting the brutal treatment of prisoners, an idea that because you committed a crime you deserve everything you get," she says. "I think it's impossible for Europeans to truly comprehend how horrible it is here."

You could take the "squirrel cages". These are used in the prison in St Tammany Parish, one of the richest districts in the New Orleans conurbation. The metal cages measure 3ft by 3ft and are 7ft high, meaning the prisoner can stand but can't lie down.

New Orleans, according to the American Civil Liberties Union (ACLU), is a city "without mental health care". The cages are therefore used for prisoners who report being suicidal, have some mental disturbance or are simply being punished for a misdemeanour.

Until August last year at least, there were six of them in the booking area of the jail. Katie Schwartzmann, an attorney with the ACLU, established that prisoners were kept

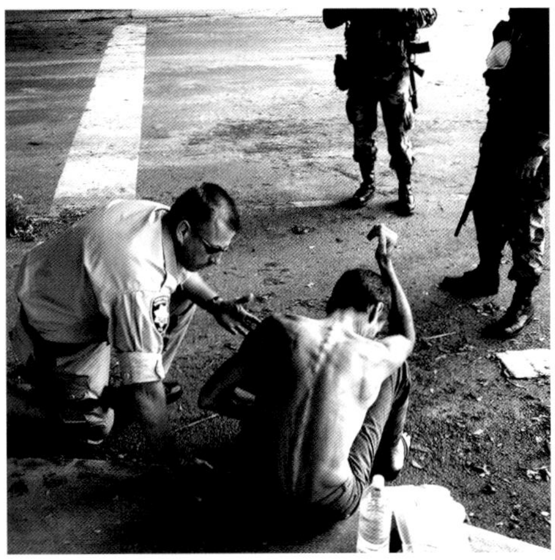

Washed up: rounding up the unevacuated homeless

in them for a minimum of 72 hours and often for "days, weeks and even over a month". She added: "I spoke to one prisoner a few days ago who went completely crazy when they put him in there. He started banging his head against the wall as hard as he could and had to have eight staples."

The ACLU sent a letter to the parish, noting that "the cages have frequently been used to hold more than one prisoner at a time and that staff often ignore prisoners' requests to use the bathroom, forcing people to urinate in discarded milk cartons". It also pointed out that the St Tammany Parish code states that dogs must be kept in cages at least 6ft by 6ft, with "sufficient space to lie down". Sick prisoners in the parish were being afforded a quarter of the space afforded to animals. Following the ACLU report, the parish said it would use the cages only in an "emergency".

> "Police in the US exceed terrorists as the greatest threat to the public"

Then there was "Camp Greyhound", a detention facility known for organised brutality – a little-known, near-exact facsimile of Guantanamo Bay, set up in the bus station in downtown New Orleans. There are few photographs of it – it came and went in a few weeks – but there is a detailed description of it in Dave Eggers's non-fiction bestseller *Zeitoun*. The book gets its name from an American Muslim, a Syrian-born building contractor who had lived in New Orleans for 11 years. Abdulrahman Zeitoun had sent his wife and their children to Baton Rouge and stayed back to check on his properties.

A boatload of goons from the various militias, government and not, that had started patrolling the city after the hurricane arrived at Zeitoun's flooded place. They arrested him and three companions, one a fellow Muslim Syrian by birth called Nasser Dayoob. The charge sheet he saw many weeks later read: "Looting". Roughed up – face in the mud, knee in the back – handcuffed and shouted at, they were taken to the Union Passenger Terminal bus station in the centre of New Orleans. A wooden sign outside said: "We're taking our city back." One of Zeitoun's companions asked a passing soldier: "Why are we here?" "You guys are al-Qaeda," was the reply.

In the car park they saw a vast construction of chain-link fences, 16 ft high, topped with razor wire stretching 100 yards. It was divided into smaller cages, all brand new. Sixteen of them. "It looked precisely like the pictures he'd seen of Guantanamo Bay," Eggers wrote of Zeitoun, noting that many of the prisoners were wearing orange jumpsuits. "Like Guantanamo it was outdoors, all the cages were visible and there was nowhere to sit or sleep."

Each cage had a portable toilet in the open. Electricity was provided by a stationary Amtrak train engine, roaring 24 hours a day. Bright floodlights lit it at night.

The detention unit was purpose-built for the maximum discomfort of its inmates. As Eggers writes: "In the cage, the men had few options: they could stand in the centre, they could sit on the cement, or they could lean against a steel rack." It was run along Gitmo rules. No one had been charged with an offence; none had or would see a lawyer.

This is where Zeitoun and his companions spent three agonising days, being subjected to humiliating strip searches, the guards pushing ham sandwiches through the wire even though they had been seen praying. They watched as one mentally handicapped inmate was tied up and pepper-sprayed in the face until "he was cowering in a foetal position wailing like an animal, trying to reach his eyes with his hands".

Anyone who complained or touched the wire was dragged out, tied up and pepper-sprayed, or shot with beanbag guns. Eventually the guards just shot at men and women through the wire indiscriminately. The worst torture for Zeitoun was not being allowed to make a phone call to reassure distressed relatives. Even after he was moved to a "normal" prison, his wife heard nothing of him for almost two weeks.

The orders were undoubtedly punitive – the prison's rules served no other purpose, and even taking a message from a prisoner was an offence. It was also a breach of the prisoners' rights. A jury ordered the city to pay out $650,000 to two white tourists who had their cellphones confiscated and who, as a result, got lost in the gulag for several weeks. They could afford bail and would have obtained it – they claimed – if they had been permitted to use their phones.

Zeitoun and the three others were moved to the Elayn Hunt Correctional Centre. Then, mysteriously, his wife got a call from ▶

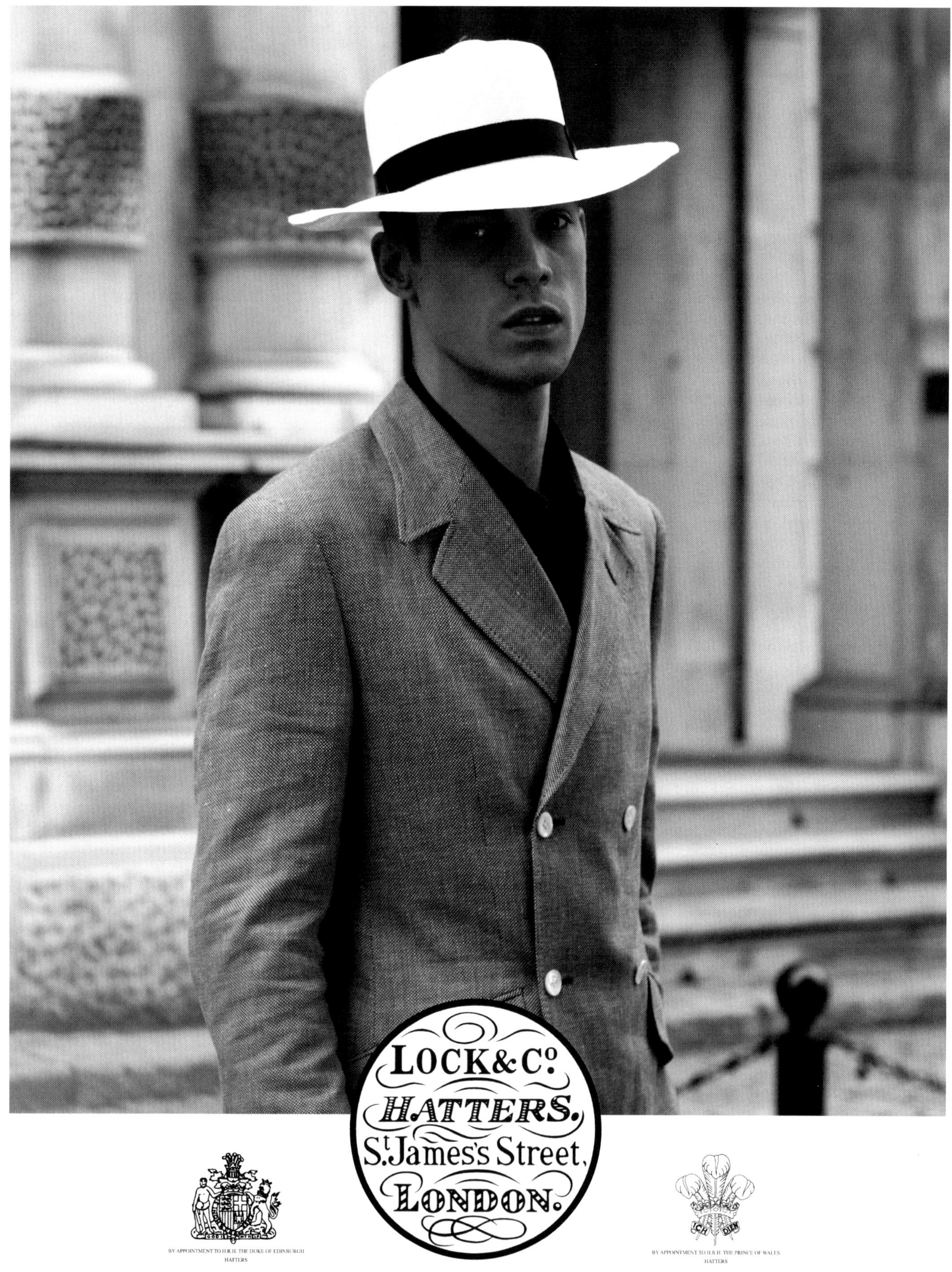

LOCK & C^O.
HATTERS.
S^t. James's Street,
LONDON.
ICH DIEN
BY APPOINTMENT TO H.R.H. THE DUKE OF EDINBURGH
HATTERS
BY APPOINTMENT TO H.R.H. THE PRINCE OF WALES
HATTERS

homeland security saying he was free to go. It still took an astute lawyer several more days to get him out on $75,000 bail. Nasser, his Syrian-born companion, spent five months in jail; of the other two, one was locked up for six months and the other eight. All charges were dropped.

How and why had Camp Greyhound been built with such speed and efficiency, with its food and portable toilets, when the rest of the stranded population had been abandoned for days by the government and was fighting for food and water? It was constructed by the inmates of Angola, the 18,000-acre Louisiana state penitentiary, a former slave plantation and the toughest of all American jails, where the average sentence is 89.9 years. Burl Cain, the warden of Angola, had brought his labour force of convicted murderers and rapists to the New Orleans bus station, where they slept overnight, and used his own equipment and supplies to construct it. He had it done in two days. "A real start to rebuilding New Orleans," Eggers quotes him as saying. Angola has some of the lowest-paid prison guards in the United States, and few of them have graduated from high school. Cain kept them at Camp Greyhound as part of the package.

Who had picked up Zeitoun and his friends? It was hard to tell. Every gun club in America had responded to the NOPD's call for help. It was the chief of police who had said that babies were being raped in the Superdome sheltering thousands of the homeless after the hurricane; his assistant who had, within earshot of many police officers, said they should "shoot looters". The mayor of the city called, farcically, for martial law to be declared where no such ordinance existed in Louisiana. It established a free-fire zone – one white vigilante, since indicted for murder, incautiously described it as being "like the pheasant season in South Dakota".

One of Katie Schwartzmann's clients was arrested by a gang called the Iowa Guard. There were also at least five mercenary outfits, all licensed by homeland security, including a firm named Instinctive Shooting International. It described itself as being staffed by "veterans of the Israeli special task forces".

"There are policy decisions that are made because of the fact that we are a largely African-American city," says Howell. "And that's something that was so shocking, that not only did the local authorities not care, [but] every level of government failed. Every level."

Camp Greyhound, when it was exposed, was the focus of much retrospective anger in the black population: it made it clear where the priorities lay – a holding jail was more important than food, water and medical help. Meanwhile, the 7,000 inmates of the main buildings of Orleans Parish Prison had been left, more or less, to drown. They very nearly did: the buildings are in the lowest part of New Orleans.

Marlin Gusman, who is still the city's sheriff, refused to evacuate the jail when the floodwaters came. As the jails started filling up with water, many deputies left their posts, abandoning the prisoners in their cells, in the dark.

Almost every prisoner reported going without food and water for days after the storm. They lived in terrible heat – with broken air-conditioners and no windows, in stinking floodwater. One said: "I witnessed several inmates with various medical conditions suffer from dehydration – we were forced to live off toilet water and lie in our own waste and body fluids. When the rescuers arrived, I was still locked in my cell and they had to pry the bars open. I walked out in chest-deep sewer water."

Abu Ghraib was a sample export of everyday abuse in the US penal system

A deputy who came back to try to release the prisoners recalled: "Before the water got to my waist, we put them all on lockdown, and the scary thing about that was the cells wouldn't open back up. We had to go under the water and try to open them manually." The rescuers only just succeeded.

Hundreds of prisoners were moved from other buildings to the prison's central lock-up area, where they remained standing in deep water for as long as 12 or 13 hours – mostly because the sheriff didn't have enough boats to transport them to higher ground. For those who went to the Jena Correctional Facility, a former juvenile prison, it was "the beginning of a new nightmare", according to the ACLU. "They were subjected to egregious physical and verbal abuse almost immediately after they arrived . . . At one point in their stay several prisoners were told to line up, place their hands behind their heads and press their groins against the buttocks of the prisoners in front of them. An officer taunted them, saying, 'Hard dicks to soft ass! I know y'all are getting hard, because I am.'"

This makes it appear that the Abu Ghraib prisoner scandal was not an aberration – it was a sample export of everyday abuse across the criminal and penal system in the US. But Sheriff Gusman dismissed the entire ACLU report. "Don't rely on crackheads, cowards and criminals to say what the story is," he said.

In 2007, two years after Katrina, when the murder rate rose again – to five times that of comparable-sized cities – there was an explosion of anger at the failure of the New Orleans criminal justice system. The people began to speak with a collective and powerful voice. Hundreds had been locked up for trivial offences and murder kept on rising. Zero tolerance wasn't working; besides, it was very expensive.

But as the *New York Times* wrote: "There are serious risks in taking on sheriffs in Louisiana, given their political heft." The jail is every sheriff's power base; it gives him one of the most influential positions in government. It gives him jobs to dispense – non-civil service, non-union jobs – and a large, pliable workforce that can be called on for any task, such as getting the vote out.

Sheriff Gusman (who is black) strongly criticised the size of Orleans Parish Prison when a councilman – before Katrina, it had the largest number of inmates per capita of any city in the US. Later he changed his tune, campaigning to build a new jail with a similar capacity, of 5,500 beds. Building such a jail would cost a quarter of a billion dollars, and involve big contracts. But then Gusman hit a snag.

Some new members had been elected to the city council in 2006, among them James Carter, a prominent young African-American attorney who wanted reform. The council had sought help from the Vera Institute of Justice, a non-profit organisation that advises governments. The leading figure behind the recommendations that Vera made was Jon Wool, its local director. He had galvanised progressive-minded government officials as well as community and activist organisations that wanted change.

"The whole story turned on the size of this new jail," he says. The counterproposal was to build a jail with 1,438 beds. To make this work, Wool proposed reforms that would reduce the jail population. He set up a pre-trial release system for non-violent crimes which has sped up processing for minor offences from 60 days to five days; summonses have replaced custodial arrests in more than half of minor cases. By December last year there was a drop of 500 inmates from the previous June. The public defender's office – crucial for poorer defendants – was reinvigorated with grants of $4m; lawyers were required to give up private practice and do public work full-time.

Further reforms are afoot which, Wool is sure, will bring the jail numbers in line with his new prison figure. On 3 February, the city council voted unanimously to pass an ordinance mandating the sheriff to build a new facility limited to 1,438 beds. It was an important turning point – and a victory for community action.

But it's not over. The sheriff is not happy, and Wool sees the window for change staying open for only a short time. Funding could be cut off. Political whimsy could put an end to all reforms. "The real question and the hard part," says Mary Howell, "is making real changes that have a prayer of lasting. We can't wait another 30 years for solutions." ●

Lives and Letters

Reach out for that dream: admirers in Baltimore, Maryland mob Martin Luther King after he won the Nobel Peace Prize, 1964

***Portrait of Percy Bysshe Shelley* (1819) by Amelia Curran**

31 MARCH 1917

Shelley the Adolescent

By Lytton Strachey

There is a story in Hogg's *Life of Shelley* of how the poet went to a large dinner party at Norfolk House. He sat near the bottom of the table, and after a time his neighbour said to him: "Pray, who is that very strange old man at the top of the table, sitting next to His Grace, who talks so much, so loudly, and in so extraordinary a manner, and all about himself?" "He is my father," Shelley replied; "and he is a very strange old man indeed!"

Our knowledge of Timothy Shelley has been hitherto mainly based upon Hogg's portrait of him—eccentric, capricious, puzzled, blustering, "scolding, crying, swearing, and then weeping again", then bringing out the old port, and assuring everybody at great length that he was highly respected in the House of Commons, and then turning in a breath from some rambling anecdote of poachers in Sussex to a proof of the existence of the Deity. But Hogg was not always accurate; he was capable of rearranging facts for his own purposes; he was even capable of rewriting letters. It seemed, therefore, difficult to accept his presentment of "the poor old governor" as literally true; the letters especially looked as if they had been delicately manipulated—even an irate and port-bibbing country gentleman of the time of the Regency could hardly be supposed in sober earnest to have been the author of quite so much incoherence and of quite so little grammar.

Now Mr Ingpen has discovered and published a collection of documents which give us a great deal of first-hand information upon Sir Timothy and his relations with his son. These documents, drawn principally from the correspondence of the Shelleys' family lawyer, William Whitton, are full of interest; and they substantiate—in a remarkable way—Hogg's account of Sir Timothy. It becomes clear that Hogg's portrait was by no means a fancy one, that "the epistles of the beloved Timothy" were in truth "very peculiar"—illiterate, confused, and hysterical to an extraordinary degree, and that his conduct was of a piece with his correspondence. Indeed, if in all the other elements of his character Shelley was the very antithesis of his father, there can be no doubt at all where his eccentricity came from.

Of course, Sir Timothy is only interesting from the accident of his fatherhood. It is one of Fate's little ironies that the poor old governor, who in the natural course of things would have dropped long since into a deserved and decent oblivion, should still be read about and thought about—that even his notes to his lawyer should be carefully unearthed, elaborately annotated, and published in a large book—for the sake of a boy whom he disliked and disapproved of, whom he did his best to injure while living, and whose very memory he tried hard to suppress. He is immortal, as the French say, *malgré lui*—an unwilling ghost caught up into an everlasting glory.

As to Shelley himself, it may be hoped that Mr Ingpen's book will lead the way to a clearer vision of a creature who still stands in need of a little understanding. It is a misfortune that the critics and biographers of poets should be for the most part highly respectable old gentlemen; for poets themselves are apt to be young, and are not apt to be highly respectable. Sometimes the respectable old gentlemen are frankly put out; but sometimes they try to be sympathetic—with results at least equally unfortunate. In Shelley's case it is difficult to decide whether the distressed self-righteousness of Matthew Arnold's famous essay or the solemn adoration of Professor Dowden's standard biography gives the falser impression. Certainly the sympathetic treatment is the more insidious. The bias of Matthew Arnold's attack is obvious; but the process by which Shelley's fire and air have been transmuted into Professor Dowden's cotton-wool and rose-water is a subtler revenge of the world's upon the most radiant of its enemies.

Mr Ingpen's book deals chiefly with that part of Shelley's life between his expulsion from Oxford and his separation from his first wife. It is the most controversial period of Shelley's career. It is the period of the elopement with Harriet Westbrook, of the sudden flittings and ceaseless wanderings to and fro between Edinburgh, York, Keswick, Wales, Ireland, Devonshire, and London, of the wild Dublin escapade, of the passionate correspondence and furious quarrel with Miss Hitchener, of the composition of *Queen Mab*, and of the elopement with Mary Godwin. The great merit of Mr Ingpen's new letters is that they show us the Shelley of these three years, neither as the Divine Poet nor as the Outcast from Society, but in the painful and prosaic posture of a son who is on bad terms with his father and wants to get money out of him.

Now there is one fact which must immediately strike every reader of this correspondence, and which really affords the clue to the whole queer history: Shelley's extraordinary youthfulness. And it is just this fact which writers on Shelley seem persistently to ignore. It is almost impossible to remember, as one watches their long faces, that the object of all their concern was a youth scarcely out of his teens; that Shelley was eighteen when he was expelled from Oxford, that he was just nineteen when he eloped with Harriet, who was herself sixteen, that he was under twenty-two when he eloped with Mary, while Mary was not seventeen. In reality, Shelley during these years was an adolescent. His restlessness, his crudity of thought and feeling, his violent fluctuations of sentiment, his enthusiasms and exaggerations, his inability to judge correctly either the mental processes of other people or the causal laws which govern the actual world—all these are the familiar phenomena of adolescence; in Shelley's case they happened to be combined with a high intelligence, a determined will, and a wonderful unworldliness; but, none the less, the adolescence was there.

That was the fundamental fact which his father, like his commentators, failed to realise. He persisted in treating Shelley's behaviour seriously. The leaflet for which Shelley was sent down from Oxford, *The Necessity of Atheism*, signed "Jeremiah Stukeley", was obviously little more than a schoolboy's prank; but Atheism happened at that moment to be the bugbear of the governing classes, and Sir Timothy lost his head. Instead of attempting to win over the youth by kindness, the old man adopted the almost incredible course of refusing to have any communication with his son, save through the family lawyer.

> "I would hollow in your ears Bysshe, Bysshe, Bysshe till you're deaf"

The lawyer, Whitton, was the last man who should have been entrusted with such a task. His letters show him to have been a formal and testy personage, with the disposition, and sometimes the expressions, of a butler. "You care not, you say," he wrote to Shelley, "for Family Pride. Allow me to tell you that the first part of the Family Pride of a Gent is to preserve a propriety of manners and a decency of expression in communication, and your forgetfulness of those qualifications towards me in the letter I have just received induces me to say," etc. "The Gent," Whitton told Sir Timothy, "has thought proper to lecture me on the occasion." "The occasion" was Shelley's innocent suggestion that he should be allowed to resign his inheritance to the family property (worth over £200,000) in return for a settled income of £100 a year. The lawyer was appalled, and easily whipped up Sir Timothy into a hectic fury. "The insulting, ungentlemanly letter to you," wrote the indignant parent, "appears the high-toned, self-will'd dictate of the Diabolical Publications which have unluckily fallen in his way, and given this Bias to his mind, that is most singular. To cast off all thoughts of his Maker, to abandon his Parents, to wish to relinquish his Fortune and to court Persecution all seems to arise from the same source."

If Sir Timothy had decided to cut off his son altogether and let him shift for himself, there might have been something to be said for him. But he could not bring himself to do that. Instead, while refusing to allow Shelley to return home, he doled out to him an allowance of £200 a year; and then, when the inevitable happened, and the inflammable youth fell into the arms of the beautiful Harriet, imagined he was rescuing her from a persecuting family, and married her, the foolish old man cut off the allowance without a word.

Shelley's letters to his father at this juncture reveal completely the absurd ingenuousness of his mind. Penniless, married, in a strange town—he had eloped with Harriet to Edinburgh—Shelley brought himself to beg for money, and yet, in the very same breath, could not resist the opportunity of lecturing Sir Timothy. "Father, are you a Christian?... I appeal to your duty to the God whose worship you profess, I appeal to the terrors of that day which you believe to seal the doom of mortals, then clothed with immortality", and so on, through page after page and letter after letter. As Mr Ingpen says, it is strange that no inkling of the mingled pathos and comedy of these appeals should have touched Sir Timothy.

Then, when the poor boy was met by nothing but silence, we see him breaking out into ridiculous invective. "You have treated me *ill*, *vilely*. When I was expelled for Atheism, you wished I had been killed in Spain... If *you* will not hear my name, *I* will pronounce it. Had I money enough I would meet you in London and hollow in your ears Bysshe, Bysshe, Bysshe . . . aye, Bysshe till you're deaf." Had I money enough! Truly, in the circumstances, an exquisite proviso!

These are the central incidents with which Mr Ingpen's book is concerned; but it is difficult to indicate in a short space the wealth of human interest contained in these important letters. They may be recommended alike to the psychologist and the historian. Mr Ingpen is able to throw fresh light on some other circumstances of interest: he shows that Shelley was arrested for debt; he gives new documents bearing upon Harriet's suicide; and he reproduces extracts from the poet's manuscript note-book. Not the least amusing part of his book is that in which he traces the relations between Sir Timothy and Mary Shelley, after the tragedy in the Gulf of Spezzia.

The epistles of the beloved Timothy retain their character to the end. "To lose an eldest son in his lifetime," he writes to Whitton, "and the unfortunate manner of his losing that life, is truely melancholy to think of, but as it has pleas'd the Great Author of our Being so to dispose of him I must make up my mind with resignation." And Whitton's own style loses nothing of its charm. After Shelley's death, one of his Oxford creditors—a plumber—applied to the lawyer for payment of a bill. Whitton not only refused to pay, but took the opportunity of pointing the moral. "The officious interference of you and others did a most serious injury to the Gent that is now no more." ●

D H Lawrence in Love

By Rebecca West

Many of us are cleverer than Mr D H Lawrence and nearly all of us save an incarcerated few are much saner, but this does not affect the fact that he is a genius. It does, of course, affect the fact of his being an artist. *Women in Love* is flawed in innumerable places by Mr Lawrence's limitations and excesses. His general ideas are poor and uncorrected, apparently, by any wide reading or much discussion; when he wants to represent Birkin, who is supposed to be the brilliant thinker of the book, as confounding the shallow Hermione with his power over reality, he puts into his mouth a collection of platitudes on the subject of democracy which would have drawn nothing from any woman of that intellectual level, except perhaps the remark that these things had been dealt with more thoroughly by Havelock Ellis in his essay on the spheres of individualism and Socialism.

He is madly irritable.

> The porter came up. "À Bâle—deuxième classe?—Voilà!" And he clambered into the high train. They followed. The compartments were already some of them taken. But many were dim and empty. The luggage was stowed, the porter was tipped. "Nous avons encore?" said Birkin, looking at his watch and at the porter. "Encore une demi-heure," with which, in his blue blouse, he disappeared. He was ugly and insolent.

We are not told anything more about this porter. This is the full span of his tenuous existence in Mr Lawrence's imagination. He has been called out of the everywhere into the here simply in order that for these two minutes he may be ugly and insolent.

This is typical of Mr Lawrence's indifference to that quality of serenity which is the highest form of decency. He thinks it natural that everybody should take their own Grand Guignol about with them in the form of an irritable nervous system and that it should give continuous performances. This prejudices his work in two ways. It makes him represent the characters whom he wishes to be regarded as normal as existing permanently in the throes of hyperæsthesia. When Gerald Crich and Gudrun stay in London on their way to the Tyrol, her reactions to London, which she does not appear to like, are so extreme that one anticipates that Gerald will have to spend all his time abroad nursing her through a nervous breakdown, which is in fact not what happened. It also shatters the author's nerves so that his fingers are often too clumsy and tremulous to deal with the subtleties which his mind insists on handing them as subjects.

But *Women in Love* is a work of genius. It contains characters which are masterpieces of pure creation. Birkin is not. The character whom an author designs as the mouthpiece of truth never is; always he is patronising and knowing, like "Our London Correspondent" writing his weekly letter in a provincial newspaper. But there is Hermione Roddice, the woman who stood beyond all vulgar judgment, yet could be reduced to misery by the slightest gesture of contempt from any servant because she has no real self and, though she could know, could not be. Mr Lawrence could always conjure imaginary things into the world of the eye, and he makes visible the unhappy physical presence of Hermione, with her long face and her weight of heavy dull hair, her queer clothes, her strange appearance that made people want to jeer yet held them silent till she passed.

> When Mr Lawrence writes of love he always soils the matter

There are also Mr and Mrs Crich, the mine-owner and his wife, though their creation is not so indisputably pure as that of Hermione. One suspects that they were called into being in consequence of Mr Lawrence's readings in German philosophy, that they are not only post but propter Nietzsche and Max Stirner. But they are great figures: the father, who loved to give to the poor out of his faith that "they through poverty and labour were nearer to God than he", until in time he became "some subtle funeral bird, feeding on the miseries of the people"; the mother, like a hawk, loathing the rusty black, cringing figures of his parasites, despising him for his perpetual indulgence in the laxer, gentler emotions, and bending over his dead body at the last in bitter contempt because his face was so beautiful, so unmarked by pride.

The persons who are most intimately concerned in the development of the main thesis of the book are not so satisfactory because that thesis deals with love. It is in itself an excellent thesis. It is a stern answer to the human cry, "I can endure the hatred the world bears me, and the hate I bear the world, if only there is one whom I love and who loves me." It declares: "No, that is not how it is. There shall be no one who loves you and no one whom you love, unless you first get in on loving terms with the world." Gerald Crich refuses to enter into an alliance of friendship with Birkin. He, the materialist, has no use for an expenditure of affection in a quarter where there is no chance of physical pleasure, and stakes his all on his union with Gudrun. This concentration itself wrecks that union. She finds him empty of everything but desire for her; he has had no schooling of altruistic love; he does not help her out of her own fatigued desire for corruption and decay, the peace of dissolution; and she breaks away from him. Thereby, because he staked everything on her, he is destroyed. It is not really very abstruse, nor very revolutionary, nor very morbid. In *Antony and Cleopatra* Shakespeare permitted himself to say much the same sort of things about the quality of love that arises between highly sexual people. But when Mr Lawrence writes of love he always soils the matter by his violent style.

Mrs Mary Baker Eddy once remarked that the purpose of the relationship between the sexes is to "happify existence". There are times when Mr Lawrence writes as if he thought its purpose was to give existence a black eye. His lovers are the Yahoos of Eros, and though Beauty may be in their spirits, it is certainly not in their manners. This is not represented as incidental to their characters, but as a necessary condition of love. It is a real flaw in Mr Lawrence's temperament; but it is so marked and so apart from the rest of him that it no more spoils the book than a crack in the canvas spoils a beautiful picture. ●

Early Recollections of Adolf Hitler

By W W Crotch

The first time I heard the name of Adolf Hitler mentioned was shortly after the end of the war, when a man named Franz Xavier Huber, a veteran who had a leg shot away before Verdun in 1917, told me the stories of a curious fellow who had been in his regiment at the front. He was a garrulous chap, and, sitting in that same Bürgerbraü Keller in Munich (where in 1923 Hitler took his first plunge into revolutionary activities by firing off his army revolver at the ceiling and declaring the morrow would see him victor or dead—although it saw him neither the one nor the other, but unscathed, a helter-skelter fugitive in the Bavarian hills), he used to tell tales tragic and humorous of his campaign experience.

The thing that had struck him about "Private Hitler" was his grandiloquence. He was neither popular nor the reverse with his fellows; they just smiled at him and his vague rambling speeches on everything in the world and out of it. He showed distinct talent in avoiding disagreeable tasks, but he knew on which side his bread was buttered. He interested himself particularly in the important question of seeing the officer's washing was done or doing it himself. This secured for him the good graces of the colonel, who removed him from the more constant dangers of the trenches and appointed him runner between regimental headquarters and the front line.

These duties brought him frequently in contact with men and he would sit for hours in a dug-out and hold forth on Socialism, of which it was evident he had only very hazy notions. Old Social Democrats used to laugh at him, but no one debated seriously with him. He could not brook contradiction and used to fly into terrible rages if anyone ventured a word of dissent. Though he got the Iron Cross of the second class, no one in the regiment ever looked upon Hitler as any sort of hero; indeed they rather admired him for the skill with which he avoided hot corners. The regimental records contain not a line concerning an award of the Iron Cross of the first class, though in latter years he has taken to wearing it prominently on his self-constructed uniform.

In those days in Munich I lived in the Thiersh Strasse and I frequently noticed in the street a man who vaguely reminded me of a militant edition of Charles Chaplin, owing to his characteristic moustache and his bouncing way of walking. He always carried a riding whip in his hand with which he used incessantly to chop off imaginary heads as he walked. He was so funny that I inquired from neighbours who he might be: most of them, owing to his Slav type, took him to be one of those Russian émigrés who abounded in Germany at that time, and they freely talked of his being probably a trifle mentally deranged. But my grocer told me it was a Herr Adolf Hitler from Braunau in Austria, and that he was leader of a tiny political group which called itself the "German National Socialist Workers Party". He lived as a boarder in the apartment of a small artisan, wrote articles for an obscure paper called the *Völkischer Beobachter*, and orated in hole-and-corner meetings before audiences of a dozen or two. Out of curiosity I bought the paper once or twice, and found it a scatter-brained collection of wild anti-Jewish stories and articles interlarded with panegyrics on the Germanic race. My obliging grocer closed his information on Hitler by remarking that he frequently purchased things in his shop and was, despite his eccentric appearance, quite a pleasant fellow, though inclined to talk sixteen to the dozen about anything and everything.

> He reminded me of a militant edition of Charles Chaplin

Some time later I became a frequent customer of a little wine saloon in the Schelling Strasse. The public in this inn was mostly composed of Bohemians, artists and art students, members of the staff of *Simplicissimus*, the famous satirical weekly; musicians and poetasters sat around of an evening and listened to Gulbransson or Thöny giving forth on art, politics and the price of a pound of meat. Discussions ensued that lasted far into the night, over tankards of beer and bottles of excellent Chianti. Hitler was an almost daily visitor; he had, I learned, been a house painter in his early days in Vienna, but he was rather sore on the subject, and posed as an artist. He was very fond of airing his views on art and architecture, which, however, were not taken seriously by any of the artists who frequented the place.

Hitler was often accompanied by one or two friends who, I was told, were members of his little political group. The most sensible of the band was a chemist named Gregor Strasser, a very sound fellow with whom I often spoke. Hitler's closest friend at that time, however, seemed to be an ex-army captain named Roehm, who later became chief of the Storm Troops, while his friend, Baldur von Schirach, was entrusted with leadership of the "Hitler Youth", the boy scout organisation of the National Socialist movement.

One thing that struck me about Hitler was his extreme abstemiousness. He ate every night a dish of vegetables, and mineral water was his only drink. He never smoked. This reminds me of an amusing incident when Hitler became Chancellor. The German vegetarians have a central organ of their league, and this paper came out with flaming headlines:

FIRST GREAT VICTORY OF
GERMAN VEGETARIANS. HITLER
BECOMES CHANCELLOR.

Sometimes instead of regaling us with chaotic speeches, Hitler would sit for hours on end in front of his mineral water, staring into space, not uttering a word, and apparently quite oblivious of his surroundings. If on these occasions someone suddenly addressed him, he would start as if out of sleep, and stroke his forehead with his hand several times before coming back to reality.

Apart from politics and art, Hitler's chief topics of conversation were Italy and clairvoyance. He had never visited Italy, but he would sometimes talk for half an hour on end about the glories of ancient Rome and the greatness of the Caesars. There was something about his talk that made one think of the prophets of the Old Testament: he spoke as if he believed himself to be inspired. The only thing that dispelled the illusion was his frequent use of words that are not found in the dictionary of a cultivated German.

One day I remember a man came in who, for the price of a plate of soup, read hands and

JULIANO GUEDES/NAOPERECIVEL.COM.BR

told fortunes. Hitler retired with the soothsayer into a corner and spent a whole hour with him in earnest conference. When he got back among us, he turned with anger upon a student who had made a slighting remark about clairvoyance, and launched out upon an eloquent defence of occultism of every kind, and especially of astrology.

He made a confidant, too, of a Jewish charlatan named Steinschneider who had taken to himself the name of Hanussen, and consulted him frequently. Hanussen, who subsequently founded and ran a weekly newspaper on astrology, devoted to indirect propaganda for Hitler, became for a few weeks after Hitler's accession to power almost as important a factor in Germany as Rasputin had been in Russia. But his end was a tragic one. He was found murdered in a field in the environs of Berlin. The incident does not appear to have shaken Hitler's faith in astrology, and one of Hanussen's chief rivals, a man named Mücke, has been appointed by Hitler "Federal Commissary for Occultism". This, I believe, is the first time in modern ages that a state has officially recognised soothsaying and turned it into a government department.

But there is one extraordinary feature about Hitler's faith in the occult which gives rise to intriguing speculation. As everyone knows, he has adopted the Swastika as the emblem of the State. But curiously enough this Swastika is reversed, and anyone acquainted with Eastern beliefs knows that this is to be regarded with positive horror. An inverted Swastika is indicative not of endless life but of the flood and flame of life leading to a violent destruction. Did Hitler know this when he foisted it upon the German nation? Is the reversed Swastika just another sign of the man's half-baked conception of things? Or is this a last vestige of the irony of his political faith?

Hitler was not without devoted adherents in the "Osteria Bavaria". Some students became seized with a sort of hero-worship regarding him, and hung on to every word he said with wrapt attention. But his chief admirers were the two waitresses, buxom Bavarian wenches, who listened open-mouthed to him and danced attendance on him in a way that formed the subject of many jokes among the habitués of the place.

Hitler's relations with women indeed are a strange and obscure chapter. I saw a great deal of him at that time, and I can certify that he was in these matters as abstemious as in regard to food and drink. The only woman he seemed to care for at all was the lady to whose villa in the hills he fled after his inglorious collapse in November, 1923. Latterly he is said to have fallen in love with Winifred Wagner, but I can hardly imagine the Hitler of 1921 in love.

Another thing that struck me was the man's utter incapacity to deal with important details. When he spoke of Italy, or the German race, or occultism, or the Jews, his talk was a succession of vague generalities, couched in attractive if flowery language, but showing in every case either complete ignorance or at least complete contempt for detail.

Though he insisted in season and out of season on the greatness of "pure Germanism", I never met a German who was so entirely un-German. His speech, his thought, his outlook were far more Slav than Teutonic. He loved everything foreign while he denounced it.

His race theories came from the Frenchman, Gobineau, and the English renegade, Houston Chamberlain. His famous phrase "the Third Reich" was the invention of the Dutchman, Moeller van den Bruck. The party salute was an Elizabethan stage convention—a subterfuge adopted by actors to imitate the Romans. His regimental standards were a pale imitation of Roman eagles. His uniforms are a sort of cocktail of French, Austrian and English uniforms with most of the bad points to all three.

But I will say this, as the result of those long evenings spent with him: he was, and probably still is, passionately, almost ferociously, sincere in all he says and does, even when it appears hypocritical and insincere. ●

The Upside-Down World of Lewis Carroll

By Virginia Woolf

The complete works of Lewis Carroll have been issued by the *Nonesuch Press* in a stout volume of 1,293 pages. So there is no excuse—Lewis Carroll ought once and for all to be complete. We ought to be able to grasp him whole and entire. But we fail—once more we fail. We think we have caught Lewis Carroll; we look again and see an Oxford clergyman. We think we have caught the Rev C L Dodgson—we look again and see a fairy elf. The book breaks in two in our hands. In order to cement it, we turn to the Life.

But the Rev C L Dodgson had no life. He passed through the world so lightly that he left no print. He melted so passively into Oxford that he is invisible. He accepted every convention; he was prudish, pernickety, pious, and jocose. If Oxford dons in the nineteenth century had an essence he was that essence. He was so good that his sisters worshipped him; so pure that his nephew has nothing to say about him. It is just possible, he hints, that "a shadow of disappointment lay over Lewis Carroll's life". Mr Dodgson at once denies the shadow. "My life," he says, "is free from all trial and trouble." But this untinted jelly contained within it a perfectly hard crystal. It contained childhood.

This is very strange, for childhood normally fades slowly. Wisps of childhood persist when the boy or girl is a grown man or woman. Childhood returns sometimes by day, more often by night. But it was not so with Lewis Carroll. For some reason his childhood was sharply severed. It lodged in him whole and entire. And therefore as he grew older this impediment in the centre of his being, this hard block of pure childhood, starved the mature man of nourishment. He slipped through the grown-up world like a shadow, solidifying only on the beach at Eastbourne, with little girls whose frocks he pinned up with safety pins. But since childhood remained in him entire, he could do what no one else has ever been able to do—he could return to that world; he could re-create it, so that we too become children again.

In order to make us into children, he first makes us asleep. "Down, down, down, would the fall *never* come to an end?" Down, down, down we fall into that terrifying, wildly inconsequent, yet perfectly logical world where time races, then stands still; where space stretches, then contracts. It is the world of sleep; it is also the world of dreams. Without any conscious effort dreams come; the white rabbit, the walrus and the carpenter, one after another, they come skipping and leaping across the mind. It is for this reason that the two Alices are not books for children; they are the only books in which we become children. President Wilson, Queen Victoria, the *Times* leader writer, the late Lord Salisbury—it does not matter how old, how important or how insignificant you are, you become a child again. To become a child is to be very literal; to find everything so strange that nothing is surprising; to be heartless, to be ruthless, yet to be so passionate that a snub or a shadow drapes the world in gloom. It is to be Alice in Wonderland.

"At this the whole pack rose up": Arthur Rackham's Alice

It is also to be Alice Through the Looking-Glass. It is to see the world upside down. Many great satirists and moralists have shown us the world upside down, and have made us see it, as grown-up people see it, savagely. Only Lewis Carroll has shown us the world upside down, as a child sees it, and has made us laugh as children laugh, irresponsibly. Down the groves of pure nonsense we whirl laughing, laughing—

> They sought it with thimbles, they sought
> it with care
> They pursued it with forks and with hope ...

And then we wake. None of the transitions in Alice in Wonderland is quite so queer. For we wake to find—is it the Rev C L Dodgson? Is it Lewis Carroll? Or is it both combined? This conglomerate object intends to produce an extra-Bowdlerised edition of Shakespeare for the use of British maidens; implores them to think of death when they go to the play; and always, always to realise that "the true object of life is the development of *character*..." Is there, then, even in 1,293 pages, any such thing as "completeness"?

28 JANUARY 1950

The Wintry Conscience of a Generation

By V S Pritchett

George Orwell was the wintry conscience of a generation which in the Thirties had heard the call to the rasher assumptions of political faith. He was a kind of saint and, in that character, more likely in politics to chasten his own side than the enemy. His instinctive choice of spiritual and physical discomfort, his habit of going his own way, looked like the crankishness which has often cropped up in the British character; if this were so, it was vagrant rather than puritan. He prided himself on seeing through the rackets, and on conveying the impression of living without the solace or even the need of a single illusion.

There can hardly have been a more belligerent and yet more pessimistic Socialist; indeed his Socialism became anarchism. In corrupt and ever worsening years, he always woke up one miserable hour earlier than anyone else and, suspecting something fishy in the site, broke camp and advanced alone to some tougher position in a bleaker place; and it had often happened that he had been the first to detect an unpleasant truth or to refuse a tempting hypocrisy.

Conscience took the Anglo-Indian out of the Burma police, conscience sent the old Etonian among the down and outs in London and Paris, and the degraded victims of the Means Test or slum incompetence in Wigan; it drove him into the Spanish civil war and, inevitably, into one of its unpopular sects, and there Don Quixote saw the poker face of Communism. His was the guilty conscience of the educated and privileged man, one of that regular supply of brilliant recalcitrants which Eton has given us since the days of Fielding; and this conscience could be allayed only by taking upon itself the pain, the misery, the dinginess and the pathetic but hard vulgarities of a stale and hopeless period.

But all this makes only the severe half of George Orwell's character. There were two George Orwells even in name. I see a tall emaciated man with a face scored by the marks of physical suffering. There is the ironic grin of pain at the ends of kind lips, and an expression in the fine eyes that had something of the exalted and obstructive farsightedness one sees in the blind; an expression that will suddenly become gentle, lazily kind and gleaming with workmanlike humour. He would be jogged into remembering mad, comical and often tender things which his indignation had written off; rather like some military man taking time off from a private struggle with the War Office or society in general.

Orwell: "fast, clear, grey prose"

He was an expert on living on the bare necessities and a keen hand at making them barer. There was a sardonic suggestion that he could do this but you could not. He was a handyman. He liked the idea of a bench. I remember once being advised by him to go in for goat-keeping, partly I think because it was a sure road to trouble and semi-starvation; but as he set out the alluring disadvantages it seemed to dawn on him that he was arguing for some country Arcadia, some Animal Farm, he had once known; goats began to look like escapism and, turning aside as we walked to buy some shag at a struggling Wellsian small trader's shop, he switched the subject sharply to the dangerous Fascist tendencies of the St John's Wood Home Guard who were marching to imaginary battle under the Old School Tie.

As an Old School Tie himself, Orwell had varied one of its traditions and had "gone native" in his own country. It is often said that he knew nothing about the working classes, and indeed a certain self-righteousness in the respectable working class obviously repelled his independent mind. So many of his contemporaries had "gone native" in France; he redressed a balance. But he did know that sour, truculent, worrying, vulgar lower-class England of people half "done down", commercially exploited, culturally degraded, lazy, feckless, mild and kind who had appeared in the novels of Dickens, were to show their heads again in Wells and now stood in danger of having the long Victorian decency knocked out of them by gangster politics.

By "the people" he did not mean what the politicians mean; but he saw, at least in his Socialist pamphlets, that it was they who would give English life of the future a raw, muddy but unmistakable and inescapable flavour. His masochism, indeed, extended to culture.

In a way, he deplored this. A classical education had given him a taste for the politician who can quote from Horace; and as was shown in the lovely passages of boyhood reminiscences in *Coming Up for Air*, his imagination was fun only in the kind world he had known before 1914. Growing up turned him not exactly into a misanthrope—he was too good-natured and spirited for that—but into one who felt too painfully the ugly pressure of society upon private virtue and happiness.

His own literary tastes were fixed—with a discernible trailing of the coat—in that boyish period: Bret Harte, Jules Verne, pioneering stuff, Kipling and boys' books. He wrote the best English appreciation of Dickens of our time. *Animal Farm* has become a favourite book for children. His Burmese novels, though poor in character, turn Kipling upside down. As a reporting pamphleteer, his fast, clear, grey prose carries its hard and sweeping satire perfectly.

He has gone: but in one sense, he always made this impression of the passing traveller who meets one on the station, points out that one is waiting for the wrong train and vanishes. His popularity, after *Animal Farm*, must have disturbed such a lone hand. In *Nineteen Eighty-Four*, alas, one can see that deadly pain, which had long been his subject, had seized him completely and obliged him to project a nightmare, as Wells had done in his last days, upon the future. ●

Stephen Spender: Lost Horizons, Brief Encounters

By Norman Mackenzie

The late Norman Mackenzie joined the New Statesman as assistant editor in 1943, after being recommended to the editor, Kingsley Martin, by Harold Laski of the London School of Economics. Here we republish a piece he believed to be one of his best: a profile of the poet, critic and essayist Stephen Spender, which originally ran as part of a series of unsigned biographical sketches in the 1950s.

In the two decades in which Stephen Spender has been a passenger in the cultural Blue Train, he has become an experienced fellow-traveller. He has always chosen the right moment to move to another compartment and new companions. He has been an orderly and undemonstrative passenger, too. In the journey which he himself described in *World Within World*, published two years ago, he admits that much of his experience has been vicarious. Through most of his 45 years he has been the witness, never the doer. He has spent his life writing his biography in various forms, because things happen to him, never because of him. He has relied, at each critical moment, upon someone else, a person on whom he has become desperately though temporarily dependent.

Spender is disarmingly frank about each of these brief encounters. One or other of them (the pseudonyms used below are those he uses) has provided the stimulus for each of his 17 books of verse, criticism and journalism. Each time the loved one has fascinated Spender because he or she has embodied much of the phase of life that he has been about to reject. He wishes his father dead, so that he may demonstrate his grief by the open grave. He can free himself of his family only by confessing his hope of freedom to his grandmother, though he suspects she continually betrays him to his uncle. Marston, at Oxford, whom he bored with his late adolescent affection, really belonged to the room-breaking rowing hearties, whose self-confidence Spender envied and hated. Auden, the recluse, made him into a popular poet in the same way that a prefect makes his fag a footballer. The spiritually hollow bronzed bodies of the New Life are personified, in Hamburg, by Joachim; the shabby stucco of the *Weimardaemmerung* is Isherwood in Berlin. In post-Dollfuss Austria, Vienna is a tragedy of political ambivalence; for Spender it is a choice between Elizabeth and Jimmy. Spain, which Jimmy's desertion from the International Brigade transformed from an heroic into a pathetically distasteful cause, was best expressed in Kerrigan, the Communist Commissar, the Father of the Family, whose insistence on moral absolutes both fascinated Spender and terrified him.

> For Spender, the aim has always been to avoid commitment

The terror sprung from a fear of commitment. In each relationship, Spender had been the passive element. When, as it always did, the moment came that the stronger partner threatened to dominate and detain him, a change of compartments became imperative. He acted when action was forced upon him; when decision demanded less than indecision. For Spender, the aim has always been to avoid commitment. He cannot state his destination, for the idea that there is an end to any journey is the greatest of all human delusions. To remain in one place is to succumb to the illusion.

Is it a sense of guilt that keeps him moving on? Is the passenger, discovering the faults of his fellow-travellers, in fact listening to the echo of his own faults? Do others seem inadequate, because he feels inadequate? Can his social guilt be expiated by making a career of his own humiliation? It is the search for such personal salvation that has driven Spender up and down the corridor looking in every compartment for someone who could tell him the facts of life. For a moment in the Thirties it seemed that he had found them.

Spender is a contemporary Puritan, and in the Popular Front he found the Puritan Revolt of the bourgeois intellectuals. The boy who, he later wrote in his autobiography, "thirsted for great injustices" could expiate his sense of guilt in the struggle for Social Justice. The adolescent from the Liberal home had "often regretted that there were no great causes left to fight for"; now, as Good and Evil struggled for possession of the Soul of Europe, the adult, moving forward from Liberalism, could enrol in the Cause of Liberty. For Spender, like many of his contemporaries, reaching manhood in the years of Depression and Fascism, this meant enlisting with temporary acting rank in the army of Communism. In the Communist Party they found the ready-made morality that clothed their naked Puritan consciences: Spender declared that "by being anti-Fascist, I created a rightness for myself beside which personal guilt seemed unimportant". Nothing could have a greater moral appeal to an intellectual with leisure and money than a doctrine that taught that salvation could be found in work; that mass-meetings, *agit-prop* and fund-raising were all signs of grace; and that sent the elect to walk bravely into death in the Jarama Valley, the Party manifesto in one hand and the obsolete rifle in the other.

Why, then, should Spender reject Communism as a means to the salvation he sought? The God failed because it demanded a moral commitment that was not only absolute, but was also external. Communists, like Puritans, knew the difference between Right and Wrong. Both types of sectarian possessed the

Against all gods: Vicky's portrait of Spender, published in the *NS*, 1954

truth that saved and saw their opponents damned in error. Their actions became Good by definition; all that stood between them and triumph was Evil. Though he became a member of the CP, Spender stopped short of the ultimate conversion to Communism. The moment that the fellow-traveller joined the Party was the first moment at which he began to break with it.

Communism had appealed to Spender because he believed that the individual should matter; that his task was no longer to interpret history but to change it. When Spender and many of his contemporaries discovered that, as a condition of salvation, the Communist Party demanded the total surrender of its converts to its own standards of truth and falsehood, they felt that they had been recruited on false pretences. Betrayed, they turned to hate what they once had loved. They could find no salvation in a movement which did not leave it to them finally to decide between Good and Evil; if temptation no longer existed, one could not find grace by resisting it.

Some of Spender's fellow-travellers from this period did not understand why the God had failed: they continued to look for a spiritual home in which guilt could be expiated by accepting a reach-me-down morality, and so, making the same mistake twice, they joined the Catholic Church. Others, including Spender, reacted differently. In the Forties they realised that every organisation demands commitments; every institution has its moral code; every God is bound to fail. Personal salvation can be found only in resisting the temptation to be saved by others. Guilt cannot be shared; the spiritual search can succeed only in isolation; the kindness, shyness and generosity which Spender displays are the defences behind which loneliness can be protected.

If Spender has become better known as a publicist than a poet, that is hard on his poetry. Never able to immerse himself in the public frustration of politics, he has skirmished on its outskirts, and allowed himself to become a symbol of ideas which have been more profoundly expressed by others. Thus he has managed to escape burial in the ruins of a Movement by leaving just before the catastrophe. The fascination of watching these escapes may blur our appreciation of his vein of talent. In the most-remembered couplet of his best poem, Spender wrote of those who "wore at their hearts the fire's centre":

> Born of the sun, they travelled a short
>   while towards the sun,
> And left the vivid air signed with
>   their honour.

It would have been a fitting epitaph for the young author of *Poems*. It seems inappropriate for the Shelley who has survived to middle age. ●

30 JUNE 1956

Jean-Paul Sartre: The Far Side of Despair

Unsigned profile

In our age, there is one besetting moral problem: what attitude to adopt towards Communism. There is, therefore, a unique and universal significance in the ratiocinations of a man whose formidable intellectual energy has been devoted exclusively to its solution. Jean-Paul Sartre is a playwright of genius, an incisive pamphleteer and controversialist, a writer of ideological novels, a schematic philosopher, an anti-Freudian psychologist, a brilliant teacher and editor, and a professional Left Bank *mandarin*. But through each and all of these activities runs a unifying thread: the search for an intellectual reconciliation with the dominant material and political force of our times.

Nobody else has made the attempt in such a systematic and determined manner, or been so ruthless in eliminating extraneous considerations. The Koestlers and Silones have surrendered to rigid moral imperatives, the Kanapas and Aragons have embraced dogmatism. But Sartre, with his fanatical—almost irrational—belief in reason, has marched doggedly on into the dark tunnel.

Somewhere within the mind of this dwarf-like sage, behind the thick spectacles, the angry eyes, the fleshy facial mask with its wide and sensual mouth, the decisive intellectual battle of our century is being fought in microcosm.

Yet, despite the single-mindedness of Sartre's aim and the logical symmetry of his intellectual development, no great thinker has been more misunderstood and provoked such violent and conflicting reactions. Sartre has been denounced as "unfathomably obscure" (Raymond Aron) and as "a deliberate vulgariser" (Merleau-Ponty). *L'Être et le Néant* was once called "the most difficult philosophical work ever written"; yet *L'Existentialisme Est Un Humanisme* has sold more copies (150,000) than any other volume of modern philosophy. The Vatican has placed his works on the Index; yet Gabriel Marcel, himself a militant Catholic, regarded him as the greatest of French thinkers. The State Department found his novels subversive; but *Les Mains Sales* was the most effective counter-revolutionary play of the entire cold war. Sartre has been vilified by the Communists in Paris and fêted by them in Vienna. No great philosopher ever had fewer disciples; but no other could claim the intellectual conquest of an entire generation.

> No great thinker has provoked such violent and conflicting reactions

Amid the bitter hatreds and controversies of which Sartre has been the centre, his principal objective—and the logical concentration with which he has pursued it—has tended to become obscured. Around the man has grown a myth; and around the myth, foggy, concentric rings of intellectual prejudice. When we strip the layers, however, we find that increasingly rare—indeed, today, unique—phenomenon: a complete philosophical system, an interlocking chain of speculation which unites truth, literature and politics in one gigantic equation.

In the late Thirties, Sartre was a young, underpaid, over-educated philosophy teacher in a smart Paris school, a member—and a typical one—of the most discontented, numerically inflated and socially dangerous group in the world: the French bourgeois intellectuals. He had studied Heidegger and Kierkegaard in Germany; he taught Descartes in France. Like all intellectuals, he asked himself the question: had his knowledge any relevance to the problems of his day? The Fascists were at the gates of Madrid; what was he supposed to do about it? Why had Blum failed? Did it matter that Stalin had seen fit to murder the Old Guard of the Bolsheviks? Why was capitalism in ruins, Hitler triumphant, the democracies afraid?

It is typical of Sartre that he began his search for the answers to these problems ▶

Henri Cartier-Bresson's celebrated portrait of Sartre on the Pont des Arts, Paris

▶ by reformulating them at an abstract level. *La Nausée* (1938), his first major work, is an imaginative inquiry into the problems of existence. Roquentin, its autobiographical and solitary hero, discovers that the bourgeois world in which he lives is senseless and incoherent. His past no longer exists, his future is unknown, his present unrelated; life has no pattern. Through Roquentin's introspective reveries, Sartre presents his fundamental metaphysical image: a loathing for the incompleteness of existence in the world as he finds it, a longing for completeness which is both intelligible and creative. If Kafka's *The Trial* epitomises the nightmare of the ordinary man in a hostile and incomprehensible world, *La Nausée* is the nightmare of the philosopher, in which physical fear is replaced by intellectual disgust.

Under the impact of the war, Sartre's view of existence acquired firmer outline and greater depth. By 1943 he had completed, in *L'Être et le Néant*, a full exposition of his Existentialist philosophy, which concluded his exploration of the problem at an abstract level. In it, he succeeded in isolating the fundamental dilemma. Like Wittgenstein, he bluntly denied the existence of value ("In the world everything is as it is and happens as it does happen. In it there is no value"), and concluded that meaning and purpose do not reside as objective facts in the world of things. Man's sense of value—which he defined as essentially a sense of incompleteness—could never, therefore, be satisfied, and value itself—stable, lived totality—could never be achieved. Yet man is a creature who requires value, "a being who aspires to be God". Despite the impossibility of his task, he continues to pursue his desire for completeness. Hence his agony, because his life is a vain quest: "*L'Homme est une passion inutile.*" Could the dilemma be solved? Sartre asked. And, if so, how? By self-destruction? By social organisation? Was there an intellectual Third Force between the extremes of resignation and despair?

Inevitably, Sartre was intellectually drawn into the world, and into its highest organisational manifestation: politics. In his plays and, above all, in his long novel-cycle, *Les Chemins de la Liberté*, he began to reformulate his problem at a concrete level. In abstract terms, he had calculated that the dilemma was insoluble, and that a Third Force was not viable. As the post-war years unfolded, he saw his calculations—like Einstein's—proved correct by empirical observation. The world polarised into the capitalist and Communist extremes. His own political group proved a noisy failure. The Socialists were prised apart from the Communists and imprisoned on the right. Sartre could not accept the intellectual limitations of Communism: "Marxist doctrine," he wrote, "has been withering away; for want of internal controversy it has been degraded to a stupid determinism." Yet neither could he accept the world as he found it. What, then, was he to do? Already, by 1948, when he wrote *What Is Literature?*, he was conscious of the impotence and isolation of his own position. "We bourgeois," he wrote, "who have broken with our class but who remain bourgeois in our moral values, separated from the proletariat by the Communist screen, remain up in the air; our good will serves no one, not even ourselves... we are writing against the current."

As the cold war progressed, Sartre found his position more and more intolerable. He slowly came round to the view that the Communist Party, despite its bad faith and intellectual sterility, was the objective personification of the workers, and this led him to the agonising conclusion, which he puts into the mouth of one of his characters: "If the party is right, I am more lonely than a madman; if the party is wrong, the world is done for." Could he remain intellectually neutral? And, if so, for how long? By 1952, when the cold war seemed to be moving irresistibly towards the ultimate catastrophe, Sartre had decided to take sides. After all, he reasoned, in Marxism, as in Existentialism, the search for truth in action is the central, reconciling feature. The Marxist vision of the world is completeness; the system it has created is evil only in so far as it is fallible. If we presuppose that the system is perfectible, any of its aspects to which we object—for non-philosophical reasons, for instance—can simply be dismissed as imperfections. By this time, Sartre was willing to make the decisive presupposition. His conversion was a piece of philosophical legerdemain—a case of the intellectual end justifying the intellectual means. But it brought his mind four-square with his moral conscience, because it satisfied his basic moral compulsion to be at one with the working class.

> Of all the fellow-travellers, he became the most impeccable

Even so, Sartre took sides in a characteristically complicated manner. He refused to join the party: on his own premises, he could not organically ally himself with a system which demanded, of necessity, absolute mental discipline and which, though perfectible, was not yet perfect. But, at the same time, he accepted the consequences of his choice in the spirit in which he had made it. Of all the fellow-travellers, he became the most impeccable. He repudiated his anti-Communist writings and disowned a new production of *Les Mains Sales*. His latest play, *Nekrassov*, is the pure, strong milk of Communist satire: the little bits of Existentialism which refused to fit into the mould were pummelled either into Marxism or out of sight.

His slavish orthodoxy, in fact, has led him into grave embarrassments. A philosophical certainty made him join forces with the Communists; but a geographical accident placed him under the intellectual suzerainty of the French Communist Party. He thus became a spokesman of the party which, above and beyond all the rest, has always been, and remains, the most Stalinist. When, therefore, the 20th Party Congress in Moscow signalised the liberating event for which Sartre, along with so many others, had waited for so long, he was placed in an impossible quandary. He, of all people, could not observe the surly silence of *L'Humanité*. But if he chose to comment, he would inevitably be forced to acclaim the news from Moscow in terms which could objectively be construed as criticism of his local hierarchs. His position was made even more difficult by the fact that a leading Communist intellectual, Pierre Hervé, had chosen to jump the gun and had been promptly expelled for his pains. Sartre should, from an intellectual—even from a doctrinal—point of view, have applauded Hervé's gesture. But his position as a French fellow-traveller—and therefore as a faithful ally of the top brass of the French CP—made such a move, from a political point of view, impossible. Nevertheless, everyone expected Sartre to comment on Hervé's book, and comment he dutifully did, struggling manfully to reconcile the irreconcilable. It was not a very happy performance, and in the weeks that have followed, the *mandarins* of the non-Communist Left have used Sartre as an easy target for some intellectual firing-practice. "Sartre," one of them commented, "is now merely a figure of fun."

Their contempt, even their pity, is understandable. For Sartre made his choice between two irreconcilable systems just before the 20th Congress made that kind of choice obsolete. Convinced that the march towards Communism could not be halted, Sartre set out to guide other intellectuals who, he believed, must follow him in seeking a reconciliation between their philosophical beliefs and the harsher realities of life under Stalin-style Communism. Rationalising his own commitment, his own misjudgment, he went over to the Communists because he thought, as Oreste remarks in *Les Mouches*, that "it is on the far side of despair that life begins".

Here lies the tragedy of his choice. In the Communist countries, the intellectuals are now seeking the road back from the far side of despair, and of all living thinkers none is so well qualified by intellect, and sympathy, to aid them as Jean-Paul Sartre. Unhappily he too has to find his way back. ●

14 JUNE 1963

The Kennedy Revolution

By Karl E Meyer

This week President Kennedy committed himself, his party and his country to a massive experiment in racial democracy. Finally the American Negro has the unequivocal support of an American President. "Now the time has come," Mr Kennedy said in a quietly eloquent speech, "for this nation to fulfil its promises." The operative word is *now*. Mr Kennedy's timing was flawless. Only a few hours before, the federal government won a bloodless victory in Alabama, once the cradle of the confederacy. Governor George Wallace vowed he would stand in the door to block admission of two qualified Negroes to the state university. He came, he stood, and he capitulated. It was the final spasm of the Civil War; Alabama is no longer the only state with a totally segregated school system.

The entire drama, redolent of magnolia and malice, came over television. Sporadic battle dispatches issued from Tuscaloosa, where the Governor arrived on the campus behind a wedge of state-troopers. Then a declamatory speech, as a Justice Department official asked Wallace four times in all to step aside. The National Guard was mobilised and, in a memorable tableau, the commander asked the Governor to yield. With a dignity worthy of a better cause, Mr Wallace surrendered; there was none of the repulsive hypocrisy of Mississippi's Governor Barnett but instead the bitter sincerity of a man who genuinely thinks Washington is an alien capital.

At eight o'clock the same evening Mr Kennedy spoke from the White House with a slight edge of tension in his voice; this was not a speech he relished making. ("He does not feel comfortable with preachy subjects," an aide explained. One feels he is almost ashamed of having a heart.) "This nation was founded by men of many nations and backgrounds," he began. "It was founded on the principle that all men are created equal..." So far, fairly safe – Americans hear this theme so often they are inured to the meaning. But it was something else when Mr Kennedy tried to get his countrymen to see life through the eyes of the oppressed one-tenth of a nation. "We are confronted primarily with a moral issue," he continued. ". . . if an American because his skin is dark cannot eat lunch in a restaurant open to the public, if he cannot send his children to the best public school available, if he cannot vote for the public officials who represent him, if, in short, he cannot enjoy the full and free life which all of us want, then who among us would be content to have the colour of his skin changed and stand in his place? Who among us would be content with counsels of patience and delay?"

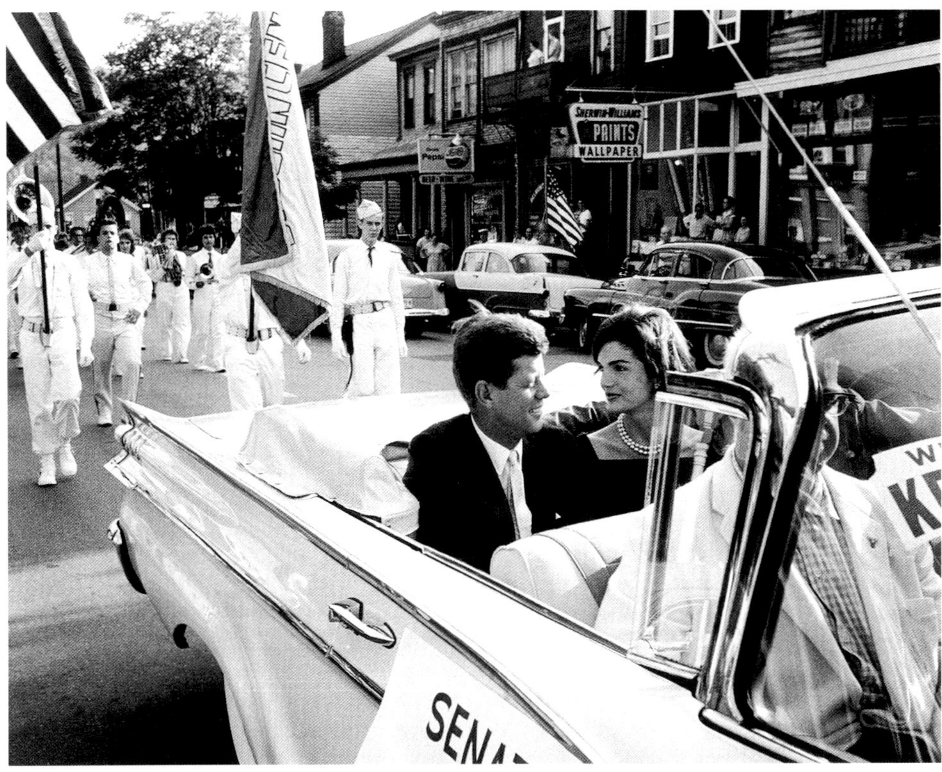

The Kennedys in Wheeling, West Virginia, during JFK's presidential campaign tour, 1959

MARK SHAW/MPTV/CAMERAPRESS

The succeeding words were those of an otherwise prudent politician who has crossed a moral divide. "That fact that we face a great change is at hand, and our task, our obligation, is to make that revolution, that change, peaceful and constructive for all. Those who do nothing are inviting shame as well as violence. Those who act boldly are recognising right as well as reality. Next week I shall ask the Congress of the United States to act, to make a commitment it has not fully made in this century to the proposition that race has no place in American life and law."

Specifically, Mr Kennedy is going to seek laws giving all Americans the right to be served at public places – hotels, restaurants, theatres and stores – and also for new powers to strengthen the government's hand in speeding school desegregation. This inescapably means that there will be a relentless struggle with Southern Democrats, a combat the President has tried to avoid.

No one can be certain of the outcome of the first deep-moving domestic crisis of Mr Kennedy's administration. But the American consensus is changing, and if the President follows through as firmly as he has begun, he can strengthen the impulse of decency among even the timid. He can also confound a fashionable school of commentary that now holds, in Hannah Arendt's phrase, that the American Revolution was an event of only local importance and deeply conservative at root. Meanwhile credit for Mr Kennedy's conversion goes to the beaten and battered Negroes of Birmingham. They have a right to be proud. So, for that matter, does the President. He has really taken on big battalions at home in a fight that matters. ●

29 NOVEMBER 1963

The Man We Trusted

By John Freeman

The most grievous assassination in modern history has transformed John Kennedy from an embattled president, deadlocked with a hostile and suspicious Congress, into the brightest legend of our time. It was inevitable. The shock and the grief are universal and so great. Emotions have poured out – and they have gilded the truth. Yet that too may be misleading, for the emotions were part of the truth; and if Kennedy is remembered, as I think he may be, along with Lincoln and FDR as one of the great presidents, it will be more because he captured the imagination of a whole generation in almost every corner of the world than because he succeeded in fulfilling the purposes to which he dedicated his presidency.

His great achievement, for which the world outside America chiefly honours him this week, was his leadership of the western alliance. When he took over, we walked in the shadow of nuclear war. Two years and 10 months later, the dialogue between the White House and the Kremlin has proceeded so far that no one can doubt the genuineness of Krushchev's dismay at the young President's death. Yet he wrought this change without any surrender of vital interest, by strength and not by weakness. He persuaded Krushchev that negotiations were practicable, because he was himself clear about what could be negotiated – and firm about what could not. The test-ban treaty and the hotline are the visible signs of a business relation between the Soviet bloc and the West, in which each side recognises the power of the other and the suicidal folly of pressing points of difference to the brink of war.

Kennedy's achievement in all this was not one-sided. Nuclear war would be as deadly to Russia as to the West, and Krushchev has played his part. But few would deny that the initiative has lain most of the time with the White House or that Kennedy's own qualities have been decisive. The three personal gifts which lifted him into the realm of international statesmanship were intellect, steadiness of nerve and the capacity to take decisions. Indeed, this week's inevitable anxiety about the future is based not on half-baked guesses about President Johnson's capacity or intelligence as a politician, but on the fact that the decision-making machine – largely extra-governmental – which Kennedy created to meet his own needs proved so uniquely well-suited to the strategic demands of the Cold War. The doubt must exist whether President Johnson, operating through more normal political channels, will be able to match the speed, logic and certainty of his predecessor. For Kennedy's decisions were his own. The professors, the soldiers, the computers, seldom the professional politicians, were detailed to provide the data and rehearse the arguments. The President listened, reflected, balanced the equation and, fortified by all that intellect and calculation could bring to bear, finally took the decision.

> He illuminated ideas by the grace of his personality

Naturally this method of government was unpopular on Capitol Hill, and the unpopularity was reflected in Kennedy's inability to secure from Congress either the money or the legislation he needed to implement his domestic policies. And this inability amounted to something like failure. Whether it stemmed fundamentally from a lack of profound conviction about liberal causes with which he was saddled by his 1960 campaign-managers, or from the intellectual's contempt for the log-rolling of the workaday politicians, or from over-caution about the electoral consequences of controversy, or from a constitutional inadequacy of Congress to live with the speed of modern decision-making will long be argued by American historians. What we can say this week is that, despite his visible achievement in foreign affairs, the quality of Kennedy's presidency as a whole – apart from the noble and historic decision to stake the whole prestige of the presidency on his civil rights legislation – is arguable.

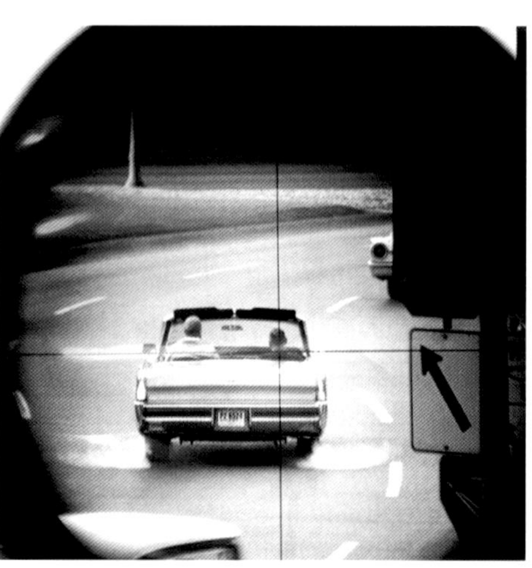

In cold blood: Kennedy was 46 when he died

His quality as a man is to me beyond argument. He brought to public life not only the hard assets of leadership which determined his actions, but the rarest capacity to illuminate ideas by the grace of his personality and the clarity of his speech. One can only guess, for instance, at the legislative outcome of his battle with Congress and his own party over civil rights. But one can be sure that individual American opinion about the cause of justice for the Negroes has been touched, as never since Lincoln, by the words he spoke.

Perhaps his greatest achievement in the end was to turn the gaze of his own people towards some of the more distant goals of political action and to infuse his pragmatic programmes with the radiant light of tolerance, idealism and purpose. If so, the glossy wrappings of the New Frontier may be remembered as a permanent landmark in the evolution of American democracy.

"And so, my fellow Americans: ask not what your country can do for you – ask what you can do for your country. My fellow citizens of the world: ask not what America will do for you, but what together we can do for the freedom of man." Those words struck the keynote of his inaugural address; they form a message which evokes a response in every radical heart. However limited his social achievement, his approach to politics was fundamentally a challenge to conservatism everywhere. That is why, with all our reservations about where his ultimate convictions lay – they certainly did not lie with the ideological left – and with all our disappointment at his comparative failure to make good the promise of 1960, the left in Britain admired and, when the chips were down, trusted him. He was the golden boy of the post-war world, and we mourn him as a friend. ●

LAWRENCE SCHILLER/CURTIS/JOHN F KENNEDY ARCHIVE/CAMERAPRESS

22 MAY 1964

Bob Dylan

By Francis Newton (Eric Hobsbawm)

From 1956 to 1966 the Marxist historian Eric Hobsbawm wrote a jazz column under the pseudonym Francis Newton. The name came from a communist jazz trumpeter who had played on Billie Holiday's "Strange Fruit". At times, the column provided a space for American music and countercultural habits largely ignored elsewhere in the magazine.

Getting the global view in New York, 1962

JOHN COHEN/HULTON ARCHIVE/GETTY IMAGES

The affluent society, realising that man does not live by bread alone, supplies him also with electric toothbrushes, but those who cannot get them or are still unsatisfied remain in a state of suspended rebellion: the outcast and coloured, the unemployable and intellectual, the old and the young. Sometimes they find a voice, and the most cheerful cultural news of our time is that for one group of the dissidents it is no longer that of the blind Samson, the self-destroyer, the rebel without cause. At present it is the nasal, flat, anti-rhetorical voice of a thin, child-faced chansonnier from the US, a cross between a curlier James Dean (minus death wish) and a politically conscious Holden Caulfield.

A rapt Festival Hall, packed with carefully informal O- and A-level dandies of both sexes between 16 and 22, demonstrated – against the competition of the Whit Sunday heat wave – that Bob Dylan is not merely a singer of formidable appeal, but a culture hero of 1964. If an unqualified rejection of western society and a decision for change are enough to justify the term, he sang mostly revolutionary songs. He also proved that the folk-song revival has been worth it.

What Dylan writes, composes and sings in an unprofessional raw amble, slowing down at critical moments to a sleepy cry of great emotional intensity, is not of course folk-song. In spite of his acknowledged debt to the blues, it has neither the musicality, nor the fun, nor the anonymous oppression, which we have lately had occasion to hear in the splendid *Blues and Gospel Caravan* concert-tour. It is interesting that no Negroes were to be seen at his concert. He cannot operate like the two blind men who converged on the stage at the most moving moment of the blues show – Sonny Terry, the travelling harmonica player and blues-shouter, and the Rev Gary Davis, the old street preacher – who cried their own sufferings to the world. Dylan sings about other people's sufferings – Davy Moore, the boxer killed in the ring, Hollis Brown, the Dakota dirt farmer, Negro militants killed in the South, or the bleak, very Brechtian, "Lonesome death of Hetty Carroll". What is more, he sings about their *causes*. His thing is political poetry for the intellectual young.

It's clear – especially from Dylan's fairly numerous bad verses – that he comes from that *Reader's Digest* mass civilisation which has atrophied not merely men's souls but also their language, confining the ordinary person to a mixture of stammering and cliché. Song however has given him the courage of speech; folk-song a vocabulary, a sense of form, and at the same time – because of its lucky association with the left – a moral frame. The music is probably little more than pastiche, though Dylan's capacity to write unassuming tunes should not be underrated: when performed by technically better musicians their possibilities are evident.

When slogans like the New Frontier have been forgotten, the desperation of men who lived in a negation of human society will still survive in the apocalyptic repetitions of "A Hard Rain". Even the hope of better times sounds real. Yet Dylan's vision remains that of a minority: Mods and Rockers were absent from the Festival Hall. ●

19 FEBRUARY 1965

T S Eliot's Dream

By Frank Kermode

It was natural that the news of Eliot's death should bring vivid memories of the dark cold day 25 years earlier when Yeats died; but on the face of it the two events seemed to have little in common beyond what is obvious. In the months preceding Yeats's death there had been an extraordinary outpouring of poetry. And there was the poet himself, masked as a wild old man or a dangerous sage; the learned half-fascist shouting about eugenics. But one didn't hate the poet for what he thought he knew. "Man can embody truth but he cannot know it," he said in his last letter; and years before, in a line which gives modern poetry its motto, "In dreams begin responsibilities." He made no order, but showed that our real lives begin when we have been shown that order ends. The time of his death seemed appropriate to the dream; in a few months the towns lay beaten flat.

History has not collaborated in the same way to remind us of the responsibilities begun in Eliot's dream. His farewell to poetry was taken only a couple of years after Yeats's. It was no deathbed "Cuchulain Comforted"; it was "Little Gidding". As a man he continues to suffer and without reward:

> Let me disclose the gifts reserved for age
>   To set a crown upon your lifetime's effort.
>   First, the cold friction of expiring sense . . .
> Second, the conscious impotence of rage
>   At human folly . . .
> And last, the rending pain of re-enactment
>   Of all that you have done and been . . .

So the ghost speaks of a Yeatsian guilt, remorse and purgation. The man who suffers is now truly distinct from the mind that creates: poems have to be, as Picasso said of a painting, "hordes of destructions".

It happened that when the death was announced I was reading through the transcripts of a series of British Council interviews with poets. They were often asked about "influences" and they named a great many poets in reply, more, I think, than any poet would have done a generation ago. When Eliot's name was mentioned it was nearly always by way of denial, usually respectful but occasionally not even that. Now it may be that, as Auden said in an obituary notice, Eliot cannot be imitated, only parodied; indeed that seems very just, because nobody except Pound more insistently taught the way of making it new, of treating every attempt as a wholly new start. The craft of poetry is no longer the imitation of what has been well made, but the return to brute elements, the matter which may have a potentiality of form; but last year's words will not find it. In consequence the writing of major poetry seems an even more ruinous and exhausting undertaking, so that nobody will blame poets for modestly not taking it on, or for coming to think of Eliot and his peers as Chinese walls across their literature.

There is, in fact, a certain rough justice in their speaking of him as he used to speak of Milton. The more we see of the hidden side of Eliot the more he resembles this poet, whom he thought of as a polar opposite. As we look at all the contraries reconciled in Eliot – his schismatic traditionalism, his romantic classicism, his highly personal impersonality – we are prepared for the surprise of finding in the dissenting Whig regicide a hazy mirror-image of the Anglo-Catholic royalist. Each, having prepared himself carefully for poetry, saw that he must, living in such times, explore also the cooler element of prose. Each saw that fidelity to tradition is ensured by revolutionary action. Each knew the cold climate of an age too late; with the Commonwealth an evident failure Milton wrote one last book to restore it, and as the élites crumbled and reformed Eliot wrote his *Notes*. If Milton killed a king, Eliot attacked vulgar democracy and shared with the "men of 1914" and with Yeats some extreme authoritarian opinions.

As poets, they wrote with voluptuousness of youth, and with unmatched force of the lacerations of age. And each of them lived on into a time when it seemed there was little for them to say to their compatriots, God's Englishmen. Eliot can scarcely have failed to see this left-handed image of himself in a poet who made a new language for his poetry yet used a venerable tradition; but Eliot at first moved away and pretended to find his reflection in the strong and lucid Dryden, deceiving many into supposing that he resembled that poet more than the lonely, fierce maker of the new, of whom he said that it was "something of a problem" to decide in what his greatness consisted.

However, a great poet need not always understand another. And Eliot certainly has the marks of a modern kind of greatness, those beneficial intuitions of irregularity and chaos, the truth of the foul rag-and-bone shop. Yet we remember him as celebrating order and it is doubtful whether many have much sympathy now with his views. His greatness will rest on the fruitful recognition of disorder, though the theories will have their interest as theories held by a great man.

Such theories, we now see, are highly personal versions of stock themes in the history of ideas of the period. They have been subtly developed and are now, increasingly, subject to criticism. The most persistent and influential of them, no doubt, is the theory of tradition. In a sense, it is Cubist historiography, unlearning the trick of perspective and ordering history as a system of perpetually varying spatial alignments. Tradition is always unexpected, hard to find, surprising; and it is emblematic that a father of modernism should call himself Anglican, for early Anglicans upset the whole idea of tradition in much this way.

He also called himself royalist, and this is an aspect of a larger and even more surprising traditionalism; for Eliot, in a weirdly pure sense, was an imperialist. The essay on Dante, which is one of the true masterpieces of modern criticism, has been called a projection on to the medieval poet of Eliot's own theories of diction and imagery; but it has an undercurrent of imperialism, and can usefully be read with the studies of Virgil and Kipling.

The imperialist Eliot is a poet of the *urbs aeterna*, of the transmitted but corrupted dignity of Rome; hence his veneration not only for Baudelaire but for Virgil. The London of *The Waste Land* is a parody of the true city, "Unreal City . . . the city over the mountains/ Cracks and reforms and bursts in the violet air . . ." And Eliot's Virgil is the prophet of the *imperium sine fine*, the central classic, the highest poet, as Dante called him. To ignore "the consciousness of Rome" as Virgil crystallised it is simply to be *provincial*: to be provincial is to be out of the historical current in which the imperial dignity flows. Virgil is the poet of the European destiny, of the empire which

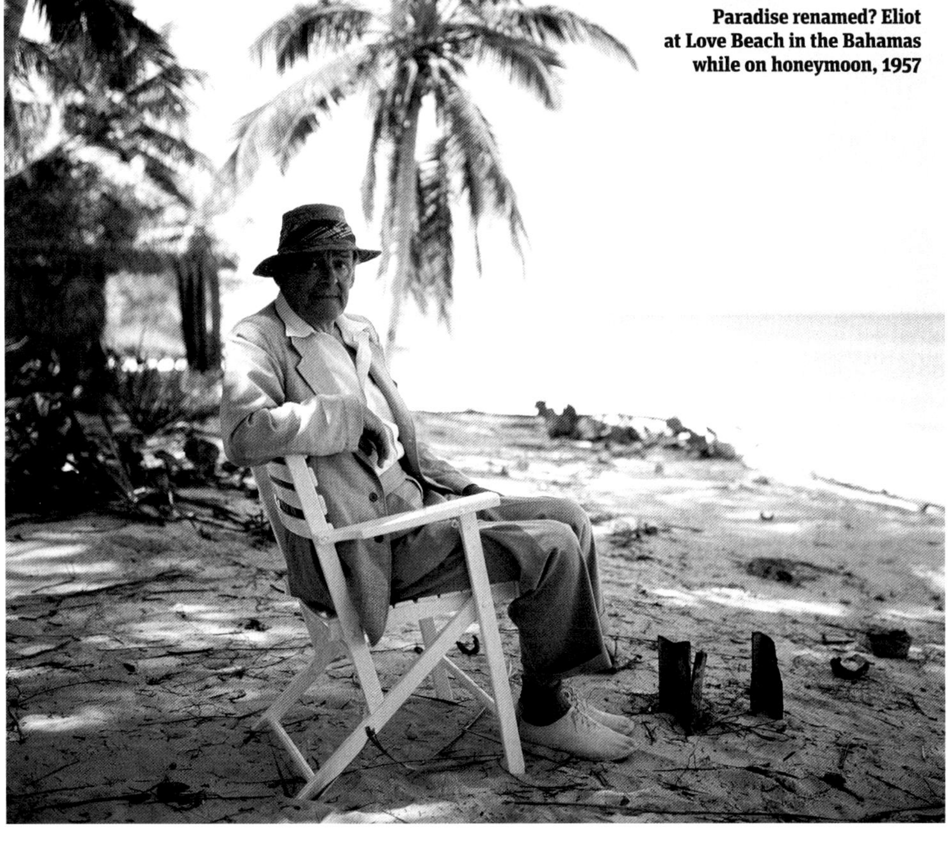

Paradise renamed? Eliot at Love Beach in the Bahamas while on honeymoon, 1957

SLIM AARONS/MASTERS/GETTY IMAGES

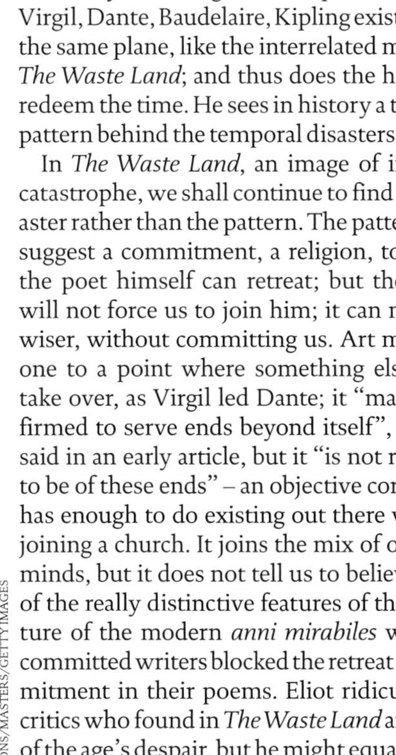

became the body of the church. But out of that came nationalism; and the task of the chosen – which is to defeat the proud and be merciful to the subject – was increasingly identified with motives of profit – a situation in which Kipling's relevance is obvious. Eliot speaks of his "imperial imagination"; given a view of history as having a sort of pictorial unity, Virgil, Dante, Baudelaire, Kipling exist within the same plane, like the interrelated motifs of *The Waste Land*; and thus does the historian redeem the time. He sees in history a timeless pattern behind the temporal disasters.

In *The Waste Land*, an image of imperial catastrophe, we shall continue to find the disaster rather than the pattern. The pattern may suggest a commitment, a religion, to which the poet himself can retreat; but the poem will not force us to join him; it can make us wiser, without committing us. Art may lead one to a point where something else must take over, as Virgil led Dante; it "may be affirmed to serve ends beyond itself", as Eliot said in an early article, but it "is not required to be of these ends" – an objective correlative has enough to do existing out there without joining a church. It joins the mix of our own minds, but it does not tell us to believe. One of the really distinctive features of the literature of the modern *anni mirabiles* was that committed writers blocked the retreat to commitment in their poems. Eliot ridiculed the critics who found in *The Waste Land* an image of the age's despair, but he might equally have rejected the more recent Christian interpretations. The poem resists an imposed order; it is a part of its greatness, and the greatness of its epoch, that it can do so.

No one has better stated the chief characteristics of that epoch than the late R P Blackmur in a little book of lectures which seems not to be much read here. It is called *Anni Mirabiles: 1921-1925*, and was published by the Library of Congress in 1956. We live, wrote Blackmur, in the first age that has been "fully self-conscious of its fictions" – in a way, Nietzsche has sunk in at last; and in these conditions we are more than ever dependent on what he calls, perhaps not quite satisfactorily, "bourgeois humanism" – "the residue of reason in relation to the madness of the senses". Without it we cannot have "creation in honesty", only "assertion in desperation". But in its operation this residual humanism can only deny the validity of our frames of reference and make "an irregular metaphysic for the control of man's irrational powers". So this kind of art is a new kind of creation, harsh, medicinal, remaking reality "in rivalry with our own wishes", denying us the consolations of predictable form but showing us the forces of our world. And the great works in this new and necessary manner were the product of the "wonderful years" – in English, two notable examples are *Ulysses* and *The Waste Land*.

> Auden said: Eliot cannot be imitated, only parodied

The function of such a work, one has to see, is what Simone Weil called "decreation"; Wallace Stevens, whose profound contribution to the subject nobody seems to have noticed, picked the word out of *La Pesanteur et la Grâce*. Weil explains the difference from destruction: decreation is not a change from the created to nothingness, but from the created to the uncreated.

One sees the use of this distinction for modern art, with its multiple manifestos and rejections; the merely destructive is useless, the decreative is what is needed. "Modern reality," commented Stevens, "is a reality of decreation, in which our revelations are not the revelations of belief."

In most of the poetry since this great age we have what neither destroys nor decreates. Hence our continuing dependence on the "modern" of 40 years ago. There is no doubt that our mental habits are deeply conditioned by it, and especially by its decreative aspect. The positives that accompanied it are of transient interest; what survives is the habit of breakdown, of analysis by controlled unreason. Much genuine anguish, and some spurious anguish, in our ways of looking can be traced to the decreative efforts of that "modern" poetry. Arnold complained that Carlyle "led us out into the wilderness and left us there". So did Eliot, despite his conviction that he knew the way; even before the "conversion" he had a vision of a future dominated by Bradley, Frazer and Henry James. But we need not complain, so long as the response to the wilderness is genuine. Of course there is a *Waste Land* myth, and this comfortable unfelt acceptance of tragedy is contemptible; not the least heartening aspect of Mr Bellow's recent book was his attack on it ("what this country needs is a good five-cent synthesis"). *The Waste Land* is in one light an imperial epic; but such comforts as it can offer are not compatible with any illusions, past, present or future.

This is not the way the poem is usually read nowadays; but most people who know about poetry will still admit that it is a very difficult poem, though it invites glib or simplified interpretation. One can think of it as a mere arbitrary sequence upon which we have been persuaded to impose an order. But, as Stevens observed, to impose an order is not to find it; and the true order, I think, is there to be found, unique, unrepeated, resistant to synthesis. *The Four Quartets* seem by comparison isolated in their eminence, tragic, crystalline in the presentation of the temporal agony, but personal, and often closer to commentary than to the thing itself. When they speak of a pattern of timeless moments, of the point of intersection, they speak *about* the pattern and the point; the true image of them is *The Waste Land*. There the dreams cross, the dreams in which begin responsibilities. ●

***Mary Wollstonecraft* by John Opie (c.1797)**

21 MAY 1971

A Fallen Woman

By Claire Tomalin

Two o'clock – My dear love, after making my arrangements for our snug dinner today, I have been taken by storm, and obliged to promise to dine, at an early hour, with the Miss —s, the *only* day they had intended to pass here. I shall however leave the key in the door, and hope to find you at my fireside when I return, about eight o'clock. Will you not wait for poor Joan? – whom you will find better, and till then think very affectionately of her.

How many novels start as well as this? It is a love letter, written in a city in revolution, from an eminent bluestocking lady of 34 to a captain in the American army. The date is 1793, the town Paris, the woman Mary Wollstonecraft; for all her professed allegiance to Reason, her letters speak of spontaneity, warmth, clinging affection and a sensibility that makes Marianne Dashwood seem a model of prudence and steadiness in comparison. As someone who has "always been half in love" with J J Rousseau, Mary gives free rein to her feelings and her expression of them.

The letters are extraordinary; they describe, directly and fluently, the sensations and emotions of love and longing, and of pregnancy and motherhood, with a frankness not equalled again in England until the 20th century. Mary possessed a melancholy temperament and her love affair was mostly a matter of separations and disappointments (hence the abundance of letters); but she could be spirited and happy, especially when talking of her baby or imagining good days ahead. Here and there she adopts a highflown manner, usually when she begins to preach to her errant lover; much more often she writes, as the best letter writers do, with the appearance of being off her guard: "when my heart is warm, pop come the expressions of my childhood into my head"; "I do not want to be loved like a goddess; but I wish to be necessary to you"; "If you do not return soon . . . I will throw your slippers out at window, and be off – nobody knows where." Missing him, she "makes the most of the comfort of the pillow", turning to the side of the bed where he lay. She meets friends who observe she is with child: "let them stare! . . . all the world may know it for aught I care! – Yet I wish to avoid —'s coarse jokes." She feels the "little twitcher" move inside her, speculates whether it sleeps and wakes, grows anxious when it is still: "I sat down in an agony till I felt those said twitches again."

The letters tell their own story, but it is as well to fill in the background. Mary, fresh from the success of her *Vindication of the Rights of Woman*, but suffering from an unreciprocated passion for the artist Fuseli, decided to visit Paris in December 1792. The French admired her and at first she admired the revolution. Her circle included Tom Paine and the Helen Maria Williams to whom Wordsworth addressed a sonnet. In the spring of 1793 she met, at the house of an English friend, Gilbert Imlay, an American who had fought in the War of Independence [and] written a still readable book on the topography of Kentucky and Ohio as well as an overblown novel, *The Emigrants*, aimed at reforming English divorce law and proclaiming the idyllic possibilities of life in the American wilderness.

Imlay has been roughly handled by Mary's biographers for his treatment of her, but I find it impossible not to have some sympathy for him; clearly he got himself into a false position; he had neither the nature to settle into matrimony nor the strength of mind to break off the affair which seemed so sacred and binding to her. Probably he was bowled over by her fame, her charm and her unusual sexual forwardness; the wooing was very swift. An early meeting place was at the Neuilly tollgate, known to them as the "barrier" (*la barrière*); the child, conceived there, was often referred to as the "barrier-girl" and Imlay's good moods as his "barrier-face".

They went through no marriage ceremony, but Mary registered herself with the American ambassador under the name Imlay (probably as a protection against imprisonment, to which English subjects became liable when war was declared). Both lovers at times referred to her as a wife, but Mary spoke cheerfully about not having "clogged" her soul by promising obedience; their arrangement was of that semi-formal variety most difficult to manage smoothly. In spite of a grumble or two, she was delighted with her pregnancy, having strong theoretical views about maternity; but already Imlay was called away on business, the first of many separations that indicate the rapid cooling of his attachment.

At least they provided us with Mary's letters: her love, her reproaches, her self-chastisement for doubting him, her joy in the child. She followed Imlay to Le Havre, where Fanny was born in May 1794, under the care of an admiring midwife. "Nothing could be more natural or easy than my labour," she wrote to a woman friend. She was out walking eight days after the birth, and suckled her child: "My little Girl begins to suck so Manfully that her father reckons saucily on her writing the second part of the R---ts of Woman."

Soon Imlay was off again, and the story grows sadder and sadder as she travels with the baby to Paris, London, and then, on Imlay's business, to Scandinavia. His infidelities drove her to desperation and she twice projected suicide, the second time saturating her clothes before walking into the Thames (Mirah's method in *Daniel Deronda*; Charles Kegan Paul suggested that George Eliot was inspired by Mary). She was rescued by friends and Imlay tried to behave "kindly" towards her; but kindness, when one looks for love, is the worst torture:

> I never wanted but your heart – That gone, you have nothing more to give. Had I only poverty to fear, I should not shrink from life. – Forgive me then, if I say, that I shall consider any direct or indirect attempt to supply my necessities, as an insult which I have not merited.
> I have been hurt by indirect enquiries, which appear to me not to be dictated by any tenderness to me. – You ask "If I am well or tranquil" – They who think me so, must want a heart to estimate my feelings by.

"I never wanted but your heart. That gone, you have nothing more to give"

But Mary's behaviour could be trying; on one occasion she rushed into a room where Imlay was sitting with some friends and thrust the two-year-old Fanny on to his lap. This was typical of one aspect of her – the impulsive, dramatising side – but equally she knew how to pull herself together again. The most important and affecting aspect of the letters is their picture of a woman refusing to accept that she is "ruined", a resourceless victim of seduction and abandonment; she goes down into the depths of misery again and again, but repeatedly determines to be rational and independent, to learn to cope with her situation both emotionally and financially and to give up her lover, in the end, without bitterness or demands. It was not easy for her, jealous, passionate, agonised for her child: "my little darling is calling papa, and adding her parrot word – Come, come!" There is something heroic in her final words to Imlay: "I part with you in peace."

The story of the publication of the letters provides a tragi-comic epilogue. Few love letters survive, and those that do generally remain unpublished for decades; but Imlay preserved these and returned them at Mary's request. In 1797 she married William Godwin and died within a few months in childbirth; whereupon this odd man, as an act of devoted homage, published her impassioned letters to her former lover. Deeply mistrustful of violent emotion at first hand, he seems to have been fascinated by the evidence of it at one remove; at any rate, though he tried to calm the Wollstonecraft temperament in Mary and later her daughters (Fanny and Mary, who married Shelley), he greatly admired it in her words to another man. Perhaps he felt safer thus. His preface begins: "The following letters may possibly be found to contain the finest examples of the language of sentiment and passion ever presented to the world."

Godwin's action in publishing them called down the satirical contempt of his opponents. Even Mary's supporters thought he had done her a disservice; an anonymous defender writing in 1803 attacked Godwin for his failure to protect her reputation by silence about her personal life. He was probably right; the eclipse of Mary Wollstonecraft in the 19th century can be partly attributed to Godwin's revelations, which shocked middle and upper classes alike: a revolutionary thinker and unchaste to boot!

Godwin expunged Imlay's name from his edition, but it was generally known: he was ill regarded and disappeared from the scene, never (as far as we know) taking any interest in Fanny; he is thought to have died in Jersey in 1828. Fanny was kindly brought up by Godwin; her step-sisters Mary and Claire Clairmont were lively girls, but she was melancholic and committed suicide, alone in a Swansea inn to which she had travelled for the purpose, in October 1816; a sadly effective repetition of her mother's efforts.

Mary's letters were reprinted in 1879 by Charles Kegan Paul and again in 1908 by Roger Ingpen. Both editors felt obliged to explain away and apologise for some of her behaviour and freedom of speech, and Ingpen quaintly dismissed Imlay as a "typical American", always dashing about on business. The only good modern biography is a long and meticulously scholarly one by another American, Ralph Wardle. Mary Wollstonecraft is not much known in this age when we are able to be more understanding of her behaviour and also of her lover's. Perhaps it is time for a new edition of her letters. ●

"Still, I'd like you to sign this non-disclosure agreement"

EMILY FLAKE

8 MARCH 1974

Lord Longford

By Gore Vidal

On election day, the Seventh Earl of Longford and I appeared together on television. As the Seventh Earl was introduced to the viewers, he swung around in his chair and looked at himself in the television monitor; it was plain that he was ravished by what he saw. And I? In those few seconds I was depraved and corrupted by the sort of blind self-love that is so communicable that one is transformed. I was – am – like Onan on a peak in Darien; the prurient theatre of my mind hopelessly dominated by the fact of the Seventh Earl who made me love him as he loves him.

In front of me now is the Seventh Earl's third volume of memoirs. On the dust jacket there is a photograph *in colour* of the Seventh Earl's head. He looks mighty pleased with himself – as well he ought. Beneath, "The Grain of Wheat, an Autobiography, Frank Longford". That's all: a vivid contrast to the Seventh Earl's billing on the slender paperback *Humility*: "Frank Pakenham, Earl of Longford". But no matter how Frank wants to be known, I find his ruling passion perfectly irresistible.

In the present volume Frank brings us up to date. He admits right off to being an intellectual. And, as he says, "my special kind of brain is well above average in literature", having produced "*Peace by Ordeal*, still the standard book on the Anglo-Irish Treaty of 1931"; while his biography of De Valera? "Sales were highly satisfactory . . . and the English reviews were very pleasing." Frank tells us that his college was Christ Church, "certainly the most aristocratic college in the world".

Frank's war was not much good; he was "invalided out with a nervous breakdown". But Frank turned this to tremendous advantage:

> With prisoners, ex-prisoners, outcasts generally and all those who hesitate to show their faces abroad, I have had one unfailing and unforeseen point of contact. I can say and mean and be believed – "I also have been humiliated." The gulf is bridged as if by magic. If my sense of compassion has been strengthened and activated from any human experience, it is from my own infirmities and the indignities I have myself undergone.

Like Henry James, Frank does not spell out those infirmities and indignities. We can only guess at his anguish. But he does share his triumphs with us: "according to the *Economist*, I was an enormously successful amateur banker". When Leader of the House of Lords, Frank spoke on Rhodesia and "Harold Wilson and other leaders crowded in to listen". Later, "when I resigned I was overwhelmed with letters . . . referring in glowing terms to my leadership". And why not? On one occasion, when Leader, *Frank spoke from the back benches!* "I can't find that a Leader of the House had ever previously done what I did."

Frank had his downs as well as his ups in politics. He was not heeded as often as he ought to have been. He might "have swayed the issue" on devaluation, but didn't. Serenely he records that Harold Wilson is supposed to have noted: "Frank Longford quite useless. Mental age of 12." Frank takes this well (after all, any *bright* 12-year-old is perfectly able to lead the Lords). But he does hope that in future Harold "will avoid such indiscretions". Anyway, "nothing in my membership of the Wilson Government became me so well – it was said at the time – as the manner of my leaving it". He "most treasures" a letter from someone mysteriously called "Bobbity Salisbury". Truly great men like Attlee thought the world of Frank who also

> Harold Wilson noted: "Frank Longford quite useless. Mental age of 12"

> treasures more than one of his letters running like this: "My dear Frank, I will look into the point you mentioned as soon as possible. Yours ever, Clem."

Yet for all the wonderful letters and compliments from his peers, "I felt, and still feel, that I was largely wasted in the Cabinet". But, Frank, that's the point isn't it? To be humiliated in order that you may be able to grow as a human being, to learn compassion so that you can help us outcasts across that awful gulf.

Frank writes a lot about sinners (loves them, hates the sin). He got to know the Kray Brothers: "talking to me that afternoon, I am sure that they had made a resolution: never again". He befriended Ian Brady and Myra Hindley, of Moors fame: "their agony is never far from my mind". Frank admits that he is sometimes criticised for his Christian treatment of murderers: "psychologists and other men assess my motives as they wish". But Frank is, simply, good. There is no other word. Best of all, he wants us to share with him through his many testaments his many good actions. That's why he writes books and gets on television programmes. By reading Frank and looking at Frank people will want to be as good as he is. Of course he can be stern. Although Frank doesn't want to put homosexuals in jail, he doesn't want people to forget that "homosexual conduct . . . remains wrongful". Pornography, on the other hand, is not only wrongful but must be rooted out and the makers and dispensers of it punished.

All in all, he has been having a super time even though he is a bit miffed that the press has not so far acknowledged that "I had an experience of inquiries which no one in politics could equal". But more fortunately,

> I was featured in the *Evening Standard* as "British worthy No 4", my predecessors being the Duke of Norfolk, the Archbishop of Canterbury and Mick Jagger. I was interviewed times without number and was chosen by the *Sunday Times* as the most caricatured figure of 1972 . . . My citation as "Man of the Year" referred to me as Crusader Extraordinary.

Then came The Garter, "a clear reminder that I was not without recognition". And so, gartered as well as belted, on to Copenhagen. TV cameras. Strippers. Porn. Jesus. Love. Compassion. Outrage. Filth. Human decency. Where will it end, Frank? I think I know, because Frank let a bit of the cat's whisker out of the bag when he quoted a journalist who wrote:

> Lord Longford is clearly a good man. If he is not actually a saint, he is certainly the most saintly member of the Upper Chamber, and I do not overlook the Bishops.

That's it. After the humiliation of the bad war, the failed career in politics, the eccentric attempt to regulate England's morals, the halo, the nimbus and translation to Paradise. And so at God's right hand, for ever and ever stands the Seventh Earl of Longford, peering happily into an eternal television monitor. Pray for us, Saint Frank. Intercede for us, teach us to love ourselves as you loved you. ●

The uncool planet

By Andrew Simms

Our addiction to fossil fuels and consumer goods has left the earth in a parlous state. It is not too late, however, to unlearn bad ecological habits

When in 1913 the British government made a barely noticed decision to take a 51 per cent stake in a private company, it set the shape of the environment and geopolitical fault lines for the century to come. The consequences of that decision and the industry it spawned still determine our future.

Winston Churchill was convinced that oil brought "more intense forms of war power". In 1912, faced with the threat of German armament, he and Admiral John Fisher persuaded Britain's principal weapon of empire, the navy, to switch from coal to oil. They were responding to lobbying by William Knox D'Arcy, who founded the First Exploitation Company, later the Anglo-Persian Oil Company (APOC), which eventually became BP.

The pattern of global warming, rooted in our dependence on fossil fuels, had already been predicted by a Swedish Nobel-winning chemist, Svante Arrhenius in 1895. But, for the ensuing century, politicians almost entirely disregarded the knowledge that what was powering their economy would also fuel climate change. It seems politicians today care equally little. Our oil-addicted flying habits also started with the leap that aviation made back in the early 20th century. In 1915, Britain had only 250 planes; by the end of the war British factories had made 55,000.

In 1913, oil was mainly refined into kerosene for home use, but the reserves that D'Arcy's company found had a high sulphur content, making it smelly and unfit for domestic use. He needed another outlet and he found it in Britain's military ambitions and insecurities.

The government took a controlling share in APOC because, as Churchill argued, we "must become the owners, or at any rate the controllers, at the source", of oil supplies. Oil brought power in an increasingly mechanised conflict, but it also fostered lasting dependence.

Western invasion of places such as Baghdad, Basra and Kirkuk bookended the 20th century; it was in 1917 that Britain captured the Mesopotamian territory from which Iraq was carved. Oil contracts signed under British government control heavily favoured the oil companies over the host country, and concessions were intended to last until the year 2000.

Fossil fuels in general allowed the global economy to expand beyond the biosphere's thresholds. As Gertrude Bell wrote from Baghdad in 1921, "Oil is the trouble, of course. Detestable stuff!" Not only did the fuel allow us to defy gravity by taking to the air, and make ever bigger tanks, trucks and ships go faster and further, they allowed our food system to defy ecological gravity, at least for a while.

> As early as 1962, it was clear the green revolution wasn't green at all

Germany's ability to fight had depended on a recent breakthrough permitting natural limits to be transgressed. A process developed by Fritz Haber and Carl Bosch from 1913 combined nitrogen and hydrogen gases to produce ammonia in large quantities. This was used to make artificial fertiliser and created the beginnings of modern intensive farming. Germany used the same method to synthesise nitrates for explosives. Without it, as Churchill remarked, the Germans "could not have continued the war" for so long once their natural supplies of nitrates were used up.

Although the contemporary left is oddly blind to the environment's importance as the basis of working people's livelihoods, it was not always so. Even the Marxist revolutionary Rosa Luxemburg railed against the impact of early industrial farming. As she once said, "I feel so much more at home even in a scrap of garden . . . and still more in the meadows when the grass is humming with bees, than at one of our party congresses."

Methane – a greenhouse gas far more potent than carbon dioxide that derives from natural gas – is central to the chemical reaction. Haber-Bosch production of fertiliser consumes about one-twentieth of world natural gas production today. Coupled with new plant varieties and synthetic pesticides, the technique led to the "green revolution" in farming, boosting food output. For several decades, on its own terms, this was a success.

Yet as early as Rachel Carson's *Silent Spring* (1962) it was clear that there was a price to pay, that the revolution wasn't green at all in the environmental sense. Soil erosion, over-extraction of fresh water, chemical pollution, loss of biodiversity, rural unemployment and depopulation, greenhouse-gas emissions and food waste pervade industrial farming.

Oil also, with the support of advertising and innovations such as "hire purchase", ushered in a kind of livelihood – late-20th-century consumerism – guaranteed to do for the environment what the Chicxulub asteroid strike did for the dinosaurs.

BP's production soared from three-quarters of a million barrels a day in 1954 to 1.5 million by 1960 and nearly four million a decade later. The firm grew so fast that it struggled to find a market for all its output. It diversified into petrochemicals and became second in size only to ICI in this industry. It was the birth of the age of plastic, disposability and waste on a previously unimaginable scale.

Like an artificial cuckoo in nature's nest, a new technosphere grew up inside the biosphere. It remains visible in drains blocked with plastic bags, birds strangled by the packaging from six-packs of beer, oceans decorated with the indestructible plastic detritus of consumer society and much more carbon released into the atmosphere.

CHRISTOPHE SIMON/AFP/GETTY IMAGES

In one wave, we surrounded ourselves with cars, fridges, freezers and TVs. Later came the age of the "upgradeable" electronic and digital device – a clever rebranding of built-in obsolescence. Between 1970 and 2009, the number of consumer electronic gadgets in a typical UK household increased elevenfold. While some individual items use energy more efficiently than before, the sheer volume increased energy consumption by household gadgets over the period by 600 per cent.

Even though renewable energy is expanding, ever more power for the ever-growing global economy will come from fossil fuels, according to the International Energy Agency. In the IEA's most optimistic scenario, which includes renewables, global warming will still push past 3° above pre-industrial levels – well beyond any notional safety level.

The effect of human pressure on the biosphere is that we are living through a mass extinction event, something that rarely happens on earth. In one previous event, the Palaeocene Eocene Thermal Maximum, the earth warmed over several thousand years. Climate zones today appear to be shifting about ten times faster.

Past a certain point, impacts work like dominoes, one thing toppling the next. Reflective ice sheets melt along with permafrost, oceans absorb less carbon, forests die back. There may be only a few years left before the odds shift against stopping irreversible upheaval.

The Nasa climate scientist James Hansen says we are on the cusp of losing the climatic conditions in which civilisation evolved. In the past century, a minority has become accustomed to disproportionate levels of consumption; if most of us were to consume at the same level it would take several planets to support humanity. And although research shows rising consumption over the past few decades has brought the rich no commensurate rise in well-being, many people are reluctant to envisage having less stuff.

Perhaps this is not surprising, when a multi-billion-pound advertising industry keeps us focused on having rather than being. The sadness is that the same research on well-being suggests that a much better life exists off the hedonic treadmill, whose baubles were lampooned by both Adam Smith and Karl Marx.

Yet, *in extremis*, societies from the UK to Cuba have been able to re-engineer their economy and change their behaviour, reducing consumption rapidly, with unexpected health, social and environmental benefits. With the will, and collective effort, it can be done.

But what big, immediate steps can we take to reshape our chances of surviving and thriving in the next century? First of all, we should be leaving three-quarters or more of already proven fossil fuels in the ground, because the best science tells us that to burn them will condemn us to catastrophic warming. Some in insurance, the actuarial industry and even a few in oil conclude that the likes of BP need a new category for their oil reserves – "unburnable". This is the signal that, more than anything, would catalyse a green economy.

Second, how do we meet the needs of millions worldwide still trapped in subsistence? Conventional growth has failed the poorest by giving them a shrinking share of its benefits and passing on its costs in pollution and inequality. If we are to sustain life within the biosphere's ultimately non-negotiable boundaries, we will be obliged to redistribute the bounty of our ecosystems, as much as money.

Third, to help ease that transition, especially in countries such as ours, we need to measure economic success differently. Instead of being hypnotised by size, measured by GDP, we need to know how good the economy is at delivering quality of life within natural boundaries. There are measures available to do this.

So, here are three tests to steer us into the next century. Will any proposal made raise or lower: **i)** our ecological impact; **ii)** inequality; **iii)** human well-being? With the right answer to all three, we may achieve what Raymond Williams once said was the precondition for being radical – we will "make hope possible, not despair convincing". ●

Andrew Simms is the author of "Cancel the Apocalypse: the New Path to Prosperity" (Little, Brown, £13.99)

Ken Livingstone's Threat to Labour

By Steve Richards

Ken Livingstone walks on to the Commons Terrace on a blazing afternoon, wearing dark glasses, a tieless shirt and jeans. He smiles wryly. "I've just had this ghastly woman on the phone from an American magazine who has spent the past 20 minutes trying to get me to say something nasty about Glenda [Jackson]. She gave up in the end. I haven't said anything nasty about Jeffrey Archer so I'm not about to slag Glenda off."

The House of Commons is in recess. Most MPs have disappeared for their holidays. But Livingstone is still beavering away. He has been reinvigorated by his campaign to be London mayor. Or, more accurately, his campaign to be allowed to stand in Labour's internal contest, in which the party's candidate will be selected. Since his election to the Commons in 1987 Livingstone has lacked a political role. After the abolition of the Greater London Council he remained famous for his appearances on TV but he has not run anything, not even a select committee. Now he has a purpose. "On my tombstone there will be one sentence: 'Abolished by Margaret Thatcher; revived by Tony Blair'," he says mischievously.

Livingstone knows that his revival could be extremely short-lived. While he is enthused by the prospect of becoming mayor, he fears that his renewed ambition could be snuffed out in the autumn. He insists he would remain in the Labour Party if the national executive stopped him throwing his hat into the mayoral ring. Obviously he has to say so in public or else he would give his political opponents in the party the killer ammunition they seek. But I believe him when he says he could not face leaving Labour in order to stand as an independent. Instead, he offers an intriguingly human response, rather than a political one, as to what would happen if his candidacy was blocked. "I know exactly what would happen. I would go into a period of depression. I would get depression with associated psoriasis, a classic stress pattern.

"I've had very few depressions in my life, but they follow a pattern, and I look and feel awful for a few months. One such depression was in 1979, when I didn't get elected to the Commons. Another was in 1983, when the NEC barred me from standing in Brent East. The other was when we lost the election in 1992, when I thought, as many here did, that we would never win again."

So that is the most likely consequence of Livingstone being blocked: after an almighty row, the martyred Ken would sink into depression. He would not stand as an independent. In the meantime he is doing all he can to avoid the possibility of either depression or defection. He wants the party to allow him to stand and almost goes as far as to project himself as the new Labour candidate. He cannot actually bring himself to mouth the words "new Labour" but he does define himself as being "not old Labour".

> "My relationship with Tony Blair has never been anything but cordial"

He says: "My relationship with Tony Blair has never been anything but cordial. According to a Downing Street spokesman, he's quite sad that there's been this waste of talent over the past 15 years or so, when I haven't been allowed to run anything. He probably realises that I'm indelibly not old Labour. He and I are different kinds of post-old Labour, I suppose. We are part of the post-1968 generation. Before, it was about the big state machine making provision, in some cases tackling genuine evils. But our generation just became conscious of the bureaucracy which went with it. It's what turned so many people away from the welfare state, for example, and why the reforms have got to make it more of a service and less an instrument of social control."

At around the time the anonymous Downing Street spokesman spoke about the "waste" of Livingstone's talent, he himself made it clear, in an *NS* interview, that he was keen to serve in the government. He is still waiting. "Offer came there none. I think Tony assumed that, because I've been critical in the past, I would refuse to play the game of collective responsibility. That's not the case. If you are a minister you have pathways to influence; in return you have to be loyal to the government. I accept the trade-off. I would happily abide by rules of collective responsibility."

Would he be as loyal if he became mayor, when he would not be dependent in the same way on prime ministerial patronage? "There are one or two really big issues on which I would take a stand. If they proposed to break the trade union link, I would fight that. If they proposed a merger with the Lib Dems, I would oppose it, although that looks as if it's off the agenda now. But on all the other issues, where's the big difference?

"My views on public transport are in line with all the worriers in No 10 who say we mustn't be anti-car. I certainly don't think you should be anti-car, but you do need to hugely improve public transport." He goes on to make a detailed proposal. "Reluctantly I would use congestion charging. It would be £5 a day to drive into central London, a figure supported by many business leaders. I would freeze fares for four years, and then you've got to get the capacity up of buses and trains. You know, people remember the one time when London transport was getting better and I was running it."

Livingstone also promises to appoint a Blairite as his deputy. Earlier in the year he suggested that Trevor Phillips would be the ideal candidate, provoking preposterous allegations of racism from the Phillips camp. Now Livingstone makes a broader pledge. "A Blairite will be my deputy. You've got to have a balanced ticket. I am not daft. It would not be encouraging to voters if I appointed Linda Bellos [the left-wing former leader of Lambeth Council] as my deputy. There are two blocks of opinion in the party and we

The man who would be mayor: the role offered him power for the first time since the 1980s

win when we work together. Also, from a practical point of view, I would have to have someone saying: 'Look, Tony would like it if we did this or that.' But if I were mayor I would make sure I had lots of contact with the Prime Minister anyway."

So there you have a central plank of the embryonic Livingstone manifesto. But that doesn't impress his critics. Earlier this year the Home Office minister and former GLC councillor Paul Boateng wrote an article arguing that Livingstone had been an incompetent leader. "Just before that article I chatted to Paul about his GLC experience, and he said they were the happiest years of his life. Some ghastly thing from the bottom of the food chain decided on a change of strategy, that they were going on the offensive, showed him the article and told him to sign it. If you're part of collective responsibility, that's what you've got to do, I suppose."

But what about the normally mild-mannered Nick Raynsford, a likely mayoral candidate? In an *NS* interview, he complained that Livingstone had not attended any of his meetings with London MPs, in which he had outlined the details of the bill introducing the new mayor. Raynsford was the architect of the bill.

"I'm a great believer that if you want to achieve something you put it in writing, rather than attend some ghastly meetings where everyone broadly makes the same point. When Raynsford published his white paper, my response was longer and more detailed than from any organisation.

"I also applied to be on the bill's committee. I was surprised that nobody ever sought my opinion directly as the leader of the last elected London authority, but I intervened with this massive document which cost me a couple of thousand pounds to put together and distribute."

Livingstone is a more complex politician than the "Red Ken" stereotype. He is a strong supporter of the single currency ("we should have joined at the beginning") and a critic of John Smith's vote-losing tax plans in the 1992 election. But he is well to the left of the Blairites and personifies a part of Labour's recent history that the modernisers view with horror.

Yet they are by no means sure how to stop him. They may still persuade Frank Dobson to stand, and Tony Banks has some supporters. But Livingstone is right to assume that Blair has not decided whether he should be blocked in the autumn. Meanwhile, the great charmer expresses a provocative appreciation. "I owe a great debt of gratitude to our boss for creating a mayor. It has brought to the fore all the issues in politics which really interest me, from transport to regional government."

As we leave the Commons Terrace, an excited family approaches. They want him in a group photograph overlooking the Thames. Livingstone's continuing prominence is remarkable. He has been in no position of power since the mid-1980s yet is better known than most of the cabinet.

Once the camera has clicked, I think of one more question. Does he still want a job in government? "Definitely. The ministerial ambition is still there. It would be just like Blair to block me from standing as mayor and then offer me a job in his government. Still, it might cure the psoriasis." ●

Christopher Hitchens: "Never Be Afraid of Stridency"

Interview by Richard Dawkins

This was Christopher Hitchens's last interview, and it was published in the New Statesman the day before his death in December 2011. As the news travelled around the globe, the piece became a media sensation.

Richard Dawkins I've been reading some of your recent collections of essays – I'm astounded by your sheer erudition. You seem to have read absolutely everything.

Christopher Hitchens It may strike some people as being broad but it's possibly at the cost of being a bit shallow. I became a journalist because one didn't have to specialise. I remember once going to an evening with Umberto Eco talking to Susan Sontag and the definition of the word "polymath" came up. Eco said it was his ambition to be a polymath; Sontag challenged him and said the definition of a polymath is someone who's interested in everything and nothing else. I was encouraged to read widely – to flit and sip, as Bertie [Wooster] puts it – and I think I've got good memory retention. I retain what's interesting to me, but I don't have a lot of strategic depth.

A lot of reviewers have said, to the point of embarrassing me, that I'm in the class of Edmund Wilson or even George Orwell. It really does remind me that I'm not. But it's something to have had the comparison made.

RD As an Orwell scholar, you must have a particular view of North Korea, Stalin, the Soviet Union, and you must get irritated – perhaps even more than I do – by the constant refrain we hear: "Stalin was an atheist."

CH We don't know for sure that he was. Hitler definitely wasn't. There is a possibility that Himmler was. There's no mandate in atheism for any particular kind of politics, anyway.

RD The people who did Hitler's dirty work were almost all religious.

CH I'm afraid the SS's relationship with the Catholic Church is something the Church still has to deal with and does not deny.

RD Can you talk a bit about that – the relationship of Nazism with the Catholic Church?

CH The way I put it is this: if you're writing about the history of the 1930s and the rise of totalitarianism, you can take out the word "fascist", if you want, for Italy, Portugal, Spain, Czechoslovakia and Austria, and replace it with "extreme-right Catholic party". Almost all of those regimes were in place with the help of the Vatican and with understandings from the Holy See. It's not denied. These understandings quite often persisted after the Second World War was over and extended to comparable regimes in Argentina and elsewhere.

RD But there were individual priests who did good things.

> "There is no mandate in atheism for any particular kind of politics"

CH Not very many. You would know their names if there were more of them. When it comes to National Socialism, there's no question there's a mutation, a big one – the Nazis wanted their own form of worship. Just as they thought they were a separate race, they wanted their own religion. They dug out the Norse gods, all kinds of extraordinary myths and legends from the old sagas. They wanted to control the churches. They were willing to make a deal with them.

The first deal Hitler made with the Catholic Church was the *Konkordat*. The Church agreed to dissolve its political party and he got control over German education. Celebrations of his birthday were actually by order from the pulpit. When Hitler survived an assassination attempt, prayers were said, and so forth.

There's another example. You swore on Almighty God that you would never break your oath to the Führer. This is not even secular, let alone atheist.

RD There was also grace before meals, personally thanking Adolf Hitler.

CH I believe there was. Certainly, you can hear the oath being taken – there are recordings of it – but this, Richard, is a red herring. It's not even secular. They're changing the subject.

RD But it comes up over and over again.

CH You mentioned North Korea. It is, in every sense, a theocratic state. It's almost supernatural, in that the births of the Kim family are considered to be mysterious and accompanied by happenings. It's a necrocracy or mausolocracy, but there's no possible way you could say it's a secular state, let alone an atheist one.

Attempts to found new religions should attract our scorn just as much as the alliances with the old ones do. All they're saying is that you can't claim Hitler was distinctively or specifically Christian: "Maybe if he had gone on much longer, he would have de-Christianised a bit more." This is all a complete fog of nonsense. It's bad history and it's bad propaganda.

RD And bad logic, because there's no connection between atheism and doing horrible things, whereas there easily can be a connection in the case of religion, as we see with modern Islam.

CH To the extent that they are new religions – Stalin worship and Kim Il-sungism – we, like all atheists, regard them with horror.

RD You debated with Tony Blair. I'm not sure I watched that. I love listening to you [but] I can't bear listening to . . . Well, I mustn't say that. I think he did come over as rather nice on that evening. What was your impression?

CH You can only have one aim per debate. I had two in debating with Tony Blair. The first one was to get him to admit that it was not done – the stuff we complain of – in only the *name* of religion. The authority is in the *text*. Second, I wanted to get him to admit, if possible, that giving money to a charity or organising a charity does not vindicate a cause.

I got him to the first one and I admired his honesty. He was asked by the interlocutor, ▶

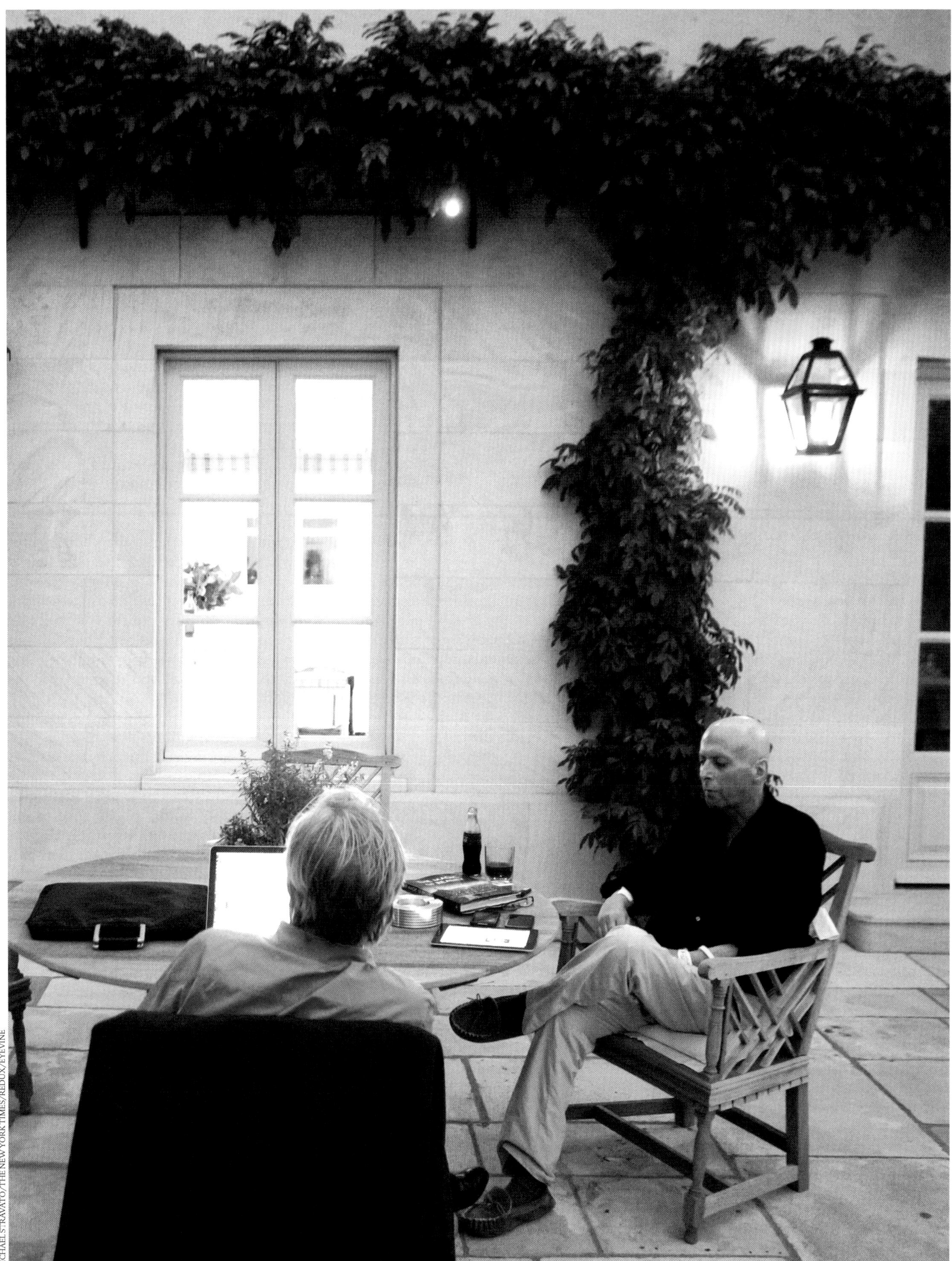

MICHAEL STRAVATO/THE NEW YORK TIMES/REDUX/EYEVINE

Dawkins and Hitchens met and talked in Texas in the late summer of 2011

▶ at about half-time: "Which of Christopher's points strikes you as the best?" He said: "I have to admit, he's made his case, he's right. This stuff, there is authority for it in the canonical texts, in Islam, Judaism." At that point, I'm ready to fold – I've done what I want for the evening.

We did debate whether Catholic charities and so on were a good thing and I said: "They are but they don't prove any point and some of them are only making up for damage done." For example, the Church had better spend a lot of money doing repair work on its Aids policy in Africa, [to make up for preaching] that condoms don't prevent disease or, in some cases, that they spread it. It is iniquitous. It has led to a lot of people dying, horribly. Also, I've never looked at some of the ground operations of these charities – apart from Mother Teresa – but they do involve a lot of proselytising. They're not just giving out free stuff. They're doing work to recruit.

RD And Mother Teresa was one of the worst offenders?

CH She preached that poverty was a gift from God. And she believed that women should not be given control over the reproductive cycle. Mother Teresa spent her whole life making sure that the one cure for poverty we know is sound was not implemented.

So Tony Blair knows this but he doesn't have an answer. If I say, "Your Church preaches against the one cure for poverty," he doesn't deny it, but he doesn't affirm it either. But remember, I did start with a text and I asked him to comment on it first, but he never did. Cardinal Newman said he would rather the whole world and everyone in it be condemned for ever to eternal torture than one sinner go unrebuked for the stealing of a sixpence. It's right there in the centre of the *Apologia*. The man whose canonisation Tony had been campaigning for. You put these discrepancies in front of him and he's like all the others. He keeps two sets of books. And this is also, even in an honest person, shady.

> "I have one consistency, which is being against the totalitarian"

RD It's like two minds, really.

CH I think we all do it a bit.

RD Do we?

CH We're all great self-persuaders.

RD But do we hold such extreme contradictions in our heads?

CH We like to think our colleagues would point them out. No one's pointed out to me in reviewing my God book *God Is Not Great* that there's a flat discrepancy between the affirmation he makes on page X and the affirmation he makes on page Y.

RD But they do accuse you of being a contrarian, which you've called yourself...

CH Well, no, I haven't. I've disowned it but I am a bit saddled with it.

RD I've always been very suspicious of the left-right dimension in politics. It's astonishing how much traction the left-right continuum [has] . . . If you know what someone thinks about the death penalty or abortion, then you generally know what they think about everything else. But you clearly break that rule.

CH I have one consistency, which is [being] against the totalitarian – on the left and on the right. The totalitarian, to me, is the enemy – the one that's absolute, the one that wants control over the inside of your head, not just your actions and your taxes. And the origins of that are theocratic, obviously. The beginning of that is the idea that there is a supreme leader, or infallible pope, or a chief rabbi, or whatever, who can ventriloquise the divine and tell us what to do.

There have been some thinkers – Orwell is pre-eminent – who understood that, unfortunately, there is innate in humans a strong tendency to worship, to become abject. So we're not just fighting the dictators. We're criticising our fellow humans for surrendering and saying, "[If] you offer me bliss, of course I'm going to give up some of my mental freedom for that." We say it's a false bargain: you'll get nothing. You're a fool.

RD One of my main beefs with religion is the way they label children as a "Catholic child" or a "Muslim child". I've become a bit of a bore about it.

CH You must never be afraid of that charge, any more than stridency. If I was strident, it doesn't matter – I was a jobbing hack, I bang my drum. You have a discipline in which you are very distinguished. You've educated a lot of people; nobody denies that, not even your worst enemies. You see your discipline being attacked and defamed and attempts made to drive it out.

If you go on about something, the worst thing the English will say about you, as we both know – as we can say of them, by the way – is that they're boring.

RD Indeed. Only this morning, I was sent a copy of [advice from] a British government website, called something like "The Responsibilities of Parents". One of these responsibilities was "determine the child's religion". Literally, determine. It means establish, cause... I couldn't ask for a clearer illustration, because, sometimes, when I make my complaint about this, I'm told nobody actually does label children "Catholic" or "Muslim".

CH Well, the government does. It's borrowed, as far as I can see, in part from British imperial policy – you classify your new subjects according to their faith. You can be an Ottoman citizen but you're a Jewish one or an Armenian Christian one. And some of these faiths tell their children that the children of other faiths are going to hell.

RD I would call it mental child abuse.

CH I can't find a way, as a libertarian, of saying that people can't raise their children, as they say, according to their rights. But the child has rights and society does, too.

Now, it would be very hard to say that you can't tell your child that they are lucky and they have joined the one true faith. I don't see

MICHAEL STRAVATO/THE NEW YORK TIMES/REDUX/EYEVINE

how you stop it. I only think the rest of society should look at it with a bit of disapproval, which it doesn't.

RD There is a tendency among liberals to feel that religion should be off the table.

CH Or even that there's anti-religious racism, which I think is a terrible limitation.

RD Do you think America is in danger of becoming a theocracy?

CH No, I don't. The people who we mean when we talk about that – maybe the extreme Protestant evangelicals – I think they may be the most overrated threat in the country. They've been defeated everywhere. Why is this? In the 1920s, they had a string of victories. They banned the sale, manufacture and distribution and consumption of alcohol. They made it the constitution. They'll never recover from [the failure of] Prohibition. It was their biggest defeat. They'll never recover from the Scopes trial. Every time they've tried [to introduce the teaching of creationism], the local school board or the parents or the courts have thrown it out. They try to make a free speech question out of it but they will fail with that, also. People don't want to come from the town or the state or the country that gets laughed at.

RD Yes.

CH And if they passed an ordinance saying there will be prayer in school every morning from now on, one of two things would happen: it would be overthrown in no time by all the courts, with barrels of laughter heaped over it, or people would say: "Very well, we're starting with Hindu prayer on Monday." They would regret it so bitterly that there are days when I wish they would have their own way for a short time.

RD Oh, that's very cheering.

CH I'm a bit more worried about the extreme, reactionary nature of the papacy now. But that again doesn't seem to command very big allegiance among the American congregation. They are disobedient on contraception, flagrantly; on divorce; on gay marriage, to an extraordinary degree that I wouldn't have predicted; and they're only holding firm on abortion, which, in my opinion, is actually a very strong moral question and shouldn't be decided lightly. I feel very squeamish about it. I believe that the unborn child is a real concept, in other words.

So, really, the only threat from religious force in America is the same as it is in many other countries – from outside. And it's jihadism, some of it home-grown, but some of that is so weak and so self-discrediting.

RD It's more of a problem in Britain.

CH And many other European countries, where its alleged root causes are being allowed slightly too friendly an interrogation, I think. Make that much too friendly.

RD Some of our friends are so worried about Islam that they're prepared to lend support to Christianity as a kind of bulwark against it.

CH I know many Muslims who, in leaving the faith, have opted to go ... to Christianity or via it to non-belief. Some of them say it's the personality of Jesus of Nazareth. The mild and meek one, as compared to the rather farouche, physical, martial, rather greedy ...

RD Warlord.

CH ... Muhammad. I can see that that might have an effect.

RD Do you ever worry that if we win and, so to speak, destroy Christianity, that vacuum would be filled by Islam?

CH No, in a funny way, I don't worry that we'll win. All that we can do is make absolutely sure that people know there's a much more wonderful and interesting and beautiful alternative. Christianity has defeated itself in that it has become a cultural thing. There really aren't believing Christians in the way there were generations ago.

RD Certainly in Europe that's true – but in America?

CH There are revivals, of course, but I think there's a very long-running tendency in the developed world and in large areas elsewhere for people to see the virtue of secularism, the separation of church and state, because they've tried the alternatives ...

RD If you look at religiosity across the world you find that religiosity tends to correlate with poverty and with various other indices of social deprivation.

CH Yes. That's also what it feeds on. But I don't want to condescend about that. I know a lot of very educated, very prosperous, very thoughtful people who believe.

RD I'm often asked why it is that this republic [of America], founded in secularism, is so much more religious than those western European countries that have an official state religion, like Scandinavia and Britain.

CH [Alexis] de Tocqueville has it exactly right. If you want a church in America, you have to build it by the sweat of your own brow and many have. That's why they're attached to them. The Jews – not all of them – remarkably abandoned their religion very soon after arriving from the shtetl.

RD Are you saying that most Jews have abandoned their religion?

WILLIAM McPHAIL

"Ideally I'd like mosquitoes to spread it ..."

CH Increasingly in America. When you came to escape religious persecution and you didn't want to replicate it, that's a strong memory. The Jews very quickly secularised. American Jews must be the most secular force on the planet now.

RD While not being religious, they often still observe the Sabbath and that kind of thing.

CH There's got to be something cultural. I go to Passover every year. Sometimes, even I have a seder, because I want my child to know that she does come very distantly from another tradition. It would explain if she met her great-grandfather why he spoke Yiddish.

And then there is manifest destiny. People feel America is just so lucky. It's between two oceans, filled with minerals, wealth, beauty. It does seem providential to many people.

RD Promised land, city on a hill.

CH All that and the desire for another Eden. Some secular utopians came with the same idea. Thomas Paine and others all thought of America as a great new start for the species.

RD I've heard another theory that, America being a country of immigrants, people coming from Europe, where they left their extended family and left their support system, were alone and they needed something.

CH The reason why most of my friends are non-believers is not particularly that they were engaged in the arguments you and I have been having, but they were made indifferent by compulsory religion at school.

RD They got bored by it.

CH They'd had enough of it. They took from it occasionally whatever they needed – if you needed to get married, you knew where to go. Generally speaking, the British people are benignly indifferent to religion.

RD Can you say anything about Christmas?

CH Yes. There was going to be a winter solstice holiday for sure. The dominant religion was going to take it over and that would have happened without Dickens and without others.

RD The Christmas tree comes from Prince Albert; the shepherds and the wise men are all made up.

CH Cyrenius wasn't governor of Syria, all of that. Increasingly, it's secularised itself. This "Hap-py Holidays" – I don't particularly like that, either.

RD Horrible, isn't it? "Happy holiday season."

CH I prefer our stuff about the cosmos.

The day after this interview, I was honoured to present an award to Christopher Hitchens in the presence of a large audience in Texas that gave him a standing ovation, first as he entered the hall and again at the end of his deeply moving speech. My speech ended with a tribute, in which I said that every day he demonstrates the falsehood of the lie that there are no atheists in foxholes: "Hitch is in a foxhole, and he is dealing with it with a courage, an honesty and a dignity that any of us would be, and should be, proud to muster." ●

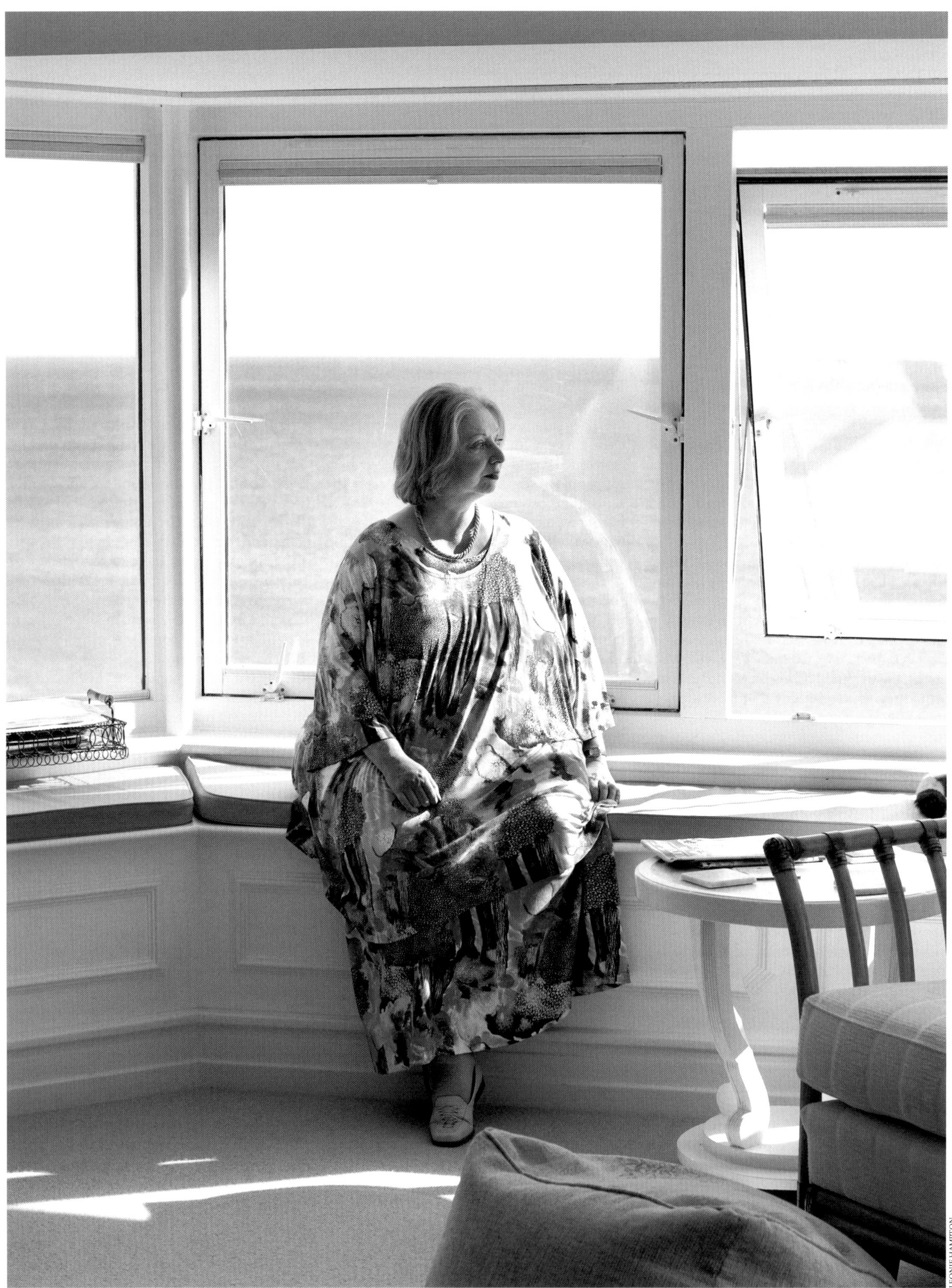

LEONIE HAMPTON

The Unquiet Mind of Hilary Mantel

By Sophie Elmhirst

The desk at which Hilary Mantel writes is pushed up against a window with a view out to sea. The sea isn't in the distance, spotted between hills. It's there, almost at her doorstep, the shingle beach just across the road. To write, she sits at her computer facing the large window and the sea can fill her vision. It's the kind of view that swallows time. There is no sign of human life; nothing except waves and clouds. On her computer desktop, Mantel has put an image: a photograph of the view from her window. "It reminds me to actually look up from the screen," she says.

****

Every summer, there is a music festival in Budleigh Salterton, Devon. From the flat where she lives with her husband, Gerald McEwen, Mantel can walk along the beach into town in ten minutes or so. Last year, once she'd realised that she was writing not one, not two, but three books about Thomas Cromwell, once she'd realised that the second was going to end with Anne Boleyn's beheading, once the title – *Bring Up the Bodies* – had struck her as she wrote the words (it echoes the Tower of London order to bring the accused to trial), once she had told her publishers that they'd have a second instalment sooner than they'd thought (you can imagine their fists punching the air), Mantel began to write.

This was not writing that can be identified as writing in the ordinary sense: spasmodic, agonised, write-delete-write-delete. These were eight-, ten-, 12-hour days, marathons of prose, a 400-page book written in five months, between May and September 2011. (Don't be encouraged. The words spilled only because Mantel had done long, professorial research into her subject. She first had the idea for a book about Thomas Cromwell in her mid-twenties; she had read everything – all the books, all the books about the books and all the original sources; she filled red Chinese chests with meticulous notes and cards and folders of information. She checked every fact, every source, every date, every letter, every name. Her Cromwell books are a combination of wild imagining and unimpeachable accuracy.)

One of her few distractions from writing was going to concerts at the music festival or going for walks along the beach: "I wasn't really listening to the music, but listening to what was going on in my head and walking along the seafront home with my head feeling as if it was wobbling with the weight of ideas and voices inside it and then coming and sitting down at my desk to catch it all down."

****

Budleigh Salterton: population 5,000, mostly elderly. It's a town of gift shops and mobility scooters. For Mantel, perfection. On a walk through the town she stops to pet a pug and tells its owner about the pugs she once had, how much she loves the breed. At a restaurant, a man comes to the table to tell her how an article she wrote has resonated with him. "Oh thank you, thank you," she says, smiling. The people are congenial here, she says. No one has the vulgarity to ask her how the next book is going.

Mantel first saw Budleigh's roofs from a clifftop when she was 16. She was escaping at the time. Along the coast, in Exmouth, her family was on holiday in a caravan, cooped up and crabby. She went for a walk along the coastal path and saw the town below her, houses falling down the hillside, and it imprinted itself on her mind as the place where she would live if she could live anywhere in the world. It became her idea of exotic, of Europe, the white houses by the sea. "I remember when I went back to school that year, telling people about it – they were all very sniffy because they were much more moneyed and sophisticated girls. They said, when you've been abroad you won't think anything of a place like this. But even when I'd been abroad very extensively, it was still in my head and actually I can see why now, because" – she points through the living-room window – "if you are up on the cliffs there looking at the view you'd be hard pushed to find a more beautiful spot anywhere."

Mantel, born the eldest of three in 1952, spent her early years living in the village of Hadfield, in northern Derbyshire, surrounded by grandparents, great-aunts, cousins. The first jolt was a move to a modern house, up the hill in Brosscroft. The second was more disruptive. One day when she was six, a man called Jack Mantel moved in. Her father, Henry, a clerk, didn't leave. The family lived like that, an awkward, unspoken configuration of three children and three adults, until ▶

▶ the shunning of the villagers moved them on to a small town in Cheshire, leaving behind all those relations and Henry, who she never saw again. She even took Jack's surname.

Mantel was desperate to grow up and get out (her principal recollection of childhood is about how little it suited her). In her memoir, *Giving Up the Ghost*, she recalls a pair of curtains from the family home. Their pattern was Mediterranean windows, with colourful blinds and pots of flowers, windows that were used to the sun shining through them, warming the house. Many years later, Mantel told her mother about how she often fantasised about living behind those windows. "My mother turned away, so that I couldn't see her face. She whispered, and I, oh so did I."

****

This is a strange, suspended moment. Two books of a trilogy down, one to go. Mantel can't wait to write it, but such is the success of the first two books that the demands on her time are overwhelming. There is no possibility of immersion, those sucked-under days or head-wobbling beach walks. For years, says her agent Bill Hamilton, Mantel said yes to every invitation to speak, every festival, every opportunity to promote one of her books, but the books never quite took off. Her subjects were odd and unpredictable: an 18th-century Irish giant, moor-dwelling nuns, a suburban social worker, performing psychics, Norfolk missionaries, the French Revolution. It took Henry VIII to usher her into the light.

She is aware – how could she not be – of how her readers have swollen in number. Before the Booker-winning *Wolf Hall*, she says, she could stand by a pile of her own books at a signing and go unrecognised. Now new readers write to her. After *Wolf Hall* many complained: it was confusing, ambiguous; why was the protagonist referred to as "he"? Amanda Craig wrote in this magazine that it was "one of those novels you either loved or hated. I belonged to the latter camp." Craig, though a fan of both Mantel's earlier work and *Bring Up the Bodies*, says now that she found *Wolf Hall* "attention-seeking . . . the combination of the historic present and the lack of clarity, the word 'he' – it gets in the way".

Mantel wondered if she was being too demanding. But then she thought that to adjust her style would be not only a loss, but patronising ("You simply cannot run remedial classes for people on the page"). Some will be lost along the way, but she doesn't mind. "It makes me think that some readers read a book as if it were an instruction manual, expecting to understand everything first time, but of course when you write, you put into every sentence an overflow of meaning, and you create in every sentence as many resonances and double meanings and ambiguities as you can possibly pack in there, so that people can read it again and get something new each time."

She can sound arrogant, Mantel, assured of her abilities and candid about them in a way that seems peculiarly un-English. But even the arrogance is purposeful. It is one of her pieces of advice to young authors: cultivate confidence, have no shame in being bullish about your ideas and your abilities. She was patronised for years by male critics who deemed her work domestic and provincial (one, writing about *A Place of Greater Safety* – the French 800-pager – dwelt on a brief mention of wallpaper). So she makes no apologies for her self-belief.

****

He, Cromwell. She knew after one page that she'd got it, the voice. "I just wanted to laugh in joy because I'd been wanting to do it for so long." Historical fiction doesn't cover it; these books are an inhabitation. Mantel, when describing how she writes, refers to a passage near the beginning of her earlier novel *Beyond Black*, about a performing medium, Alison:

> She takes a breath, she smiles, and she starts a peculiar form of listening. It is a silent sensory ascent; it is like listening from a stepladder, poised on the top rung; she listens at the ends of her nerves, at the limit of her capacities. When you're doing platform work, it's rare that the dead need coaxing. The skill is in isolating the voices, picking out one and letting the others recede.

After all the research, the reading, the note-taking, the indexing, the filing and refiling, it is a question of tuning in. Alison, she says, is how she would have turned out if she hadn't had an education – not necessarily a medium, but not far off, someone whose brain hadn't been trained, and so whose only (but considerable) powers were those of instinct, of sensing, of awareness. Mantel describes herself as "skinless". She feels everything: presences, ghosts, memories. Cromwell is researched, constructed and written, but he is also channelled. Occupying his mind is pleasurable. He is cool, all-seeing, almost super-heroic in his powers to anticipate and manipulate. Mantel relishes his low heart rate, the nerveless approach to life, a mental state unbogged by rumination. She says that when she began writing *Wolf Hall* she felt physically robust in a way she hadn't for years.

"When you write, you put into every sentence an overflow of meaning"

Mantel's mind is different. Left to her own devices, she can get caught up: "Yesterday I was enjoying a hot shower and I started thinking what it would be like if I were in prison, and I couldn't have this shower? And then I thought, 'Well, I wonder, if I were in prison, would people bully me, or would I bully them?' And then I stared thinking, 'Well actually, it's unlikely that you'd have to go to prison now, although earlier in your life you probably could very well have murdered someone . . .'."

Sorry, what? "I think there was probably a time in my life when I did have that capacity if I'd encountered the right circumstances. So by the time I've got out of the shower, I've been through this whole scenario in my head where I've gone to prison for a variety of offences at a variety of ages and of course I'm suddenly miserable and frightened. But it's like an exercise, the way a dancer would go to the barre every day and go through a routine: I think this is how you live as a writer. You wake up with some uncomfortable thought and instead of dismissing it, like a normal person, you find yourself indulging it."

****

Education is the difference between Mantel the morbid, murdering shower fantasist and Mantel the person who can trap such a fantasy on the page. Education is the difference between her and her mother, who left school at 14. If she hadn't gone to school (a convent grammar) and university, the sensing side of her, her inner Alison, "would have been the only side of me I could have used. It may be pushing it a bit far to say I'd make a living reading the cards, but what else could you do? If you're all sensibility and sensitivity but no knowledge or analytical powers."

She was always a reader, though, even before she knew how. She remembers being read to – *King Arthur and His Knights of the Round Table* on repeat – and knowing passages by heart, coloured by her imagination into something more vivid, so that when finally she came to learn to read, she was disappointed by the simplicity of children's books, with their "short, dull words". Jane Eyre was Mantel's kindred spirit in childhood; at last, a cousin on the page, a girl who was also guilty of being "unchildlike".

After school, Mantel went to the London School of Economics to study law. But then she met Gerald, a geologist, whom she married and moved with to Sheffield, Botswana, Saudi Arabia and then into the traffic-throttled towns of London's commuter belt: Woking, Windsor, Sunningdale. Early on, she worked briefly as a social worker, and this experience and the stints in Africa and Saudi Arabia fed into later novels. They also shaped a sensibility: she listens to, and writes about, the overlooked. And she knows, from spending time in places oversimplified by the west, that things are always more complicated than they seem from afar. Saudi Arabia taught her – an ardent feminist – that the women there didn't necessarily envy women in the west. She doesn't like to talk about politics, going only as far as to describe herself as a "radical"

For Mantel the lively dead are "only just out of range"

LEONIE HAMPTON

and, once upon a time, a member of the Young Communist League. Nowadays she resists signing petitions; to be a novelist is to relish uncertainty, to be shot with doubt. She makes a hopeless newspaper columnist because, she says, she is unable to "generate opinions. I have to say, wait, I have to think about that, if you could come back to me in two years . . ."

****

History breathes in Mantel's version. There is nothing closed about it, nothing finite. The Cromwell books are written in a present tense that thrums with urgency and a sense that everything is uncertain, that history could be rewritten: maybe he doesn't marry her, maybe she has a son, maybe they don't break with Rome. It lives for her, too; the membranes are thin. She remembers going to Hampton Court as a child on a hot summer's day and walking into the Wolsey Rooms "and crying and crying. But trying to conceal from my family the fact that I was crying, and I don't know what it was about. Something had hit me."

She hasn't lost that susceptibility in adulthood, though now she can control her reactions. While writing *Wolf Hall* she went to see Ralph Sadler's house in Hackney. Down in the cellar she found the original Tudor bricks, and in one she spotted the imprint of a dog's paw. Centuries ago, when the bricks were made and then laid out to dry, some unknown mutt had run across them. The sight moved her. Most of us would see a paw print; Mantel hears the dog, smells it, feels its rough fur under her fingers, watches it lope down a stinking London street.

The dead feel close, "only just out of range" – the legacy of a large Irish family who spoke of uncles and aunts long buried as though they were still living next door. Uncle Martin's house was still known as Uncle Martin's house even though he had died before Mantel was born. She sees her brother now, reading a newspaper (a brother too young to remember their real father) and she is jarred by her father's presence: the way he throws one knee over the other, how he turns the pages.

She wonders if her own brain is cross-wired. "I am prone almost to have this reminiscence, in that if you were to refer to a certain incident in my childhood, for example, I am apt to be plunged back in there in a way that feels very visceral, very real, and it doesn't feel like a memory, it feels like living . . . The memories are all-embracing, because you really are back in that room at that moment, and once you can do that for your own life, the next step is can you do it for someone who has never existed? Or someone who's been dead 400 years? I think that's the aim, to give your characters memories that are as real as yours."

****

Her books are her babies. Christmas, 1979: aged 27, after years of pain deemed imaginary by doctors who prescribed her frenzy-inducing anti-psychotic drugs and then hospitalised her in a psychiatric ward, she accurately self-diagnosed chronic endometriosis. It was confirmed by a doctor, and she went into hospital and had her womb, her ovaries and part of her bowel removed.

Things fell apart. On a 12-week break back from Botswana at the end of 1979, her first manuscript for *A Place of Greater Safety* was rejected (the book was finally published in 1992); her marriage to Gerald broke down (they divorced, and then remarried); and the potential for motherhood was cut out of her body. The only thing she knew was that life was unlikely to get worse.

You can't write about Mantel without writing about her body. From her memoir: "One of my favoured grim sports, since I became a published writer and had people to interview me, has been to wait and see how the profiler will turn me out in print. With what adjective will they characterise the startlingly round woman on whose sofa they are lolling? 'Apple-cheeked' is the sweetest. 'Maternal' made me smile: well, almost."

As a child, she was frail, thin, small, but a combination of illness and medication distorted her natural shape. For much of her life Mantel has felt she is inhabiting a stranger's body. She looks in the mirror and can, sometimes, see the ghost of the person she once was, but it is concealed by flesh. And then there are the other ghosts: those of the children she couldn't have. In all her books, but especially the Cromwell books, there are wombs, foetuses, the unborn, shadows of dead children everywhere. If Gerald and she had been able to have a daughter, they would have called her Catriona.

Does the body's collapse alter the mind? In Mantel's view, undoubtedly. If she'd had a different body, one that obeyed, she would have had a different personality. She knew from early on that she would have to predicate her life on mental effort, because she was so physically erratic. "My thoughts," she says, "have been the thing I can rely on."

****

Elusive – the word is used often by people around Mantel, even those who have known her for decades. Bill Hamilton describes how in conversation "she's always three steps ahead of me . . . I mean, I just like sort of throwing tennis balls at her and seeing what comes back. You have no idea where the ball's *gone*."

Hamilton plucked Mantel off the slush pile. She had found him, at the literary agency A M Heath, in the *Writers' and Artists' Yearbook*. She knew little about the industry, apart from its rejection of her first novel, and simply sent in a letter and the manuscript of what became her first published book, *Every Day Is Mother's Day*. Her habit now is to show Hamilton a chunk of the next book when she feels she has captured the style, to give him an idea of what to expect. (The first 40 pages of *Bring Up the Bodies* were handed over during a lunch with him and Nicholas Pearson, her editor at Fourth Estate. She had a "glint in her eye", Hamilton recalls). They exchange emails and calls regularly and when the reviews come out she merrily dismembers critics who have failed to untangle an obvious ▶

100 years of crop protection

100 years ago a single farmer produced little more than enough food to feed their family. Today's farmers have access to modern technologies that help them provide food for over 7 billion people.*

Tools such as pesticides have helped to reduce crop losses, boost crop yields, cut food waste and improve the efficient use of scarce natural resources such as land, water and energy.

The crop protection industry is proud of the role it has played in supporting sustainable agricultural production and meeting the rising global demand for food – and we will continue to rise to the challenge of protecting crops across the globe over the next 100 years and beyond.

26% - 40%
of world's
annual potential
crop production
lost
to pests & diseases

100
years ago
agriculture fed
1 billion
people
today
7 billion

70%
increase in food
production needed
by 2050
to feed
9 billion

*American Farm Bureau Federation
/ OECD-FAO Agricultural Outlook 2012

▶ metaphor. She is, Hamilton says, a lively email correspondent, sardonic and candid.

There is a gap between Mantel in person and Mantel on the page. To be in her company is to find a woman polite, wide-eyed, generous, chatty, occasionally unleashing spikes of wit. She conducts a tour of her flat – its two studies, a second bedroom that has been turned into a dressing room, the decision to paint everything cream because she was ill at the time of redecoration and couldn't think about it properly – with the formality and attention to detail of a house-proud retiree.

But on the page, there is violence and brutality: entrails, cocks, fuck, cunt. "How can I write this, I wonder?" she asks in her memoir. "I am a woman with a delicate mouth; I say nothing gross." Her writing self, she says now, is "much tougher than my everyday, operating self, much less compromising and much less afraid". It was always the way: she doesn't think she's got braver as time and books have passed; she hasn't had to steel herself gradually to write about executions and seductions in bald detail. "No. I think I started off fearless on the page."

****

Any worry Mantel has about the future of the novel is not for the form, but for its authors. "I worry about people who can't make their voices heard... People like me from working-class backgrounds could sort of weasel through and I'm not sure that applies any more." On the night of 6 October 2009, when Mantel won the Man Booker Prize for *Wolf Hall*, she sat at the Fourth Estate table with Pearson and, minutes before the announcement of the winner was due, she told him about a young writer she thought he should read. They were both anxious, hyper-aware that this was the career-transforming moment, that she was on the cusp of industry recognition long overdue, but she thought she would use the time and the opportunity to recommend a new author to her publisher.

Man Booker night awaits again. She is shortlisted this time for *Bring Up the Bodies*, and if she wins on 16 October she will be the first British author to win twice. Her plan is straightforward: get through it, press on to the end of the year, then shut up shop. Next year she wants a repeat of last summer, months of saying no to everyone, week after week lost to a book. If she can get this one right, put all the mirrors in place, catch all the reflections that she has been preparing since the first pages of *Wolf Hall*, if she can, as she puts it, "bring the third volume home in the style I would like to complete it", then she will feel something approaching satisfaction. She knows that she will look back at the Cromwell books as the central writing of her life, because "it was a book in which I felt instantly at home. I felt I'd been waiting all my writing life to get there."

****

For so long, it wasn't like this: the glory, the prizes, the money. Pearson describes the frustration of publishing, for book after book, an author who was that respected but limited thing, a writer's writer. Cromwell has propelled her. Why? A reader and fellow author of historical fiction, Sarah Waters, emails: "Well, it's tempting to be cynical about it and note that, after a respectable but underappreciated career of writing mainly about women, she was finally recognised as a literary heavyweight once she produced a novel that was all about men..."

Waters then tempers this, suggesting that perhaps it is due to the sudden surge in interest in historical fiction, or maybe the darkness and strangeness of the earlier novels put people off, or it was because she was always unpredictable in subject and style. But then, "Maybe it's more simple – maybe it's just that, with *Wolf Hall* and *Bring Up the Bodies*, Mantel has hit her stride as a novelist; that her writing, now, is too good for anyone to ignore."

> "How can I write like this? I am a woman with a delicate mouth"

There is no one else writing like her, says Pearson. "I haven't seen anything like it, not in this country." Hamilton is sure that once people have caught up with these books, once they've twigged that every sentence has a parallel text, once people reread them and grasp the extent of her achievement, then she will be acknowledged as a "first-rate writer who will be read and studied for ever, I think".

****

Mantel offers clues. We know the third book (to be called *The Mirror and the Light*) has to end with Cromwell's fall, but to get there she must weave together all the other strands and settle the fates of a ranging cast of characters. She will turn her attention to Gregory, Cromwell's hapless, kindly son, and Cromwell will realise that he has oppressed Gregory in his own way, just as his father oppressed him. It will, inevitably, be tinged with tragedy. It will end in death.

On Mantel's desk is a ring binder. She opens it and leafs through an assorted jumble of pages: a paragraph written on branded hotel notepaper in her slanting hand; a page of lined A4 paper covered in hurried scribbles; a recipe for quail, torn out of a Sunday newspaper supplement. "Jane Seymour, during her pregnancy with the future Edward, couldn't get enough quail, and they kept sending them over from Calais," she says, still amused by Seymour's cravings. "I suppose I thought, 'OK, I'll cook some quail.'"

She writes the books in collage – distinct, hermetic scenes that she stitches together to make a whole, though the overall architecture is always in her mind. History is useful like that. She sees something she has written about Seymour towards the end, pulls the rings apart, removes the piece of paper and places it towards the front, where it should be. This is Mantel making the third book.

****

For years, Mantel followed Gerald around the world. Now he follows her. He looks after the business of her authorship; the contracts and engagements and logistics. He travels with her, collects visitors from Exmouth Station and drives the car so that she can sit and think and write in her head. He brings coffee and biscuits elegantly arranged on a plate.

They agree that he will go and see her mother, who is staying in their other flat up the road. (They bought it for their pension, she says, and it's a good place to house guests so that she can control how much, or little, she sees them. Her mother is a talker, and Mantel likes to work uninterrupted in the early mornings.) As they make this arrangement, they stand opposite each other in the cream living room, holding each other's hands, one pair up, one pair down, as though caught in a still moment during a dance.

****

Not long ago, Mantel gave a talk in Sydney. She didn't go to Sydney, preferring not to travel, so the interviewer sat on the stage with a laptop on his knees on which he conducted a conversation with her which was beamed on to a large screen. The audience numbered nearly 1,000 and was, apparently, silent throughout, enthralled.

For someone who lives so much in her mind, who describes herself as a "creature in paper and ink", she can perform. She can pick a stitch from a question and unravel an answer. She has the ability, which is said of many but in her case is true, to speak in sculpted paragraphs. Here's one:

"I think if I hadn't become a writer I would just have suppressed that part of my personality. I think I would have put it in a box that I never opened. I'm not sure I would have been happy doing that. Sometimes people ask, does writing make you happy? But I think that's beside the point. It makes you agitated, and continually in a state where you're off balance. You seldom feel serene or settled. You're like the person in the fairy tale *The Red Shoes*: you've just got to dance and dance, you're never in equilibrium. I don't think writing makes you happy, not that you asked that question, I'm asking myself. I think it makes for a life that by its very nature has to be unstable, and if it ever became stable, you'd be finished." ●

Mantel won her second Man Booker Prize for "Bring Up the Bodies" on 16 October 2012

The Critical Condition

Gilded age: a literary party at George Plimpton's Upper East Side apartment in 1963, with guests including Jonathan Miller, Gore Vidal and Truman Capote

Science as an Element in Culture

By Bertrand Russell

Science, to the ordinary reader of newspapers, is represented by a varying selection of sensational triumphs, such as wireless telegraphy and aeroplanes, radio-activity and the marvels of modern alchemy. It is not of this aspect of science that I wish to speak. Science, in this aspect, consists of detached up-to-date fragments, interesting only until they are replaced by something newer and more up-to-date, displaying nothing of the systems of patiently constructed knowledge out of which, almost as a casual incident, have come the practically useful results which interest the man in the street. It is with these other reasons, especially with the intrinsic value of a scientific habit of mind in forming our outlook on the world, that I shall be concerned in what follows.

The instance of wireless telegraphy will serve to illustrate the difference between the two points of view. Almost all the serious intellectual labour required for the possibility of this invention is due to three men—Faraday, Maxwell, and Hertz. In alternating layers of experiment and theory these men built up the modern theory of electromagnetism, and demonstrated the identity of light with electromagnetic waves. The system which they discovered is one of profound intellectual interest, bringing together an endless variety of apparently detached phenomena, and displaying a cumulative mental power which cannot but afford delight to every generous spirit. The mechanical details which remained to be adjusted in order to utilise their discoveries for a practical system of telegraphy demanded, no doubt, very considerable ingenuity, but had not that broad sweep and that universality which could give them intrinsic interest as an object of disinterested contemplation.

From the point of view of training the mind, of giving that well-informed, impersonal outlook which constitutes culture in the good sense of this much-misused word, it seems to be generally held indisputable that a literary education is superior to one based on science. Even the warmest advocates of science are apt to rest their claims on the contention that culture ought to be sacrificed to utility. Those men of science who respect culture, when they associate with men learned in the classics, are apt to admit a certain inferiority on their side, compensated doubtless by the services which science renders to humanity, but none the less real. And so long as this attitude exists among men of science, it tends to verify itself: the intrinsically valuable aspects of science tend to be sacrificed to the merely useful, and little attempt is made to preserve that systematic survey by which the finer quality of mind is formed and nourished.

But even if there be, in present fact, any such inferiority as is supposed in the educational value of science, this is not the fault of science itself, but the fault of the spirit in which science is taught. If its full possibilities were realised by those who teach it, I believe that its capacity of producing those habits of mind which constitute the highest mental excellence would be at least as great as that of literature, and more particularly of Greek and Latin literature. In saying this I have no wish whatever to disparage a classical education. I am firmly persuaded that the Greeks fully deserve all the admiration that is bestowed upon them, and that it is a very great and serious loss to be unacquainted with their writings. It is not by attacking them, but by drawing attention to neglected excellences in science, that I wish to conduct my argument.

> Our whole life is built about a certain number of primary instincts

One defect, however, does seem inherent in a purely classical education—namely, a too exclusive emphasis on the past. By the study of what is absolutely ended and can never be renewed a habit of criticism towards the present and the future is engendered. The qualities in which the present excels are qualities to which the study of the past does not direct attention. In what is new and growing there is apt to be something crude, insolent, even a little vulgar, which is shocking to the man of sensitive taste; quivering from the rough contact, he retires to the trim gardens of a polished past, forgetting that they were reclaimed from the wilderness by men as rough and earth-soiled as those from whom he shrinks in his own day.

The habit of being unable to recognise merit until it is dead is too apt to be the result of a purely bookish life, and a culture based wholly on the past will seldom be able to pierce through everyday surroundings to the essential splendour of contemporary things, or to the hope of still greater splendour in the future.

> My eyes saw not the men of old;
> And now their age away has rolled.
> I weep—to think I shall not see
> The heroes of posterity.

So says the Chinese poet; but such impartiality is rare in the pugnacious atmosphere of the West, where the champions of past and future fight a never-ending battle, instead of combining to seek out the merits of both.

This consideration, which militates not only against the exclusive study of the classics, but against every form of culture which has become static, traditional, and academic, leads inevitably to the fundamental question: What is the true end of education? But before attempting to answer this question it will be well to define the sense in which we are to use the word "education". Education, in the sense in which I mean it, may be defined as the formation, by means of instruction, of certain mental habits and a certain outlook on life and the world. It remains to ask ourselves, what mental habits, and what sort of outlook, can be hoped for as the result of instruction?

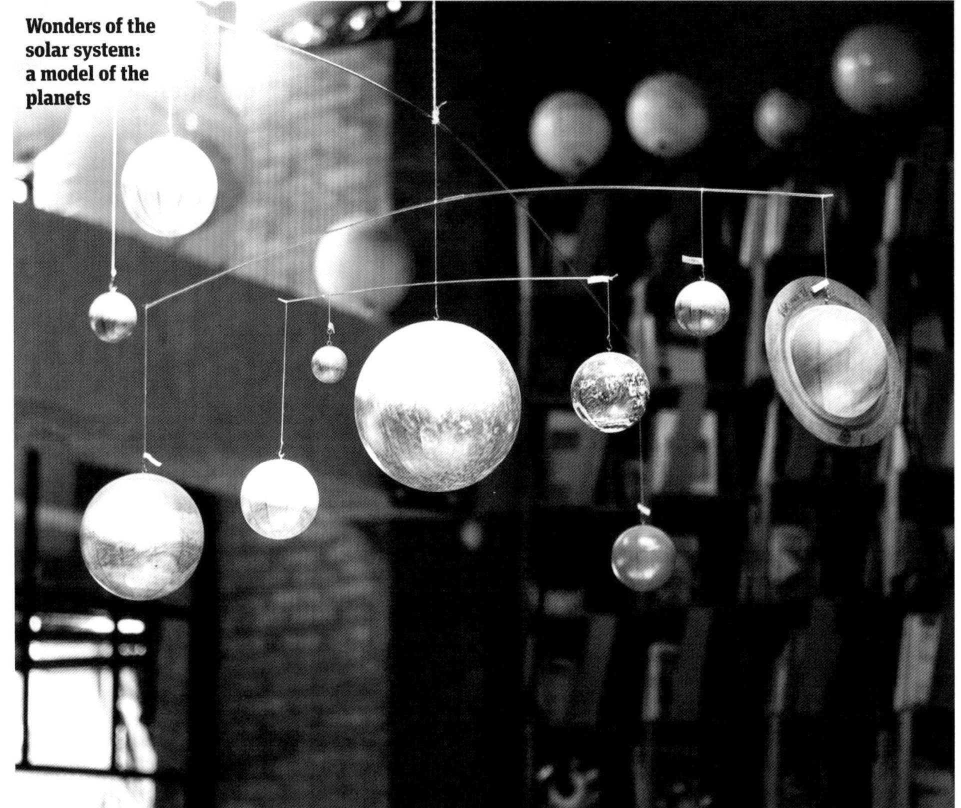
Wonders of the solar system: a model of the planets

ROC CANALS PHOTOGRAPHY/GETTY IMAGES

When we have answered this question we can attempt to decide what science has to contribute to the formation of the habits and outlook which we desire.

Our whole life is built about a certain number of primary instincts and impulses. Only what is in some way connected with these instincts and impulses appears to us desirable or important. Each of them is like a queen-bee, aided by a hive of workers gathering honey; but when the queen is gone the workers languish and die, and the cells remain empty of their expected sweetness. So with each primary impulse in civilised man: it is surrounded and protected by a busy swarm of attendant derivative desires, which store up in its service whatever honey the surrounding world affords. But if the queen-impulse dies, the death-dealing influence, though retarded a little by habit, spreads slowly through all the subsidiary impulses, and a whole tract of life becomes inexplicably colourless. What was formerly full of zest, and so obviously worth doing that it raised no questions, has now grown dreary and purposeless: with a sense of disillusion we inquire the meaning of life, and decide, perhaps, that all is vanity. The search for an outside meaning that can compel an inner response must always be disappointed: all "meaning" must be at bottom related to our primary desires, and when they are extinct no miracle can restore to the world the value which they reflected upon it.

The purpose of education, therefore, cannot be to create any primary impulse which is lacking in the uneducated; the purpose can only be to enlarge the scope of those that human nature provides, by increasing the number and variety of attendant thoughts, and by showing where the most permanent satisfaction is to be found. Under the impulse of a Calvinistic horror of the "natural man", this obvious truth has been too often misconceived in the training of the young; "nature" has been falsely regarded as excluding all that is best in what is natural, and the endeavour to teach virtue has led to the production of stunted and contorted hypocrites instead of full-grown human beings.

But although nature must supply the initial force of desire, nature is not, in the civilised man, the spasmodic, fragmentary, and yet violent set of impulses that it is in the savage. Each impulse has its constitutional ministry of thought and knowledge and reflection, through which possible conflicts of impulses are foreseen, and temporary impulses are controlled by the unifying impulse which may be called wisdom. In this way education destroys the crudity of instinct, and increases through knowledge the wealth and variety of the individual's contacts with the outside world, making him a citizen of the universe, embracing distant countries, remote regions of space, and vast stretches of past and future within the circle of his interests. It is this simultaneous softening in the insistence of desire and enlargement of its scope that is the chief moral end of education.

Closely connected with this moral end is the more purely intellectual aim of education, the endeavour to make us see and imagine the world in an objective manner. The complete attainment of such an objective view is no doubt an ideal, indefinitely approachable, but not actually realisable. Education is to be judged successful in proportion as its outcome approximates to this ideal; in proportion, that is to say, as it gives us a true view of our place in society, of the relation of the whole human society to its non-human environment, and of the nature of the non-human world as it is in itself apart from our desires and interests. If this standard is admitted, we can return to the consideration of science, inquiring how far science contributes to such an aim, and whether it is in any respect superior to its rivals in educational practice.

Two opposite and at first sight conflicting merits belong to science as against literature and art. The one is hopefulness as to the future of human achievement, and in particular as to the useful work that may be accomplished by any intelligent student. This merit and the cheerful outlook which it engenders prevent what might otherwise be the depressing effect of another aspect of science, to my mind also a merit, and perhaps its greatest merit—I mean the irrelevance of human passions and of the whole subjective apparatus where scientific truth is concerned.

In the study of literature or art our attention is perpetually riveted upon the past: the men of Greece or of the Renaissance did better than any men do now; the triumphs of former ages actually increase the difficulty of fresh triumphs by rendering originality harder of attainment; not only is artistic achievement not cumulative, but it seems even to depend upon a certain freshness and *naiveté* of impulse and vision which civilisation tends to destroy. Hence comes, to those who have been nourished on the literary and artistic productions of former ages, a certain peevishness and undue fastidiousness towards the present, from which there seems no escape except into the deliberate vandalism which ignores tradition and in the search after originality achieves only the eccentric. But in such vandalism there is none of the simplicity and spontaneity out of which great art springs.

The despair thus arising from an education which suggests no pre-eminent mental activity except that of artistic creation is wholly absent from an education which gives the knowledge of scientific method. The discovery of scientific method is a thing of yesterday; speaking broadly, we may say that it dates from Galileo. Yet already it has transformed the world, and its success proceeds with ever-accelerating velocity. In science men have discovered an activity of the very highest value in which they are no longer, as in art, dependent for progress upon the appearance of continually greater genius, for ▶

Science and Engineering – progressing the future

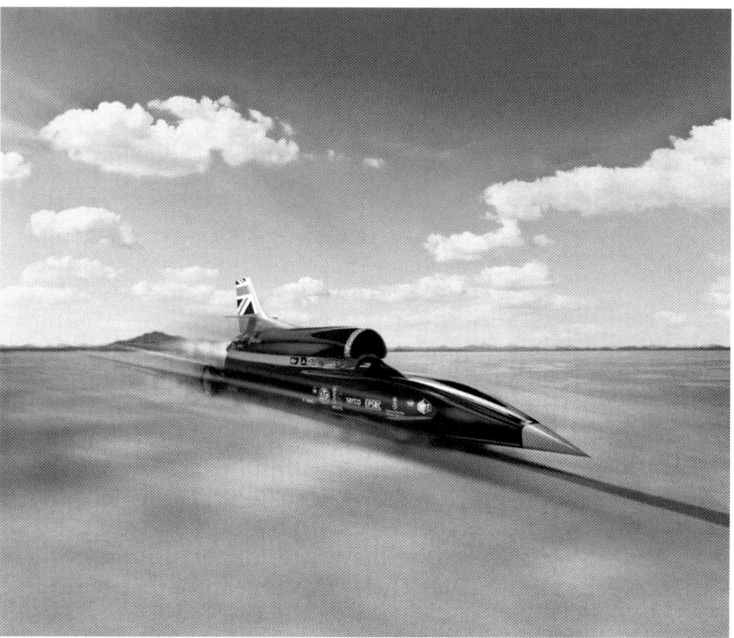

History shows us that innovative science and engineering research has an impact far beyond the original questions it set out to answer. Crick and Watson's discovery of DNA's double helix has led to regenerative medicine, stem cell research and has transformed forensic science.

Tim Berners-Lee developed hypertext years before he created the world wide web which has revolutionised how we work, shop and share knowledge. Fibre optics were developed decades ago but new uses of the technology in medical instruments are only now being realised. As Bertrand Russell said in his article, "Science can unveil secrets which might well have seemed for ever undiscoverable."

Investing in science and engineering research, therefore, is, not only a long game, but vital to the challenges faced by the UK economy and the planet. The Engineering and Physical Sciences Research Council (EPSRC) supports research in physical and mathematical sciences, engineering, and in areas such as energy, healthcare and manufacturing, including the automotive and aerospace industries. Seventy-five per cent of research funded by the EPSRC relates to the government's industrial strategy, and amply demonstrates the importance, impact and reach of the research we fund.

The UK, supported by EPSRC-funded research, has already created a strong legacy of world leading achievement in these disciplines. For instance, EPSRC-funded Andre Geim and Konstantin Novoselov's ground-breaking research into graphene led them to win the 2010 Physics Nobel Prize. Now, significant progress is being made in developing a wide array of applications for the 'super material' graphene, one of the thinnest, lightest, strongest and most conductive materials known to man.

The future for science and engineering in the UK is exciting with potential technological breakthroughs in areas ranging from telecommunications and electronics to energy generation. The development of new composite materials which are lighter, stronger and more flexible is improving fuel efficiency within the aerospace industry. Clothes that can clean up pollution, 3D printing to create building panels and improved processes to improve manufacturing of the next generation of pharmaceutical therapies are examples of recent projects from EPSRC's £800 million annual investment.

Helping solve the major issues faced by society such as energy efficiency and limited natural resources, climate change or stimulating economic growth is an essential part of EPSRC's remit, as is nurturing inspirational leaders of the future through its career fellowships and Centres for Doctoral Training. EPSRC supports a continuous pipeline of scientists and engineers. Put simply, any research is only as good as the people who carry it out.

The Bloodhound project, led by Richard Noble, to design and build a car that will be able to reach a thousand miles per hour, is leading to new advances in aerodynamics that will have benefits far beyond the motor industry. At the same time it is capturing the imagination of schoolchildren who could become our next generation of engineers and scientists.

Getting research to market and out of the so-called 'valley of death' has traditionally been an issue. Now partnerships between universities, businesses, public bodies and government departments are common with collaborative working bringing great benefits and commercial applications.

The romantic vision of the scientist working alone is less common. Now scientific teams of different disciplines, such as mathematical sciences, engineering, chemistry, software, and health often work on large scale research projects to address the challenges we face.

EPSRC has funded research that has initiated and contributed to the technology behind MRI scanners, lasers, pin code encryption, prosthetics and liquid crystal displays, for example. Developments in detecting crime, longer lasting hip replacements, improving infrastructure or software that can track the spread of epidemics, show how engineers and scientists are working together.

Sometimes it is history itself that provides the inspiration for future innovation. For instance the same computer modelling techniques that are being used to design better sounding or quieter public and domestic buildings are also being used to ascertain what sounds our ancestors would have experienced, such as a ritual at Stonehenge four thousand years ago. However, current EPSRC-funded research is also showing that the original circular bluestone construction of Stonehenge provided fantastic acoustics for an outdoor concert, something that designers are looking at harnessing for modern concert building design. It's also an example of how one generation's culture can become another generation's science, even after a gap of four thousand years!

From new technological advances that improve the design of cars and planes, mobile phones, alternative energy sources, and satellite technology, to the design of new plastics and tissue regeneration, EPSRC-funded research and scientists continue to leave a positive impact on the world in which we live. Continuing recognition of the importance of this on-going impact is also helping to ensure that UK-funded research in engineering and the physical sciences will remain at the forefront of innovation in the future.

Paul Golby
Chair of EPSRC

EPSRC
Engineering and Physical Sciences Research Council

▶ in science the successors stand upon the shoulders of their predecessors; where one man of supreme genius has invented a method, a thousand lesser men can apply it. No transcendent ability is required in order to make useful discoveries in science; the edifice of science needs its masons, bricklayers, and common labourers as well as its foremen, master-builders, and architects. In art nothing worth doing can be done without genius; in science even a very moderate capacity can contribute to a supreme achievement. In science the man of real genius is the man who invents a new method. The notable discoveries are often made by his successors, who can apply the method with fresh vigour, unimpaired by the previous labour of perfecting it; but the mental calibre of the thought required for their work, however brilliant, is not so great as that required by the first inventor of the method.

There are in science immense numbers of different methods; but over and above them all, there is something not easily definable, which may be called *the* method of science. It was formerly customary to identify this with the inductive method, and to associate it with the name of Bacon. But the true inductive method was not discovered by Bacon, and the true method of science is something which includes deduction as much as induction, logic and mathematics as much as botany and geology. The temper of mind out of which the scientific method grows is the second of the two merits that were mentioned above as belonging to a scientific education.

The kernel of the scientific outlook is a thing so simple, so obvious, so seemingly trivial, that the mention of it may almost excite derision. The kernel of the scientific outlook is the refusal to regard our own desires, tastes, and interests as affording a key to the understanding of the world. Stated thus baldly, this may seem no more than a trite truism. But to remember it consistently in matters arousing our passionate partisanship is by no means easy, especially where the available evidence is uncertain and inconclusive. A few illustrations will make this clear.

Aristotle considered that the stars must move in circles because the circle is the most perfect curve. In the absence of evidence to the contrary, he allowed himself to decide a question of fact by an appeal to æsthetico moral considerations. In such a case it is at once obvious to us that this appeal was unjustifiable. We know now how to ascertain as a fact the way in which the heavenly bodies move, and we know that they do not move in circles, or even in accurate ellipses, or in any other kind of simply describable curve. This may be painful to a certain hankering after simplicity of pattern in the universe, but we know that in astronomy such feelings are irrelevant. Easy as this knowledge seems now, we owe it to the courage and insight of the first inventors of scientific method, and more especially of Galileo.

We may take as another illustration Malthus's doctrine of population. This illustration is all the better for the fact that his actual doctrine is now known to be largely erroneous. It is not his conclusions that are valuable, but the temper and method of his inquiry. His great merit lies in considering man not as the object of praise or blame, but as a part of nature, a thing with a certain characteristic behaviour from which certain consequences must follow. If the behaviour is not quite what Malthus supposed that may falsify his conclusions, but does not impair the value of his method. The objections which were made when his doctrine was new—that it was horrible and depressing, that people ought not to act as he said they did—were all such as implied an unscientific attitude of mind; as against all of them, his calm determination to treat man as a natural phenomenon marks an important advance over the reformers of the eighteenth century and the Revolution.

> The kernel of the scientific outlook is so simple, it almost excites derision

There is, however, one study which is as yet almost wholly untouched by the scientific spirit—I mean the study of philosophy. Philosophers and the public imagine that the scientific spirit must pervade pages that bristle with allusions to ions, germ-plasms and the eyes of shell-fish. But as the devil can quote Scripture, so the philosopher can quote science. The scientific spirit is not an affair of quotation, of externally acquired information, any more than manners are an affair of the etiquette-book. The scientific attitude of mind involves a sweeping away of all other desires in the interests of the desire to know—it involves suppression of hopes and fears, loves and hates, and the whole subjective emotional life, until we become subdued to the material, able to see it frankly, without preconceptions. Now in philosophy this attitude of mind has not as yet been achieved. A certain self-absorption has marked almost all attempts to conceive the universe as a whole. Mind, or some aspect of it, has been regarded as the pattern after which the universe is to be conceived, for no better reason than that such a universe would not seem strange, and would give us the cosy feeling that every place is like home. To conceive the universe as essentially progressive or essentially deteriorating, for example, is to give to our hopes and fears a cosmic importance which may, of course, be justified, but which we have as yet no reason to suppose justified.

Until we have learnt to think of it in ethically neutral terms, we have not arrived at a scientific attitude in philosophy; and until we have arrived at such an attitude, it is hardly to be hoped that philosophy will achieve any solid results.

Cosmic dancing. Einstein by David Low (*NS*, 1933)

Human beings cannot, of course, wholly transcend human nature; something subjective must remain in all our thought. But science comes nearer to objectivity than any other human pursuit, and gives us, therefore, the closest contact and the most intimate relation with the outer world. To the primitive mind everything is either friendly or hostile; but experience has shown that friendliness and hostility are not the conceptions by which the world is to be understood. Science thus represents a higher stage of evolution than any pre-scientific thought or imagination, and, like every approach to self-transcendence, it brings with it a rich reward in increase of scope and breadth and comprehension.

I have spoken so far largely of the negative aspect of the scientific spirit, but it is from the positive aspect that its value is derived. The instinct of constructiveness, which is one of the chief incentives to artistic creation, can find in scientific systems a satisfaction more massive than any epic poem. Disinterested curiosity, which is the source of almost all intellectual effort, finds with astonished delight that science can unveil secrets which might well have seemed for ever undiscoverable. The desire for a larger life and wider interests, for an escape from private circumstances, and even from the whole recurring human cycle of birth and death, is fulfilled by the impersonal cosmic outlook of science as by nothing else. To all these must be added the admiration of splendid achievement, and the consciousness of inestimable utility to the human race. A life devoted to science is therefore a happy life, and its happiness is derived from the very best sources that are open to dwellers on this troubled and passionate planet. ●

3 MARCH 1917

Reflections on Vers Libre

By T S Eliot

A lady, renowned in her small circle for the accuracy of her stop-press information of literature, complains to me of a growing pococurantism. "Since the Russians came in I can read nothing else. I have finished Dostoevski, and I do not know what to do." I suggested that the great Russian was an admirer of Dickens, and that she also might find that author readable. "But Dickens is a sentimentalist; Dostoevski is a realist . . . one cannot read the Victorians at all!" She added that she could no longer read any verse but *vers libre*.

It is assumed that *vers libre* exists. It is assumed that *vers libre* is a school; that it consists of certain theories; that its group or theorists will either revolutionise or demoralise poetry if their attack upon the iambic pentameter meets with any success. *Vers libre* does not exist, and it is time that this preposterous fiction followed the *élan vital* and the eighty thousand Russians into oblivion.

When a theory of art passes it is usually found that a groat's worth of art has been bought with a million of advertisement. A mythical revolution will have taken place and produced a few works of art which perhaps would be even better if still less of the revolutionary theories clung to them. In modern society such revolutions are almost inevitable. An artist happens upon a method which is new in the sense that it is essentially different from that of the second-rate people about him, and different in everything but essentials from that of any of his great predecessors. The novelty meets with neglect; neglect provokes attack; and attack demands a theory.

Vers libre is a battle-cry of freedom, and there is no freedom in art. And as the so-called *vers libre* which is good is anything but "free", it can better be defended under some other label. If *vers libre* is a genuine verse-form it will have a positive definition. And I can define it only in negatives: **(1)** absence of pattern, **(2)** absence of rhyme, **(3)** absence of metre.

The third of these qualities is easily disposed of. What sort of a line that would be which would not scan at all I cannot say. Even in the popular American magazines, whose verse columns are now largely given over to *vers libre*, the lines are usually explicable in terms of prosody. Any line can be divided into feet and accents.

"Any line can be divided into feet and accents"

Scansion tells us very little. It is probable that there is not much to be gained by an elaborate system of prosody, by the erudite complexities of Swinburnian metre. With Swinburne, once the trick is perceived and the scholarship appreciated, the effect is somewhat diminished. One ceases to look for what one does not find in Swinburne; the inexplicable line with the music which can never be recaptured in other words. The most interesting verse which has yet been written in our language has been done either by taking a very simple form, like the iambic pentameter, and constantly withdrawing from it, or taking no form at all, and constantly approximating to a very simple one. It is this contrast between fixity and flux, this unperceived evasion of monotony, which is the very life of verse.

At the beginning of the seventeenth century, and especially in the verse of John Webster, one finds the same constant evasion and recognition of regularity. Webster is much freer than Shakespeare, and that his fault is not negligence is evidenced by the fact that it is often at moments of the highest intensity that his verse acquires this freedom. That there is also carelessness I do not deny, but the irregularity of carelessness can be at once detected from the irregularity of deliberation.

We may therefore formulate as follows: the ghost of some simple metre should lurk behind the arras in even the "freest" verse; to advance menacingly as we doze, and withdraw as we rouse. Or, freedom is only truly freedom when it appears against the background of an artificial limitation. Not to have perceived the simple truth that some artificial limitation is necessary except in moments of the first intensity is, I believe, a capital error.

So much for metre. There is no escape from metre; there is only mastery. But while there obviously is escape from rhyme, the *vers librists* are by no means the first out of the cave. I do not minimise the services of modern poets in exploiting the possibilities of rhymeless verse. They prove the strength of a Movement, the utility of a Theory. What neither Blake nor Arnold could do alone is being done in our time. "Blank verse" is the only accepted rhymeless verse in English—the inevitable iambic pentameter. The English ear is (or was) more sensitive to the music of the verse and less dependent upon the recurrence of identical sounds in this metre than in any other. There is no campaign against rhyme. But it is possible that excessive devotion to rhyme has thickened the modern ear. When the comforting echo of rhyme is removed, success or failure in the choice of words, in the sentence structure, in the order, is at once more apparent. Rhyme removed, the poet is at once held up to the standards of prose.

And this liberation from rhyme might be as well a liberation of rhyme. Freed from its exacting task of supporting lame verse, it could be applied with greater effect where it is most needed. Formal rhymed verse will certainly not lose its place. But the decay of intricate formal patterns has nothing to do with the advent of *vers libre*. It had set in long before. Only in a closely knit and homogeneous society, where many men are at work on the same problems, such a society as those which produced the Greek chorus, the Elizabethan lyric, and the Troubadour canzone, will the development of such forms ever be carried to perfection. And as for *vers libre*, we conclude that the division between Conservative Verse and *Vers Libre* does not exist, for there is only good verse, bad verse, and chaos. ●

CAMILLA WISBAUER/GETTY IMAGES

A coloured illustration of the Bach monument in Eisenach, where the composer was born in 1685

2 OCTOBER 1920

The God That Is Bach

By W J Turner

None of the other Arts has a god like John Sebastian Bach—not literature, not sculpture, not painting, not architecture—nor has science. The faults of Shakespeare and of Michelangelo are lingered over uncomfortably by even their devoutest admirers who cannot "away" with them—not by the most tortuous ingenuity. Even their acknowledged masterpieces are incomplete or blemished or, if flawless, of limited scope.

In music, Beethoven, the most inspired, is perhaps the most unequal of the great composers. The formlessness of his work is so distressing that it prevents many people from ever really enjoying his symphonies and sonatas. Even such a great work as the *C Minor Symphony* sounds like a series of marvellous improvisations, loosely strung together like beads on a thread. The fatal "repeats", proof of the lack of any real organic design, are sprinkled almost everywhere. Perhaps the nearest approach to a genuine organic structure in Beethoven's orchestral music is in the Leonore Overture No 3, and there the form is dictated by an external dramatic programme, wonderfully assimilated, I grant, but still external to the music. On the intellectual and constructive side Beethoven was weak, and like nearly all his successors, had recourse to a mould into which to pour his musical ideas, not having the power, the patience, the training and the temperament requisite to enable him to build them into a structure of their own.

If you take any of Bach's great organ preludes and fugues, you will find that there occur in them moments as dramatic as that pause and trumpet call in the Leonore Overture—moments that thrill your blood, but they will stand much more repetition than the Leonore Overture, and the thrill will be soberer, graver, more intense with repetition, because it is not incidental, it does not depend on the emotional value of a chance situation, eg, sympathy with a prisoner in a dungeon hearing the trumpet call of his approaching liberator. It may be argued that you can be equally stirred by the Leonore Overture if you are completely ignorant of its programme, but I say that the Overture challenges your intellectual curiosity. You *have* to invent a programme, and if you did not find one that would fit it you could not bear to listen to it, it would drive you mad in unsatisfied irritation—that is, if you had any intellectual grasp of music.

The Bach prelude and fugue, on the other hand, raises no such questions as to its ▶

The organ at St Thomas Church, Leipzig

meaning because it is complete in itself. It is that rare thing, an artistic whole; it has the unity that exalts and satisfies, that is all-embracing yet concrete, finite, yet infinite, which scientists are forever seeking and approaching in their profoundest and most comprehensive laws.

If you can imagine the sensation of a Galileo, of a Newton, of an Einstein, when they first grasp the complete idea that they have been groping for, you get some faint perception of the sensations of a musician when he hears one of Bach's great preludes and fugues, for Bach—and this is not to be said lightly—is more satisfying than Galileo, Newton and Einstein, because he is nearer the truth than they are, his imagination has flown deeper and higher and is more all-embracing.

It may well be asked what authority I have for such a statement. Well, first, even the plain man can feel for himself the inadequacy of the scientists' finest generalisations, beautiful as they are, and this feeling is supported by the scientists who will admit to sharing it themselves. But I know of no musician of acknowledged standing who could honestly say that there was anything lacking, anything imperfect in Bach's greatest works, and there is, assuredly, no other composer living or dead of whom they could say the same.

Now, I should like to go on to argue that absolute perfection is possible in Art, while it never will be possible in Science, unless science—as it very possibly may do occasionally—becomes an art and does not attempt to represent all reality except as a creation of the mind; but this would lead me away from my subject, which is Bach.

Dr Terry has done English musicians considerable service by translating and editing [J N] Forkel's famous monograph on Bach, originally published in 1802. It is true that Forkel's book had been translated and published in England in 1820, but it was badly done, and the translator added nothing by way of commentary to a book which needs supplementing very considerably. The great merit of Forkel—who as a musician and composer is now completely forgotten—was that although born in 1749, a little more than a year before Bach's death, and writing in 1802 (fifty-two years later), he was the first to proclaim Bach's supreme greatness to the world.

> Bach—and this is not to be said lightly—is more satisfying than Galileo

Dr Terry has written an introduction which tells us a good deal about Forkel that is not to be found elsewhere in English, but he has also added a complete chapter on Bach's life in Leipzig for twenty-seven years as Cantor of St Thomas' School (of which Forkel tells us nothing), a large number of notes, one hundred and fifty-six pages of appendices (giving a chronological catalogue of Bach's compositions, an exhaustive examination of the librettos of the cantatas, a full account of the monumental *Bach-gesellschaft* Editions, and a Bibliography), an index, and seven illustrations, so that two-thirds of what Dr Terry magnanimously describes as "Bach by Forkel" is Bach by Terry. My only complaint is that there is not still more Terry.

I would not have the very important rivulet of Forkel drained away. Forkel is mainly critical and explanatory and, on the whole, I think, illuminating and sound, but he tells us practically nothing personal. He is, as Dr Terry points out, extraordinarily meagre in biographical detail of which Dr Terry might well have added more than he has done. Although Dr Terry seems to think that Forkel appreciated Bach mainly as a supreme master of technique, he does not attempt to deal critically with Forkel's criticism, which therefore still remains the sole contribution to that side of the subject. This was wise, for a critical estimate of Bach would require a volume to itself. But it is impossible to read this book through without a feeling of sympathy for what Dr Terry describes as Forkel's "narrow depreciation of Haydn, Mozart and Beethoven".

To Forkel these composers, by comparison with Bach, must have seemed like inspired amateurs. In his constant reference to Bach's indefatigable application, Forkel surely hits the nail on the head.

Astounding as Bach's original genius was, it was certainly not greater than Mozart's, than Beethoven's or than Wagner's. An early death and unfavourable conditions prevented Mozart from doing himself justice. Beethoven was by temperament and mental equipment unable to cope with the greatness of his ideas. Wagner alone achieved an intellectual mastery of a wealth of material comparable to Bach's, but there was an ignoble strain in Wagner, and he never attained the sublimity of Beethoven and Bach, or the unsullied purity of Mozart. Bach alone was undivided and undistracted in his absorption in his work.

The demands made upon him were more regular, more insistent and more prolonged. His very situation and control of singers and players would have made any ordinarily gifted man a master of technique. For twenty-one years Bach composed a new Cantata every month for official use; as Dr Terry well says: "There are few phenomena in the record of art more extraordinary than this unflagging cataract of inspiration in which masterpiece followed masterpiece with the monotonous periodicity of a Sunday sermon." I would say there are none and would add this question: How can the composer of to-day, restlessly rushing from place to place, full of social engagements, without leisure, without congenial occupation, without the control of players to perform his works, without repose of mind or spirit, how can he hope to produce works of the calibre of J S Bach, even if, which is improbable, he had the genius?

REX FEATURES

6 MARCH 1926

Anton Chekhov's Music

By Desmond MacCarthy

Tchehov's drama has been coming into its own in this country lately with a rush. The same sort of play-goers who usually ask their neighbours at dinner with bright alacrity, if they have seen the latest Noel Coward or Milne play, now actually show a disposition to use Tchehov as a conversational gambit. This is indeed surprising. It is ten years since I saw a Tchehov play for the first time. It was a Stage Society performance of *Uncle Vanya*; I remember the delighted enthusiasm into which it threw me.

The spread of the taste for Tchehov has been due mainly to two causes: Constance Garnett's translations of his stories, and, above all, the delicate imaginative expertness of M Komisarjevsky as a producer. Without him neither *Ivanov*, nor *Uncle Vanya*, nor *The Three Sisters* would have made a deep impression. The attentive would no doubt have perceived that they were the works of a dramatist of genius, but they would have been forcedto intensify in their own imaginations what they actually saw and heard on the stage till it approximated to the just perceptible intentions of the author.

Tchehov follows in the steps of Turgenev: his favourite theme is disillusionment, and above the kind of beauty he creates might well be written "desolation is a delicate thing". He is fond of the same kind of settings as Turgenev; summer woods, a country house full of cultivated people who talk and talk, in fact *une niche des gentilhommes*. There you will find the idealist who melts over his own futility, the girl who clutches daily duties tighter in order to forget that youth is sliding away under her feet, the clever man turned maudlin-cynical after his failure to find a purpose, the old man who feels he has not yet begun to live, and the old woman who only wants things to go on quietly on the familiar humdrum lines. The current of their days is slow; the air they breathe is sultry with undischarged energy, and only broken by unrefreshing nerve storms. It is an atmosphere of sighs, yawns, self-reproaches, vodka, day-dreams, endless tea, endless discussion. These people are like those loosely agglutinated sticks and straws which revolve together slowly in a sluggish eddy. They long to be detached, and ride down a rushing stream, which they fancy is sparkling past them. Some day—three hundred, five hundred years hence—perhaps life will be *life*. That is the atmosphere in which Tchehov's characters live and move. It differs from that of Turgenev's generation in being a still stuffier air to breathe, and more unresponsive to effort and to hope. Tragedy is there, but it is in the form of a creeping mist which narrows the world to the garden gate.

This is a generalised picture of Tchehov's world. What, you may ask, has it in common with us that it should move us so deeply? We have more self-control and are less hysterical, 'tis true, but when examined closely do not our lives often resemble that of flies in a glue-pot? But it is not only upon this resemblance that the appeal of this drama rests. To watch a Tchehov play is to recapture one's youth, that most uncomfortable yet enviable time when there was intensity even in moments of lassitude, when self-torture did not seem vain. "Why, these people," the spectator exclaims to himself, "are suffering from an unduly protracted youth!" To all of them, except the meaner, harder sort, it seems that life would be beautiful if, if, if... With the three sisters it is "*if* we could get to Moscow", with the baron "*if* I could find my work", with Vanya "*if* Elena loved me". And to feel like that is to be, as far as it goes, young. It is young to want to prop your ladder against the horn of the moon. It is also young not to know that though we have immortal hungers in us, there are extremely satisfying properties in a little real bread; and Tchehov's characters have not learnt that. They have a wail in them responsive not only to their own particular frustrations, but to the inevitable disillusionment of life.

The artist of farewells: Anton Chekhov in 1897

MELIKHOVO/BETTMANN/CORBIS

Tchehov is the artist of farewells; farewells to youth, to our past, to hopes, to lovers. The climax of *The Cherry Orchard* is a farewell to an old home and all that can mean to the middle-aged; at the end of *Uncle Vanya* the words "They've gone", uttered by one character after another as they enter after seeing off the professor and his siren wife, are like the tolling of a bell for the burial of passion and excitement. The close of *The Three Sisters* is even more poignant. It is a goodbye to their youth. The military band is playing; the regiment is marching away from their detested provincial town; the girls will never exclaim again, either in hope or misery, "To Moscow! To Moscow!"

Yet out of this conception of life, which might be labelled "depressing", Tchehov makes a work of art which moves us and exalts us like a beautiful piece of music. It is not in a mood of depression one leaves the theatre after seeing *The Three Sisters*. How true it is that a good play should be like a piece of music! For our reason it must have the logical coherence of fact, but for our emotions the sinuous, unanalysable appeal of music. In and out, in and out, the theme of hope for the race and the theme of personal despair are interwoven one with the other. Each character is like a different instrument which leads, and gives way alternately, sometimes playing alone, sometimes with others, the theme of the miseries of cultivated exiles, or the deeper one of the longing of youth.

There have been dramatists with a wider sweep and a stronger hand than Tchehov, but none has brought to the weighing of human character a more delicate sense of justice. ●

1 JULY 1933

Picasso or Matisse?

By Clive Bell

May I make of the Matisse exhibition, open at Messrs Tooth's gallery in Bond Street, an occasion for saying something I have long wished to say on that perennial theme—Matisse and Picasso? It seems almost impossible to think of one without talking about the other. To extoll the art of Matisse is, by implication, to raise the Picasso question; and to appreciate Picasso is in the opinion of many foolish people to depreciate Matisse.

Of course, the opposition is of a Plutarchian obviousness. The painting of Matisse is a pure and simple delight: to get the best out of Picasso's pictures requires some intellectual effort. The one thing common to both is that [they] are painters born. With Matisse all is plain sailing. Here is the best painter alive, and one who takes his place neatly in the French tradition. That his pictures shocked at first is but one more example of the public's traditional stupidity. There is nothing odd about it; it is just the story of the Impressionists, with whom he has so many affinities, over again. What is odd is that he has so little influence on his contemporaries. It was not always so. There was a moment, about 1907, the stirring and scandalous moment of the Fauves, when the mark of Matisse was everywhere; on Derain, Friesz, Vlaminck, the fashionable Van Dongen even. It looked then as though we were in for an "Age of Matisse". Instead it has become the age of Picasso. Why?

If Picasso be, as I maintain, essentially but not predominantly a painter, what is he predominantly? Does he sometimes use the painter's medium to say something unpainter-like? It seems to me that the mystery of his intention may have helped to magnify his prestige. Had he expressed himself in words, his "message" might have seemed less thrilling. Picasso, I suspect, is sentimental; you have only to look first at his early work and then at almost anything he has ever done to see that it is so. Now in the depths of his heart almost everyone likes sentimentality, but crude and obvious sentimentality we of the better sort, we who read poetry and go to exhibitions and talk about books and pictures, do not like: at all events, we are ashamed of liking it. Is it possible that Picasso's abstract art is a way of being sentimental in secret?

Henri Matisse, pictured in his studio in 1950

Be that as it may, I feel pretty sure that Picasso is always interested in humanity as Zola and Dostoievsky were interested, as Poussin and Cézanne were not; as Matisse is not. Therein lies his strength. Possibly, also, we ask more of a picture than of a textile or a pot.

A painter's criticism of other painters' pictures will sometimes help to an understanding of his own. I have often heard Picasso give his opinion. What I know of Matisse's I know almost wholly at second-hand. Matisse cares passionately for his own pictures, and, I surmise, for not many others. No harm in that. Picasso, too, takes a rather perfunctory interest in other people's pictures but in other more or less formal manifestations of human desire for perfection he is interested profoundly. The doings of a house-painter or a shop-window dresser can hold him spellbound. He likes popular art, not the Maypole and the Morris, but the popular art of the street and the fair, for here he finds common life expressed in some uncommon way.

Let us make no mystery about it, Matisse is interested in what has interested painters always—his vision of things and the problem of expressing that vision. Because he is an artist the expression becomes beauty; because he is original his beauty was at first mistaken for ugliness. Now that he has taught the world to see with him, the enjoyment of his pictures comes as easily as the enjoyment of Renoir's. Matisse looking out of his window at Nice perceives simple, sensuous loveliness and renders his version of it in his own inimitable way. Picasso, on the beach in Brittany, sees otherwise, sees what is there and a string of implications as well. A vision of that sort is not to be expressed simply and sensuously. It might be expressed coldly and viciously. What is rendered is not always the joy of seeing and feeling, but, as often as not, something flavoured, at times pretty strongly flavoured, with disgust or despair; that is why the whole, in its wilful cynicism, is what I call sentimental.

Thus it comes about that Picasso is not predominantly interested in what absorbs craftsmen. It is the manifestation in craft of odd scraps of individuality, scraps which by hook or by crook have escaped industrial regimentation, that catches his eye. The embellishment of a match-box, betraying some remnant of artistic feeling, will attract him more than a Chippendale chair. He goes further, and seems to enjoy the very baseness of the contemporary urban mind once he can find an unmistakable expression of it in a place where you would last have looked for expression. A lamp-post, a public urinal, a street-vendor's toy, all or any of these may become manifestations of the spirit of the age, and as such for Picasso charged with significance. For it is not merely as curious forms that they interest him; they move him as symbols, too, as manifestations. He can be cautiously sentimental about them.

I put it forward as a hypothesis that what the journeyman, be he tinker, tailor, toy-maker or house-painter, be he ever so little individual and an artist, is crudely manifesting, Picasso is trying to express deliberately, in full and perfect consciousness, and with exquisite delicacy. It is the complete consciousness that gives the touch of cynicism. He is trying to express his sense of such idiosyncrasy and oddity as has adhered, parasitewise, to our uniform and machine-ridden civilisation. Matisse, meanwhile, is painting rapturously, as a bird sings, in the ageless garden of the French tradition. He will be admired as long as painting is enjoyed—as the last of the great Impressionists. Picasso may be admired as one of the original and inventive minds of a peculiarly inventive and harassed age. But Matisse must be admired: Picasso may. ●

13 AUGUST 1938

Twenty-Four Hours in Metroland

By Graham Greene

The little town always had an air of grit about it, as one came in under the echoing tin railway arch associated with shabby prams and Sunday walks, unwilling returns to Evensong—grit beside the watercress beds and on the panes of the station's private entrance which the local lord had not used for generations. Neither country nor city, a dormitory district—there are things which go on in dormitories…

Sunday evening, and the bells jangling in the town; small groups of youths hovered round the traffic lights, while the Irish servant girls crept out of back doors in the early dark. "Romans", the elderly lady called them. You couldn't keep them in at night—they would arrive with the milk in a stranger's car from Watford, slipping out in stockinged feet from the villas above the valley. The youths—smarmed and scented hair and bitten cigarettes—greeted them in the dark with careless roughness. There were so many fishes in the sea . . . sexual experience had come to them too early and too easily. The London, Midland and Scottish Line waited for everyone.

Rhythm of life: a hat factory in St Albans in 1936

Up on the hillside the beech trees were in glorious and incredible decay: little green boxes for litter put up by the National Trust had a dainty and doyly effect; and in the inn the radio played continuously. You couldn't escape it: with your soup a dramatised account of the battle of Mons, and with the joint a Methodist church service. Four one-armed men dined together, arranging their seats so that their arms shouldn't clash.

In the morning, mist lay heavy on the Chilterns. Boards marking desirable building lots dripped on short grass where the sheep were washed out. The skeletons of harrows lay unburied on the wet stubble. With visibility shut down to fifty yards you got no sense of a world, of simultaneous existences: each thing was self-contained like an image of private significance, standing for something else—Metroland, loneliness. The door of the Plough Inn chimed when you pushed it, ivory balls clicked and a bystander said, "They do this at the Crown, Margate"—England's heart beating out in bagatelle towards her eastern extremity; the landlady had a weak heart, and dared not serve food these days in case she went off just like that in the rush. In a small front garden before a red villa a young girl knelt in the damp with an expression abashed and secretive while she sawed through the limbs of a bush, and a woman's angry voice called "Judy, Judy", and a dog barked in the poultry farm across the way. A cigarette fumed into ash with no one in sight, only a little shut red door marked Ker Even; "the leading Cairn Terrier Farm" was noisy on the crest of the down, the dogs like the radio, never ceasing—how does life go on?

At the newsagent's in the market town below the Chiltern ridge there was a shrewd game on sale, very popular locally, called "Monopoly", played with dice and counters—"The object of owning property is to collect rent . . . Rentals are greatly increased by the erection of houses and hotels . . . Players may land in jail." The soil exacted no service and no love: among the beechwoods a new house was for sale. It had only been lived in a month: the woods and commons were held out by wire. The owners, married last December, were divorced this summer. Neither wanted the house. A handyman swept up the leaves—a losing fight—and lamented the waste. "Four coats of paint in every room . . . I was going to make a pond in that dell—and I was just getting the kitchen garden straight—you can see for yourself."

Kick these hills and they bleed white. The mist is like an exhalation of the chalk. Beechwoods and gorse and the savage Metro heart behind the Whipsnade wire: elephants turning and turning behind glass on little aesthetic circular platforms like exhibits in a "modern" shop window, behind them dripping firs as alien as themselves; ostriches suddenly visible at thirty yards, like snakeheads rising out of heaps of dung. A wolf wailing invisibly in the mist, the sun setting at 4.30, the traffic lights out in the High Street and the Irish maids putting the door on the latch. In an hour or two the commuters return to sleep in their Siberian dormitory—an acre of land, a desirable residence for as long as the marriage lasts, no roots, no responsibility for the child on the line. "The object of owning property…" ●

C&D

18 DECEMBER 1954

Tolkien's Infantilist Invasion

By Maurice Richardson

First, let me get Professor Tolkien out of my delusional system. *The Two Towers* is the second volume of his mammoth fairy tale, or, as some call it, heroic romance, *The Lord of the Rings*. It will do quite nicely as an allegorical adventure story for very leisured boys, but as anything else I am convinced it has been wildly overpraised and it is all I can do to restrain myself from shouting: Conspiracy! and slouching through the streets with a sandwichman's board inscribed in jagged paranoid scrawl in violet ink: "Adults of all ages! Unite against the infantilist invasion."

It has been compared by Richard Hughes to Spenser's *Faerie Queen*; by Naomi Mitchison to Malory; by C S Lewis to Ariosto. I can see why these three should have soft spots for its Norse and Celtic and mystical trappings. Mr Auden has also gone into raptures over it. This, too, is not unexpected, because he has always been captivated by the pubescent worlds of the saga and the classroom.

It is not Professor Tolkien's fault if he has been overpraised

Down in the Shire: tourists on the Hobbiton film set in Matamata, New Zealand

Of course one must be fair. It is not Professor Tolkien's fault if he has been overpraised. Also, coming in half-way, it is difficult to judge his story as a whole. Still, one third (200,000 words, about as long as *Anna Karenina*) should be a representative sample. My first impression is that it is all far too long and blown up. What began as a charming children's book has proliferated into an endless worm. My second that, although a great deal of imagination has been at work, it is imagination of low potential. The various creatures, hobbits, elves, dwarfs, orcs, ents are nicely differentiated. Their ecology is described with scholarly detail and consistency. But not one of them has any real individuality; not one is a character. And though their dialogue is carefully varied, from colloquial-historical for men and wizards to prep school slang for hobbits and orcs, they all speak with the same flat, castrated voice.

I also find the story-telling confusing. Interest is diffused between too many characters and groups. In this volume the hobbits, Pippin and Merry, steal too much of the picture from the chief hobbit, Frodo, the original possessor of the Ring which all the fuss is about.

Naturally there are points in favour. The battle scenes are well done; the atmosphere of doom and danger and perilous night-riding often effective. The traditional mystical confusion attaching to a quest, and a struggle between good and evil, is neatly worked into the plot. And the allegorical aspect rouses interesting speculation. How much relation is there between the world—ruined, note—of the story and our own past, present and future? To what extent, if any, does the Ring tie up with the atomic nucleus, as well as symbolising whatever rings do symbolise? Are the orcs at all equated with materialist scientists? Nevertheless, the fantasy remains in my opinion thin and pale. And the writing is not at all fresh. Here is a sample—one of the rare descriptions of a female person in a story most of whose characters appear to be sexless:

> ... Grave and thoughtful was her glance,
> as she looked on the king with cool pity
> in her eyes. Very fair was her face, and
> her long hair was like a river of gold.
> Slender and tall she was in her white robe
> girt with silver; but strong she seemed and
> stern as steel, a daughter of kings. Thus
> Aragorn for the first time in the full light
> of day beheld Éowyn, lady of Rohan,
> and thought her fair, fair and cold, like a
> morning of pale spring that is not yet
> come to womanhood ...

Observe the strange effect of pre-Renaissance literature on a distinguished scholar's style; this might almost be Michael Arlen. ●

22 OCTOBER 1955

The Keyhole Screen

By Tom Driberg

The columnist and Labour MP Tom Driberg had the auspicious honour of writing the New Statesman's first television review. He begins by asking whether the medium will ever become an art form and how one should approach writing critically about it, and he traces the beginnings of reality television.

The newcomer to television, as performer or as viewer, broods on the nature of the thing that he has got mixed up in (for even the small screen *involves* the viewer more completely than sound-radio does).

One contrast between TV and sound, at the transmitting rather than the receiving end, may be less superficial than it seems. The performer on TV is far more conscious of being in, or on the fringe of, "show business" than the sound broadcaster is. The atmosphere of a sound broadcasting studio is almost like that of a teaching hospital; no don need feel out of place. The atmosphere of a TV studio is far more like that of a film studio: the blazing lights and moving cameras, the make-up girls hovering to dab powder on sweat-prone faces, the teams of insouciant technicians, the long hours of hanging about. No don (except Mr Alan Taylor) would feel at ease here. It all seems much more contrived, because eye as well as ear has to be cozened.

Does this also mean that television is a new art-form, or indeed an art-form at all? If poetry is definable as verse that cannot be paraphrased exactly in prose, and if stage plays filmed usually make bad movies, it might be expected that TV at its best would convey an aesthetic or intellectual satisfaction new in kind—to create works of art, however slight, intrinsically different from those of radio.

It is too soon to be sure; but so far, in dramatic or feature programmes, it seems that the art of TV, in idiom and in impact, hardly differs in kind from that of the cinema. This is perhaps inevitable; many TV programmes are, of course, filmed. It is with the movies rather than with sound radio that TV should be compared, and perhaps, judged.

Of one kind of TV programme alone can it be said that it is uniquely and specially of TV. That is the programme which seeks to explore and exploit the intimacies of human suffering, the agonies of embarrassment felt by those who suddenly find themselves hauled before the cameras. I have not yet seen Mr Winn's programme, *Write to Winn*, which has had, on the whole, a good press (and actors, not "real people", are used in it), or Miss Edana Romney in *Is This Your Problem?*; but last Saturday I did see Mr Derek Roy in *People Are Funny*.

This is one of the programmes in which ordinary people are taken unawares by extraordinary intrusions into their privacy; exposed not only to the cameras but to the uproarious laughter of a large studio audience; and then consoled with gifts—pressure-cookers, washing-machines, refrigerators, all the *desiderata* of the well-conditioned modern housewife.

For one of last Saturday's items an ordinary, pleasant, middle-class couple were inveigled on to the stage of the theatre from which the programme was transmitted. Mr Roy asked the woman what she loved best in the world. "My husband," she said. "We'll soon see how much you love him," said Mr Roy. The husband was then shut in a cupboard (rather like an earth closet) with a hole in its top. A man was stationed above it with a bucket of ice-cold water. "If I give you five shillings," said Mr Roy to the wife, "may we pour the water over him?" "No," she said. "Seven-and-six? Ten shillings?" "No, no, no!" "Well, what about a dozen pairs of fully fashioned nylons ... look at them, aren't they lovely and sheer?" "Oh ... that's different!"

"When I hear the word 'culture', I reach for the switch . . ." A cartoon by Vicky (*NS*, 1955)

The water was poured: a stifled howl from inside the cupboard, the wife a picture of remorseful anxiety. The process was repeated, with more and more horrifying deposits (quick-drying cement, porridge) and ever richer bribes. The wife was almost in tears, but overwhelmed by her sudden acquisition of all these gleaming gadgets. The saving gimmick was that the cupboard had a false ceiling which caught all the muck: the husband emerged unharmed, his wife fell in his arms.

Possibly no great harm was done to the couple—though, unless she was a consummate actress, the wife had a pretty thorough emotional shaking-up. I found the programme degrading to watch—and impossible to switch off.

"Human problem" programmes deal with more serious situations than this, but their essence is the same: to expose human beings spiritually naked for the entertainment of inquisitive strangers. They are the apotheosis of the keyhole. To claim that their purpose is "to try to help people" is cant. Their purpose is to make money. Such, then, is TV's only distinctive contribution so far. It may be the raw material of a new art-form. If so, it still awaits its Griffith or its Pudovkin.

***

Listeners and viewers long accustomed to the BBC's monopoly in the word "epilogue" may have been surprised to find that, on ITV, it is used, but not to describe a fragment of late-night religion. Instead, a poem is read, rather well. This, however, is only *An* Epilogue. The BBC's is still *The* Epilogue. Both are disfigured by visual vulgarisms: on the BBC a Presbyterian university chaplain, the Rev Ian Pitt-Watson, whose voice and manner are admirably composed, fades into a pietistic still-life, a composition of shimmering cross and open Book; on ITV a peculiarly nasty olde-Englishe lettering is used for the title.

It is strange that those who are spending so much money on these services shouldn't know where to look for competent designers of such details. ●

HAPPY 65th BIRTHDAY

Wish our brilliant NHS a happy birthday and many more by joining in a 'hands around our hospital' event near you.

Len McCluskey, General Secretary | **Tony Woodhouse,** Chair, Executive Council

www.unitetheunion.org/nickoftime

Our NHS is 65 on 5 July 2013

If it's to enjoy 65 more it needs "folk with the faith to fight for it."
Aneurin Bevan

David Cameron's pro-privatisation coalition government has left our NHS fighting for survival.

Growing waiting lists, staff shortages and A&E closures reflect the chaos caused by this government in just three years.

Our NHS is at grave risk. Private companies making profit from our health is not on.

29 SEPTEMBER 1956

A Critic's Farewell

By John Berger

This, by my own request, is the last regular article I shall write for the next year. But what of the past five years? What do they add up to? The only fact of which I am certain is that I have sold three extra copies of this paper: one bought by my mother; another by a charmingly obsessed admirer; and, the last by myself in a regular fit of impatience, before my complimentary copy arrives late, to discover if and how I have been cut.

Nor am I being entirely flippant about this: for if the critic wants a personal assessment of what his effect has been, he is bound to get a dusty answer. The critic is a bastard—in more senses than one. Finally, he has no definite status. He is merely the index of the tension, the relationship between the changes taking place in art and the changes taking place in the ideas and economics of his time.

Whenever I look at a work of art as a critic, I try to follow up the threads connecting it to the early Renaissance, Picasso, the Five Year Plans of Asia, the man-eating hypocrisy and sentimentality of our establishment, and to an eventual Socialist revolution in this country. And if the aesthetes jump at this confession to say that it proves that I am a political propagandist, I am proud of it. But my heart and eye have remained those of a painter. I take it for granted that one considers and is acutely sensitive to the formal, painterly, technical qualities of a picture, as I also take for granted that an artist's political opinions may have little to do with his work. What I cannot and will not take for granted is the shameful public role that the artist is forced to play in our society: the role of a huckster amusing that small sophisticated section of the public who are queueing up in their own furry night for their own personal salvation via Culture. And this role will not be changed by getting the tones right or the forms sculptural. It can only be altered—though it hasn't always been—by Five Year Plans.

It is frequently said that the Battle of Realism has now been won, although those who, believing this, want to jump on to the triumphant band wagon almost fall off again backwards in their anxiety to explain that they don't, of course, mean SOCIAL realism. In fact, very little has been won. There will be no victory until reasonable talent, as opposed to genius, can produce satisfying works of art—and that means an alive, teachable tradition, a confident society and a broad cultural public.

Only two things have been achieved to date. First, certain young painters, encouraged to look at the life around them, are now in a position to retackle the eternal problems of image-making, and so have liberated themselves from the blind alley of shape-making, wrongly named after Cézanne. Secondly, the earlier 19th-century masters—Goya, Delacroix, Géricault, Daumier, Courbet—have been taken out of the deep freeze into which they were put by Fry, and their example can now show that there is a tradition of European art which began in the Renaissance and did *not* have to be restarted by the Post-Impressionists. But that is the entire achievement: two illusions broken.

Abstract expressionism, "action" painting or whatever you like to call it, still deceives both artists and pundits, although it is the most literal reflection of the ultimate passive hopelessness of *laissez faire*; the subjective justification of what has happened as the result of almost pure accident. Other artists, dehumanised by their isolation, still resort to Sunday sensationalism.

The Academics die on, tempting with the vision of another world. The unrealistic separation of art from architecture continues—exemplified by the waste and misunderstanding of Léger's genius.

Kingsley Martin, by Vicky (*NS*, 1957)

Yet even if all these confusions and frustrations could be overcome entirely within the studios, galleries and architects' offices (which they cannot be), there would still remain the problem of popular participation in the arts—which is a civil servant's phrase for the electric, mysterious process by which men can help each other to grow. And it is because I believe that our society now prevents at home, and actively threatens abroad, nearly all human growth, that I am with the Communists.

In the end we must await new men for a new integration of the arts, and meanwhile we can only struggle to improve the separate component parts. Admittedly the communist politician and artist have in the past stared each other out—and blindly, each expecting the other to recognise the same responsibilities. But we can fight this, knowing in the recent words of the Czech poet Seifert that "when a statesman keeps silent on a certain question that is strategy, when an artist keeps silent he is lying".

What about actual painters themselves, alone with the challenge of a white canvas? None of what I have ever said would have any meaning at all if it were not for the fact that artists still obstinately exist: if it were not for William Roberts, forgotten but bitterly continuing to work; Keith Vaughan learning small step by small step how to make a landscape yield a figure; Ceri Richards searching for the precise centre of his turbulence; Epstein, like Rodin, impregnating clay with his sense of the passing of time; Pasmore making his logical, lonely and we do not yet know whether vain experiments; Michael Ayrton experimenting to interpret psychology without any easy recourse to surrealism, and others, known and unknown—for I persist in believing that the unknown are at least the equal of the known. All their tenacity and talents should force us to generalise, to connect. Go and see Jack Smith's new canvases at the Beaux Arts and Philip Sutton's at Roland, Browse and Delbanco. Think of nothing but the pictures as you stand in front of them. But in the end they will either make you grow or they will make you shrink. And the process of growing is the process of learning to connect. And every extension of a person's awareness is a political fact. ●

Long-term treatment

By Nicholas Timmins

If the NHS is "the greatest gift a nation ever gave itself" it is also one that has undergone 40 years of "organisation, reorganisation and redisorganisation"

Year: 1913. A time of huge wealth, hideous inequality and great social reform. The last great gilded Edwardian summer before the lamps went out all over Europe. A time also when the first state pensions, the first unemployment insurance and the first state-backed insurance scheme for health were starting to take effect following the tough parliamentary battle over Lloyd George's "People's Budget" of 1909, which, by 1911, had raised the money to pay for them.

It was the start of what became known as the "ambulance state", the precursor of the modern welfare state. Winston Churchill, then still a youngish Liberal Turk, declared of it: "We have not pretended to carry the toiler on to dry land. What we have done is strap a lifebelt about him."

The health part of this was Lloyd George's "ninepence for fourpence" health insurance scheme. In return for the worker's compulsory fourpence, the employer had to add threepence while the taxpayer, through the state, chipped in tuppence. The scheme was administered by approved societies – voluntary organisations – which gave the worker access to a "panel" family doctor but no right to hospital care or medicine.

There was no cover for wives or children, other than a maternity grant. A minority of people lived on into their seventies, eighties and even longer, but such was the infant mortality rate, particularly among the poor and less well-off, that life expectancy at birth was 51 years for men and 55 for women.

Nonetheless, it was a magic moment. The scheme's arrival had in part been promoted by the chastening experience of the Boer war in the early years of the 20th century, when it was discovered that almost half of those volunteering to fight in South Africa were medically unfit to do so. Indeed, one survey of First World War conscripts found one in three not fit enough to join the armed forces. By the Second World War, one in seven was judged grade-one fit on recruitment.

Yet advance in the field of health and health services is rarely linear. The idea that there should be some form of national health service can be traced back to Beatrice Webb's 1905 *Minority Report* of the Poor Law Commission, through various reports by the great and the good and, indeed, by the British Medical Association in the 1920s and 1930s – and to the growing involvement of local authorities in the provision of health care.

> The Second World War proved that a national health service could work

Councils had long run the Poor Law workhouse infirmaries. They managed many of the great Victorian asylums for the mentally ill, later known as "the bins". They also ran fever hospitals and – in a sign of changed patterns of disease – more than 30,000 beds in sanatoriums for tuberculosis.

Following the Local Government Act 1929, however, the great municipalities and some major counties – Sheffield, Newcastle, Bristol, Middlesex – began to develop modern general hospitals. By the outbreak of the Second World War the London County Council was probably the biggest hospital authority in the world, rivalling in size the entire voluntary hospital sector, whose stars were the great teaching hospitals – St Thomas', Barts, Guy's and St Mary's in London, for example – together with their smaller provincial equivalents. These were ancient foundations (dating back, in the case of Barts, to the 12th century) where specialists charged the better-off what they could afford, or tolerate, and gave part of their time to the poor for free.

But it was the Second World War which proved that a national health service could work. It was not just that William Beveridge, in his seminal report on social security, took as one of his three "assumptions" that there would be "a national health service for prevention and comprehensive treatment available to all members of the community". It was also that the war led to the creation of an emergency medical service, and huge sums of taxpayers' money going into treating victims of war and war workers, to the point where both the voluntary and the municipal hospitals were being run largely on state cash.

It was against this background that Attlee's great reforming government and Aneurin Bevan, in particular, launched the NHS. Nationalising the hospitals provided a way of solving the problem of which of the two warring hospital sectors – municipal against voluntary – would emerge triumphant in any new dispensation. Over time, it also got medical specialists out of the confines of Harley Street in London and Rodney Street in Liverpool and more evenly spread around the country.

The result was, in the words of the historian Peter Hennessy and the former Conservative chancellor Nigel Lawson, both "the greatest gift a nation ever gave itself" and "the closest the English have to a religion".

Everyone had access to both a family doctor and hospital care, and free at the point of use. The health service "lifted the shadow of fear from millions of homes", as Bevan put it.

The NHS is now just short of its 65th birthday. Few institutions, other than the church, the courts and the monarchy, outstrip such longevity. That length, however, makes it hard to sum up its history.

There have been landmark moments. The Guillebaud report of 1956 demonstrated that the apparently sharply rising costs of the service were not running out of control. Rather, spending on it had failed to match the overall

BLOOMBERG VIA GETTY IMAGES

increase in national income. There have been repeated bursts of medical advance: the arrival of antibiotics on a large scale, antidepressants, transplants, microsurgery, spectacular forms of imaging and, now, the application of genetics and potential gene therapies.

There were the dire reports on the great Victorian asylums – Ely in Cardiff and Normansfield in Kingston, to name just two – that made care for the mentally ill and those who used to be called "the mentally handicapped" move out into the community over more than 30 years: a policy that exacted a terrible price on some individuals but produced a far better service.

In 1974, after 26 years of relative stability, the first great reorganisation of the service took place, bringing into the NHS many services that had been left with local government in 1948, including public health, a whole bunch of community services and the ambulance service. Unfortunately, 1974 proved to be just the first step in 40 years of successive reorganisations – to the point where "organisation, reorganisation and redisorganisation" might almost be said to be the English NHS disease.

Crucial moments included the Griffiths report of 1983, which got rid of what proved to be the lowest-common-denominator-type consensus management that 1974 had introduced. It brought more professional management by both clinicians and managers into the NHS. Without it, there would have been no one available to deliver Kenneth Clarke's mighty 1991 reform: the first to introduce an element of market-like principles into the service. GPs were offered budgets to buy their patients' care (roughly half took them) and hospitals were, at least nominally, made more free-standing entities and businesses.

Since then, it has been a tale of two steps forward, one step back towards a health service that has adopted an increasingly market-driven approach to the way services are delivered.

To some, this is the only way to ensure a more efficient and responsive health service. To others, particularly as the former health secretary Andrew Lansley's sweeping restructuring of the service takes effect this year, it is merely one step further down a road that will end in the privatisation of the NHS. But privatisation has a multitude of meanings. It could mean merely that more services will be supplied, at a profit, by the private sector rather than by state-owned entities: in other words, changes, possibly big ones, to the supply side of the NHS.

However, some sceptics believe that the restructuring will lead inevitably to changes on the demand side – that the ultimate goal is to require the public, in one form or another, to pay more directly towards the cost of their care, either through charges or some sort of personal insurance.

In practice it may well prove to be austerity, rather more than ideology, along with the changing patterns of life and disease, that challenge the status of the NHS as a service largely free at the point of use.

Life expectancy has rocketed. In 1948 a 65-year-old woman could expect to live about 15 years longer on average, a man 12 years. Today the equivalent figures are more than 24 years and almost 22. Whereas in 2008 there were 8.1 million people aged over 65 living in the UK, it is predicted that by 2023 this figure will have risen to 13 million. Dementia and chronic conditions have made it harder to define the boundary between "free at the point of use" NHS care and means-tested social care. And, given the need to cut the deficit, the health service faces many years in which its budget will not rise at all in real terms and may even be cut. No health system anywhere has survived such challenges unscathed.

Britain's NHS has become, in a way no other health system has, an important part of national identity, witness the role it played in last year's Olympics opening ceremony. It has passionate defenders. Significant changes to the way it is funded will not happen easily. But there must be a chance, a century on from 1913, that it may become a little more like an ambulance state, and a little less like the more or less fully comprehensive service it has been for the past 65 years. ●

6 OCTOBER 1956

The Two Cultures

By C P Snow

The scientist and novelist C P Snow first articulated his "Two Cultures" thesis in an essay for the New Statesman. He later developed the idea to compose the celebrated Rede Lecture of the same title. His contention that we need to bridge the gulf between the scientific and the "traditional", "mainly literary" cultures resonates today; but arguably it is now science and technology that have gained the upper hand.

"It's rather odd," said G H Hardy, one afternoon in the early Thirties, "but when we hear about 'intellectuals' nowadays, it doesn't include people like me and J J Thomson and Rutherford." Hardy was the first mathematician of his generation, J J Thomson the first physicist of his; as for Rutherford, he was one of the greatest scientists who have ever lived. Some bright young literary person putting them outside the enclosure reserved for intellectuals seemed to Hardy the best joke for some time. It does not seem quite such a good joke now. The separation between the two cultures has been getting deeper under our eyes; there is now precious little communication between them, little but different kinds of incomprehension and dislike.

The traditional culture, which is, of course, mainly literary, is behaving like a state whose power is rapidly declining—standing on its precarious dignity, spending far too much energy on Alexandrine intricacies, occasionally letting fly in fits of aggressive pique quite beyond its means, too much on the defensive to show any generous imagination to the forces which must inevitably reshape it. Whereas the scientific culture is expansive, not restrictive, confident at the roots, the more confident after its bout of Oppenheimerian self-criticism, certain that history is on its side, impatient, intolerant, creative rather than critical, good-natured and brash. Neither culture knows the virtues of the other; often it seems they deliberately do not want to know. The resentment which the traditional culture feels for the scientific is shaded with fear; from the other side, the resentment is not shaded so much as brimming with irritation. When scientists are faced with an expression of the traditional culture, it tends (to borrow Mr William Cooper's eloquent phrase) to make their feet ache.

It does not need saying that generalisations of this kind are bound to look silly at the edges. There are a good many scientists indistinguishable from literary persons, and vice versa. Even the stereotype generalisations about scientists are misleading without some sort of detail—eg the generalisations that scientists as a group stand on the political Left. This is only partly true. A very high proportion of engineers is almost as conservative as doctors; of pure scientists, the same would apply to chemists. It is only among physicists and biologists that one finds the Left in strength. If one compared the whole body of scientists with their opposite numbers of the traditional culture (writers, academics, and so on), the total result might be a few per cent more towards the Left wing. Nevertheless, as a first approximation, the scientific culture is real enough and so is its difference from the traditional. For anyone like myself, by education a scientist, by calling a writer, at one time moving between groups of scientists and writers in the same evening, the difference has seemed dramatic.

> About scientific culture, there is an absence of the feline and oblique

The first thing, impossible to miss, is that scientists are on the up and up; they have the strength of a social force behind them. If they are English, they share the experience common to us all—of being in a country sliding economically downhill—but in addition (and to many of them it seems psychologically more important) they belong to something more than a profession, to something more like a directing class of a new society. In a sense oddly divorced from politics, they are the new men. Even the staidest and most politically conservative of scientific veterans have some kind of link with the world to come. They do not hate it as their colleagues do; part of their mind is open to it; almost against their will, there is a residual glimmer of kinship there. The young English scientists may and do curse their luck; increasingly they fret about the rigidities of their universities; they violently envy their Russian counterparts who have money and equipment without discernible limit, who have the whole field wide open. But still they stay pretty resilient: they are swept on by the same social force. Harwell and Windscale have just as much spirit as Los Alamos and Chalk River: they are symbols, frontier towns.

There is a touch of the frontier qualities, in fact, about the whole scientific culture. Its tone is, for example, steadily heterosexual. The difference in social manners between Harwell and Hampstead, or as far as that goes between Los Alamos and Greenwich Village, would make an anthropologist blink. About the whole scientific culture, there is an absence—surprising to outsiders—of the feline and oblique. Sometimes it seems that scientists relish speaking the truth, especially when it is unpleasant. The climate of personal relations is singularly bracing, not to say harsh: it strikes bleakly on those unused to it who suddenly find that the scientists' way of deciding on action is by a full-dress argument, with no regard for sensibilities and no holds barred. No body of people ever believed more in dialectic as the primary method of attaining sense; and if you want a picture of scientists in their off-moments it could be just one of a knock-about argument. Under the argument there glitter egotisms as rapacious as any of ours: but, unlike ours, the egotisms are driven by a common purpose.

How much of the traditional culture gets through to them? The answer is not simple. A good many scientists, including some of the most gifted, have the tastes of literary persons, read the same things, and read as much. Broadly, though, the infiltration is much less. History gets across to a certain extent, in particular social history: the sheer mechanics of living, how men ate, built, travelled, worked, touches a good many scientific imaginations. Philosophy the scientific culture views with indifference, especially metaphysics. As Rutherford said cheerfully to Samuel Alexander: "When you think of all the years you've been talking about those things, Alexander,

Seeing things differently: a partial lunar eclipse

and what does it all add up to? *Hot air*, nothing but *hot air*." A bit less exuberantly, that is what contemporary scientists would say. They regard it as a major intellectual virtue to know what not to think about. They might touch their hats to linguistic analysis, as a relatively honourable way of wasting time; not so to existentialism.

The arts? The only one which is cultivated among scientists is music. It goes both wide and deep; there may possibly be a greater density of musical appreciation than in the traditional culture. In comparison, the graphic arts (except architecture) score little, and poetry not at all. Some novels work their way through, but not as a rule the novels which literary persons set most value on. The two cultures have so few points of contact that the diffusion of novels shows the same sort of delay, and exhibits the same oddities, as though they were getting into translation in a foreign country. It is only fairly recently, for instance, that Graham Greene and Evelyn Waugh have become more than names. And, just as it is rather startling to find that in Italy Bruce Marshall is by a long shot the best-known British novelist, so it jolts one to hear scientists talking with attention of the works of Nevil Shute. In fact, there is a good reason for that: Mr Shute was himself a high-class engineer.

Incidentally, there are benefits to be gained from listening to intelligent men, utterly removed from the literary scene and unconcerned as to who's in and who's out. One can pick up such a comment as a scientist once made, that it looked to him as though the current preoccupations of the New Criticism, the extreme concentration on a tiny passage, had made us curiously insensitive to the total flavour of the work, to the epic qualities in literature. But, on the other side of the coin, one is just as likely to listen to three of the most massive intellects in Europe happily discussing the merits of *The Wallet of Kai-Lung*.

When you meet the younger rank-and-file of scientists, it often seems that they do not read at all. The prestige of the traditional culture is high enough for some of them to make a gallant shot at it. Oddly enough, the novelist whose name to them has become a token of esoteric literary excellence is that difficult highbrow Dickens. They approach him in a grim and dutiful spirit as though tackling *Finnegans Wake*, and feel a sense of achievement if they manage to read a book through. But most young technicians do not fly so high. When you ask them what they read—"As a married man," one says, "I prefer the garden." Another says: "I always like just to use my books as tools." (Difficult to resist speculating what kind of tool a book would make. A sort of hammer? A crude digging instrument?)

That, or something like it, is a measure of the incommunicability of the two cultures. On their side the scientists are losing a great deal. Some of that loss is inevitable: it must and would happen in any society at our technical level. But in this country we make it quite unnecessarily worse by our educational patterns. On the other side, how much does the traditional culture lose by the separation?

I am inclined to think, even more. Not only practically but also intellectually and morally. The intellectual loss is a little difficult to appraise. Most scientists would claim that you cannot comprehend the world unless you know the structure of science, in particular of physical science. In a sense, and a perfectly genuine sense, that is true. Not to have read *War and Peace* and *La Cousine Bette* and *La Chartreuse de Parme* is not to be educated; but so is not to have a glimmer of the Second Law of Thermodynamics. Yet that case ought not to be pressed too far. It is more justifiable to say that those without any scientific understanding miss a whole body of experience: they are rather like the tone deaf, from whom all musical experience is cut off and who have to get on without it. The intellectual invasions of science are, however, penetratingly deeper. Psychoanalysis once looked like a deep invasion, but that was a false alarm; cybernetics may turn out to be the real thing, driving down into the problems of will and cause and motive. If so, those who do not understand the method will not understand the depths of their own cultures.

But the greatest enrichment the scientific culture could give us is—though it does not originate like that—a moral one. Among scientists, deep-natured men know that the individual human condition is tragic; for all its triumphs and joys, the essence of it is loneliness and the end death. But what they will not admit is that, because the individual condition is tragic, therefore the social condition must be tragic, too. Because a man must die, that is no excuse for his dying before his time and after a servile life. The impulse behind the scientists drives them to limit the area of tragedy.

They have nothing but contempt for those representatives of the traditional culture who use a deep insight into man's fate to obscure the social truth—or to do something prettier than obscure the truth, just to hang on to a few perks. Dostoevski sucking up to the Chancellor Pobedonostsev, who thought the only thing wrong with slavery was that there was not enough of it; the political decadence of the *avant garde* of 1914, with Ezra Pound finishing up broadcasting for the Fascists; Claudel agreeing sanctimoniously with the Marshal about the virtue in others' suffering; Faulkner giving sentimental reasons for treating Negroes as a different species. They are all symptoms of the deepest temptation of the clerks—which is to say: "Because man's condition is tragic, everyone ought to stay in their place, with mine as it happens somewhere near the top." From that particular temptation, made up of defeat, self-indulgence, and moral vanity, the scientific culture is almost totally immune.

It is that kind of moral health of the scientists which, in the last few years, the rest of us have needed most; and of which, because the two cultures scarcely touch, we have been most deprived. ●

CHINAFOTOPRESS/GETTY IMAGES

And Ursula undressed . . . The hero and the bimbo from *Dr No*

ALLSTAR COLLECTION

5 APRIL 1958

Sex, Snobbery and Sadism

By Paul Johnson

Paul Johnson's journey from left-wing Bevanite in the 1950s to an advocate for Thatcherism is clearly visible in his articles in the New Statesman. Whatever his target, his vitriolic rhetoric was a reliable constant. His attack on the Beatles, "The Menace of Beatlism", was one of the most complained-about pieces the NS ever published. Here he sets his sights on James Bond.

I have just finished what is, without doubt, the nastiest book I have ever read. It is a new novel entitled *Dr No* and the author is Mr Ian Fleming. Echoes of Mr Fleming's fame had reached me before, and I had been repeatedly urged to read his books by literary friends whose judgment I normally respect. When his new novel appeared, therefore, I obtained a copy and started to read. By the time I was a third of the way through, I had to suppress a strong impulse to throw the thing away, and only continued reading because I realised that here was a social phenomenon of some importance.

There are three basic ingredients in *Dr No*, all unhealthy, all thoroughly English: the sadism of a schoolboy bully, the mechanical, two-dimensional sex-longings of a frustrated adolescent, and the crude snob-cravings of a suburban adult. Mr Fleming has no literary skill, the construction of the book is chaotic, and entire incidents are inserted, and then forgotten. But the three ingredients are manufactured and blended with deliberate, professional precision; Mr Fleming dishes up his recipe with all the calculated accountancy of a Lyons Corner House.

The plot can be briefly described. James Bond, an upper-class Secret Service Agent, is sent by his sadistic superior, M, to Jamaica, to investigate strange incidents on a nearby island. By page 53, Bond's bodyguard, a faithful and brutal Negro called Quarrel, is already at work, twisting the arms of a Chinese girl to breaking point. She gouges his face with a broken flash-bulb, and in return, he smilingly squeezes the fleshy part of her thumb (described by Fleming as "the Mount of Venus", because if it is well-developed then the girl is "good in bed") until she screams. ("She's Love Moun' be sore long after ma face done get healed," chortles Quarrel.) Next, Bond's mysterious enemies attempt to poison him with cyanide-loaded fruit, and then insert a six-inch-long venomous centipede in his bed.

Bond visits the island, falls asleep, and on waking sees a beautiful girl, wearing only a leather belt round her waist ("The belt made her nakedness extraordinarily erotic"). Her behind, Bond notices, "was almost as firm and rounded as a boy's". The girl tells Bond she was raped at the age of 15 by a savage overseer, who then broke her nose. She revenged herself by dropping a Black Widow spider on his naked stomach while he slept ("He took a week to die"). Bond rejects her urgent invitation to share her sleeping bag. Then the enemy arrives – huge, inhuman Negro-Chinese half-castes, known as Chingroes, under the diabolical direction of Dr No. Quarrel is scorched to death by a flame-thrower, and Bond and the girl are captured.

There follows a vague series of incidents in a sort of luxury hotel, built into the mountain, where Dr No entertains his captives before torturing them. This gives Fleming an opportunity to insert his snob ingredient. A lubricious bathroom scene, in which the girl again attempts to seduce Bond, involves Floris Lime bath-essence, Guerlain bathcubes and "Guerlain's Sapoceti, *Fleur des Alpes*". Bond, offered a drink, demands "a medium vodka dry Martini". At last Dr No appears, 6ft 6in tall, and looking like "a giant venomous worm wrapped in grey tin-foil". Some years before, his hands had been cut off, but he is equipped with "articulated steel pincers", which he has a habit of tapping against his contact-lenses, making a metallic noise. He has a polished skull, no eyelashes, and his heart is on the wrong side of his body; he is, needless to say, Chinese (with a German mother). His chief amusement is to subject his captives to prolonged, scientific tortures. ("I am interested in pain. I am also interested in finding out how much the human body can endure.")

Bond contemplates stabbing No's jugular vein with the jagged stem of a broken wine-glass, but reluctantly abandons the idea. The girl is taken off, to be strapped, naked, to the ground and nibbled to death by giant crabs. Bond is put through an ingenious obstacle course of tortures. First come electric shocks. Then an agonising climb up a steel chimney. Then a crawl along a red-hot zinc tube, to face 20 giant Tarantula spiders "three or four inches long". Finally Bond is hurled into the sea, where he is met by a 50-foot giant squid. Having survived all these, Bond buries No alive under a mountain of bird-dung, rescues the girl and at last has a shot at a jugular vein, this time with a table-knife. He also shoots three Chingroes. The girl's feet get cut up, but they tramp to safety, "leaving bloody footsteps on the ground". The story ends with Bond biting the girl in an erotic embrace, which takes place in a special giant sleeping bag.

I have summarised the plot, perhaps at wearisome length, because a bare recital of its details describes, better than I can, how Fleming deliberately and systematically excites, and then satisfies the very worst instincts of his readers. This seems to me far more dangerous than straight pornography.

Irresistible frolics: Bond (Sean Connery) with Tatiana Romanova (Daniela Bianchi) in *From Russia, With Love*

UNDERWOOD & UNDERWOOD/CORBIS

In 1944, George Orwell took issue with a book which in some ways resembles Fleming's novels – *No Orchids for Miss Blandish*. He saw the success of *No Orchids* as part of a discernible psychological climate, whose other products were Fascism, the Gestapo, mass-bombing and war. But in condemning *No Orchids*, Orwell made two reservations. First, he conceded that it was brilliantly written, and that the acts of cruelty it described sprang from a subtle and integrated, though perverse, view of human nature. Secondly, in contrasting *No Orchids* with *Raffles* – which he judged a healthy and harmless book – he pointed out that *No Orchids* was evil precisely because it lacked the restraint of conventional upper-class values; and this led him to the astonishing but intelligible conclusion that perhaps, after all, snobbery, like hypocrisy, was occasionally useful to society.

> Fleming excites and then satisfies the very worst instincts of his readers

What, I wonder, would he have said of *Dr No*? For this novel is badly written to the point of incoherence and none of the 500,000 people who, I am told, are expected to buy it could conceivably be giving Cape 13s 6d to savour its literary merits. Moreover, both its hero and its author are unquestionably members of the Establishment. Bond is an ex-Royal Navy Commander and belongs to Blades, a sort-of super-White's. Mr Fleming was educated at Eton and Sandhurst, and is married to a prominent society hostess, the ex-wife of Lord Rothermere. He is the foreign manager of that austere and respectable newspaper, the *Sunday Times*. Fleming belongs to the Turf and Boodle's and lists among his hobbies the collection of first editions.

Orwell, in fact, was wrong. Snobbery is no protection: on the contrary, the social appeal of the dual Bond-Fleming personality has [given] an additional flavour to his brew of sex and sadism. Fleming's novels are not only successful, they are also smart. The *Daily Express*, pursuing its task of bringing glamour and sophistication to the masses, has serialised the last three. Our curious post-war society, with its obsessive interest in débutantes, its cult of U and non-U, its working-class graduates educated into snobbery by the welfare state, is a soft market for Mr Fleming's poison. Bond's warmest admirers are among the Top People. Of his last adventure, *From Russia, With Love,* his publishers claim, with reason, that it "won approval from the sternest critics in the world of letters". The *Times Literary Supplement* found it "most brilliant", the *Sunday Times* "highly polished", the *Observer* "stupendous", the *Spectator* "rather pleasant". And this journal, most susceptible of all, described it as "irresistible". It has become easier than it was in Orwell's day to make cruelty attractive. Recently I read Henri Alleg's horrifying account of his tortures in an Algiers prison; and I have on my desk a documented study of how we treat our prisoners in Cyprus. I am no longer astonished that these things can happen. Indeed, after reflecting on the Fleming phenomenon, they seem to me almost inevitable. ●

2 JUNE 1961

Beatnik-Land Blows Its Cool

By Ralph J Gleason

A full Ulysses S Grant beard, luxurious and flecked with grey, provided Bill the Beatnik with a supplementary income during his several years in San Francisco's North Beach neighbourhood, home of the original Beats.

Photographed – for a fee – by a tourist against the wall of the Co-Existence Bagel Shop, the Coffee Gallery or any telephone pole on Grant Avenue, Bill was the living symbol of modern American urban dissent, proof positive to the folks back home that the tourist had seen a Beatnik in the flesh.

Last year Bill went to Veterans' Hospital for repairs. He came back to the Beach this spring, his beard a hospital casualty. But it didn't matter really because, for Bill, North Beach is now a strange and lonely land. The tourists still throng the streets, but the regulars have gone like the ferries from the Bay. "What happened? Everybody's split," Bill complained on his first night back On the Scene. Now beardless, Bill is no longer even in demand as a model.

Bill's dilemma symbolises what has happened to North Beach, locale of Beat Generation literature from Kerouac and Ginsberg to *The Connection*. The Beatnik in his native form has all but disappeared from its alleys and cafés, like the Model T Ford from the roads of the US. When you see a Model T now, it's owned by a vintage car club member. Any surviving Beatnik on the Beach belongs to the entrepreneurial minority making a living off the tourists, selling sandals or running guided tours for Little Old Ladies from Dubuque. Or they are amateur Beats, fleeing part-time a dull office.

Beatnik-land attracted too much publicity and too many amateurs. The weekend commuters to Bohemia and the tourists increased in strength until the San Francisco police reacted. North Beach had, in the words of the Beat hipsters, "blown its cool". The great diaspora began like chunks of ice slipping away from an iceberg entering warm waters, a few at a time and then a grand rush. They went to Big Sur, to Monterey, down the coast to Santa Monica and Venice. They moved to other neighbourhoods in San Francisco. They went up-coast to Bolinas and inland to the Sierra. Mostly they went to New York.

Kerouac and Ginsberg had already left by the time the tourists and the amateurs took over (though both returned for brief visits in 1960). Bob Kaufman, known as Bomkauf and author of the Abominist Manifesto, went to New York; Pierre deLattre, the Beatnik priest, whose Bread-and-Wine Mission was a landmark but is now a laundromat ("Pierre got tired of being a housemother to the Beats, on call any hour of the night"), went to the country to write a novel. Grant Avenue now is as dark and lonesome at night as any neighbourhood street. The Cassandra (Zen soup – 20 cents) is a record store; The Place is an art-goods shop; the Coffee Gallery is open only occasionally ("They have events now," an old-timer says disgustedly); the Co-Existence Bagel Shop is a sandals-and-jewellery shop, and the Jazz Cellar is dark and empty.

> The Beatnik has all but disappeared, like the Model T Ford

The end was really heralded when the whole of Grant Avenue burst into brief flame last year with a series of tourist traps. The Surplus Store added berets and turtleneck sweaters to its staples of sweatshirts, blue jeans and GI clothing. A leather-goods shop offered "sandals for beatnik dogs". Henri Lenoir hired Hube-the-Cube Leslie, one of the authentic originals, who in recent years had existed at survival level by serving as a human guinea-pig at hospital laboratories, to sit in the window of the Café Vesuvio, an earnest of the café's authenticity.

Jack Kerouac reads at the Seven Arts Café, 1959

The City Lights Bookstore, owned by poet-businessman Lawrence Ferlinghetti, and featuring an extraordinary collection of paperback books and magazines, began to remain open to two and three o'clock in the morning. "The tourists buy books all night," says Shig Mauro, whose corduroy jacket and full beard behind the counter fit the late-night bookstore mood.

The Place, which originated Blabbermouth Night, where the customers could rise and speak at will, was the first to topple. Leo Kerkorian, the owner, recalls it as "the kind of a joint where I had a bartender who once took off his pants and worked all night with no pants. Some places he couldn't do that but in my place it was all right."

The Co-Existence Bagel Shop lasted until this winter when, under continual police harassment (once a cop even ripped down a poem from the window), its proprietor, Jay Hoppe, universally known as Jay Bagel, gave up. Jay Bagel is only one of the colourful names of Beats. Others are Reverend Bob, Dr Fric-Frac, Linda Lovely, Barbara Nookie, Mad Marie, Lady Joan, Big Rose, Groover Wailin', Taylor Maid and The Wig.

"I'm tired of dealing with a psychopathic police department," Hoppe said when he closed the Bagel Shop and left town. Hoppe also credits the police with being the basic cause of the others leaving. "Bob Kaufman gave up when he was arrested on his birthday," Hoppe says. "Everybody got tired of being rousted by the cops. In New York City, San Francisco poets are treated like visiting celebrities."

But the tourists still come; and Bill the Beatnik, a vestigial remnant of a departed era, alternates between parked cars in the day and the window of the grocery store on Broadway, across from the Expense Account Row of restaurants, at night. "They got TV in here," he says, "and I can watch it with one eye and catch the Passing Parade with the other. But it's not like it was. All the old-timers are gone and the cops never bother the tourists." ●

Rock'n'Roll Crucifixion Jazz

By Reyner Banham

There can be little doubt that Coventry Cathedral is the worst set-back to English church architecture for a very long time. Its influence, unless sternly resisted, can only be confusing and diversionary. I have known the cathedral since it was a concrete foundation-slab, and followed all Sir Basil Spence's long series of modifications and revisions since the competition results were first published, and my conviction that something was fundamentally wrong with the whole operation has grown – in parallel with my increasing admiration for the skill and astuteness with which Sir Basil has done what he set out to do.

In other words, it is the basic proposition that is adrift, not the architectural execution – there is only one fundamental point on which the architect is to be blamed, which is that he accepted the competition conditions. It is important, among all the rock-n-roll-crucifixion jazz currently being trumpeted up about "a modern cathedral for a modern age", to remember that Coventry's original intention after the war was not to have a modern cathedral at all, but a Gothic-revival one, and that when this was abandoned after public outcry, the assessors chosen to judge the competition were about as square as could be found without going grave-robbing. The cards were effectively stacked to make a modern cathedral impossible: what was wanted, and what was got, was a traditional cathedral restyled.

Coventry is trad, Dad, but has tried to give itself a new image – a medieval long plan with aisles and off-lying polygonal or circular chapels, but executed in non-medieval materials (in part) and adorned with devotional art-work in various non-medieval styles. A true modernist would have rejected this basic proposition. What was needed was an imaginative enquiry into those functions, engendered by the rites and responsibilities of episcopacy, that distinguish cathedrals from other churches. At Coventry, the emergence of certain genuinely new and progressive relationships between cathedral and town, cathedral and overseas Christendom, has resulted in no radical innovations, merely two clip-on chapels.

Given, then, that Sir Basil may be blamed for not embarrassing the diocese into genuine thought by shock tactics after he had won the competition, what sort of job has he made of executing this brief that he ought not to have accepted? A real whizz! A ring-a-ding God-box that will go over big with the flat-bottomed latitudinarians who can't stand the quiet austerities of St Paul's, Bow Common. The sheer quality, and quantity, of detailing at Coventry, the mastery of dramatic effects, the richness of the art-work, the sonority with which the note of absolutely conventional piety has been struck, all combine in an image that will have to be fought to the death by everyone who believes that church architecture is part of the mainstream of the Modern Movement, not a picturesque backwater.

Graham Sutherland's tapestry in Coventry Cathedral

> Coventry is trad, Dad, but has tried to give itself a new image

Only two things have gone wrong with Spence's scheme. The Sutherland tapestry is wrong in colour and in the scale of its elements – it dominates the east end, but fails to achieve the presence of a Byzantine pantocrator. Clearly, in attempting this unprecedented scale in tapestry, architect and artist were biting off more than the artist could chew. It is difficult, however, to understand why the failure of the west window was not foreseen. Strictly, it is a screen of clear glass occupying the entire west wall of the cathedral, some of the panes engraved by John Hutton with life-sized figures of saints and angels in a style that one associates with the Royal College of Art. However, the style of the art matters less than the amount of light that enters through it.

It was intended that the crowning moment of the entire design should be that when the communicant rises from the altar rail and turns to go back to his place, he sees the glowing ranks of stained-glass windows down either side of the nave. As it is, he is simply half-blinded by the glare of hard white light from the west. There are three reasons for this: liturgical west is, in fact, south; the glass is clear, not stained; and the successive raisings of the roof of the porch in search of a more monumental entrance have lifted it to the point where it does not shade the window at all.

So, after the first blast of light, and the first disappointment with the tapestry, one avoids looking at either. The rest exhibits a level of sheer professionalism in the creation of visual effects and the manipulation of spaces that is rare in Britain. The porch in particular is masterly. The general grouping of the exterior, with the two off-lying chapels seen against the long flank of the main building, is one of the few designs which preserves anything worth having of the South Bank aesthetics of 1951.

The main ranks of stained-glass windows are so much at home with the whole conception that one is surprised to remember that they are not by Spence himself, but by Keith New and Geoffrey Clarke and Lawrence Lee. Similarly, Stephen Sykes's mosaic relief is the perfect work of devotional art to catch and draw the eye at the end of the south aisle. This exact conjunction of architectural and artistic intentions becomes most obvious in John Piper's glass for the tall curved wall of the baptistery on the liturgical south side. Seen, unexpectedly, on emerging from the Chapel of Unity opposite, it startlingly creates the impression of the Holy Ghost descending on the font in a ball of atomic fire.

Time after time, Sir Basil gives us, in this sense, masterstrokes of architectural religious drama. The pity is that the play itself should be by Eliot at his most Establishment, not Osborne at his most probing. ●

9 MAY 1975

Life of a Myth-Maker

By Naomi Lewis

Yes, Hans Christian Andersen's life was a fairy tale – but not nearly as simple a one as popular singing comedians like to present. His devouring early wish for fame and acclaim was granted to the full, if not quite by the means he intended. But every wish has its price; the greater the one, the higher the other: and this is Andersen's story. Oddly, few good accounts can be found in print in English. So Dr [Elias] Bredsdorff's well-tempered and well-documented study [Phaidon, £4.95] agreeably supplies a need.

Andersen material is extremely plentiful: never can so essentially solitary a life have been lived so visibly. He was a tireless diarist and letter writer and in almost every one of his stories he makes an appearance, main, minor or minuscule, leaving more self-portraits than Rembrandt. Facts help to light the Andersen mysteries, but the chief enigmas are not factual. They touch on such themes as reputation; the nature of genius; what this Dane has left in the stream of English writing – and why the Andersen tales, in England, are (wrongly) thought of only as nursery fare. Most – there are 156 – are not known here at all.

One crucial point made clear by Dr Bredsdorff is the force of the barriers that Andersen crossed in life. Odense was no kindly village in his childhood, but a story-kingdom in miniature: wealth and poverty; nobility, gentry, trade, the labouring poor; royal castle, mediaeval town hall, ancient grammar school, lunatic asylum, gaol.

The people (some 5,000) belonged in their rigid feudal stations; nobody stepped outside except the washerwoman's crazy boy. For all his wrong clothes and cold reception, he pushed himself into the Dean's confirmation class for the well-to-do, instead of the curate's for the poor. The restlessness and recklessness came from the father; reader, freethinker, an indifferent shoemaker. He died when the boy was 11. To his illiterate mother Andersen owed his obstinacy and endurance – and his often baffling superstition and piety.

Still, there, at 14, was the zany innocent, newly arrived in Copenhagen, battering at doors, clowning, singing, weeping his way from patron to patron. At 17 he was sent to school like a child, from public funds, a great tall anxious scarecrow among the 11-year-olds. It was the darkest period of his life. But he had shifted class; he had even acquired a family. When his principal guardian, Councillor Jonas Collin, took on the role of father, the handsome clannish sons and daughters became his adopted brothers and sisters. They showed an amused kindness to the young troll. By 30 – what a change! – he was known as a writer; soon he would be welcomed throughout Europe for work in a new genre, begun quite casually: short tales, the first few meant for children, the rest for everyone.

> He was a mass of anxieties: fearful of dogs, of fire, of water, of being seduced

Success brings another kind of preposterousness to the story. The diaries show him touring Europe, hobnobbing with Liszt, Mendelssohn, Heine, Vigny, Hugo, Lamartine, Dumas, Wagner, Rossini, George Sand. An onlooker always, he resisted sampling ether as dinner-guest of Dr Simpson, anaesthetist. He resisted, too, the prostitutes he was offered everywhere, though they did not leave him undisturbed. Uncertain of protocol, he evaded invitations from young Victoria and Albert. But in Germany he was soon a guest of the King and Queen of Prussia, then speeding off for the court of the Hereditary Grand Duke of Weimar. "He pressed me to his bosom, we kissed one another. 'We are friends for life,' he said. We both wept." It was the world of toy theatres come to life.

Yet none of this touched the Collins. He simply could not impress them. What a relief to leave admonitory Denmark for all that intrepid travelling. But the desperate early years had left their mark. Respectable and respected, he was a mass of anxieties – hypochondriac, agoraphobic, fearful of dogs, of fire, of water, of being robbed, seduced or murdered, of losing his passport, of making a social gaffe.

Clearly, one of his troubles was that he could never learn the essential rules in the game of love. This is of less importance in his brief romances with nice sisterly girls but the really abiding love affair was with the Collin family, above all with the cool, responsible Edvard. Dr Bredsdorff's note – was Andersen a homosexual? (Answer: No) – is hardly necessary. Andersen's "crush" rose from a complex of other sources. But what letters everyone wrote and kept! Andersen begs Edvard to address him with the less formal *Du*. I will not, says Edvard calmly. Edvard writes the kind of icily devastating letter that one might set down to assuage one's feelings – then not send. Edvard's were always sent. And yet it is Edvard who deals with Andersen's affairs while he is away, writes to publishers, buys his lottery ticket, and transcribes the *Autobiography* by hand, most intimate of tasks.

What a writer can't resolve in his own affairs, he can very well on paper. The tales are Andersen's true response to life. The miniature was his scale: kitchen debris, dustbin stuff, the elf-world, even – any such things could reflect a human scene. This of course is only one aspect of Andersen's tales. Light crosses dark; dark crosses light; here is the haunted past, there, an irrepressible interest in modern invention. The stories map his past, his present, the journey of his mind.

One real injustice lasted until the end. Lack of money had made him too long a suppliant and dependant. But – with no international copyright – what he should have earned he could not get. For 30 years he was a bestseller in America without receiving a penny. He was, of course, not in need. In fact, when his lottery ticket brought him a sizeable win at last, two years before his death, he scarcely referred to it. Honours were pouring in. He was (with Hamlet) most famous of all the Danes.

The ironic reward of the mythmaker had come to him, that his myths had a life of their own. Was this his chief satisfaction? Or was it the thought of those reproving patrons of his youth? "Don't you realise," Mrs Wulff had written, "that you are on the wrong road? Supposing I had the idea that I wanted to be Empress of Brazil . . ."

"It was not easy for her to realise," commented the Andersen scholar H Topsoe-Jensen, "that she was speaking to a future Emperor of Brazil." With clothes; sometimes without: an Emperor certainly. ●

BATES LITTLEHALES/NATIONAL GEOGRAPHIC/GETTY IMAGES

A long, anxious scarecrow lost among small children: story time at the statue of Hans Christian Andersen in Central Park, New York, 1960

16 MAY 1975 AND 21 DECEMBER 1979

Godfather, Forbid

By John Coleman

John Coleman reviewed films for the NS between 1960 and 1986. In the centenary edition of the magazine, Julian Barnes remembered him with affection: "It seems to me that journalists were more colourful characters back then. The NS film reviewer, for instance, was a wonderful old boho... who in his university days had had more poems in Cambridge Poetry than either Ted Hughes or Thom Gunn – then he was sent down and went off to Paris and wrote pornography for Maurice Girodias." Here the old boho offers fresh impressions of two now classic films.

The Godfather: Part II

There is a feeling abroad that Francis Ford Coppola's *The Godfather Part II* is better, subtler, more probing than its record-breaking predecessor. And all this without that starry party of the first part, Marlon Brando. There was certainly some ground for greater expectations. "*The Godfather* made me really rich, so I'm not under financial pressure any more," said Coppola in an interview. Then he made *The Conversation*, that fascinating study of the long-distance bugger, a firm reinforcement of his credentials. And then . . . well, then he made the promised follow-up to Life and Death with the Corleones and it is 25 minutes longer than that one and about twice as confusing. Apparently Coppola's first cut ran nearly four and a half hours. The new film, once again co-written by its director and Mario Puzo, moves haphazardly in a couple of directions: backwards and forwards.

The warrant for the flashback material is largely to be found on pages 197-215 of the paperback Puzo, which details the early days of young Vito: his flight from Sicily to escape the Don who had murdered his family; his hard times and insidious rise to eminence in New York's Little Italy. The onward progression of the story, which concerns son Michael's consolidation of his father's empire, is fresh stuff, only fresh seems hardly the word.

Michael (Al Pacino again) still has a body or three to bury before he can fulfil his dream of going as legit as a Mafia boss ever may, but he is essentially en route to an American respectability. This Michael has his emotional moments ("I know it was you, Fredo, you broke my heart, you broke my heart," kissing a treacherous brother on the mouth; howling with rage when gunfire rakes his family bedroom; slapping his wife as she admits to an abortion) and Pacino is up to them. Yet it is not a memorable performance and one wonders, with hindsight, if Pacino may not have garnered a few quiet laurels on his previous outing simply by being set against the speak-your-weight appearance of Brando.

With much the same team as before, Coppola has produced a picture with much the same look, muted, brownish, unflashily composed. This pays off best in the several flashbacks. The child Vito's mother rockets back from a shotgun blast with shocking effect; the impersonal routine of immigration, quarantine on Ellis Island, an ironic glimpse of the Statue of Liberty are nicely set up; there is a fine recreation of an Italian music hall in New York. In fact, if Pacino stole the earlier film, it is Robert De Niro (Vito as a young man) who walks off with this. Nothing is more lovingly mounted than his first killing. A religious procession, with a Christ covered in dollar-bills, white-suited Fanucci (Gaston Moschin) swaggering by as a neighbourhood little big shot, Vito scrambling over rooftops, down a skylight, to blast the fat man at his front door.

> If Pacino stole the earlier film it is Robert De Niro who walks off with this

It would be wrong to give the impression that all's at sea in this second instalment. There is an ingenious twist when Michael is hauled before a Senate committee and escapes by flying in the bewildered Sicilian brother of a witness against him, who then – ah, that Mafia code – breezily contradicts earlier testimony. Coppola knows how to build from piano to fortissimo and he handles actors well. But he should have known how to be stricter with himself. There are too many loose ends here for sense. A third film? Godfather, forbid.

Apocalypse Now

In the beginning was Joseph Conrad's short novel *Heart of Darkness*. Some 10 years ago, the gun-happy surfing buff, film-writer and film-maker John Milius turned the Conrad into a script set during the Vietnam War. More recently, there was Michael Herr's book, *Despatches*, on the same conflict. Now comes Francis Ford Coppola's hectic, heralded movie, *Apocalypse Now*, which draws on these various sources with something approaching cinematic genius and with something else, too, best described as crassness.

Surely the last reels, which have loopy Dennis Hopper intoning "I should have been a pair of ragged claws" and bald, bloated Brando – as renegade Colonel Kurtz amid skulls and mad Montagnards – indulging in a kind of Eliot seminar, achieve a new high in pretentiousness. And the more's the pity, because it is the stations of the quest itself – whereby a zonked-out young veteran, Captain Willard (Martin Sheen), is sent to "terminate" Kurtz "with extreme prejudice" – which provide the edgy, pyrotechnical fascination, the awful brilliance, of Coppola's movie; and not the last maunderings of his quarry.

The true revelations of *Apocalypse Now* are essentially its tremendous audio-visual set-pieces. As Willard travels up-river in his naval patrol boat, the sort of large-scale surrealism adumbrated in *Catch 22* takes him and us over. I defy the most pacific viewer not to surrender for the moment to a helicopter strafing of a Vietcong beachhead, struttingly led by a rasp-throated Lt Colonel Kilgore (Robert Duvall superb as a sawn-off John Wayne). A dozen choppers weave and duck through a menacing aerial dance to the hugely amplified strains of "The Ride of the Valkyries"; rockets streak, flares smoke yellow and pink, bodies stagger and slump; Kilgore talks chirpily of surfing, the point of the exercise – "Charlie don't surf". Later, Willard has coldly to administer the *coup de grâce* when an innocent sampan is attacked in error. By now, Willard may be intended as no better than his raving victim; but, though nightmare-haunted, he was a hard killer from the first. Coppola furnishes a string of incidents of extraordinary impact, high-operatic, caustic, roustabout, horrifying – a Hell, you might say, of a spectacle. What worries me is that the main weight of his effort goes to support a simple and damnable proposition: war is downright exhilarating. ●

Goose-Stepping

By Julian Barnes

When the early results came through on Day One of the Moscow Olympics, we learned that Russia had won a gold medal in the free pistol shooting. Well, they would, wouldn't they, my viewing companions sneered back at the set in unison. As these morally tatty Games proceed, it's going to become harder and harder to avoid lapsing into a state of self-pitying international paranoia. Take the case of Danny Nightingale, our gold-medal hope in the modern pentathlon. He randomly selects a Russian horse for the show jumping leg, and rides it more or less impeccably round the ring, except that the daft commie nag chooses to drop its rear hooves into precisely as many fences as there are onion domes on St Basil's. Explanation? Quite obviously, a subcutaneous KGB electrode implanted in the haunches of every horse, and a belted figure high up in the stands "whispering" into his sleeve.

"Moscow 80 = Berlin 36" declared a chalk slogan near my home for the length of half a shower. Not really; but you'd think, wouldn't you, that the Russians would be keen to avoid providing for worldwide transmission too many images which evoked those earlier propaganda Games? At the opening ceremony, the Olympic flag was trooped by "eight unknown sportsmen" (ie, eight really not very good sportsmen) in pale blue lightweight suits and white gloves; they goose-stepped round the stadium to Beethoven's *Ninth Symphony*, legs sabre-dancing out and free arms flung vigorously across opposite shoulders. (Of course, the goose-step is commonplace in Eastern Europe, and doesn't have fascist connections over there; but even so, it's nothing if not martial, and looks very odd on a sportsman, however unknown.)

This queasy image had no sooner appeared than it was amplified. Behind the eight Daks stormtroopers came 22 additional high-kickers, though looking a little more Austin Reed in their blue blazers and white slacks. White gloves again – though this time they were designed to protect the strutters' hands against "accidents" from the rear ends of the white doves they carried aloft on their straightened right arms. A dove of peace on the end of a Nazi salute: was it the year's strangest image?

Lord Killanin made a tactful speech, and the only children left in Moscow duly bombarded him with gladioli as if he were Barry Humphries. Brezhnev, speaking from a panelled bus shelter, was allowed (by Olympic tradition) only one sentence in which to open the Games; but who can monitor Russian punctuation – and the result was something so long it might have been scripted by Bernard Levin. The British athletes stayed away, and the team's *chef de mission* paraded with an Olympic flag, which the Soviet TV producer craftily excised from the picture. As a result, the Russian viewer was free to conclude that the British had become so enfeebled and ricket-stricken a race after a year of Mrs Thatcher that all they could raise for the Games was a single middle-aged pole-vaulter.

One wondered what the average Muscovite in the stadium made of it: or rather, the average, sanitised, with-dissidence-removed Muscovite. Most of them, of course, couldn't see much anyway because they had to keep on holding up coloured cards to construct a kaleidoscope of insincere slogans ("O Sport Thou Art Peace", etc). Why is this form of stadium entertainment so popular behind the Iron Curtain and so antipathetic to us? Is it perhaps because it seems to us to emphasise the antishness of the participants; whereas it seems to them to prove that expressions of the popular will can be both located and pungently conveyed? But what must it feel like to be a chap with a placard, turning it over by command, never seeing the result of your endeavours, and constantly blocking out the sun? It must be a bit like singing in the chorus of the *Messiah* while wearing earplugs. Perhaps one of the card-bearers who made Jimmy Hill's face for the opening credits of *Match of the Day* will write and elucidate.

Propaganda games: the Olympics opening ceremony

The Olympics began – doubtless not intentionally – just as Gay Pride Week was ending. BBC2 acknowledged the occasion with an *Inside Story* on *Coming Out*: a useful programme at a time when there seems to be a certain mild backlash against gays. Not just among Leviticans like Sir John Junor either: a lot of heterosexuals who supported gay lib as a principle now seem less pleased with it in practice. To some, gay couples are acceptable as long as they keep house plants and do French knitting in the long winter evenings; but if they jump about on the streets, dress in leather, and (my God) *look* gay, then they're held to be overstepping the mark. *We* didn't intend for you to behave like *that* when we legalised you, is the patronising implication.

What "that" may involve was occasionally made explicit in this programme: "You then have to get across," murmured a Hammersmith press officer, softly, "that you enjoy sodomy . . . it's very pleasant, very ok." One felt the soft shuffle of tightening sphincters all across the country; but it was bravely said.

At the moment, homosexuality is legal rather as prostitution is legal, and scarcely more socially acceptable; so, as *Inside Story* made clear, all the old reality of being homosexual – of guilty suicides, shamed and bitter parents, arbitrary job dismissals – continues unabated. Gay pride is only partly about being proud to be gay; it's also about relief at surviving as such.

Russell Harty's new chat show, *Sorl Baht Booooks* (as the title song has it), will soon presumably be retitled *Sorl Baht Sex* (BBC1). Last week the Lip discussed boffing with the parents of Louise "Test Tube" Brown and with a benign Christopher Isherwood. As a relief between these two serious bits, Robert Morley was paid to plug his son Sheridan's new anthology. Memo to Russell: I've just written a book, and my dad's free any time. ●

Do You Dare Like This Book?

By Ian McEwan

In the current public debate on freedom of expression there is something not altogether free. One writer told an editor last week that she feared for her life if she spoke out for *The Satanic Verses*. Another said he felt strongly about the right to publish but if he made his views public he would only make things "worse" for Salman Rushdie. Muslims who have spoken out against book burning or banning or author murdering have been threatened by those of more straightforward convictions. Muslims of all shades of opinion have been threatened by white racists.

The poison of intimidation is infecting the free exchange of ideas. The stain of one crazed edict is spreading. What follows from intimidation is fear. Going to bed with fear, and waking up (if you've managed to sleep) with fear is hardly any life at all. But what follows from fear has direr consequences. I am talking of self-censorship. It is an invisible process, even to the one who is doing the censoring. No Muslim, Christian, atheist or whatever should feel obliged to make public statements in an atmosphere of threat. The right to silence is inalienable from the right to free expression. But fear needs to be fingered. If we name it, then we can see it. If we can see it, we might be able to do something about it.

But let's not be solemn. Since I am feeling a little fearful myself today, I think I would rather talk about Voltaire. The famous attributed remark, "I might disapprove of what you say, but I will defend to the death your right to say it," has had many airings recently. It is a fine sentiment. But just lately the remark has seemed somewhat abused. There are, after all, more difficult positions to take. Suppose I actually approve of what you say, of what you've written? Then not only might I die for your right, I might even have read your book and engaged with its ideas.

And what is it you are saying? Is Christianity the subject? It might as well be, what with the phone ringing again, and someone talking to me from a public call box. What has always puzzled me is the distance you might travel in, say, 1,500 years. You start with a man, a very special man, who claims a direct relationship with his God. His teachings are a unique blend of tolerance and compassion, forgiveness and love, and they hold out the prospect

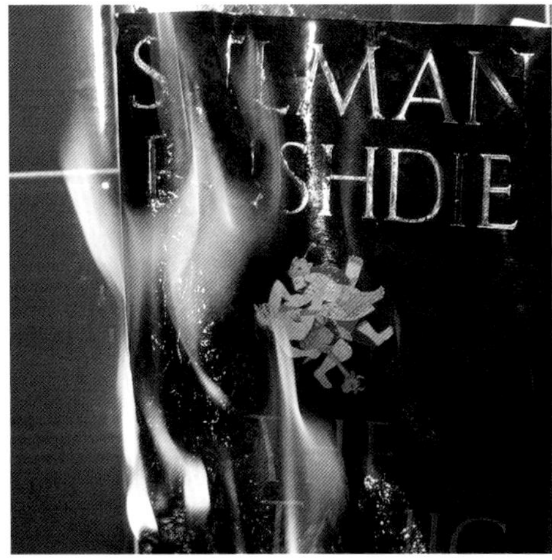

Direct lines: *The Satanic Verses*

of great joy in the afterlife. After his death, his followers continue his work. The life and teachings are written down.

But then, 15 centuries or so later, what do we have? A vast, hierarchical bureaucracy, certain members of which are aware of God's intentions and accordingly issue their edicts, fiats, decrees, canons, encyclicals, bulls and whathaveyou. How the major fourth is the devil's interval and must never be heard in church, how women are weak and unclean and less in reason, how the sun goes round the earth. *Rules about every damn thing.*

> Fear needs to be fingered. If we name it, then we can see it

From the vision of one man, to a total thought-system, impatient with dissent and ready to kill to keep the small print intact, ready to slaughter the inhabitants of Albi, or the followers of Luther, or risk the wine-dark seas to kill the infidel Muslims. And the dissenters, the Reformers, they don't seem so shy of slaughter for their cause either. The faithful are ready to kill or die bravely for their particular spin on doctrine. They hear each sound of their own Word of God, they all get their instructions direct. *From the beginning, men used to justify the unjustifiable.*

But, coming back to Voltaire, perhaps it is Stalinism we are talking about. You are asking me to fight to the end for your right to talk about that? Well, yes, there's another long hard road to travel, from an initial impulse to lift from the majority of mankind its heavy burden of hard work and ignorance, to the ministrations of Uncle Joe. Another full-nelson on thought, a total system, as happy devouring its friends as its enemies. Mock it if you dare – *It's his Word against mine.*

Or again, are we talking about the space between Danton and Robespierre? Or is this all too harsh? Am I really offering myself up to your right to talk about *any* closed system of thought, any monopoly on truth? Scientific method, Freudian analysis, structuralism, voodooism, sociology, Thatcherism, journalism? They all have their high priests with their direct line to the Highest Authority.

Have you heard, the Ayatollah has announced that his Edict, this pronouncement on your Headandballs, is not something dreamed up in the bath. It was God's Word in his ear. His Word against yours. God told the Ayatollah, and the Ayatollah told us. God made Viking publish your novel to demonstrate the international conspiracy against Iran. *You brought us the Devil himself, so that we could witness the workings of the Evil One, and his overthrow by the Right.*

But back to Voltaire. I'm getting the idea now, it's the monotheistic you want to shake your stick at. What you're wanting to hammer to the door of this here church is hardly a reasoned argument at all. It's a fairground, a carnival, a riot. It's a *novel*. You are a trouble maker.

And Ohmigod! You want to include Islam, you want me to fight to the death for your right to treat Islam as if it were only one more thought-system, one more authority, one more idea. That's a helluvalot to ask, brother. That's a wrathful world religion you're talking about there. Christ, Socrates, Buddha, Lao Tse, but not this one, baby. I'll only make things worse for you and (da!) here's the phone ringing again. It's that racist Peter Sellers imitation in the call box, so (hello? hello?) I think I'd better (you'll do what?) stop right here. ●

All italicised quotations are from Salman Rushdie's "Satanic Verses"

Comprehensive change

By Melissa Benn

Despite decades of reform, Britain still has one of the most socially segregated education systems in the world. Disadvantaged children are still waiting for politicians to learn their lesson

No public figure today would dare assert, as the poet Matthew Arnold did in 1864, that "the education of each class in society has, or ought to have, its ideal, determined by the wants of that class and by its destination". Yet in many ways our education system retains similar features to that of a century ago: a bewildering multiplicity of school types, a high level of religious influence and clear divisions along class lines, usually entailing far inferior provision for poorer children.

In the early 20th century, while other nations such as the US were laying the basis for a universal public (state) school model, education in England was divided and divisive. The upper classes were shipped off to public schools or elite day schools; the middle classes were educated at the competitive grammar schools, which based their curriculum on the public school model; and working-class children received a wildly uneven elementary education, its quality dependent on which regional school board or which church was in charge.

From the mid-19th century, legislation had begun to bring schools in England and Wales under local democratic control (Scotland has always been separately administered). This sparked off skirmishes, particularly after the Balfour Act 1902, which provided state subsidy for denominational instruction in schools.

The Second World War was an important turning point. Many schools had been closed in readiness for evacuation but a million children were never sent away, leading to scenes of delinquency as they roamed the streets. Ministers were criticised for not knowing what was happening to state education "because they educate their own children elsewhere". Even senior officials at the Board of Education conceded that full-time schooling for most children was in many ways "seriously defective – and that for 90 per cent of them, it ended too soon. It is conducted in many cases in premises which are scandalously bad."

The establishment of free universal secondary education was one of the great achievements of the wartime coalition government. It was also a lost opportunity, in two ways. The declining efficacy of some of the public schools in the 1930s, recorded with acerbic accuracy by George Orwell and Robert Graves, among others, offered a historic chance to merge private and state education, yet none of the postwar politicians – Labour or Tory – was bold enough to pursue such a step.

> Parents' opposition to selection helped bring in comprehensives

In 1938 the Spens report had also "considered carefully the possibility of multilateral schools . . . the provision of a good general education for all". Instead, a tripartite system was created after 1944. As the proposed technical schools never really took off, children were sent to either grammar or secondary modern schools, depending on the results of an eleven-plus exam, based on IQ tests devised by the psychologist Cyril Burt – whose work was later found to be fraudulent.

Grammar schools by and large took children who were already advantaged, though they propelled a small number from lower-middle-class homes into the elite universities and the professions, a narrative of class transcendence that still obsesses some of the newly powerful. Secondary moderns were under-resourced and disregarded, consigning generations of working-class children to an inadequate education, and countless lost opportunities.

Few now realise that it was, in part, widespread opposition from parents that ushered in comprehensive reform. The journalist Simon Jenkins records how, in the late 1960s, Edward Boyle, the then Tory spokesman on education, was "torn limb from limb" by Conservative voters, furious that their children had failed the eleven-plus. The intellectual firepower for a different model was provided by researchers who demolished the Burtian argument of fixed ability and believed passionately in the intellectual as well as social benefits of comprehensive education.

With cautious support from the 1964 Labour government, which merely "requested" local reorganisation on comprehensive lines rather than "required" it, a piecemeal revolution was launched. The initial reform was strongly bipartisan, winning support from many Tory and Labour authorities, though to this day one-fifth of local authorities use the eleven-plus. Research in the 1990s showed that the proportion of 16-year-olds gaining five or more A to C grades at comprehensive schools with at least one competing grammar school in the area was 29 per cent, compared to 48 per cent where schools could claim an intake that was fully comprehensive.

Despite this advance, the political history of the past 50 years has been a story of persistent counter-revolution. The Labour prime minister James Callaghan may have inaugurated the Great Debate on state schooling in 1976 but it was the work of the organised right wing, from lobbying by the Institute of Economic

PHOTOFUSION/REX FEATURES

Affairs to the notorious Black Papers from 1969 onwards, that bolstered Thatcherism's repeated attempts to dismantle the hard-won achievements of the 1960s and early 1970s.

The key notes of Thatcher's premiership in education were strengthening centralised control and a rhetoric of choice, diversity and freedom, themes taken up by every successive government. New Labour, however, distinguished itself by substantively increasing investment in schools and taking a much more positive approach, in its early years. Its academies programme boosted private-sector involvement in schools but also directed valuable resources to poorer areas and communities.

No one argues seriously today for the return of a grammar school system. An important moment in the political right's conversion to the notion of "excellence for all" came in 2007 with a speech by the then Tory spokesman on education, David Willetts, which conclusively dismissed the idea that the grammar schools of today promote social mobility. In fact, they educate a tiny proportion of all the children who are on free school meals.

The irony, and paradox, of the coalition is that it vigorously promotes comprehensives, but only for the chosen few. By watering down fair admissions and proper democratic scrutiny and ruthlessly assigns fiscal (and political) capital to one section only of the school estate (academies and free schools), the revolution being championed by the Education Secretary, Michael Gove, celebrates, confirms and extends myriad forms of selection.

The evidence from the OECD is clear: the best-performing school systems do not select, academically or geographically. Where selection exists, it does not produce higher results overall but does increase the gap between the advantaged and the disadvantaged. The UK has one of *the* most socially segregated systems. Education in England still awaits a visionary party: one that will seek to create a consensus for a truly unified system, bringing in both selective state schools and the private sector.

As to the future, a critical question concerns the administrative chaos that will be brought about by coalition policy. Given that it will be impossible for Whitehall to oversee thousands of free-floating schools, and as concern is growing about the quality and accountability of the shadowy new school chains, fresh ideas for more dynamic forms of local government are now developing.

The lesson of successful areas such as Hackney and Camden in London, confirmed by the government's research, is that high standards are created and sustained by close collaboration, including continuous monitoring of leadership, rather than fixating on school type. Most of the schools in Hackney are academies; in Camden, most schools have remained under the local authority. Will a future Labour government promote collaboration and bring place planning back under democratic control?

The second battle concerns curriculum and exam reform. Heads, teachers and academics are united in opposition to the coalition government's proposals for the curriculum, which will certainly damage prospects for a significant minority of poorer children, as will its plans for more draconian exams.

Finally, the spectre of for-profit schooling hovers. Gove has indicated that, should the Tories win the 2015 election, he will pursue this idea more enthusiastically. Polls suggest the public is against it, and rightly so. The evidence on for-profit education from other countries is decidedly mixed; it encourages a sterile "payment by results" approach and further detaches schools from their communities.

It is useful here to recall the words of the great R H Tawney, from 1917, that "education is a spiritual activity . . . much of which is not commercially profitable, and that the prevailing temper of Englishmen is to regard as most important that which is commercially profitable, and as of only inferior importance that which is not". That may well be the Tory view, yet surely a future Labour government will back a broader vision of our schools and see the need to keep them in the public realm? ●

Melissa Benn's "School Wars: the Battle for Britain's Education" is published by Verso (£8.99)

31 MAY 2010

The Double Life of Christopher Hitchens

By Terry Eagleton

The Oedipal children of the establishment have always proved useful to the left. Such ruling-class renegades have the grit, chutzpah, inside knowledge, effortless self-assurance, stylishness, fair conscience and bloody-mindedness of their social background, but can turn these patrician virtues to radical ends. The only trouble is that they tend to revert to type as they grow older, not least when political times are lean. The Paul Foots and Perry Andersons of this world are a rare breed. Men and women who began by bellowing "Out, out, out!" end up humiliating waiters and overrating Evelyn Waugh. Those who, like Christopher Hitchens, detest a cliché turn into one of the dreariest types of them all: the revolutionary hothead who learns how to stop worrying about imperialism and love Paul Wolfowitz.

That Hitchens represents a grievous loss to the left is beyond doubt. He is a superb writer, superior in wit and elegance to his hero George Orwell, and an unstanchably eloquent speaker. He has an insatiable curiosity about the modern world and an encyclopaedic knowledge of it, as well as an unflagging fascination with himself. Through getting to know all the right people, an instinct as inbuilt as his pancreas, he could tell you without missing a beat whom best to consult in Rabat about education policy in the Atlas Mountains. The same instinct leads to chummy lunches with Bill Deedes and Peregrine Worsthorne. In his younger days, he was not averse to dining with repulsive fat cats while giving them a piece of his political mind. Nowadays, one imagines, he just dines with repulsive fat cats.

The two faces of Hitchens, however, are as much synchronous as sequential. In a sense, he has become what he always covertly was. Even at the age of 20 he felt tugged between dissidence and dining out. "Hypocritchens", as he was known at Balliol, was suave, bright, fearless, loquacious, self-admiring and grotesquely ambitious. (I write as one who knew him as a comrade in the International Socialists.) He was a man who made Uriah Heep look like Little Nell. Having worked his way through everyone worth knowing in the United Kingdom, he spied a larger stage in the United States (a nation that was the stuff of his fantasies even as a student), hopped on a plane and proceeded to cultivate everyone worth knowing in Washington and New York as well. If he has not settled in Bingley or Sudan, it is because there is nobody worth knowing there.

Yet the synchrony cuts the other way, too, as something of the old lefty survives. His favourite colour, he tells us, is "Blue. Sometimes red". The tentative punctuation says it all. He still detests Henry Kissinger, despises Bill Clinton, takes a brutal swipe at Dick Cheney (while mentioning that they share a dentist) and, having lustily cheered on the invasion of Iraq, is now honest enough to write of the "impeachable incompetence of the Bush administration" and the "terrifying damage" it inflicted on Iraqi society (though he confines

> If one can swallow one's vomit, there is much in the book to enjoy

this to cultural looting). He has not made his peace with the insolence of power, simply with capitalism. Nowadays he is a political sceptic, convinced that there are "absolutely no certainties". This is the catch-22 suggested by the title of his memoirs, *Hitch-22*: the double bind of marrying a wariness of belief with a conviction that certainties are obnoxious.

It is, in fact, a false problem. Liberals ought to hold their convictions just as passionately as their illiberal opponents. Hitchens absolutely believed that it was right to unleash a murderous fury on the innocent people of Iraq. What was wrong was not the degree of his certainty, but the belief itself. It is absolutely certain that Osama Bin Laden is not a liberal pluralist. The mistake is to slip from this fairly innocuous use of the word "absolute" to a political one. But Hitchens, despite being one of the world's most renowned public intellectuals, was never very adept at ideas. In some ways, Hitchens is a reactionary English patrician, in other ways a closet Thatcherite, and in yet other ways a right-leaning liberal. The problem, in a striking historical irony, is that it is the literary-liberal guardians of the flame of tolerance and pluralism who are nowadays most likely to be cultural supremacists and gung-ho militarists when it comes to the Muslim world.

His double life as establishment groupie and swingeing iconoclast (Hitchens is to be seen smoking on the front cover of this book, the US equivalent of tearing up cobblestones) is reflected in his literary style. Take, for example, this nauseating piece of self-congratulation: "'I suppose you know,' said the most careful and elegant and witty English poet of my generation when I first took his hand and accepted a Bloody Mary financed from his slight but always-open purse, 'that you are the second most famous person in Oxford.'" Perhaps Hitchens obtusely imagines that the faint put-down of "second" will conceal the odious egotism of this vignette, as though he is wryly telling a tale against himself.

This blend of self-vaunting and perfunctory self-deprecation is a common device in his prose, as he recounts some self-aggrandising moment from his career as a war journalist while insisting that he was shaking with fear at the time, or professes to be knocked back by discovering that the great Isaiah Berlin should prefer his humble company while he is still an Oxford student to that of "much more distinguished figures". Hitchens's tutor had taken this Marxist on the make to meet Berlin, along with Noam Chomsky, at a private seminar at Oxford, and "I hope that by dropping these names I can convey something of the headiness of it". The faux candour of "dropping these names" is meant to deflect the charge that Hitchens is a fawning little name-dropper. As a speaker at the Oxford Union, he had the chance to dine and drink with senior ministers, and also to be "amazed once again at how ignorant and sometimes plain stupid were the people who claimed to run the country". The comment is intended to cloak his arriviste excitement at hobnobbing with the powerful, as well as to suggest his own intellectual superiority, even as a stripling, to the pick of the political class.

When Nelson Mandela tells him with a "room-warming smile" that a letter the youthful Hitchens had sent him had brightened his

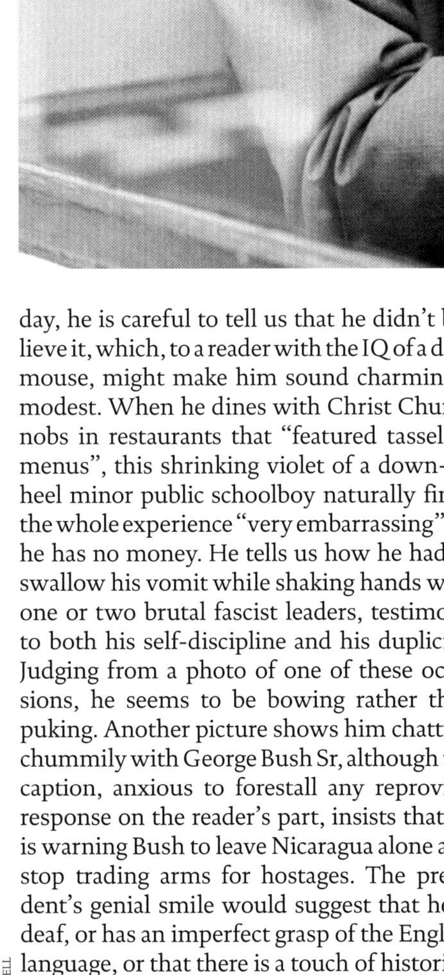

Effusions of grandeur: Hitchens in 2006

CAMERA PRESS/JASON BELL

day, he is careful to tell us that he didn't believe it, which, to a reader with the IQ of a dormouse, might make him sound charmingly modest. When he dines with Christ Church nobs in restaurants that "featured tasselled menus", this shrinking violet of a down-at-heel minor public schoolboy naturally finds the whole experience "very embarrassing", as he has no money. He tells us how he had to swallow his vomit while shaking hands with one or two brutal fascist leaders, testimony to both his self-discipline and his duplicity. Judging from a photo of one of these occasions, he seems to be bowing rather than puking. Another picture shows him chatting chummily with George Bush Sr, although the caption, anxious to forestall any reproving response on the reader's part, insists that he is warning Bush to leave Nicaragua alone and stop trading arms for hostages. The president's genial smile would suggest that he is deaf, or has an imperfect grasp of the English language, or that there is a touch of historical revisionism at work here.

Hitchens is foolishly proud of having been thwacked on the bum by Margaret Thatcher, a tale he cannot stop recounting, but then hastily notes that he could hardly believe it was happening. He is almost as eager to report that the "blind Yorkshire socialist and proletarian David Blunkett" (three of the descriptive terms are accurate) observed how a brilliant lecture by Hitchens reduced a Tribune meeting to absolute silence, but adds in a touchingly self-effacing manner that he doesn't remember the silence "being quite so absolute". He feels, he tells us, "absurdly honoured" to be grouped in the public mind with such great scholars as Richard Dawkins and Daniel Dennett. "Absurdly" because such parity is absurd, or "absurdly" because it is no more than his due?

"At the cocktail party afterwards, Norman Mailer, Gore Vidal and Susan Sontag were all vying rather comically for my attention, an undignified scramble that lowered the lot of them in my ineradicably sceptical English eyes." Hitchens did not in fact write this sentence, but it is surprising that he did not. Like "that great Cornish queen, A L Rowse", whom young Comrade H is clearly tickled pink to have sat beside at a sumptuous All Souls dinner, he is "lost in conceit".

Speaking of Gore Vidal, there is a fulsome comment by him about Hitchens on the dust jacket; but because Hitchens has fallen out with him over the downing of the World Trade Center, he has, as a man of principle, scored the comment through in proof and scribbled a "no" beside it. The dust jacket reproduces the proof. Fortunately, however, he has crossed out Vidal's remarks very lightly, which allows us still to read them.

It is not that Hitchens is blind to his own schizoid nature. On the contrary, he makes considerable play of the tension between prole-loving Chris and arse-licking Christopher, *Socialist Worker* and John Sparrow, Prometheus and Oscar Wilde (both men he would have liked to be). He is not at all coy about his life as a double agent. On one page he indulges in a curious flight of nostalgia for the working-class movement, yet in a footnote elsewhere he seems rather chuffed that he may have been the recipient of Oswald Mosley's last missive. He relishes portraying his courageous student self taking part in demos and sit-downs, being carted off by the police and hauled before magistrates, and all in the cause of a politics for which he can now scarcely conceal his middle-aged contempt.

What others would see as squalid social climbing, gross opportunism and a greedy desire to have it every possible way, he himself seems to regard as both clever and amusing. (He has it every possible way in more senses than one, boasting of having bedded two young Oxford men who became cabinet ministers under Thatcher. Sodomy can be yet another route to success.) He also trumpets how he once "toyed" with a lesbian girlfriend of the youthful Bill Clinton, no doubt the only way he can claim intimacy with a man who can't stomach him.

It is as though he sees his own double-dealing as a rather agreeable versatility – as testimony to his myriad-mindedness rather than as a privileged, spoilt-brat desire (among other things) to hog it all. One is reminded of the scatty socialite in Evelyn Waugh's *Vile Bodies* who had heard talk of an Independent Labour Party and was furious that she had not been invited.

If one can swallow one's vomit at some of this, there is much in the book to enjoy. Hitchens writes with admirable seriousness and passion about the 11 September 2001 attacks, Poland, Cuba, Iraq and a good deal more. The old bellicose champion of human liberties and decencies is still alive and well. There is a vastly entertaining account of London literary life, and a chapter on the Rushdie affair that magnificently displays all the finest qualities of a long-standing critic of autocracy and injustice.

Paul Foot, Hitchens writes, was "perhaps the person with whom it was hardest to identify the difference between the way he thought and felt and the principled manner in which he lived and behaved". And with whom is it the easiest? ●

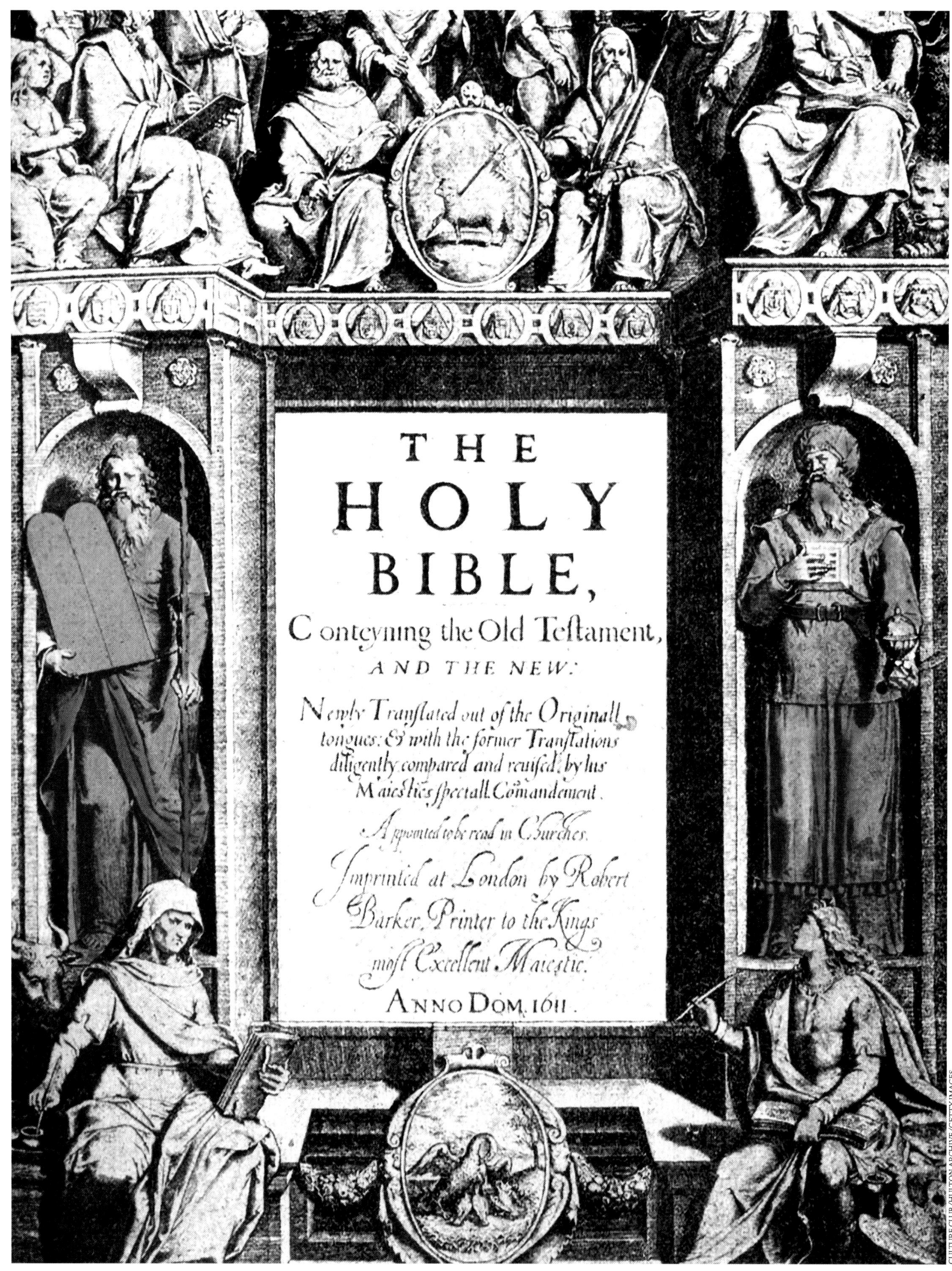

THE

HOLY

BIBLE,

Conteyning the Old Teſtament,

AND THE NEW:

Newly Tranſlated out of the Originall tongues: & with the former Tranſlations diligently compared and reuiſed, by his Maieſties ſpeciall Cōmandement.

Appointed to be read in Churches.

Imprinted at London by Robert Barker, Printer to the Kings moſt Excellent Maieſtie.

ANNO DOM. 1611.

CULTURE CLUB/HULTON ARCHIVE/GETTY IMAGES

The frontispiece of the 1611 King James Version. This is the text that followers of the Reformation recognised as the Word of God

Why I Love the Bible

By Richard Dawkins

The King James Bible occupies nearly 42 pages of the *Oxford Dictionary of Quotations*, only narrowly beaten by Shakespeare, with 45. Not just literature in the high sense but everyday speech is laced, suffused – riddled, even – with biblical phrases, the status of which ranges from telling quotation ("They have sown the wind and they shall reap the whirlwind") to cliché ("No peace for the wicked"). Although I wouldn't call the Bible my ewe lamb, and I would have to go the extra mile before I killed the fatted calf for it, you don't need the wisdom of Solomon to see how biblical imagery dominates our English.

It has to be the King James version, of course. Modern translations break the spell as surely as a sounding brass or a tinkling cymbal. Listen to this, if you can bear to, from the Good News Bible, whose clunking title matches its style:

> It is useless, useless, said the Philosopher. Life is useless, all useless./You spend your life working, labouring, and what do you have to show for it?

Older readers might hear the voice of Tony Hancock. Or is it Victor Meldrew? Anyway, now here's the real thing:

> Vanity of vanities, saith the Preacher, vanity of vanities, all is vanity./What profit hath a man of all his labour which he taketh under the sun?

Real thing? Well, let me not emulate that notorious slogan against the teaching of Spanish in Texas schools: "If English was good enough for Jesus Christ, it's good enough for the children of Texas." Hebrew, alas, is a sealed book to me (yes, that's another one: Isaiah 29:11), but poetry can gain in translation, and I believe this may have been achieved with the King James Bible.

It is often said that the Bible is not a book but a library. Obviously unable to cover it all, I shall attend to my two favourite books, neighbours in the Old Testament: Ecclesiastes and the Song of Songs. First, the world-weary Preacher's lament for the passing of youth and the privations of old age.

> Remember now thy Creator in the days of thy youth, while the evil days come not, nor the years draw nigh, when thou shalt say, I have no pleasure in them.

Compare that to the Good News version:

> So remember your Creator while you are still young, before those dismal days and years come when you will say, "I don't enjoy life."

"I don't enjoy life"? How are the mighty fallen! If I can't have poetry, I'd prefer the frankness of my godfather who died this year at the age of 93. "Richard, old age is a bugger."

My theory is that translation, and even mistranslation, can sometimes enhance the poetry. Here's an example.

> ... in the day when the keepers of the house shall tremble, and the strong men shall bow themselves, and the grinders cease because they are few, and those that look out of the windows be darkened,/And the doors shall be shut in the streets, when the sound of the grinding is low, and he shall rise up at the voice of the bird, and all the daughters of musick shall be brought low ...

Translation, and even mistranslation, can enhance the poetry

Those "grinders" have always intrigued me, and I have been especially haunted by "when the sound of the grinding is low". Some sort of ancient mill rumbled through my imagination. But the Good News Bible finds a more down-to-earth meaning of grinders and "those that look out of the windows". It's simply that the poor old chap had cataracts (darkened windows) and lost his teeth ("grinders" is kin to Wodehousian "snappers"). That may be less poetic, but it has the ring of plausibility. Hebrew scholars may correct me, but I suspect that this Good News banality may be closer to the original than my much-loved 1611 flight of poetry.

Naturally, I have to come down on the side of accuracy, even at the expense of poetry. From the religious point of view, however, I can't help wondering whether accuracy of translation is desirable. If you are trying to persuade people to follow your religion, do you really want them to understand it? When the Roman Church gave up Latin, the congregations suddenly saw, with merciless clarity, exactly what it was they had been reciting all those years.

After Ecclesiastes, my second favourite book of the Bible is the Song of Solomon (not by Solomon, needless to say):

> For, lo, the winter is past, the rain is over and gone;/The flowers appear on the earth; the time of the singing of birds is come, and the voice of the turtle is heard in our land ...

I regret the day I first learned the real meaning of "turtle" in this lovely passage, and I am not about to shatter anybody else's illusions by exposing the mistranslation. On the other hand, I admit to being curious about what the other hand is really doing in this passage:

> Stay me with flagons, comfort me with apples: for I am sick of love./His left hand is under my head, and his right hand doth embrace me.

If that means what I think it means, coupled with "My beloved put in his hand by the hole of the door, and my bowels were moved for him", it casts into an even funnier light the charming Bowdlerism that heads the page: "The mutual love of Christ and his church".

Let's celebrate the 400th anniversary of this astonishing piece of English literature. Warts and all – for I have not mentioned the carnage, the smiting, the vindictive, genocidally racist, jealous monster god of the Old Testament. Warts and all – for I have drawn a veil over the New Testament misogyny of Paul, the founder of Christianity, or the Pauline obscenity of every baby being born in sin, saved only by the divine scapegoat suffering on the cross because the Creator couldn't think of a better way to forgive everybody.

Warts and all, let's encourage our schools to bring this precious English heritage to all our children, whatever their background, not as history, not as science and not (oh, please not) as morality. But as literature. ●

The Rest of Life

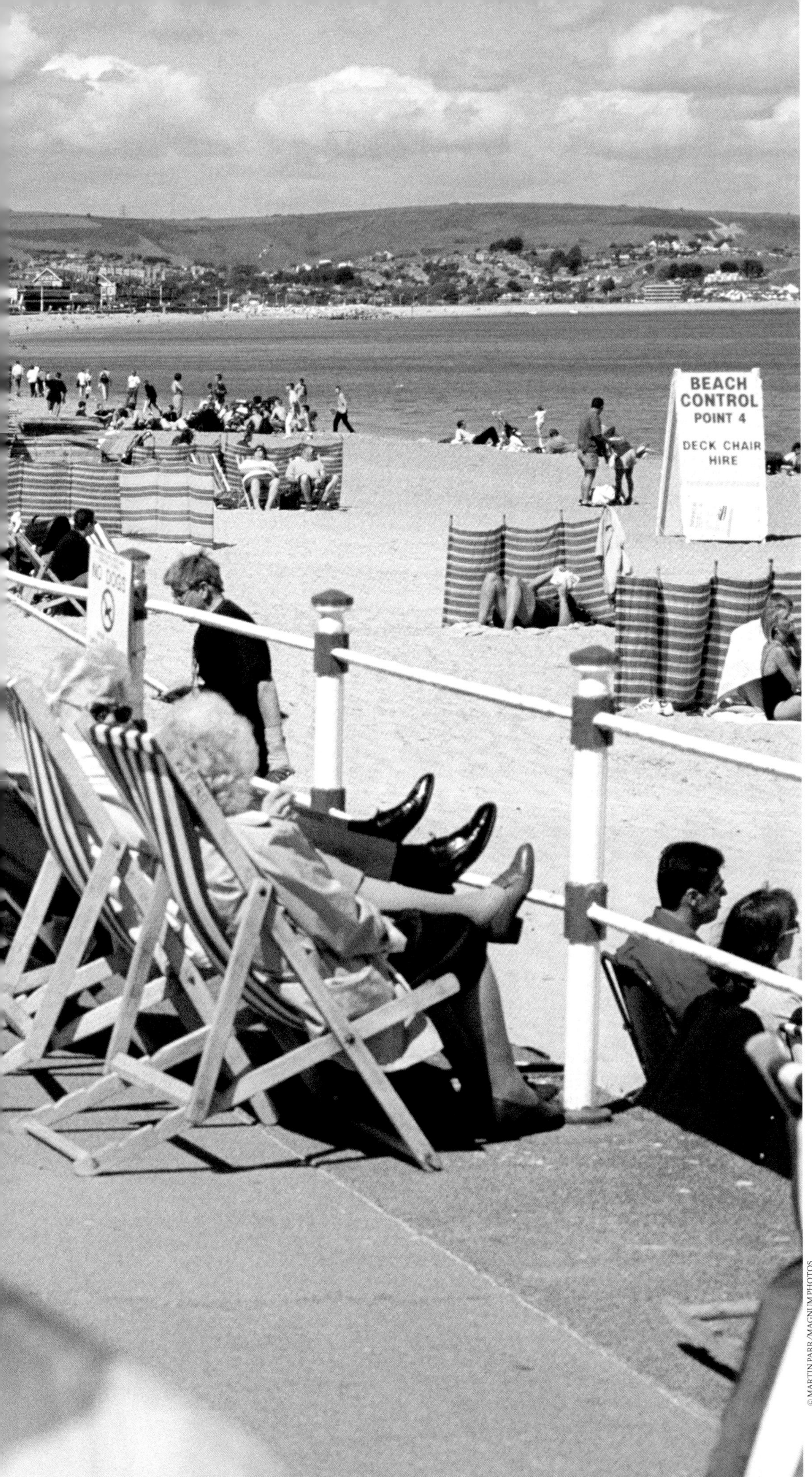

Turned out nice again: a bright day in Weymouth draws sunseekers to the beach, 2000

Nature's Verdict

By Lens

Dr Caleb Saleeby was a physician and writer, and an adviser to the ministry of food control. Writing under the pseudonym Lens, he was commissioned by the New Statesman to explain the scientific issues of the day; even when, as in this report on infant mortality, his verdict was distasteful to many readers.

Bradford offers its newcomers what would appear to be every possible advantage. The city has long been prosperous, both before the war and since 1914. Owing to the importance of wool, it has latterly become more prosperous than ever, and recent figures show that, in such matters as subscriptions to war-charities and so forth, Bradford takes the lead. In proportion to its numbers, about 300,000, it is perhaps the wealthiest community in the United Kingdom. Further, it is extremely generous. The citizens give freely to all manner of good causes, and the municipality is as generous as the citizens. It spends some £20,000 a year on infancy alone, and this sum is duplicated by the Local Government Board, so that the few babies of Bradford, born into a community of extremely high general prosperity, also have £40,000 a year spent on their special interests—this working out at the highest rate of expenditure on infancy of any part of these islands.

Given these two large facts we must ascertain only a third in this part of the picture. Is the money also spent wisely? The answer again is superlative. All things considered, it is probable that Bradford spends its money on infancy more skilfully, with more foresight, science and co-ordination than any other municipality in this country.

They have, for instance, the finest system of municipal midwifery in the country—so good that visitors from the United States and the Continent used to be sent to study it when they asked the highest authority at the Local Government Board what was really worth seeing. There is also what should perhaps logically have been named first, a splendid system of free feeding for expectant mothers. The mothers, however, are so prosperous—note this well—that they do not patronise their feeding centre, which has been converted into a national kitchen. The Infant Department is a model of its kind. No municipality or private person should attempt to set up such a place without making a careful and prolonged study of Bradford's truly admirable Infant Department in all its details of method and equipment. I hope to study such things in New York and other Transatlantic cities in a few weeks, but at the moment I do not see how Bradford could be surpassed in this respect.

> Wealthy, generous, scientific Bradford is dying out

Bradford now has a fine ante-natal equipment, and it has adopted, from the United States, the system of milk grading and certification which the Ministry of Food and Mr Wilfred Buckley, the Director of Milk Supplies, rightly desire to introduce throughout this country. What they hope for, Bradford has already done.

And now, you ask, what are the results? Well, the answer is a blow in the face—very nearly but not quite a knock-out blow. What I have described has been running for many years now, with steady improvement in principle and detail. Further, those who work for the babies have had what is almost universally proclaimed to be the immense advantage of a very low birth-rate, which has fallen from year to year, so that their task of saving the few babies that were born should have been easier each year than the year before. The upshot is an infant mortality which now stands at about 135, with no notable improvement for many years, and against a birth-rate which was only 13.06 in 1917 and probably less, according to a provisional estimate, last year. The general death-rates for those two years were, 1917, 14.6 1918 (provisional) 18.0. The influenza was a large factor of last year's death-rate and the war affected all the figures of the last two years, but when the most liberal discount is made for these exceptional factors, the conclusion remains that wealthy, generous, scientific Bradford is dying out and that these wonderful and admirable efforts to save it seem futile. The explanation that the stock is inherently defective is immediately negatived by the quality of many of the living and by the record in the war of Bradford's splendid soldiers (whose deaths are *not* included, observe, in the dreadful figures foregoing).

Before we attempt to interpret what seems an absurdity, and to show that it is really a paradox (which is a *seeming* absurdity), let us help ourselves by looking at the second picture, which I have chosen because of the extreme contrast which it offers to Bradford in every particular I have named—and, above all, in the one particular which I have designedly refrained from naming. (Have you already asked yourself, "Yes, yes, but what about—?") ▶

A young health service: (top) boys line up for a dose of medicine and (below) mothers and children queue outside a communal kitchen set up at a Bradford gas showroom, 1940

THE BECKLEY FOUNDATION PUBLIC LETTER

THE GLOBAL WAR ON DRUGS HAS FAILED IT IS TIME FOR A NEW APPROACH

WE THE UNDERSIGNED call on Governments and Parliaments to recognise that:

More than fifty years after the 1961 UN Single Convention on Narcotic Drugs was launched, the global war on drugs has failed, and has had many unintended and devastating consequences worldwide.

Use of the major controlled drugs has risen, and supply is cheaper, purer and more available than ever before. The UN conservatively estimates that there are now 250 million drug users worldwide.

Illicit drugs are now the third most valuable industry in the world, after food and oil, estimated to be worth over $350 billion a year, all in the control of criminals.

Fighting the war on drugs costs the world's taxpayers incalculable billions each year. Millions of people are in prison worldwide for drug-related offences, mostly personal users and small-time dealers.

Corruption amongst law-enforcers and politicians, especially in producer and transit countries, has spread as never before, endangering democracy and civil society. Stability, security and development are threatened by the fallout from the war on drugs, as are human rights. Tens of thousands of people die in the drug war each year.

The drug-free world so confidently predicted by supporters of the war on drugs is further than ever from attainment. The policies of prohibition create more harms than they prevent. We must seriously consider shifting resources away from criminalising tens of millions of otherwise law abiding citizens, and move towards an approach based on health, harm-reduction, cost-effectiveness and respect for human rights. Evidence consistently shows that these health-based approaches deliver better results than criminalisation.

Improving our drug policies is one of the key policy challenges of our time. It is time for world leaders to fundamentally review their strategies in response to the drug phenomenon.

At the root of current policies lies the 1961 UN Single Convention on Narcotic Drugs. It is time to re-examine this treaty which imposes a 'one-size-fits-all' solution, in order to allow individual countries the freedom to explore drug policies that better suit their domestic needs.

As the production, demand and use of drugs cannot be eradicated, new ways must be found to minimise harms, and new policies, based on scientific evidence, must be explored.

Let us break the taboo on debate and reform. The time for action is now.

Yours faithfully,

President Juan Manuel Santos
President of the Republic of Colombia

President Otto Pérez Molina
President of the Republic of Guatemala

President Jimmy Carter
Former President of the United States, ***Nobel Prize*** *winner*

President Fernando H. Cardoso
Former President of Brazil

President César Gaviria
Former President of Colombia

President Vicente Fox
Former President of Mexico

President Ruth Dreifuss
Former President of Switzerland

President Lech Wałęsa
Former President of Poland, ***Nobel Prize*** *winner*

President Alexander Kwaśniewski
Former President of Poland

George P. Schultz
Former US Secretary of State

Desmond Tutu
Archbishop, ***Nobel Prize*** *winner*

Mario Vargas Llosa
Writer, ***Nobel Prize*** *winner*

Dr. Kary Mullis
Chemist, ***Nobel Prize*** *winner*

Professor Sir Harold Kroto
Chemist, ***Nobel Prize*** *winner*

Professor John Polanyi
Chemist, ***Nobel Prize*** *winner*

Professor Kenneth Arrow
Economist, ***Nobel Prize*** *winner*

Professor Thomas C. Schelling
Economist, ***Nobel Prize*** *winner*

Professor Sir Peter Mansfield
Physicist, ***Nobel Prize*** *winner*

Professor Sir Anthony Leggett
Physicist, ***Nobel Prize*** *winner*

Professor Martin L. Perl
Physicist, ***Nobel Prize*** *winner*

Wislawa Szymborska
Poet, ***Nobel Prize*** *winner*

Sir Richard Branson
Entrepreneur, founder of Virgin Group

Sting
Musician and actor

Yoko Ono
Musician and artist

Carlos Fuentes
Novelist and essayist

Gilberto Gil
Former Minister of Culture, Brazil

Sean Parker
Founding President of Facebook, Spotify

Thorvald Stoltenberg
Former UN High Commissioner, Refugees

Louise Arbour, CC, GOQ
Former UN High Commissioner, Human Rights

Javier Solana, KOGF, KCMG
Former Secretary General, EU Council

Amanda Feilding
Director, the Beckley Foundation

For a full list of signatories, see www.beckleyfoundation.org/public-letter

▶ Let us go almost where you will in the West of Ireland or, for choice, since the figures are in my head, to County Roscommon, in Connaught. Instead of wealth here is poverty, as extreme as Bradford's prosperity. Instead of Bradford's applied science, here is ignorance—nay, the people's heads are largely crammed with active superstition. In many particulars we see Ignorance in Action, which Goethe called the most dangerous thing in the world. The public and explicit provision for infancy is really best left undescribed. No one would visit or send others to visit Roscommon in order to admire its medical, nursing, ante-natal, obstetric, housing, municipal or voluntary resources. The birth-rate, when standardised to correspond to the number of women of reproductive age, is extremely high. The figure is about 45 or more. In other words, the families are enormous. Now, in very many cases, the birth-rate and death-rate, especially the infant death-rate, go together. Where many babies are born, their death-rate is high; and conversely. This high positive correlation between birth and death-rate is exploited by the Neo-Malthusians who, begging the question, assume, and base all their anti-Socialist teaching, all their propaganda against poverty, on the assumption that *correlation* is *causation*, that the way to lower a death-rate is to lower the birth-rate. Bradford and Roscommon prove instantaneously that the Neo-Malthusians are guilty of the commonest of all fallacies—to confound correlation with causation. In this, as in hosts of cases in every domain of being, results which are causally independent may and will vary together—show a positive correlation—if, for instance, they be both due to the same cause or set of causes. I do not assert that there is never any causal relation between birth-rates and death-rates; but I do assert that the cases I have cited dispose of the fundamental Malthusian contention, which is clearly an example, supremely dangerous, of the common fallacy.

What, then, is the infant mortality of Roscommon, with its very high birth-rate and its plentiful lack of all those good things which Bradford provides so abundantly? Well, about 35, as compared with Bradford's 135. It is the most significant and astonishing contrast in all the vital statistics that I have ever seen. Omitting 1918, because of the influenza, let me give approximate figures for a typical year in juxtaposition:—

	Birth-rate	**Infant Death-rate**
Bradford	13	135
Roscommon	45	35

It may be said that this is the contrast between town and country. But that is not so; there are country places—not in Ireland—with figures of the order of Bradford's, and the figures of Huddersfield, for instance, which has the influence of Mr Benjamin Broadbent, our great practical pioneer, are very different to Bradford's, with the expenditure of very much less money. Further, the infant mortality of Germany and Holland is higher in the country than in the towns. As for the palpable nonsense which has been written about urban smoke, I have disposed of that elsewhere, and so may anyone else who compares, for instance, the respective mortalities of Jewish and English babies in Leeds or of Jewish, Irish and English babies in Whitechapel. That smoke theory ends where it began.

The world-famous student who was until recently our highest official on this subject told me that, with all my praise of Bradford, I had forgotten one omission—that there is "not enough domiciliary visitation" in Bradford. I am not an official, and will simply call that home-visiting, for the shorter word is the key to all. But why is there not enough home-visiting?

> The one thing that supremely matters is the mother

Because there are no homes—or very few. In all the foregoing I have not so much as hinted at the one thing that supremely matters—the mother, the natural saviour of the baby. I have written, in the modern style, as if we were not mammals. I have ignored the fundamental sin of Bradford and our civilisation against the laws of life. I do not use the word in a theological sense, for I am not a theologian; here it suffices to be a biologist and a mammal.

In Bradford the mothers are incomplete. Some 90 per cent of them go out to work. The home disappears. "Humanised" milk, which was cows' milk before "humanisation" and is cows' milk still—the only way to humanise milk being to pass it through a human mother—feeds young Bradford and young Bradford dies. The modern fashion in skirts has permitted me, this afternoon, in walking three hundred yards in Bradford, to see more bow-legs—that is, rickets—than I would see in a lifetime in the West of Ireland. Our Continental friends and enemies call rickets the English disease, as they may; and the Irish may call it so, too, if they will.

Here industry flourishes, and when the mills close we see the procession of mothers rushing to the hovels where they left their babies in the morning. Production is maintained, wealth aggregated, by the accursed industrial system which breaks up the home, tempts the mother or the possible mother to worship the Calf of Gold in place of the Child of Life, to prevent conception, to procure abortion, or to desert her child if, despite all her efforts, she has one. So Money is to blame after all, despite the splendid generosity of the municipality. It is the worship of the false god called Mammon, which is idolatry; and the wages of sin is racial death.

In Roscommon the mothers are mammals still. The home may not be visited, but it is a home. The housing is poor enough, but the homing is the real thing. The baby is in its poor, ignorant, ignored mother's arms, its lips are at her nipple, and it lives and thrives. If we could add what Bradford has to what Roscommon has, infant mortality and infant damage would practically disappear. (This for Mr Chesterton, who would seem to infer a condemnation of infant welfare work from a recent comment on these figures. Does he know what Mr Broadbent's admirable visitors have achieved in Huddersfield, where many homes still remain, or how welcome they naturally are in the homes they help?) I assume, of course, that the mother *can* safely be a mother—for syphilis is almost unknown in rural Ireland; whilst I need hardly say that it is rife and increasing in Bradford, as the latest dreadful figures from the Infant Department show. In a word, infant mortality and racial survival are social problems of motherhood. If the social problem of motherhood be solved, the doctor and the student and the visitor are nearly superfluous; if it be not solved, they are nearly futile.

In Bradford, as elsewhere, the manufacturers and the mothers, backed by public departments such as the Ministry of Munitions, are in favour of maintaining the system of prostituting motherhood to machinery which the war of necessity aggravated. I raise this protest against these powerful forces, to which many aggressive brands of anti-female feminism may be added. Those old figures from Birmingham, which show the scarcely astonishing fact that a baby starving to death through poverty is more likely to live if its mother goes out and earns money for food, will be cited against me but will evidently leave my withers unwrung. Survey the range of life, insect, fish, reptile, bird, mammal from monotreme and marsupial—duckmole and kangaroo—up to the tiny grey squirrel I saw in Kensington Gardens on Easter Monday, chased by a horde of horrible boys, carrying its baby in its mouth, running up a tree, jumping from a slender oscillating branch to that of the next tree, which held its nest where it left its young in high safety; and so on to cat and dog and monkey and ape and man and you cannot but be assured that Bradford expresses, like the illegitimate death-rate anywhere, the consequences of the fundamental social crime, which is to divorce mothers and children, whilst Roscommon, like the sub-human races I have named, expresses the verdict of wisdom—Whom Nature hath joined together let not man put asunder. ●

On Talking and Not Talking to People on Trains

By Hilaire Belloc

In the matter of talking (and not talking) to people in trains there would seem to be two branches, according to whether one wants to talk in trains and be talked to, or whether one doesn't. So that the subject naturally divides itself into two sciences, or arts, which may be collectively called "silentiarum vel gabbalarum cultus"—the art of making people talk to you although they don't want to—and the art of making them stop talking to you when they do.

We will begin with the simplest side, which is the art of stopping people who want to talk to one in trains. The amateur's way, which for my part I greatly despise, is to answer briefly, growl, frown, continue reading, begin writing jerkily upon the margin of the paper, and so on. You have all done it. It is ill-bred, uncharitable, leaves a bad atmosphere in the carriage and, what is worse, is often unsuccessful. There are other ways.

The first and best (but it needs what parsons call "character") is to reply by contradictions.

The enemy says, "It looks as if it were going to rain." You answer as offensively as you can, "Not it!" The meekest man will bridle up and say, "Oh, you don't think so, don't you?" Then you answer, "No, I don't!" and the chances are he dries up.

Another way, more dangerous, but exceedingly useful, is to feign madness. You need not go so far as that peer who, now not long since, would, when anyone spoke to him in a train, pull out a large Norwegian knife and begin to strop it lustily upon the window strap. It is enough to answer intriguingly.

The enemy says, "It is going to rain." You put on a cunning idiot look, you lisp and say, "Ah, that's right!" with which you smack your lips and roll your eyes. It should frighten him off. If the first check is not enough and he tries to go on nervously by asking whether you mind rain, lean forward to him with a meaning look, wink and say, "No, I like it!—and there's a reason!"

I have no room to go into the four other classic methods of stopping conversation in trains, for I have now to deal with the sister art of luring into conversation those who are determined not to talk at all. The first and sovereign method is not of my own experience at all, but was told me by another.

It seems you can nearly always get the poor blighter to break silence, however determined he may be not to talk, if you have a companion; and the method is to say to this companion (if you have no companion, any honest-faced stranger will do), "I am glad they have put Wembley on the site of the old Crystal Palace." Your companion must answer that they did not know where Wembley was but that they are glad to hear it. (If you are handling a stranger, he will deny your statement.) Then must you begin to curse and to swear, and to say that you are absolutely positive, and that you were there only yesterday and part of the remains of the horrible old conservatory were still standing. It is impossible for a Trappist to stand up against such an attack. The most silent man will burst out against your monstrous lie. Then it is for you to play him. Allow yourself to be gradually convinced; but do not gaff him into your basket until he is tired out. Get a run for your money.

> People in trains, unlike the rest of the human race, have very kind hearts

Another way is to stretch out of the window, clutch the door, stare forward and shout, "Oh, my God!" It does not work unless you put your head right out of the window. The dupe will think there is going to be an accident and will ask you in alarm what is the matter. You must then affect relief and say, "The danger is past!" making up I know not what lie, but having thoroughly shaken him up. The chances are that he will go on talking, and you must lure him to this by a detailed description of some interesting accident of which you will say that you were a witness, although you were not. He will then tell you that his uncle was in a railway accident. This also will be a lie. But you will go on to ask him whether he remembers accidents in the past, and the fire will be well alight and burning merrily.

Another way (so contemptibly easy that I hardly recommend it) is to feign sudden illness. People in trains, unlike the rest of the human race, have very kind hearts. You need not shriek; a few groans are enough, and who knows but that the fellow may have a flask upon him? When you are better, you will find yourself fast friends in full conversation.

Yet another method, savouring somewhat of the first, but in a chapter by itself, is to sit down comfortably after the train has started for a long non-stop journey (as to Bath) and say, "Well, that's all right! A fair run to Swindon!" There is no living man—no, not even though he were dumb—who will not be moved to speech by this trick. On hearing that the train will not stop at Swindon you must make a convulsive gesture to catch the little chain which runs through the carriage and costs £5. The enemy will certainly seize your wrist if you are slow enough. Allow yourself to be persuaded. Tell him in great detail the dreadful consequences that follow your failing to meet your aunt at Swindon. You will have a long and pleasant conversation all the way to Bath. You will be the more certain of this happy issue if you make the story turn upon money. For appetite, avarice and fear are the three motives of the human race. Appetite is often lulled to sleep, fear you may not be able to excite, but to avarice you can always appeal by bringing in some talk of money.

And this leads me to my last method. You can always provoke conversation in trains by the prospect of gains whether it shines or whether it rains. If the stubborn man will not yield to a hint of gain in stocks, try horses. If he will not yield to horses, tell him about a reward (offered by the railway company) for anyone who will spot cracked walls along the line. If that fails, talk of some way of doing the journey cheaper. Anyhow bring in money and you will milk conversation as by a sort of physical necessity of the noble, human mind, which is always charged with an overburdening consideration of money.

I say "my last"; but I wish to add one more. Ask your opponent for a match. When he has given it to you, let it go out and ask for another; then ask for a third. There will be objection, apology, and you will be a witless man if you cannot hook such origins on to a really interesting discussion upon the fate of the soul, the future of Great Britain, cancer, or whatever else may take your fancy. ●

We Must Drift: A Letter from Joseph Conrad

By Joseph Conrad

Joseph Conrad was born Józef Teodor Konrad Korzeniowski in 1857 to ethnically Polish parents living in western Ukraine. After a time in the British merchant navy, "Conrad" became a British citizen in 1886. The following letter was written the previous year at a time when Conrad had not yet achieved full fluency in English. The letter, addressed to a Polish friend, remained unpublished until 1935 when the naval officer and politician Oliver Stillingfleet Locker-Lampson offered it to the New Statesman with the permission of the addressee's family. H G Wells wrote in his 1934 autobiography that Conrad never quite managed to speak English without a Polish accent but, as this letter shows, at 28 he was already mastering the language in which he later wrote novels, short stories and essays. Conrad died in 1924.

Joseph Conrad in 1903, by Sir William Rothenstein

December 19th, 1885
Calcutta

My Dear Sir,

I received your kind and welcome letter yesterday, and to-day being Sunday, I feel that I could not make better use of my leisure hours than in answering your missive. By this time, you and the rest of the "right thinking" have been grievously disappointed by the result of the General Election. The newly enfranchised idiots have satisfied the yearnings of Mr Chamberlain's hoard by cooking the national goose according to his recipe. The next culinary operation will be a "pretty kettle of fish"—of an international character! Joy reigns in St Petersburg—no doubt, and profound disgust in Berlin; the International Socialist Association are triumphant, and every disreputable *ragamuffin in Europe feels that the day of universal brotherhood, despoliation and disorder is coming apace, and nurses day dreams of well plenished pockets amongst the ruins of all that is respectable, venerable and Holy.* The great British Empire went over the edge and got on to the inclined plane of social progress and radical reform! *The downward movement is hardly Perceptible yet and the clever men who started it may flatter themselves with the mistaken and delusive sense of their power to direct the great body in its progress; but they will soon find that the fate of the nation is out of hands now!* The Alpine avalanche rolls quicker and quicker as it nears the abyss—its ultimate destination! Where's the man to stop the crashing avalanche?

Where's the man to stop the rush of social, democratic idiocy? The opportunity and the day have come—and are gone, believe me gone for ever. For the sun is set and the last barrier removed. England was the only barrier to the pressure of infernal doctrines born in continental back-slums. Now there is nothing!

The destiny of this nation and of all nations is to be accomplished in darkness amidst much weeping and gnashing of teeth, to pass through robbery, equality, anarchy and misery under the iron rule of a military despotism. Such is the lesson of history! Such is the lesson of common-sense logic!

Socialism must inevitably end in Cesarism.

Forgive me this long disquistion; but your letter—so earnest on the subject must be my excuse. I understand you perfectly. You wish to apply remedies to quell the dangerous symptoms; you evidently hope yet——. I do so no longer. Truthfully I have ceased to hope a long time ago. We must drift!

The whole herd of idiotic humanity are moving in that direction at the bidding of unscrupulous rascals, and a few sincere and dangerous lunatics. Those things must be. It is a fatality!

I live mostly in the past—and in the future. The present has—you easily understand—few charms for me. I look with the serenity of despair and the indifference of contempt upon passing events. Disestablishment, Land Reform, universal brotherhood are but like milestones on the Road to Ruin. The end will be awful — no doubt! Neither you nor I shall live to see the final crash; although we may both turn in our graves when it comes for we both feel deeply and sincerely. Still there is no earthly remedy. All is vanity . . . !

This is signed,
Yours very sincerely and faithfully,
K N Korzeniowski

Mothers turn their backs on their babies and strain for a glimpse of Princess Margaret as she opens the final flats on the Tachbrook estate, Westminster, 1953

TOPICAL PRESS AGENCY/HULTON ROYALS COLLECTION/GETTY IMAGES

22 OCTOBER 1955

The Royal Soap Opera

By Malcolm Muggeridge

There probably are quite a lot of people—more than might be supposed—who, like myself, feel that another newspaper photograph of a member of the royal family will be more than they can bear. Even Princess Anne, a doubtless estimable child, becomes abhorrent by constant repetition. Already she has that curious characteristic gesture of limply holding up her hand to acknowledge applause. The Queen Mother, the Duke of Edinburgh, Nanny Lightbody, Group Captain Townsend—the whole show is utterly out of hand, and there is a much graver danger than might superficially appear that a strong reaction against it may be produced.

This attitude of adulatory curiosity towards the royal family is, of course, something quite new. *Punch* in the nineteenth century made full use, for instance, of the rich vein of satirical material provided by the Royal Dukes, and in our own time Max Beerbohm found the reigning monarch a natural subject, along with all the eminent, for caricature. All this was very healthy. It presupposed a respect for the institution of monarchy, and a sense that the incumbents were, like us all, mortal men and women. Let us beware lest, in adulating the incumbents, in insulating them from the normal hazards of public life, we jeopardise the institution. It is, of course, true that the present royal family are much more respectable than most of their Hanoverian ancestors, and therefore lend themselves less to satire. But to put them above laughter, above criticism, above the workaday world, is, ultimately, to dehumanise them and risk the monarchy dying of acute anaemia.

It may be argued that it is the general public who require this adulation of the royal family, and that the newspapers, magazines and the BBC, in catering for it, are merely meeting the public's requirement in this, as they do in any other field. Undoubtedly it is true that a picture in colour of the Queen or Princess Margaret is a circulation-builder. Equally undoubtedly it is true that the unspeakable Crawfie, and all the other dredgers up of unconsidered trifles in the lives of members of the royal family, down to and including Godfrey Winn, provide popular features. It may even be true (though there is no means of proving this) that those portentous, unctuous BBC announcements, with "the Queen and the Duke of Edinburgh" rolled off the tongue like a toastmaster at a particularly awesome Guildhall banquet—that even these are liked by listeners. Personally, I came to feel, during the recent royal tour, that it was better to sacrifice the news than endure them.

The fact remains that tedious adulation of the royal family is bad for them, for the public, and ultimately for the monarchical institution itself. Is there anything that can be done to check it? One step would be for the royal family to provide themselves with an efficient public relations set-up in place of the rather ludicrous courtiers who now function as such. This would enable information and photographs to be channelled out in a controlled, instead of haphazard, manner. It would also, if astutely conducted, check some of the worst abuses in the way of invasion of privacy and sheer impertinence. An experienced public relations operator knows how to distribute and withhold favours in such a manner as to maintain some measure of control over those with whom he deals. Also, he knows how to advise those on whose behalf he acts. When, for instance, this Townsend business first started it would have been his duty to convince the royal family that it was essential to make some sort of statement at once, frankly explaining the situation. Otherwise, he would have urged, there was bound to be an orgy of vulgar and sentimental speculation which could not but, in the long run, damage the whole standing and status of everyone concerned. After all, if we are to accept that the Crown is useful constitutionally even though deprived of all real power, it must be maintained with some dignity. A Lord Chancellor who was constantly providing material for the commoner sort of magazine and newspaper feature would soon be considered unsuitable for his high office. Likewise a Speaker of the House of Commons or a Lord Chamberlain. How much more, then, is this true of the royal family?

Of course it is not their fault, though I suspect that they develop a taste for the publicity, which, in theory, they find so repugnant. This is merely human. Even a tiny television notoriety is liable to please, or at any rate excite, when all one's conscious being finds it vulgar and odious. At the same time, the royal family ought to be properly advised on how to prevent their lives from becoming a sort of royal soap opera.

Nothing is more difficult than to maintain the prestige of an institution which is accorded the respect and accoutrements of power without the reality. The tendency for such an institution to peter out in pure fantasy is very great. It is like the king in chess. If he ventures into the middle of the board the game is lost. He has to be kept in the background and ringed round with pieces more powerful than himself. Indeed, in a sense it could be said that popularity is fatal to monarchy. The Russian monarchy was never so popular, or treated to such scenes of insensate adulation as in 1914; and even for Farouk's wedding the streets of Cairo were crammed with cheering Egyptians. Yet when, a few years later, the Tsar and his family were cruelly shot down in a cellar no one seemed to care much, and most, if not all, eyes were dry in Egypt when Farouk made off. Extremes of public emotion are always socially dangerous. Cromwell remarked to Fairfax when they were riding through cheering crowds that the same people would have turned out as eagerly to see him hanged. It was the very fatuity of adulation and sycophancy to which King Edward VIII, as Prince of Wales, was subjected which made the reaction so much the greater when the soap opera took, from the point of view of those set in authority over us, an ugly turn. The whole question of the King's relations with Mrs Simpson might have been handled sensibly if sense had prevailed before. You cannot graft a Henry James denouement on to an Elinor Glyn novel.

As a religion, monarchy is a failure; the god-king invariably gets eaten

The probability is, I suppose, that the monarchy has become a kind of *ersatz* religion. Chesterton once remarked that when people cease to believe in God, they do not then believe in nothing, but in anything. Among other solaces, like Johnnie Ray and dreams of winning a football pool, is royalty. The people one sees staring through the railings of Buckingham Palace even when the Queen is not in residence are like forlorn worshippers at one of those shrines, whether Christian or Hindu or Buddhist, which depend on some obviously bogus miraculous happening. As a religion, monarchy has always been a failure; the god-king invariably gets eaten. Men can only remain sane by esteeming what is mortal for its mortality. I dare say what really drove the Gadarene swine mad was the thought that Group Captain Townsend was at the bottom of the cliff.

The normal middle-class attitude is to blame the press, and, heaven knows, it has excelled itself in vulgarity in dealing with the Townsend story. Yet the provocation has been very great. Has even the Foreign Office ever devised a more inept communiqué than the one about no statement of Princess Margaret's future being contemplated at present? If the intention had been to give the story another shot in the arm no more effective device could have been adopted.

This sort of thing is expected of Rita Hayworth, but the application of film-star techniques to the royal family is liable to have, in the long run, disastrous consequences. The film-star soon passes into oblivion. She has her moment and then it is all over. And even her moment depends on being able to do superlatively well whatever the public expects of her. Members of the royal family are in an entirely different situation. Their role is to symbolise the unity of a nation; to provide an element of continuity in a necessarily changing society. This is history, not the Archers, and their affairs ought to be treated as such.

If there were a republican party, as in Joseph Chamberlain's time, it might get quite a few recruits. A lot of the old arguments which pointed to the great advantages of a monarchical over an elective presidential system no longer apply. The simple fact is that the United States' Presidency today is a far more dignified institution than the British monarchy. It is accepted that the President must be "put over" by all the vast and diverse apparatus of mass communications. If the result lacks elegance, at least the impression created is of efficiency and forethought. Just imagine if Princess Margaret and Group Captain Townsend, instead of being trailed about the country (which the procedure imposed on them actually encouraged, just as T E Lawrence's avoidance of publicity necessarily brought reporters scurrying after him) and thereby, incidentally, occupying a great many police sorely needed elsewhere, had called a press conference and explained simply and in their own words just how matters stood. What a relief for us all! What a saving of acres of newsprint! The objection, no doubt, would be that such a press conference would be undignified. In fact, it wouldn't be nearly as undignified as what has happened. The royal family and their advisers have really got to make up their minds—do they want to be part of the mystique of the century of the common man or to be an institutional monarchy; to ride, as it were, in a glass coach or on bicycles; to provide the tabloids with a running serial or to live simply and unaffectedly among their subjects like the Dutch and Scandinavian royal families. What they cannot do is to have it both ways. ●

Vicky reworks the Order of the Garter motto, 1960

12 OCTOBER 1962

Manchester: Bottled Beer and Jaguars

By Frank Kermode

Nobody would say Manchester gets a good press. The pseudodoxies that are epidemic concerning it ensure that few arrive there expecting much in the way of metropolitan elegance or the sweet life. Genuine Mancunians pay no attention to these doxies anyway, but the dispassionate observer might have to admit that they are not entirely pseudo; it does rain a good deal and the quickest way out of Manchester is what they say it is. It is a smoky city, the world centre of chronic bronchitis. What do people *do* in Manchester, people who don't like dog-racing and speedway or strip-clubs? There are two First Division football teams, though City is chronically insecure. There is no very good restaurant. As to theatres, the position is catastrophic. The Halle orchestra has to play about three times as many concerts as it ought to in order to make ends meet. There are fine libraries, and the Grammar School is one of the biggest and most successful in the country; but a quick look at the reading room in the John Rylands – a great library – will serve to disprove the notion that we are all devoted to learning at the expense of the lighter bourgeois pleasures.

Nor, it must be added, do we pass our time admiring the city itself. There is a green belt, but the worst thing about Manchester is that it is unstoppable – it spreads like spilt beer. It has virtually no centre. In Liverpool everything at least seems to stop and start at the Pier Head (where commuters have to cross the river to Cheshire). In Newcastle you know you are walking home when you go uphill, because all roads plunge down to the Tyne; and from such natural declivities there derive man-made things worth looking at – controlled skylines, the severe angled beauties of Grey Street. Manchester's river is the Irwell, an almost invisible stream that divides it from Salford. Along the main London road Manchester flows into Stockport, a town affording some sad smoky Victorian spectacles – steep escarpments and bold viaducts – but third-rate, it must be admitted, with Fourth Division football. This is Cheshire, densely spotted with colonies of Mancunian suburbia. The city of Manchester itself has a few acres – threatened by proliferating office-blocks – that belong to a metropolis; look for the cathedral and St Anne's church and you see it all.

> The worst thing about Manchester is that it is unstoppable

From the station across the road from the cathedral diesels hourly climb the Pennines. This is a reminder that there is "good country" all round Manchester, moorland, the wonders of the Peak, the lush southern-looking fields of Cheshire.

Manchester is the heart of our densest concentration of population, and also of money. What happens to it all? By London standards property, outside the business area, is cheap. We don't go in, as a town of this size might, for opera houses. There is, by London standards again, little conspicuous consumption – there is even a certain disregard for comfort. When I moved to Manchester four years ago I decided, after a brief reconnaissance, that we should live in the Cheshire fringe, about 10 miles out, but avoiding the handful of really rich suburbs. Since then thousands of others have made the same choice. The Urban District Council we live in is the size of a large town, but it has no cinema, no restaurant, and – in the "village" itself – only one dreary pub.

This development may be standard for all suburbias; anyway, it's an aspect of a way of life that might be called blameless. But we all live here because we work in Manchester – every morning sees my Mini fidgeting among the growling Jaguars. Great cities are expected to offer scope for living it up, as well as merely living, and indeed it is said that the city has a fantastic number of clubs, busiest immediately after office hours. I understood how little I knew of this side of life when I had, last spring, to entertain a distinguished American *littérateur* who felt, after dinner, like "seeing" Manchester. Having taken advice, we started at a noted music hall, where a handful of people who seemed to have got drunk on bottled beer were bawling pop songs into a microphone. After a bit of this I remembered reading in a Sunday paper that Professor Ross of Birmingham visits Manchester to study Trinidad dialects in the West Indian clubs. High life and steel bands! A taxi put us down at a boarded-up sweetshop in Moss Side. It seemed hopeless, but we knocked for a while and were let in.

A record-player was providing jazz for four customers, whose dignified gloom made a pleasant contrast with the lachrymose hilarity of the music hall. They drank their bottled beer and told us to try another place nearby for steel bands. There, as we ordered our bottled beer, we learned that steel bands were strictly for Friday and Saturday. Abandoning the exotic, we then proceeded to what I thought a very unlikely address, practically next door to the Vice-Chancellor's lodge; it had a French name and roulette tables. The street outside was stacked with Jaguars; inside my neighbours were sedately dancing with their wives and drinking bottled beer and whisky. The roulette tables had the odds and maximum stakes painted on them. The

"What do people *do* in Manchester?": a Lowry-like scene of street life, 1962

limit seemed to be a pound, but most people were playing for half-crowns. Every time you put on sixpence for the house. The croupier kept saying, "Make your bets, it's not gambling, just a bit of fun." I lost eight half-crowns and stopped. My guest, relaxing after his long struggles with love and death, won 16 and stopped also, perhaps unable to bear the excitement. We went home – it was after 11.

I don't doubt that half a million people could have shown him a better time, but I don't take all the blame. Knowing Manchester hardly at all, I approached it with great good will, remembering that better men than I can love it. The difficulty is to find a way in, to know where the strange heart beats. The city has powerful ejection mechanisms; you are flung to the outer suburbs and only your job induces you to force your way back. The nature of Manchester is inaccessible, therefore, like its glories; these are either part of its 19th-century heritage that you don't feel entitled to, or they have been nationalized, stripped of everything specifically Mancunian, like the title of the *Guardian*.

Provincial self-sufficiency is, sadly, less justified by the facts than it was even a generation ago. London grabs everything, including the glory. Whatever takes place there that is worth talking about is exhaustively talked about. The major public subsidies to the arts are largely spent there (we have our grudging biennial visit from the Covent Garden Opera). Somehow this affects one's reception of what there is here, though of course it shouldn't. Last season there was a Halle performance of the Verdi *Requiem* that would have echoed loudly in the weekly press had it taken place at the Festival Hall. Here it was recognised as very good, but there was no London fuss. You sat and listened in workaday clothes and were turned into an emptying Manchester at twenty-past-eight. The Left Wing Coffee House was still open, and that night we supped there; it closed a week later.

Manchester people don't give a damn what London thinks about them. Ignorant southerners – I once heard a man in a Hampstead pub complaining about the stupidity of the authorities who went on holding the Grand National at Liverpool where nobody could get to see it. I am Mancunian enough to resent this kind of talk. Yet I am twice an outsider: first because I work at the University – civic, admittedly, but the ties with the city are tenuous except at high levels – and therefore a member of an out-group. Secondly I live in the fringe country. It was a mistake to do so, I now feel; anybody moving to Manchester would do well to think seriously about the big Victorian suburbs nearer the city, largely evacuated by the rich long ago, and full of parks and large inconvenient houses, rather cheap. Didsbury, the noblest of these, is alive yet solid, cosmopolitan without ceasing to be provincial. Its shops and people might provide a few nostalgic moments to exiles from the King's Road.

It would be wrong, though, to look in Didsbury for the essential Manchester, the Manchester some reader of Cardus might want to find. Not long ago – being slow to learn – I went, on a Tuesday, to a shop in St Anne's Square. The square was empty, the parking meters hooded, the shops shut. The one-way streets were turned into two-way streets, and I was glad of a quicker way than usual out of Manchester; I usually find myself, muddled by these streets, en route for Oldham. Then I noticed that there were about as many people around as usual, quietly crammed on the pavements where, 100 yards down, the great Whit processions were to pass.

A distant brass band announced their arrival. These processions have some religious basis, and I'm told there are Catholics who think the Protestant affairs are liturgically pointless. But they have other motives that only an anthropologist could uncover.

There is so much finery on the children that it is said – I don't vouch for this – that the crime figures rise sharply every year as the payments fall due. Anyway, what the band announced was that Manchester was declaring its identity, its tutelary spirit was about to make its annual epiphany. The Mancunians were either in the procession or in the silent crowd on the pavement. It seemed unlikely that I'd be able to see much even if I joined them; so I drove off, violating the silent one-way streets, towards the suburb, towards the south. The supermarket was open and doing good business. ●

Talking shop: merchants Orthodox and unorthodox in old London

JOHN MURRAY/HULTON ARCHIVE/GETTY IMAGES

23 JULY 1965

Am I a Jew?

By Bernard Levin

Well, now. I have a Jewish name, but there is many a Gentile Isaacs, so why not a Levin? I have a Jewish nose, though oddly enough, I cannot see its Jewishness in a mirror, only in a photograph. In any case, it is a meaningless test. The good Dr Morris Fishbein, who in the course of his researches into this subject undoubtedly measured more noses than any man has measured before or since, concluded that there was no such thing as a "Jewish" nose, or that if there was, it was possessed by so many undoubted Aryans that there was no way of ensuring that the Jews would win – or lose – by a nose.

There are more persuasive, though still superficial, arguments. I like Jewish food, Jewish jokes, hold some traditionally Jewish beliefs, such as the respect for learning. (I can remember to this day the shock of incredulity I had at school when a non-Jewish friend told me that he had had a great struggle to be allowed to take up his scholarship. His uneducated father's attitude – more common then than now – had been that "What was good enough for me is good enough for my son." This attitude was absolutely inconceivable in a Jewish home.)

None of this will provide any real evidence, though. I was brought up on Jewish food, and the fact that I enjoy it is only an index to the strength of early environmental influence. Jewish jokes appeal to me because of their underlying gallows-humour, which I like because I am at heart a melancholic. I still laugh when my sister tells the story of *kreplach*, not because the *goyim* can't understand it, but because of its Thurberesque suggestion of the frailty of human happiness and the prevalence of unreason.

Of course, I am begging the question. I know perfectly well that I am a Jew; what I am really inquiring into is what this means to me. Let us start with religion. I rejected Judaism more or less as soon as I was old enough to have any understanding of what religion was about. All religions have their obsessions with form, ritual, observance. I don't know whether I feel further from Judaism than from most religions because its particular observances – the dietary laws, for instance – seem to me sillier today than their equivalent in, say, Roman Catholicism; or whether the savage monotheism of Jehovah (or Nobodaddy) repels me. I think that there are parts of the Pentateuch that are about as nasty as anything I have ever read anywhere, but you might also say the same thing about St Paul.

Of course, one would have to be very dull of spirit not to find beautiful and fine some aspects of Judaism. A well-ordered *seder* (the Passover-eve family service) is a very remarkable experience – but to me largely aesthetic. I have an uncontrollable revulsion at the sight of someone lighting a cigarette from a candle (some Jews who have long rejected Judaism feel sick at the sight of someone putting a pat of butter on a steak), because I was brought up to look upon a candle as a holy thing. I no longer believe consciously that it is a holy thing, but I do believe that it is a beautiful one and its use to light a cigarette seems to me vulgar and belittling. Such objective religious sympathies as I have are with the quietist faiths, like Buddhism, on the one hand, and with a straightforward message of salvation like Christianity, on the other. I am unable in fact to accept any of them, but can imagine myself a convert to several faiths; not Judaism, however.

Race, then. Aha. First, I accept what biology and anthropology tell me about race and its attendant oceans of nonsense. There are no innate superiorities or inferiorities; even if there were, there is no such thing as a separate Jewish race, though there may be a race of Semites. (The Jews in modern times have found their greatest antagonists in the Germans and the Arabs; with the former they have many of their most deeply ingrained characteristics in common, and with the latter their very race.) There's something in this more than natural, if psychology could find it out. Besides, suppose there was a Jewish race, and I was of it; what would follow from that? There is a Negro race; membership of it implies that you are black, but need imply nothing else. So you may be a nice Jew or a nasty one, a clever or a foolish, a generous or a mean, a clubbable or a solitary. I can list my qualities and defects; more meaningfully, I can get a candid friend to do so. I can give myself marks down the list; but for the life of me I cannot see that, whatever the total, it adds up to anything I have in common with Mr Jack Solomons or Mr Ewen Montagu QC.

Which brings me to the only point at which there can any longer be room for doubt. The concept of race is too completely exploded to provide a fair test. Let us think not of race, but of psychology and characteristics. *Have* I anything in common with Mr Solomons or Mr Montagu? If so, what? And if I have not – which is what I believe – have I entirely dissolved any meaning in my own life, indeed any objective meaning at all, for the word Jew?

There is an interesting paragraph on this point by Bernard Berenson, though it seems to me to demonstrate the opposite of what he was arguing.

> A Jew is the product of being cooped up in a ghetto for over 1,200 years. His conditioning from within and without, the outer pressure driving more and more to defensive extremes, the inner clutching to rites, to practices, to values making for union and for safety, the struggle for food and survival, the lust for pre-eminence and power: all have ended in producing the Jew, regardless of what racial elements originally constituted him.

The savage monotheism of Jehovah (or Nobodaddy) repels me

Precisely; then the Jew is nothing but a conditioned reflex to a conditioned stimulus (who could have thought the behaviourists could help us here?). And although the idea seems capable of bearing the weight of a considerable structure of generalisation, it falls down as soon as you look at Israel. If a hardy, martial, fair-haired and blue-eyed people are now the heirs of Zion, surely the case for environment is proved? When Herzl's trumpet finally felled the walls of the ghetto, Jewry won her greatest victory. Why, Israel even has her own anti-Semitism, in the discrimination of the Ashkenazim against their culturally more backward brethren from the East. Perhaps it will go like this, then. While the Jews of the Diaspora become more completely assimilated – the rate of intermarriage continues to grow, generation by generation – Israel will become more and more remote from any of the traditional concepts of Jewishness. She is still heavily influenced by theocracy; but the ultimately inevitable *Kulturkampf* must break the rabbinical power and turn Israel into a modern secular state.

This may mean that the last test of the *déracinés* will become their attitude to Israel. I think I can clear myself here, even after the severest Positive Vetting. My attitude to Israel – admiration for the incredible achievements, hope that it will continue, combined with the strongest condemnation of her crime against her original Arab population and the campaign of lies waged ever since on the subject – does not mark me off in any way from a Gentile of similar political outlook. And the other obvious crude test – one's attitude to the Final Solution – I claim to pass with marks above the average, insisting that the slaughter of Russians by Stalin in not much smaller numbers and for no less wicked and senseless reasons should be equally condemned.

And I cannot see that there are any valuable babies that I risk emptying out with the bath-water of my rejection of any concept of Jewishness. I can admire Spinoza or Disraeli or Menuhin just as much without my judgment being affected by any thought of their origins, and I have the additional advantage of being able to despise Ilya Ehrenburg without any reservations.

Has it come to this? Has an idea so old and tenacious, so provocative of generosity and malice, good and evil, responsible for such prodigious outpourings of words and deeds ceased to have any meaning at all? For me, it has. Yet I must face the last logical barrier, the same in effect as the first logical barrier that surrounds Christianity. How can such an idea have survived and conquered half the world, if it is not true? Similarly, how can Jewry have survived, how indeed can she have continued to attract the attention of anti-Semitism, if there is no such thing?

Only here am I conscious of any logical weakness in my position. For to an anti-Semite I could not bring myself to deny that I am a Jew, and I would not only not dream of changing my name, but think the less of the Courtenay-Cohens and Lipschitz-Logans for doing so. Yet time will surely take care of this problem, too (plus the fact that the antis have now got somebody else to pick on; not even Dr Fishbein can measure away the Negro's blackness). The world now has no excuse for not knowing what anti-Semitism can lead to, and actually does, on the whole, show signs of amending its attitude accordingly.

And now it is the others who will be increasingly exposed as illogical. If you do not consider yourself Jewish enough to go to Israel, and not Judaistic enough to go to the synagogue, what is left but a vague necessity to belong? And this will disappear, or at any rate be dispersed, with further intermarriage and assimilation; so, of course, will the superficialities attributable to upbringing and environment.

The proprietor of my favourite Jewish restaurant tells me that a high, and growing, proportion of his customers are not Jewish. For my part, I reserve the right to go on laughing at the story of the *kreplach* while not particularly caring for the *kreplach* themselves. ●

Coming in Handy

By Bruno Holbrook (Martin Amis)

In 1973, following the publication of "The Rachel Papers", Martin Amis wrote two columns for the New Statesman as the lusty "Bruno Holbrook". The first, "Fleshspots", was a tour of Soho strip clubs of varying distinction. In the second, he reported on the erotic bankruptcy of soft-core pornography.

Realistically considered, the nude magazine is a visual aid, designed (in Kurt Vonnegut's phrase) for lonesome men "to jerk off to". Since my own early activities in the field were confined to nocturnal, torchlit perusals of household copies of *Woman's Realm* (the underwear ads) and Littlewood's Catalogues (surprisingly good value in this respect, actually), and since I had caught only the odd *Titbits* and *Parade* during my formative years, it was with some trepidation that I fanned out the glistening cache of masturbatory material assembled for the present report. If I was once so stirred by those reticent likenesses, how would I react in the era of the full-frontal and ice-hardened nipple, of the Tampax shot and the pubic close-up?

Now I think I know why there was once an American nude-mag called *Droop. Ecce femina*:

> Our pictures help to provoke those thoughts of petals, soft and silkily smooth to the fingers . . . buds flesh pink, glistening with dew as they proudly await the warm kiss of the sun to blossom round and full. Rosie . . . a bush of magical delight.
>
> There is no doubt that Stella enjoys your stares of pleasure at her luscious body. Her expression in her poses, open and honest, prove [*sic*] it . . . So what would Stella want from you? Perhaps, the answer is exactly what you would want from Stella. But, speculate as we may, with a woman you never know.

Nor you do. These paragraphs are taken from *Soho International*, the grubbiest item I had the stomach to purchase. That Rosie has nipples like cupcakes (and no visible bush, incidentally), and the splay-legged Stella might as well be rehearsing her 13 times table, is very characteristic also. The rougher the goods, the breathier the sell.

For the most part the lower-order mags are grey, dispiriting bestiaries, in which haggard and portly persons display their charms with a combination of listlessness and unalluring candour. Legs are parted, breasts cupped, derrières hoisted towards camera, while the face – in life, the sexiest part of the naked female – remains dourly stupefied or else contorted in cynical ecstasy. Now these girls are probably much on a par with some of our own imperfect consorts, and they might even prove endearing if more modestly presented. Perhaps it's with this in mind that the pimp-like copywriters encourage you to make, as it were, the girls' acquaintance. On the one hand, the nudes; on the other, the husky, nudging captions: caught in that sensual music, presumably, the subscriber grinds himself empty.

Splay-legged Stella might as well be rehearsing her 13 times table

As the quality of the mags rises the canvassers have less work to do. A publication like *New Chance*, for example, will still gawp and gloat at its sitters but won't actually caress itself with the deliciousness of it all. Similarly, editorial pressure eases and the nymphs are allowed to speak for themselves, although one way or another they usually end up stressing their scorn for monogamy, their freedom from inhibition, their empiricism in matters sexual, their firm preference for men with a sense of humour – in short, their availability. *Girl Illustrated* is fairly typical in this respect. In the current issue the lovelies are asked to air their views on the dividing line between sex and art, a debate that naturally enough centres on the performances of their more creative boyfriends in bed: "He was the most wonderful artist I ever met. But he didn't use a brush" – thus spake Zette, and thus speak most of her colleagues.

No less detumescing in its way is the house-style of the ritzier glossies. Partial exceptions include *Penthouse* and *Mayfair*, which – despite Hopkinsian nonsense along the lines of "sea-spangled, sun-stained, Suki steps in sand-summer silence", etc – limit themselves to analyses of the playmates' careers and keep-fit programmes, only rarely probing into their life-styles (ie, sex-lives). Conversely, Paul Raymond's booming monthlies, *Club International* and *Men Only*, revert to a sophisticated version of Soho's hard sell. In *Club* the photographers are permitted to gurgle on about the cuties in a free-associative style, eloquent either of disabling vacuity ("Belle likes to take off all her clothes and file her toenails with her dad's Black and Decker") or sneering prurience. In *Men Only* the team concoct idylls round their subjects' hackneyed whims: recluse Inga strolls the Scandinavian fjords which "allow the sounds of Sibelius to haunt the penumbras of her mind"; liberated Danielle manifests her dual commitment to free love and communism by going about Nice painting "Fuck" on back-street walls. Since the posh magazines seem to be intent on letting everyone get on with being as silly and mawkish they please, the effect of the captions invariably runs counter to that of the (really very taking) studies they annotate. For by now – fair's fair – the girls are often depressingly attractive: a bit powder-puffed and idealised, but photographed with frankness, cunning, and a sound sense of what is and is not sexy. Instead of being implicit recommendations of the priestly life, these magazines actually *sex you up*.

And there's the rub. The magazines I have mentioned retail at the same price (40p). Some readers may opt for the seamy mags because of the occasional shaved vagina or sapphic snap but my guess is that they just like sex to seem monochrome, furtive, unreal. Some readers may opt for the dinkier mags because they prefer fantasy girls to everyday ones but my guess is that they like sex to seem brisk, throwaway, unreal. The only moralistic line one can take against these magazines is that they are *malum per se*: they cheapen and dehumanise; although they may not be corrupting, they are corrupt. Perhaps there's life in this argument, despite the fact that masturbation has always been a rather private thing. If television kills the art of conversation, then nude-mags kill the art of erotic imagination. Your reporter for one – meat-replete, gonad-glutted – will in future stick to the well-thumbed photographs of the mind. ●

The future is a thing of the past

By James Harkin

Only 32 per cent of us now believe young Britons will have a better life than their parents. How did the future stop being bright?

> The European response to the unprecedented changes of the time was to develop a new sense of perspective that discerned the shape of things to come in the circumstances of contemporary society. This unique understanding of the dynamic relationship between present and future is certainly the most distinctive and possibly the most extraordinary of all the changes – from bellows and steam-engines to atomic bombs and space laboratories – that separates the modern epoch from the rest of human history.
>
> *I F Clarke, "The Pattern of Expectation"*

In December 1913 Sir Vansittart Bowater, a moustachioed Tory with a combover who had only just been installed as Lord Mayor of London, laid out his predictions for how life would look in the year 2013. On the whole he didn't fare badly – tilting as he did at the rise of air travel, the population spillage into the suburbs and even the building of a Channel tunnel. All the same, it's the omissions that glare. Man landing on Mars, Bowater felt, was close to a dead cert and cancer, by 2013, would be "as much of a memory as plague and the 'Black Death' are to us today".

London's current mayor is more bullishly pro-technology than most politicians, yet even Boris Johnson would stop short of associating the Tories with a cure for cancer. Nor can he count on any photo opportunities on Mars; after half a century, America's space-shuttle programme was wound up in 2011 and its plans for Mars exploration succumbed to cutbacks the following year.

Without a doubt, 1913, the year in which Stravinsky fired *The Rite of Spring* like a warning shot over the heads of the Parisian *haute bourgeoisie*, was a giddy high point of European modernism – just before the love affair with technology and the future that had been born the previous century got snagged in the slaughter of the First World War.

The future, it's worth remembering, is a relatively recent invention; only in the late Middle Ages did the pace of technological change quicken so much that it became a reasonable assumption that tomorrow might look substantially different from today. Some date the birth of futurology to the radical pamphleteering of the French Enlightenment. Certainly by the late-Victorian period there was a chorus of confident future-thinking, much of it central to the political propaganda of the time.

> We have run out of battery. We're so chilled as to be in deep freeze

But the future isn't what it used to be. The current economic malaise has shaken our belief in a better future as never before. More than half of all Americans (55 per cent, according to a Gallup poll published in 2011) think it highly unlikely that young people of today will have a better life than their parents. It was the only time pessimists had outweighed optimists since Gallup first asked the question in 1983; a decade earlier, 71 per cent had believed that the future would be better for young people.

If anything, we Britons are even more pessimistic. Only 32 per cent of us, according to an Ipsos MORI poll also published in 2011, thought it likely that young British people would have a better life than their parents. Twice as many thought they wouldn't. Hardly surprising, because, for the time being, all of our futures have stalled. Real median household incomes in the UK are forecast to be no higher in 2015-2016 than they were in 2002-2003 – an entire decade in which average living standards don't budge at all.

Who knew that the "end of history" was going to bring about the end of the future, too? What the futurologist Francis Fukuyama called the "Mechanism" in his 1992 book – that elusive combination of reason, desire and resources that propels us into the future – now seems to have come wholly unstuck.

Yet even before then, it's now clear, the future had been pootling along at a snail's pace for decades. If the real annual income of the median American household had continued to grow at the postwar rate, it would now be well over $90,000. Instead, as the economist Tyler Cowen points out in his excellent e-pamphlet *The Great Stagnation*, it came to a halt around 1973, declined in real terms over the past decade, and is now hovering around the $50,000 mark.

It's true that in the 1980s and 1990s the future made a comeback, but only as a brand and a buzzword. Does anyone remember all those attempts to find the future in Japan, a clumsy precursor to the contemporary fascination with China? The mantra repeated by politicians and their flaky ideas men was that we were being buffeted by "an accelerating pace of change". Society, technology and culture were said to be advancing at a dizzying pace.

It was all razzle-dazzle; outside the computer industry and the internet, there was no evidence to support it. Following Bill Clinton's lead, Tony Blair shot to power in 1997 on the back of the tagline "Things can only get better". The future was so bright, we were going to need to wear shades.

Even science writers got in on the new feeling. "We know something's happening, and we're beginning to sense what it is," James

Gleick enthused in his 1999 book *Faster: the Acceleration of Just About Everything.* "Our technology is speeding up; our arts and entertainment and the pace of invention and change – it's all speeding up."

So now we know that it wasn't. It was all breezy uplift allied to economic escapism – a kind of mortgaging of the future to win kudos in the here and now. Like one of those garish "Future Home" exhibits that were fashionable at the turn of the 20th century, the narrow technological visions thrown up in the allegedly "roaring" 1990s proved to be tinny and alien – and more than a little empty.

The promised advances in biotechnology or the reproductive sciences are still at the laboratory stage and may never materialise. There is precious little investment in high-value manufacturing. The internet is great, but has been a damp squib in terms of ability to kick-start the rest of the economy.

More generally, the notion that we in the west were experiencing a rate of change comparable to that which separated Depression-era Britain from the affluence of the postwar period was more leg-pull than serious economics: the humble washing machine improved our ability to live much more than any of the cat's cradle of communication platforms we've been given in the past decade.

Even the enthusiasts are beginning to feel cheated. Neal Stephenson is a sci-fi writer and futurologist whose books have inspired a great deal of thinking about the internet. "We can't facebook our way out of the current economic status quo," he told a reporter from the *New York Times.* Peter Thiel, one of Silicon Valley's canniest venture capitalists, who got in early on PayPal and Facebook, puts it pithily. "We wanted flying cars," reads his business motto; "instead we got 140 characters."

A stagnant present is far from our only problem, however: even before our economic groundhog day, many of us were struggling to come up with a vision of how we might want to live in the future. The social changes that accompanied Fukuyama's "end of history" thesis – as traditional forms of social solidarity have declined – seem to have brought with them a fatalism about the future.

In thrall to high priests who confuse intellectual pessimism with profundity, we have also fallen victim to a sociological version of what the psychologist Daniel Kahneman would call a "focusing illusion" – a short-sightedness when it comes to predicting the future and a tendency to exaggerate just one aspect beyond all recognition.

Some time in the past few decades we have lost sight of what everyone used to know – that the future needs to be rooted in a common purpose; that it can't be an exercise in wish-fulfilment or a luxury bauble available only to the super-rich. In our approach to everything from technology to immigration, we are too sensitive to change and too easily blindsided by anything that might come around the corner.

Seduced by gadgetry, we've overlooked how expansive and transformative real technological change can be when it improves the human condition. In China, the rural migrant worker population expanded from roughly 30 million in 1989 to more than 140 million in 2008, according to its National Bureau of Statistics. Every single year now, 200 million Chinese peasants up sticks and move to the cities in search of a better life.

That, rather than the soft-focus retro-futurism of an Instagram picture, is what proper change means. Rather than accelerating out of control, the ceremonies and rituals that seep through the pores of western culture suggest that we're on go-slow, that we have run out of battery, that we're so chilled as to be in deep freeze.

We are stuck, in other words, and our inability to imagine a brighter future is only deepening our rage and our frustration with the present. The uncomfortable truth is that, without a future, the present is barely worth the effort – and that modern societies that stop moving forward, that don't open themselves to perpetual flux and that are not constantly on the move, are as good as dead. ●

James Harkin is the director of the trends agency Flockwatching. His latest book is "Niche: the Missing Middle and Why Business Needs to Specialise to Survive" (Abacus, £9.99)

Taken to Hart

By Auberon Waugh

Hatred of students stretches across the whole political spectrum in Britain, through every age group and social class, and I often wonder why no politician has thought of harnessing it to his own ends. No doubt blacks arouse stronger feeling in some parts of the country, but hatred of students is nearly universal. The traditional explanation for working-class hatred of students was that they outraged ordinary social values: they didn't work. But nor do many other people nowadays and work has lost much of its kudos. Next there was an element of implied superiority: man is born equal, but some of them pass their O-levels and some of them don't. But money is the only accepted criterion here, and coal-miners already earn more than many headmasters. Finally, of course, there was and remains the element of sexual jealousy which may always have existed between the generations but which is made particularly bitter nowadays by the apparently endless sexual opportunities available to young people, something we never knew. Oh dear, I feel a twinge of it even now as I write. And the truth is that many of these students are rather prettier than we are, an awkward fact from which we may need protecting.

So, in the popular mind, we have the stereotype Essex University or North London Polytechnic freak. He is hideous to behold; what little intellectual vitality he ever possessed has been destroyed by drugs, bombarded by mindless revolutionary jargon to inhibit any awareness of his own ignorance and social parasitism. Ingratitude, lust, idleness, hypocrisy and self-righteousness are the main characteristics of this horrible cancer in our midst which we call higher education. But what can the honest politician do with all this popular resentment? To close down the North London Polytechnic and Essex University would be to kill the geese which lay the golden eggs.

In my own experience of visiting university grads, this image of the modern student is no more or less a caricature than Lord Snow's picture of earnest, idealistic ninnies in his last novel. Most students are nice, dull people with many human qualities, just like the miners. What seems odd is that they should continue to be despised for doing no work when work is no longer thought a clever thing to do. Of course nobody resents those who do no work more than those who do practically none. It was while I was musing on this that I hit upon a way of putting the hatred to good account.

Few people will have missed the gloating reports of last week: in a ratio of nine to one, students are opting for £10-a-week supplementary benefit to tide them over the vacation rather than apply for thousands of vacation jobs available at £25-35 (less tax). Figures published in the *Times Educational Supplement* are fairly striking, if true. The student is better off in vacation on supplementary benefit than in term time on full grant. Of 650,000 students on holiday this summer, only 10,000 (1.5 per cent) will take vacation jobs, while over 91,350 (the Easter figure) will draw supplementary benefit. There has been a 450 per cent increase in students going on the dole since 1970.

Another aspect is that out of 500,000 school-leavers this year less than half are likely to find jobs (in Liverpool, Leeds and Manchester, there are jobs for only one in five school-leavers). As a preparation for life, familiarity with the ins and outs of social security is likely to prove more useful than any number of lurid experiences as courier on a coach tour to Addis Ababa, but is this really what the drafters of the 1944 Education Act had in mind when they decreed a free education for every boy and girl in accordance with his or her abilities? Under normal circumstances in the present climate of opinion, nobody (or practically nobody) would blame people for taking money to which they were entitled, especially when the only alternative is to do something so deeply repugnant to the moral assumptions of our society as *work*.

A minimalist take on the Beatles by Vicky (*NS*, 1964)

In the early days of the 1966 Labour government when Mrs Hart was Minister for Social Security I remember listening to her impassioned plea that we should never regard supplementary benefit as anything to be ashamed of. People were starving to death because they were too proud to apply for benefits which were theirs by right, she said, and I for one believed her. Perhaps there are still one or two loonies around with similar inhibitions, but I maintain it is not the major problem. No doubt furious people will write in and say I am wrong, that they know hundreds of little old women who have eaten nothing but Kit-e-Kat for months because they are ashamed to apply for any benefit which carries the stigma of being called supplementary. They can't all be liars. I can only record my own observation that Mrs Hart's little homily seems to have made a profound impression on everyone else. And nothing could better illustrate the way we are moving than the conscious decision of 92,000 students to draw supplementary benefit rather than apply for the many vacation jobs available at three times the money (less tax).

The trouble is that fewer and fewer people nowadays are prepared even to pretend that they like working, or think it a useful thing to do. Why should we, after all? Hypocrisy may be the essential glue which binds all human society together, but other people seem only too anxious to assume responsibility for holding society together nowadays and it is really none of our business . . . On the other hand, as we watch these students sauntering down to collect social security in their tight jeans and nipple-flaunting shirts, we may start remembering the days gone by when people used to say they took a pride in their work, believing in a good day's work for a good day's wage etc, etc, etc, etc, etc, etc, etc, etc, etc. When our hypocrisy is finally exhausted, only the labour camps will remain. ●

Back to the bunker: a former air-raid tunnel in London called Third Avenue

PETER MACDIARMID/GETTY IMAGES

19 DECEMBER 1980

A Christmas Party for the Moles

By Duncan Campbell

Deep below London lies a hidden maze of tunnels, part of a 1950s network established to protect the government. These tunnels may easily be entered from the public highway. We therefore chose this unusual spot for our Christmas Party for Moles, bringing cakes and gifts, decorations and Christmas trees to the very entrance of the home of the Nuclear Button. The government may not care for our sense of humour. They should be deeply grateful that we brought only Christmas stockings, and that our easily accomplished weekend visit was not a trip by terrorists with a sinister sackful of gelignite and incendiaries. Such an act would have surpassed Guy Fawkes in cutting off a large portion of Britain's communications and defence capacity for months to come. In happier spirit, we invite readers to the Moles' Christmas Party.

Who are the moles that feed the *NS* with its packages of secret documents and other bureaucratic detritus? This question, at once deeply troubling the MI5, the CIA and the KGB, will here, for the first time be answered. The underground spies in government ranks – the *NS* Mole Force – are in secret contact with our reporters at midnight rendezvous deep below our own offices.

From run-down Bethnal Green, in the East End of London, to the plush western pastures of Maida Vale, from Euston Station in the north to Waterloo in the south, runs a network of secret tunnels, built in the 1950s and 1960s to protect the machinery of government from A-Bombs and other mindless violence. Over 30 shafts and a dozen lifts connect these catacombs with the surface – most of them emerging unobtrusively in government buildings or telephone exchanges.

Implausibly disguised as a touring cyclist, I have often visited these tunnels. An access shaft emerges, usefully, on a traffic island in a public highway – Bethnal Green Road, E1. On this festive occasion, my travelling kit includes not just a bicycle but a Christmas tree, decorations, and gifts for the new stars in the Good Mole Guide.

A manhole cover, gently raised, gives access to one of the Post Office's thousands of ▶

▶ sub-surface cable chambers. But this one is different. A stout grey-painted waterproof door leads through the side of this chamber. Open it, and you are standing on the top platform of a shaft one hundred feet deep. Climb down the rung ladders, and you stand poised at the entrance to the secret network. A long ribbon of lights and cables extends into the distance, as you look into Tunnel L (St Paul's to Bethnal Green). No bustling commuters or noisy trains here, just a pleasantly warm and enveloping silence.

The tunnels have an eerie feel to them. There is no-one about after 5pm, and the Patrolmen who daily pace these subterranean corridors concentrate on checking their structure and not on keeping watch for journalistic infiltrators. There are over 12 miles of tunnel, so a bicycle does indeed make light of otherwise heavy footwork as one travels around central London on this uniquely quiet and exclusive subway. Alternatively, one may gently jog through these pleasant underground corridors, the only pollution-free running track to be found in (or under) central London. (At this point, I would stake public claim to the world record for the 1½-mile distance run 100 feet below ground: 10.8 minutes, St Paul's to Covent Garden, Tunnel M.)

Riding down Tunnel L, one passes side shafts and alleys *en route* to the first interchange, directly below Postal Headquarters close to St Paul's Cathedral. Here, tunnels shoot off in all directions: three *rise* to join the ordinary London underground Central Line, and the Post Office's own underground mail railway. Tunnel R and Tunnel A grandly circuit round St Paul's Cathedral – they lead to an underground complex with six shafts below the Post Office's Citadel telephone exchange. Citadel's workings, and shaft, are hidden behind seven foot thick concrete walls.

But Tunnel B leads on to greater things, on to Holborn, home of the *New Statesman*, and the seat of government. I ride through dense jungles of cable, and past noisy ventilator fans. The air becomes hot and fetid. We are nearing Whitehall.

The Moles' Christmas Party is to be held at the entrance to the nastiest bit of government of all. This is the Chamber Of Mass Destruction With The Nuclear Button In It. It would naturally have been more exhilarating to have partied around The Button, but this precise bit of the tunnels is undoubtedly guarded by blood-thirsty SAS men with huge, slavering Alsatians. Reliable sources speak of at least a regimental Great Dane. We made do with the doorstep of the awful place.

We pass more side turnings – Tunnel M leads off to Fleet Street and Tunnel P meanders off under Leicester Square to finish up below the Post Office Tower. Finally Tunnel S heads left across the Thames to Waterloo, and the bizarre roadsign, such as are to be found at every intersection, warns ominously that we are now travelling down a Dead End. There is "No Exit" from Whitehall. Do we have no hope, if pinned down by the SAS? Three hundred yards on and we halt at the start of the Whitehall Bunkers. The main tunnel is 20 feet wide, and leads through double doors to the first of the Bunkers, a Post Office lair called Q-Whitehall. Q is Post Office jargon for hush-hush. Down the Q-Whitehall tunnel, narrower eight feet wide tunnels lead off to the bowels of the great Departments of State. There's one for the Ministry of Defence, one for the Admiralty, one for the Old War Office, one to No 10, one to the Treasury.

> An access shaft emerges on a traffic island in Bethnal Green Road, E1

At the end of each side tunnel a worn spiral staircase and mini-lift reaches up into the corridors of power. The air is fusty. It is being piped in, along great metal ducts, from the new offices of nice Mr Heseltine's Department of the Environment.

The whole of Whitehall, virtually, is interlinked through this central tunnel, which dog-legs around the Houses of Parliament (needless to say, these are *not* connected) finishing up in the gigantic underground complex below the DoE. This area, like the original small tunnel network, was first constructed as a Second World War "citadel" to resist 1,000lb bombs and V-weapons. The tunnels and the DoE citadel were enormously extended during the 1950s as an A-bomb shelter. The greater power of H-bombs has made them vulnerable and so the major government bunkers are now outside London.

But there's still one of these metaphysical buttons, in the Ministry of Defence Operations Centre. Another shaft leads to the Cabinet Office, with its famed COBRA Cabinet Office Briefing Area, HQ of Mr Whitelaw and his heroes of the Iranian Embassy Siege. Close by COBRA is the one piece of Whitehall bunkery which may be visited by the ordinary tourist – Winston Churchill's underground headquarters opposite St James's Park.

Also opposite St James's is the Institute of Contemporary Arts, which tunnel enthusiasts believe to conceal a small but significant part of this system. A ventilator fan, linked to the Admiralty's bit of the bunkers has been tucked in – beside the Gents, to be precise. The fan may be heard and observed by taking a discrete footing on the ICA's sanitary ware. The odours then detected may well be naval.

Back to Trafalgar Square for the underground mole party. We have gathered at the start of Q-Whitehall. At this point we are about 40 yards south of Nelson's Column and 100 feet below it. Festivities ensue, a 12-month of uncovering bureaucratic skulduggery is celebrated, and the Mole Force is inspired with further Principle and greater Moral Courage, the better to combat Fear and Loathing instilled by the notorious Civil Service Estacode and the no-longer-quite-so-dreaded Official Secrets Act.

I have abandoned the cunning disguise as a passing cycle tourist, and dressed formally for this occasion. Christmas tree and decorations are set out with gifts and consumables for many moles. At the end of the celebration the moles disperse through the tunnels, our last lingerings undisturbed by Patrolmen, SAS guards, slavering Great Danes, or itinerant Post Office cable-laying persons.

I pedal off slowly on the trusty tunnel-cruiser, away from the Dead End of Whitehall, and must now choose a route out. A right turn into Tunnel M offers the prospect of a jaunt 100 feet below Drury Lane. A little sign indicates that Fleet Street's own shafts to the surface, Shafts NA and NB, might be suitable ways out. But no mole has ever spoken of these mysteries, and precisely where these underground accesses go.

At the far end of Tunnel G, there is another interchange. We venture into Tunnel C, a bombproof highway to Euston. But a giant illuminated red sign warns *Danger*. This tunnel, a notice explains, is unventilated and has no air in it. Continuing this trip might perhaps provide a happy ending to the tale for the Post Office. Turning back, one climbs a steep staircase to the catacombs below our own Holborn office. Close at hand, shafts GA and BC, complete with lift, now emerge in Holborn Telephone Exchange, and the entrance to this building is a mere 30 yards from our Great Turnstile offices. This geographical good fortune has already been communicated to other staff, and plans are in hand for commandeering the place as a People's Nuclear Shelter (with especial reference to journalists) should the Worst happen.

This article, no doubt, will result in the tunnels and the shafts of this extraordinary network being knee-deep in persons from MI5, MI6, the Special Branch, the Post Office, and Health Inspectors. They will find no moles: a new rendezvous has been arranged. They will, of course, be disturbed by the Big Question. Who was the Great Festive Mole who, last Christmas, instructed me to lift the manhole cover on the traffic island between Bethnal Green Road and Sclater Street E1, and thus opened up this underground world. Does he or she even exist? My lips should remain sealed but the position of this handy hole may be discovered from public sources.

To MI5 and the Special Branch, a Happy Christmas and a trying and unstable New Year for '81. ●

The House of Slaves

By Andrew Stephen

Flipping through some dusty files at my local library in Georgetown the other day, I made a horrifying discovery. I was looking up the deeds of my nearby house, which I already knew was built in 1795, and which is therefore – by American standards – almost literally a historic monument. My least favourite task in the house is crawling into a crude, darkly mysterious space beneath the basement to remove the bodies of huge rats when their stench becomes unbearable on hot summer days. Crouching inside a crawl space, I would carefully peer in and around ancient brickwork and cavities that served, I vaguely assumed, some long-forgotten purpose.

But that day when I looked up the records all these mysteries became clear. The owner of the house in 1807 was one Thomas Turner, and the value of his belongings at the property was fully listed, viz:

> 2 negro men $300
> 1 ditto woman $150
> 4 ditto girls $150
> 2 horses $200
> 2 cows $30

Put simply, I discovered that the occupants of the crawl space under my house, before the rats, were slaves: fellow human beings, living in surreal degradation beneath a household in which more monetary value was put on the ownership of two horses and two cattle than the ownership of a black man, or woman, or four girls. The brickwork, I belatedly realised, was the remains of an old oven where the slaves cooked for Turner and his family; the cavities, barely more than two feet high, were probably where they slept. The discovery brought home to me (literally) yet another reality of American history that says so much about the country today: this time, the roots of racial hatred and shame, and why their legacies persist well into the 21st century.

I could not leave it there. Who were these people? How did they come to be in my house? Why are there five all-black churches flourishing in Georgetown today but fewer than ten black inhabitants left in the current population of 4,800? We read so much about the fashionable four square miles that make up Georgetown and why they are so important in the nation's history; how Georgetown nestles on the Potomac that symbolically separates the historic south from the north; how successive presidents and congresses introduced unique legislation for such a tiny place because it was so important to them; how Abraham Lincoln went to church there; how John F Kennedy and his wife made it the chicest place on earth.

Yet we see or hear little of black people in Georgetown, save those who empty our dustbins or serve us, often surlily, in the drugstores. The only exception to this rule is on Sundays, when carfuls and busloads of well-dressed blacks pour into Georgetown to fill those five black churches. Walk past them on a Sunday morning and you hear the kind of gospel singing and choruses of "*Yessir!*" and "*Right!*" in response to the exhortations of the preacher that you expect to hear only in the Deep South, and certainly not in genteel, white Georgetown. Indeed, few inhabitants today know that black people once made up more than a third of Georgetown's population, or how a combination of consciously initiated legislative, social and economic pressures gradually forced them out so that Georgetown could become not only chic and expensive but exclusively white.

Subhuman Treatment

Lest we forget, neither blacks nor whites lived at all in Georgetown – then known as Tahoga – until British settlers went ashore there in 1696. In those days, it was a peaceful village inhabited by Algonquin Indians, but they were soon expunged by the settlers. Then, in the 18th century, white entrepreneurs realised that huge sums of money could be made from an insatiable demand in Europe and elsewhere for the tobacco cultivated in Virginia and Maryland (of which Georgetown was then part). So black slaves, as US history textbooks have only recently started to tell American kids, were forcibly transported into labour in the tobacco fields.

Its geographical position made Georgetown an ideal port from which ships laden with tobacco could sail to Europe; by the end of the 18th century it had become the largest tobacco port in the US, an economic powerhouse to which slaves were brought in (mostly from the existing tobacco fields but some direct from Africa) to provide labour and to service the households of the white tobacco merchants. The blacks were treated as subhuman in just about every conceivable way, while the more successful of their white owners started to amass huge fortunes.

Perhaps, indeed, those white merchants included Thomas Turner? In peculiarly personal ways like this, the sheer evil of it all somehow makes me feel complicit. I shudder, for example, when I realise that just two minutes from where I now live a white man called John Beattie set up a highly successful slave-trading business that continued well into the second half of the 19th century. In my research odyssey, I found a newspaper ad from the time that read:

> NEGROES WANTED: Persons wishing to dispose of Negroes from 10 to 25 years of age, (both sexes) can obtain the cash for them, by applying to the subscriber, two doors east of the Union Tavern Stage Office, Bridge street, Georgetown. NB A smart likely [*sic*] GIRL, 11 to 13 years of age, would be desirable.

Black people had thus become essential economic tools in Georgetown, but were simultaneously rejected and feared socially. To the whites, it was as though dangerous wild animals were roaming the streets. The first law designed to keep them out of sight came as early as 1795, when Georgetown had already become part of what was then known as the Federal City (later the District of Columbia), but was still separate from Washington. The town passed a law forbidding black people from congregating in Georgetown in groups of seven or more. The 1800 census showed that, in a population of 5,120 in Georgetown, there were already 1,449 slaves and 277 "free blacks" – those technically not the property of white people, but who were treated as only marginally less dangerous animals.

Against all the odds, a handful of "free" black men in Georgetown managed to distinguish themselves – but then, crucially, remained oppressed and their achievements unrecognised. Benjamin Banneker (1731-1806) was of Ethiopian descent, but played an important role in surveying the new boundaries of Washington. He still had to sleep in a ▶

tent in Georgetown, and even the supposedly enlightened president Thomas Jefferson – who wrote later that black people were "improvident, sensual, extravagant and weak in faculty" – told a friend that, in reality, Banneker had "a mind of very common stature indeed" (he did not mean it as a compliment).

Jefferson would have been equally unimpressed by Yarrow Mamout (circa 1736-1823), a Muslim who was born in Guinea but brought to Georgetown to serve nearly 50 years in slavedom. In his old age, Mamout was given his "freedom" by a relatively benevolent owner and somehow managed to amass enough money to buy a tiny house, an achievement so extraordinary that he attracted the attention of the celebrated portrait painter Charles Willson Peale (1741-1827).

Rigid Segregation

By this stage in my research, I was beginning to get a glimmer of what life must have been like for the former residents of my crawl space – though it was going to get worse. There was one exception to that 1795 law forbidding them from congregating, however: they could go to church on the Sabbath, which explains why those five churches remain the one potent black force in Georgetown today. But blacks were kept rigidly segregated from whites, and when St John's Episcopal Church was established in 1815 – it's still there, only a five-minute walk away for me – it had an outdoor staircase built specially for blacks.

The following year, hardly surprisingly, a handful of "free" black men managed to raise a little money to start their own breakaway house of worship, which was to become the Mount Zion Methodist Church, one of the five black churches still thriving today. But the white Methodist church, at which Lincoln later worshipped, insisted that black churchgoers have white ministers in charge; it took half a century before Mount Zion was allowed to appoint its own black minister. On the secret "underground railroad" through which slaves were later smuggled north from the South, the Mount Zion burial vault was used as an important hiding place.

Knowing what I now know, I found it strangely moving when the Reverend Robert E Slade, chief pastor at Mount Zion today, who does not even live in Georgetown himself, told my son and me that "when we didn't have anything, the church was our everything . . . When there was nothing and no place to go, [it] was the one place to go." Those words alone explained why the emotional bonds to the black churches in Georgetown remain so strong for the black descendants of slaves who attend today, even though the vast majority of them have never lived in Georgetown itself.

I imagine that at least the girls who lived in my crawl space in 1807, if not the adults, were still alive in 1848 – a year that should make every white resident of Georgetown today hang his or her head in shame. It was the year when just about the most despotic legislative measure imaginable, known as the "Black Code" of the Corporation of Georgetown, was passed into law.

I have the ten pages in front of me as I write, and it is hard to know quite how to convey the flavour of the legislation. Chapter XCIV, maybe, which ordered that "if any slave shall, before the hour of nine o'clock, PM, and after the hour of five o'clock, AM, bathe in the Potomac or Rock Creek . . . he shall be publicly whipped"? Or Chapter XCVIII: "if any slave shall fly any kite or kites . . . such offender may be punished by whipping"? Or perhaps Chapter CII, which insisted that "if any free negro or mulatto person, living in this town" should have in his or her possession "any written or printed paper . . . of a character calculated to excite insurrection or insubordination among the slaves or colored people" he or she should be fined or "committed to the work-house"? That if a mere slave was to do the same he or she should receive up to 39 lashes and his or her white owner fined? And that if the owner refused to pay the fine, the slaves would then receive another 39 lashes? And so on, ad infinitum.

> "When we didn't have anything, the church was our everything"

I went on to discover that in the same year 77 black slaves tried to escape this kind of oppression by sailing from Georgetown harbour on a ship called the *Pearl*. Furious owners sent a posse on a steamer called the *Salem* to recapture them, and they caught up with the *Pearl* 140 miles downriver. Though this attempt was unsuccessful and the slaves returned to their owners, the black flight from Georgetown was already beginning.

The atmosphere was such that black people were still being bought and sold as property in Georgetown as late as November 1861 – even though President Lincoln signed a local law the following year to free slaves eight months before his landmark Emancipation Proclamation of 1862. The white slave owners of Georgetown, DC (as it was then known, because it was not officially absorbed into Washington, DC until 1895) demanded compensation, and an "Expert Examiner of Slaves" was brought in – this was a local phenomenon that did not happen elsewhere in the country – who, after examining the slaves' teeth and health in general, assessed their overall value at $300,000.

Meanwhile blacks from the South, anticipating freedom following Lincoln's Emancipation Proclamation, poured into both Georgetown and Washington. Between 1865 and 1870 the black population of Georgetown increased from 1,935 to 3,271. Yet white residents voted against the Negro Suffrage Bill 1866 by a majority of 712 to 1, declaring that giving "the elective franchise to persons of color is wholly uncalled for, and an act of grievous oppression against which a helpless community can have no defense". That helpless white community was still paying supposedly free blacks $6 per month to work for them.

The records at the local library showed that my house was undergoing renovations at that time – and it was then, I suspect, that the brick kiln was abandoned and the human occupants of the crawl space finally moved to somewhat better housing. With hindsight, we can now see that the next two or three decades were a golden age for blacks in Georgetown: a skilled working class able to earn a reasonable living started to emerge, as did a handful of professionals such as doctors.

But there were countless laws and regulations that prevented true economic or social emancipation. Only white passengers were allowed to ride on Georgetown's new electric streetcars, for example, thus enabling them to commute in to Washington for high-paying jobs that were in effect denied to blacks. The forces of racism were still raging, too: I came across one news item in the *Washington Post* of 1 September 1897, headlined "Mammy's White Mistress Was Fond of It, and Neighbors Objected". It told of how a white "philanthropic lady" of Georgetown had taken a shine to the "nigger baby" of one of her servants, leading to fierce protests from white neighbours, who objected to what the *Post* amusedly described as the baby's "osculatory performances" on the front porch of the white woman's house.

The Depression and Dispossession

This kind of vicious racism, combined with such repressive legislation, was already driving black people out of Georgetown – but it was a series of economic blows that then started to seal their fate. The Potomac silted up, virtually ending the industrial effectiveness of Georgetown's harbour. The Chesapeake and Ohio Canal, which flowed through Georgetown and was crucial for many businesses such as flour and paper mills, flooded disastrously in 1889; black people were the first to lose their jobs when firms went bust. By 1910 the black population of Georgetown had peaked, and when the Great Depression struck, 19 years later, more and more black workers found themselves displaced by white people forced to take their menial jobs.

I discovered, however, that FDR's New Deal then perversely began to work *against* black people in Georgetown. It was intended to lift the poor out of poverty, but the effect in DC was that thousands of new, white and relatively well-paid civil servants flooded into the area to implement the new legislation.

Leafy white town: a Georgetown resident admires a dogwood tree in full bloom, 1930

Their arrival had a knock-on effect on housing prices in Georgetown, putting homes hopelessly and finally out of the economic reach of black people. "The dispossession of the Negro residents [of Georgetown]," the Conference on Better Housing Among the Negroes reported at the time, "is jointly managed by the city's leading realtors and their allied banks and trust companies."

In the 20th century, two acts passed by none other than the mighty US Congress were the final straws for Georgetown's blacks; both were covertly racist pieces of legislation aimed specifically at Georgetown. The ostensible purpose of the District of Columbia Alley Dwelling Act 1934, for example, was to get rid of slums in Georgetown – but to a House of Representatives that had only one black member and a Senate that had none at all, slums were synonymous with black people. And many of the white members of Congress lived in Georgetown, after all.

Then the US Congress passed the Old Georgetown Act 1950 "to preserve and protect places of historic interest", but its real purpose was to make white gentrification legally enforceable. In 1972 the *Washington Post* reported that there were fewer than 250 blacks left, "so few that some Georgetown residents are unaware they are there".

Going Full Circle

The truth is that racism in the heart of America's capital had become so casually institutionalised that even such iconic Democrats as the young senator John F Kennedy voluntarily signed a "restrictive covenant" when he bought his house on N Street – close to mine – which specified that the home should not "ever be used or occupied or sold, conveyed, leased, rented, or given to Negroes or any person or persons of the Negro race or blood". The likes of the Kennedys, Pamela Harriman and Kay Graham joined forces to create those Georgetown social salons of ludicrous legend, but the only black face I can recall ever seeing in such a place since I moved to Georgetown is that of Vernon Jordan, super-lawyer and Mr Fixit for Bill Clinton.

Which brings us full circle to 2006. I went to the Reverend Slade's church the other Sunday – I have rarely felt more welcome anywhere, even though few white Georgetowners would even think of setting foot in the place – and spoke to an 84-year-old black parishioner called Carter Bowman, born in Georgetown but who long since moved out.

With neat serendipity, I met three generations of Bowmans, because his son and grandson, who attends university in England, happened to be visiting. It was chilling to realise that if you go back another three generations, you find that all of Carter Bowman's great-grandparents were born and raised when slavery was at its most wickedly intense in Georgetown. They were all subject to the Black Code of 1848. The birthplace of only one is recorded, and it was Madagascar. They could have been residents of my crawl space.

Who, knowing all this, should be surprised that present-day black employees of drugstores in Georgetown are so often surly when they serve white customers? I have to have blood tests every month and have become chummy with the young black nurse who draws the blood; as she plunged her needle in the other day, I told her of my shock and disbelief reading the Black Code 1848 of Georgetown. "It can't be worse than the Willie Lynch letters," she responded. I had no idea what the Willie Lynch letters were and nor did any white American I asked; white Americans, after all, prefer to forget about their country's systematic oppression of black people.

But that gentle woman knows her black American history only too well – and she and her children and grandchildren and subsequent generations will not, I suspect, ever forget that their forebears were treated like rats. Nor should they, and nor should any of us. ●

©DAN MURRELL

11 APRIL 2011

The Bugger, Bugged

By Hugh Grant

When I broke down in my midlife crisis car in remotest Kent just before Christmas, a battered white van pulled up on the far carriageway. To help, I thought. But when the driver got out he started taking pictures with a long-lens camera. He came closer to get better shots and I swore at him. Then he offered me a lift the last few miles to my destination. I suspected his motives and swore at him some more. (I'm not entirely sympathetic towards paparazzi.) Then I realised I couldn't get a taxi and was late. So I had to accept the lift.

He turned out to be an ex-*News of the World* journalist and paparazzo, now running a pub in Dover. He still kept his camera in the car's glove box for just this kind of happy accident.

More than that, he was Paul McMullan, one of two ex-*NoW* hacks who had blown the whistle on the extent of the paper's phone-hacking, particularly under its former editor Andy Coulson. This was interesting, as I had been a victim – a fact he confirmed as we drove along.

He also had an unusual defence of the practice: that phone-hacking was a price you had to pay for living in a free society. I asked how that worked, but we ran out of time, and next thing we had arrived and he was asking me if I would pose for a photo with him, "not for publication, just for the wall of the pub".

I agreed and the picture duly appeared in the *Mail on Sunday* that weekend with his creative version of the encounter. He had asked me to drop into his pub some time. So when Jemima [Khan] asked me to write a piece for this paper, it occurred to me it might be interesting to take him up on his invitation.

I wanted to hear more about phone-hacking and the whole business of tabloid journalism. It occurred to me just to interview him straight, as he has, after all, been a whistle-blower. But then I thought I might get more, and it might be more fun, if I secretly taped him, the bugger bugged, as it were. Here are some excerpts from our conversation.

Me So, how's the whistleblowing going?

Him I'm trying to get a book published. I sent it off to a publisher who immediately accepted it and then it got legal and they said, "This is never going to get published."

Me Why? Because it accuses too many people of crime?

Him Yes, as I said to the parliamentary commission, Coulson knew all about it and regularly ordered it . . . He [Coulson] rose quickly to the top; he wanted to cover his tracks all the time. So he wouldn't just write a story about a celeb who'd done something. He'd want to make sure they could never sue, so he wanted us to hear the celeb like you on tape saying, "Hello, darling, we had lovely sex last night." So that's on tape and so we can publish . . . Historically, the way it went was, in the early days of mobiles, we all had analogue mobiles and that was an absolute joy. You know, you just . . . sat outside Buckingham Palace with a £59 scanner you bought at Argos and get Prince Charles and everything he said.

Me Is that how the Squidgy tapes [of Diana's phone conversations] came out? Which was put down to radio hams, but was in fact . . .

Him Paps in the back of a van, yes . . . I mean, politicians were dropping like flies in the Nineties because it was so easy to get stuff on them. And, obviously, less easy to justify is celebrities. But yes.

Me It wasn't just the *News of the World*. It was, you know – the *Mail*?

Him Oh absolutely, yeah. When I went freelance in 2004 the biggest payers – you'd have thought it would be the *NoW*, but actually it was the *Daily Mail*. If I take a good picture, the first person I go to is – such as in your case – the *Mail on Sunday*.

Did you see that story? The picture of you, breaking down . . . I ought to thank you for that. I got £3,000. Whooo!

Me But would they [the *Mail*] buy a phone-hacked story?

Him For about four or five years they've absolutely been cleaner than clean. And before that they weren't. They were as dirty as anyone . . . They had the most money.

Me So everyone knew? Would Rebekah Wade have known all this stuff was going on?

Him You're not taping, are you?

Me [*slightly shrill voice*] No.

Him Well, yeah. Clearly she . . . took over the job of [a journalist] who had a scanner who was trying to sell it to members of his own department. But it wasn't a big crime. [*Ed*: Rebekah Brooks has always denied any knowledge of phone-hacking.]

It started off as fun – you know, it wasn't against the law, so why wouldn't you? And it was only because the MPs who were fiddling their expenses and being generally corrupt kept getting caught so much they changed the law in 2001 to make it illegal to buy and sell a digital scanner. So all we were left with was – you know – finding a blag to get your mobile [records] out of someone at Vodafone.

Me So they all knew? Wade probably knew all about it all?

Him [. . .] Cameron must have known – that's the bigger scandal. He had to jump into bed with Murdoch as everyone had, starting with Thatcher in the Seventies . . . Tony Blair . . . Maggie openly courted Murdoch. So when Cameron, when it came his turn to go to Murdoch via Rebekah Wade . . . Cameron went horse riding regularly with Rebekah. I know, because as well as doorstepping celebrities, I've also doorstepped my ex-boss by hiding in the bushes, waiting for her to come past with Cameron on a horse . . . before the election to show that Murdoch was backing Cameron.

Me What happened to that story?

Him The *Guardian* paid for me to do it and I stepped in it and missed them. They'd gone past – not as good as having a picture.

Me Do you think Murdoch knew about phone-hacking?

Him Errr, possibly not. He's a funny bloke given that he owns the *Sun* and the Screws . . . quite puritanical. Sorry to talk about Di- ▶

▶ vine Brown, but when that came out . . . Murdoch was furious: "What are you putting that on our front page for? You're bringing down the tone of our papers." [*Indicating himself*] That's what we do over here.

Me Well, it's also because it was his film I was about to come out in. It was a Fox film.

[*A pause here while we chat to other customers, and then –*]

Him So anyway, I was sent to do a feature on *Moulin Rouge!* at Cannes, which was a great send anyway. Basically my brief was to see who Nicole Kidman was shagging – what she was doing, poking through her bins and get some stuff on her. So Murdoch's paying her five million quid to big up the French and at the same time paying me £5.50 to fuck her up . . . So all hail the master. We're just pawns in his game. How perverse is that?

Me Wow. You reckon he never knew about it?

Him [*pause*] I don't even think he really worried himself too much about it.

Me What's his son called?

Him James. They're all mates together. They all go horse riding. You've got Jeremy Clarkson lives here [in Oxfordshire]. Cameron lives here, and Rebekah Wade is married to Brooks's son [the former racehorse trainer Charlie Brooks]. Cameron gets dressed up as the Stig to go to Clarkson's 50th birthday party [*Ed*: it was actually to record a video message for the party]. Is that demeaning for a prime minister?

So basically, Cameron is very much in debt to Rebekah Wade for helping him not quite win the election . . . So that was my submission to parliament – that Cameron's either a liar or an idiot.

Me But don't you think that all these prime ministers deliberately try to get the police to drag their feet about investigating the whole [phone-hacking] thing because they don't want to upset Murdoch?

Him Yeah. You also work a lot with policemen as well . . . One of the early stories was [*and here he names a much-loved TV actress in her sixties*] used to be a street walker – whether or not she was, but that's the tip.

Me and Chum MLTVA?!

Me I can't believe it. Oh no!

Chum Really??

Him Yeah. Well, not now . . .

Chum Oh, it'd be so much better if it was now.

Him So I asked a copper to get his hands on the phone files, but because it's only a caution it's not there any more. So that's the tip . . . it's a policeman ringing up a tabloid reporter and asking him for ten grand because this girl had been cautioned right at the start of his career.

And then I ask another policemen to check the records . . . That's happening regularly. So the police don't particularly want to investigate.

Me Do you think they're going to have to now?

Him I mean – 20 per cent of the Met has taken backhanders from tabloid hacks. So why would they want to open up that can of worms? . . . And what's wrong with that? It doesn't hurt anyone particularly. I mean, it could hurt someone's career – but isn't that the dance with the devil you have to play?

Me Well, I suppose the fact that they're dragging their feet while investigating a mass of phone-hacking – which is a crime – some people would think is a bit depressing.

Him But then – should it be a crime? I mean, scanning never used to be a crime. You're transmitting your thoughts and your voice over the airwaves. How can you not expect someone to stick up an aerial and listen in?

Me So if someone was on a landline and you had a way of tapping in . . . do you think that should be illegal?

Him I'd have to say quite possibly, yeah. I'd say that should be illegal.

Me But a mobile phone – a digital phone . . . you'd say it'd be all right to tap that?

Him I'm not sure about that. So we went from a point where anyone could listen in to anything. Like you, me, journalists could listen in to corrupt politicians, and this is why we have a reasonably fair society and a not particularly corrupt or criminal prime minister, whereas other countries have Gaddafi. Do you think it's right the only person with a decent digital scanner these days is the government? Are you comfortable that the only people who can listen in to you now are – is it MI5 or MI6?

> "Cameron gets dressed up as the Stig . . . Is that demeaning for a PM?"

Me I'd rather no one listened in. And I might not be alone there. You probably wouldn't want people listening to your conversations.

Him I'm not interesting enough for anyone to want to listen in.

Me Ah . . . I think that was one of the questions asked last week at one of the parliamentary committees. They asked Yates [John Yates, acting deputy commissioner, Metropolitan Police] if it was true he thought the *NoW* had been hacking the phones of friends and family of those girls who were murdered . . . the Soham murder and the Milly girl [Milly Dowler].

Him Yeah. Yeah. It's more than likely. Yeah . . . It was quite routine. Yeah – friends and family is something that's not as easy to justify as the other things.

Me But celebrities you would justify because they're rich?

Him Yeah. I mean, if you don't like it, you've just got to get off the stage. It'll do wonders.

Me So I should have given up acting?

Him If you live off your image, you can't really complain about someone . . .

Me I live off my acting. Which is different to living off your image.

Him You're still presenting yourself to the public. And if the public didn't know you . . .

Me They don't give a shit. I got arrested with a hooker and they still came to my films. They don't give a fuck about your public image. They just care about whether you're in an entertaining film or not.

Him That's true . . . I have terrible difficulty with him [*points to pap shot of Johnny Depp*]. I was in Venice and he was a nightmare to do because he walks around looking like Michael Jackson. And the punchline was . . . after leading everyone a merry dance the film was shot on an open balcony – I mean, it was like – he was standing there in public.

Me And you don't see the difference between the two situations?

Chum He was actually working at this time? As opposed to having his own private time?

Him You can't hide all the time.

Me So you're saying, if you're Johnny Depp or me, you don't deserve to have a private life?

Him You make so much more money. You know, most people in Dover take home about £200 and struggle.

Me So how much do you think the families of the Milly and Soham girls make?

Him OK, so there are examples that are poor and you can't justify – and that's one of them.

Me I tell you the thing I still don't get – if you think it was all right to do all that stuff, why blow the whistle on it?

Him Errm . . . Right. That's interesting. I actually blew the whistle when a friend of mine at the *Guardian* kept hassling me for an interview. I said, "Well if you put the name of the Castle [his pub] on the front page, I'll do anything you like." So that's how it started.

Me Have you been leant on by the *NoW*, News International, since you blew the whistle?

Him No, they've kept their distance. I mean, there's people who have much better records – my records are non-existent. There are people who actually have tapes and transcripts they did for Andy Coulson.

Me And where are these tapes and transcripts? Do you think they've been destroyed?

Him No, I'm sure they're saving them till they retire.

Me So did you personally ever listen to my voice messages?

Him No, I didn't personally ever listen to your voice messages. I did quite a lot of stories on you, though. You were a very good earner at times.

Those are the highlights. As I drove home past the white cliffs, I thought it was interesting – apart from the fact that Paul hates people like me, and I hate people like him, we got on quite well. And, absurdly, I felt a bit guilty for recording him. And he does have a very nice pub. The Castle Inn, Dover, for the record. There are rooms available, too. He asked me if I'd like to sample the honeymoon suite some time: "I can guarantee your privacy." ●